Routledge Handbook of Internet Politics

The internet is now a mainstay of contemporary political life, and captivates researchers from across the social sciences. From debates about its impact on parties and election campaigns following momentous presidential contests in the United States, to concerns over international security, privacy, and surveillance in the post-9/11, post-7/7 environment; from the rise of blogging as a threat to the traditional model of journalism, to controversies at the international level over how and if the internet should be governed by an entity such as the United Nations; from the new repertoires of collective action open to citizens, to the massive programs of public management reform taking place in the name of e-government, internet politics, and policy are continually in the headlines.

The *Routledge Handbook of Internet Politics* is a collection of over 30 chapters dealing with the most significant scholarly debates in this rapidly growing field of study. Organized in four broad sections: Institutions, Behavior, Identities, and Law and policy, the Handbook summarizes and criticizes contemporary debates while pointing out new departures. A comprehensive set of resources, it provides linkages to established theories of media and politics, political communication, governance, deliberative democracy, and social movements, all within an interdisciplinary context. The contributors form a strong international cast of established and junior scholars.

This is the first publication of its kind in this field; a helpful companion to students and scholars of politics, international relations, communication studies, and sociology.

Andrew Chadwick is Professor of Political Science and Founding Director of the New Political Communication Unit at Royal Holloway, University of London. He is the author of *Internet Politics: States, Citizens, and New Communication Technologies* (Oxford University Press), which won the American Sociological Association Communication and Information Technologies Section Outstanding Book Award.

Philip N. Howard is Associate Professor in the Department of Communication at the University of Washington, and directs the World Information Access Project (www.wiareport.org). He is the author of *New Media Campaigns and the Managed Citizen* (Cambridge University Press), which won book awards from the American Sociological Association and the International Communication Association.

Routledge Handbook of Internet Politics

Edited by
Andrew Chadwick and
Philip N. Howard

Routledge
Taylor & Francis Group
New York   London

Routledge is an imprint of the
Taylor & Francis Group, an informa business

First published 2009
Paperback edition first published 2010
by Routledge
2 Park Square, Milton Park, Abingdon, Oxon OX14 4RN

Simultaneously published in the USA and Canada
by Routledge
270 Madison Avenue, New York, NY 10016

Routledge is an imprint of the Taylor & Francis Group, an informa business

Transferred to Digital Printing 2010

Typeset in Bembo by
Taylor & Francis Books

British Library Cataloguing in Publication Data
A catalogue record for this book is available from the British Library

Library of Congress Cataloging in Publication Data
Routledge handbook of Internet politics / edited by Andrew Chadwick and
  Philip N. Howard.
    p. cm.
  Includes bibliographical references and index.
  1. Internet – Political aspects. 2. Political participation – computer network resources.
  3. Communication in politics – computer network resources. I. Chadwick, Andrew.
  II. Howard, Philip N. III. Title: *Handbook of Internet Politics.* IV. Title: *Internet Politics.*
  HM851.R6795 2008
320.0285'4678 – dc22   2008003045

ISBN10 0-415-42914-5 (hbk)
ISBN10 0-415-78058-6 (pbk)
ISBN10 0-203-96254-0 (ebk)

ISBN13 978-0-415-42914-6 (hbk)
ISBN13 978-0-415-78058-2 (pbk)
ISBN13 978-0-203-96254-1 (ebk)

Contents

Figures

Tables

Contributors

Nick Anstead is a doctoral candidate in the New Political Communication Unit in the Department of Politics and International Relations, Royal Holloway, University of London, U.K.

Sandra J. Ball-Rokeach is a Professor of Communication and Sociology at the University of Southern California, U.S.A., and Principal Investigator of The Metamorphosis Project.

Jody C Baumgartner is an Assistant Professor of political science at East Carolina University, Greenville, U.S.A.

W. Lance Bennett is Professor of Political Science and Ruddick C. Lawrence Professor of Communication at the University of Washington, Seattle, U.S.A., where he also directs the Center for Communication and Civic Engagement.

Bruce Bimber is Professor of Political Science and Communication at the University of California, Santa Barbara, U.S.A.

Jennifer Brundidge is a doctoral candidate in the Department of Communication at the University of California, Santa Barbara, U.S.A.

Andrew Chadwick is Professor of Political Science and Founding Director of the New Political Communication Unit at Royal Holloway, University of London, U.K.

Derrick L. Cogburn is an Assistant Professor of Information and Director of the Center for Research on Collaboratories and Technology Enhanced Learning Communities in the School of Information Studies, Syracuse University, U.S.A.

Stephen Coleman is Professor of Political Communication and Co-Director of the Centre for Digital Citizenship at the Institute of Communications Studies, University of Leeds, U.K.

Richard Davis is Professor of Political Science at Brigham Young University, Salt Lake City, U.S.A.

Ronald J. Deibert is an Associate Professor of Political Science and Director of the Citizen Lab at the Munk Centre for International Studies, University of Toronto, Canada.

William H. Dutton is Professor of Internet Studies at the University of Oxford, U.K., where he is Director of the Oxford Internet Institute and a Fellow of Balliol College.

Greg Elmer is Bell Globemedia Research Chair and Director of the Infoscape Research Lab, Ryerson University, Toronto, Canada.

Kenneth Neil Farrall is a doctoral candidate at the Annenberg School for Communication, University of Pennsylvania, Philadelphia, U.S.A.

Andrew J. Flanagin is an Associate Professor in the Department of Communication at the University of California, Santa Barbara, U.S.A.

Kirsten A. Foot is an Associate Professor of Communication at the University of Washington, Seattle, U.S.A.

Jane E. Fountain is Professor of Political Science and Public Policy and Director of the National Center for Digital Government at the University of Massachusetts, Amherst, U.S.A.

Peter L. Francia is an Assistant Professor in the Department of Political Science at East Carolina University, Greenville, U.S.A.

Oscar H. Gandy, Jr. is Emeritus Professor of Communication at the Annenberg School for Communication at the University of Pennsylvania, Philadelphia, U.S.A.

Rachel Gibson is Professor of Political Science at the Institute for Social Change, University of Manchester, U.K.

Kathleen Hall Jamieson is the Elizabeth Ware Packard Professor of Communication at the Annenberg School for Communication and Walter and Leonore Annenberg Director of the Annenberg Public Policy Center at the University of Pennsylvania, Philadelphia, U.S.A.

Bruce W. Hardy is a doctoral candidate at the Annenberg School for Communication, University of Pennsylvania, Philadelphia, U.S.A.

Philip N. Howard is Associate Professor in the Department of Communication at the University of Washington, Seattle, U.S.A.

Nicholas W. Jankowski is a Visiting Fellow, Virtual Knowledge Studio for the Humanities and Social Sciences, Royal Netherlands Academy of Arts and Sciences, Amsterdam, The Netherlands.

Yong-Chan Kim is an Assistant Professor of Health Communication in the Department of Community and Behavioral Health at the College of Public Health, University of Iowa, Iowa City, U.S.A.

Randolph Kluver is Director of the Institute for Pacific Asia and Research Professor of Communication at Texas A&M University, College Station, U.S.A.

Brian McNair is Professor of Journalism and Communication at the University of Strathclyde, U.K.

Helen Margetts is Professor of Society and the Internet at the Oxford Internet Institute and Professorial Fellow at Mansfield College, both at the University of Oxford, U.K.

Christopher May is Professor of Political Economy and Head of the Department of Politics and International Relations, Lancaster University, U.K.

Daniel Milton is a doctoral candidate at the Florida State University in Tallahassee, U.S.A.

Jonathan S. Morris is an Assistant Professor of Political Science at East Carolina University, Greenville, U.S.A.

Karen Mossberger is an Associate Professor in the Graduate Program in Public Administration, University of Illinois, Chicago, U.S.A.

Zizi Papacharissi is a Professor and Head of the Department of Communication at the University of Illinois-Chicago, U.S.A.

Malcolm Peltu is an Editorial Consultant to the Oxford Internet Institute, University of Oxford, U.K.

David J. Phillips is an Associate Professor of Information Studies at the University of Toronto, Canada.

Justin Reedy is a doctoral candidate in the Department of Communication at the University of Washington, Seattle, U.S.A.

Ronald E. Rice is the Arthur N. Rupe Professor of Communication and Co-Director of the Carsey-Wolf Center for Film, Television and New Media at University of California-Santa Barbara, U.S.A.

Jason Rittenberg is a doctoral candidate in Speech Communication at the University of Illinois, Urbana-Champaign, U.S.A.

Kenneth S. Rogerson is Lecturer in Public Policy Studies at the Sanford Institute of Public Policy at Duke University, U.S.A.

Steven M. Schneider is Professor of Political Science and Interim Dean of the School of Arts & Sciences at the SUNY Institute of Technology, U.S.A.

James Stanyer is Lecturer in Communication and Media Studies at Loughborough University, U.K.

Cynthia Stohl is Professor of Communication at the University of California, Santa Barbara, U.S.A.

David Tewksbury is an Associate Professor of Speech Communication at the University of Illinois, Urbana-Champaign, U.S.A.

Amoshaun Toft is a doctoral candidate in the Department of Communication at the University of Washington, Seattle, U.S.A.

Jan A. G. M. van Dijk is Professor of Communication Science at the University of Twente, The Netherlands.

Niels van Doorn is a doctoral candidate at the Amsterdam School of Communications Research and Junior Lecturer at the University of Amsterdam, The Netherlands.

Liesbet van Zoonen is Professor of Media and Popular Culture at the Universities of Amsterdam and Oslo.

Stephen Ward is a Senior Lecturer in Politics, European Studies Research Institute, University of Salford, U.K.

Chris Wells is a doctoral candidate in the Department of Communication at the University of Washington, Seattle, U.S.A.

Deborah L. Wheeler is Assistant Professor of Political Science at the United States Naval Academy in Annapolis, U.S.A.

Kenneth Winneg is Managing Director of the National Annenberg Election Survey, a project of the Annenberg Public Policy Center of the University of Pennsylvania, U.S.A.

Michael Xenos is an Assistant Professor in the Department of Communication Arts at the University of Wisconsin, Madison, U.S.A.

Preface to the paperback edition

The hardback edition of the *Handbook of Internet Politics* went to press just as the internet's role in politics took center stage with the victory of Barack Obama in the U.S. presidential election of November 2008. Several of the chapters in this volume deal explicitly with the causes and consequences of Obama's victory. Many offer insights and conceptual frameworks that will undoubtedly inform the scholarly analyses of the coming years. Still others remind us that, for all the glitz, excitement, and global media attention, understanding the political and policy implications of new media goes far beyond a single U.S. electoral contest. Yet however one chooses to look at it, the Obama campaign was a genuine phenomenon. The internet's role in creating and sustaining a modern political brand took many scholars, journalists, even the politicians themselves, by surprise. And the new administration has continued to innovate, sparking off a series of transparency reforms and online consultations that are reshaping the U.S. federal government.

Precisely one year on from voting day in 2008, it remains to be seen whether the Obama campaign and administration will provide a lasting or exportable model for political leaders in other countries. The fragmented and pluralistic institutional structure of the United States is unusual, even if only viewed in the context of the "first wave" democracies. A glance further afield, to authoritarian and semi-authoritarian contexts, presents even greater challenges for those who seek to generalize about the liberating effects of new media, as the failed 2009 uprising in Iran—fueled in part by dissidents' coordination via the online social network site Twitter—attests. We await the empirical detail—on Obama and on Iran—but it seems clear that the foreseeable future of political communication in many countries, including the United States, lies not in a single, easy-to-grasp model, but in hybridity: the blend of old and new behaviors, organizations, regulatory strategies, technologies, media forms and genres; the simultaneous concentration and dispersal of power; the complex adaptation of actors and institutions; reactions to, but also the shaping of the new, partly, but not wholly, in the image of the old.

The paperback edition was made possible by healthy sales of the hardback but it provides an opportunity for this book to reach a much broader readership. When we assembled the 31 specially-commissioned chapters, we anticipated that the volume would be adopted for courses and we designed a structure that we hoped would prove intuitive. A year on, we believe that the four broad thematic sections: institutions, behavior, identities, and law and policy, stand up well as a means of capturing the breadth, the diversity, and the emerging coherence, of scholarship on the internet and politics.

Andrew Chadwick
Philip N. Howard
London and Seattle
November 3, 2009

Acknowledgments

A handbook is impossible without the generosity and cooperation of its authors. We would like to thank all of the contributors for delivering their chapters and for responding so positively to our editorial recommendations. Thanks also to Craig Fowlie, commissioning editor at Routledge, as well as Natalja Mortensen and all of the publishing staff who worked hard to make this book happen.

Our home departments at Royal Holloway, University of London and the University of Washington have been generous in providing the time and space required to complete this project. The Whitely Center at the University of Washington's Friday Harbor Labs provided a quiet intellectual home for Howard to work, while the New Political Communication Unit at Royal Holloway provided Chadwick with a stimulating scholarly context.

Nick Anstead at Royal Holloway and Justin Reedy and Chris Wells at the University of Washington gave substantive feedback on over half of the contributions to this collection. Several anonymous external reviewers read chapters in draft form and gave useful commentary, often at very short notice, for which we are very grateful. Special gratitude must go to Nick Anstead, who provided crucial editorial assistance during the closing stages.

Lee Rainie at the Pew Internet and American Life Project has been a generous scholar, sharing data for the varied interests of several handbook contributors. The contributors to this collection have used data sets from many research projects, including Pew, but these projects bear no responsibility for the interpretations or conclusions made by contributors.

Last but by no means least, we would like to express immense gratitude to our wives, Sam Turner and Gina Neff, for their invaluable support, patience and tolerance of the occasionally crazy working schedules of two editors divided by eight time zones.

Introduction

New directions in internet politics research

Andrew Chadwick and Philip N. Howard

The politics of the internet has entered the social science mainstream. From debates about its impact on parties and election campaigns following momentous presidential contests in the United States, to concerns over international security, privacy and surveillance in the post-9/11, post-7/7 environment; from the rise of blogging as a threat to the traditional model of journalism, to controversies at the international level over how and if the internet should be governed by an entity such as the United Nations; from the new repertoires of collective action open to citizens, to the massive programs of public management reform taking place in the name of e-government, internet politics and policy are continually in the headlines. Welcome to the *Handbook of Internet Politics*: a collection of 31 chapters dealing with the most significant scholarly debates in this rapidly growing field of study.

About this book

This volume is concerned with the contemporary expression of voice and citizenship, political institutions and practices, and how the internet creates new policy problems or reinforces old ones. The volume is pluralistic in content but coherent in its thematic structure. Chapters are organized in four broad parts: Institutions, Behavior, Identities, and Law and Policy. This is the first publication of its kind to focus on the politics of (and on) the internet.

A handbook provides an excellent means of summarizing and criticizing contemporary debates but it should also point out new departures from the established literature. First, this collection provides a thematically organized overview of as many important areas of internet politics and policy as possible. Second, it presents readers with a survey of the state of the art in this field. Third, it functions as a means of punctuating the field's development—a chance to take stock and reflect on developments to date and future challenges for research. Fourth, it provides linkages to established theories of media and politics, political communication, governance, deliberative democracy and social movements, all within a context that is both interdisciplinary and focused on political phenomena. Finally, the contributors form a strong international cast and a mix of established and junior scholars.

The process of producing the book was designed to foster a blend of editorial guidance and author autonomy. As editors, we first defined the broad contours of the areas to be covered. We then approached authors for submissions. Once the final list of contributors had been established, we proceeded through a four-stage review process. Authors were invited to submit abstracts, and these were the subject of editorial feedback and suggestions. Next, first drafts were submitted. These received detailed editorial commentary, not only involving us as editors but also colleagues in our respective departments at Royal Holloway, University of London, and the University of Washington. Following this, authors submitted complete drafts. A final editorial exercise shortly before completion of the whole manuscript led to further alterations in the case of some of the chapters.

Our approach throughout has been to encourage authors to reflect upon the existing literature in their chosen area but also to advance their own arguments and analyses. An ideal handbook will push ahead with distinctive, original arguments and the discovery and manipulation of new data. In such a fast-moving area, it is essential to provide readers with a scholarly context but also a sense of how developments are unfolding and undermining received wisdom. Indeed, there is very little received wisdom in this field, and this is arguably what makes it so exciting.

The growth of a field of study

Over the last decade or so, scholarly analyses of the relationship between the internet and politics have grown at a remarkable rate. Figure 1.1 shows the results of a simple Boolean search against text contained in titles, abstracts or indexing keywords in the world's most important scholarly article database—the

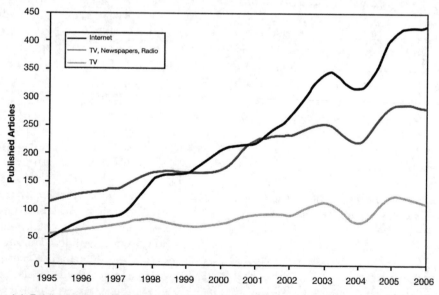

Figure 1.1 Published scholarly articles on political communication, 1995–2006.

Source: Authors' calculations from Boolean searches of article title, abstract and keywords: TS = (Internet OR web) AND TS = (politic* OR govern*); TS = (television OR newspaper* OR radio) AND TS = (politic* OR govern*); TS = (television) AND TS = (politic* OR govern*) in ISI Web of Science scholarly article database 1995–2006, November 8, 2007.

ISI web of science index. The chart shows the number of articles whose subject matter is the internet *or* web *and* politic★ *or* govern★. For comparison, results are also shown for the number of articles on television *or* newspapers *or* radio *and* politic★ *or* govern★, and for television *and* politic★ *or* govern★. The truncated words politic★ and govern★ are used to capture the range of words that have these as their root, such as politics, political, government, governance, and so on.

The first point here is that these are the results of tightly controlled searches against a highly specialized database of published articles in mainstream academic journals. Leaving aside the fact that many journals are not covered by the ISI, the index also does not include the thousands of books, book chapters, reports, working papers, and conference presentations that have been produced in this area over the last decade. Similarly explosive growth can be seen in searches of the press and periodicals database LexisNexis, as well as open search engine results, but these are not reported here because we cannot control for companies' decisions to change their indexing coverage.

The second point about Figure 1.1 relates to the comparator of new information and communications media: broadcast media and the press. While scholarship in these fields is vibrant, the rate of overall growth has been substantially slower than for the internet. The number of articles on the internet and politics exceeded those on broadcasting, the press, and pol-ics for the first time in 2000. By 2006, overall difference was substantial and inues to grow. The middle line nts article counts for three different television, newspapers, and radio) . Focusing on television alone, t is even greater. In 2006, 113 with television and politics, ere concerned with the litics. Opinion surveys still

report television
political medium,
popular medium of

This is, of course,
ready analysis. But ove
for those working in th
you are part of a rapidly
of scholarly endeavor, in
relative terms.

New directions in internet politics research

Despite this huge growth in scholarsi
when the internet first emerged as
popular communication medium (in the
developed world) few seemed to take it
seriously. It was often dismissed as a passing fad, a minority pursuit too dependent
upon specialist forms of technical knowledge, of far less importance than television
and the press, or a simple manifestation of
irrational exuberance in the financial
markets. Many commentators were intrigued by the new medium's capacity for
self-expression and its potential for disrupting social, political, and economic
relations, but there was a palpable "let's
wait and see" quality to the academic
discourse of the mid-1990s. Some scholars
dismissed this domain of research as seemingly without effect on the traditional
evidence of political science such as campaign spending, voter turnout, and public
opinion formation.

But over the course of a decade, this
context has arguably changed, as appreciation has grown of deeply rooted changes
in social, economic, cultural, and political
life in the advanced democracies. Many of
these changes are now rippling out to the
less wealthy regions of the globe, albeit in
highly uneven patterns.

In the developed countries, particularly
the Anglo-American world, important
subterranean shifts occurred as the internet
continued to diffuse at a remarkable rate

in th
duct
onli
po
to
b
a

early 2000s. People started to con-
important aspects of their lives
ne, as internet shopping, social sup-
t networks, and public services began
proliferate. All of this was underpinned
a reduction in the costs of computers
nd other networked devices and an
ncrease in the capacity of broadband telecommunications.

The first inkling that the political role
of the internet had been underestimated
came in late 2002 and early 2003. This
awareness was not caused by but coincided with the increasing frequency of the
word blog, both online and in the traditional media. While the roots of the blog
format date back to Dave Winer's Radio
UserLand self-publishing platform launched in 1997, it was not until 2002 that
blogging started to grow under the influence of new platforms such as WordPress
and Moveable Type.

The spectacular growth of blogging
and its associated offshoots soon led to the
invention of another term: Web 2.0.
Looking back over the last five years it
seems clear that there have been significant shifts in political uses of the
internet. Some may recoil at the adoption
of a term conceived by the entrepreneurial and technology community of Silicon
Valley, but even if they do not con-
sciously use the label, there is little doubt
in the minds of the majority of contributors to this volume that Web 2.0
does have substantive meaning and serves
as a useful term for a number of significant developments.

Politics: Web 2.0

Space limits preclude a full discussion of
Web 2.0 here, but this section highlights
its central features by building upon Tim
O'Reilly's (2005) seminal approach. For
good or ill, this is arguably the most
influential discussion of the term to date.

O'Reilly is regarded as the first to
publicly coin the term Web 2.0 in 2003.
This primarily technology-focused approach
defines it in terms of seven key principles
or themes. Some of these are more relevant to internet politics than others, and
some require extra theoretical work to
render them amenable to social science
investigation. Nevertheless, the seven principles are: the internet as a platform for
political discourse; the collective intelligence emergent from political web use; the
importance of data over particular software and hardware applications; perpetual
experimentalism in the public domain;
the creation of small-scale forms of political engagement through consumerism;
the propagation of political content over
multiple applications; and rich user experiences on political websites.[1] How might
these principles work as a means—both
literal and metaphorical—of sketching out
a first take on new directions in the realm
of internet politics research?

First, the internet as a platform for
political discourse. In essence, this theme
relates to the idea that the web has moved
from the older model of static pages
toward a means of enabling a wide range
of goals to be achieved through networked software services. The archetypal
Web 2.0 web as-platform service
course Google, whose value
almost entirely on its ab
wealth from the interf
advertising netwo
and its huge
Two ke
2.0

an
its s
Th
2006)
tribution

content creation and distribution. Traditionally, movie studios, publishers, and record companies tend to try to create small numbers of big-hit products because the sunk costs of developing a film, book, or album can be more quickly and predictably recouped. Similarly, real-space retail outlets (cinemas, city-center record stores, booksellers) can only afford to sell "hit" products because the relatively high cost of providing shelf or screen space for low-selling niche products makes it risky. Online distribution significantly reduces these costs, resulting in a sales/products curve with a large "head" and a long "tail" of niches. The internet thus contributes to a more diverse and pluralistic media landscape.

These web-as-platform principles can be seen at work in a range of political arenas. Elsewhere it has been argued that the 2004 primary and presidential campaign in the United States saw the emergence of a model of campaigning that relied upon a range of online venues loosely meshed together through automated linking technologies, particularly blogs, as well as face-to-face meetings coordinated via the user-generated Meetup site (Chadwick, 2007; Hindman, 2005). However, nowhere is the idea more strongly embodied than in the recent shift towards online social networking on platforms such as Facebook and MySpace. The symbolic moment came in January 2007, when John Edwards announced his candidacy for the Democratic presidential nomination via a brief and informal video posting on YouTube, but the U.S. midterms of November 2006 had already witnessed an explosion of political activity on social networking sites as well as the intensification of blogging by candidates and the long tail of amateur pundits.

The second theme of Web 2.0 is collective intelligence. The core idea here is that a distributed network of creators and contributors, the majority of them amateurs, can, using simple tools, produce information goods that may outperform those produced by so-called authoritative, concentrated sources. Examples of this abound, but two stand out as having caught the political imagination: free and open source software projects and user-generated content sites. The underlying model of online collaboration that produces these vast collections of human intelligence has been much debated. Opinions differ, for instance, over the extent to which hierarchy matters in these environments. Some, such as Weber (2004) suggest that it accounts for a great deal, while others, such as Weinberger (2007), downplay its importance. These debates aside, this theme points to the growth of a deeply voluntarist model of content creation and knowledge aggregation.

At a basic level, many of the most interesting and significant developments in online collective action have been enabled by free and open source software creations. This provides a perfect example of the elective affinity between political values and technological tools. Wikipedia itself has become a political battleground, as supporters of candidates, causes, groups, movements, even regimes, engage in incessant "edit wars" over entries. Beyond this, the principle animates politics in a variety of arenas. The blogosphere has enabled ongoing citizen vigilance on a grand scale. Political actors and media elites now exist in an always-on environment in which it is impossible to escape the "little brother" surveillant gaze of citizen-reporters. From Flickr photostreams of marches and demonstrations ignored by the mainstream media to bloggers such as Connecticut Bob, who took to the streets with his home movie camera to film Senator Joseph Lieberman's off-the-cuff remarks in the 2006 U.S. midterms, the media environment for politics has shifted.

The third principle of Web 2.0 concerns the importance of data. The central claim here is that the Web 2.0 era is characterized by the aggregation of huge amounts of information, and those who can successfully mine, refine, and subsequently protect it are likely to emerge as dominant. Most of these data have been created from the concentrated labor of volunteers (Andrejevic, 2002) or they may simply be the by-products of countless, coincidental interactions. But the key point is that informational value emerges from the confluence of distributed user-generated content and its centralized exploitation.

When used as an analytical lens for internet politics, this principle points to the ongoing importance of longstanding controversies surrounding privacy, surveillance, and the commercial and political use of personal information (Howard, 2006). The irony is that the celebrated freedom of political expression via self-publishing and the ease of connection facilitated in the social networking environments of Web 2.0 also offer a multitude of possibilities for automated gathering, sorting, and targeting. In the early days of the web political actors would often be heard complaining that they had "no control" over the online environment or that they did not know how to target particular groups or supporters (Stromer-Galley, 2000). The applications of Web 2.0 arguably render these tasks much more manageable, as individuals willingly produce and reveal the most elaborate information about their tastes and preferences within enclosed, proprietary technological frameworks. In the realm of political campaigns, social networking sites thus offer many advantages over the open web. For governments seeking to filter or control internet content, the advantages are also plain.

The fourth theme is perpetual experimentalism in the public domain. As indicated above, the attraction of O'Reilly's model is that it captures literal, quite narrow developments in technological practice but it can also be used at a metaphorical level to capture social and political behavior. Web 2.0 applications have been characterized by an unusual amount of public experimentalism. This is most obviously illustrated by the "perpetually beta" status of many of the popular services. While this is a reflection of the requirements of building and testing scalable web applications on meager resources, it also reflects something of a value shift away from tightly managed development environments towards those characterized by fluidity and greater collaboration between developers and users.

This sense of democratic experimentalism has of course been one of the driving values of the internet since its earliest days (Chadwick, 2006: 38–48). But Web 2.0 has seen it proliferate across a surprising range of political activities. Election campaigns in the United States are now characterized by obsessive and continuous recalibration in response to instant online polls, fund-raising drives, comments lists on YouTube video pages, and blog and forum posts. But perhaps a better example of the impact of the permanent beta in politics is the British prime minister's e-petitions initiative, "launched" in November 2006. At the time of writing, the site remains in beta, and will probably do so for some time to come, or until it metamorphoses into another application. Adding the beta stamp to an e-government initiative at the heart of the executive machinery of one of the world's oldest liberal democracies tells us just how far the penetration of internet values and working practices has gone.

The next two Web 2.0 themes—the creation of small-scale forms of political engagement through consumerism and the propagation of political content across multiple applications—are more specialized but still reveal important aspects of the new politics. Many data cannot be sealed off from public use because it would be politically unacceptable, or a business model might depend upon open access. A celebrated aspect of Web 2.0 is the mashing together of different data in pursuit of goals that differ from those originally intended. In political life, this practice often grants increased power to citizens. For example, British activist volunteer group mySociety has launched a number of sites, such as TheyWork ForYou.com and FixMyStreet.com, that combine publicly accessible government data with user-generated input. Theyrule. net allows users to expose the social ties among political and economic elites by mapping out the network structures of the corporate boards of multinational firms. Meanwhile, mobile internet devices are increasingly important, again with a distinct user-generated inflection through practices such as video and photoblogging, as well as mainstream news organizations' increasing reliance on amateur "witness reporters" as Stanyer argues in this volume.

The final theme is rich user experiences on political websites. In the narrow technical sense this refers to the development of applications designed to run code inside a web browser in ways that facilitate interactivity and the rapid retrieval, alteration, and storage of data. Most of the successful Web 2.0 applications combine such capabilities with back-end databases that store user generated content that can be modified by others. While valuable information is created by such actions, these are often not the result of heroic individual efforts but of aggregated small-scale, low-threshold forms of behavior: seemingly "happy accident" outcomes of thousands of individual interactions (Chadwick, 2007: 290). But these are not entirely accidental: many Web 2.0 systems are deliberately designed to capture aggregated data from even the most minimal of user activities. This occurs on sites that encourage users to create original content but which also offer readers the chance to rate it. To take just a couple of examples, highly rated pieces rise to the top of the recommended diaries feature on the *Daily Kos* home page, while MoveOn.org's Action Forum contains a similar mechanism for prioritizing issues.

Perhaps the most significant aspect of Web 2.0 politics as rich user experience has emerged in the form of online video. The explosion of user-generated video content in 2005 took most commentators by surprise. Past predictions of media convergence generally argued that an abundance of bandwidth would make the internet a more televisual, large-screen experience. There are developments in this area, with IPTV applications such as Joost and the BBC's iPlayer launching in 2007 on the basis of deals to stream large-screen quality video across adapted peer-to-peer networks. However, the main event in online video to date is the user-generated site YouTube, initially an independent company established by two individuals, but acquired by Google in early 2007 for $1.65 billion. YouTube may eventually metamorphose into a fully converged large-screen online "broadcasting" network, but the indications so far are that it will not. This is primarily because it has generated a huge regular user base that savors its small-screen, DIY format.

In the political sphere, YouTube has made a sizeable dent in earlier predictions of the emergence of slick, professionalized televisual online campaigns able only to be resourced by wealthy candidates and their campaign teams (Margolis and Resnick, 2000). This is clearly wide of the mark when both political elites and citizens perceive that the visual genres of an effective YouTube video do not depend upon professional media production techniques. The cynical may decry the rise of YouTube political campaigning on the grounds that it is inauthentic "spin" based on manufactured folksy imagery. In the United Kingdom, the Conservative Party leader David Cameron was widely criticized by the mainstream media for this approach on his site Webcameron, launched in 2006. And yet the impressionistic evidence suggests that the method attracts members of the public, evidenced by 28,000 postings within five months of that forum's launch in May 2007 (Webcameron.org, 2007). And in important ways, each new digital technology that captures public attention quickly becomes politicized. YouTube has become one of the most popular online applications, essentially a tool for content distribution by political campaigns.

Technologies may possess inherent properties that shape and constrain political norms, rules, and behavior, but these must be situated within political contexts (Chadwick, 2006: 17–21). The seven themes of Web 2.0 discussed above are by no means exhaustive and only begin to provide analytical purchase on the huge changes currently underway in internet politics. Yet it would be a mistake to dismiss Web 2.0 as the creation of marketing and public relations. All of the chapters in this collection provide tools for making sense of the sometimes remarkable pace of these recent changes, yet they do so while also recognizing the continuities with the internet's earlier phases. It remains for us to provide a brief outline of the book.

Outline of the book

In Part 1, on political institutions, Davis et al. chart the evolution of election campaigns in the United States and identify Web 2.0 networks as a new means of reaching out to voters. Ward and Gibson argue that the net is amplifying broader individualization and disaggregation trends—now obvious traits of the internet environment. Foot et al.'s work on elections outlines web production practices among political actors. Highly significant is that three of these—involving, connecting, and mobilizing—are explicitly interactive and feature politicians habitually integrating citizens into their campaigns in novel ways. Anstead and Chadwick provide a comparative institutional explanation for the proliferation of new styles of interactive campaigning in the United States and its fitful development in the United Kingdom. Bimber et al.'s communicative theory of collective action rests upon the huge diversity of organizing strategies now available to citizens and political leaders alike, while Coleman finds inspiration for e-democracy in the subversive data-mashing approaches of Web 2.0. Fountain considers interesting problems with interactive computer-mediated networks in government, while Margetts identifies, among other trends, the growing assumption that the storage of information produced by citizens themselves in the consumption of public services is of far greater value to government than top-down "second guesses."

Part 2 of the handbook examines political behavior. Hardy et al. focus on the internet's effects in enabling citizens to verify candidate statements via online fact checking—widely lauded as a central feature of the political blogosphere. Brundidge and Rice, and Reedy and Wells tackle its other much-discussed characteristics—balkanization of opinion and citizen engagement with political issues. Mossberger reminds us of the persistence of the digital divide but also highlights the huge changes in this area among the young and connected. Tewksbury and Rittenberg suggest how the diversity of news outlets available in the contemporary era leads to greater individual-level filtering of content, though not to the extent that had earlier been predicted. Finally in this part, Stanyer highlights the impact of citizen journalism on the production and consumption of news.

In Part 3, the focus shifts to political identities. McNair picks up where Stanyer left off but broadens the scope to illustrate the flattening hierarchies of global political communication in an era characterized by "cultural chaos." Papacharissi highlights the problematic but also liberating nature of citizen participation in Web 2.0 environments that subvert the solemnity of traditional political deliberation. Bennett and Toft suggest that the presentation and organization of political narratives is central to collective mobilization online, but citizens are still feeling their way in exploiting the potential of networks to leverage such narratives. Van Doorn and van Zoonen discuss shifts in gender representation and the rise of a participatory ethos but they also suggest that this is unlikely to require a wholesale reappraisal of gendered computer-mediated communication. Kim and Ball-Rokeach offer a nuanced understanding of the multiplicity of individuals' local and transnational connections by focusing on the case of immigrant communities. Van Dijk reminds us that persistent digital divisions shape life online in terms of motivation, physical access, skills, and usage, irrespective of the latest celebratory claims, while Wheeler outlines how citizen-produced content may be steadily reshaping daily life in Arab countries.

The final part of the volume deals with law and policy. Deibert's chapter punctures the new mythology of the participatory net by outlining how states monitor and control content. In a similar vein, Phillips reveals the infrastructure of mobile surveillance and the policy instruments and vertical controls that overlay seemingly horizontal information networks. Gandy and Farrall suggest how new modes of economic and social organization increasingly require new types of legal analysis in an environment in which traditional understandings of privacy and property are increasingly inadequate. May's chapter focuses on one of the central driving forces of the democratization of creativity: free and open source software, while Elmer highlights how older styles of online political communication such as the White House website, still of major importance for citizen information, are open to strategic manipulation by political elites. The final three chapters, by Dutton and Peltu, Cogburn, and Rogerson and Milton deal with the extent to which decisions taken in global forums or national policy bodies shape the kinds of online environment citizens are able to experience. The handbook ends with an editorial chapter summarizing the main findings and pointing out some potential areas for future inquiry.

Conclusion

In little more than a decade, the internet has evolved from a collaborative tool for scientists to become a fundamental part of our system of political communication. The production and consumption of politics today differs significantly from that of the 1990s, as does the scholarly vocabulary used for understanding contemporary political life. The 31 chapters in this handbook together offer a panoramic perspective on these new domains.

Note

1 O'Reilly's original principles are: "the web as platform"; "harnessing collective intelligence"; "data is the next 'Intel inside'"; "the end of the software release cycle"; "lightweight programming models"; "software above the level of a single device"; and "rich user experiences." See O'Reilly, 2005.

Part I

Institutions

2

The internet in U.S. election campaigns

Richard Davis, Jody C Baumgartner, Peter L. Francia, and Jonathan S. Morris

In recent years, candidate websites and other internet-based innovations have dramatically altered political campaigns for national office in the United States. The internet has improved the ability of campaigns to inform citizens, mobilize voters, and raise money from political donors. Websites have become only one of several weapons in a candidate's online arsenal. Blogs, podcasts, social networking sites, and YouTube also have become additional means to reach voters, particularly those who would not visit the website or have their name appear on an e-mail list. We explore the immediate implications that these and other changes have had for national campaigns, as well as the possibilities for the future.

The advent and popularization of the internet has generated a great deal of hype about its potential to invigorate electoral politics. Dick Morris, former advisor to President Clinton, suggested that a "fifth estate" of internet politics would alter the balance of political power in the United States by linking people together (Morris, 1999). The early success of Howard Dean's campaign on the internet led one journalist to ask in 2003, "what will happen when a national political machine can fit on a laptop?" (Ehrlich, 2003). Dean's campaign manager, Joe Trippi, claimed that the internet would do nothing short of revolutionize electoral politics (Trippi, 2004). Indeed, by 2006, the internet had changed the way candidates conduct campaigns. Congressional candidates were using the internet for fundraising, blogging, creating online communities, making video and audio clips available, and much more. In January of 2007, Hillary Clinton announced her run for the presidency on her website by way of a short video titled "Let the Conversation Begin."

This chapter examines the specific ways in which candidates and parties have used the internet in their campaigns. The main focus is on candidates for national office in the United States. The subject is important for several reasons. First, because it is a considerably less expensive medium than television, the internet holds the potential to level the playing field for outsider candidates and minor parties. Although major party candidates are still advantaged in terms of their ability to carry their message to the public (Margolis, Resnick, and Levy 2003), the existence of the internet as a campaign tool offers citizens more choice, thus potentially enhancing candidate options. Second, as an unfiltered medium, candidates and parties are able to "get their message out" through bypassing traditional media gatekeepers in order to reach groups of interested voters (Graber, 2006). The internet is also a sophisticated and relatively inexpensive communications tool that like-minded citizens, candidate, and party organizations can use to interact with each other and mobilize support.

To begin, we review the short history of internet campaigning, focusing on how the use of the medium has evolved. We divide this discussion into three sections, each corresponding to a particular phase of the development of internet campaigning. In the discovery phase, which dates from about 1992 until 1999, candidates, parties, and groups began experimenting with the internet and exploring its possible electoral uses. By the presidential campaign of 2000, the internet campaign had reached a maturation phase. At that point, the vast majority of major-party candidates for federal elections, and many state-level candidates, maintained websites throughout the campaign. Political campaign websites no longer lagged behind their commercial counterparts in terms of interactivity, integration of server-side and database technologies, and aesthetic sophistication.

Internet campaigns entered yet another phase in the 2006 congressional election cycle and this continued through the 2008 presidential campaign. By this time, virtually all serious candidates for national political office had fairly sophisticated websites that professionals maintained. In this new phase, candidates, parties, and interest groups have turned their attention beyond their own websites to other venues. Campaign organizations, in particular, have begun to carry the campaign to blogs, social networking sites such as Facebook, and other quasi-media forums such as YouTube.

Discovery: experimentation and exploration

George H. W. Bush and Bill Clinton were the first presidential candidates to make use of the internet during their 1992 campaigns. During the election, the White House Communications Office e-mailed approximately 200 Bush speeches and position papers, and distributed them to several commercial bulletin boards (Bradley, 1993). Clinton was more aggressive in his use of the medium, distributing speeches, position papers, and biographical information on various newsgroups and a Clinton Listserv. He also made his e-mail address for the campaign available through commercial internet service providers, such as Compuserv (Sakkas 1993; Bimber and Davis 2003: 23). However, the reach of these electronic campaign efforts was limited, as few citizens used or relied on the internet for their political information.

In March of 1995, the Republican National Party registered the domain name "rnc.org," and the Democrats followed with "dnc.org" the following month. During that same year, several Republican candidates for president, including Lamar Alexander, Phil Gramm, and Steve Forbes, built websites for the primary campaign. The eventual nominee, Bob Dole, and the Clinton–Gore re-election campaign had websites, although their internet campaign operations were still under the radar in most respects. This changed after the first presidential debate, when during his closing statement, Dole invited viewers to become involved in the campaign by giving the address of his campaign's website. Although technically he erred by saying "www.dolekemp96org" rather than "www.dolekemp96.org," the site received more than two million visitors in the following 24 hours (Cornfield, 2004a: 3).

By 1998, more than two-thirds of all congressional candidates maintained websites for their campaign, and many state party organizations had established an online presence as well. Most of these early campaign websites were little more than "brochureware." They offered little interaction and were not updated often (Bimber and Davis, 2003: 24). However, they did offer a wealth of information (for example, platforms, issue positions, and so on) through a new and growing medium (Francia and Herrnson, 2002).

In addition to websites, campaigns began to make greater use of e-mail communications. Former professional wrestler Jesse Ventura drew from existing networks of professional wrestling fans and Reform Party activists to build an e-mail network of more than 3,000 supporters. His Minnesota gubernatorial online campaign was able to facilitate registration and get-out-the-vote efforts, and the coordination of campaign events and rallies. While this was not exactly interactive web technology, it did suggest the potential for using the internet to mobilize support.

Maturation

By the election of 2000, political campaign websites were no longer a novelty, and by 2004, the overwhelming majority of congressional, gubernatorial, and presidential candidates maintained websites (Howard, 2006: 26–8). In this maturation phase, campaign websites began to include many of the features that sophisticated commercial websites offer. For example, in 2000, the Gore–Lieberman site featured an "Instant MessageNet" for online chatting. In 2004, George W. Bush allowed visitors to ask questions to his campaign staff in real time in the site's "State of the Race." Many campaign websites now routinely include interactive features or games. Bush's 2004 site included a "Kerry Gas Tax Calculator" that allowed visitors to see how much John Kerry's proposed 50 cent per gallon gas tax would cost them. Within this maturation phase, the internet supplemented campaign efforts in four different functions: campaign operations, communication, mobilization, and fund-raising.

General campaign operations

The internet allows the campaign to gather various types of information that are useful to the campaign effort. This includes possibly damaging information about the campaign's own candidate (Baumgartner, 2000: 1), background material on the opponent (personal and public life, voting, speeches), as well as developments in polling, endorsements, statements by other public figures, and information about the various legal and technical requirements associated with running for public office. Campaign staffs previously acquired this information by other, less efficient means. With the rise of the internet, however, the process has become much easier and more convenient. Campaign information sources include news services such as LexisNexis, as well as standard internet news monitoring techniques like RSS news feeds and search engines.

Another aspect of general campaign operations conducted via the internet is the distribution of various campaign materials, such as posters, buttons, bumper stickers, and clothing. In 2000, for example, Al Gore's online store for these materials was called "Gore Stores." In 2004, Kerry sold campaign products from a section of his website labeled "Kerry Gear." President Bush had a section called "Wstuff," which in addition to traditional campaign materials, included a reading list, computer screen-savers and wallpapers, and a section to create and print a customized campaign poster.

Campaign communications

Political campaigns are fundamentally exercises in communicating a simple message: "vote for me," or, "don't vote for my opponent." Candidate home pages serve multiple purposes in this regard. Most home pages post the candidate's personal and professional biographies and information about the candidate's family. Under a heading labeled "Get to Know Us," the front page of the 2000 Gore–Lieberman website (algore.com) featured small photos of each of the candidates and their wives linked to their respective biographies. Front pages typically include contact information for the campaign, including toll-free telephone numbers and e-mail addresses. Most also have other standard website features, including, for example, a way for visitors to search the site or to send a link to the site to someone.

Candidate home pages further allow for more targeted advertising. Sites typically have links to related or friendly campaign organizations, such as party affiliates or major interest or advocacy groups. Presidential candidate websites can provide state and local information about campaign events, as well as disseminate unique information about voter registration and early voting in all 50 states. In another form of targeted advertising, the major-party presidential candidates in 2004 allowed users to select Spanish versions of their website. Both campaigns had sections on their websites dedicated to demographic groups they were courting. Kerry called these groups "Communities." Bush referred to them as "Coalitions," devoting sections on the site to the concerns of women, African Americans, Catholics, educators, first responders, health professionals, Hispanics, seniors, small business owners, sportsmen, students, veterans, and more.

Campaign websites also provide information about the policy positions of the candidate, which include statements of issue positions, rebuttals of charges from the opposition, speeches, and campaign pamphlets. Frequently these materials are made available in printer-friendly or downloadable formats, reminiscent of campaign books of previous eras. Howard Dean's December 2003 "Common Sense for a New Century," an eight-page manifesto "addressed to the Citizens of America," was one such example. It is also common for campaign websites to have a section devoted to why voters should *not* vote for the opposition. In 2004, for example, John Kerry's "Bush–Cheney: Wrong for America" section, which was linked to a "Rapid Response Center," outlined his case for why voters should oust the incumbent president. Bush's "Kerry Media Center" performed a similar function and included rebuttals to Kerry's positions.

Another way the internet aids in campaign communication is via e-mail. One reason e-mail is invaluable is because it allows campaigns to communicate *internally*. Of course, there are other technologically advanced communications (cell phones, text messaging), but an e-mail from a campaign manager can reach thousands of employees and volunteers easily, quickly, and cheaply.

E-mail also can keep supporters informed about the campaign, alert them to upcoming events, candidate appearances, and circulate rapid rebuttals in response to opposition attacks or press reports. For example, in his 1998 bid for Governor of Minnesota, Jesse Ventura relied on e-mail to his supporters to debunk a rumor that had been spread that he supported legalized prostitution (Cornfield, 2004a: 67–8). In early January of 2000, John McCain e-mailed supporters requesting that each make ten phone calls to registered independents or Republicans in New Hampshire; more than nine thousand did so. McCain also used e-mail to ask supporters to preview radio ads before they aired (Cornfield 2004a: 69–70). It is now standard for campaign organizations (candidates, parties) to maintain lists of e-mail addresses of supporters. Visitors to the campaign website can opt in or "subscribe" to a campaign newsletter, entering an e-mail address and other information (for example, name, mailing address, phone number, age). Michael Turk, Bush's 2004 e-Campaign Director, claimed that the campaign collected more than seven million e-mail addresses using this method (Jenkins, 2004). With the additional information, campaigns can "narrowcast" messages, personalizing them to groups of individuals based on various characteristics.

Mobilization

Mobilization is a specialized form of political communication, an attempt to do more than just inform, but to engage supporters to act. One mobilization tool that political campaigns employ is the blog. Blogs connect supporters with the candidate, the campaign, and each other, providing them with an arena in which to voice their opinions. In addition, the hypertext format allows writers to link to other stories relevant to the campaign. The most well publicized use of blogs in a campaign effort was Howard Dean in 2003. The Dean campaign directly or indirectly supported and moderated several blogs throughout 2003 and into 2004, including "Dean Nation" (dean2004.blogspot.com), "Change for America" (www.changeforamerica.com), "Howard Dean 2004 Call to Action Weblog" (deancalltoaction.blogspot.com), and what was to become his main blog, "Blog for America" (blogforamerica.com). Dean even parlayed his blog into a forum for decision-making in his campaign.

Dean's blogs were updated daily (and sometimes more often) with journal entries, photos, audio, and video clips (Trippi, 2004: 16–17). On a single day in late December 2003, the Dean campaign posted roughly 400 messages to their "Blog for America," which in turn prompted more than 4,000 comments over the next 24 hours (Stromer-Galley and Baker, 2006). This activity helped propel Dean from a largely unknown candidate in early 2003 to the presumed front-runner for the nomination by the end of 2004. By the time polling began in the Iowa caucuses, the Dean campaign estimated it had the support of approximately 600,000 online activists (Manjoo, 2003; 2004).

The Dean campaign ultimately did not win the nomination. In fact, Dean won a primary in only one state—Vermont. The Dean campaign's failure illustrated the drawbacks of using online discussion as a substitute for outreach to undecided voters. Even though Dean was able to appeal strongly to his online supporters, his base was simply too small a proportion of the primary electorate.

Dean's initiatives, however, did affect other campaigns' use of blogs. George Bush and John Kerry had official blogs linked from their campaign websites in 2004 (Trammell, 2006). Many of the candidates for president in 2008 also had blogs up and running as early as March 2007.

Another way that the internet aids in mobilization is by helping supporters find local campaign events, ways to volunteer on a local basis, or other ways to become involved in the campaign effort. In 2000, Al Gore had a section on his website called "Take Action," which provided visitors the opportunity to select their state and their "coalition" (group), and returned suggestions about how they might help the campaign based on those selections. Gore also gave supporters the opportunity to build their own Gore-for-president web page by joining the "Gore I-Team." The 2004 campaign website of John Kerry featured a section labeled "Get Local," in which visitors could get state-specific information on how to get involved in the campaign (Postelnicu et al., 2006). Likewise, the Bush campaign had a "Grassroots" section on its website, designed to build networks of people who would canvass their neighborhoods

(Ceasar and Busch, 2005: 133–4). The efforts were based on a model used in the 2000 Iowa caucuses and the 2002 congressional elections in South Dakota. Volunteers were given the opportunity to become a "team leader" by recruiting ten additional people. Daily communications from national team leaders supported and informed these local leaders (Lowry, 2004). Approximately 1.4 million volunteers were recruited in this manner (Lizza, 2002).

Fund-raising

The presidential primaries of 2000 demonstrated the potential of using the internet as a fund-raising tool. New Jersey Senator Bill Bradley, a candidate for the Democratic Party presidential nomination, was the first candidate to raise one million dollars online. Even more impressive was the internet fund-raising of John McCain, who was vying for the Republican Party nomination. At the time of the New Hampshire primary, McCain was virtually out of money. His surprising win, however, coupled with the publicity generated from it and an online appeal for donations, helped him raise more than one-half million dollars in online donations in a single day (Bimber and Davis, 2003: 38–9).

Online donations have become increasingly important because the current campaign finance system encourages small donations from a multitude of sources. The small donations McCain received from online donations after his New Hampshire victory, in conjunction with federal matching funds, enabled him to raise a large amount of money very quickly. While McCain eventually lost his bid to secure the Republican nomination, he raised $6.4 million online, or about one-quarter of the total amount the campaign raised (Cornfield, 2004b: 66–7; Howard, 2006: 13–14). In 2003, Howard

Dean raised an enormous amount of money through internet donations. Altogether Dean raised approximately $20 million solely online, roughly 40 percent of his entire campaign funding (Postelnicu *et al.*, 2006: 105). What makes these totals more impressive is that his campaign was over fairly early in the primary season. George Bush raised approximately $14 million online, only about 5 percent of his total campaign funding. John Kerry, on the other hand, raised $89 million online, a healthy one-third of his total (Postelnicu *et al.*, 2006: 105).

In terms of their demographic profile, online donors tend to be middle-class, fairly well educated, and politically active. Disproportionate numbers of online donors, for example, attended a house party or Meetup.com event. Online giving seems to have become the preferred method of donating to a campaign. Significantly better than half of both small and large donations were made online by all age groups except seniors (those over 65). Small donors between the ages of 18 and 34 overwhelmingly gave online (87 percent) (Graf *et al.*, 2006).

In terms of online fund-raising strategy, some lessons can be gleaned from the presidential campaign of 2004. One comprehensive study suggests that Democrats were more successful at raising money online. Twice as many donors who gave $500 or more gave to Democratic rather than Republican Party candidates (64 percent to 31 percent), and the disparity between the two parties was even greater with respect to those who contributed $100 or less (54 percent to 19 percent). The study speculates that this was in part due to the fact that many of Dean's supporters migrated to Kerry's candidacy after the primaries. In addition, Kerry was forced to be somewhat more aggressive in his fund-raising efforts given the financial advantage of the incumbent President Bush (Graf *et al.*, 2006).

However, online giving remains unpredictable. Approximately half (46%) of all small donors and more than one-third (39%) of large donors contributed without being asked (Graf *et al.*, 2006). The implications of this for future fund-raising strategy are unclear. It does seem safe to conclude that candidates who can capture the imagination of the electorate (e.g., underdog candidates Bill Bradley and John McCain) or appeal to a politically active base (e.g., Howard Dean or Ned Lamont in 2006) will enjoy more success raising money online.

Post-maturation: beyond the candidate website

Since the initiation of candidate websites, campaigns have realized the limited reach of this medium. Websites reach those who actively visit them, and those who visit them are a relatively small percentage of the electorate. Moreover, those who visit candidate websites are existing supporters rather than the "undecided" voters who can often swing an election (Bimber and Davis, 2003). While e-mail has the potential to expand beyond the narrow reach of a website because it does not rely on a site visit and "pushes" its message, it is constrained by a subset of supporters (spam blockers prevent widespread distribution of e-mail messages, and, if they do not, candidates face the wrath of voters who punish spammers).

How, then, do candidates go beyond the self-selection problem that limits exposure to their message to those who already intend to vote for the candidate? What are the means by which they can reach voters—and even activists—who are not site visitors or e-mail recipients?

Campaigns have reached out beyond their own websites to two other types of internet-based political communication tools: media controlled and user controlled.

The next section describes each of them, as well as their variations, and then discusses how candidates are using them to present themselves to voters.

Media-controlled online communication

Media-controlled online communication refers to websites disseminating news and information to a relatively large number of voters, but which a third party controls. One type is the traditional news media website (for example, ABCnews. com, Foxnews.com). In terms of the news functions, candidates approach the online versions much as they do the traditional print or broadcast versions.

A growing area of interest for candidates is advertising on media-controlled sites. internet advertisements cost only a fraction of what advertising on television costs. Because the audiences for such sites are likely voters, candidates have steadily increased the share of their advertising budget devoted to online advertising. In 2004, both presidential candidates produced and distributed many of the "banner" ads (small rectangular advertisements that appear on a web page that lead visitors to the advertiser's website). For example, by the spring of 2004, the Republican National Committee placed banner ads that attacked John Kerry's war record on more than 1,000 different websites (Kaid, 2006). Both the Bush and Kerry campaigns directed most of their internet ad buys to local news organizations (television, radio, newspaper). One study suggests that almost 70 percent of Bush's internet ads, and 60 percent of Kerry's, appeared in venues like these (Cornfield, 2004b). Also popular were the websites of national periodicals and blogs.

Online campaign advertising increased by more than 700 percent between 2002 and 2006 (PQMedia, 2006). Twenty-nine candidates or party organizations advertised online in the last week of 2006, but the number of online ad impressions bought (approximately 4 million) was small compared to 2004. However, the 2006 election lacked a presidential race (Kaye, 2006). The 2008 presidential campaign featured early advertising, including online advertising, by major contenders.

A newer relationship is between candidates and another form of media-controlled website, the blog. In addition to candidate-controlled blogs or blogs started by an individual, there are also more popular and well-known political blogs such as Daily Kos or InstaPundit. These blogs constitute a new type of online information that is beginning to rival some existing traditional media sites in readership size and loyalty. Moreover, much like traditional media, many of their writers—bloggers—have journalistic status, gaining special entrance to political events such as national party conventions, and candidate and policy-maker press briefings. These bloggers serve a political news dissemination function, and, most importantly, candidates court them regularly.

Politics is not the primary topic in the blogosphere, but national political blogs have acquired a niche and an expanding readership. Some national political blogs reach hundreds of thousands of people, and political blog readership is approaching the size of the traditional news media audience. Daily Kos has approximately one half million visits per day. InstaPundit, Eschaton, and CrooksAndLiars each have more than one hundred thousand visits daily. By comparison, the daily circulation of the *Los Angeles Times* is 775,000 (Ahrens, 2006b).

Political blogs offer the opportunity to reach well beyond the campaign's website. By placing information with blogs or, even better, currying the support of high-profile bloggers, candidate campaigns hope to tap into the millions of Americans who read blogs. Candidates have started to

learn to give exclusives to blogs in order to gain the goodwill of bloggers who see themselves as the underdogs in competition with the traditional news media.

However, candidates do not treat political bloggers quite like other media. Unlike journalists, bloggers sometimes join campaigns as consultants. In return for a consulting fee, bloggers become advocates of a particular campaign. Much like the partisan press of the late 1700s and early 1800s, bloggers are willing to establish a relationship with candidates that traditional journalists would eschew. One current debate in internet campaigning regards the ethical question of whether bloggers should reveal any financial connection to a campaign when writing about that candidate and their opponents.

Candidates must be wary of establishing relationships with bloggers, given that blogging can be quite shrill and feature extreme and flagrantly abusive language. Even when a blogger tones down rhetoric to accommodate the campaign, another problem is the transparency of the past history of blog posts. Many blogs include archives on their sites, allowing easy access to journalists, interest groups, or other campaigns that wish to locate material that a blogger has written, which might embarrass the candidate through association.

Indeed, candidates already have faced such a situation. For example, in 2006, a Catholic group accused two bloggers, working for presidential candidate John Edwards, of posting anti-Catholic statements on their personal blogs. At first, the Edwards campaign made a decision not to terminate the bloggers, although it did separate itself from their statements. Eventually, however, both bloggers resigned as the controversy continued to swirl around them (Broder, 2007).

Relations with bloggers can be especially problematic for a moderate candidate. A candidate with rather extreme political views can appeal to a larger blogging community than a candidate with centrist positions. One example is the contrast between Joseph Lieberman and Ned Lamont. Lieberman aroused the wrath of liberal Democrats, including bloggers, when he supported the Iraq war and continued to do so even when Democrats (and even some Republicans) had largely abandoned that position. Lamont, Lieberman's primary opponent in the Connecticut Democratic Senate primary, acquired broad support from liberal bloggers who favored Lamont's liberal stances. When Lamont won the primary election, many political observers credited the activities of liberal bloggers for his victory. Although Lieberman later defeated Lamont in the general election, the primary election outcome suggested that bloggers may be helpful to more ideologically polarizing candidates within intraparty nomination contests.

User-controlled online communication

One of the features of the internet is the potential for self-publishing. At its inception, this was one of its much-heralded characteristics. However, the audience for an individual's website was rarely more than family or friends. But a new medium for self-publishing—the social networking site—has enhanced the reach of the practice. Online forums such as YouTube, Flickr, MySpace, and Facebook have centralized self-publishing efforts and brought large audiences to such portals. These types of sites have recently begun to have an impact on political campaigns.

Perhaps the best known online site for self-publishing is YouTube, a website that allows people to upload videos for general viewing. The growth of YouTube's audience has been phenomenal. In a six-month period in 2006, the number of unique site visitors grew by 300 percent.

In July 2006, an estimated 19.6 million visitors went to the YouTube website ("YouTube U.S. Web Traffic Grows 75 Percent Week over Week"). A visit to YouTube usually is not a quick one; because site visitors spend time browsing videos (many of them lengthy) the average visit is 28 minutes (Cornfield, 2006).

YouTube has become the one-stop source for popular videos about politics. The site even created a separate section for political campaign videos for the 2008 presidential campaign (Vargas, 2007a). Videos posted there largely consisted of candidate ads from the campaigns themselves. The most popular candidate videos seem to be those in which the candidate says or does something not intended for viewing (e.g., videos of Hillary Clinton singing the national anthem off-key, or John McCain sleeping through the State of the Union address). Controversial advertisements, such as actor Michael J. Fox's appeals to voters to reject candidates who were against government funding for stem cell research, or the racially charged negative advertisement against Senate candidate Harold Ford in Tennessee, were also popular.

Of course, journalists have sought to catch candidates in embarrassing positions for years. Examples from an earlier era include a comment made by 1968 Republican candidate George Romney to a television journalist that he had been brainwashed by the U.S. military while visiting Vietnam (Sabato, 1991), Ronald Reagan's 1984 joke caught on an open mike that "we start bombing [the Soviet Union] in fifteen minutes" (Taylor, 1984), or news stories that emphasized George H. W. Bush's mistake in calling September 7 Pearl Harbor Day in 1988 ("Bush Trips in Speech" 1988).

Ever-present video recording devices have increased candidate exposure to an unprecedented level, and the existence of YouTube democratizes "gotcha journalism" by allowing anyone who catches a candidate or politician off guard to self-publish the gaffe. The problem is not limited to a candidate doing or saying something in an off moment. An old video could highlight the candidate making a speech or speaking in a debate and contradicting his or her position on an issue. An example is a YouTube video of Mitt Romney giving a speech in an earlier campaign touting his pro-choice position on abortion and his support for gun control (Finnegan, 2007). By 2008, presidential candidate Romney had changed his positions, but YouTube has been there to remind voters of his previous position.

Campaigns can, it should be noted, use YouTube to their advantage. They can, for example, upload videos touting their own candidate (Jalonick, 2006). Placing a campaign ad on YouTube enhances audience exposure at no cost to the campaign. Campaigns also are using the reality characteristic of YouTube to trip up their opponents. Campaigns now hire staffers to follow their opponent with a video camera to record candidate gaffes and post the video online (Jalonick, 2006). The most famous example in 2006 was the Jim Webb staffer who followed Senator George Allen and became part of the story himself. When Allen made reference to the Webb staffer by using the term "macaca," the staffer was recording Allen's remarks. The staffer uploaded the video to YouTube, and then the campaign informed local and national journalists on where to view it. With journalists' assistance, the "macaca" video was able to reach millions of Virginia voters, as well as tens of millions of others watching around the nation. The video became a national story that forced the Allen campaign into defensive mode from which it never recovered (Lizza, 2006). Ultimately, Allen lost the race.

Another forum within user-controlled media is one commonly called a "social networking site." These are web portals where users can create their own web pages and link to the "profiles" of others. Social networking sites are used to conduct conversations, express opinions, keep journals, display photos, and so on. Many such sites exist, but the two best known of this growing genre are MySpace and Facebook. These have acquired a large following, particularly among young people. According to the Pew Research Center, 54 percent of young people aged 18–25 have used one or more of these sites. In addition, 76 percent of young people visit them at least once a week (Pew Research Center for the People and the Press, 2007), and spend an average of about two hours per visit (Noguchi, 2006).

The growth of online social networking has been dramatic. In its first 30 months of existence, MySpace filled to 124 million profiles. Facebook (the newer site) acquired nine million members in two years and was already the target of a billion dollar buyout offer by a media conglomerate (Ahrens, 2006a).

Candidates have discovered the political uses of these sites. In 2006, several candidates created profiles on MySpace and Facebook including Sherrod Brown, Claire McCaskill, and Ned Lamont. All the major presidential candidates for 2008 did so. Not only do candidates create their own sites, but supporters also create sites and groups in support of their favored candidate. At about the time Barack Obama announced his candidacy for president, there were already more than 500 Obama groups on Facebook. These groups devoted their space to discussing the Obama campaign, posting photos of Obama, and spreading news about their favored candidate (Vargas, 2007b). While candidates may not control such sites, they can benefit from them. Chris DeWolfe, one of the founders of MySpace, called them "digital yard signs, for lack of a better term" (Williams, 2007).

Supporter networks also becomes a gauge for others (such as the press and other site visitors) to measure the appeal of a candidate. While candidates popular with young people, such as Barack Obama or John Edwards, gain widespread support, more traditional candidates appear to lag in attractiveness to this audience. For example, when the 2008 presidential campaign began with a flurry of announcements in early 2007, Barack Obama already had 64,000 "friends" on MySpace, while Hillary Clinton's site only registered 25,000 (Williams, 2007).

One problem with online social networking as a campaign tool, however, is the demographic of the audience and their potential to affect the candidate's chances of victory. These sites attract the least participatory age group (18–24) in terms of voter turnout. However, they can be effective for volunteer recruitment given that young people often become the foot soldiers for political campaigns.

The social networking concept has migrated onto official candidate websites as well. For example, on Barack Obama's site, visitors can create their own profile, link to friends, and join groups just as they would on a commercial site. In addition, user-controlled media are even linked from candidate websites. The Obama campaign linked YouTube, Facebook, and Flickr, while the Edwards campaign linked all of those in addition to MySpace, Gather, del.icio.us, and a dozen others. The Edwards campaign's site made a point of saying the candidate had a presence on all of these social networks.

Conclusion

The internet is not television. Despite the hype, it has not changed campaigning in the same way. For example, unlike television ads that reach potentially tens of million of voters in the midst of entertainment programming, an average campaign website attracts a relatively small audience that chooses to go to and use that resource. However, that does not mean the internet has no value in a campaign. By using the internet for research, communicating with supporters and activists, mobilizing voters, and raising funds, campaigns have carved out a critical niche for the website. The modern campaign for president and Congress relies on the website to perform tasks such as volunteer mobilization, fund-raising, and supporter reinforcement more efficiently and inexpensively than other means in the past.

As this chapter has shown, websites have become only one of several weapons in a candidate's online arsenal. Blogs, podcasts, social networking sites, and YouTube also have become additional means to reach voters, particularly those who would not visit the website or have their name appear on an e-mail list. Of course, beyond some anecdotes, it is still largely unknown whether these new technologies can play a decisive role in determining the success or failure of a campaign. However, what is clear is that candidates and their campaigns will continue to experiment with these new technologies in order to discover if they are capable of having a major impact on election outcomes.

Guide to further reading

Since the mid 1990s, there has been a plethora of published works that examined the effects of the internet on campaigns and political participation in general in the United States. Some of these works have operated as instructional guides for how citizens can use the inherently democratic nature of the internet to circumvent traditional forms of political participation (see Browning, 2001; Davis *et al.*, 2002; Kush, 2000). A wide range of work then examined whether the internet had an effect on political participation. Some argued that participation had been positively influenced and that the prospects for the future of internet democracy were bright (Grossman, 1995; Morris, 1999). Other work (often grounded more in empirical data), found the internet to be much less consequential (Davis, 1999; Margolis and Resnick, 2000; Wilhelm, 2000), or even dangerous (Putnam, 2000; Sunstein, 2001) regarding the public's influence on democratic engagement. More recent research has also examined virtual political participation via blogs, chat rooms, and instant messaging (see Davis, 2005).

The debate surrounding the broader participatory influences of the internet gave way to empirical research that specifically has examined the medium in the context of campaigns. From the American national perspective, Bimber and Davis (2003) offer an overview of this topic, as does Chadwick (2006) and Foot and Schneider (2006). Williams and Tedesco (2006) also provide a comprehensive view of the internet's role in the 2004 presidential election. On a wider scale, Kluver *et al.*'s (2007) recent edited volume takes a cross-national comparative look at the internet and elections, and concludes that the internet has had significant electoral influences worldwide.

3

European political organizations and the internet

Mobilization, participation, and change

Stephen Ward and Rachel Gibson

Much has been written about the supposed decline of the traditional vehicles of political activity in European democracies, especially parties and trade unions, and the corresponding rise of new forms of political organization: single issue campaigns, new social movements, and radical direct action protest. This chapter explores the impact of the internet on such trends. In particular, it analyzes the role of information and communication technologies (ICTs) in the intra- and interorganizational arenas. In the case of the former, it examines the use of ICTs to mobilize support and sustain activism through helping organizations reach new audiences and deepen levels of engagement. In the case of the latter it analyzes the impact of ICTs on organizational competition, to see how far it is increasing pluralism and changing the traditional parameters of representative democracy. To date, the empirical evidence outside North America has been somewhat limited, but it suggests that new technologies are facilitating changes in both arenas, though not necessarily in a uniform manner. Early evidence indicates a deepening of activism among the already engaged, but only a marginal mobilization role in relation to new audiences. Overall, ICTs appear to be accelerating some of the trends of the pre-internet era such as individualization and disaggregation. Finally, the chapter discusses the drivers of, and barriers to, organizational responses to new technologies.

This chapter discusses the role of European political organizations (parties, trade unions, pressure groups and new social movements) in mobilizing the public and how far the arrival of new ICTs is helping to reshape such organizations, both in terms of their internal organization and, more broadly, as vehicles for political participation.[1] In particular, the chapter has three aims. First, it provides a context for organizational development in the internet era by discussing trends in organizational mobilization. It assesses how far traditional collective forms of mobilization are in decline and whether new forms of collective participation via loose protest networks and direct action are replacing traditional representative politics. Second, it examines the potential impact of the internet on political organizations from both an intra- and interorganizational perspective. Have new ICTs provided for additional organizational pluralism by allowing fringe causes a louder voice in European political systems? Do new technologies streamline organizational hierarchies and provide for greater internal democracy? Third, it analyzes the factors shaping the strategies underlying political organizations' ICT usage. Since ICTs can be used for a variety of different purposes, ranging from information storage to promoting interactive participation, the chapter seeks to develop an explanatory framework from which expectations of organizational behavior can be derived: what types of political organization will use the technology most extensively, and to what ends?

Representative democracy and political organizations: decline and crisis?

Increasingly, the idea of representative democracy is being questioned from a variety sources. While some talk excitedly of a new era in politics (Mulgan, 1997), others bemoan declining interest and engagement in democratic politics (Putnam, 2000). Critics and supporters of representative democracy have noted apparently declining levels of political interest, electoral turnout, participation, and trust in the system (Dalton, 2004; Putnam, 2000; Gray and Caul, 2000). It has been suggested that increasing individualism, freedom of choice, and the rise of a consumer society has meant that citizens have become more demanding and less willing to allow others to make decisions on their behalf. European publics have become used to being offered choices and products to match their individual preferences, but political systems have been slow to catch up in many liberal democracies. In short, critics of representative democracy have suggested that it is failing to promote opportunities for direct input from the public.

Yet others have suggested that this rather pessimistic picture is overly simplistic (Norris, 2002). Political organizations are not necessarily in crisis but in flux; they are evolving rather than dying. Countervailing trends in political participation can also be identified, which challenge the logic of decline and point to a more complex situation.

Political participation and organizational change

Central to arguments about the performance of representative political systems are the functions of collective political organizations. While we have noted that traditional participatory organizations have been said to be in decline, the literature on their participatory role in modern democracies is somewhat contradictory. Four areas of debate are worth highlighting.

First, survey evidence has revealed a considerable fall in party and trade union memberships and activism across Western Europe over the past 30 years. This has also led to an increasingly ageing membership (Mair and Von Biezen, 2004; Ebbinghaus and Visser, 1999). Among the wider public, an increasing lack of knowledge or interest in such organizations, especially among younger generations, has been noted (Klingemann, 1999; Pharr and Putnam, 2000; Coleman, 2005b). However, some of these trends need to be viewed with caution. Statistics for party and union membership have not been particularly reliable until quite recently. Also as Norris (2002) has pointed out, decline is not a global phenomenon and parties still remain a popular organizational form—witness the number of new parties that have emerged over the past 30 years. Moreover, there is a danger that the notion of decline is based on a mythical golden age of collective representative organizations that never really existed (Fielding, 2001).

Second, it has been suggested that overall levels of participation in Western societies are not necessarily declining, but that the public is now more willing to support single-issue campaigns and engage in unconventional forms of protest activity, rather than join broad-based catch-all parties. The proliferation of environmental, animal-rights and social-welfare organizations since the 1960s has been seen as a significant counter-trend to the decline of established parties and older social movements (Kriesi *et al.*, 1995; Jordan, 1998). Social movement scholars have also pointed to increasing cycles of protest and direct action politics since the 1960s (Dalton, 1994). Initially, this was through anti-Vietnam war protests, then anti-nuclear campaigns and green protest, and latterly the emergence anti-capitalism/globalization networks. These loose coalitions or global networks of protest are difficult to categorize as political organizations, since they often have no formal memberships or recognizable organizational structure (Pickerill, 2000, 2003; Wall, 1999, Doherty 2002). Accurate figures on the growth of cause organizations and the number of protests are also difficult to establish: many networks are informal, ephemeral and wither away (Putnam, 2000).

A third debate centers on the role of the individual member within large political organizations. Common patterns can be detected in political parties, trade unions, and, in some cases, large non-governmental organizations (NGOs). The notion of the mass organizational model has been challenged by the individualization of participation within organizations. For example, since the 1980s many trade union and party members have been given more formal rights to participate through direct postal ballots on policy issues, leadership, and candidate selection. Centralization and professionalization of campaigning within parties, unions, and some NGOs, has also occurred (Farrell and Webb, 2000; Diani and Donati, 2001). Traditional local campaigning activities of activists and branches have been somewhat superseded by national campaigning particularly through the media. As television has become more important in communicating the organizational message

this has in turn promoted the rise of a new professional class of media relations personnel. A further trend is the growth of "checkbook members." In the NGO sphere, Jordan and Maloney (1998) note the rise of what they refer to as protest businesses. Here, for the most part, the vast majority of supporters simply donate funds, rather than participating actively in protest or internal decision-making. Such donations support a professional class of activists who undertake participatory action on behalf of the organization. Finally, there has been erosion of the concept of formal membership. In European parties the lines between formal party members and informal supporters are blurred, with parties encouraging donations, and participation, from non-party members (Margetts, 2006). In a more radical sense, many of the newer direct action networks have simply removed the concept of membership altogether since there are no hierarchies or structures, just activists (Pickerill, 2003).

A fourth area of debate concerns internal democracy, where the impact is mixed. Certainly, individual members have increased their formal rights to participate, most often as voters in internal selection processes. In some instances, power has been dispersed from unrepresentative activist cliques to the wider membership. However, this does not necessarily make leaders more accountable or the process more democratic. Often the participative agenda and candidate choice is restricted or controlled by organizational elites as part of a top-down approach. Moreover, it can be argued that atomized organizational members are unlikely to build a stable platform to challenge elites. Indeed, organizational elites have often been keen to pursue an individualized model of participation as means of legitimizing their own position by bypassing activists and appealing to the more passive and moderate members.

Overall, though, it is difficult to detect a clear picture: there is no uniform trend towards citizen disengagement. While older forms of collective participation have undoubtedly withered to some extent, collective organizational participation is still taking place, albeit in different and sometimes more ephemeral forms than before. In addition, we must not assume the existence of a golden era of traditional representative organizations.

The arrival of the internet into the midst of these upheavals has added a further layer to debates about the role of political organizations. The internet has been viewed as both savior and executioner of the current political system and its organizational infrastructure. Much of the remainder of this chapter therefore discusses the differing scenarios that surround the role of new ICTs in the intra- and interorganizational arenas.

The internet and intraorganizational change

The intraorganizational debate has so far tended to focus on contested claims within three key aspects of internal organizational life: recruitment and the use of ICTs to gather additional members and supporters; activism and the use of the net to increase supporter activity and commitment; internal democracy and the use of the new technologies to avoid the so-called "iron law of oligarchy" (Michels, 1915).

Extending organizational reach? The internet as a recruitment tool

Information and communication technologies have been viewed as means of attracting additional supporters for political organizations and also diversifying the social base of membership, bringing new life to traditional political organizations but also sustaining new political forms. At one level, the basis for the internet as recruitment tool can be seen in terms of administrative gains and increased marketing potential. New technologies allow parties and NGOs to become more administratively efficient in processing recruitment. The collection of e-mail databases of addresses of supporters now allows organizations to make streamlined, regularized, and swifter appeals at less cost. Requests for donations or membership forms can be sent out to thousands of supporters at the touch of a button. Once members have been recruited, e-mail can enable organizations to keep track of their supporters more effectively.

The internet and e-mail are in some senses a continuation of direct mail targeting and computer database packages that have been deployed by parties and large NGOs since the 1980s, both of which have allowed organizations to target and track sympathizers (Doherty, 2002). However, the internet and e-mail have also been seen as more effective marketing devices. The combination of the traditional printed media with audiovisual tools and interactivity make websites, in particular, an attractive medium with which to advertise and canvass support. Furthermore, the ability to gather information on website visitors and the narrowcasting potential of the technology of the internet provide increasingly sophisticated opportunities to target sympathizers (Bowers-Brown, 2003). Similarly, viral marketing techniques can be used to extend the range of the organizational message still further, as e-mail, web pages, and video clips can be easily forwarded by existing supporters to their friends, family, and work colleagues.

Beyond simple administrative efficiency, one relatively straightforward way in which organizations can extend their reach is geographically. It is now much easier than in the past for organizations to appeal to a broader global audience (Rodgers,

2003; Clark and Themudo, 2003). The internet has facilitated the rise of new, virtual, global protest networks, such as Avaaz.org, which focuses on global justice issues, organizes around internet tools, and targets multinational companies. It is not just new networks that have used the internet for global activism; traditional party and trade unions have also extended their campaigns beyond national boundaries. One good example of this is the emergence of virtual overseas party branches where parties can gather support from expatriate communities. Similarly, in the trade union movement some have suggested that the net is supporting a new form of internationalism by linking workers' campaigns across the world (Lee, 1997; Hodkinson, 2004). One further benefit for organizations is the ability to attract members in areas where they have no or weak physical infrastructures on the ground. Supporters can join virtually, even where the organization has no local presence, and still be a part of the organization nationally. This is a particular advantage for small organizations with geographically dispersed memberships.

The internet has also, arguably, formed a new virtual sphere in which organizations can campaign to attract new types of supporter. One of the main debates in internet politics literature is how different the web sphere is for recruitment: is there actually a new audience for organizations to target that might not be reached through the traditional media? In particular, many organizations have seen the web as means of targeting younger supporters, so-called "digital natives", who are hard to reach through the traditional media but who have grown up with computer technologies as part of their everyday lives.

Despite these advantages to online recruitment, one significant problem limits the net's potential as a recruitment tool. Essentially, the internet is a "pull"

technology. It is difficult to get one's message across to a general and often more passive audience. Before people visit political websites they generally need pre-existing knowledge and some degree of political interest. Simply because an organizational website is available, it is unlikely to make those uninterested in, or unfavorable towards, an organization, visit it. Many visitors to political sites are already politically active (Norris 2001b, 2002; Gibson et al., 2003a, 2005). While empirical data on audiences for political websites outside the United States are still limited, the balance of most general surveys across Europe to date tend to support a reinforcement rather than a mobilization story (Norris, 2003). Nevertheless, our own case study evidence suggests that where organizations do deploy resources and technology creatively then they can, at least modestly, extend their reach. For instance, the pro-hunting Countryside Alliance in the United Kingdom successfully used new technologies to mobilize a wider support base among young people and in urban areas (Lusoli and Ward, 2006). We found similar results among U.K. parties with online recruitment aimed at the young, particularly students (Lusoli and Ward, 2003, 2006). As yet, though, research on the internal angle remains limited because of the difficulties of gaining access and the cost of data collection. There remains considerable scope to analyze how and why online recruitment campaigns succeed or fail.

Deepening supporter engagement? The internet as an activist tool

Beyond the simple argument about reinvigoration of organizations through additional members is the idea that the internet could allow organizations to deepen their engagement with supporters on a more regularized basis. For example, organizations now have more potential to create additional opportunities for participation. Virtual discussion forums, intranets, online surveys, e-mail links, blogs, and social network sites such as MySpace or Facebook could all provide for more regular and in-depth supporter input. While traditional participatory opportunities might be limited to monthly meetings, annual conferences or one-off events, new online spaces could allow for ongoing dialogue between members and between organizational elites and members. While one might dismiss this as simply an updating of traditional participatory channels, the net has also created a range of new protest repertoires, notably electronic civil disobedience and hacktivism where online activists have targeted government and corporations through the defacing of websites, publishing of private information, and through swarming and denial of service attacks that tie up websites and networks (Jordan, 2001).

One positive knock-on effect of additional electronic channels is to create stronger links to the organization and between organizational supporters. This can help build levels of trust and commitment. Most studies of participation conclude that the more contact that members have with an organization the more they are likely to feel efficacious and the more they participate (Jordan and Maloney, 1998).

One further benefit from the perspective of organizations is the ability to use the technology to enable their supporters to campaign more effectively against governments or opponents (Galusky, 2003). Buxton (2002) notes that the Jubilee 2000 campaign, (to end developing world debt), used the web and e-mail to provide information and campaign material for activists. Such information would previously have remained within the domain of professional NGO staff. The result was the professionalization of activists who could then more confidently lobby governments and parliamentarians with high-quality information.

The emergence of so-called Web 2.0 campaigns, however, suggests even more radical consequences whereby supporters and activists help shape campaigns and even reconfigure them, potentially reducing the control organizational headquarters has over campaigning. Greenpeace's recent "green my apple" campaign targeting the Apple company provides an early indicator of such novel elements in campaigns. Greenpeace supporters were encouraged to create their own online banners and also remix video and images placed on the Greenpeace site.

Again, however, these positive benefits have been questioned not only by scholars but also by political activists themselves. Some within the activist community, especially those engaged in direct action, have criticized online activism as a distraction from real-world activities or as a relatively shallow form of participation with negligible impact (Pickerill, 2000, 2003).

Moreover, studies have even suggested that far from stimulating activism, the internet is more likely to create passivity (Putnam, 2000). For example, Nie and Ebring (2000) found that precisely because the internet removes social setting, place, and time, it becomes a much more isolating experience than television. While people may connect online, the more they surf, the less time they spend socializing with others. Diani (2001) has further questioned whether virtual networks can engender enough trust between participants to support high-risk radical activism. This sort of activity, he argues, requires collective identification that is dependent on face-to-face interaction.

One may join organizations online but without the real-world connections to other supporters or local networks the net is more likely to encourage a passive chequebook membership with limited long-term ties (Lusoli and Ward, 2004).

Flattening hierarchies? The internet as a democratic tool

Even if we accept that the internet assists with increasing their recruitment and deepening membership engagement, would this necessarily alter the internal dynamics of organizations? Much has been made of the supposed democratizing influence of new technologies that weaken oligarchy and institutionalization and promote more flexible, grass-roots, decentralized modes of behavior (Washbourne, 2001; Greene et al., 2003). But how far are ICTs really likely to override pre-existing practice and culture? Their role in intraorganizational democracy can best be conceptualized along two dimensions (Gibson and Ward, 1999).

The first dimension is vertical, member-to-elite relations. It has been argued that the creation of intranets, internal discussion forums, e-mail lists, blog networks, and the like might make organizational elites more accountable to ordinary members. The greater volume and speed of information flows offered via ICTs, combined with its interactivity and presence in homes means members/supporters can have more frequent and direct access to elites. This would promote increased accountability of elite-level decision-making.

The second dimension concerns horizontal, member-to-member relations. The independent adoption of new media technologies by either individual members or internal groups arguably allows them to communicate their views to local, national, and global audiences more effectively. Moreover, they can communicate with one another more easily and network independently without the need to go through official channels. Washbourne (2001:132–3) notes the growth of "translocalism" in Friends of the Earth, where local branches and activists have used technology to facilitate decentralized action without the need for going through

headquarters. Furthermore, organizational elites find it harder to control internal flows of information and dissent. Potentially, therefore, it makes it easier for elites to be challenged from below (Greene et al., 2003).

Often underlying such arguments are normative assumptions that flattening hierarchies will increase the power of grass-roots members and create a more participatory form of internal democracy. Skeptics however, have questioned whether technologies facilitate such unidirectional changes. Simply providing electronic tools for participation is not the same as actually empowering members. The existing participatory context is clearly important: who controls the agenda for electronic discussion? What are the rules for access? How do existing organizational rules incorporate electronic channels? And is participation even viewed as important? (Burt and Taylor, 2001). Several studies have indicated that due to their resource and power advantages organizational headquarters are more likely to dominate the e-agenda and use it to strengthen their position of power (Pickerill, 2001; Ward and Gibson, 2003). At a basic level, beyond the headquarters of many parties and pressures groups, access and use of new ICTs is often more patchy (Gibson and Ward, 1999). Similarly, there is little guarantee that use of new technology within organizations, even if it challenges existing hierarchies, will not simply create new divides. As Grignou and Patou (2004: 178–9) conclude in their study of ATTAC, a French originated social movement, electronic tools maintain and even enlarge gaps between expert and non-experts, and active supporters and non-active supporters.

In short, therefore, it is not clear that any particular model of internal democracy may emerge. Information and communication technologies do not automatically promote internal democratization. Much is clearly dependent on the participatory ethos of the organization in question.

The internet and interorganizational change

Beyond ICT-facilitated internal change, commentators have suggested that such technologies may eventually alter the organizational landscape of democracies and that certain types of organizations can more readily adapt the technology and benefit from it. A variety of possibilities have been advanced, from radical dein-stitutionalization through to a "politics as usual" scenario.

Direct democracy: disintermediation and erosion?

One of the most radical scenarios, particularly from early accounts, is the idea that the internet may hasten the demise of traditional representative democracy by producing a process of deinstitutionaliza-tion as organizational hierarchies are flat-tened and displaced by direct input from citizens (Rheingold, 1995; Leadbeater and Mulgan, 1997; Morris, 1999). At its most revolutionary, a return to the classical model of unmediated direct democracy has been envisaged. New technologies allow for much more regular and direct input from the individual. Electronic forums, discussion areas, e-voting, and referenda all make it easier for citizens to have a direct say in governing themselves, thus bypassing mediating institutions and organizations, such as parties, pressure groups, and even Parliaments. The orga-nization and administration of direct democracy in a mass society is, therefore, no longer untenable (Budge, 1996). While practical details are somewhat limited, normative debates about the benefits or drawbacks of direct democracy have flour-ished. While proponents see technology-enhanced direct democracy as heralding a new, more responsive system of govern-ance replacing the outmoded organiza-tions and rules of the pre-modern era

(Morris, 1999), critics point to the possi-ble rise of electronic populism or dema-goguery open to abuse and manipulation (Barber, 2004).

Nevertheless, the idea of the removal of organizational frameworks in politics seems fanciful, for several reasons. An unwritten assumption in these type of accounts is that political organizations are powerless to defend their positions against the tide of technological change. Yet, as historical studies of the arrival of new technologies remind us, most organiza-tions tend to adapt and adopt the tech-nology (Wring and Horrocks, 2001). Moreover, direct democracy proponents perhaps underestimate the extent to which people wish to participate on an individual basis. From a rational choice perspective, citizens may lack time, skills, resources, and interest to be involved on the scale required. Even if the technology is available, some citizens may prefer to see experts and professionals in pressure groups participate for them.

An outsiders' medium: equalization?

A second school of thought suggests a more differentiated impact for the inter-net and a less deterministic approach. Notions of accelerated pluralism or equalization indicate that outsider, oppo-sitional, or fringe organizations are likely to benefit disproportionately from the rise of new ICTs and potentially pose more of a challenge to the mainstream political establishment. In short, new ICTs could help level the campaign communication playing field. Equalizers point toward the apparent rise of protest activity, direct action campaigns, and global networks all making use of the technology to organize and mobilize (Doherty, 2002; Bennett, 2003; Clark, 2003; van de Donk et al., 2004). The media have been quick to highlight the use of the internet in a range of protest campaigns, from the anti-fuel tax campaigns in the United Kingdom, anti-globalization protests at Seattle, Prague, Milan, and the anti-Iraq war campaign (Kahn and Kellner, 2004).

The equalization case tends to rest on arguments about costs, disintermediation, and internet culture. While newspapers require journalistic and printing skills and the costs of producing one's own television or films are still relatively expensive in equipment terms, the internet is seen a cheap and open publishing source. It can significantly lower communication and start-up costs for resource-poor organizations and networks (Dalton and Wattenberg, 2000). Even obscure political groups with very little resources can create a website that can sit alongside the mainstream political establishment. Similarly, the low cost and viral quality of e-mail can also generate rapid connections and momentum in campaigns, promoting flash protests. Whereas television and newspapers have limited space and editors can control and edit out fringe concerns, websites, blogs, and YouTube provide an unlimited platform with which to get one's message across. They effectively help decentralize control of the communication process.

Given that control and authority are decentralized, it is often difficult for a web surfer to gauge the size, legitimacy, or authenticity of organizations by simply looking at a website. Hence, small and fringe organizations can create an amplification effect with a web presence. As Copsey (2003) notes in relation to far right parties, their professionally designed, often slick sites give the impression of much larger, more representative, organizations than they are in reality.

It has also been suggested because of the way the internet developed, its initial audience, (techies and academics), and its decentralized nature has led to a particular ethos or online culture. The original,

supposedly rather anarchic environment of the net with its free flows of information and a common space, relatively unregulated by governments would seem to benefit flexible, non-hierarchical types of organization outside the mainstream. Thus direct-action protest campaigns, anarchistic and libertarian networks are those whose values are supposedly best reflected in cyberspace (Scott and Street, 2001).

However, the equalization thesis is less precise over which specific organizations will benefit. Bimber (1998) argues that all organizations may well benefit from the use of new ICTs but that single-issues campaigns, new social movements, and protest networks are likely to benefit most. Others have suggested that not all parties will be disadvantaged: some fringe outsiders, such as the far right or the greens, may in fact gain as much as non-party organizations (Ward et al., 2007). While a number of studies have suggested that environmental organizations may be best placed to develop a lead with the technology because of their supposed participatory culture and their ability to link global issues with local campaigns facilitated by the net (Pickerill, 2000, 2003; Doherty, 2002). Yet it could also be argued that not all such single-issues groups are likely to prosper. Large pressure groups or new social movements, as much as parties, may find themselves increasingly challenged by looser *ad hoc* protest networks or virtual campaigns with no identifiable leaderships or clear structures (Mobbs, 2000; Lebert, 2003).

Politics as usual: normalization?

At the other end of the spectrum, other writers have expressed considerable skepticism that the rise of the internet will bring about any significant changes in the nature of democratic politics. Resnick (1998) argues that although it was originally a playground for the alternative and anarchic increasingly the internet has been normalized. In the political sphere, this means that the large traditional political forces will come to predominate as they do in other media. This so-called normalization thesis is built on four main assumptions: commercialization, fragmentation, new skills, and increasing regulatory control. First, as the net has developed, cyberspace has been increasingly commercialized and dominated by business interests in particular (Margolis and Resnick, 2000). As commercialization has occurred so the space for alternative politics has been squeezed. Indeed, the space for politics as a whole is being crowded out. The main uses of the internet have become the leisure activities of sex, sport, and shopping.

Second, normalizers have also questioned the idea of the increased reach of the net. As we have already noted, the net is a pull medium, in which it is difficult to reach the politically uninterested. More fundamentally, skeptics have argued that the internet has contributed to a further fragmentation of the media. While theoretically the consumer has more choice, in reality this is likely to mean that more choose not to be exposed to political coverage (Sunstein, 2001; Norris, 2001b; Scott, 2005). Unlike the traditional terrestrial broadcasting era, during which the public was regularly exposed to political news, even if only as passive consumers, in the era of web portals and digital TV packages citizens can easily filter out news and politics.

Third, far from being a cost-free exercise, normalizers argue that to produce a sophisticated web strategy involves considerable investment (Lebert, 2003). Again, established organizations have more resources to devote to creating websites and using ICTs creatively. They can afford to pay professional web designers and full-time staff to maintain their sites and respond to voters, whereas, smaller, volunteer-run organizations are reliant on the goodwill of members or supporters who lack the time and skills to manage websites on a continuous basis.

Finally, while the internet is often depicted as uncontrollable, it is clear that governments and established interests are devoting increasing effort to trying to regulate and control online communication. In authoritarian regimes, this has meant attempts by authorities to limit online opposition through restrictions on access, as well as surveillance and arrests. Even in European democracies attempts have been made to restrict the online activities of far right groups (Copsey, 2003) and also monitor the activities of a range of protest campaigns (Pickerill, 2003).

So far, changes in the interorganizational arena are somewhat mixed. Information and communication technologies have yet to upset the balance of power between organizations in European countries. Nevertheless, they have undoubtedly lowered the start-up costs for campaigns and are facilitating the growth of new networks and organizations operating in ways that were previously impossible. In short, as we have argued elsewhere, the internet is widening the political playing field and accelerating established trends such as the growth of direct action and single-issue politics that pre-date its arrival (Ward et al., 2003; Ward and Vedel, 2006). New technologies have not revolutionized or destroyed traditional collective organizations, but such entities have benefited less than new social movements, protest campaigns, and flexible, decentralized supporter networks.

Explaining levels of activity and strategies online: developing a framework[2]

Much of the literature on organizational ICT use has focused on rather oversimplified two-dimensional approaches—

equalization versus normalization, or centralization versus decentralization. We reject such "one size fits all" explanations and argue that social and political shaping are crucial to understanding the development of an organization's approach to new technologies. As Burt and Taylor (2001: 72) have suggested: "the extent to which technologies are exploited and the ways in which they are appropriated are shaped by the social conditions, philosophies and value systems within which the technologies are immersed."

The remaining section in this chapter explores what more specific factors could shape organizational ICT strategy and choice. Drawing on the literature, we propose that three sets of factors (systemic opportunity structures, organizational capacities, and organizational incentives) may hold the key to explaining organizational activity.

Systemic and technological opportunity structures

Systemic and technological opportunity structures provide the broad political and technological parameters within which political organizations operate. In short, especially within national boundaries, they can alter the extent and the style to which technology is used by organizations. For example, the idea of political opportunity structures has long been used to explain and compare protest movement strategic choice (Kitschelt, 1986; Kriesi et al., 1995). The arrival of a new communication channel adds further dimension to those opportunity structures. One can envisage opportunity structures as falling broadly into two categories:

■ Media environment: both the shape of the old media environment, as well as the development of internet infrastructure, are important here. In a number of European countries, (see for example

Italy), parties and social movements have traditionally owned newspapers or television channels, which arguably slow the need to develop online channels (Gibson et al., forthcoming). The extent of fragmentation of media and the role of public broadcasters can also have an influence. The fragmented, highly volatile U.S. media-market seems to have produced an environment conducive to the creation of partisan new media channels. Alternatively, where there is a dominant and comparatively trusted public service provider, such as the BBC in the United Kingdom, it has arguably ameliorated the development of a partisan websphere. More directly, the spread of internet technology and the speed of connection within countries or regions clearly provides incentives for all organizations to move online (Norris, 2).

■ Political environment: the basic political system framework (federalism, party system, electoral system, etc.) will also shape the use of new ICTs. Arguably, presidential, candidate-centered, federal systems are more likely to be responsive to interactive online technologies than highly centralized polities because multilevel government with large numbers of independent actors is likely to result in wider experimentation and innovation in terms of campaigning (Gibson and Rommele, 2005; Zittel, 2003). Moreover, the extent to which such institutional frameworks are entrenched may also influence technological uptake. As March (2006) suggests, newer democracies, (in Eastern Europe for example), where political communication and political systems are less fixed, could allow a greater role for new technologies.

Overall, therefore, we might expect to see greater and more innovative uses of internet technology in countries with relatively fragmented and less trusted media systems, high internet penetration rates, along with decentralized, personalized, and less fixed political systems.

Organizational capacity

Organizational capacity determines the extent to which organizations can use ICTs for a variety of purposes. Capacity can be understood in terms of three resources: staff time, skills, and finance.

- Staff time: to run an effective website it requires time, not least to keep the site fresh, innovate with the technology, and deal with the information gathered through the site. Even small political organizations have found that a website can end up generating an off-putting amount of e-mail demanding information and answers.
- Skills: basic web technology is not necessarily difficult to understand, but it still requires a degree of knowledge and training to create the more sophisticated and innovative online features.
- Finance: websites are comparatively cheap to design and manage compared with making TV broadcasts or placing large press ads. Nevertheless, small organizations with limited finances may have a somewhat different perception of such costs. In short, generally, the more sophisticated the website, the more money is required.

Overall, we would expect organizations with greater organizational capacity to develop more sophisticated and multi-purpose strategies than those with limited capacity.

Organizational incentives

While resources are clearly important, organizational incentives are likely to be the key factors not only in increasing or decreasing the willingness of organizations to use ICTs, but also the purpose for which they are used—consumerist or grass-roots participatory approaches, for example. Organizational incentives include the following:

- Organizational ideology: organizations on both the right and the left of the political spectrum have claimed the web to be their "natural" medium. The participatory, communitarian politics and even anarchic tendencies of the green movement provide a fit with the internet ethos and the possibilities of online grass-roots activism. Equally, though, the radical libertarian right see the web as their medium due to the possibilities for the free market and free speech it offers.
- Target audience: access and use of the web, while growing rapidly in Europe, is still skewed toward the more affluent and educated sectors of society. Hence, organizations with a predominantly working-class membership, or audience among socially excluded groups, may well develop ICT strategy more slowly than those organizations with affluent web-oriented supporters. Similarly, organizations that have a geographically dispersed audience may also have greater incentive to develop an ICT strategy.
- Organizational age: the age of an organization may have some impact

on the willingness to adopt the technology. Organizations founded in the 1990s are more likely to accept the technology as mainstream because they have grown up in the internet age. Similarly, longstanding political organizations with well established communication and bureaucratic structures might face more internal hurdles in grafting new technologies onto existing administrative frameworks.

- Organizational status: because they may lack sufficient exposure in the traditional media and access to official channels of publicity and websites, opposition parties, outsider pressure groups, or challengers in a political system are likely to have the greatest incentive to use new media.

In sum, incentives are likely to be greatest among young, oppositional network-style organizations with a dispersed, internet-literate, and participatory support base.

Conclusion

One of the weaknesses of internet studies is a failure to link research to existing literatures or place it within current political and social contexts. To understand the political role of the internet, it should be clear that we need to relate it to existing trends within participatory politics. Hence, at the start of the chapter, we referred to three contested trends: declining membership within established organizations, the changing role of the member, and the disputed rise of alternative organizations and protest. What impact is the internet having in these areas?

Those organizations with significant capacity are already using the technology to try and broaden their support base. This is not dissimilar to the way that large

pressure groups and parties have adopted marketing techniques and direct mail. This may help widen participation at the margins, but it is unlikely to radically alter internal democracy. In terms of intraorganizational democracy, the technology may strengthen existing trends within political parties and large organizations. Individual members of traditional political organizations may be provided with more information, more opportunities to input opinion direct to organizational elites, and even more plebiscitary voting rights, but the net is unlikely to foster more collective participation within these types of organization. Unless organizations have particular incentives for using ICTs for participatory and innovative purposes, the technology alone will not change existing organizational goals. Such organizations are likely to use ICTs for supplementary purposes, although the emergence of Web 2.0 campaigns and tools may place further pressure on large organizations to allow a degree of decentralization in their campaigns.

More innovative online activity and participatory strategies are likely to emerge from protest networks and radical grass-roots organizations that have some of the greatest organizational incentives to use ICTs for these purposes. This should not be a surprise, since in the "offline world" it is these types of organization that have tended to extend the range of protest behavior. The internet further allows such networks the opportunity to gain a foothold and mobilize support, at least in the short term. Hence, mobilizing one-off protests or creating rapid but ephemeral networks is where the internet may make the biggest impact. Sustaining those networks may be more problematic since they often lack organizational capacity.

The evolution of organizations in the internet era also raises methodological questions. The traditional metrics of political participation and organizational success (voter turnout and organizational membership, for example) are too narrow and require expansion. As we have seen, the internet has already fostered the growth of informal supporter networks and blurred the boundaries between formal membership and more ephemeral supporters. Notably, partisan blogs and social networking supporter sites are now fostering participation outside formal organizational structures and impacting on formal organizational policy agendas. Studies of organizations and mobilization arguably need to take account of new forms of online participation. For example, the unofficial use of online humor that has become increasingly popular in political campaigns through spoof websites, blogs, and YouTube videos, could be seen as a participatory activity (Shifman et al., 2007).

Moving from the changes that take place within organizational types, to the broader systemic level, competing democratic visions are emerging from consumerist to web network models. Nevertheless, contrary to talk of decline, we should not forget that representative organizations have actually been remarkably resilient. The deployment of new ICTs may be used to modernize representative democracy on a consumerist model, rather than sweeping it away (Bellamy and Taylor, 1998). Here citizens are viewed more as consumers of public services and the focus is on value and efficiency and providing individuals with increased choice through access to information (Hoff et al., 2000). This in itself is likely to create increasing challenges for organizations and networks dedicated to a cyberdemocratic approach. In short, while the extent of systemic developments is shaped in different countries by different opportunity structures, we may be moving towards a more fragmented and more contested democratic model.

Guide to further reading

There is a growing general literature on the internet, political organizations, and participatory politics, but it is still limited in a number of respects. Much of the early work draws on North America and, to a lesser extent, Northern Europe. It also tends to be limited to single country studies. Second, methodologically, much of the initial focus has been on the content of organizational websites and small-scale case studies. There is still a dearth of studies looking at the internal organizational angle and little from the user perspective or on internet political audiences (members, supporters, and the broader general public).

With these limitations in mind, however, there is a range of work that forms a useful basis for study. In relation to the broader ideas of democracy and the internet and the role of political organizations, Budge's (1996) early speculative work sets out the arguments for a more direct democracy enabled, in part, by technology. Although based on the U.S. experience, Bimber's (1998) idea of accelerated pluralism, is a useful conceptualization of the potential reshaping role of the net. Margolis and Resnick's (2000) "politics as usual" approach presents perhaps the best account of why politics and mainstream actors are likely to retain their power in the internet era. The more conceptual and theoretical work of Stephen Coleman on democracy in the internet era, particularly his idea of direct representation (Coleman, 2005b) provides an interesting argument for how the participatory potential of ICTs could be harnessed by representative organizations and institutions. From a more empirical, but still general, approach, Zittel's (2003) article is one of the few that lays out the comparative potential impact of the systemic political environment on the influence of the internet.

Useful introductory chapters on participation, democracy and the net, as well as case studies of organizations can be found in Webster and Lin (2002), Hoff *et al.* (2000), Gibson *et al.* (2004), and Oates *et al.* (2006). More specific studies of political organizations (especially in Europe) have tended to skew towards parties in the electoral context (Gibson *et al.*, 2003c; Kluver *et al.* (eds), 2007; Davis *et al.*, 2008) and case studies of campaign activity among groups and new social movements. Among the latter, see Van de Donk *et al.* (2004) and McCaughey and Ayers (2003). Literature on trade unions and ICTs is sparser, although a special issue of the *Journal of Industrial Relations* 34 (4), 2003, contains a number of good European case studies.

For empirical studies of internal organizational democracy or activity beyond the national or collective level, see, in the party context, Lusoli and Ward (2003, 2004) on the United Kingdom, and Pederson and Saglie's (2005) study of Danish and Norwegian party members. There is also corresponding work by Greene *et al.* (2003) on trade unions, ICTs, and activism. Work on the internal organizational side of mainstream pressure groups is more difficult to locate. Pickerill's (2000, 2003, 2006) research on a range of environmental organizations from Friends of the Earth to radical direct-action protest networks contains some excellent insights on the way ICTs have been incorporated in ways reflecting differing organizational cultures.

Notes

1 Parts of this chapter are based on Ward, S. J. and T. Vedel (2006) The potential of the internet revisited, *Parliamentary Affairs*, 59 (2):1–16.
2 This section draws on and expands two chapters dealing with parties and internet strategies (Nixon *et al.*, 2003; Ward *et al.*, 2008).

4

Electoral web production practices in cross-national perspective

The relative influence of national development, political culture, and web genre

Kirsten A. Foot, Michael Xenos, Steven M. Schneider, Randolph Kluver, and Nicholas W. Jankowski

To what degree are websites produced during an election shaped by a country's political culture, level of development, and the type of actor producing the site? Surprisingly, the websites produced during 19 elections in 2004 are more consistent across types of political actors than within political cultures. When analyzed for four communicative functions—informing, involving, connecting, and mobilizing citizens—political actors' sites are remarkably consistent regardless of which country they are operating in. Data from the Internet and Elections Project (Kluver et al., 2007) reveals that, controlling for levels of national development, a significant amount of the variation in web production practices can be explained by differences in political culture even among democratic nations, and even more is explained by genre effects associated with five types of political actors: candidates for election, government agencies, political parties, news media, and civic groups such as labor unions and non-governmental agencies. This suggests that along with the diffusion of internet technologies comes a diffusion of genre practices, causing institutional isomorphism among political actors around the world.

The phenomenon of transnational technology diffusion has received significant attention among scholars of innovation, technology, and development (cf. Howard and World Information Access Project, 2006; Rogers, 1995; Wilson, 2004). However, cross-national similarities and differences in the adoption and adaptation of information and communication technologies by political actors in the context of democratic politics remain understudied.[1] Studies of technology diffusion have demonstrated a transnational flow of notions about technological affordances for political and other human activities, technological expertise, and technology-related practices, including web production practices (Howard, 2006; Kamalipour, 2006; Wilson, 2004). Patterns of transnational technology diffusion indicate a globalizing trend among economic, political, and intellectual elites in different countries toward similar technology-related practices (Wilson, 2004). One manifestation of this trend in the political arena is the international circuit traveled by American political technology consultants in between U.S. elections, as they advise political parties and campaigns in other countries on strategic uses of internet technologies (Howard, 2006).

On the other hand, differences in political culture underlie the varying ways that political practices—including those that involve technologies—take shape in different countries (Ho *et al.*, 2003; Kluver, 2005; Kluver and Banerjee, 2005; Ott, 1998). This literature suggests that the particularities of political culture "localize" technology, that is, national political cultures contextualize technology adoption and adaptation in politics within countries. Different assumptions within national cultures regarding the relationship between citizens and the state and regulations lead to variance in expectations of political actors and in patterns of engagement by various types of actors across countries.

Foot and Schneider (2006) have demonstrated that the structure of a *web sphere*, defined as website features produced in relation to an event or topic by a range of sociopolitical actors within a particular timeframe, can either enable or constrain the range of actions available to internet users. Web sphere structure affords users with opportunities to act and to associate. For instance, on political party sites, the provision of features enabling e-mailing messages to the editors of local newspapers enables site visitors to voice their political opinions quickly and easily, while at the same time linking party sites with the press sites. Electoral web spheres take shape as various types of actors engage in web production practices reflecting their respective political roles and goals, both individually and in (hyperlinked) relationship to each other.

The overarching aim of this chapter is to shed light on the relative influence of web genres, national development, and localizing political culture on the web production practices of political actors active in national electoral web spheres. Prior work on technology appropriation across countries has indicated that political culture and several aspects of national development play important roles in the

ways technology is employed. However, the findings of this study suggest that web producers are more likely to adopt transnational genre markers in producing their sites, than to employ culturally specific patterns in the online structures they produce.

This analysis is based on data from 19 national electoral web spheres spanning Europe, North America, and Australasia collected in the context of the internet and Elections Project (Kluver *et al.*, 2007). The project was designed to facilitate the collection of comparable data on one facet of the internet and political life: how a wide range of political actors in democracies around the world engaged in the web during national elections in 2004–5. With research teams in each country, the overall project examined the web production practices of political parties, campaigns, news producers, government bodies, and non–governmental organizations, in nations with varying levels of technology penetration, economic power, and styles of democratic governance, and with different political cultures.

Very few large-scale cross national studies of the web in elections have been conducted to date with a common methodological framework that enables strong comparisons across political, economic, and cultural contexts. Prior cross-national comparative studies on political uses of digital information and communication technologies (ICTs) have shown that levels of economic development and technological development, and national political structure, are significant predictors of the deployment of ICTs in politics (Norris, 2000, 2001b). A collection of case studies on the online activities of political parties in several countries shed light on some of the ways parties were experimenting with ICTs both in election and governance contexts (Gibson *et al.*, 2003b), and a close comparison of online campaigning in the United Kingdom and the United States suggested interesting

41

differences between candidate-centric and party-centric elections (Gibson *et al.*, 2003a).

These studies and others have contributed significantly to our understanding of the issues related to particular ICTs, political structures, and electoral, advocacy, and governance activities. However, in our view, insufficient attention has been paid to the role of political culture in the deployment of ICTs in politics, and to political actors other than parties and campaigns in the context of elections. Political culture has been defined as the symbolic environment of political practice, shaped by political institutions, historical experiences, and philosophical and religious traditions (Kluver, 2005; Martin and Stronach, 1992). This broad description includes the assumptions, expectations, mythologies, and mechanisms of political practice within a country and addresses the ways values and attitudes influence political behavior. Most research on the political use of the web has overlooked political culture, which may constrain use of the technology. Norris (2001b), for example, seems to disregard the role of cultural issues in her analysis of the internet in global politics when suggesting that electronic infrastructure may be the primary predictor of internet deployment in political campaigns.

Addressing these gaps in the literature was one of the principal goals of the Internet and Elections Project. It was hoped that by looking across national contexts during a period in which elections were held around the world, a greater sense of the diversity of ways in which various types of political actors employ web technologies with regard to elections in a wide variety of contexts could be gained. The aim of this chapter is to contribute to scholarship on the web and electoral politics through a large-scale, cross-national comparative analysis of the relationships between the web production practices of a wide range of

political actors, and political culture as well as political, technological, and economic development. This analysis was guided by three overarching research questions. First, to what extent do the patterns in the production of election-related resources online observed in the present study compare with prior research in the field (notably Norris, 2000, 2001b)? Second, how do aspects of national development and political culture correspond with the production of election-related resources online? Third, to what extent do particular political actor types engage in the same web production practices across national contexts? Some extant scholarship demonstrates that national development and political culture influence technology appropriation. Other scholarship suggests that technology adoption patterns have some remarkable similarities cross-nationally. This study compares the explanatory power of all three on the web production practices in national electoral web spheres.

Electoral web practices: informing, involving, connecting, and mobilizing

Four indices were constructed to analyze systematic variations in political web practices across a variety of web spheres, corresponding to four types of communicative functions addressed in the study. The creation of the indices was primarily guided by theoretical concerns related to distinct differences in the types of features observed on all of the various sites in the study. Extending and modifying conceptualizations of web production practices developed in earlier research (Foot and Schneider, 2006), we thus used functional differences to associate features with four practices, each representing a key dependent variable in the analyses that follow. The first practice, *informing*, concerns the most basic function of political communication online. Features that fall into the informing category convey basic information about the central figures in each electoral web sphere, the substance of their public discourse, and the election process itself. The second practice, *involving*, is evidenced in features that serve as a point of entry into a more interactive relationship between site visitors and site producers. The third practice, *connecting*, concerns the ways in which a site producer creates the means for site visitors to interact with other political actors and with websites produced by other political actors. Finally, *mobilizing* entails a set of features through which site producers enable visitors who are supporters of a candidate, party, or cause to become advocates for that candidate, party, or cause.

A clearer understanding of the complex nature of the variations explored here, however, comes from an examination of how the electoral web spheres studied rank in terms of the prevalence of each practice. In preliminary examinations of these rankings, a complex set of patterns suggests a number of different explanations for differing levels of political web practices across the spheres. For example, countries known for their economic status, such as the United States and the United Kingdom, display some of the highest levels of connecting and mobilizing, while Finland—whose residents also enjoy a relatively high standard of living—consistently ranked near the bottom for all four practices. Korea and Italy both consistently rank among the top three web spheres in the areas of informing, involving, and mobilizing, suggesting that all three factors—technological development, transnational technology diffusion within particular types of actors, and political culture—may all play important roles in explaining web practices. And yet, there are also a number of

other countries near the top of the four ranked lists that are known neither for their economic strength, their political cultures, nor their technological infrastructures, e.g. Slovenia (with the second highest prevalence of informing features), Portugal (with the second highest rate of connecting features), and Indonesia, (with the second highest rate of mobilizing features). This spread of adoption patterns for the four web practices examined suggests the need for a multivariate model, including a wide variety of potential explanatory variables.

Explaining variation in web practices: national development, political culture, and producer types

To build this multivariate model, several independent variables were employed.

Based on the results of prior comparative analyses of political websites (Norris, 2000, 2001b), indicators of economic development, on the one hand, and technological development, on the other, were selected. By exploring the degree to which observations of political actors' web practices in electoral web spheres correlate with either or both of these variables, the notion of a global "digital divide" may be tested and reconsidered (van Dijk, 2005; Norris, 2001b) with respect to political uses of internet technology in the context of elections. These variables enable the comparison of web observations as directly as possible to prior international investigations of politics online.

However, to further extend and develop understanding of international patterns of diffusion of online politics, two additional concepts were added to the analyses. Moving beyond traditional material predictors of the online actions of political actors, this portion of the analysis

43

was designed to test the notion that variations in national political contexts may provide substantive insight into international variations in political actors' web practices. Specifically, the two different aspects of the political contexts in the countries included in this study were political development, and political culture. The first of these, *political development*, relates to the variations in the political institutions and political structures within which the elections of 2004 took place. Although each country included in the study is, in some measure, democratic by virtue of having elections at all, there are still a number of vitally important variations between them in terms of constitutional, legal, and administrative characteristics associated with democratic governments. With the concept of *political culture*, the extent to which online political practices may be driven by demand factors associated with the citizenry itself is explored. Thus, the variables related to political culture are based on variations in the temperament, attitudes, and behavior of potential voters in each country, as evidenced through available secondary survey data.

A final set of variables included in the analyses that follow arises from previous research on web production in general, and the production of campaign websites in particular (Crowston and Williams, 2000; Foot and Schneider, 2006; Yates and Orlikowski, 1992; Xenos and Foot, 2005). This research into the production of various kinds of websites, political and otherwise, revealed patterns of what Foot and Schneider (2006) called genre effects. That is, sites produced by the same type of actor and/or sharing a similar purpose often reflect certain regularities of form and function that become associated with the genre of the site by both producers and visitors alike. As Burnett and Marshall (2003) explain, genres develop as a constantly cycling interplay between audience expectation and producer delivery of audience expectation. In the case of personal web pages, for example, common or expected features include personal photos and contact information. In the case of campaign websites, the standard list of features begins with the candidate biography, and typically includes other informational features related to political or policy goals of the candidate. Recognizable and stable sets of site features, produced by the same type of actors, carry elements of genre comparable to genre markers in other media (Vedres *et al.*, 2004; Xenos and Foot, 2005). Site genres create pressure on would-be site producers to conform to others' expectations by employing the pertinent genre markers in their web production practices, and at the same time, provide tracks from which to improvise and diverge. In addition, the transnational dissemination of political web production strategies and practices through networks of political actors in different countries (cf. Howard, 2006) are likely to catalyze similar web production practices among the actors of the same type, regardless of their national political context.

Since the sites analyzed in each web sphere studied in the Internet and Elections Project were produced by a variety of political actors, the producer types themselves were included as variables for two reasons. First, based on known relationships among and between various types of political actors and different kinds of communicative activities on the web, the inclusion of site producer type variables was anticipated to improve the explanatory power of the models. More importantly, the inclusion of such genre variables also enables a further test of competing theoretical interpretations of the impact of the web as a communication medium on political activity. Specifically, such variables enable estimation of the relative proportion of variation in political web production that is related to domestic factors such as economic and political development or culture, or more universal forces such as a particular style of communication and presentation using the internet that transcends such geographical, economic, and political differences.

To summarize, this comparative analysis of variations in web practices across the international elections project centers on an explanatory model that compares three distinct kinds of web production strategies employed by political actors, along a number of dimensions. The focal practices are informing, involving, connecting, and mobilizing. The explanatory dimensions include economic, technical, political development, political culture, and genre effects.

Measurement of web production practices and explanatory dimensions

The data from which each of the four dependent variables was drawn consisted of feature coding observations from 19 national election web spheres. After completing training exercises on five English-language sites, all participants were required to code the same set of ten archived English-language sites as a means of measuring agreement among coders. Four response options were provided for each item: (1) Yes, present on a page produced by this site producer; (2) Yes, but present on a page produced by a different site producer; (3) No; and (4) Not clear. Since our comparative analysis is based on the simple presence/absence of features, these response options were collapsed into three responses (Yes, No, and Not Clear) for the purpose of calculating inter-coder agreement. Because the display of archived websites can be problematic, participants had been instructed to

use the Not Clear option when technical problems prevented them from viewing the archived page. Thus, coordinators assumed that a Not Clear response in the reliability test was due to technical archival display difficulties and disagreements between coders that involved a Not Clear response were not counted as disagreements in the reliability assessment. Percent agreement was calculated between each individual coder in the internet and Elections Project and a set of master codes agreed upon by the project coordinators. Percent agreement was also calculated between the coders within each sphere, relative only to the coders working within each sphere, to account for differences in interpretation of the measures due to language and political cultural differences across coding teams.

Inter-rater reliability was evaluated according to percent agreement among coders based on two important characteristics of the data. First, the primary concern in the systematic coding conducted for this study was with either the presence or absence of certain types of features and information, and did not incorporate continuous variables. Neuendorf (2002) notes percent agreement is particularly appropriate in such instances, "wherein each pair of coded measures is either a hit or a miss." Second, the distributions of the measures in this study were skewed in that fewer than half the sites sampled for reliability testing offered half of the 24 features included in the coding schemes. Such distributions force lower reliability calculations of agreement beyond chance even when coding is reasonably reliable (Potter and Levine-Donnerstein, 1999). For these reasons, a requisite threshold of 80 percent agreement was established both between each participant's codes and the master codes and between members of the research team for each electoral web sphere to create the cross-national data set for this comparative analysis. That

45

is, there was at least 80 percent agreement between each of the coders and the master codes, and between the coders for the given web sphere, for each of the web sphere data sets employed in this analysis. For each web sphere, a variety of producer types were represented in the collections of websites for coding. Table 4.1 contains a list of the 19 countries included in this analysis, the proportion of sites from each producer category included, as well as the total number of functional sites included in the sample for each web sphere.[2] Dougherty and Foot (2007) provide a more detailed overview of the research design and data collection methods employed in the Internet and Elections Project, within which this study was conducted.

Comparing web practices

To operationalize each of the four practices of informing, involving, connecting, and mobilizing as dependent variables, indices of features were constructed representing these practices. As the number of features associated with each practice is not identical, the indices were created by calculating the proportion of the features for any given practice that were present on a site.

Informing

The informing index comprises five distinct and relatively straightforward features. The first is a biography or "About Us" text. On campaign sites, biographical information typically takes the form of pages where candidates provide their personal stories and backgrounds. On sites produced by other types of organizations, a description of the organization was treated comparably to a biography. The second feature is information about issue positions held by political actors within the web sphere, whether that actor was

the site producer or some other actor in the political system, as when the site producer is a press organization or political party. The third is information about voting, such as registration information and the location of polling sites. A fourth feature included in the informing index is general information about the campaign process. This includes information about the campaigning rules and possibly governmental regulations on campaigning in the country in which the elections are being held. Finally, the fifth feature used to construct the informing index is the presence of speeches, either in the form of audio files, video files, or simple transcripts. The mean value of the informing index across all 1,219 sites included the study was 0.40, with a standard deviation of 0.23.

Involving

The index for involving also comprises five features. First, the involving measure includes the presence or absence of features enabling the site visitor to join the organization or group sponsoring the site. Distinct from volunteering, which is also a part of the involving index, joining refers specifically to explicit membership of an organization or campaign. The second feature is the ability of the site visitor to sign up for an e-mail distribution list. A third involving feature is the provision of forms or other materials that enable visitors to volunteer in the electoral process in some capacity. In the case of campaigns and parties, this typically takes the form of teams of canvassers and phone bank operators, while for less partisan non-governmental organizations, volunteering can take the form of more general efforts related to the election process. The fourth feature in the involving index is the provision of a calendar of events, typically sponsored by the site producer. Such calendars are a

Table 4.1 Political content online and development measures for 19 countries with elections in 2004

Country	Websites sampled, by political actor type							Social, technological, and political development				
	Candidate (%)	Government (%)	Party (%)	Press (%)	NGO/ Labor (%)	Other (%)	Total Number	Human Development Index	New Media Index	Democracy Index	Participation Index	Engagement Index
Australia	15	1	27	8	14	36	89	0.95	1.37	6	1.81	6.91
Czech Republic	27	9	33	12	7	11	70	0.87	0.55	6	1.68	7.08
Finland	51	10	15	10	7	7	72	0.94	1.32	6	1.67	5.90
France	31	15	17	10	17	10	48	0.93	0.81	6	1.90	6.03
Hungary	7	30	22	11	6	24	54	0.85	0.44	4	1.27	—
India	5	36	26	14	3	16	88	0.60	0.04	2	1.53	6.30
Indonesia	11	7	15	33	7	28	77	0.69	0.07	1	1.24	6.52
Ireland	23	20	43	3	3	7	30	0.94	0.92	5	1.70	6.11
Italy	41	6	24	10	6	13	63	0.92	0.68	7	1.74	6.11
Japan	61	14	5	4	9	7	77	0.94	1.10	3	1.63	7.32
South Korea	44	8	12	7	7	21	72	0.89	1.37	4	—	6.89
Netherlands	48	8	24	5	6	10	63	0.94	1.29	6	1.80	7.32
Philippines	31	8	4	11	10	36	83	0.75	0.10	3	1.21	6.94
Portugal	3	3	41	35	7	10	29	0.90	0.76	4	1.49	5.53
Slovenia	3	45	24	10	8	10	38	0.90	0.81	4	1.64	5.79
Sri Lanka	0	14	25	49	2	10	49	0.74	0.02	3	—	—
Thailand	5	32	8	34	3	18	93	0.77	0.16	2	—	—
United Kingdom	50	8	15	10	5	12	60	0.94	1.00	5	1.76	5.78
United States	43	16	11	5	13	13	63	0.94	1.85	5	1.92	7.29

Source: Internet and Elections Project, 2006; International Telecommunications Union, 2005; United Nations, 2004; World Values Survey 2000; Vanhanen, 2003.

key line of communication between the organizers of political events, and those that may be drawn to participate in them through political communication online. Finally, the involving index also includes the presence of features used to allow site visitors to donate money either to the site producer, or to other political actors within the system that may be distinct from the site producer. The average level of involving across all sites in the study was 0.25, with a standard deviation of 0.26.

Connecting

The connecting index is based on three features by which a site producer creates bridges for visitors to other political actors. These bridges may be either cognitive, that is, invoking cognitive processes to make the connections between the actors, or transversal, incorporating and going beyond cognitive bridges by facilitating movement and a shift of attention from the connecting actor to the "connected to" actor (Foot and Schneider, 2006). The first feature associated with the practice of connecting is the presence of an endorsement or endorsements of particular candidates or parties in the upcoming election by the site producer. The second is the presence of information that facilitates a direct comparison of parties or candidates on particular issues. Typically, this takes the form of an issue-grid, which provides either a simple tabular entry or a link to information on the positions taken on various issues by a number of different candidates or parties. Finally, the third feature included in the connecting index is the presence of information or links that enable the site visitor to register to vote in the upcoming election. Across all sites included in the study, the mean level of connecting was 0.15, with a standard deviation of 0.23.

Mobilizing

The mobilizing index is based on four features and, as indicated earlier, reflects the efforts of a site producer to enable supportive site visitors to become advocates. The first is the potential for, and encouragement of, users to access materials on the website for their reproduction and distribution offline. For example, this would include the ability to download images of posters or flyers to copy and distribute at meetings or rallies. A second feature associated with mobilizing is e-paraphernalia. E-paraphernalia serves a similar function to offline distribution, but as the name implies the communications that are encouraged and enabled by the site are electronic in nature. A common form of e-paraphernalia is the downloadable screen-saver, which communicates an affiliation or message to one's co-workers or others that share one's computer space. The third feature in the mobilizing index is the presence of features facilitating the making of public statements in support of a candidate or other political actor by site visitors. For example, site producers may encourage visitors to write letters to newspaper editors, or attach their name to a petition or endorsement in support of a policy agenda or political actor. In some cases, visitors may be able to enter their location and receive the contact information for all opinion page editors in their area. The fourth feature associated with mobilizing is a web-to-e-mail application for a site visitor to send a link to someone else's e-mail address. The average level of mobilizing among the sites included in the study was 0.13, with a standard deviation of 0.20.

Together, these four indices make up the principal dependent variables in this analysis of variations in political web practices across the web spheres included in this comparative analysis. As described earlier, the independent variables consist of a number of factors and conditions that display noticeable differences across the cases in the study, and are believed to be related to variations in the ways that political actors use the internet. Specifically, the primary independent variables are measures of levels of human, technical, and political development, as well as political culture.

Comparing nations

Human development

The Human Development Index (HDI) produced annually by the United Nations is the data source on economic or human development in this study.[3] The HDI is a metric that provides a representation of general quality of life, that is comparable across the countries whose web spheres were examined in this analysis and thus sensitive to variations in general conditions. In addition to measuring economic development by including an index of gross domestic product within its general formula, the HDI also combines economic productivity data with measures of literacy and average life expectancy. In doing so, it produces a more comprehensive picture of development across various countries than a mere reliance on GDP figures alone. Across the full cross-national data set, the average HDI score was 0.85 ($SD = 0.11$, $N = 1,219$).

Technological development

A second variable in the models described below is the level of technological development present in the web spheres in which sites included in the study originate. Following Norris (2000, 2001b) three different proportions are combined to measure technological development, creating a new media index. The three proportions are the percentage of persons online within a given country, the proportion of personal computers per capita, and the proportion of hosts per capita. Data from the 2003 edition of the *CIA World Factbook* on the percent online in each country, and population sizes contemporaneous with the electoral web spheres studied, were used to calculate proportions for this analysis.[4] Data on the number of PCs and hosts in each country are drawn from data sets publicly available through the International Telecommunications Union for the same year.[5] The mean value of the new media index observed in these data is 0.75 ($SD = 0.56$, $N = 1,219$).

Political development

As mentioned earlier, in addition to measures of human, economic, and technical development, the analyses are supplemented with variables designed to test for the possible influence of political conditions on the patterns observed concerning political campaigning online. Several indicators were employed to obtain measures of political development. The first of these was the Freedom House ratings, which summarize assessments of civil rights and liberties into a simple index. However, since the present project is automatically limited to countries holding elections, Freedom House ratings displayed almost no variability across the countries included in this comparative analysis, making them unsuitable for use as independent variables in our regression analysis. Thus, another measure was employed—the Index of Democratization developed by Tatu Van Hannen—to provide a slightly more detailed assessment of political development that captures the subtle variations in structural political conditions that may be related to variations in political web practices across the web spheres included in the study.[6] Van Hannen's index provides a detailed metric of what he defines as the preconditions to healthy democratic governance that is comparable across a wide variety of countries. The principal ingredients in this index are the level of electoral competition (calculated by subtracting the proportion of votes garnered in the last election by the largest party in the country from 100) and a measure of political participation (based on the proportion of the total population that voted in the last election). Scores were obtained for all countries in the project that were available from the latest published figures, based on data collected in 2000, and then those scores were converted to an index ranging from 1 to 7. Across all observations, the mean Van Hannen rating was 4.19 (SD = 1.73, N = 1,219).

Political culture

A second dimension of overall political conditions is political culture, defined as the ways in which values and attitudes influence political behavior, including political participation, mobilizations, and actions (Kluver, 2004). To capture variations in political culture across the different web spheres, data from the World Values Survey (WVS) were employed.[7] Although these measures are certainly imperfect, they represent the most reliable—and most importantly—the most comparable set of indicators related to the general political temperaments and possible demand functions that may be working in various web spheres. In this area two specific facets of countrywide political temperament are explored, political participation (beyond mere voting, which is captured in the Van Hannen index), and another variable termed political engagement for the purpose of this study.

Political participation is a simple additive index based on responses to items in the WVS querying respondents as to whether they have engaged in five types of political or civic engagement activities. The five activities were: signing a petition, participating in a boycott, participating in a public demonstration, engaging in a "wildcat" strike, and taking part in a "sit down" strike. The sum of the activities was then aggregated by country to create a metric of the rate of non-voting political or civic participation in each of the web spheres under study.

A similar approach was taken with the *political engagement* index. The items used for this measure consisted of three questions from the WVS dealing with respondents' level of objective and subjective involvement with politics as a matter of daily concern. The first is a simple measure of the rate of political discussion. ("When you get together with your friends, would you say you discuss political matters frequently, occasionally or never?") Responses to the discussion item ranged from 1 (never) to 3 (frequently). The second item simply asks, "How important is politics in your life?" Responses for the importance item range from 1 (not at all) to 4 (very important). Finally, the third item is a classic measure of political interest ("How interested would you say you are in politics?") with responses ranging from 1 (not at all) to 4 (very interested). As with the participation index, responses were summed, and then aggregated by country to provide means, by web sphere, of political engagement. Across all observations for which these data are available, the mean value of the participation index was 1.62 (SD = 0.22, N = 1,000) and the mean value of the political engagement index was 5.53 (SD = 0.56, N = 1,018).

Together, the five measures explained here provide the best available indicators of the concepts implicated in the model introduced earlier. The indicators constituting the independent variables employed in this study are summarized by country in Table 4.1; for more detail see Foot *et al.* (2007).

Site producer types

As discussed earlier, the explanatory model also includes variables for site producer types as a way to capture the known relationship between political website genres and constellations of features. Information on producer types was originally gathered by those who compiled the original site populations for each web sphere. As an added precaution, the categorization of each site as belonging to a particular producer type (candidate, government, party, press, NGO/labor, or other) was also confirmed at the coding stage. Before proceeding with coding on a site, coders were provided with the category of site producer initially selected by whomever identified the site as having been produced by an entity with a role or voice in the election, and were asked to either confirm this, or correct it. In cases of conflict, we deferred to the assessments of the trained coders. For the purpose of increasing comparability across spheres, we excluded sites that were noted as lacking related content at the time of coding.

Results: the power of genre in electoral web spheres

As explained above, there were three central questions motivating our comparative analysis of the data. First to be examined was the extent to which the patterns in online political communication observed in the present study compare with prior research in the field. Second, extant scholarship was extended further, through adding factors into the model related to aspects of political development and political culture. Third, the extent to which particular types of political actors engaged in the same web production practices across national contexts was examined. Overall, a number of notable patterns emerged from these analyses, which took the form of hierarchical regression models that explored the relationships between our dependent variables and a series of explanatory variables introduced into the model in succession. The results of the fully specified models, which include the site producer variables, while controlling for the national development and political culture variables, are displayed in Table 4.2.

The first pattern was seen in the models that only included the human and technological development variables. The findings from those analyses did not, by and large, neatly correspond to the findings of prior comparative research on online political communication. Although the relationships between the New Media Index scores and the web practices of informing, involving, connecting, and mobilizing were all significant and in the expected direction, the results for human development were somewhat puzzling. That is, in nearly all cases, the observed relationship between human development and each of the web practices under study appears to be negative or non-significant.

The second pattern was revealed in the next group of models tested, which probed for the influence of political culture, while controlling for the effects of national development. Based on these models, the addition of variables related to political development and political culture made a distinct contribution to the model. For example, though small, the effect of political development on the practice of involving was statistically significant. And, as seen in the results reported in Table 4.2, remains significant even after the site producer variables are added to the analysis. Furthermore, in this series of regressions, the participation index was found to be significantly related to the practice of informing, again remaining so even after the genre effects are taken into account. Finally, we also

51

Table 4.2 Explaining web production practices: development, political culture, and producer types

Predictor variable	Informing	Involving	Connecting	Mobilizing
Human development				
Human development index	0.08	−0.16	−0.31*	−0.06
Technological development				
New media index	−0.04	0.05	0.12***	−0.01
Political development				
Democracy index	0.01	0.02*	−0.03***	−0.01*
Political culture				
Participation index	0.13*	0.02	0.13*	0.05
Engagement index	0.00	0.00	−0.01	−0.01
Genre effects				
Candidate site	0.17***	0.12***	0.07***	0.06**
Government site	0.14***	−0.08**	0.00	−0.07*
Party site	0.22***	0.23***	0.14***	0.12***
Press site	0.03	−0.03	0.04*	−0.01
NGO/Labor	0.11***	0.09**	0.07*	0.01
Adjusted R^2	0.13	0.22	0.09	0.08
Unweighted N			946	

Source: Internet and Elections Project, 2006; International Telecommunications Union, 2006; United Nations, 2004; World Values Survey, 2000; Vanhanen, 2003.

Notes:
* = $p < 0.10$; ** = $p < 0.01$; *** = $p < 0.001$

saw a significant relationship between the participation index and connecting practices. This relationship also remains significant after the genre variables are controlled for in the fully specified model. Thus, some support was found for the idea that elements of political context, such as institutional characteristics and emergent demand functions, appear to be related to variations in online political communication across different web spheres. This suggests that at least in the case of democracies, models of online politics that only take into account human and technological development may be incomplete.

The third and most striking pattern within these data concerns genre effects. As explained earlier, the inclusion of genre variables to the model reflects our interest in understanding the transnational diffusion of web production practices

within actor types. Each set of results suggests that these political actor/site producer categories explain a large share of variations in features observed across the web spheres subjected to systematic comparative analysis. Indeed, once the genre variables are entered into the analysis, significant increases in the overall variance are explained (as indicated by the adjusted R^2s). Specifically, for the involving and connecting regression analyses, over half of the variation explained can be attributed to the site producer variables, and in the analyses for informing and mobilizing, virtually all of the explanatory power lies in these variables. This suggests that among democratic nations, the influence of a website's producer type (e.g. campaign, political party, press organization) tends to outstrip the influence of factors specific to the geographic and political web sphere from which it originates.

Discussion

There are a number of possible interpretations regarding the first pattern in these findings, that is, the non-significant or negative relationship between human development and each of the web practices under study. It could be that the exclusive focus in this study on countries with elections during 2004 masks or distorts the relationship between the level of human development and the likelihood that site producers engage in the web practices examined. Another possible factor influencing the observed relationship is the study's focus on electoral web spheres; other web spheres, perhaps those produced by government agencies or for commercial purposes, might yield the expected relationship. Further research is required to examine these relationships more closely.

There is an interesting tension between the second and third patterns in these findings. On one hand, the strong similarities discovered between the web production practices of political actors of the same type cross-nationally support patterns of international diffusion of innovation in the realm of politics and internet technologies from the U.S. and the U.K. to other countries in Europe and Asia found by other scholars (Howard, 2006; Wilson, 2004). On the other hand, the fact that political development and political culture factors had statistical significance in predicting web production practices across this sample of 19 election-holding countries merits further attention. Even though these relationships are not as strong as those found for producer types, and indeed for one practice (connecting) the relationship is negative, on the whole this finding is remarkable considering the relatively narrow range of political cultures represented in the sample. Most of the nations studied are parliamentary democracies; in addition to the U.K., the

U.S., and Australia, the political cultures of several other countries included in the study have historically been shaped by Anglo-American influences, including the practice of hiring political consultants, who often bring their experiences in one nation to another.

Contrary to some prior studies indicating that levels of national development determine technology appropriation, and other work suggesting political culture would trump transnational flows of expertise, the findings of this study indicate that political actors in various countries are more likely to model their sites on those produced by similar political actors from other countries rather than modeling them on sites produced by other types of political actors within their own country. There are a number of possible reasons for this, including the aforementioned role of political technology consultants working transnationally, the desire to establish international legitimacy, the particular needs of the political actors as web producers, and the purposes for the sites they produce.

Political culture and political development are difficult to define operationally and assess quantitatively (Verba et al., 1987; Pye, 1985). While the measures employed in this study—Van Hannen's development index and aggregate indicators of political participation and political engagement—are important indicators of some aspects of political culture, they are by no means comprehensive, and undoubtedly fail to capture some of the more nuanced differences between the different countries. Furthermore, survey data related to political culture that could enable comparison across all the countries included in this study were limited. In addition to displaying relatively little variation across the countries in this study, survey data were not available for a few of the countries included in the analysis, as indicated by the lower Ns for the Model 2 and Model 3 results.[8] More fine-grained studies of political culture are needed to develop additional measures, and cross-national surveys on political attitudes and actions need to be implemented more broadly across regions.

Conclusion

Systematic cross-national comparative research is challenging to design, fund, and conduct on a large scale—and it holds much value for the pursuit of knowledge. Only this type of research allows for the exploration of questions affecting great numbers of people in many countries. This study has focused on teasing out the complicated relationships that explain the tendencies of a wide variety of political actors to engage in different types of web practices, across Europe, Asia, and the U.S.

In summary, for the countries included in this analysis, the type of political actor producing a site was more potent than human development, technological development, and political culture variables in explaining web production practices. The production of a national electoral web sphere happens in a global context: the production practices of one type of actors in a national electoral web sphere are more likely to be like those of the same type of actors in other electoral web spheres than like those of other types of actors within the same national electoral web sphere. For example, websites produced by political parties in the Philippines are more likely to be similar to websites producer by political parties in the United States than they are to be similar to websites produced by advocacy groups in the Philippines.

At the same time, political culture was determined to exert significant influence on how web production practices are implemented within national contexts. Even within the relatively narrow range of democratic nations included in this study, differences in political participation and political engagement among the citizenry corresponded with differences in political actors' web production practices.

Aside from the findings on genre effects and political culture, the positive relationship between technological development and each of the web practices confirms the association between overall level of technical development within a country and the types of web practices in which producers engage. As expected, countries with more diffusion of media technology, greater access to the media technology, and greater use of media technology, included producers who engaged in more types of web practices. Additional research is necessary to examine the observed negative relationship between level of human development and level of web practices.

Further research would be useful to both confirm and shed further light on these findings. Such research efforts could include a finer grained analysis of the specific types of web practices found in websites produced by specific types of political actors. For example, a cross-national study of political party websites, focused on the particular functions and needs of political parties, could highlight those aspects of party websites that were common across political cultures, as well as identify aspects of party websites that were distinctive across political cultures. In addition, a cross-national study of a particular practice across multiple types of political actors—for example, the ways in which information is solicited from site visitors—could explain the relative influence of actor type and political culture.

Guide to further reading

An increasing array of scholars from diverse fields, including political science, communication, sociology, psychology, information science, and rhetoric, have studied the use of the web by political parties and campaigns, particularly in the U.S. and the U.K. The foci of scholarly analyses ranged from the integration of the web into campaigns' day-to-day operations (cf. Howard, 2006), to the range of features provided by producers of campaign websites and campaigns' web strategies (cf. Williams and Tedesco, 2006), to the ways in which citizens, journalists, and others have used the web to obtain political information during campaigns (cf. Bimber and Davis, 2003), to the impacts of web campaigning on civic engagement as well as campaign processes and electoral outcomes (cf. Valentino *et al.*, 2004). A considerable literature has developed examining online campaign activities outside the U.S. and the U.K. (cf. Gibson and Rommele, 2003; Gibson and Ward, 2002; Park *et al.*, 2000; Thach-Kawasaki, 2003). Some of this research on the internet in elections has been explicitly comparative (Gibson *et al.*, 2003b; Ward and Voerman, 2000). Chadwick's (2006) book provides an excellent overview of the internet and politics in the U.S. and the U.K. Other scholars have studied technology appropriation cross-nationally, but not necessarily in explicitly political contexts (cf. Norris, 2000, 2001b; Wilson, 2004).

Notes

1 An earlier version of this chapter was published by Foot, Schneider, Kluver, Xenos, and Jankowski as "Comparing Web Production Practices Across Electoral Web Spheres," in *The Internet and National Elections: a comparative study of web campaigning*, Kluver, Jankowski, Foot, and Schneider (eds.), Routledge, 2007, pp. 243–60.

2 Electoral web spheres analyzed in this chapter consist of 2004 European Parliamentary elections in the Czech Republic, Finland, France, Hungary, Ireland, Italy, the Netherlands, Portugal, Slovenia, and the United Kingdom, the 2004 congressional election in the United States, the presidential and/or parliamentary elections held in 2004 in Australia, India, Indonesia, Japan, Philippines, South Korea, Sri Lanka, and the 2005 parliamentary election in Thailand.

3 http://hdr.undp.org/reports/global/2004/?CFID=1548133&CFTOKEN=71996467. Accessed August 16, 2007.

4 www.cia.gov/library/publications/the-world-factbook/docs/notesanddefs.html. Accessed August 16, 2007.

5 www.itu.int/ITU-D/ict/statistics/. Accessed August 16, 2007.

6 Polyarchy Dataset: www.fsd.uta.fi/english/data/catalogue/FSD1216/ VanHannen's Codebook: www.fsd.uta.fi/english/data/catalogue/FSD1216/FSD1216_variablelist.txt. Background materials: www.fsd.uta.fi/english/data/catalogue/FSD1216/bgF1216e.pdf www.prio.no/files/file42501_introduction.pdf. All accessed August 16, 2007.

7 http://data.library.ubc.ca/datalib/survey/icpsr/3975/03975–0001-Codebook.pdf. Accessed August 16, 2007.

8 World Values Survey data on political culture were not available for Hungary, Thailand, and Sri Lanka.

5

Parties, election campaigning, and the internet

Toward a comparative institutional approach

Nick Anstead and Andrew Chadwick

This chapter argues that a comparative approach to analyzing the relationship between technology and political institutions has the potential to offer renewed understanding of the development of the internet in election campaigning. Taking the different characteristics of political parties and the norms and rules of the electoral environment in the United States and the United Kingdom as an illustration, it suggests that the relationship between technology and political institutions is dialectical. Technologies can reshape institutions, but institutions will mediate eventual outcomes. The chapter outlines five key variables: degree of systemic institutional pluralism; organization of membership; candidate recruitment and selection; campaign finance; and the "old" campaign communication environment. This approach has the potential to generate a theoretical framework for explaining differences in the impact of the internet on election campaigning across liberal democracies.

Since the mid 1990s, it has been widely predicted that the internet will have a decisive influence on election campaigning. This prophecy has, in part at least, been fulfilled in the United States, especially since Howard Dean's blog-fueled campaign for the Democratic presidential nomination in the 2003–4 primary season, the widespread impact of online video during the 2006 midterm elections, and the proliferation of Web 2.0 social media during the 2007–8 contest.

It is tempting to think that this "success story" has been driven by the diffusion of the internet. By 2005, 76 percent of Americans were recorded as being online (International Telecommunication Union, 2005). And, despite ongoing divisions in patterns of use, the overwhelming majority of people have integrated information and communication technologies into their everyday lives (Horrigan, 2007). Since the public get their news, do their

shopping, and communicate with friends online, it is hardly surprising that they are also being citizens.

However, technology diffusion explanations of changes in election campaigning only tell part of the story. There are other countries with high levels of internet diffusion, in which it has yet to have such a significant impact. In the United Kingdom, while more than 60 percent of the population are now online (International Telecommunication Union, 2005), there is consensus that the internet has had only a marginal influence on elections, a fact noted on numerous occasions during both the 2001 and 2005 national polls (Coleman and Hall, 2001; Ward, 2005). It seems perverse, therefore, to suggest that once internet penetration reaches some kind of critical mass (whatever that may be) a decisive political impact somehow becomes inevitable. Given the unevenness of the role played by the net in electoral contests across even the liberal democratic world, we must look for additional explanations for national differences.

One element of such an explanation may be found by considering how the internet interacts with the relevant political institutions that pre-date its existence: in particular, the organization of political parties and the norms and rules of the electoral environment. These vary greatly across political systems. Different types of party organization and electoral environment have the potential to catalyze or to retard the development of internet campaigning because they render new communication technologies more or less useful to candidates and parties seeking office. When viewed in comparative context, American parties are unusual political organizations, and quite dissimilar to those found in other, notably European, liberal democracies. Such differences may help explain the quantitative and qualitative differences in internet campaigning across countries.

This is not to suggest that research on internet campaigning has lacked an international orientation. Rigorous individual country studies are growing in number. But, to echo the opening comments of Foot et al.'s chapter in this volume, with a few exceptions (for example, the editors' conclusion in Gibson et al. (eds), 2003c; Newell, 2001; Tkach-Kawasaki, 2003), very little of the research on parties and internet campaigning is grounded in cross-national comparison of relevant political institutions. Gibson et al. (2003) conducted a comparative survey of candidate websites in the United States and the United Kingdom, but excluded variables related to parties and the electoral environment. Zittel (2004) focused, not on campaign dynamics, but on individual legislators' adoption of the internet. Again, this involved a survey of legislator websites in three countries, correlated

with independent variables: age of legislator, constituency demographics, the electoral system, and type of government. The latter was not disaggregated but defined in basic terms as "presidential" versus "parliamentary". Foot et al.'s highly illuminating chapter in this volume, while focusing on a wide range of political actors and featuring sophisticated dependent variables that signal the growth of online campaign "web spheres"—nevertheless downgrades political institutions in the overall analysis. The closest of several independent variables, termed "political culture" is, understandably given the scale and ambition of the *Internet and Elections Project* from which it is drawn, defined and measured solely in terms of individual citizen attitudes and self-reported behavior.

Institutions proximate to election campaigns can have a direct impact on the mobilization of resources, acting as catalysts and anti-catalysts. At their most extreme, institutional structures may act as complete barriers. Examples include the ban on the purchase of television advertising in the United Kingdom, or on podcasting in Singapore. Most of the time institutions may simply make the process of deploying resources unattractive, as would be the case if stringent regulatory hurdles had to be overcome to set up a political website, for instance. Opportunity costs are also entailed in choosing to deploy a particular resource. A large billboard purchase may cut the number of mailings a party can send; dedicating campaign staff to a blogging campaign may remove them from face-to-face roles. The internet may reconfigure or reduce opportunity costs but it does not destroy them. The benefits political actors are able to derive are thus strongly influenced by the institutional environment (March and Olsen, 1989).

This chapter argues that a comparative approach to analyzing the relationship between technology and political institutions has the potential to offer renewed understanding of the development of the internet in election campaigning. Taking the different characteristics of political parties and the norms and rules of the electoral environment in the United States and the United Kingdom as an illustration, it aims to show that the relationship between technology and political institutions is best perceived as dialectical. Technologies can reshape institutions, but institutions will mediate eventual outcomes. This approach has the potential to generate a theoretical framework for explaining differences in the impact of the internet on election campaigning across liberal democracies.

Normalizers, optimists, and institutions

The lack of comparative institutional research on internet campaigning is perhaps best explained by the terms of reference that have dominated discussion of internet politics more generally. Since the net's early days, analysis of its political impact has been dominated by two distinct schools of thought: the normalizers, who claim that current political relationships and power distributions will ultimately be replicated online, and the optimists, who claim that the internet will reform politics and radically redistribute political power. These two camps are descendants of an older debate between sociological and technological determinisms: between those who claim that the impact of technology is shaped by social and political institutions and those who believe technology has the power to shape society and politics. While the debate between normalizers and optimists has been useful in creating much of the significant early analysis of the internet, it has also proved limiting. Both sides have generally paid insufficient attention

to the complex interaction between technology and political institutions.

While institutions have often been neglected by the normalizers and the optimists, they have at least had an implied significance. Normalization theory argues that the broader resources available to political actors, such as money, bureaucracy, supporter networks, or an interested mainstream media, will heavily condition their ability to make effective use of the internet for campaigning (see, for example, Davis, 1999; Margolis and Resnick, 2000). Online advantage accrues to the strongest offline actors. In their influential book, *Politics as Usual*, Michael Margolis and David Resnick (2000: 2) argue that cyberspace "will be molded by the everyday struggle for wealth and power."

The relationship between normalization and political institutions can be critically understood in two ways. First, the theory is socially determinist. It assumes that pre-internet power brokers will come to define the online world, autonomously of technological change. It therefore neglects important differences between old media of political communication, particularly the paper press and television, and new, low-cost, low-threshold interactive and participatory media. Second, in normalization theory, existing institutions offer a framework for the explanation that political behavior will remain *normal*. The problem is that, when situated in a cross-national comparative context, it is best seen not as a universal truth but as a matter for investigation. The question we must ask is: what *kinds* of institutional features are more likely to have affinities with the particular technological affordances of internet communication? A comparative approach allows us to hypothesize what may, or may not, gain traction in different political systems.

The relationship between institutions and the case made by internet *optimists* is more difficult to disentangle, largely because they do not form a single school but can be divided into two broad categories according to their attitudes to representative democracy. Most applicable to the American experience is what can be termed *representative democracy optimism*. This approach does not argue that the internet will destroy all representative institutions, but instead claims that it has the potential to reform and rehabilitate indirect vehicles of democratic participation, most notably political parties and elections (for example, Trippi, 2004). This approach has been accompanied by a second: the view that the internet will actually undermine representative political institutions (Morris, 1999).

This distinction between representative democracy optimists and direct democracy optimists is significant. However, both posit a monocausal relationship between technology and politics: existing political institutions will either be reformed or entirely replaced under the weight of technological change. This is grounded in how the characteristics of the internet differ from previously dominant media of political communication, most notably television. The necessities of the television age political campaign are said to have made parties centralized and steeply hierarchical, and grass-roots activism and civic life are said to have become emaciated (Trippi, 2004: 37–40, 214–15). The televisual form is one-to-many; the internet offers rapid, distributed, multidirectional, interactive, many-to-many communication.

Criticisms of technological determinism are of course manifold, and cannot detain us here (see Roe Smith, 1994). But from our perspective, devaluing the role of non- or pre-internet organizational structures, norms, and rules, in mediating technological forces, and how these processes may vary across political systems, renders such an approach problematic as a framework for the explanation of the development of internet campaigning.

In summary, normalization and internet optimism approaches do not adequately consider the possibility that *some* political institutions, as currently arranged, are likely to act as a catalyst for the integration of the internet into election campaigning, while *others* may not.

America's online success story

While the chronicles of headline-grabbing examples of internet campaigning now feature several countries, it is on the United States that most interest, both popular and academic, has focused. This is unsurprising: the country can claim to be the birthplace of the internet; it is the only global hyperpower; its elections are followed throughout the world; and interest in its politics is strongly linked to the idea of Americanization, which suggests convergence in electoral politics, especially in styles of campaign communication (see, for example, Farrell *et al.*, 2001; Kavanagh, 1995, Negrine and Papathanassopoulos, 1996).

The internet's potential has long been apparent. In the 1998 Minnesota gubernational contest, Independent candidate Jesse Ventura, running against well-established Democratic and Republican candidates, used the net to organize and publicize campaign rallies in the hours before polls closed (Greer and LaPointe, 2004: 117; Klotz, 2004: 71). In the Republican presidential primary contest in 2000, following his unexpected win in New Hampshire, John McCain was able to raise $3 million in donations in ten days (Klotz, 2004: 77), an unprecedented feat at the time. During the presidential contest that year, Al Gore organized an innovative series of online "town hall" style discussion forums.

However, it was Howard Dean's candidacy for the Democratic nomination for the presidency in 2004 that really seemed to fulfill the early promise of the internet as a campaigning tool. Dean was little known nationally, though his continued opposition to the war in Iraq did give him a platform distinct from the other candidates in the Democratic field. During the early phase of the primaries, Dean struggled to get his campaign off the ground: his opinion poll ratings were within the margin of error of zero and he was woefully short of cash and known supporters. At the end of 2002, Dean's campaign team restructured its online presence, in order to test the networking and fundraising potential of the internet. By the end of 2003, Dean had gone from being an unknown candidate with very few financial resources to the leader in the race and the most successful primary fundraiser in the history of the Democratic Party (Chadwick, 2007; Hindman, 2005; Trippi, 2004).

Following on from Dean's success, the eventual winner of the Democratic nomination, John Kerry, while relying mainly on large donors to get him through the primaries (defined by Hindman, 2005 as those who give the federal maximum of $2,000), nevertheless used the internet to raise a large number of small donations during the main campaign. This allowed Kerry, in a situation unprecedented for a Democrat, to achieve near financial parity with his Republican opponent, George W. Bush, by the close of the 2004 campaign (Dwyer et al., 2004).

The 2006 midterms continued to offer effective demonstrations of the power of the internet. During the Democratic primary for the Senate seat in Connecticut, three-term Senator and former candidate for the vice presidency, Joe Lieberman, was defeated by journeyman candidate Ned Lamont, who had only previously held local office. Lieberman was an outspoken defender of the Iraq war, a stance that put him at odds with many grass-roots Democrats, while Lamont worked to portray himself as an anti-war candidate. Lamont's attempt to defeat Lieberman was embraced by high-profile Democratic bloggers, the so-called "netroots," who promoted his candidacy, raised money, and even starred in celebrity-style campaign commercials. The internet was important in creating momentum for Lamont: he convincingly defeated Lieberman in the primary (Murray, 2006; Ned Lamont for Senate, 2006).

The main midterm election period of 2006 continued to feature extensive use of the net. The most notorious episode came during the race for the Virginia Senate seat. Republican incumbent George Allen was expected to comfortably retain his position, as the precursor to a possible presidential run in 2008. However, some months before the election, Allen was filmed referring to Democratic opponent Jim Webb's campaign worker as a "macaca", a racist term. The DIY video of this event was immediately uploaded onto media-sharing site YouTube, and soon became a viral sensation, leading to Allen's views on race being questioned both online and, crucially, in mainstream newsprint and television media. From being 20 points ahead in the polls at the end of April, Allen went on to lose (CNN, 2006; NOI, 2006; YouTube, 2006). By the time of the close of the 2006 elections, it was also clear that the netroots movement MoveOn, by campaigning in support of several successful Senate and House candidates, had exerted influence on the Democratic takeover of Congress. Soon after the election, MoveOn's website displayed a table of statistics for the pivotal districts, including margin of victory, financial contributions, and number of phone calls to voters. It mobilized volunteers to make seven million calls and host 7,500 house parties

(MoveOn, 2007). Although hard data are lacking, it seems fair to suggest that Allen's defeat in Virginia was caused by the viral effect of the YouTube video. Certainly a Republican online campaigning guidebook for the 2008 elections suggested that this was the case (National Republican Senatorial Committee, 2007). And, as Davis *et al.* reveal in their chapter in this volume, the 2006 midterms and the early stages of the 2007–8 primary season witnessed the growing use of online social networking sites such as MySpace and Facebook, with Hillary Clinton and Barack Obama amassing hundreds of thousands of members in supporter networks.

From this very brief depiction of high-profile cases it is evident that the internet plays a great many roles in the American campaign environment, whether it be creating political networks, promoting discussion of politics, raising funds, or storing, retrieving, and automating information (Howard, 2006).

Britain's online non-events?

Observers of British elections have long been wondering if the internet campaign phenomena witnessed in the United States will make their way across the Atlantic. United Kingdom campaign managers eagerly followed the 2000 presidential contest in an effort to "learn lessons" (Gibson *et al.*, 2003a: 51). Overall, however, the net had little impact on the 2001 general election. Only 7 percent of citizens claimed to have used it to look for election information, compared with 74 percent for newspapers and 89 percent for television (MORI, 2001). It appears to have played only a marginal role in influencing how individuals decided to vote, and candidates' online presences, though improving, were not as developed as those of their American counterparts.

By the 2005 British general election, evidence was emerging that internet campaigning was shaping political behavior. Some British MPs were using the net to reach out to supporters outside the traditional structures of party, via e-mail distribution lists, for example, which performed some of the functions performed by blogs (Jackson, 2004). Around 50 parliamentary candidates blogged during the 2005 campaign (Kimber, 2005). While the internet presence of candidates was an improvement over 2001, it was clear that the internet did not play the role it did in the 2004 U.S. campaign. Blogging remains very much a minority sport among British parliamentarians (Ward and Francoli, 2007).

In the period following the 2005 election, as social media and social networking trends reached Britain, politicians began to experiment with YouTube, MySpace, and Facebook. A handful of prominent politicians, including government minister David Miliband, began high-profile blogs. In the spring of 2006, Labour Party leader Tony Blair ordered a rethink of the party's approach to web campaigning. This led to the creation of the Labor Supporters Network, an e-mail list designed to appeal to those who were not willing or able to become fully paid-up party members, and MpURL Membersnet, a social network site that provides each party member with a blog, each local constituency Labour Party organization with an online discussion forum, and a number of general policy-related forums. Meanwhile, the Conservative Party's new leader, David Cameron, pioneered the use of viral online video in mainstream British politics, with his Webcameron video blog. Labour's deputy leadership contest in the spring of 2007 saw all candidates engage with Web 2.0 platforms such as Facebook and MySpace. Thus there are some tentative signs that British parties are integrating the net. But does this mean that they will converge on the

American model? And, if so, to what extent? The next section seeks to provide a framework for answering such questions through a consideration of the differences between the United States and United Kingdom party and electoral environments.

Party organization and electoral environment: catalysts and anti-catalysts for internet election campaigning

The British and American party organizations and electoral environments have much in common. When it comes to national elections, both are historically embedded two-party systems: only two parties have a realistic chance of securing executive power; single-party executives are the norm at the national level (not at the devolved level in the United Kingdom); and parties "take turns" in controlling the executive. Both countries have simple plurality electoral systems based on geographical constituencies, and this reinforces the two-party system.

But there are highly significant differences between the two countries. For the purposes of this chapter, these may be mapped along five distinct, though interrelated, dimensions: the degree of systemic institutional pluralism; the organization of membership; candidate recruitment and selection; campaign finance; and the "old" campaign communication environment. The aim here is to show how differences between the United States and the United Kingdom in each of these areas may be used to hypothesize the distinct characteristics of online election campaigning in each political system.

Degree of systemic institutional pluralism

Federalism and the separation of powers, both key constitutional values in the United

States, guarantee substantial institutional pluralism. This weakens national party integration (Epstein, 1980; Harmel and Janda, 1982; Key, 1964). The separate electoral bases of the presidency and Congress provide few incentives for party cohesion. Parties have state and local committees but their influence and level of organization differs significantly from state to state. Many state committees are flimsy, and where there are traditions of strong party organization, such as in New York state or Pennsylvania, these are still only weakly integrated with the national committees in Washington. Parties are important for government formation and affiliation remains a very strong predictor of congressional behavior, but away from the capitol, state and local party structures have few direct policy-making roles. National party committees are institutionally separate from the party organizations inside Congress, and while there are differences between the states, much the same can be said of the relationship between state legislatures and state-level party committees. The national committees have grown in influence since the 1970s, yet they are still of less importance during presidential races than the staff and infrastructure built up by candidates themselves during both the primary season and the main campaign. Even the most nationally-oriented electoral contest—for the presidency—necessarily becomes a matter of localized campaigning in targeted key states, due to the electoral college system. In the lexicon of Samuel Eldersveld (1982), the American party system is stratarchical rather than hierarchical. Layers of party organization, driven by factionalism along several dimensions, are only loosely joined.

Contrast this with the United Kingdom, where the separation of powers is strictly circumscribed by the near-fusion of the legislature and the executive (Lijphart, 1984) and where, despite recent devolution reforms, the state is unitary. The prime minister and Parliament share an electoral base, incentivizing party cohesion in the interests of policy success for the government and re-election for MPs. British parties are characterized by greater levels of national coordination and integration, and while there are different political traditions associated with party activism in localities, the party structures are internally uniform. Local constituency organizations enjoy policy-making influence but despite recent trends toward internal democratization, national headquarters exert close control over the whole party. While some local associations can and do deviate from the leadership's script, national party organizations nevertheless have a major influence on the election campaign by channeling resources, coordinating activity, and applying sanctions (Ware, 1996). British parties are comparatively integrated and hierarchical rather than stratarchical.

How do these characteristics interact with the technological affordances of the internet? The pluralistic environment in the United States necessitates building campaign networks composed of horizontal and vertical connections that mesh with the fundamentally stratarchical basis of the system. Integration can be achieved in a way that leaves intact the operative norms of federalism and the separation of powers, but which provides lines of communication between levels of party organization and activists. The internet provides for granular communication that allows party staff to quickly switch from local to state to national focus and vice versa. It also reinforces the trend, since the 1970s, towards a more active coordinating role for the national party committees. Yet, in a system where state party organizations often jealously guard their autonomy, the open, looser networks afforded by internet communication fit well.

Compare this with the United Kingdom, where, as we have noted, the separation of powers is weak, federalism absent, and parties comparatively integrated and hierarchical. There, though constituency-level organizations can be rebellious, the lines of communication are more vertically oriented, more firmly drawn, and are based in long-established formal structures with accompanying bureaucracies. The internet's technological affordances for creating loose horizontal networks have fewer affinities with this set of arrangements. We can hypothesize that it is more likely that British parties will deploy the internet in ways that jell with internal routinized institutional traits. This is evidenced, for example, by the MpURL Membersnet, which is a members-only layer of web applications that map onto longstanding internal party structures.

Organization of membership

In his classic work on party systems, Duverger (1954) suggested that British (and other European) parties were organizationally "superior" because they developed durable mass membership and participation infrastructures. Revisionists such as Epstein (1980) have suggested that the weaker American party model is better suited to the age of leader-focused, televisual politics. Either way, American parties do not have a system of individual membership, though there is a chance for ordinary party supporters to play a role in the selection of candidates through the primary system (see below). Nor do they have a leader embedded in their structure, but instead rely on a successful presidential candidate to lead the party once elected. Parties in Congress are often described as "headless": there is no concept of permanent opposition (Janda, 1993: 164). The once decisive role of the party convention in policy discussion and nomination has, since the 1970s, been hollowed out. And, as we have seen, the difficulty of coordinating solidary resources in American parties is affected by federalism and the separation of powers.

The lack of a permanent membership necessarily makes American parties heavily campaign focused. Candidates seeking office are required to develop their own campaign infrastructure, based around personal support for their platform. This is reinforced by the primary system, which features a large-scale campaign from which elements of the party's organization, such as national and state committees, are sometimes marginalized. United States politics is candidate centered.

In the United Kingdom, parties have an organic existence outside of election campaigns; they are organs of policy and participation and have (currently declining) memberships. National party conferences differ in terms of policy influence from party to party, but conferences do retain a residual policy-making role. Local, regional, and national policy forums provide opportunities for rank-and-file activists to participate. While campaign machinery does tend to deteriorate during the periods between elections, greater institutional presence and continuous membership do not create pressures to continually rebuild from scratch. There is a strong tradition of organized opposition in British politics, spearheaded by the permanent party leader of the second largest party in Parliament and his or her shadow cabinet. In Britain, parties have pre-formed structures containing activists inherited by successive leaders. United Kingdom politics is party centered.

The often temporary and short-lived associations that constitute the American campaign offer strong incentives for using the internet. The most successful and publicized examples, for example Howard Dean's use of Meetup or Barack Obama's creation of Facebook groups (Goldfarb, 2007) in the earliest possible stages of the campaign are attempts to construct an online network of supporters and activists at the lowest possible cost and often well in advance of organization on the ground. We may also consider this from the perspective of activists themselves, who seek policy influence and expressive benefits from political participation. For such individuals, the internet provides these earlier and, for some it seems, with greater intensity than in the "old" campaign environment.

In the United Kingdom, while volunteer activists are hardly in abundant supply, the party membership is at least a pre-existing resource that can be tapped in more routinized and predictable ways by party elites, candidates, and members alike. Party elites often engage in administrative reform of internal structures to realize political or bureaucratic goals (Webb, 2000), but the sense of fast-moving organizational fluidity, even chaos, that often characterizes American candidates' attempts to mobilize support is not evident.

Recent developments in Britain do, however, suggest that the internet may be catalyzing some aspects of party membership organization. The permanent membership base of British parties has been eroding for several decades. This incentivizes parties to seek alternative models. As mentioned in our brief description of election campaigning, the Labour Party's new "supporters' network" and its internal social networking model, MpURL Membersnet, deliberately seek to attract those who do not commit to old-style party membership, or those who do not engage with traditional face-to-face participatory structures. This is not to suggest that British parties are converging on the U.S. model. Significant differences will persist, as British parties mold the technology in their own ways. Hence, Labour's Chair Hazel Blears' view that "We don't want a U.S.-style party with a loose coalition of supporters, rather than an active membership" (Blears, 2007). Our assumption is that technology can shape institutions but institutions will mediate eventual outcomes.

Candidate recruitment and selection

In the United States, mechanisms for the recruitment and selection of candidates offer an institutional framework for sanctioned dissent (Bogdanor, 1984: x). Distrust of the corruption and patronage of urban party machines led to the early twentieth century reforms specifically designed to weaken party bosses and increase citizen influence via devices such as the initiative, the referendum, and the recall, but most significantly, primary elections. While practices have differed across the states, since the 1970s, primaries have become fundamental to U.S. politics. Uncertainty and risk are much greater for both party elites and candidates than their equivalents in Britain. Participation in primaries is restricted, but the thresholds are low. One must simply register as a Democrat or Republican, in some cases only a few weeks before the ballot. While caucus selection has not entirely disappeared, many caucus votes are in any case characterized by the same degree of fluidity and openness as witnessed during primaries (McKay, 2005: 93).

Primaries are absent from the British party system. Internal competition between contenders takes place in arenas sealed off from direct participation by the general public. United Kingdom parties do have internal procedures, which, to varying extents, involve mass memberships in the selection of national leadership positions, and permanent local constituency associations select their local party candidates, subject to the final approval of central staff. But electoral rules guarantee party elites a significant power bloc in national leadership contests, parliamentary candidates are heavily vetted by central party elites, and the committees of local constituency activists are usually small and exclusive. The environment for candidate selection is much less open and fluid, much more tightly managed, and more nationally-oriented than is the case in the United States.

It is notable that in the United States, most of the internet campaigning innovations (McCain during 1999–2000; Dean during 2003–4; Lamont during 2006; Obama during 2007–8) have occurred during primaries. Primary elections may be influenced but cannot be controlled by the parties themselves. Resources permitting, any individual may run for the nomination and those without "establishment" party backing have found the internet particularly attractive for garnering support. In Dean's case, an outsider candidate found that he could use the net to quickly ratchet up a campaign in the early primary stages in an attempt to reduce the costs of overcoming sheer geographical scale and the complexity of the different state-level contests. The uncertainty of the primary environment forces candidates to cast around for opportunities to build what are often fragile and fleeting coalitions of support. In some respects, candidates can use the internet to try to reduce this uncertainty and risk. When the risks are high but the costs of organizational innovation are low, candidates are more likely to experiment, for example by trying to tap into multiple online networks. During the 2007–8 primary campaign, John Edwards' campaign was notorious for spreading its bets across practically *all* of the important Web 2.0 sites and applications, including 43Things, Del.icio.us, Essembly, Facebook, Flickr, Gather, MySpace, Partybuilder, YouTube, Ning, Metacafe, Revver, Yahoo! 360°, Blip.tv, CHBN, vSocial, Tagworld, Collectivex, Bebo, Care2, Hi5, Xanga, and LiveJournal (Edwards, 2007).

This conjuncture of institutions and technological affordances may be especially applicable to the Democratic Party, for whom the institution of the primary was created, in its modern form, with the goal of empowering activists. The disagreement between much of the party elite and its base over the Iraq war has fueled the most prominent web campaigns, most notably those of Dean, Paul Hackett, and Lamont. Institutions (the primary) and technology came together to form a mutually reinforcing environment for grass-roots dissent. At the same time, however, it still needs to be recognized that factors such as the lack of a fully "national" campaign domain, the complexities of different state-level contexts, and the command of territorial scale required of a successful U.S. primary candidacy are important institutional constraints. These may be softened but cannot totally be overcome by the internet. Dean found this to his cost when it actually came to the ballots.

Lacking primaries and having much greater control over candidate recruitment and selection, British parties operate within a radically different environment. Factionalism, dissent, and risk are important factors in British party selection processes (Webb, 2000), but they are deliberately managed, or are not permitted such blatant institutional expression (Ware, 1996). The "selectorate" is a combination of party elites and members, but those members are fully paid up. It would be unusual to see large numbers of citizens join a British party just to participate in an internal election campaign: the threshold is too high. And while candidates must be seen to be impressive in the face of broader public opinion, they nevertheless know that the internal electoral rules and timetable are fixed and nationally uniform, and that there will (literally) be no outsider candidates. In this environment, there are fewer incentives to take advantage

of the internet for lowering costs and reducing uncertainty and risk by spreading a campaign across a wide range of networks.

Campaign finance

The campaign finance environment differs significantly across the two political systems. We focus here on three factors, all of which mediate the internet as an aid to fund-raising.

First, there is the matter of scale and significance. American politics, by the standards of anywhere else in the world, is expensive. Indeed, there is much talk of 2008 being the first $1 billion election (Malbin and Cain, 2007: 4). In contrast, in the 12 months preceding the 2005 British general election, the combined spending of the Labour and Conservative Parties was just £90 million ($185 million) (Phillips, 2007: 13). Furthermore, the acquisition of money is central to success in American politics. Electoral primaries, for example, are preceded by what is termed "the money primary", where candidates' electoral viability is assessed by their ability to raise funds from donors (Adkins and Dowdle, 2002). This process received a great deal of coverage in anticipation of the 2008 presidential primary season, with much comment being made on Barack Obama's success as a fund-raiser and the relative failure of John McCain to gather the funds considered necessary for a successful nomination bid (Heileman, 2007; MacAskill, 2007). There is no comparable institution in British politics. The importance of financial resources to American politics ensures that political actors are quick to exploit the potential of new revenue streams. This has certainly been the case online, where candidates, most notably Democrats, have proved to be adept at raising vast sums of money (Dwyer et al., 2004). Through the institution of the money primary, it is possible for American citizens to have quite a direct impact on political outcomes. For this reason, it is a far more rational course of action for Americans to make political donations. The internet has made this more apparent, by lowering the barrier to participation and making it easier for citizens to contribute to their preferred candidate.

Second, the American political system exhibits a diverse range of donation opportunities. This is a direct consequence of the pluralistic nature of American parties. Even the national parties each contain three committees to which donations can be sent: the national committee, the house party, and the senate party. Then there are party organizations at state and regional level. Money can also be given directly to candidates for office, both during the primary season (when givers will have a choice between many candidates), and then in the main electoral contest. In contrast, the centralized nature of British parties offers far fewer opportunities for individuals to donate. The vast majority of political donations in Britain are given to the national headquarters of a party. In 2005, nearly 85 percent of the £38 million of cash contributions given to the Conservative and Labor Parties and itemized by the U.K. Electoral Commission went straight to the central party organization, with only the remaining 15 percent going to sub-national bodies (U.K. Electoral Commission, 2005).

Third, the two countries employ vastly different regulatory systems, based on diametrically opposed principles. This has historically been the case, but has been further reinforced by recent legal decisions and legislation. In America, attempts to regulate political finance have focused on declaring and capping donations. The 1971 Federal Election Campaign Act required disclosure of donations to candidates, while a 1974 amendment to the act, passed in the aftermath of the Watergate scandal, imposed a donation cap of $1,000. This law was upheld by the Supreme Court in *Buckley* v. *Valeo* (1976).

However, the same hearing also ruled two significant provisos, both of which were to have huge implications for campaign finance in the United States. While caps on donations were deemed legal, any caps on spending were deemed unconstitutional, on the grounds they would breach the first amendment right to free speech. The Supreme Court also ruled that only donations made directly for the purpose of election campaigning would fall under the auspices of donation limits. In reality the distinction between electoral campaigning and issue advertising proved to be very fine, and it was this element of the ruling that led to the distinction between hard and soft money in American politics. Hard money donations to candidates fell under the remit of the Federal Election Commission and were limited by the Federal Election Campaign Act. In contrast, soft money existed outside this regulatory framework and, provided it was not used to directly endorse a candidate, could be gathered in unlimited quantities, either by issue advocacy groups or by central committees within political parties (Sorauf, 1992).

The most recent attempt to close this loophole in the law was the 2002 Bipartisan Campaign Finance Reform Act (often referred to by the names of its Senate sponsors, McCain and Feingold). At the same time as raising the hard money donation limit to $2,000 per candidate, this legislation also prohibited political parties or committees within parties from gathering soft money donations. However, in-keeping with the *Buckley* v. *Valeo* ruling, the act allowed organizations campaigning on issues to receive unlimited donations. Many of the 527 groups (so-called because their status was defined under clause 527 of the U.S. tax code) that were created after the

67

passing of McCain–Feingold are highly partisan and only quasi-autonomous from electoral campaigns, although barred from having direct contact with candidates seeking office. The internet lends itself to this type of loose political association. For example, Moveon.org is a 527 group, and thus legally defined as non-partisan. However, through its base of internet supporters, it is able to organize large-scale campaigns to aid Democratic causes and candidates. Through the network structures of online organizations, it becomes possible for "separate" organizations to coordinate their actions more effectively, to become virtually if not actually interlocking, and, in some cases, to have a significant impact on elections (MoveOn, 2007).

In contrast, in Britain, there are no caps on donations to political parties. Individuals and organizations are legally able to give any sums they wish. As a result, a significant proportion of donations to British political parties come from a small number of large donors. It has been estimated that a donations cap of £5,000 (approximately five times the cap imposed by McCain–Feingold in the U.S.) would deny British parties nearly 90 percent of their current income (Grant, 2005: 390). Instead, British legislation on campaign finance has sought to curb spending. The Corrupt and Illegal Practices Act 1883 imposed constituency spending caps on candidates, in an effort to prevent the purchase of office. The advent of organized and wealthy political parties with mass memberships during the twentieth century led to calls for a similar national spending cap. Such a cap was only introduced by The Political Parties, Elections and Referendum Act 2000 (PPERA), which limited a party's national spending based on the number of constituencies it was contesting (Kelly, 2005).

In the U.K. then, unhindered by donation caps, politicians are able to rely on fewer, large contributions to fund their electioneering (as well as still receiving significant sums from party members). They have fewer incentives to develop support from large numbers of small donors. In contrast, in the U.S., candidates necessarily need to solicit contributions from a large number of supporters. The internet has proved to be the perfect environment for this element of electoral campaigning. Indeed, there is some evidence that the internet is changing the types of donations being received by candidates. In particular, the 2004 presidential election saw an increase in the number of small donations (usually defined as less than $200, the level at which they must be reported individually to the Federal Election Commission), a change for which the internet was seen as partially responsible (Graf et al., 2006). In total, 61 percent of Dean's funds came from donations of less than $200 (Hindman, 2005: 124). Some have even gone as far as to argue that the internet, as a mechanism for giving, is creating a new era of "small dollar democracy" (Schmitt, 2007).

"Old" campaign communication environment

Our final dimension concerns how the older campaign communication environment, particularly the roles of television and targeted marketing, shapes incentives for political actors when it comes to the internet.

Internet campaigning does not exist in a media vacuum. Since the 1970s in the United States, paid-for television advertising has been one of the most important and most expensive aspects of the campaign. Advertising is largely unregulated. Candidates may buy as many slots as they are able to afford or calculate the public will bear. In addition, quasi-independent organizations affiliated with a candidate may also purchase airtime. As is well known, the United States was in the vanguard of the so-called professionalization of political campaigning. The campaign industry, with its pollsters, consultants, speechwriters, and direct marketers was, long before the arrival of the internet, strongly attuned to the role played by television in shaping electoral opinion and has ruthlessly packaged political campaigns for indirect dissemination via mainstream news media. It has equally ruthlessly developed strategies for direct marketing via old technologies (phone and mail) especially in key swing states during presidential campaigns.

Party-controlled television content is a mere sideshow in the United Kingdom, where such political advertising is outlawed. British parties are allotted a handful of regulated "party election broadcasts" during a campaign and while the audiences for these are reasonably large, they are of short duration. However, the rise of the professional campaign in Britain during the 1980s and 1990s has led to the U.S.-style "packaging" of candidates for the mainstream news media, which is of greater importance for citizens' political information in the United Kingdom (Farrell *et al.*, 2001; Franklin, 2004). Similarly, direct marketing strategies have grown in importance.

Theorizing differences across our two countries in this area is more complex. In general, the internet seems to be less effective than television in reaching undecided voters (Klotz, 2004: 64). Such voters are less likely to be motivated to seek out political information using a purposive medium (Bimber and Davis, 2003). Winning elections is about raising candidate visibility among undecided voters in key marginal constituencies. Television and direct marketing have obvious benefits when compared with online campaigning in this regard, because they can be targeted to specific

sets of voters. internet phenomenon MoveOn used TV advertisements and phone canvassing to great effect in the 2006 midterms, as its website proudly proclaims (MoveOn, 2007).

A further disincentive to devoting professional campaign resources to the internet is its unpredictability and risk when compared with older methods, as the Virginia "macaca" incident revealed. Equally, though, these things are not down to pure chance. Jessica Vanden Berg, the campaign manager of Jim Webb, George Allen's Democratic opponent, revealed a detailed account of the carefully managed campaign that launched the video, involving leaks to the mainstream media and to favored bloggers (NOI, 2006). Such events require dedicated, skilled, and well-connected campaign teams. The internet campaign also produces opportunity costs that must be paid for by comparative neglect of other aspects of campaign communication. A characteristic response in the United States has in part been to try to mold the use of information and communication technologies to reflect the norms of the old communication environment. Political actors have looked for ways to have the internet do the old jobs, only smarter. Howard (2006) has demonstrated the centrality to the online campaign of the storage, retrieval, and automation of vast quantities of information, the targeting of individual voters, and geodemographic data mining.

Similar factors are shaping British developments. The Labour Supporters Network and MpURL Membersnet are unobtrusive means of gathering data on party members. Targeted e-mail and mobile text messaging are now familiar features of the campaign landscape. However, the British experience also reveals a growing exuberance among politicians who see the potential of the internet to bypass the constraints of mainstream media and the heavily regulated television environment. This was precisely the reasoning behind the creation of the Conservative Party leader David Cameron's video blog, Webcameron, according to campaign staff. Thus we see a mix of potentialities in this field. The predominance of television and old-style direct marketing, and its benefits for targeting undecided voters in key marginals, are shaping the adoption of internet campaigning in both countries. Interestingly, however, the weaker role of candidate-controlled television exposure in the United Kingdom may act as more of a catalyst there.

Conclusion

This article aimed to suggest how we might move beyond some of the assumptions that have hitherto dominated discussions of online campaigning. The optimists' belief that the internet would remodel every existing institution has clearly not occurred as predicted. The normalizers' prediction that power arrangements within existing institutions would simply be exported to the online environment is only partially accurate. Both focus on power and resources, but both do not take into account those elements of the institutional environment that influence the utility of new technology. Existing institutions can act as catalysts or anti-catalysts.

High levels of systemic institutional pluralism in the U.S., created by the separation of powers and federalism, ensure that American political parties remain much looser affiliations than their British counterparts. The lack of a permanent membership in American parties makes them more heavily election focused than those in Britain, and candidates do not find a *ready-made* campaign organization when they seek office. The internet

is emerging as a powerful tool for undertaking these tasks. These tendencies are even more acutely demonstrated in the primary system, which, with its low thresholds for entry and potential for mass participation, allows for internal party debate and dispute. The primary and the internet are mutually reinforcing. Indeed, it could be argued that the reforms instigated within the Democratic Party in the 1970s have now taken on a whole new significance.

Campaign finance is another area where pre-existing institutions have an impact on internet-based campaign strategies. In the United States, the primary system, particularly the money primary, give donations a greater influence on political outcomes. The internet has made this process easier, and may, if the claims of the advocates of small-dollar democracy are accepted, be democratizing the process.

This article is only the starting point of a discussion of the relationship between institutions and the internet. There is more work to be done in examining differences *within* political systems. Why, for example, do the Democrats seem to be "better" at using the net than the Republicans? There are also questions about institutional development and design. In the U.K., for example, there is currently some unease about the way political parties are funded and a discussion of a range of options, including donation caps and state funding. Likewise, the Conservative Party is experimenting with primary contests for the London Mayoral elections in 2008. Clearly these and other relevant institutional changes would have ramifications for online politics that will need to be considered and understood.

The approach suggested here has the potential to help us better understand the complex interaction between institutions and new technology. The differences between British and American campaigning provide a compelling crucible, though the approach could be used to frame the comparison of other political systems. The five dimensions outlined—the level of systemic institutional pluralism, the organization of membership and supporters, the processes through which candidates are recruited and selected, the financial demands and regulations surrounding campaigns, and existing campaign communication structures—will play a role in explaining differences in internet campaigning across a wide variety of political systems.

Guide to further reading

The growing importance of comparative approaches to online election campaigning can be gleaned from Foot *et al.*'s chapter in this volume, as well as the larger Internet and Elections Project (Kluver *et al.* (eds.), 2007).

Good representatives of the normalization approach include Davis (1999) and Margolis and Resnick (2000). The distilled essence of internet optimism can be found in Morris (1999) and Trippi (2004).

Janda's (1993) is an excellent overview of the literature on comparative party systems, while Eldersveld (1982) is the classic statement of stratarchy in the United States. Ware (1996) is strong on comparing party organization across countries, from a British perspective.

For an overview of online campaigning in the United States and the United Kingdom see chapter seven in Chadwick (2006). Bimber and Davis (2003), Foot and Schneider (2006), and Howard (2006) provide excellent detail and interestingly divergent perspectives on the U.S. case. Chadwick (2007) attempts to theorize the significance of the Dean campaign and put it in a wider context. For the U.K., which awaits a comparable book-length study, see Ward (2005).

6

Technological change and the shifting nature of political organization

Bruce Bimber, Cynthia Stohl, and Andrew J. Flanagin

Underpinning the study of politics is an understanding of organizational dynamics and their relation to collective action. This chapter addresses ways in which new communication technologies enable the development of a diverse array of organizational forms in the pursuit of collective interests. Taking advantage of the internet's ability to reduce transaction costs, blur private and public boundaries, and enable accessibility to information and new types of knowledge management systems, actors have available new strategic possibilities for organizing. These options are no longer dependent upon the complex array of material resources and formal coordinating mechanisms needed in the past. We propose an integrative theoretical approach to this rich variety of collective action and forms of organizing. Toward this end, we advance a conception of collective action as communicative in nature, and offer a two-dimensional model of collective action space, comprising dimensions for (a) the mode of interpersonal interaction, and (b) the mode of engagement that shapes interaction. Conclusions address the implications of this new theoretical framework for contemporary organizations, organizing, and organizational membership.

It should come as little surprise that so many aspects of politics have been touched in some way by the internet and related technologies. Much of politics, from the highly democratic to the rigidly authoritarian, is fundamentally communicative and informational in nature, and the internet is central to changes in the environment of communication and information that are of historic proportions. In the disciplines where politics is studied, questions of change and stasis associated with the internet appear across many topics: public opinion and behavior, campaigns and elections, political institutions, social movements, global political economy, security studies, and democratization, to name only a few.

Among the most compelling topics associated with the internet and politics is political organization and its relationship to collective action. Because so many political dynamics involve collective action, from voting for city council to adopting a global warming treaty, and because so much political action is achieved through some form of organization, the nexus of organization and collective action is one of the underpinnings of the study of politics.

Indeed, over the past 35 years, the organizational nature of collective action has been a recurrent subject of research (Davis *et al.*, 2005; Oberschall, 1973; Tilly, 1978). Formal organizations provide the mechanisms through which political issues are articulated, participants are recruited, targets, locations, and timing of collective actions are determined, complex tasks and strategies are coordinated, and methods and tactics are selected. To varying degrees, these elements of collective action appear in research on topics from social movements (Nagel, 1981) to political parties (Aldrich, 1995). Across political systems, organizational affiliations and identification provide underlying motivations for individuals to respond positively to incentives and sanctions that help ameliorate the ubiquitous free-rider problem found in collective action efforts (Olson, 1965).

In the decade following the mid 1990s, research on organization and collective action associated with the internet focused on several topics, for example, demonstrating the efficacy of "online" collective action, documenting the appearance of novel forms of organizing not associated with traditional interest groups (Gurak, 1996, 1997), and describing changes in the strategy or structure of traditional interest groups, non-governmental organizations (NGOs), and social movements (Bennett, 2003; Bimber, 2003). Because the internet and related technologies reduce transaction costs of all kinds, blur boundaries between public and private realms (Bimber *et al.*, 2005), and make information-intensive tasks and communicative processes and products readily accessible, those actors pursuing the organization of collective action have available to them many alternative forms and strategies. These alternatives are less dependent than in the past on constraints associated with material resources, expertise, location, and target of the organizing.

A dominant theme to emerge from the first decade or so of this research might be described as "organizational fecundity." In their examination of the history of civic association in the U.S., Crowley and Skocpol (2001, 819) describe the Progressive Era as the most "organizationally fecund" period in American history, because of the profusion of various civic groups in response to the structural changes in society at that time. The recent literature on organizing and collective action employing the internet suggests that the current period, close to a century from the height of that wave, may well surpass it with regard to the proliferation of organizations and groups.

The fecundity of contemporary political organization is addressed in several literatures that have heretofore remained relatively distinct. For example, organizational and management scholars have explored the technological, social, and economic contingencies associated with the development of organic, self-organizing, postbureaucratic, and networked organizations (Ghoshal and Bartlett, 1990; Heckscher and Donnellon, eds., 1994; Monge and Fulk, 1999). Globalization theorists have identified underlying dynamics of time/space compression, disembeddedness of events, and increased global consciousness that are associated with a plethora of contemporary organizational forms (Castells, 1996; Giddens, 1999; Stohl, 2005). Theories of social capital, particularly the work of Putnam (2000), acknowledge the emergence of new forms of social interaction and association and lament the decline of traditional organizations, which by virtue of providing regularized face-to-face interaction among known others have a politically beneficial effect that other classes of organization do not.

There are two chief contributors to the proliferation and productive nature of new organizing forms, as described in the literature on the internet. The first is the growth of uncountable instances of civic association and organization online, through e-mail lists, discussion groups, common-interest groups at social networking sites such as MySpace, MeetUp, and the like. The focus of many of these groups is political and oriented toward problems of public goods. The second contributor is the expanding portfolio of strategies, linkages, and ways of engaging citizens on the part of traditional interest groups and political organizations, many of which date to the period described by Crowley and Skocpol (2001). Long-established groups are attracting online "members," and some of those rooted in historically anonymous forms of membership now facilitate citizens engaging with one another personally in discussion boards, or face-to-face. Clusters of smaller face-to-face groups can now sometimes readily band together to engage in larger scale action, creating new types of alliances across time and space. In these and other ways, the landscape of political organization and collective action shows change: many new types of organizations are doing new things in new ways, old organizations are doing old things in old ways, and old organizations are doing new things in new ways. These developments raise a number of theoretical questions about how organizations are conceptualized and categorized, how variation in structures is explained, and about what underlying processes may be giving rise to these developments.

Across theoretical frameworks, organizational fecundity presents a central problem of explaining organizational heterogeneity and efficacy. Researchers lack a vision of organizing that sufficiently accounts for the variety of contemporary membership groups in existence, and that also accommodates the multiple perspectives addressing collective engagement and interaction. In this chapter, we propose a model that reformulates and synthesizes a variety of relevant theoretical perspectives, while also taking into account the diversity of organizational forms used to achieve collective action efforts today. We then situate existing work on various forms of collective action within this integrative model, and draw conclusions about contemporary organizations, organizing, and organizational membership.

Organizational fecundity in the contemporary media environment

The issue of increased organizational fecundity emerges in several literatures, including work on collective action, organizational structure and form, social capital, and interest groups. Developments since the internet's emergence have drawn some theories in sharper relief than ever, but have also in some cases presented some empirical exceptions. In others the internet highlights tantalizing connections among theories. Synthesizing observations and findings across these literatures yields a new perspective on the nature of interaction and engagement among organizations and their members.

Collective action

Theories of collective action are central to politics of all kinds, appearing in explanations of social movements (Tarrow, 1998), voting behavior (Acevedo and Krueger, 2004; Downs, 1957), membership in interest groups (Berry, 1984; Olson, 1965), and the operation of the NATO alliance (Olson and Zeckhauser, 1966). These and many other phenomena share the problem of the free rider: namely, that under certain common conditions, individual actors with an interest in an outcome can enjoy its benefits regardless of whether or how much they contribute to it. Actors in such situations may be an individual citizen favoring one candidate over another in an election, or a nation favoring a treaty reducing global carbon emissions. The body of theoretical work defining conditions under which free-riding occurs is enormous, as is empirical work debating its extent in real politics.

One of the original elements of collective action theory as formulated by Olson (1965) is the proposition that organizations are central to the achievement of collective goals. Organizations serve to locate and contact potential participants in collective action efforts, motivate them to make private resources publicly available, persuade them to remain involved despite short-term setbacks and long-term risks, and coordinate their efforts appropriately. That is, the chief way that free-riding is overcome and collective action achieved is through the action of organizations. Indeed, Olson argued that "most (though by no means all) of the action taken by or on behalf of groups of individuals is taken through organization" (p. 5).

Over the decades, a great deal of work on collective action theory has come to take its organizational character for granted, or has focused on more controversial aspects of the theory, such as the assumption that human behavior is dominated by self-interest. Yet the role of organization in collective action is in many ways a resurgent problem in light of new technologies of communication and information. Researchers have increasingly been reporting instances of collective action that appear not to rely on formal organization. A plethora of communication and information tools, including electronic mail, the web, chat rooms, weblogs, bulletin board systems, databases, portable computing devices, and mobile devices, are increasingly being invoked to create and sustain collective efforts among a diversity of interest groups, formal and informal, enduring and ephemeral.

Uses of technology in novel collective actions have been reported in many contexts around the world, from Indonesia to the Middle East (Kalathil and Boas, 2003; McCaughey and Ayers, 2003) to Iraq (Arieanna, 2005) to Mexico (Ferdinand, 2000). These cases appear to challenge the old tenet of a fundamental nexus between formal organization and the solving of free-riding problems, a tenet that at this point has become part of the background of much social science theory. Use of the

internet in politics suggests that, at the very least, the scope of collective action addressed by theory should be expanded sufficiently to incorporate these efforts alongside the more traditional actions that are typically the focus of the literature, such as writing to public officials, displaying yard signs or bumper stickers, volunteering, and joining interest groups. Of particular interest is self-organized political action in the absence of a previously defined interest group or other central coordinators, and participation in online organizations in the absence of well-defined "membership" boundaries. No less important is the voluntary contribution of informational goods, which includes posting of civically useful information on websites, contributions to wikis, sharing of music, imagery, or other cultural goods, and the creating of metadata through tagging and social network-building. In many such cases, organizing for collective action is not associated with formal organizations dedicated to the specific collective goal at hand (Bimber et al., 2005).

One prominent example was the 1999 "Battle in Seattle," in which a far-flung network of groups from several nations interested in everything from human rights to the environment to women's issues used e-mail, the web, and chat rooms to engage in a largely self-organizing protest against the policies of the World Trade Organization (Bimber, 2003; Kahn and Kellner, 2004). This case involved a loosely coupled network without central financing or a fixed structure for leadership, decision-making, and recruitment. Instead, the network employed low-cost communication and information systems to focus attention on the objective of protesting the WTO meeting and to sustain practices of self-joining and horizontal coordination. As the literature describing events such as these has grown over the last ten years or so, it has become clear that many cases exist that strain the explanatory capacity of traditional collective action theory, if not violating one or another tenet outright (Lupia and Sin, 2003).

One key theoretical issue that arises in these cases of internet politics is that the classic binary free-riding decision metric is not obvious, such as in the posting of publicly useful information online and participation in various groups and public forums where people's useful contributions emerge from an interactive process rather than the explicit pursuit of a goal. In these cases it is difficult for an observer to identify a discrete choice to contribute or to free-ride, which confounds collective action theory. Another key issue is the pursuit of collective action either completely or largely in the absence of formal organization, such as the WTO protest, and the global anti-Iraqi war marches in February, 2003 (Bimber et al., 2005; Flanagin et al., 2006). The theoretical challenges go beyond the longstanding debate over the extent of rationality of people's action (Green and Shapiro, 1994).

Organizational structures

The theoretical issues raised by the internet for organization theory are somewhat different from those in the collective action literature, and they help point the way toward a synthesis. The last several decades have drawn increasedattention to the interaction of technologies and organizational structure. Understanding contemporary forms of mobilization and collective action requires understanding the ways in which organizing processes and structures are being transformed in response to rapidly changing social, task, and technological environments. Nonetheless, for the most part the organization literature has not explicitly considered collective action despite the centrality of the proposition that collective action requires organization.

Traditionally, organizational theories of convergence posit mechanisms that explain how and why organizations are becoming similar worldwide (e.g., DiMaggio and Powell, 1983; Hickson et al., 1974; Scott, 1995; Scott and Meyer, 1994). Depending upon the theory, convergence mechanisms are rooted in the increased competitiveness and interconnectedness of the global market, the dynamics of globalization, and/or the institutional mechanisms related to legitimacy (coercive mechanisms), modeling behavior (mimetic mechanisms), and the increasing professionalism and standardization of professional norms (normative mechanisms).

However, the contemporary media environment provides many opportunities for emergent forms that combine the characteristics of traditional organization forms with non-hierarchical networks resulting in new forms of relations among members, leaders, and other stakeholders. A theory of collective action organizing must simultaneously account for the efficacy of bureaucratic as well as network forms of organizing and the possibility that organizations exhibit several types of structures across time and constituencies.

Indeed, in the case of the internet and politics, there is mounting evidence for the coexistence of a myriad of organizational structures. For example, new organizations are emerging that have few organizational levels, simple management and coordination structures, and yet have large memberships that exert considerable political power. Other organizations have retained their formal structures, hierarchical management techniques, and traditional emphases. In yet other cases, hybrid forms of organizing have emerged: large bureaucratic organizations are reconstituted as networked forms where coalitions and alliances cross organizational sectors, types, and domains (Chadwick, 2007). The fluidity, blurring of boundaries, and diverse membership inherent in these dynamic networks are evidenced in the rapid appearance, transformation, and dissolution of organizations and organizational relationships across the political spectrum.

Contingency theories of organizing help address the variability in organizational forms associated with social mobilization, by focusing on strategies organizations develop to best fit the environmental conditions they face. In brief, contingency theory posits information as the critical organizational problem (Stinchcombe, 1990) and asserts that the way to cope with diverse and uncertain information is to create appropriate variety in organizational structures. By means of sufficient "requisite variety" (Ashby, 1956) in organizational structure, organizations are able to accommodate a variety of perturbations within the environment. This leads to the expectation that as the environment becomes more complex, organizational structures and growth strategies will become more diversified. This proposition, which like collective action theory dates to a time well before the current revolution in media technology, offers a potentially helpful theoretical grasp on the internet in politics. Addressed to a class of organization not typically within its purview, namely the membership organization or interest group, it suggests a way to account for some of the problems in collective action theory with respect to organizational form by offering an explanation for why the kinds of organizations involved in collective action should be diversifying.

Social capital

The literature on social capital constitutes a kind of conceptual crossroads where a number of theoretical traditions intersect. Early work on social capital took a dubious stance toward questions of the internet and politics. Robert Putnam explored the hypothesis that people's use of the internet might contribute positively toward social capital, and twice returned equivocal but skeptical answers (Putnam, 2000; Putnam, Feldstein and Cohen, 2003). Yet a number of studies relying on individual-level measurement of attitudes have shown that internet use can generate social capital (Jennings and Zeitner, 2003; Kim *et al.*, 2004; Lin, 2001; Mossberger *et al.*, 2008; Shah, Kwak and Holbert, 2001).

Of particular concern for problems of political organization are two propositions in this literature. The first is that greater stocks of social capital help people overcome free-riding challenges and achieve collective action; the second is that social capital is built in organizations and forms of association of a particular kind (Putnam, 2000). The classic argument by Putnam that generated so much discussion can be restated only slightly as follows: American society has undergone a shift in dominance from one class of participatory organization to others. The class in decline provides regularized face-to-face interaction among known others, and thereby exerts a remarkable and obvious variety of socially and politically beneficial effects, including fostering collective action and the achievement of political goals. At the same time, classes of organization in ascendance, especially the anonymous membership groups that came to dominance in the U.S. in the mid and later twentieth century, contribute to collective action in other ways but do not build the rich, community-based stocks of social capital formed in face-to-face associations. Social capital theory therefore returns us to the connection between organization and politics via a different route, raising the question of how the internet shapes forms of political organization.

Interest group mobilization

A fourth body of literature relevant to these questions is that dealing with interest groups. It is a commonplace observation that interest groups and related associations grew extremely rapidly in the U.S. during the last three to four decades of the twentieth century, prior to the rise of the internet. Baumgartner and Leech (1998) reported that the number of groups grew from about 5800 in 1950 to over 23,000 in 1995. Some of the important foci in this literature, in addition to the longstanding problem of inequality, are the presence of interest niches and networks, the extent of competition and response of groups to variations in competitive pressure, various tactical and strategic choices among groups, and the distribution of activity across policy areas (Baumgartner and Leech, 1998, 2001; Goldstein, 1999; Gray and Lowery, 1996; Heinz, 1993; Walker, 1991).

While this literature has a great deal to say about how groups represent publics, respond to their environment, compete, occupy niches, and engage the policy-making institutions they seek to influence, it has given only perfunctory notice to technology. The development of computerized direct mail in the 1970s is well recognized as a boon to interest group activity, since it facilitated medium- to large-scale communication with memberships and potential recruits. Yet this literature has treated communication technology as simply one of an organization's tools, rather than conceptualizing information and communication as central features of politics that might be fundamental to the reasons for the existence—or transformation—of groups in the first place. Perhaps for this reason, the literature on interest groups has had little of theoretical note to say about the internet, viewing it as simply a less expensive means for accomplishing an old task, and indeed a means whose efficacy is not yet demonstrated. Not the least of the questions posed by the internet for interest group theory is the problem of specifying

the conditions in which a traditional interest group is more effective or successful than other organizational forms. Another problem is that people's use of the internet in collectivities sometimes confounds the distinction between "interest group" and "civic association" that has been so crucial in the literature on social capital, interest groups, and collective action. Large, anonymous interest groups sometimes now offer their members ways to interact in personal ways with others online, or even to find and meet other members located nearby. And discussion groups online, which can attain a substantial level of personal familiarity, readily convert to advocacy groups when relevant issues arise.

Theoretical integration across perspectives

We believe that common underlying dynamics connect these various problems, and that the use of the internet in politics brings these dynamics into greater relief for researchers. Understanding better how these phenomena may reflect common processes is likely to provide a promising terrain for theoretical development in the social sciences for years—at least as much as further elaboration of each intellectual domain in relative isolation. We advocate several steps in that direction.

Organizing and organization

We begin by drawing a distinction that is simple but that provides immediate purchase on several theoretical issues at once: the distinction between organizing and organization. The central challenge of organizational fecundity for researchers is the proliferation of categories by social scientists for describing types of organization. A list of only a few types described in the various literatures would include the following: membership organization, civic organization, civic association, bureaucratic organization, post-bureaucratic organization, collective action organization, interest group, secondary and tertiary associations, and online organization. The multiplication of categories in an attempt to contain the profusion of online and traditional organizations creates a need for greater theoretical clarity. By distinguishing between the fundamentals of *organizing*, which are common to most classes of organization in politics and the specific forms of *organization* that manifest themselves in specific cases, it is possible to see linkages across theoretical domains. For many problems connected to the internet and politics, organizing human action and interaction is the fundamental process. Organizing involves a set of informational and communication functions: identifying interested people and their concerns, contacting them for purposes of developing common identity or trust or for purposes of sending appeals and requests, establishing agendas, and coordinating action or engagement.

It should be clear that organizing can occur through a number of organizational forms, and even in some cases without an organization. Given the variety of organizational forms now possible, it becomes facile to claim, as Olson (1965), Walker (1991), and others have, that collective action requires "organization." As we have argued elsewhere (Bimber *et al.*, 2005), the classic argument that collective action requires "organization" is in fact a special case of the more general claim that collective action requires organizing. Various conditions give rise to different organizational forms. The type of interest group typically envisioned in the literature on that topic represents the manifestation of organizing suited to conditions of high costs of information and communication, few avenues for horizontal interaction among citizens who are not proximate to one another, and targets for organizing that involve large, slow-moving, policymaking institutions. But all these conditions can vary: costs of information and communication can be low, for example, and the targets of organizing may not be cumbersome institutional processes. In such case, and in others, we would expect organizing to take on other organizational characteristics.

One important feature of the distinction between organizing and organization is that it focuses attention on the individual's experience of organizing or of being organized, rather than on the particular attributes of the organization that might happen to be at hand. Regardless of organizational form, all people engaged in instances of collective organizing must encounter at least two dimensions of experience, which we call mode of interaction and mode of engagement (Flanagin *et al.*, 2006). These are important to mapping the main concerns of the literature described above.

Interaction

Mode of interaction can be thought of as a dimension describing the extent to which people's interaction with others is personal. Personal interaction involves repeated, organized interaction with known others over time. Its chief characteristic is the development of interpersonal relations where the identities of others matter, and where relational development and relationship-sustaining activities are important to participation. Personal interaction may itself be the collective action of interest, or it may entail skills and norms important to other actions.

Interaction lacking entirely these attributes is impersonal. In such cases, interaction entails communication and exchange of information about goals, concerns, interests, strategies, or logistics of participation. Entirely impersonal interaction involves no personal, direct interaction with known others, who therefore remain unknown despite shared affiliation. In cases of impersonal interaction, occasional face-to-face contact might occur at events, or online interaction may occur among people who know one another, but this is incidental to the goals of the group and its members.

Traditionally, theories have maintained relatively sharp distinctions between personal and impersonal interaction. The social capital literature, for example, emphasizes personal interaction as generative of trust and norms of reciprocity that constitute social capital. It is, indeed, a literature about personal interaction. The interest group literature, on the other hand, describes interaction that is impersonal: citizens join groups, and the relevant relationships are between each member as an individual and the central group.

Especially within the collective action literature, a distinction between groups brokering one or the other mode of interaction is typical. Yet many collective action efforts feature elements of both interaction modes. This is especially true of federated organizations, such as Amnesty International, the Sierra Club, and the American Legion. In such cases, members may be organized by the group to become involved in large-scale activities that are anonymous to other group members, such as letter-writing campaigns and making individual financial contributions. At the same time, local chapters often have volunteer events, social get-togethers, fund-raising activities, and chapter meetings characterized by substantial personal interaction. The existence of hybrid personal–impersonal groups suggests the presence of a continuum rather than discrete categories. In practice groups may be more or less personal in the kinds of interaction they offer members, and indeed may offer a range of modes of engagement. Conceptualizing interaction as a dimension rather than a pair of categories is helpful for modeling change and innovation in groups, and it is especially useful for considering organizing practices associated with the internet. Doing so allows consideration of collective action organizing at any point along the continuum, and facilitates analysis of continuous change over time, as organizations adapt and shift.

Engagement

Similar features of continuous variation are associated with the second dimension of organizing: mode of engagement. This dimension represents the degree to which participants' individual agendas may be enacted within the group context. We use the terms entrepreneurial and institutional to describe the extremes of this dimension. Typically, analysis of interest groups and collective action assumes that mobilizing organizations are centralized, leadership-driven structures that accumulate resources and make decisions hierarchically (Johnson, 1998; Walker, 1991). This we label institutional, in order to highlight what it means for the experience of participation enjoyed by members, namely the paucity of opportunities for individual members to shape the agenda of the organization, and institutional structures that are generally hierarchical and bureaucratic (Bimber, 2003).

In groups with institutional engagement, central leadership makes decisions and rules for the group, and typically is in control of resource accumulation and expenditure, mobilization, and other classic aspects of organization. Institutional engagement is also typically well bounded, in that membership is clearly defined, and distinctions between staff and members are sharp. The interest group is a classic example. It presents members with opportunities for engagement, through donating, contacting public officials, or participating in events; members decide whether to participate, and how much, but the opportunities are created by the institution rather than organizational members. Members of the NRA, for instance, traditionally respond to, rather than create, the organizational calls for action intended to further the collective interests of members.

Many forms of organization deviating from the bureaucratic type are well known (Davidow and Malone, 1992; Drucker, 1988; Galbraith and Kazanjiam, 1988; Heckscher and Donnellon, eds., 1994; Nohria and Berkley, 1994; Powell, 1990). Key features of these are a diversity of organizational roles that may change over time and space, flexible leadership, a high degree of horizontal communication (Monge and Contractor, 2003), boundaries arising from communication patterns rather than institutionalization, and in some cases network-based forms predominating entirely over bureaucractic forms (Fulk, 2001). In instances of collective organizing with many such features, participants have greater opportunities to shape the agenda of action, by defining and creating opportunities for action rather than responding passively to agendas created centrally. They may even produce collective action not sanctioned by a central authority.

We refer to this as entrepreneurial engagement. It is illustrated by students who mobilize "friend" networks on MySpace or Facebook to accomplish a collective action, such as protesting a proposed change to U.S. immigration policy. It is also illustrated by participants in MeetUps, who use the informational power of the internet to propose and organize face-to-face meetings of people interested in some local or national public good. Organizing occurs with both institutional and entrepreneurial features as well. Protests and demonstrations against social injustices connected with globalization provide a number of examples, typically combining the agendas of institutionalized actors, such as fair trade organizations, with the self-organizing aspects of both community groups and international online networks.

It is theoretically useful to align mode of engagement and mode of interaction as orthogonal dimensions. The resulting two-dimensional area we call "collective action space" (Flanagin et al., 2006), which is illustrated in Figure 6.1. In this space, we designate mode of interaction the horizontal dimension, with increasing values representing more personal interaction. On the vertical axis, increasing values represent more entrepreneurial engagement. We use the standard convention for numbering quadrants in a Cartesian system, starting with I in the upper-right and proceeding counterclockwise to IV.

A number of theoretical traditions and claims can be placed in relation to one another in the collective action space. The observation in the interest group literature about the rapid growth of membership groups in the American political scene constitutes an observation that quadrant IV was largely populated in the U.S. during the second half of the twentieth century. The diversification of political interests in the U.S., the structure of parties and policy-making institutions, and the legacy of industrialization and the growth of the state, created conditions whereby a great deal of organizing and collective action occurred in the institutional–impersonal modes. This makes the increasing population of quadrant IV in the twentieth century an important characteristic of American political development.

Similarly, the development of quadrants II and III, which entail more personal forms of interaction, can be placed historically. Quadrant II represents the Tocquevillian ideal of small-scale civic associations of the early nation, where personal, community-level bonds were

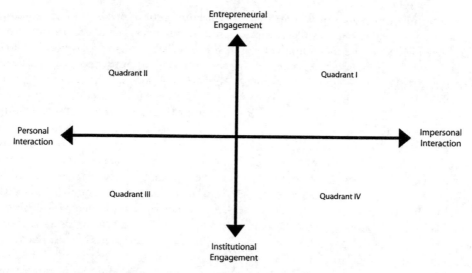

Figure 6.1 Collective action space.

formed and reinforced through local association. Tocqueville's discovery of the rich array of civic associations embedded in American public life in the early nineteenth century constitutes a comparative observation between the U.S. and Europe with respect to quadrant II. Habermas (1962/1991) similarly recognized the importance of the citizenry articulating their goals and desires, through direct dialog guided by collective interests, toward influencing acts of the state. Later sociological and historical literature describing the dislocations and alienation associated with the industrial revolution, urbanization, and modernization of the late nineteenth century and early twentieth century (e.g., Toennies, 1887/1980) entails an argument about drift toward more impersonal, institutionalized social relations. In collective action space, modernization appears as drift away from quadrant II, both downward toward institutionalization and rightward toward more impersonal forms of civic association. Putnam's argument about the decay of social capital groups in the twentieth century extends that observation. Finally, organizational theories have also articulated

shifts downward along the vertical axis, as organizations succumb to pressures of institutionalization over time (Scott, 1995; Scott and Christensen, 1995; Scott and Meyer, 1994).

The internet, interaction, and engagement

Because it depicts variation in the individual-level experience of organizing, rather than in specific organizational categories, the collective action space suggests that a wide range of literatures that have been intellectually adjacent to one another in the social sciences are in fact describing a common set of phenomena: two-dimensional variation over time and issue space in people's interaction with others and with agendas of collective action. This variation drives the highly variable forms of organization that researchers observe at the group and aggregate level of observation.

With this in mind, the dynamics of the internet in politics can be placed in context. In collective action space, the internet does not lead to wholly novel forms of organizing or organization. Like other sociotechnical developments before it, the internet would appear to alter the distribution of collective action in this space. The hallmark of the internet as a medium relevant to politics is its lack of specialization with respect to interaction and engagement. It facilitates personal and impersonal interaction, from small, intense discussion groups to "viral" e-mail that expands among unknown lists of citizens. It facilitates hierarchical control by permitting the gathering and sense-making of vast amounts of information by the central leadership of globe-spanning organizations, just as it permits decentralized, self-organizing coordination among loose networks of people. Where political organizing is concerned, this flexibility is what distinguishes the internet from previous media. It is why we see the internet aiding large, anonymous membership groups in finding members and mobilizing them toward centrally directed goals, while also helping small groups of citizens with common interests to find one another and act together in a personal way.

The flexibility of this medium makes it theoretically distinct in politics from earlier technologies: broadcasting, databases and direct mail, telephony, and the newspaper. To take one example, databases and direct mail are often described as crucial to the rise of interest-group politics. In our terms, these technologies are particularly well suited to institutional engagement and impersonal interaction. Operating a direct-mail operation requires centralized resources and expertise, and it permits "downward" or outward communication from a center to a membership, but not the reverse. These technologies provide essentially no opportunity for citizens to interact with one another, and only limited opportunity to contribute to collective agenda-building and decision-making in the group. These are technologies specialized in quadrant IV.

It would be impossible to conduct a census of forms of organizing across collective action space, and to compare this to historical baselines from, say, a decade ago or a half-century ago. However, the thesis that the internet facilitates organizing across all of collective action space is consistent with the observation of organizational fecundity. Increasing variety of organizations and heterogeneity of forms of organizing within individual organizations would be precisely the tendency one would expect to be produced by the widespread, rapid adoption throughout society of a set of technologies with the properties of the internet with respect to interaction and engagement.

If this thesis is correct, then the internet can be understood in relationship to previous historical trends in forms of organizing. Whereas previous trends have tended to be associated with shifts across quadrants and to involve growth that is comparatively localized in collective action space, the tendency of the contemporary media environment involves greater diffusion and spreading across all quadrants. New organizations with entrepreneurial styles and informal structures, such as FreeRepublic, represent growth in the upper quadrants. Meta-organizations such as MeetUp, which facilitate the formation of informal groups by citizens, also contribute to quadrants I and II, as do social networking sites, such as MySpace, which provide a means for people to interact with friends and known others and also to form large networks of thin, impersonal ties, in the absence of a centralized agenda. Efforts to recruit and mobilize members via e-mail by advocacy groups such as Environmental Defense constitute classic quadrant IV activity.

To observe that the affordances of the internet can contribute to forms of organizing located across all of collective action space is useful, but insufficient. Of course, many factors bear on the strategies, boundaries, success, and shape of organizations. Forces for organizational homophily tend to cause similarity among groups facing similar local circumstances, and therefore might lead to clustering of groups facing similar organizational "fields" or environments (DiMaggio and Powell, 1983). Competition among groups may provide returns from innovation and experimentation, leading some groups successfully to differentiate themselves in collective action space, as well as along other dimensions. Some organizations face institutionalized constraints on their form and boundaries, as in the case of political parties, which are tied by a rich web of electoral laws to the structure of states. To the extent that collective action goals involve common targets, such as a national legislature, the organizational forms that groups adopt are likely to cluster in ways that have proven historically successful.

The affordances of the internet therefore interact with such factors in affecting the overall distribution of collective action, just as such forces have shaped previous eras of organizing. On the whole, the kind of conditions generally that should contribute toward organizational variety would include low levels of constraints on organizational innovation generally; the absence of strong selection mechanisms weeding out less successful organizational innovations; conditions whereby it is difficult for groups to learn from one another, as in cases where success is distinguished from failure by non-linear, chaotic, or path-dependent mechanisms; and perhaps most importantly, by the complexity of operating environments. It is quite possible that the internet promotes organizational fecundity and variety via mechanisms both internal and external to organizations. Within them, it permits a broader range of interaction and engagement, with the result being a tendency for greater organizational variety. Externally, it contributes toward greater complexity in the organizational environment.

Conclusion

In just over a decade of its meaningful presence in politics, the internet has shown that questions about the form organizations take, and why, are key not only to organizational theory, but also to theories of collective action, social capital, and interest groups. In those literatures, the topic "organization" has been to a surprising degree a settled issue for years, yet in each case settled in isolation from the others. The ways people are using the internet in politics now is unsettling to those theories, and that is theoretically useful. We have argued that the best way to view organizational form in politics is as a reflection of the environment for communication and information, rather than seeing formal organization as fundamental or as a given. In other words, processes of communication and information give rise to organizations, just as organizations give rise to communication and information. The underlying communicative and informational features of many organizational forms can be understood in terms of engagement and interaction: the personal character of people's experience with one another as individuals, and the nature of their experience with the process of organizing. From these two ingredients arise the familiar organizational forms of civic associations and interest groups, hybrid forms of organization, and cases that are better understood as processes of organizing than as organizations.

The research road ahead is therefore not simply about technology, or media, or organizations. The crucial questions are: when many of forms of organizing are open to many kinds of actors, who chooses which ones, and how do their choices affect who wins and loses in democracy? Which factors tell us the most about how politics is organized: idiosyncratic and path-dependent features of organizations, the environment of institutions, culture, or characteristics of participants in collective action themselves? Technology itself can not constitute the answer to these questions, but understanding the relationship between technology and organizing can focus questions in new ways.

In some ways, the historically abrupt emergence of the internet in politics represents what economists might call an "exogenous shock." The internet has perturbed many parts of political systems, and responses illuminate aspects of systems that were more hidden in times of greater stability. The research agenda presented by the internet is not so much filled with novel problems as with new opportunities to resolve old theoretical problems, by taking advantage of the near ubiquity of the technology to see how common processes connected with communication and organizing may lie beneath a wide range of research topics.

This material is based on work supported by the National Science Foundation under Grant No. 0352517. The authors are equal contributors to this chapter.

Guide to further reading

This chapter integrates three distinct areas of research relevant for understanding contemporary political organization: collective action, new media, and organizational studies. Within the collective action literature, our work builds upon the pioneering treatise of Olson (1965), which functionally introduced the topic of collective action to social scientific exploration, and on Marwell and Oliver's classic text (1993), which served to synthesize work across various disciplines toward a coherent micro-social theory.

These foundational works helped to articulate the core concepts and dynamics of collective action efforts.

In the last decade or so, the work of a number of scholars has expanded the literature on collective action to accommodate changes in the new media environment. Fulk et al. (1996) are particularly helpful in moving the study of public goods into the context of the new media environment. More recently, Lupia and Sin (2003) explicate several ways in which evolving technologies may affect the logic of collective action, and Bimber et al. (2005) and Flanagin et al. (2006) articulate a number of theoretical and practical modifications suggested by the contemporary media environment. In addition, the theoretical, organizational, and political implications of changes in core technologies can be found in Bimber (2003) and the work of Bennett (2003) is not only useful for identifying the practical implications of organizing within the contemporary media environment but also brings a global perspective to the issues of politics and new media. Finally, Melucci (1994) engages globalization dynamics and moves beyond the traditional concerns of organization and leadership to examine the roles of technology, identity, language, and meaning in collective action.

More generally, the potential contribution of organizational theory to the study of collective action in the global system can be found in Davis et al. (2005). In addition, Monge et al. (1998) examine multiform, alliance-based interorganizational communication and information public goods, and Fulk et al. (2004) and Yuan et al. (2005) test the individual action component of the collective action model as applied to individual contributions to organizational information commons.

7

Making parliamentary democracy visible

Speaking to, with, and for the public in the age of interactive technology

Stephen Coleman

It has become increasingly difficult for elite institutions to preserve an aura of impenetrable secrecy. The hypermediated twenty-first century is an age of ubiquitous visibility, leaving few institutions unexposed. This chapter explores the ways in which the new visibility has been negotiated and contested in the context of British parliamentary democracy. The chapter discusses the representation of Parliament to the public and the representation of the public voice to Parliament. Parliament has attempted to manage the terms of its own visibility, but that is a losing battle, as the data-mashers of Web 2.0 are demonstrating. In seeking to become present to their representatives, citizens have colluded with managed consultations, but these are no substitute for a trusted civic space in which the public can deliberate under its own auspices. Finally, the chapter considers the implications of digital communications for representative democracy. It outlines an argument for "direct representation": a democratic system in which citizens are spoken for. This assumes that citizens do not want to examine and vote upon every area of policy and every piece of new legislation, but they do want to be consulted and involved in the decisions that affect their own lives. Citizens are entitled to feel that their contributions will make a difference to legislators' behavior.

In a moment of political madness during the spring of 2007, the British House of Commons voted for a bill, which, had it not been subsequently blocked by the House of Lords, would have exempted Members of Parliament (MPs) from the scope of the Freedom of Information Act. In effect, the bill would have prevented requests for details of MPs' expenditure from being disclosed and would have kept secret any correspondence between MPs and public authorities regarding matters of general policy. Symbolically, the bill reinforced public distrust for an institution that has come to be popularly regarded as remote, recondite, and self-serving. A small group of MPs from all

three main parties actively opposed the passage of the bill. Norman Baker, a Liberal Democrat MP, declared that:

> The argument has been won that secrecy tends to benefit only those who are corrupt, those who are incompetent or those who are careless with public money. We should not protect the people in any of those categories. The freedom of information regime that now applies to public authorities, and to this House in particular, and which we are discussing in respect of this group of amendments, has led to the beginning of a change in

culture in this country and in this House as to how we deal with information. The role of the House of Commons in how we approach these matters is central.

This minor, but highly significant battle between institutional secrecy and democratic visibility was but the latest in a long history of parliamentary resistance to the probing gaze of the public. Until 1803, scribes were prosecuted for writing reports of parliamentary proceedings; MPs regarded print as a dangerous means of stirring public excitement about issues best left to the political elite. When reporters were finally admitted into Parliament they were allowed entry on strict terms, as members of an officially regulated press lobby.

The emergence of broadcasting in the twentieth century met with similar resistance. In 1923, John Reith, the Director General of the BBC, sought permission to broadcast the King's Speech at the State Opening of Parliament, but this was refused. It was not until 1975 that the House of Commons finally agreed to an experiment in public sound broadcasting. Initial assessments of the effect of letting the public hear the proceedings of their elected representatives were negative. This was made permanent in 1978, followed by television coverage of the Lords in 1985 and the Commons in 1989. As with the press lobby before it, broadcasters were allowed into Parliament as long as they were prepared to accept strict rules of coverage—limitations that broadcasters would refuse to accept in any other institutional context.

In recent times, it has become increasingly difficult for elite institutions to preserve an aura of impenetrable secrecy. The hypermediated twenty-first century is an age of ubiquitous visibility, leaving few institutions unexposed. Political life is conducted under the gaze of an ever-present media, driven by a 24/7 demand for revelation, making it harder than ever before for politicians to manage their own images or maintain secrets. As Thompson (2005: 42) has argued:

Whether they like it or not, political leaders today are more visible to more people and more closely scrutinized than they ever were in the past; and at the same time, they are more exposed to the risk that their actions and utterances, and the actions and utterances of others, may be disclosed in ways that conflict with the images they wish to project. Hence the visibility created by the media can become the source of a new and distinctive kind of *fragility*. However much political leaders may seek to manage their visibility, they cannot completely control it. Mediated visibility can slip out of their grasp and can, on occasion, work against them.

For politicians, uncontrolled visibility constitutes a threat to their traditional backstage operations in which in times past policies could be negotiated, supporters appeased, and personal lives conducted away from public scrutiny. From the citizens' perspective, ubiquitous visibility provides a potential democratic opportunity, allowing anyone capable of setting up a website, operating a digital camera, constructing a database, or sending out a mass e-mail to engage with and represent political institutions from their own perspective. Digital information and communication technologies (ICT) have played a particularly important role here, lowering the barriers to abundant information, many-to-many communication, and media production. In pre-digital times, political institutions, ranging from parliaments to political parties to government departments, were well placed to manage the flow of public information. This is no longer the case. As political institutions have discovered to their cost, digital communication is dangerously porous.

This chapter aims to explore the ways in which the new visibility has been negotiated and contested in the context of British parliamentary democracy. It builds upon an emerging academic literature on the relationship between digital media and the legislative process (Chen, 2002; Coleman, 2006; Coleman *et al.*, 1999; Dai and Norton, 2007; Ferber *et al.*, 2005; Filzmaier, 2004; Frissen, 2002; Hoff, 2004; Leston-Bandeira, 2007; Macintosh *et al.*, 2002; Norton, 2007; Setala and Gronlund, 2006; Shahin and Neuhold, 2007; Ward and Lusoli, 2005; Zittel, 2003). Most of this literature has had an empirical focus, examining the extent to which legislatures have adapted to the conditions of a more transparent and interactive communications environment. Important though it is for analysis to be rooted in empirical observation, there is also a need for theory to be developed about the normative requirements of representative democracy and the changes that parliaments will need to undergo if they are to escape from the currently widespread perception that British parliamentary politics are irrelevant to everyday life. A key aim of this chapter is to link empirical observations about the changing nature of parliamentary communications to questions that are traditionally considered by democratic theorists.

The British Parliament is discussed in this chapter as an example of the Westminster legislative model, as well as an indicative account of what is facing representative democracies in many countries, even where the Westminster model does not prevail. Of course, nationally-specific references do not automatically translate across political borders and conclusions drawn from this account may not apply in every detail to other political cultures. The next two sections of this chapter consider parliamentary visibility from two perspectives: the representation of Parliament to the public and the representation of the public voice to Parliament. These are followed by a more theoretical discussion of the implications of digital communications for representative democracy.

Making Parliament visible to the public

The British Parliament was not entirely unprepared for the digital "information revolution." It had been through at least two information revolutions in its earlier history: the printing press and broadcasting. Faced with the emergence of the internet, in 1995 Parliament established an Electronic Publishing Group (EPG), chaired by the editor of *Hansard*. The group had three key decisions to make. First, what sort of information should the public have a right to access online? Second, should online information be provided freely or at a cost? Third, how should information be stored and retrieved?

The first decision seemed to be an obvious one: citizens should have electronic access to daily reports of the proceedings of both Houses of Parliament. In fact, this constituted a specific policy intended to control what might and might not be accessed. For example, the EPG might have decided that citizens were entitled to a record rather than a report of proceedings. Technically, there is no reason why the transcription of speech on the floor of both chambers should not appear online almost immediately; but the convention that allows parliamentarians to "correct" what they have said creates an artificial filter between utterance and dissemination. More importantly, the decision to make available the report of proceedings, as well as written and oral questions and answers to ministers and committee reports (research papers were added in 1998), assumed that the public would only ever need to know about parliamentary events after they had happened. One could also envisage other areas of parliamentary life that could be made visible online, but have not been for political reasons. For example, the working of the party whips' offices, in which policy deals are struck and MPs are pressurized to vote in certain ways; the Speakers' office, in which the mysterious "usual channels" decide upon questions of constitutional propriety and inter-party compromises; the voting lobbies, where backbench MPs mingle with government ministers and endeavor to promote particular causes. One can think of many political reasons for parliamentarians to want to keep these areas of political life secretive, but the fact that they have never even been considered as candidates for online visibility suggests that such decisions have been based upon institutional rather than democratic norms.

The EPG's second decision concerned whether online information should be provided freely or at a cost to users. The cost of a paper copy of *Hansard* in 1995 was £12 ($24) a day and electronic access was only available commercially at prohibitive prices in the order of £2500 a year. The Campaign for Freedom of Information (CFOI) complained that "The public is being denied access to *Hansard* and to Britain's laws on the internet because of HMSO's policy of commercially exploiting Crown and Parliamentary copyright … the Campaign wants HMSO to waive this unacceptable restriction and permit free on-line access to these essential materials." (Campaign for Freedom of Information, 1995.) The EPG agreed with the CFOI, arguing that "As a law-making body, Parliament needs to ensure that those subject to its laws have easy access to them and the law-making

process, and the group believes that there is a clear public right to unfettered access to this material." It recommended that "the full text of parliamentary publications be published free of charge on the internet." However, the EPG qualified its recommendation in two significant ways: first, by insisting that parliamentary papers should be made available internally to members before they were made freely available to citizens via the internet (thereby preventing immediate online publication), and second, by stating that any external body wishing to use material published under parliamentary copyright for the purpose of added-value processing or selling on could only do so by applying and paying for a license agreement.

The third task facing the ECG was to create an online space for the storage and dissemination of parliamentary information. A domain name was acquired (www.parliament.uk) and this, since 1996, has been the representational site of the British Parliament: its virtual manifestation. Establishing a single parliamentary site implies an indexical relationship between the virtual space and physical place of Parliament as an institution. The metaphorical depiction of "parliament online" conjures into being an image of Parliament as an integrated, bounded space with an inside and outside, members and visitors, and official knowledge possessing an elevated status in relation to everyday experience. By designing its own virtual representation, Parliament remains free to impose rules about what constitutes parliamentary politics. The absence of links to political parties, social movements, or sites of counter-information gives rise to a non-agonistic conception of democracy in which the political is institutionally insulated from wider flows of power. Visitors to Parliament via its website, like visitors to the parliamentary estate in Westminster, enter as outsiders who may not challenge the information that is presented or enter into the debates that are conducted. Parliament online is a political spectacle rather than a site of public deliberation.

That this was not the only model for Parliament's web presence is indicated by the remarkable growth of e-commerce. During the same period that Parliament was beginning to represent itself online, online commerce witnessed a radical change from supplier to demand-based online operations. Taking the travel industry as an illustration, in the mid 1990s most major companies launched sites intended to sell package holidays to online consumers. But consumers wanted to use the internet in other ways: to compare deals between competing companies; learn about consumer experiences of traveling to particular places; and ask the kind of questions that one would prefer to have answered by an impartial expert than by a corporate agent. By using publicly accessible websites that collate disparate reserves of consumer knowledge, travelers have become increasingly liberated from dependence upon single corporate or institutional information stores. Instead of going online to buy holidays, people are increasingly using the internet to construct their own travel plans by mixing and matching data from a variety of sources. The travel industry has been transformed by these trends, with up to a quarter of all U.K. holidays now being booked via the internet. This has weakened corporate power and at the same time expanded consumer choice. Could the same sort of opportunities be offered to online citizens, as distinct from consumers? Might it be to citizens' advantage to move away from institutionally controlled websites and towards knowledge-sharing networks?

In their report on social networking technologies, Mayo and Steinberg (2007: 12–13) refer to "two new groups" of internet users: people who create online information and those who "take information from various sources, including government, and mix it together to make new tools and services." The latter group, referred to as "data mashers" are people "who want to mix and combine information to generate valuable new forms of information and new services." An example of data-mashing from e-commerce is the American retail website, Zillow, which combines information on local land value and house price sales with mapping data to create a service that estimates the value of properties at any given address.

If data can be customized to meet consumer demand in the context of e-commerce, can parliamentary data be remixed in ways that liberate it from institutional control in order to provide citizens with a needs-based account of the day-to-day workings of democracy?

This was the question addressed by the founders of TheyWorkForYou, a site launched in 2004 by independent social hacktivists with the aim of aggregating content from the official *Hansard* reports so that they could be more accessible to the lay public. The site (www.theyworkforyou.com) allows users to track a particular issue or MP, comment on parliamentary proceedings, and register for regular updates on selected themes. Since 1996, TheyWorkForYou has been part of the mySociety project, which, according to its website, aims to "give people simple, tangible benefits in the civic and community aspects of their lives" (MySociety, 2007). By acting as an independent intermediary, mySociety can ignore the silos, routines, and hierarchical sensitivities of institutionally-bound information provision. Rather than Parliament sending a message that "We are your representatives; you may observe us from a distance," they are saying "We are the citizens and want to hear from you, our elected representatives." The mySociety model changes the terms of democratic visibility, using digital technologies to establish a citizen-centric, needs-based approach to parliamentary transparency. This marks a break with institutionally managed approaches to political communication that have hitherto dominated parliamentary information systems and could, if allowed to develop, lead to a greater degree of public understanding and ownership of the legislative process.

Making the public visible to Parliament

For Parliament to be democratic it must both connect with and represent the values and interests of the citizens who voted it into being. Relations between British citizens and their Parliament leave much to be desired. Most British citizens (88 percent) have had no face-to-face contact with their MP within the past year. Three-quarters claim that within the past year they have never seen their MP on television, 80 percent that they have not written to their MP, and 84 percent not to have visited their MP's website (Coleman, 2006).

Not surprisingly, parliamentarians have looked towards the internet as a way of reinvigorating their weak relationship with the public. In 2002, a report of the House of Commons Information Committee set out five principles that should guide Parliament's use of the internet, three of which relate specifically to its relationship with members of the public:

- The House is committed to the use of ICT to increase its accessibility and to enable the public, exercising its right to use whatever medium is convenient, to communicate with Members and with Committees of the House.

- The House is committed to the use of ICT to increase public participation in its work, enabling it to draw on the widest possible pool of experience, including particularly those who have traditionally been excluded from the political and parliamentary process.

- The House recognizes the value of openness and will use ICT to enable, as far as possible, the public to have access to its proceedings and papers.

In its 2004 report entitled *Connecting Parliament with the Public*, the Modernization Committee endorsed these principles and concluded that "There have now been several experiments with on-line consultation on an ad hoc basis, both by select committees and by all-party groups (House of Commons Select Committee on Modernization, 2004). They have generally been successful and have proved effective as a way of engaging members of the public in the work that we do and of giving a voice to those who would otherwise be excluded. We urge select committees and joint committees considering draft legislation to make on-line consultation a more regular aspect of their work." In its 2006 report, the Puttnam Commission on the Communication of Parliamentary Democracy, recommended that the "parliamentary website should be radically improved. At a minimum, it should be consultative, interactive and easily navigable." (Puttnam Commission on the Communication of Parliamentary Democracy, 2006).

Parliament's commitment to e-democracy was not confined to these modest declarations of intent. Since 1998, a number of parliamentary select, pre-legislative, and all-party committees have collaborated with the Hansard Society, an independent body, to organize a series of online consultations designed to involve members of the public in various parliamentary inquiries on subjects as diverse as domestic violence, tax credits, stem-cell research, hate crime in Northern Ireland, and diabetes care. These entailed establishing a forum in which members of the public could recount their own experiences, advise MPs to adopt particular policy positions, and interact in online dialogue. These consultations were intended to be deliberative in nature. Generally speaking, participants contributed only one opinion, but a minority of them entered into discussion with one another and with those MPs who chose to participate (Coleman, 2006). An outstanding question for research concerns the extent to which the presence of the public, as an entity comprising diverse values, interests, and preferences, expressed in a range of cultural modes, is really being made visible by these consultations. To what extent do online parliamentary consultations allow citizens to become visible on their own terms?

To answer these questions, I worked with the Hansard Society to construct pre- and post-consultation surveys, which were sent to registered participants in the five online consultations that took place in 2004–5, run on behalf of the House of Commons Science and Technology Committee, Modernisation Committee, Northern Ireland Select Committee, and the House of Lords' Select Committee on the Constitutional Reform Bill. A key aim of these surveys was to find out whether participants believed that they were being acknowledged, heard, and respected in this consultation process. A total of 650 people completed pre-consultation surveys and 212 (33 percent) also completed the post-consultation survey. Since the analysis sought to explore participants' experience of the entire consultation process, only the responses from the 212 people who completed both pre- and post-consultation surveys were analyzed.

When asked in the pre-consultation survey, 44 percent of participants felt that parliament was "out of touch" with people like them and only 20 percent thought that MPs were "interested in listening" to them. In the post-consultation surveys, 73 percent of participants reporting that they had "learned from other posters" and almost one in ten participants (8 percent) reported that they made new contacts with other people as a result of participating. Seventy-two percent of respondents said that they found the consultation in which they participated "worthwhile," of whom 79 percent said that they had learned something new from reading other messages that were posted. Interestingly, 43 percent of those who found the consultation "worthwhile" posted no messages at all, suggesting that the value of these exercises is not purely expressive.

Over half (52 percent) of respondents who regarded the consultation as "worthwhile" had indicated in the pre-consultation survey that "Parliament was out of touch" with them. And over half (60 percent) of those who had regarded Parliament as out of touch in the pre-consultation survey *disagreed* in the post-consultation survey with the statements that "There is not much I can do to change the way the country is run." A small but noteworthy group of respondents (17 percent) not only stated that they had learned from others, but that participating in the consultation had "changed their mind or opinion" in some way. Half of these people had previously expressed (in the pre-consultation survey) that Parliament was "out of touch," which was reversed after participation, with 75 percent of them taking the view that MPs were "listening to them", and 40 percent believing that the consultation process would "make a difference." The attitude changes of this group suggest that meaningful deliberative exchanges can occur in the setting of a well-run online consultation.

But not all participants in these consultations were convinced that by posting their views on a website they would become visible to their elected representatives. In response to an open-ended question about the value of participating, one respondent stated that:

> I think it is important at the start to declare openly how exactly the online consultation will feed into the final conclusions of those who have asked for it to be conducted. At no time was it clear whether the participants' contribution would have any real significance in the final outcome ...

Another respondent suggested that:

> There should be a clear response from parliamentarians to those who took part in the consultation, otherwise after spending hours on an online consultation there is a feeling that it has been a waste of time.

Clerks and specialist advisors to the committees involved in the online consultations were asked whether they thought that the internet had given them access to a greater range of experience and expertise than they would have received from the usual pool of witnesses. Responses were generally quite positive:

> We undoubtedly got some views that we wouldn't otherwise have heard, some of which were worth hearing and some of which missed the point ... (clerk)
> ... It did prove to be an avenue in which people could contribute who otherwise might not have done so ... All I can say is that the

nature and experiences mediated through the contributions were quite often of a different nature from the, sort of, institutional contributions we would normally expect to get. (clerk)

> I think with the online consultation you lower the threshold of effort that's required to participate in the inquiry, so the people that you bring are the people who wouldn't go to the trouble of drafting a memorandum and editing it and printing it out and posting it in and so on, but might just post a few sentences on a message board. (clerk)

> I think it was a useful exercise, primarily, in giving myself, managing the inquiry, and to a lesser extent, I think, the members, a good grounding in the issues and some of the sensitivities that were involved. (specialist advisor)

Despite this recognition by officials that online consultations were broadening the range of people giving evidence to Parliament, several were of the view that these particular online consultations had a very limited impact upon MPs' deliberations. In one case a committee was unsure about how to regard the status of this kind of evidence:

> ... it turned out that one of the members objected quite strongly to what were essentially anonymous comments ... And, therefore, it became difficult to actually directly draw upon that evidence, so in a sense its contribution to the report was indirect rather than direct ... (specialist advisor)

Some interviewees took the view that the consultations were limited by the absence of interaction between consultees and MPs:

I think for it to have more effect, for it to impact on them and on the way they [MPs] conduct the inquiry, and the conclusions they come up with, I think they need to be exposed to it directly. And it's a difficult thing. Engaging members at all is difficult. You are actually asking them to do something that's beyond what they would normally be prepared to do. So I think you would have to ... maybe identify a small number of individuals who would be prepared to take on a more active role. (specialist advisor)

The evidence here is mixed. Clearly, both participants and officials who experienced the parliamentary consultations recognized that a process of mutual visibility was occurring, but there was little confidence in the prospect of this having a tangible political impact. Virtual participators are still outsiders whose political presence can be overlooked precisely because they are physically absent.

Speaking for ...

The reality is that the citizens of a representative democracy *cannot* be truly present at the point of policy formation and legislative decision-making. That is why they need to be represented. Political representation becomes necessary when citizens are removed—physically, cognitively, or otherwise—from the locus of public decision-making and their interests, preferences, and values have to be expressed via an aggregating medium. If all could be fully present and attentive within the political sphere at all times representation would be theoretically unnecessary. Speaking *for* the public entails mediating between the absent and the present.

Democratic theorists' thinking about representation has tended to revolve around two apparently opposed versions of democracy: ancient and modern, direct and indirect, participatory and representative, Burkean and Rousseauan. On the one hand, democracy is seen as empowering people directly, and on the other, it is seen as investing power in professional governors or politicians who represent the people. The history that goes with this dichotomy is as familiar as the contrast itself. Ancient democracy offered direct rule by the people. But the emergence of large, pluralistic nation states, along with a liberal, negative conception of freedom, resulted in a transition to representative forms of democracy. Direct rule was replaced by indirect governance. This transition ushered in an enduring quarrel between those who sought to recover direct democracy by giving power back to the people, or by at least closely circumscribing the initiative of representatives, and those who argued that representatives should be left to govern as their judgment dictates.

The partisans of direct democracy see the representative as the ventriloquist's dummy: an aggregate channel for all the collective voices being represented. As democratically represented citizens, say direct democrats, our task is to control the representative dummy and slap it when it assumes to speak on its own. We are represented because our representative speaks as if we were speaking ourselves. The advocates of "representative democracy" see the representative as the ventriloquist and the people as the dummy. The representative speaks, but in the people's name. We are represented because our representatives speak on our behalf. They are the trustees of our collective interests. We do not elect them to do what we might do ourselves; we elect them because we do not have the time—or maybe the competence—constantly to make policy decisions for ourselves. For indirect democrats, the notion that it is the people who speak is something of a pretence, just as the notion that the dummy speaks is a pretence. It is the representative, like the ventriloquist, who is really in charge.

A striking feature of this enduring quarrel is that the two sides have tended to share an understanding of representative democracy itself, disagreeing about its value, but not about its empirical attributes. Both positions in democratic theory tend to understand representative democracy as being an etiolated version of normative democracy, according citizens the right to depose or re-elect a leader every few years, but not much more. As Joseph Schumpeter (1976: 284), a famous defender of indirect democracy, put it: "Democracy does not mean and cannot mean that the people actually rule in any obvious sense of the terms 'people' and 'rule'. Democracy means only that the people have the opportunity of accepting or refusing the men who are to rule them."

Direct democrats, quoting Rousseau, contend that contemporary representative democracy is but a parody of self-rule. Democracy, they argue, must directly involve citizens in all decision-making or it is nothing. The Burkeans and the Schumpeterians reply that representative democracy might not be wholly democratic, but it is the closest approximation we can get in the modern world to the real thing—and has some crucial advantages insofar as it ensures that well-educated specialists, rather than the mob, are really in charge.

For all its pedigree, the theoretical debate between direct, inclusive democracy and indirect, constitutionally balanced representation is hardly compelling, for it totally ignores the possibility of the options in between: systems of democratic rule that, while preserving the representative framework, ensure that, through ongoing dialogue, debate, and argument, the public

retains a degree of authority over representatives, even between elections.

In fact, the Rousseauan characterization of modern representative government as no more than the chance to elect a master every four years was always something of a caricature. A range of channels have given representatives and the represented opportunities to connect with each other. Demonstrations, petitions, letters, and pamphlets have allowed the public to express their view to representatives. Press conferences, TV and newspaper interviews, phone-ins, speeches, and parliamentary debates have allowed representatives to become more democratically visible to the public. Public meetings, political parties, and MPs' surgeries have allowed citizens and representatives to exchange views with each other. But this relationship has never been anything like an easy, equal one. The public has generally been spoken at, rather than with. Though not ignored as such, citizens were not invited to join the club. The public has been traditionally patronized, feared, or seduced.

As citizens have become less deferential, society more diverse, and technologies of communication more interactive, citizens are coming to demand a less distant, more direct, conversational form of representation. Techniques based on the broadcast-megaphone model simply do not provide the requisite depth and richness of political interaction between representatives and represented in the age of the internet. While acknowledging that representation must entail being spoken for, there are clear signs that the contemporary public demands from its democracy something closer to a full-blooded, two-way relationship. For this relationship to be satisfied, democratic theorists and practitioners might need to turn their attention to a hybrid between direct and indirect models of democracy, which I would refer to as direct representation: a democratic system in which citizens are spoken for. Citizens do not want to go through the time-consuming process of examining and voting upon every area of policy and piece of new legislation, but they do want to be consulted and involved as individuals in the decisions that affect their own lives, and they are entitled to feel that their contribution will be valued and might at least make a difference.

Hanna Pitkin, in her magisterial survey, *The Concept of Representation*—one of the few notable works on representation to have been written in modern times—understood well the necessity for democratic representation to be rooted in two-way communication (Pitkin, 1967: 209–10):

> representing … means acting in the interest of the represented, in a manner responsive to them. The representative must act independently; his action must involve discretion and judgment; he must be the one who acts. The represented must also be conceived as capable of independent action and judgment, not merely being taken care of. And, despite the resulting potential for conflict between representative and represented about what is to be done, the conflict must not normally take place. The representative must act in such a way that there is no conflict, or if it occurs, an explanation is called for. He must not be found persistently at odds with the wishes of the represented without good reason in terms of their interest, without a good explanation of why their wishes are not in accord with their interest.

The kind of democratic representation that Pitkin describes is clearly different from what exists at present. Politicians are not generally seen as being "responsive" to citizens and conflict is not usually avoided as a result of clear "explanation" being given. Although politicians are more visible to citizens than they have ever been before, and vice versa, the impressions of one another received via the mass media create and reinforce crude caricatures rather than anything resembling a communicatively rich relationship. Digital ICT could play a vital role in changing the terms of that relationship, transcending the distances that have traditionally made it impossible to think of representation in conversational terms. But this role is unlikely to be played out within the institutionally managed space of the official parliamentary website.

As with e-commerce, the most empowering developments are likely to occur in spaces opened up by opportunities to remix information and shift the balance of communication in the direction of citizens. The nature of these putative democratic spaces must remain largely speculative at the moment, for, with the limited exception of the mySociety sites, such as TheyWorkForYou discussed earlier, there are few working examples to which we can point.

But what form might digitally enabled parliamentary communication take, if citizens are to become more visible and audible in the democratic process? First, it could take a more joined-up form. Most citizens are not particularly interested in Parliament, as such, but in policies that affect their lives. As political scientists have been suggesting for some years, governance has become increasingly decentered: it does not take place within bounded institutions, but among and between them. Professional lobbyists, working on behalf of well-resourced elites, do not track policy formation and decision-making on an institution-by-institution basis, first looking at government departments, then Parliament, then specific agencies. Policy is best understood as a process in which power flows in several directions at once, often ignoring or circumnavigating constitutional boundaries and cycles. For citizens to be politically informed, they need information that tracks issues rather than reports on specific institutions. In the U.K., some people are represented by local councils, the Westminster Parliament, a devolved parliament or assembly, and the European Parliament, not to mention the many other intermediary agencies rooted in bureaucracies and civil society. Effectively informed citizens need tracking systems that can map the political process for them, showing them where issues have reached and how and when they can intervene with a view to affecting decisions.

As well as information tracking, citizens need to be able to track the flow of public communication. At the moment, most people have to rely upon media reports of what the public thinks (usually derived from crude opinion polling) or casually produced vox pops, phone-ins, or television-studio discussions (Coleman and Ross, 2008). Attempting to monitor public opinion by going to most political chat rooms or blogs is rather like going into a pub before closing time to get a sense of public discourse. Fortunately, new digital tools, such as Issue Crawler, which searches the web to establish where issues are being discussed and how those discussions are linked, are able to map the communicative landscape, which makes it easier to sense where a debate has come from and where it is leading before entering into it (Bruns, 2007). Few political researchers, lobbyists, or politicians would expect to be able to contribute to serious debate without having a sense of how issues have emerged and which actors are most engaged in pursuing them. Why should we expect lay citizens to do so?

Linked to these tools of political information-gathering and communication-mapping is a need for legitimate online spaces in which political representatives and represented citizens can exchange views and seek clarification from one another. Jay Blumler and I have argued the case for the establishment of an online civic commons in which public deliberation on local, national, and global issues can take a visible form (Coleman and Blumler, 2001; 2008). Unlike the present U.K. parliamentary website—and that of almost all other national legislatures—to which citizens are invited as a passive audience, contemporary democracy, if it is to meet the challenge of direct representation, needs to find imaginative ways of realizing active and interactive citizenship. For, as Hannah Arendt argued, the "political realm rises directly out of acting together, the 'sharing of words and deeds'" (Arendt, 1958: 198).

Conclusion

It would be glibly deterministic to posit a democratizing relationship between the internet as a communication technology and Parliament as an institution. One might just as reasonably regard the internet as a social institution and Parliament as a political technology. The relationship between one and the other is shaped by political culture, which is in turn shaped by the varied and unpredictable interplay of institutional needs and technological capacities.

Contemporary representative democracy is played out within the dialectics of visibility. How can power make itself seen, felt, and understood by the public? How can the public, as the legitimizing basis of parliamentary power, make sure that its presence is acknowledged and respected by its representatives? And how can representation come to perform the subtle trick of appearing to embody as well as act in trust for the public? As I have tried to show in this chapter, digital technologies are implicated in each of these dialectical strategies. In seeking to be visible to the public, Parliament has attempted to manage the terms of its own visibility, but that is a losing battle, as the Web 2.0 data-mashers are demonstrating. In seeking to become present to their representatives, citizens have colluded with managed consultations, but these are no substitute for a trusted civic space in which the public can deliberate under its own auspices. The challenge of representing the public, long argued over in sterile debates between indirect trusteeship and direct plebiscites, is met by the feasibility of direct representation. Of course, there is nothing inevitable about these outcomes; the path between democratic potential and realization is rarely a smooth one. The rather sad tale of the attempt to exempt British MPs from freedom of information legislation does not augur well for e-democratic anticipations. But the technologies are there, becoming more ubiquitous all the time. Representative democracies must either engage with them or face the risk of being sidelined.

Guide to further reading

To follow up ideas raised in this chapter, there are two areas of literature to be consulted. First, there are relevant collections of research on the changing role of legislative institutions, including Giddings (2005); the special issue of *Parliamentary Affairs* on "Parliament in the Age of the Internet" 52(3) (1999); the special issue of *Information Polity* on "the use of ICT by members of parliament" 9(2) (2004); and the special issue of the *Journal of Legislative Studies* 13(3) on "legislatures and e-democracy" (2007). On the representation of Parliament to the public, see Setala and Gronlund (2006); Shahin and Neuhold (2007); Coleman (2006). On the representation of the public voice to Parliament, see Coleman (2004) and Albrecht (2006).

A second area of research that might be pursued in relation to this chapter considers the changing nature of political representation. The classic text is Pitkin (1967). See also Norton (2007); Coleman and Blumler (2001); and Coleman (2005).

8

Bureaucratic reform and e-government in the United States

An institutional perspective

Jane E. Fountain

Technology enactment, an analytical framework that focuses on the processes by which new information and communication technologies come to be used by organizational actors, is distinctly institutional in orientation. An institutional perspective provides a challenge to researchers to integrate attention to structure, politics, and policy into studies of e-government. It also invites attention to the roles and relationships of formal and informal institutions. Formal institutions—laws, regulations, budget processes, and other governmental procedures—are central to legitimation and shaping incentives for the use of ICT as an integral and inseparable set of elements in the administrative state. Informal institutions—networks, norms, and trust—are equally influential. Challenges in the development of e-government stem from core issues of liberty, freedom, participation, and other central elements of democracy. Structurally, however, such challenges may be viewed through an institutional lens in terms of the adequacy of formal and informal institutions to support e-government. An institutional perspective, drawing primarily from economic sociology as well as from the institutional turn in economics, provides a path to deepening studies of information and communication technologies in government in ways that can illuminate state development and capacity. In addition, this chapter describes key institutional developments in e-government during two presidential administrations in the United States as well as key developments in state and local U.S. government.

The study of institutions is central to politics and governance, hence to internet politics and e-government. E-government research has focused predominantly on government information provision online, on public service delivery online, and on the attitudes and use patterns of citizens. An essential complement to these streams of research is one that examines the internal structures and processes of what theorists of the state term "state capacity" and "state structure," and what others have called the administrative or bureaucratic state. I argue in this chapter that an institutional perspective on e-government can provide important insights into bureaucratic reform, political development, the policy-making process, and the role of civil servants in information societies.

This chapter summarizes key elements of an institutional perspective and then briefly describes institutional developments associated with bureaucratic reform using e-government across two presidential administrations in the United States. Throughout, I sketch developments in budgeting, governance, management, oversight, and legislation that have been central to e-government. Similarly, I highlight several informal institutional arrangements such as management processes, culture, the structure of working groups, and informal norms. In addition, the chapter briefly summarizes key developments in state and local e-government in the United States. It concludes with a challenge to researchers to probe more deeply the emergent institutional correlates of increased internet and web use in government.

Institutions: formal, informal, and middleware

The term "institution" refers to regularized patterns and processes that simplify and order cognition and behavior at the individual, group, organizational, and societal levels of analysis. I focus here on institutional perspectives on organizations (for key conceptual formulations and critical overviews see Meyer and Rowan, 1977; DiMaggio and Powell, 1991; Scott, 1987). By definition, institutions are widely shared and socially agreed upon, regularized, and, in many cases, taken for granted. Institutionalists (including neo-institutionalists) have sought to account for strategic behavior and entrepreneurship in institutionalized contexts (see, for example, DiMaggio, 1988; Beckert, 1999; Garud et al., 2002; Maguire et al., 2004); institutionalization in interorganizational networks and fields (DiMaggio and Powell, 1983; Baum and Oliver, 1992; Brint and Karabel, 1991; Leblebici et al., 1991; Starr, 1982); and institutional change (Greenwood et al., 2002; Dacin et al., 2002; Hargadon and Douglas, 2001; Hoffman, 1999; Greenwood and Hinings, 1996).

Formal governmental institutions include legislation, regulation, budgetary processes, and the structures and regularized practices of the U.S. executive, legislative, and judiciary branches of government.

Informal, micro-level institutions include those social processes that have been studied as "social capital": trust, norms, and networks of individuals (Putnam, 1994; Fountain, 1998; Nahapiet and Ghoshal, 1998; Burt, 2005). Mediating between formal and informal institutional elements are organizational and interorganizational level structures and processes including management practices, task structures, and operating routines. The connection to e-government, in which ICTs are used to regularize and rationalize a host of information and communication flows, should be obvious.

Government information flows can be conceptualized across these three levels of institutionalized processes. First, micro-level interactions at the individual and small-group level structure and continually restructure ongoing social relations and comprise the locus of shared information and sense-making. For example, civil servants regularly contact trusted colleagues to interpret new information, to compare notes on accepted and promising practices, and to ask or give advice, support, and referrals. In the process of these interactions, individuals reflexively monitor and update their assessments of those they can trust, those with whom to communicate, and to share knowledge.

At a middle level, functioning like "middleware," organizations and inter-organizational arrangements, including networks, also codify and routinize information through systems, routines, and processes. Routinized information is, in part, what is meant by organization. Innovation often comprises a rethinking and restructuring of organizational and interorganizational processes (Nahapiet and Ghoshal, 1998). At a highly formalized and macro-level, the rules of the state—institutions such as legislation and regulation—constrain the behavior of government department and agencies, as well as economic and societal actors.

Formal institutions also include broad societal agreements on such matters as property rights and appropriate accountability, oversight, and resource allocation structures and practices. Thus, a multi-level integrated information system (MIIS) influences behavior directly and indirectly in government (Fountain, 2007; Nee and Ingram, 1998). Organizational change occasioned by information and communication technologies often perturbs—and is influenced by—all three layers producing unanticipated effects. I have called this combination of institutional, organizational, and new technological elements "technology enactment" (Fountain, 2001).

In sum, an institutional perspective on e government focuses attention on the internal workings—the structure and capacity—of the state. It draws out the role of the widely shared, regularized patterns of professional behavior of civil servants and other government officials working within institutionalized roles and settings. The study of e-government, using an institutional perspective, provides an opportunity to observe the collision of stable practices and traditions with technological innovations.

Weberian bureaucracy and the American state

The modern American bureaucratic state is a child of the industrial revolution. Although the term "bureaucracy" has been used by neo-liberals to connote inefficiency and ineffectiveness relative to market-based mechanisms, bureaucracy as an organizational form in government largely replaced patrimonial systems (including widespread use of patronage appointments) with a professional civil service. Through a protracted series of political negotiations over decades, bureaucratic government came to substitute

merit for political loyalty as the key measure of fitness for employment in the professional public service. The American bureaucratic state was built from a young nation of parties and courts. Although temporal delimiters over-simplify complex political development patterns, the American administrative (or bureaucratic) state was born during the final decades of the nineteenth century and the first two decades of the twentieth century. Innovations in state structure and processes, although deeply contested, were meant to align the government more closely with the results of enormous changes in the structure of the economy, rapid shifts in transportation and communication, and ensuing crises in banking, finance, and, not least, conditions and prospects for labor (Skowronek, 1982).

By analogy, one would expect to see changes in the structure and capacity of the state over a 50-year period as actors seek to re-align government with key dimensions of the information economy and network society. The institutional context in which long-term change efforts are embedded, however, is structured for stability. Thus, an institutional perspective draws attention to structure and process as well as the play of bureaucratic inertia, habits of mind, and the relative stability and durability of institutionalized forms and arrangements in the context of new capabilities occasioned by technology.

The development of information and communications technology (ICT) use by governments in the United States has by no means followed a predictable technologically determinist path. Nor could rational actor accounts predict the shape of bureaucratic reform through e-government. The technology enactment framework has been used to explain the successes and failures of ICT-based bureaucratic reform in the federal government during the Clinton administration (Fountain, 2001). Yet many other frameworks and models used in e-government research draw from institutional perspectives as well (Gasco, 2003; Danziger, 2004; Wiklund, 2005; Heeks and Bailur, 2007).

Where are we now?

Since 1993, two presidential administrations in the United States have focused bureaucratic reform initiatives in part on e-government. This section draws from empirical and archival research conducted by the author and summarizes those initiatives and the institutional developments associated with them (Fountain, 2001, 2006). More briefly, the section that follows sketches some of the major bureaucratic reform developments at the state and local government levels. Throughout, I highlight key institutional developments.

The emergence of the internet and the World Wide Web (the web) during the early 1990s led U.S. governments to begin to develop web-based government information and public services in order to align governments with societal and economic systems and expectations. Government agencies increasingly have made information available online including laws, rules, and regulations as well as policy and practical information for citizens concerning retirement, disability, health, education, housing, agriculture, transportation, and the environment. In addition, interactive public services increasingly are available including tax filing for individuals and businesses, licensing, registration, and permitting. Beyond the provision of information and services, bureaucratic reform also entails agency and inter-agency reorganization meant to leverage new capabilities made possible by ICTs.

"Reinventing government" during the Clinton administration

The Clinton administration (1993–2001) coincided technologically with early societal and economic euphoria that attended the beginning of open access to the internet through the web. Politically, President Clinton's was the first Democratic administration since the Franklin Roosevelt administration during the 1930s to win a second term. Economically, national unemployment rates and inflation were low, and the federal budget was briefly in surplus. Although Democratic, neo–liberalism was a hallmark of the administration. Clinton (1996) declared in an address to Congress that "the era of big government is over."

The beginnings of e-commerce and societal uses of the internet and web in the U.S. focused on development of web portals to simplify citizen and business search for information by integrating access to several websites. Before the internet was publicly accessible, bureaucratic reforms had been undertaken that focused on simplification of forms and procedures and service integration, notably, "one-stop shopping," to make government information and organizations easier to navigate. These efforts mirrored standard business practice in the service sector. In one sense, digital tools merely enhanced the power of a set of reforms already underway and accepted as legitimate and appropriate by civil servants. Yet the extraordinary power of the internet to allow citizens to access government "anytime, anywhere," greatly increased accessibility and made abstruse government documents and procedures, now online, more glaringly unresponsive to citizens.

In the mid 1990s, some large government agencies began to develop what the administration called "virtual agencies," or cross-agency web portals, in an effort to re-organize information and services by client type rather than agency jurisdiction. The U.S. federal government first organized students.gov, seniors.gov, and business.gov portals oriented toward three key voter groups, to provide these citizen subpopulations with a "single point of contact" with government. The term "virtual state" has been used by the author as a metaphor meant to capture the organization of government information increasingly in terms of virtual organizations such as these.

Launched on March 3, 1993, during the first phase of the National Performance Review (NPR), the bureaucratic reform effort begun during the Clinton administration was led energetically and visibly by Vice President Al Gore. The *Gore Report on Reinventing Government* was presented to the president on September 7, 1993, followed by a national tour to promote the reform effort (National Performance Review, 1993; Office of the Vice President, 1993). Information technology use was only one element of the larger bureaucratic reform initiative. The strategy for its use was underpinned by radical re-engineering methods and heroic assumptions regarding the potential disintermediation effects of the internet (Hammer and Champy, 1993). Initial steps of the NPR included cutting the federal workforce, primarily middle management positions, by 252,000 employees; passage of the Government Performance and Results Act (GPRA), which requires agencies to develop strategic and performance plans; dramatic reduction of internal regulations (or red tape); and a requirement for agencies to develop "customer service" standards and strategies.

The NPR staff published a report, "Reengineering through Information Technology," in September 1993 that included 13 recommendations combining general directions with specific projects:

strengthen leadership in IT; implement nationwide, electronic benefits transfer; develop integrated digital access to government information and services; provide government wide e-mail; improve government's information infrastructure; ensure privacy and safety; improve IT acquisition; provide incentives for innovation; provide training and technical assistance in IT to federal employees; create a national environmental data index; establish an international trade data system; provide an intergovernmental tax system; establish a national law enforcement and public safety network (National Performance Review, 1993). In 1998, the reform initiative was renamed the National Partnership for Reinventing Government.

Approximately 30 virtual agencies were developed throughout the U.S. federal government during the Clinton administration. Moreover, a single government-wide portal, FirstGov.gov, was designed to connect to all federal agency web pages. At this writing, it remains one of the largest repositories of web pages in existence.

The strategic direction of this early bureaucratic reform effort was encapsulated in the subtitle of the Gore report: "building a government that works better and costs less." The phrase echoes American public administration themes and objectives dating from the late nineteenth century. Early efforts, during a period in the 1990s when the federal budget actually was in surplus, focused publicly on government service enhancement, then referred to baldly as "customer service," rather than cost cutting. Yet during the same period, the federal government, following the example of U.S. businesses, cut the federal workforce by 250,000 jobs, primarily in middle management positions. This dramatic reduction indelibly connected use of ICTs with downsizing in the psyche of the federal workforce.

Early federal government websites in the United States allowed taxpayers to interact with government in ways similar to interactions using e-commerce following a historical pattern of alignment of state and economy that characterizes the marketized culture of the American state. By 1999, for example, 20,000 citizens used credit cards to pay their federal taxes online. The Environmental Protection Agency provided environmental and regulatory data to the public over the web and estimated that it saved approximately $5 million annually by digital provision of information. Public health agencies at the community, state, and federal levels began to provide access to previously centrally held information through centralized sites such as the Information Network for Public Health Officials (INPHO) housed within the Centers for Disease Control and Protection in the U.S. Public Health Service.

Proliferation of government websites and interactive information systems during this time period mirrors the highly fragmented and relatively autonomous nature of central departments and agencies in the U.S. federal government and the highly federated structure of the American state. Beyond the White House team of political appointees, staff, and consultants leading the National Performance Review and the Reinventing Government programs, there was no adequate oversight body for the reform effort because institutional arrangements and formal institutions simply did not exist at that time. The strategy explicitly called for a decentralized approach to innovation, to allow federal employees to use and develop their ideas without overarching coordination and control. The e-government program of the Clinton administration followed closely the zeitgeist in the U.S. of the early days of the internet and web.

On the negative side, the highly political nature of the Vice President's reform efforts linked development timetables to political timing so that events could become showcases for new technological innovations. These temporal pressures were both catalytic in terms of speeding up new developments and problematic in terms of contorting the actual time required to manage such complexity. Structurally, the formal institutions required to govern digital projects lay in the future. The White House-based bureaucratic reform team had strong support at the highest levels of the administration. But they lacked funding, management and oversight methods, and procedures adequate for governance and operations of fundamental technological innovation and change throughout the government. The naïve beliefs that the internet is self-organizing, self-correcting, and infinitely flexible reflected the euphoria of the time and substituted for hard analysis and planning. Severe cuts in the federal workforce shifted resources to the private sector, with increasing use of contracting and IT assistance from outside the government.

On the positive side, the experiments and flexibility allowed to public servants broke through old, well-worn routines and mental frameworks for how governance should work. Civil servants were told to be "grass-roots activists," and gained important experience with IT management, with envisioning the possibilities for governance and operations using web-based operations, and, not least, with interagency working groups and projects. At the same time, other formal institutions required for legitimation developed, including legislation, oversight bodies and procedures, regulation, and emergent changes in congressional committees and oversight.

The "Presidential Management Agenda" of the Bush administration

Beginning in January 2001, the Bush administration continued to use e-government as a tool of bureaucratic reform following many, but not all, of the broad outlines developed during the Clinton administration. The strong role of professional civil servants in the detailed design and implementation of reforms has much to do with this continuity of effort. Yet major discontinuities between the two administrations reflected, first, the need to reduce ICT costs during a much more constrained budgetary environment; second, a desire to evaluate and consolidate a plethora of disconnected, grass-roots reinvention efforts, which had produced a fragmented e-government landscape; third, heightened awareness of security and privacy challenges, post-9/11; and, finally, the Republican administration's desire to *manage* by strengthening business methods, and specifically by instituting strong control, accountability, and performance objectives.

The central strategy for bureaucratic reform through e-government was articulated in the "The President's Management Agenda" (http://www.whitehouse.gov/omb/budget/fy2002/mgmt.pdf). The reform blueprint consists of five "government-wide initiatives" including e-government. This enterprise, or government-wide, approach to bureaucratic reform is isomorphic with enterprise strategies in business.

The Government Performance and Results Act of 1993 became law during the Clinton administration and mandated agency strategic planning including annual performance plans and reports. The Clinger–Cohen Act (the Information Technology Management Reform Act of 1996) requires agencies to treat IT acquisition, planning, and management as a "capital investment" in order to focus IT investments strategically. These and other legislative mandates began to institutionalize e-government systems management. The Bush administration continues the trend toward rationalization and control of ICT management.

The President's Management Agenda is premised upon the economics of ICT and its potential to improve productivity. It notes that:

> The federal government is the world's largest single consumer of information technology (IT). IT has contributed 40 percent of the increase in private-sector productivity growth, but the $45 billion the U.S. government will spend on IT in 2002 has not produced measurable gains in public-sector worker productivity.
>
> (U.S. Executive Office of the President, 2001: 22)

Bush administration staff attributed lack of productivity gains to lack of strategic IT development; that is, to a failure to align IT systems development with agency performance goals. They cited a tendency toward automation of "pre-existing processes" rather than strategic use of IT for innovation, a central finding of institutional perspectives on e-government. Moreover, they noted lack of consolidation across IT systems developed for generic functional areas such as finance, procurement, and human resources. To remedy these problems, the administration focused on performance strategies and performance gains at the enterprise level, "across agency boundaries" using the budget process as a key tool for project management. Put simply: those projects that do not produce results do not receive funding, have management replaced, and are noted in high-visibility reports. In spite of consolidation efforts, both the Clinton and Bush administrations have remained dedicated to providing government information and services through multiple channels: face-to-face, telephone, and web based. Managing across multiple channels, however responsive to the public, increases the cost and complexity of e-government bureaucratic reform.

The President's budget for 2002 proposed $20 million for e-government in 2002 and $100 million for the period between 2002 and 2004 to develop "collaborative E-government activities across agency lines" (U.S. Executive Office of the President, 2001: 23). Yet congressional appropriations during this period were markedly less generous. Thus, most e-government projects have been funded largely through existing agency program budgets. Among the projects specifically singled out in the "President's Management Agenda" were further development of Firstgov.gov; development and implementation of digital signatures, which are needed for online transactions; a single e-procurement portal, with the ungainly name www.FedBizOpps.gov to allow businesses to access notices of solicitations over $25,000; government-wide federal grants application and management (grants.gov); and greater transparency and access to administrative rule-making in regulatory agencies (regulations.gov).

Cross-agency initiatives and shared services

The Bush administration's e-government plan, initially called "Quicksilver" and based upon a set of projects developed during the Clinton administration, evolved to focus on the infrastructure and management of 25 cross-agency initiatives. The e-government plan also includes a Line of Business strategy, discussed below, and calls for a Federal Enterprise Architecture, an effort to align information architecture within agencies with respect to strategic planning and to align architectural components for similar functional areas across agencies.

The 25 projects are grouped into four categories: government to business, government to government, government to citizen, internal efficiency and effectiveness, and a project that affects all others, e-authentication. Government-to-business

projects include: electronic rule-making, tax products for businesses, streamlining international trade processes, a business gateway, and consolidated health informatics. Government-to-government projects include: interoperability and standardization of geospatial information, interoperability for disaster management, wireless communication standards between emergency managers, standardized and shared vital records information, and consolidated access to federal grants. Government-to-citizen projects consist of: standardized access to information concerning government benefits, standardized and shared public recreation information, electronic tax filing, standardized access and processes for administration of federal loans, and citizen customer service. Projects focused on internal efficiency and effectiveness within the central government include: training, recruitment, human resources integration, security clearance, payroll, travel, acquisitions and records management. (For further information concerning each project see www.e-gov.gov.)

The 25 projects were selected from more than three hundred initial possibilities by a task force working with IT specialists from the Office of Management and Budget (OMB). The plethora of possibilities was developed during the Clinton administration and they continue as e-government projects although they lie outside the rubric of the "President's Management Agenda". In all cases, such projects focus attention on the development of horizontal relationships across government agencies. In this sense, they advance beyond what some have called the first stage of e-government typically entailing information provision online to citizens. They also progress further than so-called stage-two e-government, or putting transactions online such as payments to government. In a sense, the evolutionary stage three of e-government might be cross-agency initiatives built on shared systems.

Ironically, such efforts reinvigorate management developments from the 1970s by using proprietary intranets to develop shared databases and information systems using electronic data interchange. The public accessibility of the internet, flexibility of open standards, and web-based programming mean that the technological and systems development challenges differ significantly from the previous efforts, but many of the organizational and institutional challenges are similar. These institutional developments mirror supply-chain integration in vertically integrated firms and industry networks. They are not being invented whole cloth by governments; they exemplify structural isomorphism (DiMaggio and Powell, 1983). As processes and systems are incorporated into government from business, however, they become embedded in a distinctly different environment from their original setting in business.

The point of the Quicksilver effort was to find "quick wins," functional management areas in which an IT system had been developed that could be used as the basis for a government-wide system and for which the benefits would be significant. But the opportunities to develop government-wide IT systems to consolidate management functions obscured the challenges of institutional change. The effort was—and continues to be—led largely by IT professionals. It has suffered in many cases from lack of program management and the involvement of seasoned civil servants with program management experience. Experienced program managers, for example, understand subtle differences in seemingly generic management functions based on program and policy characteristics, history, and legislation.

Governance and oversight

The current e-government projects are overseen and supported by the OMB Office of E-government and Information Technology, a statutory office established as part of the E-Government Act of 2002 (Public Law 107–347). The Administrator for E-government and IT, at the apex of the organization, is an associate director of OMB reporting to the Deputy Director for Management, who reports to the OMB Director. The position initially was held by Mark Forman, a political appointee, and is currently held by Karen Evans, a former career civil servant and now a political appointee. The Associate Administrator for E-government and Information Technology, who reports to the Administrator, is responsible for the 25 cross-agency projects. Five portfolio managers have specific responsibility to oversee the cross-agency initiatives. A management consulting group (private contractors) has been responsible for most of the day-to-day communications and reporting for the programs. In effect, they serve as staff and liaisons between OMB and the cross-agency projects that are based in government agencies.

The new organization within OMB signals a major institutional development in the U.S. federal government. Before passage of the E-Government Act of 2002, which established the federal CIO and OMB structure, there was no formal capacity within OMB to oversee and guide cross-agency initiatives. This structural gap formed a major impediment to the development of networked governance during the Clinton administration. In terms of political development and fundamental changes in the nature of the bureaucratic state, we see here the emergent institutionalization of a structure for the direction and oversight of cross-agency, or networked, governance.

The projects themselves are not part of the OMB hierarchy. Oversight and guidance of the projects is exercised by portfolio managers, but the lead agency—or managing partner—for each project is

107

a federal agency. Each managing partner agency appointed a program manager to lead its project. Program managers are typically senior career federal civil servants. They have been responsible for developing a consultative process among agencies involved in each project and, in consultation with OMB, they are responsible for developing project goals and objectives. In most cases, program managers were also required to devise staffing and funding plans to support their project. Neither funds nor staff was allocated as part of the president's agenda.

The E-Government Act provided for federal funding for the projects of approximately $345 million over four years. But an average of only $4 million to $5 million per annum actually has been appropriated by Congress. Strategies developed by each project for funding, staffing, and internal governance vary widely and have been largely contingent on the skills and experience of the program manager. So far, the legislature has not adapted organizationally to networked government. This lag in institutional development makes it difficult to build networked systems because appropriations of funds continue to flow to individual agencies and programs within them. As John Spotila, former director of the Office of Information and Regulatory Affairs in OMB, remarked: "Even without homeland security absorbing most of the IT dollars, cross-agency projects have never been a favorite of Congress, where appropriations are awarded through a 'stovepipe system' of committees that makes a multi-agency approach difficult" (quotation in Frank, 2002). Appropriations for the cross-agency initiatives were $5 million in financial years (FY) 2002 and 2003 and only $3 million in FY 2004. John Scofield, a spokesman for the House Appropriations Committee was quoted during the 2004 budget negotiations as saying: "We have never been convinced that the fund [requested to support cross-agency initiatives] doesn't duplicate what already exists in other agencies or performs unique functions ... It has never been well-justified, and we don't have a lot of spare cash lying around" (Scofield quoted in Miller, 2004).

Lines of business: building a shared services environment

In 2004, the Bush administration launched the Lines of Business initiative to further consolidate and streamline functional management across the federal government. The original five lines of business, identified by virtue of shared enterprise architecture, include human resource management, financial management, grants management, federal health architecture, case management and information systems security. In 2005 the Information Technology Security task force was added as a sixth line of business. The initiative also now includes a seventh, the budget formulation and execution line of business.

Consolidated systems, or "centers of excellence," in President's Management Agenda parlance, may be operated either by agencies or private vendors. Competition is to be fostered by maintaining approximately four IT systems for each line of business. Agencies then choose the system that best meets their needs and budget. For example, the grants management centers of excellence, selected by competition, include the Department of Health and Human Services, the National Science Foundation (primarily for research grants), and the Department of Education, which has yet to build its system. The centers are to compete for agency business and to develop competitive pricing for shared services.

Yet funding shared services is difficult at times to align with congressional appropriations and oversight, which remain agency based. Congressional committees increasingly have demanded that approval for budget transfers across agencies be approved by Congress. The authority of "lead agencies" over agencies within lines of business networks is collaborative and negotiated, and, even when negotiated through Memoranda of Understanding, remains highly contingent and informal relative to statutory authorities. The coordination costs of such arrangements remain "off the books" in the sense that they fail to show up on budgets and in performance documents.

Developments in state and local e-government

A substantial gap in U.S. e-government collaboration exists between levels of government in the highly federated American system. For example, local and federal initiatives seldom collaborate with each other. This does not mean, however, that government leaders are unaware of initiatives outside their immediate level of government. In fact, "[due] to their variation in geography, demographics, and infrastructure, [the 50] states serve as laboratories of experimentation for e-government. Federal policy-makers may find aspects of state e-government planning and implementation useful examples for future decisions regarding the integration of federal information and services" (Seifert and McLoughlin, 2007, p. 1).

Currently all 50 states in the U.S. have e-government or IT departments or divisions. However, the degree and types of activity in each department and the level of support for each initiative vary widely from state to state. West ranks the websites of states of Delaware, Michigan, Maine, Kentucky, and Tennessee as the top five with respect to access, privacy, and the availability of services and other resources. He notes that the Delaware

website is designed for efficiency and ease of use, and, because most pages can be translated into multiple languages, the information is also widely accessible (West, 2007). By contrast, state websites for Arkansas, Mississippi, New Mexico, West Virginia, and Wyoming were ranked as the bottom five.

In addition to the number of services available, West (2006, 2007) examines the types of services available online. For example, in 2006, Iowa and Massachusetts allowed citizens to pay traffic tickets online; Alaska installed webcams at the field offices of the Department of Motor Vehicle to allow citizens to gauge wait times at offices. In 2007, Virginia and Vermont allowed online donations to military troops and charities; Georgia provided a searchable list of gas prices; and South Carolina provided closed captioned legislative broadcasts. Common problems among state websites include outdated information; inconsistent web page structures or URLs; and inconsistent color schemes and layouts that make it difficult for users to know whether they have left the "official" state web page when they click into a page that contrasts visually with others (West, 2006).

While the importance of an online presence is critical, e-government is much more than the existence of a website. E-government programs must have strong management and leadership and clear strategies in place in order to be effective. The majority of state government chief information officers (CIOs) surveyed by the National Association of State Chief Information Officers (NASCIO) have adopted an enterprise architecture as a way to structure e-government initiatives across an entire state government. Most states have designated a chief enterprise architect to lead their programming, although the official title varies from state to state (NASCIO, 2005). All 50 states have CIOs, but the management of e-government initiatives extends beyond the CIO to include finance and accounting offices, IT departments, and information resources departments (Seifert and McLoughlin, 2007).

As with federal e-government programs, state-level e-government strategies seek to exploit the value of cross-agency collaboration for integration of existing services. Similarly, all such projects affect organizational structures and agency cultures. The challenge of building sustainable collaboration was ranked a high priority for state CIOs in a 2005 survey by NASCIO (NASCIO, 2006b). State CIOs sought to consolidate and share models in several arenas—from procurement to security and disaster recovery. Communication services and online payment engines are reported to be the most commonly completed initiatives; standardized log-ins and identity authentication were the most commonly proposed new initiatives (NASCIO, 2006b). Those CIOs who responded to the survey cited cost savings and increased information sharing as the most common reasons to begin a consolidation program. Seventy-seven percent of CIOs also cited a pervasive stovepiped, agency-based culture as the greatest human resources barrier to implementing any consolidation effort. Moreover, 80 percent view resistance to change in their workforces to be the major obstacle to successful implementation of consolidation projects (NASCIO, 2006b).

Some of the "best practices" in bureaucratic reform through e-government at the state level reported by NASCIO are not necessarily transferable to other states due to geographic, political, social, and fiscal disparities. Yet they signify innovation and change, act as benchmarks, and point to institutional developments. For instance, in 2006, NASCIO recognized the California Statewide Information System (SIS) for Prenatal and Newborn Screening Program as one of two best practices in cross-boundary collaboration. Led by the California Department of Health Services (CDHS), the system allows physicians statewide to test newborns for 36 more genetic diseases than without the SIS. The program brings together labs, case coordinators, counselors, physicians, and staff of the CDHS for better control of testing, reporting, and follow-ups so that diagnosis and treatment is better administered and more successful. A second example is Washington D.C.'s Safe Passages information system. Safe Passages allows caseworkers to look through the district's information systems to see if their clients have case histories with other caseworkers or agencies. The program saves time and produces higher quality client services because caseworkers do not have to duplicate client histories and may quickly access previous case decisions.

Bureaucratic reform using e-government at the local level in the United States is highly varied, somewhat slower to have developed, and less often studied than at the state and federal levels. At the county level, a survey of 3099 county governments in the U.S. indicated that 56.3 percent of counties have adopted e-government portals. Portal development is positively correlated with population size, population growth, racial diversity, income, employment opportunities, and education levels (Huang, 2006). A 2004 analysis of 1873 city government websites in the 70 largest metropolitan areas found 60 percent of the cities did not offer *any* online services (West, 2004a). This shows little change from a previous study in which researchers observed that a "striking" number of cities studied did not offer e-government services (Kaylor *et al.*, 2001) and from Edmiston's (2003) finding that although most local governments have developed websites, there has been little change in local government operations or practice. However, using surveys from

2002, Norris and Moon (2005) reported "enthusiasm" for e-government at the local level and claim that plans for e-government developments were being made. They also noted the increasing rate of growth in the number of local government websites.

Bureaucratic reform through e-government at the local level has lagged for several reasons. Local governments find it difficult or impossible to finance new IT systems given fiscal constraints and local budget processes. Small local governments tend to lack IT expertise and leadership of staff. Vendors already have packaged several e-government service delivery vehicles for local governments, including vital records processes (Edmiston, 2003; Kaylor *et al.*, 2001; Norris and Moon, 2005).

Forward-looking state and local governments typically innovate before larger central governments whose systems are more difficult to change. However, local and state governments vary dramatically in the extent of electronic information and services available primarily because such governments range from small, poor, rural communities with little access to the internet to large metropolitan areas with extensive infrastructure and a range of conditions in between. The American federated system and the size and scale of the United States make e-government in the U.S. more heterogenous, fragmented, and variable than perhaps in any other country. Local governments tend to be less highly institutionalized in the sense that staff are not always professionalized, routines and procedures are less closely codified, turnover may be greater in employees and officials, and smaller scale allows for greater informality.

Conclusion

The future of e-government research can be greatly strengthened and enhanced by importation of several streams of institutionalist inquiry and methods. Institutional studies, building on a rich base of theoretical and empirical research, should be able to go further than stating that "culture matters," or that the organizational and political issues in e-government are more difficult than the technical issues. Such research is not meant to supplant studies of information and service provision or studies of citizen attitudes and uses of e-government, but to complement them by examining institutional and organizational structures and processes and their role in structuring the context within which bureaucratic reform is envisioned, designed, and implemented.

The list of institutional research dimensions is rife with possibilities for e-government research. Among the key topics is the role of formal institutions. What type of legislation seems to be most important for bureaucratic reform to move forward, assuming that the goals of the bureaucratic reform are agreed upon by major stakeholders? Is there a discernible sequence, roughly speaking, to the legislation enacted to support e-government across countries? Might there be some predictive or practical value in answers to such questions? What institutional arrangements provide the necessary oversight and overall guidance for e-government reforms?

At the root of this work are normative questions. The number of services available online or the cultural shifts in civil service attitudes toward cross-agency arrangements are important and interesting. Yet, our principal motivation in the study of government typically is to ask whether the government being created is more democratic, along some dimension, than the government being left behind. Hence, normative inquiry, informed by strong scholarly foundations in political philosophy and theory and in the canonical writing of political science and political sociology, is greatly needed in the subfield of e-government.

Of great importance also are changes in relationships among government agencies across local, state, federal, and national jurisdictions and between public, private, and non-profit organizations. Currently, institutional arrangements such as the budget process, oversight functions, and the committee structure within legislatures reinforce agency autonomy and operations at the level of a single agency or an agency working in partnership with private sector or non-profit sector organizations. Such institutional arrangements are likely to be modified as policy-makers respond to communities of interest, strengthened by the internet, that cross agency boundaries.

Potential near-term technological changes include greater use of wireless communication, personal digital devices, instant messaging, ubiquitous computing, and increased reliance on visual communications media. As these next-generation technologies become more dominant compared with personal computers, bulletin boards and chat rooms, and computer-mediated text communication, they are likely to exert as yet unknown effects on e-government. Similarly, Web 2.0 tools are likely to have an effect on bureaucratic policy-making processes.

Finally, among the important and as yet unanswered research questions for the future are the following puzzles. What are the effects, if any, of e-government on the quality of policy-making and policy implementation? What are the effects of increased transparency and power to manipulate and analyze information on the ability of governments to serve society and economy? What are the unanticipated consequences of governmental cyber-infrastructure? Government officials and policy-makers may use information and communication technologies for government reform, in part by restructuring government agencies, operations, and relationships across agencies and with non-governmental organizations. But do they? And what are the principal goals of such reforms? Perhaps the most elusive, and certainly the area of highest speculation, is the degree to which the internet is likely to prove "transformative" for governance in the twenty-first century.

Acknowledgments

The author acknowledges the research assistance of Michelle Sagan Goncalves. This material is based upon work supported by the National Science Foundation under Grant Numbers 0131923 and 0630239. Any opinions, findings, conclusions, or recommendations expressed in this material are those of the author and do not necessarily reflect the views of the National Science Foundation.

Guide to further reading

The author developed the technology enactment framework and presents detailed case studies of bureaucratic reform using e-government in the United States during the Clinton administration (Fountain, 2001a). A research agenda for the study of ICT and governance was generated through dialog at a workshop of approximately 30 researchers resulting in a monograph (Fountain, 2002). Darrell West (2005) has compared information and services available on government websites in state and local U.S. governments as well as in and among federal agencies. Patrick Dunleavy, Helen Margetts, Simon Bastow, and Jane Tinkler (Dunleavy *et al.*, 2007) compare e-government developments in the United States, with specific attention to the role of the IT industry and the costs of projects, to those in several other countries including Canada, the United Kingdom, and Australia. An assessment of cost savings in e-government is to be found in Fountain and Osorio-Urzua (2001). Finally, David Lazer's and Viktor Mayer-Schönberger's (2007) edited volume features several chapters on the role and importance of information in e-government.

9

Public management change and e-government

The emergence of digital-era governance

Helen Margetts

Contemporary government is reliant on the complex networks of information systems and websites that make up "e-government." Such systems are critical to government operations and open up new policy options. This chapter first discusses how they have been downplayed by mainstream public management research. With widespread use of the internet, a field of e-government research has emerged that focuses on digital technologies. But many authors argue that they are not an instrument for administrative reform, nor do they bring fundamental change to governmental operations and institutional development. The chapter goes on to explore an alternative perspective: that it now makes sense to view public management change with reference to digital modes of operating. Governments in developed countries have varied in the extent to which they implemented New Public Management (NPM) reforms in the 1990s and have prioritized e-government initiatives in the 2000s. The chapter examines the relationship between e-government and public management reform more generally, suggesting that "digital-era governance" (DEG), which reverses or cuts across NPM styles of management, is a useful way to view contemporary administrative reform. It outlines the three main themes of DEG: reintegration, needs-based holism, and digitization, and shows how the pervasive use of digital technologies by governments, firms, and society more generally provoke organizational responses in government organizations. The study of contemporary public administration, therefore, requires a "mainstreaming" of e-government research.

E-government may be defined as the use by government of digital technologies internally and externally, to interact with citizens, firms, other governments, and organizations of all kinds. Defined so, the phenomenon of e-government can be traced back to the 1950s, when computers were brought into government departments in the United Kingdom and United States, first in defense and science-intensive areas and later in the largest administrative transaction processing departments such as tax and social security. The widespread use of computers for holding financial information developed in government from the 1960s and combined with the development of networks and PCs with processing power opened the way for computers to begin to penetrate a wider range of "front" offices or mainstream administrative settings, instead of being concentrated only in self-contained "back-office" enclaves. But the real changes for government—and indeed the emergence of the term "e-government" came with the internet in the second half of the 1990s. Earlier government information technologies were largely internally facing, with a clear potential for transforming administrative tasks and reducing costs but few possibilities for changing the way that government communicated with citizens. As citizens began to witness the transformation of their relationship with many private sector agencies (banks, shops, and travel agents in particular) they also began to expect to interact with government electronically.

Governments too began to perceive the potential for new forms of government–citizen interactions. The development of the internet and the web presented a key opportunity for government to provide higher quality services directly to citizens in innovative ways at lower cost. It facilitated improvements in the provision of information to the public, especially allied with "open government" and "freedom of information" policies. Information can be made available via the web 24 hours a day, from whatever location people access it. Customers who know their own personal circumstances in detail can search for exactly the information they require. There is scope for many citizens to conduct most of their business with government electronically. Web-based technologies can also be used to facilitate "joined-up" government. Websites can provide virtual front-ends or entry points to otherwise fragmented organizational arrangements, allowing citizens to transact with several departments and agencies and across different tiers of government simultaneously. Someone newly out of work, for example, can use government websites to look for and apply for a job, but also claim and receive benefits, obtain information about starting up a small business, or find out about retraining and apply for educational courses. In general, governments have been slower than commercial firms to realize the potential of the internet and associated technologies, but from 2000 onwards the potential of e-government has been evident too, particularly given the phenomenal rise of e-commerce over the period 2000 to 2005.

With widespread use of the internet, IT policy rose much higher up the political agenda in those countries and regions where internet penetration was high (such as Canada, the United States, Singapore, Japan, Scandinavia, and Australia) and reached the attention of policy-makers as it never had before. By the start of the twenty-first century, governments in most of these countries had some kind of e-government initiative. For example, Singapore was an early leader and the United States, Australia, and Canada were particularly quick off the mark, while in the United Kingdom a low-key initiative in 1996 was transformed into a major government commitment by the new Labour administration in autumn 1997. In the Netherlands, an effective government portal was operating by 2001. Japan picked up the need for some e-government activity in 1999 as part of any effective "e-society" push, but progress was slow.

E-government research

The field of e-government research has grown up at very different rates in different sectors and at different times. Before the internet, the academic community showed little sustained interest in the phenomenon, particularly the relationship between information technology and public administration reform. Until the 2000s, academic visions of e-government tended to range from the highly utopian to the severely dystopian, with a lack of empirical research filling the middle of the spectrum. Most of these visions revolved around the modernist notion that technology will somehow lead government to become more rational and efficient, with strong parallels to Weber's predictions for bureaucracy and his analogy of bureaucratic organization as a "machine." So-called "hyper-modernists" (Margetts, 1999) argued that as the internet and associated technologies become ubiquitous, government will become more and more efficient and therefore smaller, until eventually governmental organizations themselves will become increasingly irrelevant. While also believing in transformation for government through technology, "anti-modernists" concentrated on the negative effects, believing that e-government would be more powerful, and more intrusive in the lives of citizens than traditional bureaucracy. Writers such as Burnham (1983) argued that the increased possibility for surveillance and control offered by information and communication technologies would lead electronic governments to "the Computer State" or the "Control State," whereby governments use CCTV cameras, "smart" identity cards, satellite navigation systems, electronic tracking devices, and centralized databases with sophisticated search capabilities to maintain an ever-closer eye on the activities of their citizens.

Outside the modernist tradition, there were a few localized examples of rigorous, empirical e-government research in the United Kingdom (such as Margetts, 1999; Bellamy and Taylor, 1998), the Netherlands (van de Donk *et al.*, eds., 1995) and the United States (Laudon, 1974; Kraemer and Kling, 1985; Kraemer and King, 1986). But in general, mainstream public administration research remained remarkably oblivious to and untouched by the potential implications of information technologies for government (see Margetts, 1999: Chapter 1 for a discussion).

With rising societal use of the internet, there was far more widespread interest in the possible implications of digital technologies for government. Many organizations directed substantive sums of research funding towards e-government, particularly the European Commission, which defined e-government as a priority in the eEurope 2005 Action Plan and its

successor, the i2010 initiative, both geared at creating "an information society for all." There sprung up a plethora of international rankings of e-government, produced by private sector consultancies vying for government business and international organizations providing information across a wider range of countries (see for example Accenture, 2001–5; UNPAN, 2004). But most of these studies are based on questionable methodologies and suffer from a number of weaknesses. The dominant way of picturing the development of e-government in IT-industry thinking in the United Kingdom and internationally that underpins all these rankings is the so-called "stages model" (for an example, see UNPAN, 2001; for a full explanation see Dunleavy and Margetts, 2002: 11). This model delineates a number of stages, which each government is said to go through over time. The first stage is basic electronic publishing where most government agencies have websites but there are few linkages with internal legacy systems or interactions with citizens, while in the second stage agencies develop more interactive and transactional websites, where users can undertake more sophisticated dealings with the agency online. Eventually, the government achieves some kind of "joined-up e-governance," where the website facilitates one-stop services for citizens across a whole range of services across central government agencies and tiers of government. Different rankings ascribe different titles to the stages. Accenture, for example, appears to choose the names carefully so as not to offend potential customers placed in the lower categories: "online presence," "basic capability," "service availability," "mature delivery," and "service transformation." But across the rankings there is strong similarity between the definitions of each stage. As with the work outlined above, this stages model of development is inherently modernist, with an inbuilt assumption that a government (or an organization, or an individual) will only proceed forward through the "stages" before reaching some kind of "e-government nirvana."

Academic research and theoretical development, however, has not kept pace with these huge volumes of practitioner activity, which remain unintegrated into the mainstream of public management research. Even by 2007, many leading texts on public management reform contain only a few isolated references to the internet or e-government; for example, the 2004 edition of Pollitt and Bouckaert's central cross-national study of *Public Management Reform* has no references to the internet or information technology.

However, as in the pre-internet era there have emerged a few key works on e-government that do investigate the empirical reality of e-government while aiming to incorporate mainstream theoretical and methodological perspectives for further study in the field. Leading journals in public administration such as *Public Administration Review, Governance,* and the *Journal of Public Administration Research and Theory* contain a smattering of articles discussing e-government issues (for example, Norris and Moon, 2005; Bretschneider, 2003; Chadwick and May, 2003). Fountain (2001) applies an institutional approach to the study of U.S. e-government, arguing that the real challenge for the "virtual state" will be to overcome entrenched organizational and political divisions within government. West (2005) uses multiple methods to identify some of the factors determining the breadth of e-government adoption across a wide range of countries. Dunleavy *et al.* (2006a) use fuzzy set methods to make a detailed comparison of seven countries in terms of their e-government performance and a range of potential factors contributing to performance, with the power of the IT industry in relation to the government emerging as the most important.

In contrast to the earlier modernist agenda, the key theme that links much of this post-internet e-government research (for example, Fountain, 2001; Moon, 2002; Norris and Moon, 2005; West, 2005) is that digital technologies are used to reinforce existing organizational arrangements and power distributions rather than to change them; that information technology cannot be an instrument of administrative reform (see Kraemer and King, 2006 for a full discussion, references, and argument). Such authors argue that, at best, IT has been an enabler of reforms; that IT has had little effect on organizational structure; and that the primary beneficiaries of e-government have been the dominant political–administrative coalitions in public administration. Although they make some acknowledgment of the potential influence of the internet in the future, there is no argument that digital technologies will set the agenda for administrative reform.

In contrast, Dunleavy *et al.* (2006a) outline the potential for e-government or, more broadly, digital-era governance (DEG) to emerge as a new paradigm for public administration. It is not argued that reform will necessarily be technologically driven in this direction; rather that the changing technological environment both inside and outside government creates demands and choices to which government agencies must respond. In so doing, the approach explores a range of scenarios for the internet and digital technologies to impact upon government and public management reform and for this reason, is discussed below.

Before e-government: the new public management

So what might we be able to predict for government in the age of digital technologies—and what is the relationship between e-government and administrative reform more generally?

The dominant theme of public management reform across many developed nations throughout the 1980s and 1990s, to strongly varying degrees, was the movement known as New Public Management (NPM). In its early days NPM was often represented as introducing modern business management methods into public administration, which was often taken to include more use of IT instead of paper-based channels. But this pro-IT theme was never really a distinctive feature of NPM, partly because all public sector organizations increased their use of IT and changed the character of the IT they were using around that time (Dunleavy et al., 2006a). So from the mid 1980s onwards, the NPM movement can be characterized as a cohort of organizational restructuring changes based on importing concepts from business practices and public choice-influenced theory into the public sector. Within this macro-level change, there were three chief themes of NPM, as below.

Disaggregation

This involved splitting up large public sector hierarchies, together with strong flexibilization of previous government-wide practices in personnel, IT, procurement. and other functions (Barzelay, 2000). Examples of changes that brought disaggregation included the separation of public sector agencies into "purchasers" and "providers"; the breaking down of large departments into small core departments and multiple agencies; the creation of quasi-government agencies; the separation out of micro-local agencies; and the dividing up of privatized industries. New forms of performance measurement and league tables and rankings of agency performance further emphasized organizational boundaries.

The enthusiasm with which these strategies were pursued in the 1980s and 1990s in some countries (such as the United Kingdom and New Zealand) has left important organizational legacies. Most importantly for the development of e-government is organizational fragmentation, typified by New Zealand where NPM change left a government consisting of over 300 separate central agencies and 40 tiny ministries, in addition to local and health service authorities, for a country of only four million people.

Competition changes

These involved introducing purchaser/provider separation into public structures so as to allow multiple forms of provision to be developed and to create (more) competition among potential providers. Increasing internal use was made of competition processes to allocate resources, in place of hierarchical decision-making. The "core" areas of state administration and public provision were shrunk and suppliers were diversified. Specific competition components included the introduction of quasi-markets into public agencies, particularly health and social services; voucher schemes; outsourcing and compulsory market testing of previously governmental activities; intra-government contracting; deregulation; and consumer-tagged financing.

Much of the competition agenda has stalled in recent years, but again leaves problematic legacies with particular relevance for government IT strategies. The most important is the almost complete outsourcing of government IT functions to private sector systems integrator firms in Australia, the United Kingdom, and New Zealand (see Dunleavy and Margetts, 2006a).

Incentivization

This involved shifting away from involving managers and staffs and rewarding performance in terms of diffuse public service or professional ethoses, and moving instead towards a greater emphasis on pecuniary-based, specific performance incentives. This shift was achieved via capital market involvement in projects such as the United Kingdom's Private Finance Initiative (PFI); privatizing asset ownership; the de-privileging of professions, such as teachers; performance-related pay; public–private partnerships; unified rate of return and discounting; the development of charging technologies; the valuing of public sector equity, in ways analogous to the private sector; and imposing mandatory efficiency dividends on public managers.

Incentivization is the most resilient of the NPM themes, including some relatively detailed rationalization changes with relevance for e-government. Of particular relevance was capital market involvement, which proceeded furthest in the United Kingdom with the PFI, under which contract providers were supposed to undertake a share of the risk in large-scale projects. Yet PFI also created new risks of catastrophic failure. In late 2003, after more than a decade of experimentation, the U.K. Treasury banned PFI for government IT specifically, reflecting a checkered history of ineffective risk-transfer to contractors and high scrap rates for IT projects.

From a comparative perspective, governments can be assessed in terms of their openness to NPM ideas and changes along these three dimensions. The United Kingdom and New Zealand emerge as core NPM countries, although with different emphases. In the United Kingdom, NPM was strongly orientated towards developing major projects and systems involving private finance and large corporations in public service delivery. In the far smaller New Zealand, a more conservative and risk-averse approach combined with the fragmentation effect meant that

IT projects tended to be small and piecemeal, although large corporations were still involved. Other countries were more ambivalent to NPM. Australia was an early NPM leader, pioneering some distinctive NPM reforms, but under Labour governments the initially radical impetus faded into a more humanist style by the mid 1990s, with less of the "private sector good, public sector bad" ethos and the negative image of public sector staff that was built into the NPM reforming culture elsewhere. Likewise, both the United States and Canada implemented parts of the NPM agenda but resisted other parts. The United States made some concerted NPM-style changes during the 1990s, as part of the Clinton–Gore National Performance Review reforms, but the style was more akin to Australia than the United Kingdom (Margetts, 1997). And it never embraced the whole agenda proactively, partly because many NPM ideas were already long in play across U.S. federal, state, and highly fragmented local governments. Other countries, such as Japan and the Netherlands, were predominantly resistant to NPM. In Japan, core central government administration remained organized on orthodox public administration lines up until 2003 and so far, changes are small scale. The Netherlands implemented some detailed NPM ideas at local levels, but these changes were made without a strong or concerted political push for NPM as such, and by the early 2000s NPM was largely viewed by officials as something that "has been tried," but was now "over."

The emergence of digital-era governance

New Public Management change proceeded, or didn't proceed, more or less independently of technological change. But as noted above, by the early 2000s

119

most countries were implementing or at least discussing some kind of e-government initiative which formed a central part of the administrative reform agenda, although with considerable variation across countries in terms of the type of changes envisaged. Dunleavy *et al.* (2006a, 2006b) have summarized the possible menu of changes as "digital-era governance" (DEG), which have IT and information handling changes at their center but which spread much more widely than was the case with previous IT influences. For the first time the authors argue, it now makes sense to characterize the broad sweep of current public management regime change in terms that refer to digital modes of operating. The advent of the digital era is now the most general, pervasive, and structurally distinctive influence on how governance arrangements are changing in advanced industrial states. This is not to argue that all these changes have or necessarily will occur in any given country, any more than did NPM, but they remain on the menu of administrative reform for contemporary government agencies.

Digital-era governance involves a range of organizational changes resulting from the need to accommodate important shifts in modes of operation, including the use of e-mail in internal and external communications; the rising salience of the internet and intranets in organizational information networks; the development of electronic web-based services for different client groups; and a fundamental transition from paper-based to electronic record-keeping. Societal changes in communications and information seeking also push governments towards further digitalization. As consumers' and corporations' behaviors in the private sector change, so there are direct demands for government information and transaction practices to shift in parallel ways (although there may be time lags). In countries where NPM influences have been high, there is an additional driver

for organizational change—the impact of large-scale contractor involvement in delivering IT-related administration processes on the organizational arrangements and cultures of the agencies they supply.

The impact of DEG practices can be considered under three main themes, summarized from the book of the same title (Dunleavy *et al.*, 2006a) as below (and also see Dunleavy *et al.*, 2006b). All three of these themes can be considered in terms of how they contrast with the dominant approaches (and emerging problems) of NPM.

Reintegration

New Public Management-driven fragmentation is a key barrier to governments wishing to maximize the potential benefits of digital-era technology. Reintegration components stress gathering back together the disparate functions and clusters of expertise that under NPM were fragmented into single-function agencies and spread across complex interorganizational networks. However, the forms of reintegration are different from pre-NPM structures and some new patterns (such as shared services) are emerging.

In the United Kingdom, the rollback of agencification and fragmentation was achieved in part via departmental mergers, reformation of cohesive departmental groups of agencies, and culls of quasi-governmental agencies, all of which were prominent features of Labour government policies from 1997 onwards. Joined-up governance was also a central element of reintegration in the United Kingdom under the Blair government (see 6 *et al.*, 2002; Pollitt, 2003; 6, 2004). Major departmental amalgamations at central or federal levels occurred in both the United States and the United Kingdom, such as the creation of the Department of Homeland Security in the United States, responding to the previous deficiencies of agency fragmentation highlighted by the 9/11 terrorist massacre (Wise, 2002) and the merging of employment service and welfare benefits operations in the U.K.'s Department of Work and Pensions. These changes rely on massive IT convergences; the merger of two previously separate U.K. tax agencies into one (HM Revenue and Customs) in 2005, for example, was completely reliant on an extensive integration program of two huge systems networks managed by different suppliers under separate contracts.

Reintegration also comes from re-establishing central processes. New Public Management's focus on creating new or enhanced corporate management processes across dozens of agencies meant duplicating on a smaller scale some similar generic functions, such as non-standard procurement, recruitment and human relations, or e-government operations. Varied initiatives have begun to re-impose a degree of order on this NPM legacy, especially in the IT area with the Canadian and U.S. Federal Enterprise Architecture Programs (FEAP). In the United Kingdom, centralized e-change programs have been extensively funded and from 2005, the e-government unit began trying to reduce duplication in areas like the over-provision of websites. However, these large-country initiatives lag years behind effective government-wide programs launched by small countries like Singapore and Finland that were more resistant to NPM influences in the past, and hence have had stronger central processes from the outset.

Re-engineering back-office functions is another form of re-integration which realizes the productivity improvements offered by newer IT, consolidating "legacy" labyrinths of discrete mainframe facilities and associated administrative units, which grew up piecemeal in the 1970s and 1980s and were never simplified in the 1990s. In the NPM countries, where problematic IT systems tended to be outsourced "wholesale" rather than being modernized or redesigned, there is considerable potential for re-engineering in this way. Reaping the benefits of re-engineering acquired political prominence in the United Kingdom in 2004 when both the Labour government and the main opposition parties outlined plans for quantum reductions of at least 80,000 civil servants (out of a total of 530,000) over a five-year period (see Gershon, 2004). The big reductions were concentrated in high IT-use departments, with 30,000 staff targeted in the Department of Work and Pensions and 15,000 from the merging of two national tax agencies.

A government-wide focus on procurement is also a move towards the re-integration of outsourced elements, particularly IT. Procurement concentration and specialization has long developed in the United States, especially with the growth of Government-Wide Acquisition Contracts (GWACs), contracts established by one agency with one or more suppliers under which other agencies can purchase products and services without tendering anew. Government-Wide Acquisition Contracts accounted for 39 percent of American public sector civil IT procurement by 2003. But in the NPM core countries these ideas were neglected and a huge increase in the number and range of contracts was not accompanied by a concurrent professionalization of procurement. In New Zealand, government outsourced its key competencies in contracts-drafting to private sector lawyers and consultants, as chief executives on short-term contracts themselves covered their positions against risks, more concerned with ensuring process-proofing and a clear audit trail than with contracting innovatively. In the United Kingdom, the NPM era produced a considerable duplication of procurement functions across departments and agencies. A 2004 efficiency review conducted for the Treasury concluded that £20 billion of cost savings could be made within four years from a range of measures, including a shift to smarter procurement carried out by a few major procurement centers, instead of independently by 270 departments and agencies at national level (Gershon, 2004).

Shared services initiatives also contribute to re-integration, encouraging smaller departments and agencies to use commonly provided back-office or more policy relevant services, like human relations, IT services, or financial services. Agencies with a proven capability in one area are encouraged to provide the same service on a contract basis to other agencies with similar needs, with multiple providers ensuring that a customer agency experiencing poor levels of service can always switch to an alternative supplier. In the United States, the GWACs for procuring simple IT were an early version of shared services. In the United Kingdom, a "mixed economy" model may develop under the Gershon review process, with a few central government "hubs" for procurement and other services competing with a limited number of major outsourcing operations run by consultancies or big IT providers who can sell more wholesale "business process outsourcing" solutions.

Network simplification is another way to resolve another problematic by-product of fragmentation; complex top tiers of regulatory or guidance agencies for networks of public agencies and quasi- or non-governmental bodies (see Hood et al., 2000). The multi-way fragmentation of the U.K. rail industry provides one of the most exaggerated NPM outcomes, with at one time in the late 1990s three separate regulators covering rail infrastructure investment, rail safety, and the licensing of train companies. Streamlining regulatory overview and simplifying underlying networks can stop the creation of multiple management teams in highly balkanized policy areas like this, each partly making more work for others to handle. The "small worlds" literature on network connectivity suggests that network simplification can be achieved when a regular lattice of local links between close neighbor organizations is supplemented by a relatively small number of random or cross-cutting, long-range links joining up further apart or even remote policy sectors (Watts and Strogatz, 1998).

Needs-based holism

In contrast to the narrow joined-up-governance changes included in the reintegration theme, holistic reforms seek to re-engineer the entire relationship between agencies and their clients. Needs-based holism involves moving away from the NPM stress on business process management and towards a citizen-based, services-based, or needs-based foundation of organization (see 6 et al., 2002). Interactive information-seeking and giving is fundamental for the emergence of all the other needs-based holism elements. This discovery was a long time coming in the public sector. Governments have tended to accept uncritically the five-phase "stages model" of e-government's development described in the first section, in which passive information-giving was dismissed as an elementary first phase, a "billboards" phase that should be bypassed as swiftly as possible en route to the "golden" applications of e-government in transactional uses (Dunleavy and Margetts, 2002). It took more than a decade for the government sector to follow the private sector in different countries in realizing that information-seeking is a crucial part of service delivery just as it is of most commercial transactions and that search applications and sophisticated information arbitrage would be every bit as critical in public sector applications. A further realization—that citizens and enterprises themselves have far more information about their own situations than government could ever acquire (just as patients know most about their condition, and consumers about their needs and desires)—is vital to the design of effective e-government services. The job of government information systems then is to maximize the potential for using this information, by recording users' actual behavior for example, in the provision of public services, rather than taking a top–down approach, which tries to "second-guess" what people want or need.

One-stop provision is another form of needs-based holism. It takes various forms, including one-stop shops (where multiple administrative services are provided by the same co-located staff), one-stop windows (where only the customer interface is integrated), and web-integrated services (where the customer transparency and cross-services integration is primarily electronic). The impulse in all one-stop provision is for government agencies to proactively mesh together provision across erstwhile separate fiefdoms, so as to resolve "lead agency" and duplication problems and to reduce the previously high cognitive burdens and compliance costs placed on citizens or businesses in the NPM heyday. Key examples have been the pulling together of previously separated employment and benefits services for working-age people in the United Kingdom, again in a new kind of client-focused agency, Job Centre Plus, following a pattern initiated much earlier by the pioneering Australian Centrelink agency. "Ask once" methods involve a commitment by government to reusing already collected information, rather than recursively gathering the same information many times, as happened under NPM's fragmented administrative systems.

Another holistic approach is end-to-end service re-engineering, involving a complete redrawing of service-provision models. Under previous public management regimes, agencies often had perverse incentives to differentiate their services and processes. Despite moving the administrative furniture around a great deal, NPM reformers were actually reluctant to undertake more fundamental questioning of administrative processes, because of the focus on short-term managerialist savings. Indeed, in the fragmented New Zealand system, re-engineering would pose impossible demands, for instance requiring agency chiefs to envisage their own organization's amalgamation or to contemplate a change program extending far beyond their own short term of office. In contrast, the migration of key government information systems to the web can emphasize the interconnectedness of provision and the potential for re-engineering. An end-to-end approach ensures that project teams focus through the whole process without artificially demarcating their analysis at existing agency boundaries.

Digitization changes

To realize contemporary productivity gains from IT and related organizational changes requires a far more fundamental take-up of the opportunities opened up by a transition to fully digital operations. Instead of electronic channels being seen as supplementary to conventional administrative and business processes, they become genuinely transformative, moving towards a situation where the agency "becomes its website," as a senior official in the Australian Tax Office described this process (Dunleavy and Margetts, 1999). Organization and cultural changes are triggered by the impacts of web, internet, and e-mail on public agencies as well as behavioral shifts by civil society actors outside.

The most obvious digitization change comes from electronic services delivery (ESD), as most paper-based administrative processes are converted to e-government processes. As noted above, many post-NPM governments have adopted relatively ambitious programs and targets, as with the U.K.'s pledge to put 100 percent of central and local government services online by the end of 2005, backed by a £1 billion investment (Dunleavy and Margetts, 1999, 2002). In fact, citizens' take-up of e-services in the United Kingdom has lagged considerably behind growth in e-commerce, but once initiated has generally shown rapid growth as with online applications for the paying of income tax and road tax, for example. Rising internet penetration acts to strengthen the business rationale and customer impetus for further ESD.

Other digitization changes include using "zero touch technology" (ZTT), pioneered in the private sector by companies like CISCO, where the ideal is that no human intervention is needed in a sale or administrative operation. There are huge areas of potential application in public agency operations. For instance, the surveillance and control system for the London congestion charge is an almost ZTT process. Once the entry of a particular car has been paid for, its number plate is automatically counted as valid in the monitoring machinery, or turned up as an apparent exception if not paid for, with the vast majority of cases not requiring staff attention. Likewise, speeding fines or traffic violations in many countries that are photographed in real-time and sent to the owner of the vehicle with address details obtained from a vehicle licensing database have the potential to be dealt with automatically in this way. In other sectors there are also many applications for auto monitoring, like immigration, where borders are electronically monitored by automatic sensors, and environmental management, where cheap mobile phone-based auto sensors (costing as little as $15 each) can

monitor water levels and replace manually inspected gauges and instrumentation.

Such technologies also facilitate disintermediation; that is, the potential for web-based processes to allow citizens, businesses, and other civil society actors to connect directly to state systems, without passing through gatekeepers in the form of civil service or agency personnel as was previously always the case. Of course, such systems in practice need substantial back-up and help-desk systems. But disintermediation changes can allow civil society actors who know their own situations very well to autonomously sift and select what they may receive from government. Disintermediation works only when government agencies facilitate changes in behavior by citizens or consumers of public services. A good example is the public transport system in London, where transport authorities introduced charging technology in underground rail stations and buses for using a smart card (called Oystercard), which allowed users to put credit on their card and then pay for any form of mass-transit journeys by swiping it past an automatic reader. Card users grew in four years from 350,000 (the original holders of paper season tickets) to more than 2.2 million, with large cost savings in ticketing staff, big reductions in peak-hour queuing times, and increased use of mass transit by passengers, who no longer had to buy tickets when traveling. Adding a web-based card-issuing service and the ability to "top-up" card credit online completed the disintermediation picture for customers.

Digitization changes also involve governments developing customer segmentation processes as strongly in the public sector as in the private business sector, where the internet is used to differentiate firmly between customers (in contrast to the NPM focus on discrete business processes). For example, for those citizens that interact with government online the internet provides unprecedented opportunities for government agencies to understand their behavior (from sophisticated usage statistics for example) and redesign electronic services accordingly. For those citizens that do not use the internet, research suggests that a significant proportion (more than 70 percent) could find an intermediary to do so for them, and formalizing online channels with intermediaries could be a key way for government agencies to interact with this major sub-section of the population. Government agencies have to employ quite different online strategies to reach these distinct groups.

Customer segmentation is also an essential step in active channel-streaming, namely incentivizing people to switch by providing e-services with lower costs or greatly improved functionality. Multichannel access is often just too expensive to provide, so rather than adding electronic service channels to existing capacity, many agencies move to a strategy of actively managing displacement of service users to electronic channels. For example, in 2006, the mayor of London heavily promoted the use of pre-pay versions of the Oystercard (see above) by dramatically increasing prices on conventional ticket sales but keeping those on electronic transactions at the previous year's prices. The logic here is that strong incentives are needed to overcome the "transaction" costs to consumers of moving from a familiar but expensive to operate payment system to a new but much cheaper alternative. Once this step transition has been encouraged the incentives for electronic customers can be reduced, and none are likely to switch back once they have actually experienced the convenience of the new methods. Mandated channel reductions or legally compelling people or businesses to change how they transact with government agencies remains an option in other areas, especially for regulatory compliance or tax payments for enterprises, as many tax and customs departments have already done (see Margetts and Yared, 2003).

All these digitization changes have the potential to bring a shift towards self-government, from agency-centered to citizen-centered (or business-centered or stakeholder-centered) processes, where citizens or businesses play more of a role in running their own interactions with government. Re-orientation around the citizen implies a move away from "closed files" government to a more "open book" model, where citizens can look at their own medical files and monitor their own treatment, or actively manage their own tax account. Such a shift involves bringing citizens "into the front office," so that they are "co-producing" or even "co-creating" public services. In some areas of government the principles of citizens co-producing services are already well appreciated; for instance, in public health where active cooperation is the key for any communicable diseases control and in "e-health," where citizens use the internet to become far more informed about their own condition than was ever possible in the pre-digital era. And in environmental services, essential innovations like differentiated waste disposal are co-produced throughout—citizens actually do all the sorting of different types of household waste prior to its being simply collected by agencies or contractors. Such a shift might be greatly accelerated if governments were to move towards using so-called "Web 2.0" applications, characterized by user-generated content (such as testimonials), the mixing of information sources ("mash-ups"), and social networking technologies, a growing societal trend discussed elsewhere in this volume. At the time of writing government use of such applications was relatively rare across even leading e-government countries, but the potential was already clear.

125

The future of digital-era governance and e-government research

This chapter has discussed the potential for "digital-era governance" to emerge as a new paradigm for public administration, and has suggested some key themes of such a movement that might be used to chart e-government change in the future. The evidence presented in this chapter suggests that there will be substantial variation across countries, just as was the case after 20 years of a public management reform agenda dominated by NPM. Countries vary in the extent to which they are responding to digital-era changes in public management, ranging from radical, transformative change or more modest changes lagging behind other sectors. And they also vary according to the level of NPM influences and the extent to which DEG processes are being used to reverse NPM change in public organizations.

By the mid 2000s, there were signs that the wave of enthusiasm for e-government from the practitioner community discussed in the first half of this chapter had died away, analogous perhaps to the "dotcom bust" of the earlier years of the decade. Hefty expenditure and e-government programs remain, but public officials were reluctant to label them as such, with both practitioners and academics arguing that we should "drop the 'e-'." In 2006, Accenture's annual e-government ranking did not even refer to e-government in its title (although most of the indicators of performance remained the same) and the U.K. government's e-government strategy was renamed "Transformational Government," while the e-government unit in the Cabinet Office was also renamed. To some extent, policy-makers seemed keen to move on even while e-government was still in its infancy, particularly compared

with e-commerce, and to return to an era where general improvement and "good government" are the mantra of public management reform.

There is certainly nothing inevitable about the "digital-era" changes outlined above. Indeed, many of them, particularly those under the "re-integration" theme but also elements of need-based holism, work against the dominant thrust of NPM reform in countries where it has been implemented. Furthermore, for any governmental organizations to make the most of the internet and related technologies, they may have to shift towards networked (rather than hierarchical) ways of working, involving a wider range of non-governmental and private organizations (the "para-state") in previously governmental tasks. One-stop shops, for example, long promoted as a benefit of IT in both the United States and the United Kingdom, have in the past proved to necessitate a degree of collaborative working that many government agencies found it difficult to attain (Margetts, 1999). Web-based technologies make collaboration easier, but some degree of back-end cooperation is still required. Policy-makers also have to recognize that making use of advanced search capabilities (often wielded by citizens themselves) combined with chaotic forms of information storage can be the most efficient way to provide information. And capitalizing on newer applications (such as those using "user-generated content" or "Web 2.0" technologies) involves drawing citizens into the front office of public services production. All these developments tend to work against the culture of traditional public administration (see Dunleavy and Margetts, 2002 for an early discussion), so can be challenging even for "low-NPM" countries. So, public organizations wishing to be at the forefront of innovation may well have to overcome considerable internal cultural resistance.

This chapter has also pointed to many gaps in e-government research. While pre-internet research tended to be dominated by a modernist agenda, oscillating between strongly determinist utopian "hyper-modernist" or dystopian "anti-modernist" accounts, post-internet work in the institutionalist tradition has tended to downplay the implications of digital technologies for government and particularly public management reform. Meanwhile, the issue has still failed to penetrate the mainstream of public administration research and has not received sustained attention from a variety of theoretical frameworks. From the evidence presented here, it should be clear, however, that the centrality of digital technologies to public management, their pervasive impact on society at large, and the necessity for organizational responses on the part of government, will ensure that to some extent, technological innovation will drive bureaucratic reform in the future. "E-government" or "digital-era governance" (or whatever it is labeled) should become a critical area of public management research.

Guide to further reading

A cross-national comparative analysis of e-government and an argument for a new framework for understanding public bureaucracies can be found in Dunleavy et al. (2006a, 2006b). West (2005) also takes a comparative approach. Fountain (2001) provides a detailed account of e-government's emergence in the United States during the 1990s. Kraemer and King (2006), and Norris and Moon (2005) provide useful statements of the reinforcement perspective. Hood and Margetts (2007) update the classic "tools of government" perspective for the digital age.

Part 2

Behavior

10

Wired to fact

The role of the internet in identifying deception during the 2004 U.S. presidential campaign

Bruce W. Hardy, Kathleen Hall Jamieson,
and Kenneth Winneg

This chapter asks whether during the 2004 presidential general election the internet enabled citizens to differentiate fact from deception. Like past elections, the one in 2004 included deceptive claims and misleading rhetoric by both the Republican and Democratic camps. Past research has suggested that traditional news sources such as newspapers and television news are not living up to their role as custodian of fact. Some forms of journalistic practice may in fact foster cynicism and depress learning among citizens. Using data from the 2004 National Annenberg Election Survey that asked respondents about 41 campaign statements—claims that were vetted by FackCheck.org of the Annenberg Public Policy Center—we found that accessing campaign information online promoted a command of facts contested in the election campaign, above and beyond the influence of traditional news media. The chapter also discusses failings of the traditional press and ways in which accessing information on the internet may overcome them.

The amount of political information available to voters in today's media environment is seemingly endless. The internet provides data on demand from news sites, both mainstream and not mainstream, ideologically driven websites, blogs of all political stripes, candidate, campaign, and party websites, and video-sharing sites such as YouTube.com, where anonymous individuals or groups can post videos related to candidates and campaigns. Some of this information is vetted by gatekeepers, some not. And when a gatekeeper is supervising, the norms under which that function is performed are not necessarily either clear or disclosed.

Does this cascade of potential information confuse users or help them make sense of contesting political claims? Can these new information technologies provide information to enable users to protect themselves from misleading campaign rhetoric? This chapter examines the effectiveness of the internet in providing the tools to enable citizens to distinguish fact from deception in the 2004 presidential general elections, above and beyond the tools afforded to them by the traditional news media.

In the 2004 U.S. presidential election, citizens turned to the internet for campaign information at unprecedented levels (Rainie *et al.*, 2005). By one estimate (that of the Pew Research Center for the People and the Press), 75 million Americans looked to the web during the election, "to get political news and information, discuss candidates and debate issues in e-mails, or participate directly in the political process by volunteering or giving contributions to candidates" (Rainie *et al.*, 2005, p. i). The number of citizens going online for political news increased from 18 percent of the general public during the 2000 election to 29 percent in 2004 (Rainie *et al.*, 2005, p. i). Similar percentages were found in the National Annenberg Election Study (NAES). Over the course of the campaign, from October 2003 through November 2, 2004 we found that 26 percent of registered voters accessed the internet for political information during the 2004 election. As election day neared (September 7 through November 1, 2004), the proportion of registered voters with internet access who reported going online for political information averaged 34 percent (Winneg and Stroud, 2005).

Like past elections, the one in 2004 included deceptive claims and misleading rhetoric by both the Republican and Democratic camps (Jackson and Jamison, 2004; Milbank and VandeHei, 2004; Winneg *et al.*, 2005). Misleading attacks on opponents' vote records, military service, and proposed policies found their way into Democratic and Republican advertisements and stump speeches.

None of this would make much difference if the public were immune to its effects. However, Winneg *et al.* (2005) found at the end of the 2004 primary season that a majority of the American public living in battleground states in which political advertisements aired, mistakenly believed that "George W. Bush favors sending American jobs overseas" and "John Kerry voted for higher taxes 350 times." These were, of course, central claims in attack ads.

The press is supposed to sort fact from fiction. If it does, an attentive public would not be deceived. Put simply, "when those seeking office offer discordant facts, the public should expect the press to weigh in to make sense of the discrepancies" (Jackson and Jamieson, 2004, p. 229). The press, however, seems to be failing in its role as the "custodian of fact" (Jamieson and Waldman, 2003; Jamieson and Hardy, 2007). Nor is the public holding up its end of the bargain. Relatively low consumption of traditional news combines with a reluctance on the part of the press to adjudicate fact to all but ensure that the presumed protection against campaign distortions expected of the press is less effective than democratic theorists would like.

Confounding such an ill-fated combination is the press's reliance on "horse-race" campaign coverage that focuses on strategy and politicking and, as some have argued, leaves citizens cynically sitting on the sidelines (Cappella and Jamieson, 1996, 1997; Jamieson, 1992; Patterson, 1993). Studying the race for mayor in Philadelphia in 1991 and the 1993–4 health-care reform debate, Cappella and Jamieson (1996) found that such coverage significantly increased cynicism and suppressed the likelihood that participants in their study could accurately report the information present in strategically framed news stories. Those experiments, however, took place in the old media environment. In the early 1990s citizens did not have any other functional alternative for accessing political information besides the traditional news outlets. Back then, citizens who were exposed to information about the gaming of self-interested politicians through traditional news, and as a result became more cynical and learned less than they otherwise might have, had little recourse. Today, however, the internet presents a viable alternative.

Here we examine the following questions. Do failures of the press lead individuals to turn to the internet in search of political information? Does the internet enable them to discern fact from deception in presidential elections, above and beyond the tools afforded to the citizens by the traditional news media? Does the use of the internet affect citizen's overall knowledge of facts?

These questions require that we explain what we mean by fact. Campaigns are contests over completing claims. Some are simple matters of opinion. "John Kerry *betrayed* his country by testifying against the Vietnam War before the Senate Foreign Relations Committee upon his return home," is a statement of opinion. One might believe that any critique of an ongoing war is an act of disloyalty, while another might believe that it is a citizen's duty. However, as Senator Daniel Patrick Moynihan was fond of noting, "Everyone is entitled to his own opinion; no one is entitled to his own facts."

The fact that John Kerry is a Democratic Senator from Massachusetts who served in Vietnam and testified before the Senate Foreign Relations Committee upon returning home is not a matter of opinion. If one holds that Kerry is a Senator from Iowa, for example, there are widely accepted sources to which one can appeal to demonstrate to a reasonable observer that the person is incorrect. For practical purposes what we mean by fact is what Jamieson (1992), in *Dirty Politics: deception, distraction and democracy,* called "consensual fact." Whether a person voted for or against a specific piece of legislation and how many votes a person cast for a certain position are matters of fact as well.

To draw up the battery of factual and false claims from the 2004 presidential campaign, this study relied on the reports of the Annenberg Public Policy Center's FactCheck.org.[1] That source was cited approvingly by both Democratic and Republican campaigns in 2004, most notoriously by Vice President Dick Cheney during his debate with Democratic Vice Presidential contender John Edwards.

This research focused on widely disseminated claims—those found in political ads and discussed in news. They included such central questions in the campaign as the extent of job loss or gain during the first Bush term, whether Bush proposed cutting current Social Security benefits for seniors and the level, timing, and extent of support for intelligence operations by Senator Kerry.

The scholarly literature raises doubts about the likelihood that internet use would positively correlate with command of political fact. After all, scholars have found that "[although] the possession of 'facts' is related to citizens' media exposure, the correlation is weak, particularly in the case of television news. And once one controls for education level, the correlation nearly disappears" (Patterson and Seib, 2005, p. 191; see also Becker and Whitney, 1980). Exposure to local news actually predicts a drop in political knowledge (Jamieson and Hardy, 2007; Prior, 2003). Newspaper readership, however, is a reliable positive predictor (Becker and Dunwoody, 1982; Chaffee and Frank, 1996; Chaffee, Zhao, and Leshner, 1994).

The press, information, and democratic society

The press is constitutionally protected because it has important functions in a democratic society. "[To] the press alone, chequered as it is with abuses," wrote Thomas Jefferson, "the world is indebted for all the triumphs which have been gained by reason and humanity over errors and oppression."

The importance of the press is magnified by the fact that most citizens experience politics second-hand. Very few directly observe political actors and policy decisions. A functioning democracy is dependent on the press to inform. As

Herbert Gans wrote, "The country's democracy may belong directly or indirectly to its citizens, but the democratic process can only be truly meaningful if these citizens are informed" (Gans, 2003: p. 1).

The role of information in democratic society

In modern democracies, citizens elect or appoint others to represent their interests. One peril in such a system is that uninformed citizens may delegate to those who could "transform democracy into a *tyranny of experts*" (Dahl, 1967; Lupia and McCubbins, 1998). Low levels of citizen knowledge (Delli Carpini and Keeter, 1996) raise the question: has such a tyranny of experts become a reality?

Political scientist Phillip Converse (1990) outlined two simple "truths" about the distribution of political information in the U.S. electorate: "the mean is low and the variance is high." However, Converse points out that these truths are relative to "naïve expectations" of the level of political information the average citizen holds and that the naïve observer is the one alarmed and shocked by low scores of the "political knowledge" tests found in many studies. "It is important," he argued, "not to leap from these low scores, as is often done, to an assumption that the substantial portions of the electorate know virtually nothing about current national politics ... even those who fall in the bottom deciles of political information tests still may have a substantial set of apperceptions about the national political world, such that with proper interviewer probing could talk non-repetitively about it for significant spans of time" (p. 372). To address the concerns raised by Converse's conclusions, researchers developed questions to ensure that they captured issues of importance to voters (e.g., Iraq, guns, Social Security, jobs) and also central to the Democratic and Republican presidential campaigns. Being incorrect on many of these questions would have led a voter to inaccurately predict how the elected candidate would govern.

As a practical matter, political scientist Samuel L. Popkin (1994) notes the "voter as an investor and the vote as a reasoned investment in collective good, made with costly and imperfect information under conditions of uncertainty" (p.10). The solution, according to Popkin, is citizens' use of heuristics or cognitive shortcuts. Of course, cognitive shortcuts can compensate but only when they prompt accurate inferences. The notion that citizens are capable of making rational choices with limited information assumes that the limited information on which they rely is accurate.

The research shows ample evidence that both campaigns relied on heuristics to mislead the public in 2004. Sixty-two percent of those surveyed after the election found very or somewhat truthful the false Bush claim that Kerry's tax increase would have hurt 900,000 small-business owners. The reason is simple: the public is inclined to see Democrats as tax raisers and anti-business. That "business bias" heuristic was also at play, perhaps, in the finding that 66 percent believed the false Kerry claim that "the new jobs created since George W. Bush became president pay, on average, $9,000 a year or less than the jobs they replaced." Republicans are expected, or so the heuristic says, to favor business over labor. More jobs at lower pay would advantage employers at the cost to employees. Misuse of the heuristic that says that Republicans are more likely to cut social programs led the public to accept as credible the notion that Bush would actually cut Social Security for those now receiving it while the heuristic that suggests that Democrats are weak on defense led it to accept the false statement that "John Kerry voted for cuts in intelligence after September 11th."

As presidential campaigns progress, voters do become more informed (Johnston, Hagen, and Jamieson, 2004). Gelman and King (1993; see also Holbrook, 1996; Campbell, 2000) for example argued the main purpose of presidential campaigns is to illuminate the differences between candidates so that voters can figure out which of the candidates are more in line with their predispositions. Additionally, overall levels of political knowledge found in the electorate seem to have increased as well. By the end of the 2004 election issue knowledge was higher than it had been at the same point in 2000 (Winneg and Stroud, 2005). Yet that increase did not signal the demise of serious forms of misinformation (Kenski and Jamieson, 2006). The bottom line remains: it is difficult to sort through misleading claims by the two political parties and their nominees. Can new information technologies, such as the internet, provide information to help citizens sort through the confusing political world of contested claims?

Past research on the civic consequences of internet use

A growing body of scholarly literature addresses the effects of the internet on democratic society. However, researchers of political communication have yet to agree on the extent to which access to, and use of, the internet promote active citizenship. Some—often labeled "cyber-optimists"—suggest that the internet can turn around waning levels of political knowledge and political participation. In this view, citizens will access information and coordinate political activism via the web (e.g., Bimber, 1998; Davis, 1999; Kaid, 2002; Rheingold, 1993).

Others suggest that the internet's prospect for civic renewal is limited; at best, it complements traditional media channels (e.g., Althaus and Tewksbury, 2000; Hardy

and Scheufele, 2005; Margolis and Resnick, 2000). Some researchers have even suggested that the internet may negatively affect community involvement by replacing social interactions with solitary activities (Nie, 2001; Nie and Erbring, 2000). Alternatively, insulating uses of the internet may limit exposure to diverse opinions thus undercutting the rational—critical decision-making resulting from the integration of opposing viewpoints (Sunstein, 2001).

Much of this work has been troubled by an over-generalized conceptualization of internet use. Specifically, much of the research focusing on the internet's influence on the electorate has looked only at an online/offline distinction instead of patterns of internet use. A study by Moy et al. (2005) found that the online/offline distinction has little explanatory power in examining the civic consequences of the internet when controlling for specific dimensions of internet use. Moy and her colleagues demonstrated that a "time spent" measure did not have any significant effects on levels of civic engagement when more specific uses of the internet are included in an explanatory statistical model. Similarly, Shah et al. (2001) concluded "Studies on the psychological and sociological consequences of internet use have tended to view the internet as an amorphous whole, neglecting the fact that individuals make very different uses of this emerging medium" (p. 142). Thus, "trying to assess the political impact of the internet ... involves shooting at a moving target" (Jennings and Zeitner, 2003, p. 311).

The lack of research focusing on the versatility of the internet and the variety of different uses invited by this new medium leave political communication researchers with only a partially painted picture of the civic consequences of internet use. Only a few studies (e.g., Moy et al., 2005; Shah et al., 2005) have looked at the civic effects of the different types of information available online while controlling for other communication variables such as traditional media use. In sum, a review of the scholarly literature on the informational effects of the internet suggests the need for a more nuanced understanding of likely patterns of use.

The notion that the public might learn information online that it has not been able to learn from traditional media presupposes that there are forms of information on the web not found in the old media or that the modes of presentation or types of access permitted online are more effective in communicating political fact. Unfortunately, there are not many systematic content analyses of political information available online partly because content analyses of web content present unique challenges for the researchers (Weare and Lin, 2000). Specifically, a main challenge is the construction of a sampling frame to study this massive, decentralized network of hyperlinked multimedia that contains over 4 billion web pages on 400 million hosts (Internet Systems Consortium, 2004). Most analyses looking at online content compare traditional print newspapers to their online counterpart (e.g., Harper, 1996; Hoffman, 2006; Peng *et al.*, 1999). Many of these studies suggest that the online counterpart simply mirrors the offline version.

Does the internet produce different effects? An experiment conducted by Kaid (2003) found that, unlike traditional news media, the internet "was very successful in encouraging voters to seek out additional types of sources of information." (p. 688). Additionally, other direct comparisons between traditional media and their internet counterpart have shown that online sources are deemed more credible than traditional news media (Johnson and Kaye, 1998a)

The next section presents a telegraphic defense of the notion that trying to learn central political fact in the old media is a somewhat futile exercise.

The traditional news is failing as the custodian of fact

Some have argued that the press is not fulfilling its democratic functions (e.g., Bennett, 2001; Bennett and Serrin, 2005; Patterson, 1980, 1993). When politicians succeed in deceiving the public, journalists fail, for example, in acting as a "custodian of fact" (Jamieson and Waldman, 2003). But how does the press fail in its coverage of politics? Two interrelated explanations account for the press's failure as the custodian of fact. First, news about campaigns is dominated by tactical and strategic coverage (Cappella and Jamieson 1996, 1997; Patterson, 1993) and, second, there is an over-reliance on "he-said-she-said reporting" (Jamieson and Hardy, 2007).

Patterson (1993) noted that "election news, rather than serving to bring candidates and voters together, drives a wedge between them" because of the news focus on the horse-race and politicking of the campaign. Cappella and Jamieson (1997) found that strategic news coverage—coverage focused on the political moves and the electoral game rather than issues—depressed learning and activated cynicism toward politics and the political actors covered. By "reporting about politicians and their policies repeatedly framed as self-interest and seldom in terms of the common good—whether such characterizations are correct or incorrect," they note, "the public's experience of their leaders is biased toward attributions that induce mistrust" (Cappella and Jamieson, 1997, p. 142). Similarly, Neustadt (1997) argued that the press is an "actor in today's political drama, conveying a steady stream of unambiguously negative cues about government and politics" (p.97). Lost in strategic news coverage is a focus on adjudicating fact.

Nor is "fact" central to "he–said–she–said" reporting. When reporters adopt a horse-race frame, they rarely draw any conclusions about the existence or extent of deception in a campaign. In most cases, if deceptive tactics are being used more by one camp than the other, reporters will make broad general claims such as in a *New York Times* article by Jim Rutenberg (2004), titled "Campaign ads are under fire for inaccuracy." Writing in his blog, *Press Think*, on June 4, 2004, media critic and New York University Professor of Journalism Jay Rosen commented that this type of "he–said–she–said" reporting "makes Rutenberg a chronicler of the will to deceive in politics, presented as part of the reality of politics."

In 2004, an Annenberg Public Policy Center poll asked professional mainstream journalists a question that presupposed a hypothetical campaign in which reporters knew that one side was more deceptive than the other (see Jamieson and Hardy, 2007; Jamieson *et al.*, 2007 for more information on this poll). The poll found that even when reporters believe that one candidate's campaign is more deceptive than their opponent's, the reporters are reluctant to report it. When asked "In a political campaign, if one side is using deceptive tactics more often than the opponents, do most journalists usually report the greater use of deception by one side, just report that both sides are using deception or avoid the matter completely?" a majority, 58 percent, of the journalists surveyed stated that they believe journalists usually report both sides are using deception. Seventy-nine percent of those journalists acknowledged that this creates the impression to the public that each side of the campaign is engaging in similar amounts of deception. The avoidance of comparative judgment, which is part of the he-said-she-said approach rooted in norms of objectivity, creates a sense of moral equivalence between the two campaigns. Instead of being able to make comparative judgments on the accuracy of individual candidate claims, the citizens can only surmise that both sides are lying.

As past studies have shown, such failure of the traditional news media fosters political cynicism and stunts learning about politics. If the over-reliance on strategic coverage and he-said-she-said reporting are making it difficult for citizens to find politically useful information, are they shunning tradition news media and turning to the internet during elections for campaign information? Such a hypothesis is consistent with studies that have shown that those who hold low levels of political trust use the internet to access political information (Johnson and Kaye, 1998b, 2003). Does the use of the internet lead to a better command of facts and assessment of the accuracy of campaign claims?

2004 National Annenberg Election Survey

Data from the 2004 NAES will help determine whether this is the case. Following the 2004 general election, the Annenberg Public Policy Center conducted a survey of a random sample of 3400 citizens to assess the extent to which they believed the many claims made by, or on behalf of, the Bush and Kerry campaigns. Respondents rated the accuracy of the claims on a four-point scale ranging from "very truthful" to "not truthful at all," in order to test the knowledge of 41 claims made by the major party campaigns in 2004. All were offered in the course of the campaign. All were checked for accuracy by FactCheck. org. The claims that are analyzed here were aired in advertisements, made in stump speeches, or brought up in the debates. The importance of these claims lay not only in their centrality to the campaign but in the significant assertion they made about the character and competence of the candidates. For example, the claim that John Kerry voted for cuts in intelligence after September 11 was promoted in the Bush campaign ad titled "Wolves"; the claim that George W. Bush's Social Security plan would cut benefits 30 to 45 percent was suggested both when Kerry told seniors in Florida on October 18th that Bush plans to cut their benefits by as much as 45 percent and in the Kerry ad called "January Surprise." A person who would cut intelligence after September 11, in many voters' eyes, would be deemed unqualified to serve as commander-in-chief. And one who would cut the benefits of those currently receiving them would be prepared to break a central social compact.

Important for our purposes, both claims are false. If a belief in either false claim shaped a voting decision, the voter was misled. If a person believed either and nonetheless voted for the candidate then that belief sundered the relationship between campaigning and governance.

The questions on the survey that asked respondents about central, significant facts from the 2004 campaign were cumulated to construct an overall index of respondents' knowledge of the claims. The higher a respondent scored on this scale the more claims he or she correctly identified as true or false. The volunteered "don't know" responses were coded as incorrect. This may seem problematic because such a response could refer to not knowing the truthfulness of the claim or a fact that the respondent never heard such a claim. As a check on the coding procedure, the statistical analyses reported in the chapter were also conducted with the "don't knows" coded as "missing values." This, however, did not affect the estimates of model.

Due to a split-ballot design of the survey, each individual respondent was asked about

half of the questions. Those who received form A were asked about 21 claims with a mean of 8.86 correct and a standard deviation of 2.91. Those who received form B were asked about 20 claims with a mean of 8.38 and a standard deviation of 2.57. As can be seen from these means the overall level of knowledge of the truthfulness of the campaign claims is moderate. On average, respondents correctly identified a little less than half of the claims. This is probably a reflection of political orientation. Citizens are more likely to believe their candidate than the opponent and more likely to hear about and believe the inaccuracies flagged by a favored candidate.

Respondents' use of the internet to access campaign information was tapped by a single question that asked respondents how many days in the past week did they access information about the presidential campaign online. The mean for this variable is 1.26 days with a standard deviation of 2.26. For those 788 respondents (23.2 percent of the sample) that reported access campaign information at least once in the past week the mean is 3.98 days with a standard deviation of 2.29.

Table 10.1 provides some examples of the campaign claims that were on the survey as well as percentages of correct identification of the truthfulness of these claims by all respondents and those who accessed the internet for campaign information at least one day in the past week of being surveyed. Consistent with our hypothesis, internet users show higher percentages of correct identification of the truthfulness of claims compared to all respondents (which include the internet users) and lower percentages of respondents reporting "don't know."

To answer the specific questions asked above, multivariate statistical analyses were conducted. These models included a variety of controls and traditional media use measures.[2] Political cynicism, for these analyses, was not measured in a general lack of confidence in institutions as is usually done in political communication research. Instead a more focused set of questions was used to tap respondents' beliefs that the presidential candidates are deceitful. A measure of respondents' belief that candidates always lie was combined from two rotated questions on the survey that were reverse coded: "How often do you think John Kerry told the truth about George W. Bush's record?" and "How often do you think George W. Bush told the truth about John Kerry's record?"—(1) none of the time, (2) some of the time, and (3) all of the time. This combined variable was then dichotomized where respondents who reported a belief that at least one of the

candidates never told the truth received a score of one (30.1 percent) and respondents that believed that both candidates always or sometimes told the truth received a score of zero.

Statistical analyses and results

The first statistical model is a logistic regression model predicting the belief that candidates always lie. As Table 10.2 shows, reading the newspaper and watching 24-hour cable news are both positively and significantly related to the belief that during the 2004 campaign George W. Bush and Democratic challenger Senator John Kerry never told the truth, while controlling for demographic and political identification variables. What these odd ratios suggest is that for every additional

Table 10.1 Correct assessment of campaign claims during 2004 presidential election in the United States, by respondents and internet users

Campaign claims	Correct answer	Percent of respondents answering "don't know"		Percent of respondents answering correctly	
		All	Internet users	All	Internet users
George W. Bush's plan to cut Social Security would cut benefits for those currently [2004] receiving them	False	8.1	6.7	46.2	52.6
The unemployment rate is now [2004] about where it was in 1996 when Bill Clinton ran for a second term	True	12.4	8.1	42.3	45.5
Senator Kerry voted to ban pump action shotguns and deer hunting ammunition	False	23.7	20.8	39.1	45.5
When George W. Bush took office as President there was a budget surplus, and now [2004] there is a deficit	True	4.9	1.3	80.6	87.0
Dick Cheney has profited from the contracts Halliburton has in Iraq	False	13.5	5.7	27.1	34.8
Saddam Hussein played a role in Sept 11	False	5.6	2.0	46.9	62.5
George W. Bush has promised to nominate Supreme Court Justices who will overturn Roe versus Wade	False	15.8	8.3	35.1	38.5

Source: Authors' calculations based on data from the National Annenberg Election Survey (2004).

day of reading the newspaper or watching 24-hour cables news a person becomes 1.04 times more likely to believe that the candidates never told the truth. Similarly, accessing campaign information online also produced a positive and significant relationship. Although these effects are not uniform across all news media, there are no significant competing results in our model that suggest that any news media use, including using the internet, promotes the belief that candidates were truthful during the 2004 campaign. These are not strong relationships, yet they are detectable relationships that support the hypothesis that some news media coverage of presidential campaigns promotes cynicism in the electorate.

Does the internet present a new avenue for the cynical voter to find information? The second model presents the results from an OLS regression model predicting accessing the internet for campaign information. Consistent with the above theorizing, the more respondents believe that the candidates never told the truth in the 2004 election the more likely they were to turn to the internet to access campaign information. As found in many studies on internet use, education, age, and gender all produced significant relationships. Specifically, educated younger males were more likely to access campaign information online. The only news media variable to be positively and significantly related to relying on the internet to access campaign information is 24-hour cable news use. Local television news use, however, was negatively related to going online for campaign information.

The final statistical model details the impact of accessing campaign information and the correct identification of the truthfulness of campaign claims. Accessing such information online significantly increases citizens' command of fact. Watching national broadcast television news, 24-hour cable news, and newspapers all had

significant and positive relationships with correct identification of truthfulness of campaign claims during the 2004 election. However, the relationship between accessing campaign information online and sorting fact from fiction produced the largest regression coefficient of all of the media variables in the model. Therefore, accessing campaign information had an overall larger net impact on citizens' ability to identify deception than any other news media.

In the model, local television news appears to have a detrimental impact as it produces a negative relationship in the model.[3] This finding is consistent with a recent study by Prior (2003) who noted "local news ... is the real villain in our story ... the effect of liking local news is actually negative for most of the hard news items" (Prior, 2003: 164). This could be, in part, a result of differences in content driven by local news' role as a "good neighbor" and not as a watchdog (see Poindexter *et al.*, 2006).

Overall, these findings suggest that the internet, in comparison with traditional press campaign coverage, has an informing effect similar to that of such major campaign events as conventions and debates (Chaffee and Frank, 1996; Kenski and Jamieson, 2005). A citizen learns about issues from watching these events. On the other hand, media coverage of these events is dominated by strategic coverage. For example, Sears and Chaffee (1979) observed that television coverage of the 1976 presidential debate focused much more on candidates' characters, leaving little room for coverage on the content of policy debate.

One plausible counter-explanation of results presented here would be that internet users are accessing mainstream news organization's websites. If so, the traditional press is actually not failing. Its venue of influence has simply changed. In 2004, over six in ten respondents cited a

Table 10.2 Regression models predicting the belief that presidential candidates always lie, that respondents accessed the internet for campaign information, and the correct assessment of campaign claims

Predictor variable	Model 1: Binary logistic regression model predicting the belief that presidential candidates always lie		Model 2: OLS regression model predicting accessing the internet for campaign information		Model 3: OLS regression model predicting correct assessment of campaign claims	
	Odds ratio	Standard error	Standardized B	Standard error	Standardized B	Standard error
Female	1.070	0.101	−0.055*	0.100	−0.149***	0.135
Age	1.013***	0.004	−0.078***	0.004	0.043*	0.005
Education	0.965	0.024	0.110***	0.024	0.128***	0.032
Income	0.987	0.028	0.056*	0.028	0.098***	0.037
Republican	1.062	0.128	0.015	0.125	−0.093***	0.168
Democrat	1.478**	0.123	0.049*	0.124	0.056*	0.167
Ideology (Conservative coded high)	0.969	0.059	−0.071**	0.058	−0.123***	0.079
National broadcast TV news	0.983	0.022	−0.025	0.022	0.075***	0.030
Newspaper	1.036*	0.018	0.029	0.018	0.042*	0.025
24 hour cable news	1.038*	0.018	0.135***	0.018	0.073***	0.024
Local TV news	0.991	0.020	−0.053*	0.020	−0.045*	0.027
Access campaign info online	1.071***	0.021	–	–	0.131***	0.030
Belief that candidates always lie	–	–	0.071***	0.108	0.019	0.146
Nagelkerke R²	3.8		–		–	
R²	–		6.5		16.6	
Unweighted N			3,400			

Source: Authors' calculations based on data from the National Annenberg Election Survey (2004).

Notes:
* = $p < 0.1$; ** = $p < 0.01$; *** = $p < 0.001$

news organization as the source for online political information (Winneg and Stroud, 2005). This argument relies on the assumption that websites of mainstream media and their offline counterparts present similar information, an assumption that has been supported by past research (Hoffman, 2006). However, this alternative explanation is unlikely because if it had explanatory power, the analytic model in this chapter would not feature differential gains in knowledge of fact from different news media channels.

Additionally, the new informational environment of the internet transforms the nature of access to the mainstream in ways that may increase the likelihood that use of these sites will produce an effect unlikely in the offline world. Specifically,

at low or no-cost web searchers can read multiple newspapers and check multiple news sites in very short order. If factual information is available in any of these sites the searcher now has an access to it unlike, for example, if the cost were subscriptions to a handful of newspapers.

Importantly, while the content of the traditional media can be found online, the websites run by traditional media contain richer, more interactive, and more timely additional material. A visit to any mainstream news media website reveals that visitors are presented with a variety of links and other interactive tools that allow them to explore informationally rich resources. With access to this information comes the possibility of additional learning.

At the same time, there are sources of factual information available only online. Outside the traditional media online, the "blogosphere" presents an interlinked net of political information with "track-back" capacity for reciprocating links and RSS feeds that breeds cross-fertilization of political messages and an organic vetting process of such information. Sites such as FackCheck.org and others, whose mission it is to keep campaigns in check, further provide internet users with tools that are all but missing in traditional news.

Another plausible competing interpretation for the results presented here is that those who are politically knowledgeable are more likely to access the internet for political information; is the causal direction correct? The knowledge questions that we use for this study, deceptive claims, are particular to the 2004 presidential election. Such reverse causation would be more plausible if we were examining general political knowledge. Due to the specificity of our dependent measure, modeling the internet as an antecedent variable is more plausible than positing that identification of the truthfulness of claims leads to accessing political information online.

Conclusion

This chapter examined the relationship between accessing the internet for political information and citizens' ability to distinguish deception from fact during the 2004 U.S. presidential election. The statistical models presented here support the suppositions that the failings of the traditional news to adjudicate fact in presidential campaigns increased cynicism toward politicians and this, in turn, may have resulted in a reliance on the internet. Such reliance led to better command of fact. The more one accessed political information online the better one was at distinguishing fact from deception.

Distinguishing accurate from false claims about key issues is important if a voter is to make a decision based upon his or her own preferences. Knowing which campaign claims are misleading can safeguard voters from drawing false conclusions from mistaken evidence. If a voter cannot sort fact from fiction during campaigns then misleading claims may lead to misguided voting. Political actors, their respective camps, and supporters deceive because they benefit from it (Kenski and Jamieson, 2005) and by so doing maximize votes. This is problematic as meaningful participation in democratic life requires that there be some consistency between citizens' own issue stances and their votes. The ability to pick up on dishonesty can also permit the citizen to penalize the deceptive candidate and campaign. Knowledge of the relative level of deception can also factor in voting decisions by increasing the likelihood that the voter will penalize the offending campaign.

The traditional press *does* have the ability to provide the information that citizens need to separate truthful campaign claims from false one. Unfortunately, journalistic norms and trends in campaign coverage have undercut the watchdog role of the press, which in turn has fostered cynicism and depressed learning among citizens. As many scholars (e.g., Cappella and Jamieson, 1996; Jamieson and Hardy, 2007; Patterson, 1993, 2000) have illustrated, the traditional press, in its ordinary distribution channels, is not sufficiently protecting citizens. Scholars and press critics have called on the traditional news media to devote less time to discussions of strategy and he-said-she-said reporting and spend more time providing substantive news and pointing out discrepancies and discordant facts offered by political candidates. As this research shows, the internet does provide the voter with a functional alternative.

Guide to further reading

For those interested in the general performance of the press, Geneva Overholser and Kathleen Hall Jamieson's edited volume, *Institutions of American Democracy: the press* (Overholser and Jamieson, 2006) and the Annenberg Democracy Project's *Institutions of American Democracy: a republic divided* (Jamieson *et al.*, 2007) offer detailed reports on the functions and performance of the press and tensions between the press and other institutions of democracy. For those interested in deception, the press, and political strategy in U.S. campaigns, Jamieson and Paul Waldman's (2003) book *The Press Effect* illustrates instances in which reporters simply analyzed the strategies employed by opposing sides rather than sorting out the facts behind the issues. Jamieson and Brooks Jackson's (2007) book *Un-Spun: finding fact in a world of disinformation* provides a crash course in identifying misleading and deceptive campaign claims.

Notes

1 FactCheck.org "is a nonpartisan, nonprofit, 'consumer advocate' for voters that aims to reduce the level of deception and confusion in U.S. politics. We monitor the factual accuracy of what is said by major U.S. political players in the form of TV ads, debates, speeches, interviews, and news releases. Our goal is to apply the best practices of both journalism and scholarship, and to increase public knowledge and understanding." From www.FactCheck.org.

2 Gender (54 percent female), age ($M = 48.35$, $SD = 16.58$; measured in years), education ($M = 14.26$, $SD = 2.50$; measured in number of years of completed school), and income (Mode = \$50,000 to \$75,000) are included in the models as sociodemographic control variables. Political orientation variables such as party identification (31 percent Republican and 33 percent Democrat) and political ideology ($M = 3.18$, $SD = 0.99$; measured on a five-point scale where 1 represents "very liberal" and 5 means "very conservative") are also included in the models as control variables. Traditional news media use was tapped by asking respondents how many days in the last week did they: "watch the national network news on TV" ($M = 2.59$, $SD = 2.67$), "watch a 24-hour cable news channel" ($M = 2.97$, $SD = 2.85$), "watch local TV news" ($M = 3.85$, $SD = 2.81$), and "read a daily newspaper" ($M = 3.70$, $SD = 2.96$).

3 Interestingly, a recent initiative, the Engaging the Electronic Electorate (E4) project, helped local broadcasters use the internet to engage their audiences in civic issues. The objective was to help increase citizens' knowledge about politics and participation in civic life. The Annenberg Public Policy Center developed and refined a number of online election templates that local news broadcasters could use to inform the public and meet the objectives of the project. As part of the project stations were required to integrate their on-air and online election coverage. Examples were ad watches and debate watches (Meltzer *et al.*, 2004).

11

Political engagement online

Do the information rich get richer and the like-minded more similar?

Jennifer Brundidge and Ronald E. Rice

A new area for research is the extent to which the internet contributes to one particular form of political engagement: political discussion among heterogeneous networks of citizens. While it may be that the information rich continue to get richer, it is far less clear that the politically similar continue to become more similar. This chapter thus discusses research on the extent to which internet use affects individual-level political engagement and examines the possible role of the internet in exposing people to politically dissimilar others. A sample analysis follows, which finds that online political discussion is significantly and positively associated with politically heterogeneous individual discussion networks. Finally, the discussion considers normative implications and future research concerning political landscapes with varying interactions between knowledge gaps and heterogeneous political discussion.

An established tenet of U.S. political culture is that the democratic process should be "firmly anchored in the judgments of the demos" (Dahl, 1989: 338). By this standard, there is reason to suspect that Americans are living in democratically troubled times—a period of history characterized by a persistently under-informed citizenry, substantial declines in traditional indicators of civic and political engagement (Althaus, 1999; Bartels, 1996; Converse, 1990; Delli Carpini and Keeter, 2003), and reduced political self-efficacy (Brody, 1978; Miller and Shanks, 1996). While connections between the state of democracy and technology have always existed, advances in information and communication technology just prior to the onset of the new millennium have made these connections all the more salient.

In particular, the internet has instigated wide speculation about its potential to reinvigorate political community and democratic life (Harrison and Falvey, 2001). internet enthusiasts have pointed to the possibility that the medium could lead to increased political engagement and to direct democracy, with an unprecedented potential to reach young, isolated, and minority citizens; to weakened boundaries between the public and private sphere; and to an increase in direct links to policy-makers (Etzioni, 1997; Norris, 2001b; Porter, 1997; Rheingold, 1993).

Other observers have been more skeptical, arguing that at the individual level, the internet is more likely to reinforce established patterns of political communication, widening the knowledge gap and digital divide between elites and non-elites. They note that opportunity is a necessary but not sufficient criterion for political engagement, and that information abundance does not mean that all, or even most, individuals will take advantage of it in ways that advance their roles as citizens (Bimber, 2003; Norris, 2001b). In other words, the information rich will get richer while the information poor will remain relatively poorer. Indeed, the vast majority of empirical evidence suggests that internet use has stimulated relatively few, if any, participation effects at the individual level (Bimber, 2001, 2003; Bimber and Davis, 2003; Katz and Rice, 2002; Scheufele and Nisbit, 2002).

However, in recent years, researchers have become more circumspect, acknowledging that, as with older media, the effects of the internet on political engagement may be more subtle and indirect than previously assumed (e.g., Hardy and Scheufele, 2005; Howard, 2003: 216–19). Further, traditional indicators of political engagement (e.g., factual political knowledge, voting) are not the only normatively compelling issues presented by an increasingly connected citizenry.

One particularly compelling issue is the extent to which internet use promotes exposure to political disagreement and deliberation among citizens—a phenomenon long considered essential to a vibrant and pluralistic public sphere, producing a "high scale of mental activity" (Mill, 1859/1998), an "enlarged mentality" or more sophisticated opinions (Arendt, 1968), and prompting greater interpersonal deliberation and personal reflection (Habermas, 1989). Empirical research has furthermore demonstrated that it has several tangible benefits, such as increased accuracy about the distribution of public opinion (Huckfeldt and Sprague, 1995)—which is likely to promote a sense of legitimacy for democratic outcomes (Price, Cappella, and Nir, 2002)—increased political

learning (Price, Cappella, and Nir, 2002), and the ability to differentiate among ideologically distinct attitudes (Gastil et al., forthcoming). Recent research has even indicated a stimulus effect on political participation when discussion among heterogeneous networks is combined with hard news media use (Scheufele et al., 2003; Scheufele et al., 2004).

Yet in spite of a good deal of theoretical speculation on this issue (e.g., Galston, 2003; Sunstein, 2001), the impact of the internet on exposure to political difference remains unclear. On one hand, the personal control provided by the internet creates the possibility that people will exercise an increasing tendency for selectivity in discussion partners, reinforcing their perceptions and attitudes. On the other hand, the internet may weaken traditional social, informational, and political boundaries, which could potentially lead to increased exposure to disagreement.

Do the information rich get richer? Hard news media use, political discussion, and political participation

News media use

In retrospect, the hope that the internet would stimulate mass political engagement at the individual level seems a bit historically naïve. With the exception of the newspaper, which for the first time allowed for the mass distribution of political information, historical advances in information technology have done little to advance political engagement (Bimber, 2003; Scheufele and Nisbet, 2002). Yet from an intuitive perspective, the current information environment would seem to be the perfect antidote to the more informationally and geographically challenged mass media audience (Sey and Castells,

145

2004)—an environment that is able to transcend time, space, and possibly ideologies. Indeed, classic explanations of political behavior at the individual level, rooted in rational choice theory, would seem to point in this direction (Downs, 1957; Verba *et al.*, 1995). A rational choice involves a form of cost–benefit analysis, which may be applied to strategies involved in choices to engage in political participation, information seeking, and the acquisition of political knowledge, or decisions to participate in political deliberation. If technological developments, such as the internet, reduce the cost of both providing and accessing information, provide more convenient and less demanding forums for political deliberation, and on many occasions reduce the cost of political participation to the click of a mouse, individuals with access to the internet, who might not otherwise find the time, will be more likely to participate.

Yet human beings are not always rational creatures—the internet is not somehow a utopia where psychological predispositions do not apply (Katz and Rice, 2002; Neuman, 1991). Any technology, and especially the internet, is shaped not only by its potentially rational uses, but also by the ways in which people actually use it. As it applies to news and other elite discourse, human psychology suggests that as the cost of information falls and as sources increase, the already information rich will get richer, while the information poor will remain relatively poorer (Bimber, 2003). This is the fundamental proposition of the knowledge gap hypothesis (Donohue *et al.*, 1975). The psychological basis of this proposition draws on schema theory and related research, arguing that individuals with more complex cognitive schema are better able to process and incorporate new information. The knowledge gap hypothesis is somewhat more sociological,

arguing that pre-existing educational, income, and other social resources allow some to not only gain access to, but also to internalize and apply, new knowledge faster and better.

Indeed, a long line of media–effects research reveals that mere exposure to news does not account for the influence of news content on individuals (McLeod and McDonald, 1985). Eveland and colleagues (Eveland, 2001, 2002; Eveland *et al.*, 2003), for example, found that attention, cognitive involvement, and news elaboration serve as important contributors to political learning. Attending to news involves the selection of a subset of information for processing, while elaboration involves a more intensive and integrative process of making cognitive associations between new information and information already held in memory. Thus, more knowledgeable individuals learn more from broadcast and print news and subsequently have more differentiated constructs and higher quality arguments in essays about policy issues (Rhee and Cappella, 1997). A media–uses and gratifications approach further supports the knowledge gap hypothesis. People with more knowledge about political and civic life should seek out more political information because they are able to process it with greater ease and find it more gratifying. For example, newspapers are more gratifying to more sophisticated and knowledgeable citizens to the extent that they facilitate purposive control (Chaffee and Kanihan, 1997).

In recent years, the internet has become an increasingly important news resource. By the end of 2005, nearly 50 million people in the U.S. obtained some of their news through the internet on an average day (Horrigan, 2006). Yet it appears that the information rich have been most able to harness the abundance of information provided online. In general, those people who were politically engaged before the internet are the very same people who are politically engaged on the internet—those high in socioeconomic status, political efficacy, and political knowledge (Bimber, 2001, 2003; Scheufele and Nisbet, 2002), have an interest in politics and are more likely to be skeptical of information (Bimber, 2003: 219; also see Shah *et al.*, 2005). Those engaged in political participation online tend to be disproportionately young, educated, and affluent (Cornfield and Rainie, 2006; Rainie *et al.*, 2005). The more people read about campaigns in newspapers or learn about them through news broadcasts, the more likely it is that they will also attend to such information online (Bimber and Davis, 2003).

Political discussion

Yet news media and other elite discourse are not the only way to garner knowledge and form public opinion. Through political discussion, citizens may elevate their thinking, reveal private information, learn to justify their claims, and thereby achieve more sophisticated opinions (Fearon, 1998; Price and Cappella, 2002). Political discussion and news use may work in tandem, one solidifying the other. Tarde (1899/1989), for example, argued that newspaper reading triggers political discussion, political discussion influences public opinion, and opinion in turn stimulates political action (Katz, 1981; Kim *et al.*, 1999).

The trouble with political discussion, however, is that the processes involved tend to be biased toward those with extensive civic skills, including a good vocabulary, the ability to communicate in English, a sense of personal efficacy, the ability to write or speak well, and the cognitive wherewithal to draw on previously existing political knowledge. The most educated members of society disproportionately tend to have these skills (Verba *et al.*, 1995). Those people with

the most requisite political knowledge tend to be the most attentive during political deliberation and are therefore likely to get more out of it (Kwak *et al.*, 2005). Thus deliberation can just as easily become a lesson in unidirectional political persuasion and opinion reinforcement as it can become a mutual uplifting of minds.

The internet offers a novel forum for political deliberation, enabling anyone with internet access to communicate via chat rooms, website bulletin boards, e-mail, wikis, videos posts, or weblogs (or blogs). Nevertheless, engagement in online forums of deliberation is greater under conditions of high political motivation, high socioeconomic status, opportunity (Price *et al.*, 2002), and strong connections to local communities through political activities (McLeod *et al.*, 1999). In a field experiment using a nationally representative panel, Price *et al.* (2002) found that individuals who participated in scheduled online discussions conformed to a hierarchical model of participation—they were older, highly educated, predominantly white, more politically knowledgeable, more politically interested and active, and had higher levels of social trust. They also found that while political deliberation online significantly improved opinion quality, those participants who benefited the most were higher in social capital, more educated, and had higher incomes.

Political participation

Political learning and the subsequent desire and means to participate are highly contingent upon the setting of political agendas and on the framing of political events and issues by elites (Bimber, 2003). Agenda-setting and framing research has demonstrated that the media influence which political issues are treated as important by focusing the public's attention on certain events and by framing those events in particular ways (McCombs *et al.*, 1997;

Wanta, 1997). They are able to serve this function by making certain news topics more salient than others, while putting a particular perspective or spin on these topics (Entman, 1991, 1993; Gitlin, 1980; Iyengar, 1990; Shoemaker and Reese, 1996; Tuchman, 1978). According to framing theory, the spin and the salience of particular news items are then transferred to (and through) the audience. Some observers have speculated that the ways in which news media tend to frame political topics, in particular though their emphasis on sensationalized political conflict as opposed to political consensus, may alienate certain segments of the citizenry and lead to a spiral of cynicism (Cappella and Jamieson, 1997). By influencing the kinds of issues that citizens think about and the way that they think about them, the media may additionally influence whether or not people choose to participate politically and which activities they choose to participate in. Furthermore, those people with the least well-developed cognitive schema are the least likely to attend to information at all, but the most likely to be influenced by the ways that the news media and other elites frame the information (Bimber, 2003).

However, as Delli Carpini and Williams (2001) point out, the internet complicates and disperses the framing and agenda setting processes. During the "mass audience" era, the political agenda had been largely shaped by a mutual relationship between dominant political actors and mainstream news outlets—the gatekeepers. The current information environment has changed this two-way system into a "multiaxial" one for at least two central reasons. First, the multiplication of political news media and the blurring of the boundaries between entertainment and news have lead to competition within the media for the role of the gatekeeper. Second, the internet with its attendant destruction of normal news cycles and rise

of news blogs and online newspapers has created novel opportunities for non-mainstream political actors to contribute to the setting and framing of the public agenda. No longer do two elite groups, the press and government institutions, hold virtually sole domain over the framing of news stories and the setting of agendas. Yet all of this simply suggests a more chaotic information environment for individuals to make sense of, not the end of framing and agenda-setting itself.

Howard (2003, 2005, 2006) argues that beyond the typical effects at the individual political participation level, and at the campaign media and funding level, an entirely new and generally unknown influence has emerged—that of hyper-media political campaigns, run by non-traditional entities using a wide range of technology and data. Digital technologies, databases, and networks have fostered the rise of hypermedia political campaign organizations, outside the control of major media and major political parties. From grass-roots activism to elite political campaigns, these organizations—often a small group of consultants and firms—collect a wide variety of information on personal demographics and consumption, polling and voting data, online and other media use. They use this information along with a wide array of techniques, such as very quick, targeted online polls, and data mining of combined and integrated databases, to shape what potential citizens are exposed to, aware of, and think about. As a result, Howard (2005: 153) argues, while democracy is becoming deeper— that is, a wider "diffusion of rich data about political actors, policy options, and the diversity of actors and opinion in the public sphere"—citizenship is thinning— that is, increased political expression with less substantive engagement, and less shared text in the public sphere.

Taken together, individual biases influencing news use and political discussion, media agenda setting and framing effects, and new forms of media and political consulting, all suggest that while political knowledge is a consistent predictor of political participation, political learning and participation are highly contingent processes, both online and offline. For example, political discussion via e-mail has been found to be a positive predictor of political participation (Brundidge, 2006) and of civic participation (Shah *et al.*, 2005) while political discussion via chat rooms is a negative predictor of political participation (Brundidge, 2006). Others have found that, as with face-to-face deliberation, it is the interaction between media consumption and online political discussion that predicts political participation (Hardy and Scheufele, 2005).

Overall, research findings have been consistent with a psychological as opposed to a rational model of political behavior. While information is easier to come by and while political participation requires less effort than ever before, the new information resources provided by the internet are more likely to be used by people who are politically knowledgeable and high in socioeconomic status. At least for the time being, the information rich continue to get richer.

Do the like-minded become more similar? The contribution of the internet to the heterogeneity of political discussion networks

While the information rich may indeed get richer, do the like-minded become more similar? Research on traditional face-to-face forums of political discussion suggests that exposure to political disagreement is not well predicted by traditional individual-level antecedents of political engagement, including political knowledge and socioeconomic status. One

theoretical explanation is that tendencies toward selective exposure to politically similar individuals may be especially strong for those who consider politics central to their lives and identity (i.e., partisans, politically knowledgeable people). Certain political attitudes, on the other hand, such as low partisanship, ideological liberalism, as well as structural-level factors, such as the forum of discussion (e.g., the workplace), seem to be better overall predictors (Huckfeldt, Johnson, and Sprague, 2004; Mutz, 2006). Exposure to disagreement online then should not then conform to the knowledge-gap or rich-get-richer hypothesis.

Yet the contribution of online forums of discussion (e.g., chat rooms and e-mail) in facilitating the creation of heterogeneous political discussion networks has been relatively neglected by research. Those studies that do examine the role of the internet tend to examine the online world as essentially separate from the offline world (e.g., Wojcieszak and Mutz, 2007). This research helps to specify the mechanisms by which people are exposed to political disagreement online, which is an essential piece of the puzzle, but does not suggest the extent to which these mechanisms contribute to the collective heterogeneity of people's political discussion networks. Because online political discussion has either been overlooked or studied in isolation from people's whole experience of the public sphere, a number of fundamental theoretical arguments about the impact of the internet are unresolved. Perhaps the most important of these is whether internet use is adding to the overall diversity of people's entire political discussion networks, having no impact, or somehow even leading to increased selective exposure and political fragmentation. Other internet related studies employ experimentally controlled settings (e.g., Price *et al.*, 2002) or tend to focus on the heterogeneity of news and information rather than heterogeneity of interpersonal discussion (e.g., Bimber and Davis, 2003; Garrett, 2005; Tewksbury and Althaus, 2000).

Broadly speaking, scholars have suggested two seemingly contradictory mechanisms that could potentially influence online exposure to political disagreement: selective exposure, which leads to narrowed domains of political discourse, and weakening social boundaries, which broaden opportunity for exposure to political disagreement.

Selective exposure

There are several processes by which use of new media may lead to narrowed domains of political discourse. In one way or another, most of these processes constitute variations on a general claim that as people gain increasing control over communication and the flow of information, they will exercise an increasing tendency for selectivity in discussion partners and exposure to information. This view invokes the longstanding theory of selective exposure from the political communication literature (e.g., Festinger, 1957; Frey, 1986; Huckfeldt and Sprague, 1995; Katz, 1981) and simply maps it onto the internet, hypothesizing an amplification in selectivity due to the increased control derived from the purposive way that the internet is used.

Bimber and Davis (2003), for example, rank-order various media environments as to their tendency to promote selectivity on the basis of the volume of information they provide, the diversity of viewpoints, and the extent of control given to the individual. They conclude that when compared with television news, newspapers, and talk shows, the internet actually offers the conditions most conducive to selective exposure. Another factor leading to increased selectivity are structural aspects of the internet that require

individuals to actively search for and click on links to information sources, which could lead to them to exclusively expose themselves to information they have been searching for or information that seems particularly personally relevant.

This line of thought is supported by some recent research. Mutz and Martin (2001) found that as individuals are given increasing control over the selection of news media sources, they become more likely to expose themselves to information more compatible with their own viewpoints. Bimber and Davis (2003) report that audiences for campaign websites during the 2000 U.S. presidential election were likely to consist of knowledgeable, interested, and partisan supporters of the candidate, as opposed to non-supporters of the candidate. Tewksbury and Althaus (2000) contrast the effects of the print edition of the *New York Times* with the effects of the online edition. Rather than attending to the most prominent or important news stories, the users of the online edition were more likely to attend to personally relevant news. Two studies of political blogs furthermore support the selective exposure/homogeneity of political discussion networks thesis. Tremayne *et al.* (2006) found that the network of links among a small number of blogs reporting on the Iraq war consisted of two distinct clusters—liberal and conservative blogs—although there were some central blogs linking the two clusters. Adamic and Glance (2005) provide quite similar results from studying relations among the posts of 40 A-list blogs over the period of two months preceding the 2004 U.S. presidential election. Liberal blogs linked primarily to other liberal blogs, and conservative blogs linked primarily to other conservative blogs (more frequently and more densely than among liberal blogs), with only a few cross-listings.

The macro-level consequences of such selectivity and subsequent "personalized realities" fostered through the internet may be substantial (Bennett, 1998: 741). These personalized realities represent a dynamic and pervasive social adjunct to Putnam's (2000) concern with the ill effects of bonding (brings homogeneous people together) as opposed to bridging (brings heterogeneous people together) social capital (see Norris, 2004 for an application to online communities). The most prominent advocate of this position is Sunstein (2001), who writes that the internet will foster enclave communication among politically homogenous citizens, yielding polarization of opinions, widening political divides between extreme sides on public issues, and encouraging cyber-cascades of unsubstantiated and sometimes false information.

Yet whatever its online implications, the theory of selective exposure has itself received only mixed support. Rooted in cognitive dissonance theories, selective exposure suggests that when individuals are exposed to information that conflicts with their political belief system, they become cognitively uncomfortable, which causes them to look for conforming messages and avoid conflicting messages (e.g., Festinger, 1957). However, despite some evidence that people seek supportive messages, research has generally been unable to consistently demonstrate that people avoid contradictory messages (Festinger, 1957; Rhine, 1967; Sears and Freedman, 1967; see also Chaffee et al., 2001). A further amendment to the original theory of selective exposure suggests that selectivity is not a common activity among all or most individuals. Rather, it is the most politically sophisticated individuals who are most likely to selectively attend to information, reinforcing previously existing beliefs and knowledge (e.g., Graber, 1984). Some observers have concluded that selective exposure is not nearly as pervasive as once suggested (e.g., Kinder, 2003). Zaller (1992: 139), for example,

suggests: "Most people ... are simply not so rigid in their information-seeking behavior that they will expose themselves only to ideas that they find congenial. To the extent selective exposure occurs at all, it appears to do so under special conditions that do not typically arise in situations of mass persuasion."

In line with amendments to the original theory of selective exposure, there is some evidence to suggest that despite the increased control provided by the internet, people are not using it to weed out certain partisan perspectives. Garrett (2005), for example, finds from a combination of survey research and laboratory experiments that the online environment facilitates people's seeking of viewpoints that reinforce existing positions, but does not comparably promote avoidance of challenging viewpoints. He argues that the internet is imperfect in its ability to weed out certain partisan perspectives. Typing in the phrase pro-choice as a search term, for example, yields results both for and against this position. Rainie et al. (2005) furthermore find that 36 percent of internet users report encountering campaign news and information on the internet not as the result of a directed search but by accident, while online for an altogether different purpose.

Weakened social boundaries

Further facilitating potential exposure to political disagreement and possibly countering the influence of online selective exposure is the potential of internet use to weaken social, political, and ideological boundaries through interactive communication technologies, such as website bulletin boards, chat rooms, e-mail, and feedback loops to news organizations and politicians (Price and Cappella, 2002; Shah et al., 2005). New media may reduce or overcome the costs and environmental or structural constraints traditionally associated with political discussion and other forms of civic engagement by blurring and making more porous the boundaries between the private and the public sphere, and between different ideological groups.

First, perhaps most obviously, geographic borders that mark and support the homogeneity of a particular population do not bind the internet. Whether or not people take advantage of it, there is ample opportunity for people to expose themselves to political difference that they might not otherwise encounter offline within their usual physical boundaries. People may be exposed to different political perspectives online simply by chance (Garrett, 2005). This possibility is well illustrated by Wojcieszak and Mutz (2007), who find that exposure to political disagreement is most likely to take place in non-political, as opposed to explicitly political, chat rooms, suggesting that it happens somewhat unexpectedly, while people are meeting to discuss topics other than politics. Second, the internet allows people to develop broader and lower density networks or weak ties (Granovetter, 1973) that potentially allow for increased exposure to novel information and political disagreement. Boase and colleagues, for example, found that the internet may actually be transforming the shape of communities from small tightly knit associations to far-reaching social networks (Boase et al., 2006: 55). Rather than relying on one or two communities for socializing, help, and information, internet users are tending to use a variety of appropriate people and web resources.

Clearly, politically heterogeneous communities can and do exist online (e.g., Barber, Mattson, and Peterson, 1997; Dahl, 1989; Downing, 1989; London, 1993). Moreover, some online political discussants actually appreciate and enjoy engagement in heterogeneous spaces of deliberation (Stromer-Galley, 2002). In 2002, about a quarter of the U.S. adult population visited

websites that provided information about specific issues or policies that interested them; while 8 percent said they visited sites that share their point of view, 13 percent said they visited websites that have different views (Howard, 2005: 159).

Overall then, tendencies toward selective exposure may constrain people's exposure to political disagreement online. While an overwhelming amount of political diversity may exist online, people may not be overly enthusiastic about exposing themselves to it. Conversely, limits on selective exposure processes and weakened social boundaries seem to facilitate inadvertent, if not intended, exposure to political disagreement online, potentially leading to an overall increase in the heterogeneity of people's political discussion networks.

Analysis of individual-level influences on heterogeneous political discussion

As a preliminary exploration of the relationship of internet use and exposure to political difference, this section provides just an example, overall summary test of several of the influences discussed above, using a national survey sample.[1]

Measures

Table 11.1 provides the descriptive statistics and operationalizations of the items and scales appearing in the final regression model—the explanatory variables of age, offline political discussion, online political discussion, ideological polarity, ideology, political knowledge, and the dependent variable of politically heterogeneous discussion.[2]

Results

In order to provide context to the particular role of the internet, a combination of sociodemographic controls, traditional predictors of exposure to disagreement, and discussion variables were entered into a hierarchical multiple regression analysis (first block: education, race, age, sex, discussion at work, discussion with family, social ideology, political knowledge, and ideological polarity; second block: online discussion).

As Table 11.2 shows, age, political knowledge, ideological polarity, social ideology, discussion at work, discussion with family, and importantly, online discussion, were significant influences on heterogeneous political discussion, explaining 34 percent of the variance. Concerning heterogeneous political discussion, the information rich, at least in terms of how

they are usually conceptualized, are not necessarily getting richer. Consistent with the results of prior research, political discussion network heterogeneity was not significantly predicted by socioeconomic status, an important predictor of most forms of political engagement. Interestingly, age was an inverse predictor, suggesting that this particular form of engagement is actually more common among younger individuals. In contrast with prior findings, political knowledge was a very small, yet significant positive predictor (however, previous research examined the ratio of like-minded to non-like-minded voices, whereas this analysis examined overall political discussion network heterogeneity).

Table 11.1 Descriptive statistics for the variables of a model explaining political discussion network heterogeneity

Variable	Mean	Standard Deviation
Frequency of political discussion at work	3.6	2.9
Frequency of political discussion with family	5.8	3.0
Frequency of online discussion (mean of two items)	1.3	1.6
Age	50.1	17.2
Social ideology	4.0	1.7
Ideological polarity	1.3	1.0
Political knowledge ($\alpha = .89$, sum of four items)	2.6	1.2
Heterogeneous political discussion (mean of four items)	2.5	1.6
Unweighted N		440

Source: Author's calculations based on data from Scheufele (2003).

Table 11.2 Hierarchical multiple regression explaining political discussion network heterogeneity

Predictor variable	B coefficient
Age	−0.11**
Ideological polarity	−0.21***
Social ideology (conservatism)	−0.14***
Political knowledge	0.09*
Political discussion at work	0.31***
Political discussion with family	0.27***
Political discussion online	0.10*
Adjusted R^2	0.34
Unweighted N	440

Source: Author's calculations based on data from Scheufele (2003).

Notes:

* = p < 0.1; ** = p < 0.01; *** = p < 0.001; online discussion was entered as a separate, second block.

While traditional forums of political discussion (i.e., at work and with family) emerged as the most powerful predictors of network heterogeneity, the internet does appear to play an important role in exposing people to political diversity. In particular, online discussion may facilitate discussion with politically dissimilar individuals. In line with prior research findings, social ideology (conservatism) and ideological polarity were furthermore inversely related to heterogeneous political discussion.

Conclusion

For the most part, research findings on the internet and political participation have conformed to the rich get richer hypothesis. New information resources provided by the internet are more likely to be used by people high with socioeconomic status and political knowledge—those individuals who are less subject to the framing and agenda setting functions of the media and who are already likely to participate politically. These tendencies help to explain why the internet has exerted little effect on individual level political participation—this, in spite of the vast array of democratic opportunities that the internet provides (Bimber, 2003). The results from the sample analysis do, however, suggest that unlike many traditional predictors of political engagement, online discussion does contribute slightly to the heterogeneity of political discussion networks.

One general potential implication of increased or decreased knowledge gaps, and increased or decreased heterogeneity of political discussion, are four different kinds of political environments. An environment where political knowledge gaps are decreasing, and exposure to political disagreement is increasing, may be the sought-after political environment of deliberative democracy. However, decreasing knowledge gaps in environments where exposure to disagreement decreases may result in polarized enclaves, each knowledgeable and politically active but at best unaware and at worst hostile to any difference. When political knowledge gaps increase but exposure to disagreement decreases, ideological domination may arise, whereby minority and less educated groups are not even aware of alternative perspectives. Finally, when political knowledge gaps continue to increase, but exposure to disagreement also increases, elite demagoguery may arise, whereby knowledgeable political elites can manipulate meanings and salience of alternative perspectives.

This final possibility of elite demagoguery receives the most support from the research findings and analyses presented in this chapter. As reflected in the observations of Bennett and Manheim (2001), this possibility suggests that as the boundaries between the public and the private sphere become increasingly porous, and as more and more political mobilists transcend them, citizens may become exposed to more numerous and more varied competitive bids for their attention. In such an environment, the formation of coherent and stable public opinion is likely a greater challenge, as opposed to a lesser one. Moreover, the current mobilization tactics used by the majority of elites exacerbate this challenge—tactics that seem to suppress the identities and motives of mobilizers, as well as the complete implications of their objectives, as a means to achieving instrumental political goals (Howard, 2006). Howard *et al.* (2005: 61) further argue that knowledge gaps make it very difficult for the lower educated and information poor to assess online claims and information during campaigns, leading to increased manipulation by political messages.

According to Dahl (1989: 338), if democracy is to move beyond a state of capture by policy elites, or quasi-guardianship, and become more "firmly anchored in the judgments of the demos," there needs to be a free flow of information in the policy process. To do this, Dahl contends that independent reliable knowledge must be transmitted to citizens in clear and transparent ways that facilitate inclusive deliberation on policy issues.

Future research should continue to explore how the internet and related new forms of discourse and sources of information, such as blogging, affect political engagement, especially political discussion among heterogeneous networks of citizens. Future research should also consider the differential likelihood and strength of each of the four political environments associated with the combinations of knowledge gaps and exposure to political disagreement.

Guide to further reading

Much has been written about the multi-layered potential of advances in information and communication technology to improve, reinforce, or perhaps exacerbate the supposed state of society and the public sphere—there are a few texts that stand out as particularly seminal. A good starting point, for a broad look at the social consequences of internet use, such as its impact on community and the digital divide, is Katz and Rice (2002). For books relating specifically to the impact of the internet and related information technology on political and civic engagement, the authors recommend Neumann (1991) and Bimber (2003), both of which theoretically and historically situate these processes; Bimber and Davis (2003) is also relevant here, which looks at the impact of the internet on political campaigns. Iyengar (1990), Putnam (2000) and Zaller (1992), are suggested for broader discussions about the civic and political

consequences of media use. In terms of the specific issue of political discussion network heterogeneity, Mill (1859) and Habermas (1989) are required reading for normative perspectives, whereas Mutz (2006) and Huckfeldt, Johnson, and Sprague (2004) take more empirical approaches, investigating the particular mechanisms that govern exposure to political disagreement. Finally, for a more thorough discussion of the macro-level consequences of selectivity, Sunstein (2001) is an essential source. Prior to examining the impact of information and communication technology on civic engagement, however, it seems essential to understand just what civic engagement is, how it might be conceptualized, the processes governing it, and why it might be desirable. Toward this end, Verba *et al.* (1995) specify the particular variables and mechanisms involved with different types of civic engagement, and Dahl (1989) provides a contemporary interpretation of democratic theory, which includes a defense of the normative value of political engagement.

Notes

1 The Cornell University Survey Research Institute collected national level survey data used in this analysis in October and November of 2003, using CATI methods (N = 781). Dietram A. Scheufele was the principal investigator for the original study and generously shared the data. The response rate was 55 percent based upon AAPOR definitions. The survey was based on a carefully constructed probability sample that reduces sampling errors. The analyses use these data and some of the scales created by Dr. Scheufele, and other scales based on the current authors' conceptualizations and analyses. For the current chapter, only internet users were included in the analyses (N = 440).

2 Offline political discussion was assessed through the use of two separate items measuring the frequency of political discussion at work and with family (from 0 = never to 1

= very rarely, up to 10 = all the time). Online political discussion was assessed by computing the mean of two separate ten-point items that asked about frequency of political discussion via chat rooms, and e-mail. Social ideology was measured with a seven-point scale, with 1 being "very liberal" and 7 being "very conservative." The measure for ideological polarity also used this item. The farther along the scale in either direction indicated higher polarity. Factual political knowledge was an additive index of four items tapping correct identification of public figures and knowledge of current events (wrong answers were coded as 0, correct answers were coded as 1)—correctly naming the Vice President, describing the role of the Supreme Court, identifying how many votes are necessary to override a presidential veto, and naming the majority party. Heterogeneous political discussion was computed based on a ten-point scale, assessing how frequently respondents discuss politics with (1) people with extreme right views, (2) people with extreme left views, (3) people who are Democrats, and (4) people who are Republicans. Collectively these items create a total discussion heterogeneity scale, with higher scores on this scale indicating greater heterogeneity in political discussion partners in terms of ideology and political party identification. Prior to the creation of this scale, however, some changes were made to the original items. Ideology and political party preference were recoded, with discussion with partners of the same ideological preferences recoded as 0. Ideological heterogeneity was assessed using respondents' self-placement on two seven-point ideological scales (economic and social) ranging from "very liberal" to "very conservative." Likewise, political heterogeneity was evaluated through the use of an item assessing political party membership that asked respondents if they were registered Democrats, Republicans, or Independent/Other Party. Democrats who discussed politics with other Democrats were coded "0" for that discussion item, as were Republicans who discussed political issues or candidates with other Republicans. The ideological and political (party) items were then totaled into a combined index of overall heterogeneity of political discussion, based on the respondents' standardized differences between their own characteristics and those of their discussion partners. The following variables were not significant influences in preliminary analyses so are not described here: race, sex, education, income.

12

Information, the internet, and direct democracy

Justin Reedy and Chris Wells

Over the past several decades, the global use of ballot initiatives and referendums at both federal and provincial levels across a range of political systems has increased dramatically. Today, decisions made by direct democracy regularly impact issues of critical importance to governments and societies, from taxes, public spending, and environmental regulations to immigration, minority rights, and foreign policy and international relations. Considerable research on direct democracy has attempted to understand how voters cope with the unique demands of direct democratic situations, which differ significantly from electoral campaigns. Surprisingly, very little research to date has investigated the impact of internet use on this important and growing political arena. This chapter explores the potential for research in this area by reviewing research on the unique information environments of direct democracy and the political impact of the internet in candidate elections, suggesting new theoretical directions. We also offer original data from case studies of three direct democratic contests: ballot initiatives in a state-wide election in a typical American state, a nation-wide American survey on internet use and ballot measures, and data on referendum voting from Europe. Comparing data from these three sources, we find that internet use predicts knowledge of both facts relevant to direct democracy and the positions of opinion leaders. Internet use also predicts improved opinion quality, and there are signs of its potential as an organizing tool in ballot initiative and referendum campaigns.

In a referendum on May 29, 2005, voters in France soundly rejected the European Constitution, dealing a severe blow to the progress of European integration and to President Jacques Chirac (Sciolino, 2005). Three days later, Dutch voters rejected the constitution with even more gusto, and although the referendum in the Netherlands was technically a non-binding consultation with voters, with turnout at 62.8 percent and a "no" vote of 61.6 percent, Prime Minister Jan Peter Balkenende said he would respect the preference of the overwhelming majority (BBC News Online, 2005). The French and Dutch referendums were only the latest in the decades-old progression of

European integration, but voters' sound rejections of a treaty generally supported by their elected officials demonstrated clearly the powerful role that ordinary Europeans will play in determining the future of their continent (Hobolt, 2007).

Voters' direct power over policy in the modern world is not limited to momentous occasions of international integration. In 1978, voters in California enacted Proposition 13, a citizen-initiated amendment to the state constitution, which permanently capped property taxes at a maximum of 1 percent of the property's value. The impact Proposition 13 has had on politics and governance in California—and, later, in many other states—would be difficult to overstate. It has deeply reshaped California's tax structure, and severely constrained local officials' options for raising money for public projects, especially in education (Staples, 2003). It also has centralized political power in the state as the proposition targeted the property taxes relied on by local governments (Qvortrup, 2002). Further, Proposition 13 demonstrates that American direct democracy is not a backwater or localized political process: after its passage in California, the "tax revolt" spread to other states (Gerber, 1999), and taxes remain one of the most popular targets of American initiative campaigns.

These examples illustrate the major impact decisions made by direct democracy—processes in which questions of policy are decided directly by voters—have had and continue to have in contemporary politics. Ballot initiatives and referendums are used to decide policies controlling billions of dollars and affecting millions of citizens, and are being used by more and more states and countries around the world (Matsusaka, 2004).

Surprisingly, despite several solid research programs investigating the practices and characteristics of direct democracy (for a review of the literature on American ballot initiatives, see Lupia and Matsusaka, 2004; for a review on the European context, see Hobolt, 2006), and the wealth of interest on the political and social consequences of internet use to which this volume attests, the use of the internet in direct democratic situations has remained unexplored. This gap is unfortunate, and this chapter will make the case that research on internet use in direct democratic situations is an important and potentially fruitful area for research.

In addition to the growing importance of direct democracy on the world stage, another argument for studying the internet in this context is that the information flows of ballot initiative and referendum campaigns are significantly different from those of candidate elections (Hobolt, 2007; de Vreese and Semetko, 2004b), which have so far received the attention of internet research on political campaigns (e.g., Bimber and Davis, 2003). They are thus unique environments in which to observe political internet use, and in which our assumptions about how voters use information may not apply. This chapter will thus offer two arguments for the study of the internet in direct democracy. First, studying internet use in direct democracy may shed light generally on how people use the internet to gather, use, and distribute political information. Studies of voter decision-making in direct democracy have already contributed to our more general understanding of how voters process information (e.g., Lupia, 1994). Second, as the examples above illustrate, the increasing importance of direct democracy for policy-making combined with the increasing prevalence of internet use make direct democracy in itself an important area for internet research. For the foreseeable future, direct democracy will be an increasingly integral part of democratic government. Likewise, the internet's role as a source of information, discussion, and citizen mobilization is only likely to grow.

In this chapter, we explore ways of thinking about the internet's possible impacts on voters in direct democratic contests. Does it increase access to information and thus voter knowledge? Is it used as a forum for deliberation and can it therefore improve voter opinion quality? Does it take the place of other political news sources, which may or may not provide substantial coverage of ballot initiatives and referendums?

There is good reason to think that the answers to these questions in ballot initiative and referendum campaigns may be different from their answers in candidate elections, because of the ways in which the two types of campaigns differ. Voters in direct democracy do not have the luxury of easily voting by party preference (Hobolt, 2007; Lupia, 1994), since, unlike candidates, ballot measures rarely appear with built-in party labels. Direct democracy also poses extremely complex questions of policy to voters, rather than simply offering a choice of candidates. Further, direct democratic contests may vary widely from candidate elections in terms of the amount of media coverage they receive and in their perceived importance to citizens.

These differences suggest that internet use in direct democracy might be different from internet use in candidate elections. The lack of explicit partisan cues attached to ballot measures may encourage voters to use the internet to learn how favored elites stand on the measures, or they may take the opportunity to assess the views of non-partisan interest groups, such as environmental, labor, or religious organizations. The complexity of propositions may push voters away from candidates' sites and conventional news sites and toward issue-specific sites, or government sites that present factual information. The low level of media coverage that some ballot measures receive may encourage voters to turn to the internet for information. Use of the internet may consequently boost knowledge of ballot measures more than knowledge of candidate races because some measure-related information is only available online. The perceived importance of a ballot measure may be more influential than voters' impressions of candidate races, since those are so fully defined by level of government. More generally, citizens online may have much more opportunity to define the meaning and terms of a direct democratic campaign, especially a citizen initiative.

The aim of this chapter is not to develop a detailed theory of the internet and direct democracy. It is intended instead as a starting point for research in this area. The chapter begins with general observations about direct democracy—its origins, spread, and place in the world's contemporary democracies. After considering the informational uniqueness of direct democracy, we present three recent case studies of internet use in direct democratic situations. We then contemplate the results of those case studies in the context of what is already known about related uses of the internet. We develop a research agenda in three domains:

- the *informational* impact of the internet—how it impacts the way voters seek and find information;
- the internet's *deliberative* impact—the opportunities it offers citizens to deliberate in preparation for plebiscites;
- and the internet's *organizational* impact—how it creates new opportunities for supporters and opponents of ballot measures to identify, contact, and organize supporters.

We conclude the chapter with calls for further research in a number of areas.

Mechanisms of direct democracy in contemporary politics

Direct democracy in the United States

The United States Constitution contains no provision for direct democracy at the federal level, and neither did any of the state constitutions before the late nineteenth century. In a time of rapidly shifting economic conditions, progressives responded by challenging political structures and demanding reforms such as the direct election of senators, women's suffrage, and the power of the public to enact legislation without the approval of state legislatures. Interestingly, the concerns of the early American supporters of direct democracy are familiar to modern ears. Reformers argued that representative democratic bodies were beholden to powerful, moneyed interests, and that the concerns of the common people were too often forgotten when decisions were made. As a result, the public had lost faith in the political system (Piott, 2003). Borrowing from the Swiss experience with direct democracy, advocates of the initiative and referendum organized at the state and federal level, coordinated with the Populist party, and won the first state constitutional amendment providing for the initiative and referendum in South Dakota in 1898 (Piott, 2003). Other states soon followed suit (Matsusaka, 2004).

The turn of the twenty-first century is also a time of high demand for public influence in government and skepticism about the ability of representative government to govern in the public interest, and we have seen a new rise in the use of direct democracy. Today, 70 percent of Americans live in a city or state that has provisions for referendum or initiative, and no state that has adopted direct democracy has later repealed it (Lupia and Matsusaka, 2004). In addition to the growth in the availability of direct democratic mechanisms, the *use* of those mechanisms has increased substantially in the last two decades. After declining use from peaks in the 1910s, the 1990s were a record-setting decade for direct democracy in the United States, with 378 total measures voted on in that decade (Matsusaka, 2004).

Direct democracy in Europe

Europe's recent explosion of direct democracy has been largely in the form of national referendums concerning European integration. France held the first such referendum in 1972, and the use of direct democracy in Europe grew steadily through the end of the twentieth century, with 40 more referendums being held concerning the issue (Hobolt, 2007). A common explanation for the growing use of the referendum in Europe is the need for political elites to legitimize international agreements by putting them to a vote. Particularly because economic globalization and the growth of the European Union have left many Europeans feeling powerless to shape their nations' futures, many leaders fear undertaking international projects without popular consent, even when they may be constitutionally empowered to do so (LeDuc, 2003).

Thus, referendums in most European countries are national, and concern major national or international issues. However, a few use them regularly for policy-making. Switzerland stands out as the world's pre-eminent nation for direct democracy; while elected representatives still make a majority of public decisions, voters have easy recourse in repealing unpopular legislation, and can pass legislation independent of legislative action. Thus, public policy is regularly put before voters, who vote in plebiscites three or four times a year (LeDuc, 2003; Treschel and Kriesi, 1996). Besides Switzerland, Ireland and Italy are the only other European countries to hold referendums on general public policy with any frequency (LeDuc, 2003).

The problems and prospects for direct democracy

While it remains solidly popular with voters (Matsusaka, 2004), direct democracy is not without its critics. Detractors have argued that the ballot initiative process imprudently delegates the power of complex policy-making to citizens who know little about the details of the issues and are unable to devote sufficient time or attention to making an informed choice. Consequently, say critics, voters are as open to manipulation through direct democracy as the representatives the process is meant to circumvent (Broder, 2000). Whatever their empirical merit (they are contested by, e.g., Matsusaka, 2004), these criticisms are intriguing because they highlight direct democracy's political uniqueness. More than anything else, it is questions about the amount, availability, and flow of information—what de Vreese and Semetko (2004b) have termed the "information environment"—that sets direct democracy apart from candidate elections and that have enflamed its critics. In this section, we describe four features of direct democratic information environments that make them unique. The first two, lack of partisan cues and complexity, set nearly all direct democratic choices apart from candidate elections. The latter two, the degree of media coverage and citizen appraisal, vary widely among different direct democratic situations, but deserve mention because of the peculiarly influential roles they may play in ballot initiative and referendum campaigns.

Setting direct democracy apart from candidate elections

It has been noted that ballot initiatives and referendums lack a tool heavily used by voters in candidate elections: explicit partisan affiliations (Lupia, 1994). The absence of this decision-making resource might suggest that citizens vote haphazardly, unable to connect any of the choices on the ballot to a preferred ideology. But Lupia (1994) demonstrated that even voters with little knowledge of a set of California initiatives were able to cast their ballots much like better informed voters by knowing the position of a key political actor or organization

(Lupia, 1994). Findings of this type have led to optimism about the ability of low-information voters to cast "appropriate" votes (e.g., Bowler and Donovan, 2002; Lupia, 2001). But voters' abilities to gather the basic information needed to make these inferences may vary widely with media exposure, attentiveness, the perceived importance of the issue, and other factors. And referendums in which parties have been divided or formed unusual alliances—often the case, especially in the referendums over European integration—may confuse voters attempting to express partisan preferences (de Vreese and Semetko, 2004a). As Hobolt (2007) shows with data from a Norwegian referendum, voters with knowledge of partisan cues but little other information may be able to vote "competently," but mere reception of those cues is insufficient; she emphasizes the importance of having a particular type—rather than a particular amount—of information (Hobolt, 2007). This is an intriguing point for the study of internet use in direct democracy. Relative to consumers of one-directional mass media, are internet users better able to control the type of information they receive, perhaps via internet searches, in order to shore-up their limited information store for competent voting?

The second characteristic that distinguishes direct democracy from the process of electing representatives is the complexity of the choices faced by voters. In contrast to the relative simplicity of choosing between candidates—however complex their platforms—citizens voting on ballot initiatives or referendums are faced with an intricate policy question with dense text, often written in legal language that is inaccessible to even educated citizens (Leib, 2006). Some ballot measures have been created to intentionally mislead and confuse (Leib, 2006). Further, ballot initiatives and referendums may allow for surprisingly confusing

161

situations—a "Yea" vote may actually be a vote to repeal a policy, leading some citizens in favor of a program to unintentionally vote to end it (Gastil *et al.*, 2007). Here again the internet may play an important role. If citizens find conventional news coverage of complex ballot measures insufficient, the internet likely offers voters the opportunity to visit information-rich sites.

Variation within direct democratic contexts

Two further characteristics of direct democratic information environments tend to differ from those of candidate elections, though they also may vary widely among different direct democratic contexts. These include the media attention directed to ballot measures and citizens' assessment of the importance of ballot measures. Here, a generalization can be made between those polities that use direct democracy frequently and for general public policy— a majority of the American states and Switzerland—and those in which direct democracy is rare and usually of major significance—most of the European countries. In the former, ballot initiatives and referendums are often the victims of habituation or voter fatigue. They often share media attention and ballot space with higher profile candidate races (Bowler and Donovan, 2002), and usually receive turnout lower than candidate elections (LeDuc, 2003). In contrast, referendums in the latter frequently concern major questions of national identity and sovereignty, attract exclusive media attention, and receive turnout comparable to elections (LeDuc, 2003).

As an illustration of this difference, de Vreese and Semetko (2004b) describe the campaign over the Danish vote to introduce the Euro, in 2000, as "very visible," with extensive campaign coverage on television, airtime allotted to the political parties for campaigning, and debates

dedicated to the issue (de Vreese and Semetko, 2004b). In contrast, as LeDuc notes, in the U.S. elections in 2000 there were more than 200 direct democratic measures on ballots in 41 states; in Oregon, voters faced 26 direct democratic decisions (LeDuc, 2003).

On the American side, it has been taken as an article of faith that ballot initiative campaigns offer voters little information on which to base their decisions (Branton, 2003). Voters consequently display little factual knowledge of ballot measures. For example, in the case of the major, statewide ballot initiative in Washington State in 2003, only a quarter of respondents could correctly estimate the number of Washingtonians impacted by the initiative. In Europe, Qvortrup suggests that Swiss voters may be comparably poorly informed (Qvortrup, 2002). What is more revealing is his comparison of Swiss voter knowledge of referendums on general issues with Danish voter knowledge of the major Maastricht treaty referendums in 1992 and 1993. Only 9.2 percent of Danish voters then had "poor" knowledge of the political issues at stake, while 19.4 percent of their Swiss counterparts did (Qvortrup, 2002). The Danes' better knowledge of a high-profile and important referendum than the Swiss' knowledge of mundane public policy referendums illustrates one of the consequences of the different information environments at play in different direct democratic contexts. This again begs questions about the possible role of the internet in these different contexts. In low-profile, low-importance campaigns, will internet use provide information not provided elsewhere? Might low-profile direct democracy offer bloggers and users of online bulletins unique opportunities to define public issues usually usurped by bigger media? And what will be the role of the internet in high-profile referendum campaigns that receive plentiful attention from other media?

The conclusion to be drawn here is that although direct democratic contexts are far from uniform, their informational characteristics make them distinct from candidate campaigns (Bowler and Donovan, 2002; Hobolt, 2007; de Vreese and Semetko, 2004a). This reveals direct democracy as a particularly interesting political context in which to explore the effects of a new and revolutionary medium of information flow: the internet. It is to the internet's impact on voters facing direct democratic votes in three case studies—a single American state, a cross-section of Americans, and a sample of Europeans—that we now turn.

Three case studies

Washington State: online political communication and three state-wide initiatives

Our first case study examines internet use and voter knowledge of three state-wide ballot initiatives in Washington State in 2006. Initiative 920 would have repealed Washington's state estate tax; Initiative 933 would have required the state to compensate landowners for the expense of complying with land-use regulations; and Initiative 937, the only of the three to pass, mandated that particular percentages of the state's energy come from renewable sources. The 2006 election offered Washington voters a typical mid-term ballot, with a single high-profile U. S. Senate race, House races, and state legislative and local races. The three ballot measures concerned issues typical for state-wide initiatives, and all three received at least some coverage from news outlets and were discussed on the editorial pages of newspapers.

A few days before the election, the Washington Poll surveyed several hundred voters around the state about issues in state and national politics, and were asked a battery of questions about the initiatives. The questionnaire included items that asked respondents if they had ever used the internet and if they had used it the day before (Washington Poll, 2006). We analyzed the data for patterns of internet use and initiative-specific knowledge.

For each of the three initiatives, respondents who had used the internet were better able to give correct answers to initiative-specific knowledge questions than those who had never used the internet. As shown in Figure 12.1, when plotted by the number of total correct answers to knowledge items, the distribution of internet users was shifted toward a higher number of correct answers relative to the distribution of non-users. Regular internet users also fared better than occasional users: Figure 12.2 shows that the distribution of intermittent internet users was centered around five correct answers out of fourteen total initiative questions, while the distribution of regular users was centered around a mean of eight correct answers. Similar distributions were seen when the sample was split into college graduates and non-graduates, indicating that the effect of internet use on voter knowledge was more than a proxy measure of formal education.

To control for confounding demographic variables, the data were also analyzed through a linear regression. As shown in Table 12.1, general political knowledge had the largest effect on referendum knowledge, followed by income, regular internet use, and intermittent internet use, which approached statistical significance. Education level had a negligible, non-significant effect.

Finally, the data were analyzed to determine how internet use might help voters access electoral cues, such as endorsements from major parties or community groups. A linear regression tested the effects of internet use, political knowledge, and demographic variables on

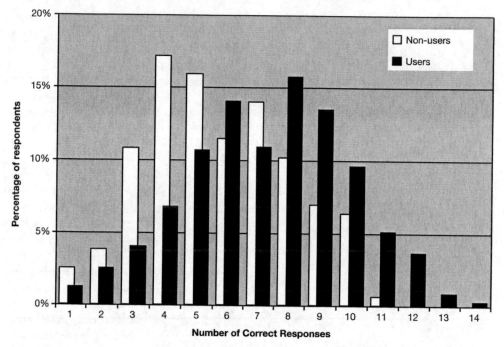

Figure 12.1 Referendum knowledge among internet users and non-users, Washington State, 2006.
Source: Author's calculations based on data from the Washington Poll (2006).

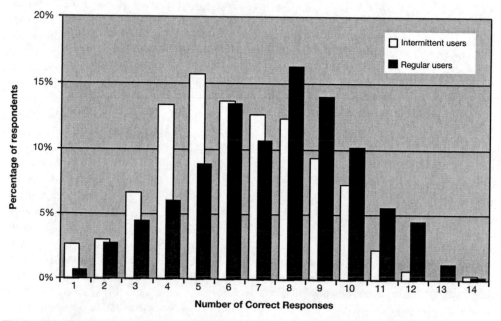

Figure 12.2 Referendum knowledge among regular and intermittent internet users, Washington State, 2006.
Source: Author's calculations based on data from the Washington Poll (2006).

Table 12.1 Linear regression models predicting referendum and political endorsement knowledge in Washington State, 2006

Predictor variable	Model 1: Linear regression model predicting referendum knowledge		Model 2: Linear regression model predicting endorsement knowledge	
	B	Standard error	B	Standard error
Constant	3.192	0.297	0.673	0.264
Education	0.015	0.220	0.314	0.195
Income	0.161*	0.066	0.108*	0.058
Political knowledge	0.489***	0.079	0.502***	0.070
Internet use	0.538*	0.310	0.518*	0.275
Regular internet use	0.348	0.247	−0.074	0.219
Adjusted R^2	0.137		0.150	
Unweighted N		616		

Source: Author's calculations based on data from the Washington Poll (2006). Public Policy Attitudes – Oct.–Nov. 2006. Seattle, Washington.

Notes:
* = $p < 0.1$; ** = $p < 0.01$; *** = $p < 0.001$; variable is education scale collapsed into two categories: college graduate and non-graduate.

a voters' knowledge of political endorsements on the initiatives. As seen in Table 12.1, political knowledge was again the strongest predictor, this time followed by internet use, then income; education had a predictive effect and approached statistical significance. In this case, the effect of regular internet use was negligible compared to overall internet use.

American direct democracy and internet use: election 2004

In the 2004 American election, President George W. Bush was challenged, unsuccessfully, and won re-election. All seats in the House of Representatives were up for vote, as were a number of Senate seats, and many local offices. Most Americans thus faced a fairly typical ballot for a Presidential election year, with races from the President down to local candidates, followed by state and local ballot measures.

The second case study presents data from the Pew Internet and American Life Project's 2004 Post-election Survey, which took place shortly after the election. The survey asked respondents numerous questions about political internet use,

including whether they had used the internet to learn about "ballot measures or initiatives," (Pew, 2004). In order to compare respondents with roughly equal likelihoods of learning about ballot initiatives online, we restricted our analysis to respondents who lived in the 34 states that had measures on the ballot in 2004 (Initiative and Referendum Institute, 2004), and those who used the internet for campaign news. Of that group, nearly a third, 28.5 percent (weighted value), reported using the internet to gather information about initiatives or ballot measures.

We explored five types of possible predictors of using the internet to find information about ballot measures. They included eight demographic variables; three political internet use variables; seven online news use variables; four variables describing reasons for internet use; and seven variables describing interactive uses of the internet relevant to the campaign. Those 29 variables were included in a regression predicting use of the internet to learn about ballot measures. All eight demographic variables, and the significant predictors from the other groups are listed in Table 12.2.

Most of the general demographic variables were predictive in the typical ways—being younger, being white, being male, being richer, and being more educated. Years of internet use and regularity of use were not significant predictors, however. All three variables concerning political uses of the internet were also significant: learning about the campaign online and learning about state-wide races online were slightly predictive, while learning about House or local candidate races online was one of the most significant predictors of learning about ballot measures online.

In terms of online news habits, going to candidate sites to learn about the campaign was marginally predictive, while going to issue-oriented sites was strongly predictive. From the set of variables describing the reasons that respondents

went online, using the internet because desired information is not available from other sources was significantly—and negatively—predictive of going online to learn about ballot measures. Using the net to obtain additional information was also marginally and negatively predictive.

From the set of variables describing actions respondents had taken online, having one's own blog was negatively predictive, while having sent or received online invitations to a party or event, and undertaking "other" campaign-related activities online were both predictive, albeit weakly.

European referendums and online politics

At the time of the 2004 U.S. election, the nations of the European Union were

Table 12.2 Linear regression models predicting use of the internet for information about ballot measures or initiatives, United States, 2004

Predictor variable	B	Standard error
Constant	−0.032	0.094
Demographics		
Age	−0.035*	0.017
Ethnicity (white)	0.071*	0.033
Sex (female)	−0.055*	0.027
Income	0.020**	0.008
Education	0.046*	0.018
Conservative	−0.016	0.014
Internet use		
Years of access to the internet	−0.002	0.006
Regular internet user	0.037	0.031
Internet Activities		
Getting campaign news online	0.027**	0.010
Learning about state-wide or Pres. race online	0.084*	0.034
Learning about House or local race online	0.303***	0.031
Going to issue-oriented sites for campaign news	0.254***	0.063
Uses internet for news not available elsewhere	−0.128**	0.048
Uses internet for additional information	−0.068*	0.036
Has started own blog	−0.112*	0.052
Has sent or received invitation to event/party	0.099**	0.036
Involved with "other" online campaign activities	0.109**	0.039
Adjusted R^2	0.257	
Unweighted N		1,897

Source: Author's calculations based on data from the Pew Internet and American Life Project (2004) Post Election Tracking Survey – November, 2004. Washington, DC.

Notes:
* = p < 0.1; ** = p < 0.01; *** = p < 0.001

debating a draft European Constitution. The document would have installed a permanent president of the EU council, replacing the six-month rotating post already in place; created a position of foreign affairs minister for overseeing foreign policy and representing the EU internationally; made changes to how the EU council made legislative and policy decisions; codified a method for member nations to leave the union; and instituted a charter of fundamental rights for EU citizens and nationals (Economist, 2007).

The constitution was controversial and widely debated in the public sphere, but it was also a topic of confusion for voters, who were being asked to weigh in on what amounted to many major policy decisions in one vote (Rennie, 2005). Even politicians and leading commentators found the 300-plus-page document difficult to decipher and fraught with potential policy pitfalls (Bush, 2005).

In October and November of 2004, the Eurobarometer poll asked citizens for their opinions on the draft constitution and quizzed them on their knowledge of the policy changes it would bring about. Respondents were asked, for instance, whether they knew that the constitution would create a foreign minister position with oversight of EU foreign policy—which it would—and if the document would allow for the direct election of the EU council president—which it would not. They were also asked about their use of telecommunication technology, including the internet, and the importance of those technologies to their personal and work lives (Eurobarometer, 2004).

In the analysis, each respondent received a referendum knowledge score reflecting the number of correct answers they provided on the EU constitution questions. Each person also received an internet use score that measured their personal use and whether they listed the internet as one of the three most important technologies in their personal lives. Linear regressions were used to determine the predictive effects of the internet use score and demographic variables, such as age, education, and political ideology, on referendum knowledge. Table 12.3 shows the results of that regression. Education level had the strongest effect on a respondent's knowledge of the referendum, followed closely by personal use of the internet. Political ideology had a very small effect on referendum knowledge, and age had a non-significant effect.

The data was further analyzed to determine the effects of internet use on respondents' ability to recall arguments in support of their view on the EU referendum. To test this, we employed the concept of argument repertoire, designed to measure a person's engagement with an issue; being able to recall more arguments for or against a policy suggests that the respondent has received and digested information from the debate on that policy (Cappella et al., 2002). As indicated in Table 12.3, age, education, and personal internet use all had modest predictive effects for argument repertoire on the EU referendum, but only for arguments in favor of the constitution.

The internet and direct democracy

The results of these analyses paint a portrait of internet use in direct democracy as sharing several features with general political use of the internet, while also distinguishing itself as unique. In this section, we explore the findings from three perspectives on the possible impact of the internet in direct democracy: the internet's informational impact, its interactive impact, and its organizational impact.

Table 12.3 Linear regression models predicting referendum knowledge and argument repertoire in Europe, 2004

Predictor variable	Model 1: Linear regression model predicting referendum knowledge		Model 2: Linear regression model predicting pro-EU argument repertoire	
	B	Standard error	B	Standard error
Constant	1.716	0.057	1.721	0.078
Age	0.036**	0.012	0.053**	0.053
Education	0.397***	0.018	0.133***	0.024
Conservative	0.013*	0.013	−0.012	0.008
Internet use index	0.311***	0.311	0.076**	0.024
Adjusted R^2	0.051		0.005	
Unweighted N		24,787		

Source: Author's calculations based on data from the Eurobarometer survey (2004).

Notes:

* = $p < 0.1$; ** = $p < 0.01$; *** = $p < 0.001$; education variable is index based on respondent's age level when formal education stopped; internet use index based on respondent's reports of personal internet use and perceived importance of the Internet to their personal life.

Informational impact

The political ideal for the internet is of a technology that improves the social knowledge base and leads to a more informed citizenry (Polat, 2005). Empirical studies tend to be cautious about viewing the internet as a panacea, showing, for example, that the political knowledge benefits of using the internet tend to be focused on those already enjoying greater knowledge resources (Bonfadelli, 2002). In this section, we explore the implications of the case studies' results for internet users' pursuit and acquisition of information in ballot initiative and referendum campaigns.

Knowledge of ballot measures

The data from the case studies show both that income and education predict knowledge of ballot measures—as in the Washington State and EU case studies—and that income and education predict using the internet to learn about ballot measures—as seen in the U.S. national study. The regression used in the U.S. case study controlled for frequent internet users and users who learned about campaign

information online; this echoes Bonfadelli's finding that information-seeking web tasks are associated with people who tend to already have greater information resources (Bonfadelli, 2002). In this case, those users tend slightly to be wealthier and better educated. At the same time, the fact that internet use was significantly edifying for both the high- and low-education groups from the Washington Poll—as well as in regressions from both the Washington Poll and EU case study—suggest that people with less formal education will benefit from using the internet in direct democracy situations.

Another explanation for the independent effects of both formal education and internet use on referendum knowledge is that direct democratic elections, which have been shown to encourage civic and political engagement (Smith, 2002), provide a context for normally unengaged citizens to connect with politics and gain information about ballot measures. While hopelessly complex, many ballot measures are also relatively discrete political events. They may provide opportunities for people mostly unaware of the political context of referendums to still cast meaningful votes. Together with the internet—

which allows for the easy retrieval of information on any particular ballot measure—direct democratic elections may sometimes bridge the information and engagement gap between privileged voters and those who are traditionally disadvantaged. What role the internet may play in engaging those citizens through ballot measures should be further explored.

Ultimately, the answer to the question of whether people are better informed about ballot initiatives and referendums as a result of their internet use, according to the Washington Poll and EU case studies, is a fairly clear "yes." In both cases, internet users were better able to answer factual questions about the direct democratic decisions they were facing, a finding with parallels in the literature on the internet and candidate elections (e.g., Drew and Weaver, 2006).

Knowledge of endorsements

As noted above, one of direct democracy's most unique characteristics is that voters make their decisions in direct democratic contests without the aid of explicit partisan cues. A major question is whether the internet aids voters in connecting their votes to preferred parties' positions. The findings of the Washington State case study suggest that it does. There, internet use trailed only general political knowledge in its power to predict knowing the endorsers of the three initiatives. This finding implies that the spread of internet use could improve voters' abilities to connect their votes to those of favored parties or political actors, by making specific types of information more plentiful and easier to retrieve (Hobolt, 2007). Future research should explore this in more detail. It might ask how citizens use the internet in deciding their votes. Do they attempt to learn everything they can about ballot measures and in the process learn about endorsements? Or do they

quickly log on to the website of a preferred group to find an endorsement? Does such a group tend to be a party, an interest group, or an online community?

Ballot measures and online news consumption

In addition to understanding who uses the internet to learn about ballot measures, what they learn, and how much, the data allow us to explore how people go about that learning. Here, the unique characteristics of direct democracy manifest themselves. The Pew data show that people who use the internet to access sites with issue-specific news are particularly likely to use the internet to learn about ballot measures, suggesting a very strong connection between ballot measures, using the internet, and seeking information specific (we might assume) to the measures on the ballot. Mysteriously, the variables for seeking online for information not available elsewhere and seeking online for additional information were both negatively predictive of learning about ballot measures, suggesting that users were not visiting issue-specific sites because they felt the conventional media were covering ballot measures inadequately. Future research investigating this seeming incongruity could tell us much about online information seeking in direct democracy.

Deliberative impact

The internet is much more than just a one-way medium of transferring information from media outlets and political elites to media consumers. On the web, consumers of information may also be producers (Polat, 2005). It is thus an arena of diverse opinions and perspectives, but it remains to be seen whether the internet can improve the character of public discussion on political issues in general or initiatives in particular (see Sunstein,

2001, for a pessimistic view, and Horrigan et al., 2004, for a refutation).

One model for evaluating the quality of political discussion is deliberative democratic theory, which calls for respectful and open deliberation of issues (see, for example, Barber, 1984; Cohen, 1997). True deliberative democracy is discussion-centered, promotes an equality of viewpoints, a free discussion, and inclusion of both fact- and emotion-based arguments (Burkhalter et al., 2002). Through deliberation, citizens make better and more informed policy decisions, promote compromise among people with differing views, and stimulate engagement in civic life (Delli Carpini et al., 2004; Gastil, 2000; Luskin et al., 2005).

At first glance, the internet may seem ill-suited to deliberation, since users are not engaging with one another face-to-face as in other deliberative settings. But scholars have proposed alternatives to in-person deliberation, such as situations in which a deliberating group offers a policy or candidate recommendation for the wider public (Gastil and Crosby, 2003), or those in which media and political elites debate the pros and cons of policy alternatives (Page, 1996). The internet may be a special case of mediated deliberation in which users interact in a virtual world, but are exposed to a wide range of viewpoints and consider many different arguments and opinions. A study of internet users in Chile, for example, described the use of an online forum to debate a highly contentious issue: the detention of Augusto Pinochet, the country's former dictator (Tanner, 2001). The forum discussions featured many elements of a deliberative discussion, such as the use of informational and emotional arguments, and the discussion of larger issues surrounding Pinochet's regime. Another study of a government-instituted online information center and forum in Denmark found that users engaged in respectful, well intentioned

discussions of policy options with each other and with political leaders, though only a small portion of the citizenry participated (Jensen, 2003). A review of the online deliberation literature indicates similar mixed results: some studies have found strong evidence of deliberation (Kim, 2006), while others have found few or no benefits to online political discussion (Janssen and Kies, 2005). Do citizens discuss ballot measures online? What role does online deliberation play in the process of voter decision-making?

One indicator of deliberation, explored by Cappella et al. (2002), is argument repertoire (AR), which refers to the number of issue-relevant reasons a person has for holding their own opinion, as well as the number of reasons they know for holding the opposite. Argument repertoire has been found to be indicative of online deliberation and has been suggested as a measure of "opinion quality" (Cappella et al., 2002). The data from the Eurobarometer offered the opportunity to assess respondents' AR on the referendums they were facing, and internet use was found to be slightly predictive of AR—but only slightly, and only for reasons in favor of the European constitution. Nonetheless, this finding suggests the deliberative potential of the internet in direct democratic contexts, and deserves further attention.

It also bears asking whether the existing concept of democratic deliberation is insufficient to describe the fledgling online public sphere. Dahlgren (2005), for example, argues that the internet is continuing a process of destabilization and dispersion of power that began with the advent of modern telecommunication technology. Analyzing the mechanisms and effectiveness of the online public sphere may require an adaptation of deliberative democratic theory to understand this destabilized setting (e.g., Edwards, 2002; Bekkers, 2004).

Organizational impact

A final potential impact of the internet on direct democratic campaigns is its potential to increase opportunities for citizen groups to support initiatives. Several scholars have argued that the internet provides unprecedented low-cost opportunities to organize many people toward a goal (Bimber et al., 2005; Rheingold, 2002). Though their history and formal structure suggest unique opportunities for average citizens to influence policy-making, critics note the heavy use of direct democracy by special interests (Broder, 2000; Gerber, 1999) and the modern cost of direct democracy. How might the internet reduce the costs of effective campaigning on ballot initiatives and referendums?

Bimber (2003) offers several observations about the internet's role in politics and collective action that suggest new forms of organization and opportunities for low-resource groups to mobilize. He notes that because the primary medium for political messages is still television, the internet may be most influential in lower profile races, because a greater portion of the effort in high-profile races is dedicated to communicating through television (Bimber, 2003). In the American and Swiss contexts, ballot measure campaigns may be just the sort of low-profile events in which savvy internet communicating has a great effect. Another of Bimber's observations is that the internet reduces the need for organizations to maintain members and replace leaving members; participation might be less "interest-based" as it becomes more "event-based." And as costs of communication decrease, organizations become more free to "form and disband at will" (Bimber, 2003).

Several findings from the Pew data set suggest ways these ideas might be applied in the direct democratic context. The strong associations between consuming issue-specific news online, learning about local races online, and learning about ballot measures online have already been noted. But people who gave or received invitations to events or parties, and people who engaged in "other" campaign activities online were also more likely to learn about ballot measures online. Future studies should explore the uses of the internet in direct democracy. Is it used as an alternative to scarce television coverage? Is it used to organize quick and temporary coalitions, as Bimber (2003) suggests?

Conclusion

Our findings show that while several of the general trends described in the literature on internet use in elections apply to direct democratic contexts, several also appear to be unique to direct democracy. These include the tendency of people using the web to learn about ballot measures to visit issue-specific websites, the association between learning about ballot measures and learning about local, as opposed to state-wide or national races, and the relative likelihood that people who use the internet to organize their social and political activities will also use it to learn about ballot measures. Our more general findings—from very different contexts—that internet use is associated with greater knowledge of ballot measures and the endorsements of political actors also deserve more study.

Both the internet and direct democracy are unique products of our era. The internet was developed over the last two decades, just as direct democracy's resurgence has boomed. Both have been heralded as new forums for expressing political will and potential salves for modern democracy's problems, especially the estrangement of the public from political processes. The study of the internet in the unique context of direct democracy is thus an important endeavor.

It offers insights on the political possibilities of internet use for a political environment with features and characteristics that set it apart from candidate elections.

Perhaps more important than contributing to our general understanding of political internet use, however, studying the internet in direct democracy reveals the impact of a tremendously important communication medium on a political process that will continue to shape the world in which we live. Direct democracy is not going anywhere any time soon—on the contrary, publics around the world are likely to increase their demands for opportunities to influence policy and check the power of wayward elites. As rates of internet use become strong majorities in the developed world, and as they approach sizeable numbers in other parts of the globe, this is a research program that will benefit our understanding of politics and the changing roles of citizens in modern democracy.

Guide to further reading

Because the subfield of the use of the internet in direct democracy has not been explored, the more general fields of direct democracy and the internet's impact on voter information would be the most helpful for readings looking for other works.

In the field of American direct democracy, the work of Shaun Bowler and Todd Donovan stands out. Their *Demanding Choices: opinion, voting and direct democracy* (Bowler and Donovan, 1998) and their edited volume *Citizens as Legislators: direct democracy in the United States* (Bowler, Donovan, and Tolbert, 1998) are excellent sources on voting in direct democracy. John G. Matsusaka's (2004) *For the Many or the Few: the initiative, public policy and American democracy* is a spirited defense

of the initiative process against charges that it has been corrupted by special interests. The Initiative and Referendum Institute, which Matsusaka directs, at the University of Southern California, also has plentiful information about direct democracy in the U.S. It is online at: www.iandrinstitute.org/. (The Intitute's European page is: www.iri-europe.org/).

The Referendum Experience in Europe, edited by Michael Gallagher and Pier Vincenzo Uleri (1996), offers a good selection of articles about experiences with direct democracy around Europe. For a study of referendums in the course of European integration, see Simon Hug's *Voices of Europe: citizens, referendums and European integration* (Hug, 2002). A solid literature review on the topic of EU referendums is Hobolt (2006). Claes de Vreese and Holli Semetko (2004b) emphasize the importance of information in *Political Campaigning in Referendums: framing the referendum issue*. De Vreese's (upcoming) edited volume, *The Dynamics of Referendum Campaigns: an international perspective*, also promises new research by top scholars. Online, C2D, the Research Center on Direct Democracy at the University of Geneva, is a clearing house for information on European and worldwide direct democracy. It is at: http://c2d.unige.ch/.

For books considering direct democracy globally, Lawrence LeDuc's (2003) *The Politics of Direct Democracy: referendums in global perspective* is very helpful. David Butler and Austin Ranney's (1994) edited collection *Referendums Around the World: the growing use of direct democracy,* provides a good historical overview of direct democracy in Europe, the Americas, and much of the rest of the world. Also see Matt Qvortrup's (2002) *A Comparative Study of Referendums: government by the people.*

13

Toward digital citizenship

Addressing inequality in the information age

Karen Mossberger

Despite the growth of the online population in the United States, substantial inequities in the capacity to use the internet remain. Some scholars claim time and market forces will effectively resolve the issue, and official policy has declared the problem essentially solved. This misrepresents the underlying issues in technology inequality. The concept of digital citizenship—the ability to participate in society online—highlights the continued need for policy that promotes effective use of the internet, including literacy, skills, and regular access. Educational competencies are crucial for digital citizenship, just as they are for political participation both online and offline. Race and ethnicity continue to matter for digital inequality, despite evidence that African-Americans, and in some cases Latinos, have even more positive attitudes toward technology than similarly-situated whites. Research suggests that structural disadvantages, including unequal educational opportunities, link technology disparities to other inequalities in society. Politics online exhibits substantial benefits for participation and greater access to government, especially in its ability to mobilize younger people. Indeed, the internet may enable participation in new ways both online and offline for some, while raising greater barriers for others. Without greater attention to fostering widespread digital citizenship, society risks creating even greater political inequality.

Systematic inequalities in the capacity to use information technology persist. internet use has increased exponentially over the past decade, but is certainly not universal, for approximately 30 percent of Americans do not use the internet. Still fewer—less than half—use the internet on a daily basis. Many of those who are counted by surveys as internet users do not have the skills to find or use information online effectively, or may use the internet infrequently. More than a decade into the information age, many Americans remain disconnected or are only tenuously connected, and variations in the ability to use technology are based on education, income, race and ethnicity, as well as age.

This chapter argues for a reframing of the issue from the narrow concept of the digital divide as a problem of simply having some access to technology, to the concept of digital citizenship, or the capacity to participate in society online (Mossberger *et al.*, 2007).

What does it mean to be a digital citizen? Participation in society online requires regular access to information technology and the effective use of technology. Digital citizens can be defined as those who use the internet every day, because frequent use requires some regular means of access (usually at home), some technical skill, and the educational competencies to perform tasks such as finding and using information on the web, and communicating with others on the internet (Mossberger *et al.*, 2007). Because of the explosion of political information and opportunities on the web, digital citizenship is an enabling factor for *political citizenship*, whether practiced online by responding to Listserv solicitations for campaign contributions or offline at the voting booth. In much the same way that public education has long been linked to civic republicanism and democratic values, the internet has the potential to facilitate the membership and participation of individuals within society.

This chapter reviews research on who is involved in politics and government online in the United States, comparing it to evidence on internet use more generally. A brief history of public policy and research on the issue reveals that many of the causes of digital inequality have not been adequately addressed. The latter part of the chapter considers possible policy solutions and examines the implications that online disparities have for democratic participation and governance in the future.

The growth and impact of politics and government online

How does the internet influence the exercise of democratic citizenship, both in terms of political participation and also access to government information and services? Opportunities for politics and government online are burgeoning and emerging evidence demonstrates that they have important impacts.

During the 2006 U.S. mid-term elections, 31 percent of all internet users engaged in some campaign-related activity online. This included viewing online news, sending or receiving e-mails about the election, or posting content online regarding the campaign. Fifteen percent

of internet users relied on the internet as their most important source of news, and 8 percent posted a blog or online comments (Rainie and Horrigan, 2007). A larger percentage—54 percent of internet users—reported ever having looked at news or information about politics or campaigns on the web (Pew Internet and American Life Project, 2007).

All U.S. federal and state agencies (West, 2005) and most local governments currently host a website (Norris and Moon, 2005). The development of "e-government"— the delivery of government information and services through the internet—(West, 2000) has implications for social inclusion and political participation. Information posted online may include e-mail addresses for contacting officials, policies, research, agendas and minutes of meetings, issues advocated by elected officials, and publicly available databases as well as information about services. Online transactions are another common use of websites, for activities such as filing taxes, applying for permits, paying tickets or fines, requesting birth and death records, renewing driver's licenses, registering to vote online, or submitting complaints. Although information and service delivery predominate on government websites (Chadwick and May, 2003; West, 2003a, 2003b) there are also examples of more participatory uses of the internet. The city of Berkeley, California has solicited online comments on the comprehensive plan (Mossberger *et al.*, 2003), for example, and Seattle lists ways to get involved in neighborhood groups and links to neighborhood websites. As of August 2006, two-thirds of internet users reported visiting a government website (Pew Internet and American Life Project, 2007).

Evidence on the democratic benefits of internet use

The prevalence of politics and government online is insufficient, however, to make the case that digital citizenship is central to citizenship in the traditional sense—for political participation and for inclusion in the polis. There is evidence, however, that access to politics and government online has important social benefits. Research has established a positive association between internet use and participation, including voter turnout (Bimber, 2003; Tolbert and McNeal, 2003; Graf and Darr, 2004), campaign contributions (Bimber, 2001, 2003; Graf and Darr, 2004), and citizen-initiated contact with government (Thomas and Streib, 2003; Bimber, 1999). Research using two-stage models suggests that these results can be partly explained by the influence of online news on civic engagement, stimulating greater political interest, knowledge, and discussion (Mossberger et al., 2007). Like print media, the internet offers in-depth coverage and facilitates recall of information, encouraging the acquisition of political knowledge (Healy and McNamara, 1996; Kyllonen and Christal, 1990). Its diverse content and convenience are valued by citizens and interactivity facilitates political discussion and mobilization. Two-stage models show that political uses of e-mail, chat rooms, and online news all increase the probability of voting. Those who have visited government websites have more positive attitudes toward government (Welch et al., 2005; Tolbert and Mossberger, 2006; West, 2005). These outcomes are evident even controlling for other factors, including the positive relationship that education has with both internet use and political participation or e-government use.

Who is involved in politics and government online?

The internet has truly become a new civic arena, but not all citizens are equally present in this venue. Those who pay attention to politics or government on the internet tend to be the young and the educated, holding other factors constant (Bimber, 2003: 218; Wilhelm, 2003; Alvarez and Hall, 2004). Some studies have concluded that men are more likely to be e-government users (West, 2005: 125) and are more interested in internet politics, including online voter registration and participation in an electronic town meeting (Mossberger et al., 2003: 100). Fuller (2004) has found that gender tends to influence the types of politically oriented websites that respondents visit rather than political interest per se. Yet, socioeconomic influences are more powerful than gender for predicting political engagement online.

The internet holds promise for engaging the young

Politics online differs from voting and many other forms of political participation insofar as young people are more likely to participate. It is well-known that political participation increases with age, under most circumstances (Campbell et al., 1960; Wolfinger and Rosenstone, 1980), and in fact political interest and activity are traditionally most visible after the age of 45 (Alvarez and Hall, 2004). The greater presence of young people in internet politics increases political participation among the young, and if these trends are sustained, they may result in greater overall levels of political interest and activity in the future. Krueger (2002, 2006) demonstrates that the internet has the ability to engage some individuals who otherwise would not be involved in politics, and that this pattern is most evident among younger individuals. Reading online news has a greater effect on political knowledge among young people, controlling for the use of traditional media and other factors (Mossberger et al., 2007).

The internet magnifies existing political disparities

In other ways, however, those who pay attention to politics online are the same individuals who are involved in politics more generally. Education emerges repeatedly across these studies as a key consideration for political involvement on the internet as well as political participation offline (Campbell *et al.*, 1960; Verba *et al.*, 1995; Wolfinger and Rosenstone, 1980). As can be expected, political interest and political efficacy play a role in online politics as well (Bimber, 2003: 218; Mossberger *et al.*, 2007: chapter 4). Online politics largely replicates existing patterns of participation, with the exception of its attractions for young people.

Moreover, prior disparities may be exacerbated online. Research that demonstrates heightened political interest and activity based on internet use would also suggest an intensification of existing disparities

rooted in education (and income) if those who are mobilized are predominantly more advantaged citizens (Alvarez and Nagler, 2002). The potential effects on civic participation among racial and ethnic minorities pose particular concern. Among *internet users,* there are no significant differences in most political activities online based on race or ethnicity, once we control for income and education. Yet race and ethnicity *do* have statistically significant influences on the population of internet users.

Descriptive statistics (simple percentages) show this pattern as well. As Figure 13.1 indicates, the percentage of African-Americans in the population who read about politics online is consistently lower than the percentage of whites for the years 2000–6. This is primarily because of lower rates of internet access rather than great differences in political engagement by race for internet users. Trends for Latinos are difficult to interpret from

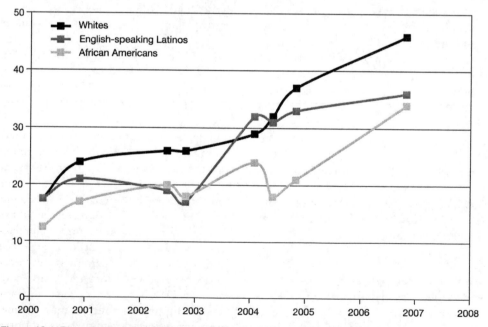

Figure 13.1 Percentage of United States' citizens who read about politics online.
Source: Author's calculations based on data from the Pew Internet and American Life Project Trends in Internet Adoption and Rainie and Horrigan (2007).

these figures, however. They include only English-speaking Latinos, and the Pew surveys from which these data are derived have consistently depicted this group as having similar internet access to white respondents. Research that includes both English and Spanish-speaking Latinos clearly demonstrates that this group overall is significantly less likely to use the internet (Fox and Livingston, 2007). At the same time that the internet promises to increase political participation for some, minorities and less-educated individuals are trailing behind. Is it probable that this will change in the near future, simply because of further diffusion of the internet?

Evolution of an issue: defining the digital divide

Understanding these trends and the prospects for change necessitates a closer look at how the issue has been defined. Complex, multi-dimensional issues are often simplified on the public agenda (Cobb and Elder, 1983) and issue definitions may pay attention to certain aspects of policy problems while neglecting others (Jones, 1994; Jones and Baumgartner, 2005). Technical solutions such as internet connections and hardware have tended to dominate policy debates since the issue of the "digital divide" first emerged on the agenda in the early 1990s. Federal policy has emphasized internet connections in schools and libraries rather than affordable home access. Relatively little money has been available for training and support services, even in schools and libraries.

The largest federal program is the E-Rate program, which provides wiring and internet connections for schools and public libraries in low-income communities. This has defined the predominant role of government as a matter of lowering the cost of access for institutions in areas with high-poverty populations, and

is analogous to the social construction of the issue of universal telephone service, where subsidies have reduced the cost of telephone connections for rural residents. In contrast with universal telephone service policy, however, the federal E-Rate program has assisted public institutions rather than reducing the cost of the service for individuals. During the Clinton administration, some smaller programs funded training and innovation using technology, but the Bush administration eliminated federal grants for the Community Technology Centers and the Technology Opportunities Program. Some limited funding is available for technology use in schools as part of the No Child Left Behind Act, but the Bush administration cuts have further narrowed the scope of federal policy. The federal E-Rate program has endured because it is embedded in legislation.

Evolution of research on digital inequality

The federal government has been an important source of data on information technology use, although this role has declined as well in recent years. Federal influence on the terms of the debate has been exercised through its research reports, issued by the National Telecommunications and Information Administration (NTIA), which is the same agency that administers the E-Rate program. During the Clinton administration, the first "Falling Through the Net" report described disparities in home computer ownership (U.S. Department of Commerce/NTIA, 1995), and later editions included home internet access as well (U.S. Department of Commerce/ NTIA, 1998). The reports regularly provided valuable information and kept the issue on the national agenda for a number of years, but shifting political priorities influenced the way in which the federal government defined the issue in later research. The 2002 NTIA report written during the Bush administration included use anywhere rather than home access. It emphasized the growing internet population, declaring that the problem was receding. A subsequent study was issued in 2004 regarding broadband use, but the U.S. Department of Commerce no longer tracks the issue. The non-profit Pew internet and American Life Project has since become a central source of current data on information technology use in the U.S.

What factors drive digital inequality?

For several years there was a dearth of studies capable of showing what factors were really driving these inequalities— whether, for example, race and ethnicity matter when controlling for income and education. Some research using bivariate analysis produced contradictory results. Hoffman *et al.* (2001) showed that African-Americans who were poor and less educated were technologically disadvantaged in comparison with whites in the same income or education categories. On the other hand, Nie and Erbring (2000) asserted that differences were based on age and education alone. Neither study used multivariate controls.

As more researchers began to use multivariate regression analysis to examine the issue, a consensus emerged among studies using different sources of data, and across years. Age and education generally account for the most variation, but income, race, and ethnicity also exercise independent effects (Neu *et al.*, 1999; Fairlie, 2004; Mossberger *et al.*, 2003). Katz and Rice (2002) examined data between 1995 and 2000 and found some diminishing effects of race by the turn of the millennium, but other research with more representative samples of minorities has revealed continued disadvantage among African-Americans and Latinos, controlling for other factors.

Using the large-sample 2000 Current Population Survey, Fairlie (2004) found that occupation, income, and education explained a good deal, but not all of the inequalities in home access for African-Americans and Latinos. The gender gap in access has closed over time, but other inequities have remained even as internet use has grown in the U.S.

Mossberger *et al.* (2008) describe "digital citizenship" as daily use, assuming that those who use the internet on a daily basis have required skills as well as regular access. Reviewing Pew data from 2000–5, they find that only about 60 percent of internet users go online on a daily basis. Holding all other factors constant, whites have a 15 percent higher probability of being daily internet users than Latinos, and a 13 percent higher probability than African-Americans, according to data from the 2003 Current Population Survey of the U.S. Bureau of the Census (2003). In contrast, there is a 28 percent difference between 63-year-olds and 29-year-olds in their probability of daily use, and a 22 percent difference for high school graduates compared to those holding associate's degrees, or for those who make $20,000–$25,000 per year compared to those earning between $75,000–$100,000 annually (Mossberger *et al.*, 2007). Daily use mirrors the disparities in access, but it serves as a proxy for skill as well as regular access.

Studies examining broadband use have found similar patterns of disparity, with the exception that rural residents are also disadvantaged because of a lack of broadband availability in less-populated areas (Ayres and Williams, 2003; U.S. Department of Commerce/NTIA, 2004; Horrigan, 2004). Broadband use is important for full connectivity, as campaign websites and news sites (among many others) use complex and interactive graphics, video streaming, and other features that require higher speeds to download. Slower speeds can be frustrating, especially for novices. High-speed connections are associated with more frequent use and more diverse uses online (Horrigan, 2004; Mossberger *et al.*, 2007).

Will time close all gaps?

As public access and occasional use have increased over the years, some observers have assumed that the problem is fading away. The most common assumption among academics who take this position is that internet adoption will merely follow the "s-curve" typical for the diffusion of many innovations (Rogers, 1995), and that later adopters will be more representative of the population as a whole (Compaine, 2001). There has indeed been real growth in occasional use, from 46 percent of Americans in 2000 to 70 percent in 2006 (Pew Internet and American Life Project, 2007). Yet, as the preceding section showed, disparities still remain. Furthermore, one analysis of respondents aged 16–32 shows that race, ethnicity, and education account for statistically significant divisions among young people as well. Current gaps are therefore not likely to close of their own accord in the near future (Mossberger *et al.*, 2007).

Some analysts have contended that the problem of digital inequality will diminish with the rapidly decreasing prices for information technology brought about by the market (Thierer, 2000; Compaine, 2001). But, the affordability of home access is still a hurdle for some individuals. The United States ranks 15th in broadband adoption in part because it is relatively expensive in comparison with countries where government has subsidized its costs as part of the national infrastructure (Organization for Economic Cooperation and Development, 2006). Income is still a significant barrier for acquiring home access for many of those who remain offline, as more than 20 percent of African-

Americans and Latinos cited costs as the major reason for not having home access in the 2003 Current Population Survey, in comparison with only 9 percent of the general population. There are also reasons to believe that certain disparities will not simply be erased by time or even cheaper technology, because they involve fundamental educational gaps rather than affordability, and these are entwined with race, ethnicity, and class.

The role of race and ethnicity: apathy or disadvantage?

The causes for racial and ethnic disparities in technology in the United States have been the topic of some debate. One possible explanation is that African-Americans and Latinos are particularly unaware of or disinterested in the potential benefits of the internet. Kretchmer and Carveth (2001) have hypothesized that minorities perceive that content on the internet has little relevance to their needs and interests. Van Dijk (2005: 40) asserts that the difference must be cultural and cites a case study of poor African-American men in one city who associate the internet with women's work rather than the manual labor they view as appropriate for men (Stanley, 2001). African-American women do indeed use the internet somewhat more frequently than their male peers (Fallows, 2005; Mossberger *et al.*, 2007), but this hardly accounts for the differences between minorities and whites.

Minorities have more positive beliefs about technology

In contrast to the common narrative about apathy, survey research demonstrates that attitudes toward internet use are even more positive among African-Americans (and to a lesser extent, Latinos) when they are compared to similarly situated whites.

179

This is particularly true for African-American attitudes toward information technology across a range of issues such as the importance of the internet for economic opportunity, and reported willingness to use public access or to learn new technology skills in a variety of ways (Mossberger *et al.*, 2003). There is evidence that race and ethnicity influence online behavior as well as attitudes. African-Americans and Latinos are considerably more likely to search for jobs online than whites, despite lower rates of access, and African-Americans are more likely than whites to take online classes for credit (Pew Internet and American Life Project, 2007; Mossberger *et al.*, 2003; U.S. Department of Commerce/NTIA, 2002). Just as African-Americans were more likely to take advantage of the GI Bill after World War II (Hacker *et al.*, 2005), the internet has been attractive for its potential to overcome discrimination in the labor market. This poses a contradiction, however: why is it that these positive attitudes fail to lead to higher rates of internet access and use?

Segregation and concentrated poverty

Research indicates that community-level factors influence the opportunities that individuals have to learn about and to use technology. African-Americans are most at risk for living in areas of concentrated poverty. The percentage of Latinos who live in segregated, high-poverty communities is also high in comparison with whites (Massey and Denton, 1993: 12). Structural barriers for technology use in poor communities may include public institutions, social networks, and labor markets. Poor communities often lack the resources to support technology use in schools and libraries, and social networks may not include many who are technology-savvy. The "spatial mismatch" thesis

argues that inner-city residents do not possess the skills or networks to obtain knowledge-intensive jobs that could provide exposure to technology (Kain, 1968; Kasarda, 1990). Mossberger *et al.* (2006) discovered that living in poor communities significantly decreases technology access and use for individuals of all backgrounds in a study that used multilevel models and data from a national survey merged with 2000 census data. Differences between African-Americans and whites at the individual level are no longer statistically significant after introducing environmental factors such as zip code median income and the percentage of high school graduates. In other words, the persistence of segregation and concentrated poverty account for the lower rates of access and use among African-Americans. African-Americans residing in more affluent areas are marginally more likely than whites to have a home computer, and just as likely to be frequent internet users. Place effects do not entirely explain technology disparities for Latinos.

Language and limited education contribute to lower use for Latinos

Some studies have indicated that Spanish-language dominance among Latinos decreases internet use, controlling for other factors (Fairlie, 2004; Fox and Livingston, 2007). However, lower levels of education among Latinos have a high impact on internet use as well (Fox and Livingston, 2007). Individuals from Mexico or of Mexican descent have the lowest rates of computer access and internet use among Latinos (Fairlie, 2004; Fox and Livingston, 2007). Second-generation, better-educated, English-speaking Latinos are more likely to resemble the population as a whole (Fox and Livingston, 2007).

Both Latinos and African-Americans have a higher probability of reliance on access outside the home in order to use the internet (Fox and Livingston, 2007; Mossberger et al., 2007). One study of three communities in Northeast Ohio found that about 20 percent of internet users in a very poor, nearly all African-American community had no access at home or at work. Primary access at the homes of friends and relatives was most common, followed by public libraries as the most frequent place of use. Poor African-American neighborhoods stood out in comparison with other low-income communities because of the effort that residents showed in going online in the absence of home access. Social networks in poor communities may be a positive force for resource sharing. The problem, however, is that individuals who lacked home or work access used the internet much less frequently, often only a few times a month. This does not provide a firm foundation for participation online, and such infrequent users are less likely to acquire the skills they need to use the medium effectively (Mossberger et al., 2006).

A varied picture of access and ability

For these reasons, it is important to recognize differences in access and capacity among internet users. Katz and Rice (2002: 75) discovered that about 10 percent of internet users lose their computer or internet connection or stop going online because of frustration or lack of interest. Internet dropouts are likely to be younger, lower-income and less-educated than those who continue to use the internet. Although Pew regularly reports figures on occasional internet use, more detailed studies issued by Pew have also acknowledged that there is a wide continuum of use ranging from those who are highly wired, tenuously connected, or truly disconnected (Lenhart, 2003; Fox, 2005).

Frequency of use and activities online

Some studies have shown a link between frequency of use and internet activities and skills. Jung et al. (2001) create an internet "connectedness index," which includes years of experience, number of places where an individual connects to the internet, goals for internet use, activities online, and self-reported dependency on the internet. Length of experience online and frequency of home use are the most important determinants for predicting different types of internet users, according to Howard et al. (2001a). They create a four-part typology ranging from newcomers to "netizens," with newcomers being more absorbed with games and social activities. As experience and frequency of use increase, internet users are more likely to engage in politics online or visit a government website, among other activities. Similarly, DiMaggio and Celeste (2004) find using other survey data that frequent use, experience, and education contribute to the deepening of activities online, including a higher likelihood of political engagement.

Technical skills and information literacy

In recent years, a number of scholars have drawn attention to skill requirements for internet use (Van Dijk, 2005; Warschauer, 2003; Mossberger et al., 2003). The ability to use hardware and software is often the focus of technical support and computer training, but for some of these technical skills at least, practice may be more important than formal education (Van Dijk, 2005: 90).

Internet use demands other skills as well, which blend educational competencies with internet-specific knowledge. These include information literacy (Mossberger et al., 2003; Warschauer, 2003) or the ability to search for, locate, evaluate, and use information online. Information literacy applied to the online context requires the ability to ask good questions, to understand search engines and search strategies, to think critically about the validity of information, and to apply the information to solve problems (American Library Association, 1989). One study of a hundred randomly recruited participants observed their ability to search online for information on political candidates, tax forms, and jobs, among other topics. Fully 15 percent failed to complete three or more of the tasks, despite being given all the time they needed to find the information (Hargittai and Shafer, 2006). In national surveys, 37 percent of respondents have said that they need help finding information on the internet. Respondents who reported needing help to use computers or locate information online were the same groups that were least likely to have home access (and therefore, frequent access)—the poor, less-educated, older individuals, African-Americans, and Latinos (Mossberger *et al.*, 2003).

Reading skills are critical

Even more fundamental for following or participating in politics on the internet is basic literacy or the ability to read and write. The internet is a reading-intensive medium similar to print media. This partially accounts for its potential richness and depth as a source of political information, but it also makes information use challenging for those with limited reading comprehension. Despite the multimedia environment online, Warschauer (2003) has pointed out that writing dominates content on the internet, and that the ability to use technology effectively also requires the management of online communications (including writing skills).

Variation in literacy could be expected to affect politics online even more than some other activities on the internet that require less reading and background knowledge.

National surveys from the early 1990s estimated that nearly a fifth of the U.S. population operated at the lowest level of literacy (able to do little more than to locate the appropriate line for a signature or to locate an item in a short passage). At least another quarter of the population has limited comprehension of longer and more complex text (Kaestle *et al.*, 2001; Kirsch *et al.*, 2002). Half of the American population reads at eighth-grade level or less, although content on government websites requires an average eleventh-grade reading-comprehension level (West, 2005: 54). As Warschauer (2003) has argued, information technology disparities are interwoven with other inequalities in society, including educational disparities.

Policy solutions beyond limited access

The predominant frame for public policy has failed to address these questions of skill as well as the regular use needed for digital citizenship. To date there have been real achievements in terms of extending internet connections and public access computing to 99 percent of the public libraries in the United States and to 92 percent of the schools (Gates Foundation, 2005; Kleiner and Lewis, 2003). Public access sites may offer resources for technical assistance and training, and have increased the ranks of those who have had some experience online. But, frequent internet use occurs most often at home, and use in places other than home or work is often intermittent (U.S. Department of Commerce/ NTIA, 2002).

The potential of municipal broadband

The movement toward free or very low-cost municipal broadband in the United States holds out the possibility of extending regular access to both rural and urban low-income communities, as well as the opportunity to study the effects of increased access in these communities as natural experiments. Bills for monthly internet services are often a greater obstacle for connectivity for low-income households than the one-time purchase of a computer (Schement and Scott, 2000), and so municipal broadband should help to expand the percentage of those who have internet access at home, as well as to upgrade connections for many others.

Comprehensive approaches to broadband opportunities

The provision of municipal broadband alone, however, may be insufficient to promote digital citizenship. Philadelphia, Chicago, and other major cities are also considering additional initiatives in low-income communities that will provide used computers, training, and support services for computer novices, and these are precisely the steps that are needed to make the most of increased connectivity (Mayor's Advisory Council, 2007). Currently, non-profit organizations such as One Economy have taken advantage of high-speed internet provision in some subsidized housing sites to offer a comprehensive array of technology-focused services. They provide training, support, a website with online content that is created by residents, and other information for low-income families, including information on job search, and the earned income tax credit (see www.thebeehive.org).

Federal funding has been cut for Community Technology Centers and other programs that once provided technology support and training. The diffusion of municipal broadband may bring in a new wave of internet users who could use such services, and there is reason to justify a government role in terms of access to e-government services as well as enabling political participation. The British government has announced that local authorities will provide universal local access to the internet by 2008, that public sector service delivery will be transformed through e-government, and that the internet will be used to address social exclusion more generally. The British government has identified persistent disparities, including the lack of necessary skills, as a barrier to economic development and realizing the full benefits of moving government services online. Plans include the expansion of U.K. Online Centres throughout the country, low-cost laptop leasing for students, and a Digital Challenge prize for local authorities (eGovernment News, 2005; U.K. Prime Minister's Strategy Unit and Department of Trade and Industry, 2005).

Tackling educational inequality is complex but necessary

Education is important for participating in the information-rich environment of politics both offline and online. The continued significance of race and ethnicity and the role of place also suggest the entanglement of technology inequalities with segregation, concentrated poverty, and unequal opportunities in education in the United States. While there are some who remain offline or sporadically connected because of a lack of interest in the technology, it is the poor and less educated who have limited choices in this regard. Inequities in poor schools must be addressed if all are to have a chance to participate equally in the information age. Adult education, literacy programs, and post-secondary programs in community colleges are also part of what will be needed to promote digital citizenship.

Conclusion

More Americans are online and are increasingly using information technology to engage in politics and to interact with government. Yet, there is wide variation in the ability to participate online, structured by age, education, income, race, and ethnicity. Age differences may diminish over time as have those based on gender, but other digital disparities are embedded in larger patterns of social inequality. Without addressing this unequal capacity for digital citizenship, the internet portends greater political inequality, mobilizing and engaging some while further marginalizing others. This may redouble the disadvantages of lower income and less educated individuals, who are already less likely to participate, and who have less influence on public policy than other citizens (Norris, 2001b; Jacobs and Skocpol, 2005). At the same time, however, the engagement of young people online indicates the exciting potential of the internet to reinvigorate politics after decades of declining participation and trust and confidence in government.

Contributions to this book and previous research demonstrate why widespread digital citizenship is crucial for the democratic process and for equality of voice and representation. Information is a critical resource for participation both online and offline, and as Bimber (2003) has argued, the growing abundance of political information online raises the costs of exclusion from the medium. Networks facilitate political participation (Verba et al., 1995), and the internet offers these in new forms, with the possibility of transcending geographic location and forming new communities of interest (McFarland, 2007).

Those who cannot effectively use the internet are politically disadvantaged. They are cut off from sources of information about politics that differ from other media in their richness and diversity. They are barred from electronic networks that can encourage mobilization, discussion, and information exchange in ways that are demonstrably significant for civic engagement, voting, and other participation. Low-income individuals have greater need for public services, and their isolation from the benefits of e-government may mean that they are less aware of available resources or are less able to take advantage of services. Access to politics and government on the internet offers a compelling rationale for attention to internet use as a policy issue in a democratic society. Research on the consequences of online politics and e-government also must pay attention to the effects of unequal capacity to utilize this important medium of communication, mobilization, and information.

Guide to further reading

Information on digital inequality in the United States is rapidly changing because of new surveys that are frequently available showing increases in the exact percentages of the population online; still, as this chapter has showed, many patterns of disparities have remained over time. Some older scholarly work is still worth examining for the concepts or theoretical arguments presented, although the survey data are now dated. Norris' (2001b) book on the *Digital Divide* is interesting for its cross-national, comparative approach and for linking technology disparities to civic participation. Katz and Rice (2002) present a good overview of the early diffusion of the internet from the mid 1990s and employ multivariate statistics to examine these trends. Their discovery of internet dropouts is also a contribution to the literature. Using more recent data from a variety of sources and multivariate methods, Mossberger et al. (2003) examine the idea of digital citizenship and evidence of its impact on civic engagement, political participation, and economic opportunity. The chapter on technology inequalities includes a detailed analysis of patterns within subgroups of the population. This shows variation in factors that influence technology use among African-Americans or Latinos, for example, as well as among low-income, less educated, older, and younger Americans. Warschauer (2003) discusses internet use as social inclusion, and has an excellent chapter examining multiple literacies needed for internet use. He employs qualitative case studies from a number of places, including Egypt and India as well as Los Angeles to argue that internet use must be placed in a meaningful social context for individuals if they are to adopt the technology. Van Dijk's (2005) book lacks the original quantitative or qualitative data of the other studies cited here, but his discussion of a deepening divide based on unequal capacities online is worthwhile. The Pew Internet and American Life Project (www.pewinternet.org) has continually updated survey research on online activities and attitudes toward information technology in the U.S. Many of the reports do not include multivariate analysis, but they have a gold mine of relevant reports and trend data.

14

Online news creation and consumption

Implications for modern democracies

David Tewksbury and Jason Rittenberg

This chapter examines how citizens acquire political information using the internet. For some time, researchers have been looking at the form of news online and how news audiences find (or at least encounter), consume, and retain political content there. The available literature suggests that major news outlets rarely create content exclusively for the online audience. In fact, news online is often similar to what one finds in print newspapers. Internet audiences are increasingly likely to seek news online, but there is little evidence thus far that this has resulted in replacement of print newspapers and television news. Online audiences tend to limit their reading to topics of special interest to them, though not to the extent that some observers expected. There is some evidence that learning from the news is different online than off. The reviewed research on learning from online news suggests that the national news audiences may become fragmented if they rely on the internet for their news consumption. This finding has implications for understanding the distribution of political knowledge and issue agendas within nations today and in the future.

Contemporary versions of democratic theory tend to hold citizens to a relatively high standard. As the keystone of democracies, citizens are expected to pay attention to local, regional, national, and international public affairs and to acquire information they can use to formulate opinion (Berelson, 1952; cf., Schudson, 1998). The strongest version of this requirement suggests that citizens should be ever-vigilant; responsibility for acquiring information primarily rests with them. A more moderate expectation acknowledges that news is selectively presented by media sources and that public affairs information vies with other information for public attention (Lippmann, 1922). This contest is most visible in newscasts, front pages, and other news venues. A reasonable set of expectations of citizens recognizes that their selection of public affairs news is a partial function of what is available and how it is presented.

Recent normative and research treatments of news audiences have focused on how people respond to expanding content options, particularly those options that have multiplied with the introduction of high-bandwidth media. If audiences were to choose content at random, heedless of cues and enticements offered by media producers, the large number of content options online would decrease the probability of any one option being selected. Of course, few audience members choose entirely at random; content producers (e.g., news editors) exercise substantial influence over what people choose to read in print and online (Graber, 1988; Eveland and Dunwoody,

1998). Basic processes of media development suggest that online content providers will develop focused sites containing content of interest to a small segment of the news audience (Merrill and Lowenstein, 1979). This segmentation strategy could result in audience members consuming only a fraction of the range of possible current affairs information. The internet provides opportunities for users to pre-select their news preferences such that they are able to avoid entire categories of news online. The ultimate version of this process is what Negroponte (1995: 153) dubbed "*The Daily Me.*" Some researchers have suggested that specialized news sites and delivery options will fracture the national news audience into internally homogeneous groups (Sunstein, 2001). The result will be a polarized nation, with divisions in knowledge and opinions becoming increasingly prevalent.

Writing about the segmentation of audiences through cable television and other high-bandwidth media, Katz (1996) put a decidedly normative spin on changes in audience knowledge. He suggested that segmentation of the audience in modern democracies was part of larger patterns of increasing social segmentation in these countries. He decried this development, suggesting that common public spaces where ideas and issues are discussed for a general audience can be highly functional for democratic nations. As a result of audience fragmentation, common public perceptions and agendas are less likely to emerge (Chaffee and Metzger, 2001). Thus, any development toward segmentation (and, therefore, fragmentation) could ultimately weaken modern democracies (Katz, 1996).

At the same time, some observers have suggested that online news media may give audiences more independence in choosing what news to view and more power over processes of news production and presentation (Corrado, 1996; Havick,

2000). The wealth of news content online available on traditional and internet-only outlets and the high levels of selectivity and interactivity these sites provide are often thought to free citizens, at least partially, from the hierarchical power of news editors and to increase citizen's involvement with political information and the public sphere.

This chapter provides a review of both the recent literature on news on the internet and the concepts researchers use to define the potential effects of the medium. Our goal is to identify a set of findings and ideas that researchers, critics, and policy-makers can use to think about certain effects of the internet. The review begins with some background on how media effects researchers have thought about comparing the effects of exposure to news in different media. We turn from there to the growing literature on the presentation of news online. Our goal here is to identify whether and how news on the internet is different from what audiences may find in the traditional media (for a discussion of the structure medium comparisons, see Eveland, 2003). The focus then turns to how people are using the internet for news consumption and whether that consumption has an effect on what and how people learn about public affairs. Finally, we will draw on the literature dealing with online news reading to discuss a set of concepts that we hope will help readers of this handbook consider and study how online news consumption operates in contemporary society.

The content and form of online news

The internet is clearly technologically distinct from the traditional news media (Eveland, 2003). Even online news sites differ significantly from each other (Deuze,

2003). Our review focuses on the main-stream news sites, which have the most traffic of news content providers (Alexa Web Service, 2007). Research differentiating online news from traditional news has emphasized three facets: creation, content, and design; we adopt that approach.

Creation

Editors play a crucial role in the production of news for any medium (White, 1964). Research shows that web editors mostly reproduce stories from the print version of their papers (Singer, 2003), with additional content coming from wire services or interactive features (Boczkowski, 2004b). Comparatively small staffs (Singer, 2006) and the success of reproducing stories (Houston, 1999) contribute to this practice. However, surveys of editorial staffs suggest an ongoing interest among editors in providing additional perspective pieces online (Cassidy, 2005), which may encourage users to view the online version as a supplement to print. Research suggests web editors make content choices with such a goal in mind (Garrison, 2005). A study of Colorado newspapers found editors recognizing a disproportionately local audience by including proportionally more local news than the print version (Singer, 2001). Again, research thus far has identified few attempts to generate original content, even for local stories.

Theoretically, news sites should publish more stories and run them with more updates than would be the case in the offline media (Dessauer, 2004), and some studies have found evidence that audiences specifically go online for news when big events occur (Salaverria, 2005; Tewksbury, 2006). Cohen (2002) suggests that the haste to publish breaking news online may warrant a re-thinking of the concept of newsworthiness. Faster publication times appear to give websites an agenda-setting advantage, and ongoing

research is evaluating whether online papers are leading traditional media, or simply beating them to the punch. For example, a study of South Korean news agendas found an online paper influencing a wire service (Lim, 2006).

Agenda building can also occur through opportunities people have for requesting and generating content (Deuze, 1999). In a review of public journalism research, Witt (2004) notes that the public appears to exert some influence over news content, and Zhou and Moy (2007) demonstrate the ability of online public discussions to shape issue frames in the news. Weblogs (blogs) are perhaps the most discussed channels for this ground-up communication (Pavlik, 2001). Some researchers (for example, Shah et al., 2005) suggest that user discussions should produce comparatively strong mobilizing effects, and American Presidential campaigns have used blogs to generate excitement among supporters (Lawson-Borders and Kirk, 2005). Lynch (2005) has reported a similar community forming around blogs and chat rooms in the Middle East, with the former being particularly used by violent political minorities.

Perhaps the image of the audience is different for mainstream and alternative sites, which has led to the mainstream's limited acceptance of new formats (for a discussion of alternative sources, see Davis, 2005). Some mainstream news sites encourage editorialists and reporters to maintain blogs and utilize discussion (Imfeld and Scott, 2005). However, research by Boczkowski (2002) suggests they have a limited impact on the creation of the news. Another reason for hesitancy is posited by Lowrey and Anderson (2005), who suggest that the increase in public journalism may undermine perceptions of mainstream news and even change what counts as news. However, successful community-building around news topics most likely has positive implications for society, and the implications of public journalism and alternative news formats should be a subject of further research.

Content

Predictably, content analyses of online newspapers have found few differences from print versions (Barnhurst, 2002). However, even subtle differences in content are worth noting; research by Eveland and Dunwoody (2001a) suggests learning occurs differently for online news. Early observers expected internet sources would eagerly provide mobilizing information (i.e., information that allows or encourages audiences to act on issues and events in the news), at least as a means of attracting an audience (Hume, 1996). Instead, studies have found few differences between the offerings of print and online papers (Hoffman, 2006), with the main variation coming in the form of additional community information (Singer, 2001). Print and web editors alike report valuing mobilizing information online (Cassidy, 2005), potentially explaining the limited variation. A more encouraging study suggests that online news fosters more discussion than print news (Shah et al., 2005), which indicates increased public participation with the news.

Design

The availability of space and opportunity for interactivity online suggests that the design of news sites should provide the biggest differences between traditional media and online news. The aesthetic design of news sites has received little attention from research. Li (1998) found major news sites emphasizing text and leaving most of the graphic space to advertisers, creating a product little different from a newspaper. Remediation theory (see Bolter and Gruisin, 1999) and

interface development (Manovich, 2001) predict visual convergence for all news media. In fact, a study of news presentation by Cooke (2005) found print papers increasingly using thumbnail-sized pictures during the 1990s, and both TV and online news adopting modular layouts.

The strongest diverging point for online news is the use of interactivity. This term has been applied loosely, despite attempts to explicate the concept (Kiousis, 2002). Interactivity is typically divided between categories such as control over content, customization, and participation (Dessauer, 2004). Alternatively, Deuze (2003) advocates discussing news in terms of connectivity, encompassing hypertext, multimedia, and interactivity as distinct components.

Hypertext plays a significant role in the interpretation of political information (see Sundar et al., 2003). Tremayne (2004) finds that linked stories become both more episodic as related information is removed from the stories, but also more contextual as relevant materials are embedded as links within the text. The result is better information only if the user follows the links. Research has also identified increased presentation of other interactive elements. Photograph slide shows and user polls became more common with coverage of the 2000 presidential campaign (Singer and Gonzalez-Valez, 2003), while personalized information such as interactive maps or itemized candidate comparisons were popular during coverage in 2004 (Singer, 2006). Such additional content may make up for the lack of original news stories online (Palser, 2004). Massey and Luo (2005) find that sites use as much interactivity as their resources allow, but other research finds editorial perceptions of the target audience a strong predictor (Boczkowski, 2004b). Anticipating audience desires may be a rather complex determinant; however, as research suggests personality types predict enjoyment of interactive features (Chan and Leung, 2005).

Research results are mixed about the potential benefits of interactive news formats. Eveland and his coauthors have found mixed results for online learning. Similarly mixed results have been found for interactivity, which is capable of increasing return rates but also of decreasing recall (Sundar, 2000). Perloff (2003) does note that video games, which are highly interactive can increase message effectiveness, but this is not necessarily a benefit in the context of the news. A realistic, but optimistic, viewpoint suggests two implications of multimedia and interactive elements on news sites. First, there is a significant chance that these elements will provide better educated audiences with more information, potentially worsening knowledge gaps (Prior, 2005). Second, online news is perhaps akin to soft news as it is not especially informative but may do well in attracting otherwise disinterested audiences. More research is certainly required to assess the changing nature and subsequent implications of online news features.

Online news, at least as it is presented in the mainstream sites, is not yet significantly different from traditional news. This lack of distinction is particularly disappointing in the area of mobilizing information. On the positive side, interactivity has improved over time, and there are more (potentially) useful features now included with stories. The onus lies with the reader to make use of the available benefits of online news, because the additional content is not in a readily scannable format. It appears that in the near future the important question regarding online news is not "what?" but "how?"

Audience use of online news

Recognizing the importance of user control as a primary characteristic of the internet, understanding public use of the web for news requires answering several questions. First, why do people use the internet for obtaining political information? Second, how do people read the news online, including both site and content choices? Technological characteristics and individual factors play a role in each level of choice.

Getting news online

The likelihood of using the internet for political information gain has increased over time. The internet audience was on the rise before 2000 (Norris, 2001a), but the events of September 11, 2001 seem to have been a catalyst for online news use. September 12 was a record day of internet news access, but other events during the following months drove traffic to news sites in similar patterns (Rappoport and Alleman, 2003). Horrigan and Rainie (2002) show that internet users turn to the medium first for most types of information. Although the news environment has changed drastically over the last decade, the internet is only part of the story. Cable news and talk radio have also risen, while print and broadcast news use have dropped (Norris, 2001a). These patterns suggest replacement of traditional sources (Dimmick *et al.*, 2004). Other research indicates that users follow complementary patterns (Dutta-Bergman, 2004), using online papers only to get updates or to use interactive features (Rathman, 2002).

Part of the decision to use online news is the belief that the internet is a credible source of information. Relatively early studies by Sundar (1999) suggest the complexity of online credibility, based on more considerations than merely evaluations of traditional media. A series of studies by Johnson and Kaye (see 2002) found that online news was viewed as more credible than the traditional media, although both were rated no better than "somewhat" credible. Other studies have looked at credibility ratings of online news by particular groups of users. Choi et al. (2006) found opponents of the war in Iraq rating online news as more credible than traditional media. Johnson and Kaye (2004) found blog readers rating these sites as most credible, with other online news performing no better than the traditional media. The findings highlight the significance of site selection once the user is online.

Reading the news online

As a medium that allows a high level of user control, the internet requires many more decisions from the user, including what source to select. Factors that play a role in source selection include browsing skill (Hargattai, 2002), site popularity (Webster and Lin, 2002), structure and information (Richard, 2004), in addition to personal choice. For example, Best et al. (2005) found that about 25 percent of all news users access foreign sites, with those most opposed to the Bush administration most likely to look abroad for information.

Once on a site, selection can again determine news exposure (Eveland and Dunwoody, 1998). Part of the determination is the user's goals for the browsing session (Sanchez-Franco and Roldan, 2005). For example, New York Times online traffic patterns suggest an audience with an atypical interest in international affairs (Wu and Bechtel, 2002). Structurally, sites can influence story selection by incorporating recommendation systems, which are most effective when "other users" choose stories (Sundar and Nass, 2001), and the "others" ratings are linearly related to selection (Knobloch-Westerwick et al., 2005). In this way, features of contemporary new sites give users the ability to bypass or supplement the traditional gatekeeping power of editors.

The importance of selection suggests that uses and gratifications theories of media are appropriate for internet effects research (Chaffee, 2001), but the current glut of definitions is problematic. Tewksbury and Althaus (2000) found support for applying traditional news gratifications: entertainment, surveillance, and passing time. Kaye and Johnson (2004) studied entertainment and information-seeking, as well as guidance-seeking and convenience. Information-seeking, but not entertainment, was supported by Flavian and Gurrea (2006). LaRose and Eastin (2004) found status-seeking a strong motivator of web use. Until consistent results are established, the best lesson from these studies is that people select websites at least partially based on personal motivations (Tewksbury, 2005a).

Specialization is another promising line of research for understanding of how people select news, particularly by exploring the choice to limit oneself to a few sources and topics. An analysis of naturally occurring online news reading patterns found that audiences of different news sites tend to be relatively distinct from one another (Tewksbury, 2005a). A parallel analysis of reader behavior at popular online news sites suggests the presence of reader clusters who limit their exposure to a small number of topics (Tewksbury, 2005b). Not all people specialize their reading, however. Some clusters sample broadly from the available news (Tewksbury, 2005b). Thus, the evidence gathered thus far suggests some element of site and audience specialization.

The research on internet use suggests the choice to get news online has been a function of time. The more exposure people have to the web, the more likely they are to get news there. There is debate over the nature of cross-media use in the public, but complementary uses seem well-supported by research. Once online, the user has the freedom to select sites and stories based on personal goals and design cues, but the nature of these motivations remains unclear. Ultimately, it is the impact of these choices that most interests media effects scholars.

The effects of reading news online

A number of effects of citizen use of online news services have been studied empirically. Much of the research has examined what people learn online and offline and how that learning influences issue agendas. This research typically examines the impact of users' online behavior and how the relationship between news content and citizens' normative roles may be changing over time.

Survey-based studies of learning effects

Survey studies have produced mixed assessments of the potential for learning from online news. Measures of general internet use (Johnson *et al.*, 1999) and online news seeking (Scheufele and Nisbet, 2002) have failed to correlate with domestic U.S. political knowledge. However, online news seeking has been shown to predict international affairs knowledge (Kwak *et al.*, 2006). More developed measures of news content sought online may improve future research. After all, the most prominent attribute of the internet is that it can be all things to all people.

While much research has focused on intentional learning from news, some studies have suggested that people can accidentally receive information from traditional media (Zukin and Snyder, 1984) and the internet (Tewksbury *et al.*, 2001). The Pew Research Center for the People and the Press (2004) reports that as many as half of internet users report coming across news (at hub sites like Yahoo! and

America Online, presumably) when going online for other purposes. Tewksbury *et al.* (2001) report that these people, with other news exposure controlled, know a bit more about current affairs in the news than do other internet users.

Incidental contact with the political news at internet hubs cannot compensate for users' focused attention on content that fits their particular non-political information or entertainment preferences. Looking at diversification of content on cable television and on the internet, Prior (2005: 580) reports that surveyed people with a "relative entertainment preference"—the extent to which people will choose entertainment over news—take advantage of the diversity of content on newer media to focus on entertainment and, by extension, avoid news (however, the pattern was not consistent across a number of tests). Prior observes that because people with political knowledge are less likely to prefer entertainment to news, the diversity of content online may exacerbate existing knowledge gaps.

Experiment-based studies of learning effects

Two experiment-based studies examined the connection between what news people choose online and their knowledge of current affairs. Tewksbury and Althaus (2000) found that online news readers select public affairs topics less frequently than their print newspaper counterparts. Looking at current affairs in terms of both national and international news (Althaus and Tewksbury, 2002) and the prominence of the news (Tewksbury and Althaus, 2000), the online readers acquired less of the political content in *The New York Times* than did the print readers of the paper.

A replication of this study failed to observe differences between readers of print and online versions of two prominent Dutch newspapers (D'Haenens *et al.*, 2004; see also Eveland *et al.*, 2002). The striking feature of the outlets examined in the Dutch study is that the print versions of the papers contained more stories than did the online versions and some categories of news (international news) were better represented online than offline. Thus, it does not appear that online versions offered the diversity of content that researchers have identified as a key component of audience distraction from political information online. This result highlights the difficulties inherent in predicting the effects of internet use when the medium does not have the constraints and traditions that define and limit the structure of news on television and in print newspapers. One online news source can be very different in its inclusion and presentation of public affairs news from another. As a result, it can be difficult for one to know, on average, how the stories will be presented when people look at news online.

The psychology of learning online

From a theoretical perspective, there is some reason to expect people will learn more from web-based news presentation than from traditional print news. Web-based news gives users more control over the flow and presentation of news, and the hyperlinked nature of news online may mimic the associative network structure of human memory (Eveland and Dunwoody, 2001a). Perhaps surprisingly, empirical research has not supported these expectations. Indeed, research in this area suggests that the online environment may not be particularly conducive to acquiring information. For example, Sundar (2000) observed that the addition of audio and video downloads to print stories online lowered news recall and recognition.

Eveland and Dunwoody's work on news processing online provides some explanations for studies showing lower recall of online news. Eveland and Dunwoody (2002) suggest that separating the extent to which people cognitively elaborate on the news they read online from the amount of selective scanning of online content they do ("picking and choosing among information" 2002: 38) should isolate the factors that can encourage and discourage learning from online news. They find that people reading news on a website engage in both more elaboration of the news and selective scanning of the presented information. The former process leads to greater learning of information and the latter tends to suppress it. These tendencies partially counteract each other, leading to a net effect of reduced learning online (see also, Tremayne and Dunwoody, 2001).

Eveland and colleagues have subsequently suggested that exposure to online news may have benefits beyond the recall of factual news information. Eveland *et al.* (2004) suggest that news sites' use of hyperlinks in stories may encourage readers to consider the connections between bits of information. The result is that online readers may develop structures of knowledge more dense than their linear (i.e., non-hyperlinked) news reading counterparts. Indeed, Eveland *et al.* (2004) find that linear online news readers learn more from a story than readers of hyperlinked stories, but the latter exhibit more dense knowledge structures regarding the news topics. Thus, there are suggestions that researchers looking at citizen acquisition of information from online news sources should be conscious of the way they conceptualize information. The density of knowledge structures may carry very different normative weight in terms of what and how people learn about public affairs.

Agenda building and agenda setting

If mainstream news sites are largely replicating their traditional media versions, then clearly these sites are not uniquely involved in setting the public agenda, at least not in a meaningful way. One area of note is the influence of alternative sites, particularly blogs, on public and media agendas. Anecdotal evidence offers several notable examples, particularly blog activity regarding U.S. Senator Trent Lott's comments about Strom Thurmond in 2002 (Lawson-Borders and Kirk, 2005). Blogs are relatively good at maintaining and developing interest in under-served stories (Pew Research Center, 2005), particularly when those stories are partisan, previously discussed, or from non-elite sources (Lowrey, 2006). The practice of posting snippets and linking leaves many stories fragmented but still able to offer worthwhile material (Wall, 2005). In fact, an analysis of external linking practices suggest that blogs are well suited to complement mainstream media, by both building stories and by channeling readers back to mainstream sites (Reese et al., 2007).

Related to the impact of the new media on the traditional media agenda is the question of whether readers of online news may develop issue agendas that differ from those of audiences of the traditional media. One expectation researchers have suggested is that readers of online news outlets may be exposed to a smaller variety of issues by virtue of their ability to focus their news selection (Schoenbach et al., 2005). Using a survey approach, Schoenbach et al. find that online newspaper use *increases* the number of social topics readers consider important, but only for the most educated members of the sample. Thus, an overall agenda shrinking effect was not observed. Althaus and Tewksbury (2002) tested a weaker version of the effect in their experiment with *New York Times* readers. They found that online readers care less about the sorts of topics that show up in the public affairs sections of the paper.

The overall normative tone of this research is mixed. Some studies of the learning effects of news media are decidedly pessimistic. Online news readers may learn less about public affairs than do their offline counterparts, and a similarly dystopian view is advanced in the research on audience agenda acquisition. However, an expanded view of online learning suggests that, to the extent that online news readers choose public affairs news, they may acquire more densely structured knowledge than if they had read a print newspaper. At the same time, a number of studies have shown that frequent use of the internet (e.g., news reading, e-mail, etc.) is positively associated with online and offline political participation (Hardy and Scheufele, 2005; Tolbert and McNeal, 2003). What is more, there is mounting evidence that citizen online political activity (e.g., blogging) may influence mainstream and online news agendas and so indirectly influence the political process.

This seeming normative paradox is illustrative of a basic feature of advanced media, of which the internet is perhaps the most extreme case. The internet, broadcast radio, magazines, and cable television, to varying degrees, allow their users to focus their exposure on topics and activities that interest them. For the bulk of Americans, the internet offers the opportunity to choose their own news, as it were, to the exclusion of political information (Tewksbury, 2003). Thus, these advanced media at the end of their natural evolution as media forms (Merrill and Lowenstein, 1979) give perhaps too much freedom, some researchers seem to assert. At the same time, the politically interested can take the reins of the abundance of political information online to build their engagement with politics and become more efficacious than may have been possible some 20 years ago.

Online news audiences: united, divided, and empowered

Our review of the literature suggests that developing an understanding of how online news distribution may influence individuals and society can be profitably undertaken by looking separately at how news is organized online (on its own and in contrast to how it is organized offline), how people use the internet, select sites, and choose individual news stories, and what they learn from the news they consume. This multi-part analysis nicely parallels what researchers and other observers have said about the potential effects of the internet on American society. There is a fair number of terms used in the literature to describe how the internet today and in the future may be affecting political knowledge, agendas, and, possibly, opinion. What follows is a review and integration of these normatively based concerns. The resolution and integration of the terms should provide researchers with some tools to apply to ongoing research regarding the political effects of internet news consumption.

Specialization

Content selection and specialization figured prominently in this review. *Specialization is what people do.* It is their tendency to focus their reading on specific topics. It can take many forms relevant for the development of segmentation, fragmentation, and polarization. Specialization in online selection can take the most direct form of audiences failing to read news content at all. Indeed, relative to what

one finds on television or in a newspaper, news online represents a substantially smaller portion of the total content the medium offers. It may be easier than ever before for citizens to omit news reading and not be reminded of that fact (this assumes low levels of the incidental online news learning online described above). Even when users seek the news, their site choices can be based on selecting sources known for specific categories of news. Thus, selection at the level of websites could result in an overall reduction in political knowledge in specialized audiences.

Specialization can also take the form of audiences selecting specific news topics when they go online, a phenomenon for which researchers have found some evidence (Tewksbury, 2005b). Specialization of news selection may be conceptualized on three dimensions. The first is the consistency of topic selection. For example, someone who occasionally selects international news is less specialized than someone who selects international news each time he or she gets news online. The second dimension is the depth of exposure. This is essentially the quantity of reading a person does on a selected topic. The amount of focused learning that comes from specialization should be different for a reader who selects one story on a favored topic than for one who reads all available stories on a topic. This difference is all the more relevant in the happy chance (from a normative view) that the selected topic concerns public affairs. The final dimension of specialization is the exclusivity of exposure. The issue here is whether specialized internet users are focused on one, two, or more topics when they choose news stories. It is easy to think of the one- or two-topic reader as specialized, as most readers do not specialize on a large number of topics (Krosnick, 1990). One could still consider a citizen who focuses on a half-dozen topics or more as specialized, but the meaning of the term begins to collapse. Specialization at that point does not carry the same implications for the distribution of political knowledge as it does were we to imagine that all news readers focused exclusively on one topic. Thus, it may be necessary to set some a priori standard for when specialization by news readers becomes normatively relevant.

Segmentation

If specialization is what users do, *segmentation is what content producers do*—inasmuch as these are separate roles online. Segmentation is the tendency for sites to tailor their content to specific groups (typically defined by demographic characteristics) of interest to advertisers or others willing to provide sites with revenue (cf., Katz, 1996). Theories of media history argue that systems progress from a stage in which most media outlets serve large, heterogeneous audiences to one in which most outlets serve smaller, internally homogenous audiences (Merrill and Lowenstein, 1979). To the extent that specific demographic groups are drawn to separate sites, one can talk about the range of online content being segmented (of course, a website can segment users within subdivisions of the site, as well).

Fragmentation

Fragmentation is the outcome of people specializing their news exposure and/or site producers segmenting the audience. Fragmentation is the lack of widespread public exposure to some content of interest. When fragmentation in a group or society is advanced, information is distributed over the population but is not widely shared by its members. It is what occurs when fewer people than before or desired receive a given piece of information. Thus, fragmentation may be best considered a social-level term that refers to the

likelihood that any one person knows any one piece of information. By definition, fragmentation is assessed relative to some past, desired, or optimal level of uniformity of political information holding.

Polarization

When fragmentation takes hold, polarization is one potential consequence. The possible segmentation of the news audience suggests that political knowledge in the population will not be reduced or fragmented in a random fashion. Rather, "to the extent that one subset of the audience comes to use [a] class of content whereas others tend not to use it, the mass audience can be said to have polarized" (Webster and Phalen, 1997: 111). The polarization of the news audience may come as the result of specialization in news reading. People may spend quite a bit of time online reading news, but they may focus entirely on sports, business, or some other content (Tewksbury, 2005b). If so, they may rarely seek public affairs content. As a result, they will not know as much about public affairs as the news readers who choose current events content. An even more focused type of polarization may result from people choosing content from within the public affairs domain. In this case, a yet unstudied possible tendency for people to specialize their news selection within political topics means that people may come to know quite a bit about one area (for example, international affairs or environmental policy) but little about some other domain (for example, education policy or health care policy).

The presence of issue publics in America is one bit of evidence to suggest that some people come to specialize their political information exposure (Converse, 1964; Krosnick, 1990). A recent study supports this suggestion. A combined observation of online information seeking and survey data collection showed that people concerned about a political issue are more likely to seek online information about the issue than are others (Kim, 2007). Similarly, a study of the personalization of internet portal sites found that when given a chance to select their own information pages, the selection of content and its placement on a page were determined, in part, by predispositions to seek certain kinds of content (Tewksbury and Maddex, 2001). In particular, that study showed that some people are quite willing to set up personalized news pages that omit such core public affairs content as international and political news.

Information democratization

At the same time that the internet provides opportunities for fragmentation and polarization—normative concerns based, perhaps, on the desirability of the mass public—it makes possible new avenues for citizen independence from mainstream news media and larger social forces. The depth of information that can be found on online news sites and the variety of content in blogs and other interactive sources gives users access to substantially more information than is available in other media. Once online, any user has access to essentially the same range of content as any other (subscription sites aside). Few would argue that knowledge gaps are impossible online. However, in many ways, the information-access advantage of economic status common offline is practically erased once someone obtains internet access. In addition, many online news sites give users the ability to post content online and interact with journalists through blogs and other forums, encouraging involvement with the news and, ultimately, politics. Finally, there is some evidence that citizen activity online may affect the agenda of news in the offline and online media, thus weakening the centralized gatekeeping role of mainstream news editors.

These elements of the internet suggest there is evolving *a democratization of the creation, dissemination, and consumption of news and information.* This information democratization comes from some of the forces that may also lead to fragmentation and polarization, but it suggests a very different normative perspective on internet news. As people seek and encounter a greater range and depth of information online, they are less likely to rely on centralized content producers. In effect, the marketplace of ideas, as an ideal and tool, is found more easily online than off. In that way the availability and structure of news online may be serving democratic ideals more effectively than are the features of the traditional media.

The bulk of the data suggests that online news readers have the ability to specialize their news reading to the point of both fragmenting and polarizing the news audience. There is less evidence to suggest that popular news sites are being designed to segment the audience, a pattern that appears to limit the likelihood of polarization occurring. Instead, polarization seems most likely to come from audiences taking advantage of personalization options on existing news services (e.g., internet hubs such as Yahoo! and AOL) and from actively focusing their reading on a select set of news topics. Sunstein (2001) has suggested that this pattern of use can result in a polarization of opinion. Were that to happen, divisions and conflicts over political parties, figures, and policies may become increasingly common. Accompanying processes of fragmentation and polarization is information democratization, a broadening of citizen control of, and access to, news and information. Thus, as people know less about what mainstream news editors think is important, they may know more about what other citizens think is important. The effect of a marketplace of ideas that is both large and diverse may be citizens more engaged with current events and politics but perhaps not as uniformly informed.

Conclusion

Almost all of the topics examined in this review require more investigation. The comments here are focused on areas with substantial normative weight and the greatest likelihood of future importance. More research is needed on the potential effects of online news presentation and selection on media and public issue agendas. The bulk of the findings on news content suggest few differences between online and offline outlets of the same organizations. Future research in this area might focus more attention on features of news presentation (for example, page placement, daily cycle and the movement of news on a site, or headline size) that might distinguish online news from offline and which might have some effect on audience agendas. The research reviewed here suggests the presence of some differences in the type of current affairs information people select online and off (Schoenbach et al., 2005; cf., Dutta-Bergman, 2004), but there is much more we can do in this area. If future audiences devote more time to reading news online than they do today, what the field knows about news availability and organization online suggests that basic agenda setting processes are in for some changes. One area of developing interest is the extent to which online discussion (for example, chat or blogs) may influence news content and agendas (Hopkins and Matheson, 2005). Thus, processes of agenda building as well as setting are potentially undergoing change.

Future research may profit from the application of the five concepts defined here. Researchers can conceptualize specialization as what audiences do in response to (or as the ultimate origin of, to some extent) the structure and content of news online. Segmentation is what websites do. Some news producers may fashion their sites to serve specific news audiences rather than follow the mass public model of traditional newspapers and television news. If so, they are essentially choosing to serve only segments of the citizenry. If people specialize and/or if news producers segment audiences, the results may be fragmentation and polarization. Fragmentation is the distribution of information over smaller segments of the public than is normatively desirable. Once that information is fragmented, polarization—the separation of information and opinion in relatively homogenous, isolated groups—is a likely outcome. Filling in some of the gaps created by fragmentation is a trend toward information democratization. By permitting the decentralization of information control online, relative to the traditional media, and by increasing the opportunities for citizens to access a range of political content, the internet may be enhancing political involvement and debate.

Future research might profitably examine more dimensions of the mobilizing potential of online news. The main findings reviewed here (Shah et al., 2005; Hoffman, 2006) suggest that there are not many differences in the amount of mobilizing information provided online and in print. Shah et al. (2005), however, suggest that interpersonal interaction options available online at news and other sites may have a larger impact on citizens than the presence of similar mobilizing information in print. Future research looking at online news might examine how news sites are continuing to integrate blogs and other means for citizens to interact among themselves and with news producers. It may be that the combination of the presence of mobilizing information and these interpersonal interactions may be particularly likely to activate citizen participation in politics.

Finally, there appears to be a need for investigation of whether online news reading patterns have implications for the presence or development of opinion polarization. Sunstein's (2001) discussion of polarization focuses on the segmentation of opinion groups online. The question for researchers is whether news reading online may play a role in such a process. It is certainly possible that specialized news reading may result from pre-existing audience polarization. Kim (2007) shows that when members of an issue public (not identified by partisanship, to be sure) go online for campaign information, they go to sites that focus on their pet issues. If citizens limit their exposure to opinions and information supporting their side of the issue, the widespread availability of that information online may foster greater opinion polarization. The field could use more research that examines whether people engage in that sort of selective exposure online. Research suggests that people are very selective on some occasions for some topics (Knobloch et al., 2003). The pivotal question is whether the online environment encourages and facilitates greater selectivity of this sort.

The evidence reviewed here suggests that audiences are willing to engage in some specialization of their news use online. Most internet news receivers appear to be using the medium to supplement their exposure to other news media, and this may leave them free to seek out their focused interests online. However, there is also evidence that many people use the internet as they use other media. If that is the case, there is little reason to expect that people will be particularly willing to specialize. At the same time, there is ample reason to suspect that

online news sites will increasingly be willing to engage in audience segmentation. Reviews of the history of media suggest that maturing media and outlets almost inevitably follow a path of increased segmentation. On the basis of these two considerations, there is reason to expect a substantial amount of fragmentation and—perhaps inevitably—polarization in the public. These trends are unlikely to be universal, of course, but they may noticeably affect the operation of democratic nations in the future. Fortunately, information democratization is also likely to expand in the near future. It is always threatened by seemingly inexorable forces of centralization and homogenization, but if any medium seems suited to the reduction of those threats, it is the internet. In sum, information democratization may be the more important long-term development facilitated by the internet.

Guide to further reading

This review focused, in part, on how the particular attributes of online news presentations affect which stories people select. Researchers looking at what people learn once they select the news could profit from the research on learning from hypermedia text. Eveland and Dunwoody (2001b) provide an excellent review of that literature. Webster and Phalen's discussion of the fragmentation and polarization potential of online new consumption proved a significant resource for this chapter. For background on those topics, and for a detailed discussion of conceptions of the mass audience in twentieth century media research, see Webster and Phalen (1997). Opinion polarization has received less attention in the recent research looking at online news media than have specialization and fragmentation. For a good discussion of the normative implications of opinion polarization, see Sunstein

(2001). In order to remain succinct, this review has focused on studies of online mainstream news since 2000. For a review of research on the production, use of, and interactivity in earlier online newspapers, see Boczkowski (2002). Davis (2005) provides insight on the social and political uses of chat rooms and blogs. Finally, readers may have found the discussion of technological characteristics of the internet (and the computer) limited. Please see Bolter and Grusin (1999) for a theoretical development of remediation and the strategies of immediacy and hypermediacy and Dessauer (2004) for a discussion of technology's implications for the development of online news.

15

Web 2.0 and the transformation of news and journalism

James Stanyer

The news environment in advanced industrial democracies is undergoing a tremendous series of changes driven by the emergence, spread, and evolution of the internet. The once ubiquitous scenario of a string of national, regional, and local news outlets with largely captive audiences and secure revenue streams is being reshaped. In a period of 15 years, the net has helped to further de-territorialize news markets, reconfigure media competition, fragment audiences, transform news reception and content production, and it has forced a reassessment of journalistic roles. At the same time, the big traditional news players have adapted to life online. It is this rapid period of evolution and its consequences for news and the wider democratic public sphere that forms the main focus of this chapter. Concentrating mainly on the United States, it considers: the degree to which the new digital news environment provides a greater diversity of information for citizens; the extent to which it enhances the expression of public opinion; and, finally, whether it democratizes the news-making process.

In just over a decade the news website has become a familiar feature of the news environment. There is no consensus about exactly when the first news outlet went online. Some suggest it was as early as 1990 in the United States, when seven newspapers could be accessed over the internet (Gunter, 2003). Others put forward the slightly later date of 1992 (Li, 2006). Much of the initial expansion, though, took place after the emergence of the World Wide Web and the dotcom boom of the late 1990s, which saw established news organizations invest millions of dollars in their web operations. An indication of the rapid expansion can be given through a quick survey of some figures. In 1994, 60 newspapers in the United States had websites. By 1998, depending on the source, there were between 1,600 and 2,000 newspapers with their own sites (Greer and Mensing, 2006;

Li, 2006), and all of the main news organizations had a website displaying news content by 1995 (Scott, 2005; Sparks, 2000). By 2002 the number of newspapers online had grown to 3,400 in the United States and 2,000 outside the United States (Gunter, 2003), although some put the figure higher. Li (2006), for instance, suggests that there are as many as 4,000 newspapers online in the United States, not counting other news outlets.

At the same time as the number of internet news sites expanded so has the audience for online news (see Deuze, 2003). Table 15.1 shows that the proportion of people who regularly consume news online grew by 29 percent from 1996 to 2006, while those using traditional offline outlets declined, though it should be noted that for many the internet complements offline news consumption and is not a substitute for it (see Ahlers, 2006).

Table 15.1 Regular news consumption in the United States by outlet, 1993–2006 (percent who regularly consume)

Medium/Year	1993	1996	2000	2004	2006
Evening network news	60	42	30	34	28
Local television news	77	65	57	59	54
Newspapers	58[1]	50	47	42	40
Cable television news	–	–	33[2]	38	34
Online news	–	2	23	29	31

Source: Compiled from Pew Research Center data, cited in Stanyer, 2007.

Notes:
1 = 1994 Figure; 2 = 2002 Figure.

Such developments are not limited to the United States. In the United Kingdom, for instance, during the first part of 2002, an average of 10.6 million people per month were accessing news websites, up by 3.5 million on November 2000 (Hargreaves and Thomas, 2002). In 2005, other research showed that 61 percent of British net users relied on it for news (Dutton *et al.*, 2005).

Over this time period the internet has also evolved. Currently, news outlets are adapting to what has been called Web 2.0. There is no agreed definition of this term, first popularized by O'Reilly Media. However, in the context of this chapter, it is taken as short-hand for a variety of changes relating to the look of content, speed of access, mobility, and content reception and production. Web content has evolved from largely text and graphics to include video and audio streaming. This is a result of a boost in network capacity due to the emergence and spread of broadband, meaning larger amounts of data can now be transferred at ever faster speeds. Further, wireless technology (wi-fi) has resulted in an increase in mobility. While Web 1.0 was mainly computer based and static, the public can now browse the web through mobile devices. Finally, not only can content be viewed on a variety of platforms, internet users can now more easily upload and disseminate text, audio, video, and digital photographs over the web. User-generated content sites such as Facebook, YouTube, and MySpace have become one of the most visible characteristics of Web 2.0 (Project for Excellence in Journalism, 2007).

News and Web 2.0

It is important to explore what these developments mean for the news. The most visible impact of Web 2.0 has been in the appearance of online news. News websites are no longer solely text and photograph based and video streaming has become a widespread feature. For example, a survey of over 80 newspaper websites in the United States in 1997 found that only 7 percent of websites had video content and 16 percent had audio content, but by 2003 44 percent of sites had both (Greer and Mensing, 2006). By 2005, online video had become a common feature on U.S. news websites (Project for Excellence in Journalism, 2006). Visitors to most of the leading news sites can view a whole bulletin or particular extracts. For instance, those browsing the main networks' websites can watch breaking news and segments from the evening news bulletins. In 2007, 37 percent of internet users said they watched news videos online (Madden, 2007).

The way news is accessed is also changing. News can be downloaded as a podcast from news websites and watched at the user's convenience. A survey in the United States found that 12 percent of internet users had downloaded podcasts from various news websites in 2006, compared with 7 percent in 2005 (Project for Excellence in Journalism, 2007). Although the numbers regularly downloading news output are small, these surge during important news events. In the United States, in the wake of Hurricane Katrina, in 2005, there were more than 10 million video clip downloads from the MSNBC website and 9 million from CNN (Project for Excellence in Journalism, 2006). Wireless technology is transforming news viewing, news bulletins can be sent to personal digital assistants or cell phones. In 2007, a survey found that 30 million internet users in the United States accessed the web from a mobile device (ComScore, 2007), with phone users regularly upgrading their cell phones these figures are certain to rise.

These changes mean that the time-linear appointment-to-view news bulletin is being replaced by a more bespoke service where the audience has the ultimate say about when and how information is consumed. Audience members can assemble their own mix of stories to suit their interest. This has empowered audiences to filter what they see/read to an unprecedented extent, facilitating the emergence of what Nicholas Negroponte has termed the *Daily Me*: "a communications package that is personally designed with each component fully chosen in advance" (Sunstein, 2001: 7). While new providers, like online news aggregators, might have pioneered personal newscasts, it is not just these new players that provide such facilities. A survey of over 80 newspaper websites in the United States found that the number of sites that allow audiences to customize their news consumption rose from 10 percent in 1997 to 24 percent in 2003 (Greer and Mensing, 2006)—a figure that is likely to have grown further.

While most of the major news sites now have well established interactive facilities such as message boards and e-mail the ability of audiences to contribute to news content has generally been more limited. However, Web 2.0 is transforming this situation. User-generated content has become a common feature of mainstream news outlets. Audiences are encouraged, and sometimes paid, to submit video footage and other material to news sites. Inspired by the success of user-generated news sites, like *ohmynewsinternational*, *wikinews*, and *digg*, some news outlets allow readers to write their own stories, particularly on local issues (Project for Excellence in Journalism, 2007). The professional staff reporter has been joined by the freelancers, compilers, amateur enthusiasts, and members of the public: the so-called "witness reporters" or "citizen journalists." Increasingly, as Dahlgren and Gurevitch (2005) observe, a large amount of the information in the online news environment does not originate from professional journalists but from amateurs.

In sum, online news has evolved from "shovelware" into increasingly sophisticated interactive output. In the world of Web 2.0, news can be accessed by a variety of portable devices. Through these different platforms audiences can not only view the stories they want at their convenience but also post content, even break news. These changes in news consumption and production, however, need to be seen as part of a wider series of developments in the news industry, as the next section will elucidate.

The reconfiguring of news markets

The geographical isolation, technological difference, and national regulation that for decades characterized the offline news environment are fast disappearing and this is altering radically the nature of competition between news organizations. This section explores the changing competitive dynamics of the online news environment.

Converging media sectors

Increasingly the old distinctions between media sectors no longer hold. Newspapers and news broadcasters now compete for the same audiences online (Sparks, 2000). For example, the television news networks ABC, CBS, Fox, and NBC and their affiliates vie not only with each other and cable providers, such as CNN, but also with a variety of regional and local newspapers. Those news providers with monopoly positions offline, like the city newspapers, have found themselves with new competitors online (Sparks, 2000). While the regional newspapers' monopoly is under threat, the news broadcasters have lost their competitive advantage in breaking news. During the aftermath of the Oklahoma City bombings in 1996, the importance of the net for breaking news became apparent. Local newspaper websites were able to relay the latest developments (Allan, 2006). Online, newspapers now break news live on a regular basis, and newspapers and broadcasters compete to be the first destination for audiences seeking news. These changes are not confined to the United States. In the United Kingdom, the television news networks BBC and ITN compete with the national press. British newspapers have invested in video streaming technology. For example, the *Guardian* now runs its own daily video news bulletin as well as producing a weekly show. The *Guardian* was also the first newspaper in Britain to run a "web first" policy, and now breaks foreign and business news on its site.

New niche news providers

As technology has reduced the cost of publicizing and distributing information—

traditionally a key entry barrier to the news and information market—the number of small news providers has increased (Anderson, 2006; Sparks, 2000). After what some observe as a "shake-out" of news providers in 2000—when new start-up news ventures went bust—there has been a growth of niche outlets that offer specialist news and information (see Scott, 2005). Some of these are low-budget independent news organizations run by amateurs, while others are commercial operations managed by professionals.

In local news markets, there has been a growth of so-called hyperlocal citizen media outlets, which make use of neighborhood user-generated content. One survey put their number at between 700 and 800—60 percent having started in 2005 (Project for Excellence in Journalism, 2007). Local websites or place blogs such as *Backfence, H20town, wadeonbirmingham. com,* and *Village Soup* provide what has been described as a fusion of "news and schmooze" (Project for Excellence in Journalism, 2007). In some cases it is not specific locales that internet-only news providers service, but linguistic minorities. California, Florida, and New Mexico have seen a flourishing of Spanish-language news websites that provide for a growing Hispanic immigrant audience. There are some 18 Spanish-language newspapers online in Florida alone.

There has been a growth of sites that cater for specific audience interests on business, sport, politics, and many lifestyle trends. For example, a recent survey of the top 100 blogs in the United States found that 34 percent were devoted to technology, 26 percent to culture, 25 percent to politics, and 3 percent to other issues (Project for Excellence in Journalism, 2007). There has also been an expansion of outlets serving audiences who want their news and information with a liberal or conservative flavor. There are news magazines such as *Salon, Slate,* and *CNet* to name a few, many bank-rolled by venture capital or owned by other media (Scott, 2005). In addition, there are one-person operations. Individual blogs such as the *Daily Kos, MyDD, Wonkette, Andrew sullivan.com, Littlegreenfootballs, Instapundit,* and *Powerline* offer comment and information for liberal and conservative audiences, including journalists and politicians. For example, the left-leaning *Daily Kos,* started in 2002, has steadily built an audience. According to Compete.com, between May 2006 and May 2007 it attracted a monthly average of around 300,000 unique visitors (see also Project for Excellence in Journalism, 2007).

Another particularly well documented group of internet-only providers, on the left of the political spectrum, are the so called "independent" news organizations (Deuze, 2003). Outlets such as *the Guerilla News Network, the Alternative Press Center,* and *Indymedia* are among the most well known of the alternative web-based operations, which seek to cover issues neglected by mainstream news (see Deuze, 2003; Scott, 2005). For example, *Indymedia* or the Independent Media Center was formed in 1999, to provide an alternative perspective on the anti-World Trade Organization (WTO) protests in Seattle. It is a network of around 150 media centers in roughly 45 countries (Allan, 2006). Its coverage of the WTO protests in Seattle, in 1999, attracted some 1.5 million unique hits (Allan, 2006).

Online news aggregators

Another type of internet-only outlet is the news aggregator. These sites do not produce their own unique content but instead allow audiences to access material from news agencies and other news outlets. Non-news producing internet service providers and search engines have taken advantage of their first destination status to provide their visitors with access to

wide variety of news content produced elsewhere. The most high-profile names include Google, AOL, and Yahoo! (Project for Excellence in Journalism, 2006). While most allow visitors to access the latest breaking news from a range of editorially selected sources, Google News, launched in 2001, provides its audience with access to the most popular news stories as determined by algorithmic software and not a team of editors. The site searches over 10,000 news sources from around the world before compiling information for its users (Allan, 2006).

In sum, the news markets of the pre-internet era are being reconfigured. The old geographical and technological divides are disappearing and the once dominant position of the main national news providers is coming to an end. The emergence of news aggregators, niche providers, and non-U.S. outlets means competition to be the first news destination is intensifying and internationalizing.

Market leaders

While the numbers of news and information providers online has increased dramatically, precisely how citizens use these sources is far from clear. While it is difficult to gain a definitive picture of the habits of American news audiences, Nielsen data provide some insight into their behavior. Table 15.2 shows the most popular news websites in the United States, as judged by average monthly visitor numbers.

It reveals that eight out of the top ten most popular news websites, between 2004 and 2006, belonged to, or were associated with, traditional news organizations. The table also shows that news aggregators, Yahoo!, AOL, and Google, have become popular sources for the public to glean news, Yahoo! being the most widely used over the three-year

205

Table 15.2 The ten most popular news websites in the United States, 2004–6

News website	Monthly average visitors in millions		
	2004	2005	2006
Yahoo! News	21.4	24.1	28.4
MSNBC	20.9	23.4	25.6
CNN	23.1	22.0	24.3
AOL News	14.6	16.2	16.8
Gannett[1]	11.3	11.8	12.9
IBS	10.2	11.4	12.2
New York Times.com	9.3	11.0	12.4
Knight Ridder	9.9	9.9	–
Tribune	8.8	9.9	11.3
USAToday.com	8.2	9.4	10.0
Google News	–	–	9.4

Source: Compiled from Nielsen/NetRatings cited in Project for Excellence in Journalism (2006, 2007).

Notes:

1 = the figures for Gannet, IBS, Knight Ridder, and Tribune represent aggregates for all their titles; – represents a position outside the top ten.

period. Google News just registered outside the top ten in 2005, with a unique monthly audience of 7.8 million, making tenth place in 2006. The popularity of aggregators is not just confined to the United States. In the United Kingdom—based on a share of total visits to news sites in 2005—Google News ranked the sixth most popular site and Yahoo! the ninth (Hopkins, 2006).The small independent news websites, mentioned in the previous section, not only did not feature in the top ten, but neither did they appear in the top twenty most popular sites for news according to Nielsen/ NetRatings (Project for Excellence in Journalism, 2006, 2007). The majority of those online in the United States, and other democracies, routinely seem to access the websites of the main news organizations and news aggregators, a point confirmed by other research (see Freedman, 2006; Sparks, 2000). But why might this be the case?

The first reason relates to audience desires for convenience. The most popular sites seem to be those that allow their visitors to check the headlines or catch the latest news quickly, in between surfing the web for other reasons (see Ahlers, 2006). In a recent survey by the Pew Center, 71 percent cited convenience as the main reason for getting news and information online during 2006 (Rainie and Horrigan, 2007). The big brand aggregators' popularity is in no small way due to the fact that they allow audiences to access a wide range of news stories easily and reduce the cost to the consumer in terms of time spent browsing. The second reason has to do with brand strength (see Sparks, 2000). With a vast amount of information online, audiences often turn first to the sites they know—namely the big online and offline news brand names.

A third reason has to do with the credibility of information. Audiences may not only turn to brands they recognize but also to ones they trust (Gunter, 2003). For example, in the United States, 56 percent of those surveyed in 2006 considered the information provided by newspapers and television news organizations to be "believable" most of the time, compared with only 12 percent that considered blogs believable most of the time (Project for Excellence in Journalism, 2006).

Using alternative sources

However, while the smaller independent news websites do not feature in the top twenty, this is not to say they were not visited or accessed indirectly via an aggregator. For example, the news blog, the Huffingtonpost.com, is regularly in the top ten most visited blogs, between May 2006 and May 2007, according to Compete.com, it attracted a monthly average of around half-a-million unique visitors. These sites also seem to be particularly attractive at particular times or during specific events. A recent survey by the Pew Center found that 53 percent of internet users went to web sources other than those fed by the traditional news media to get information about the 2006 U.S. mid-term election campaign (Rainie and Horrigan, 2007). For example, 19 percent, in the same Pew survey, said they got campaign news and information specifically from satire sites such as *The Onion* and the *Daily Show* (Rainie and Horrigan, 2007).

The main U.S. news providers are also not necessarily the first destination for American internet users, especially in the area of international news. For example, U.S. audiences seeking latest developments on a story in Europe are not reliant on their traditional U.S. channels. They may be taken indirectly to a British news site by a news aggregator such as Yahoo! or Google News. Research has shown that U.S. internet users are regularly referred to U.K. sites via aggregators (Thurman, 2007). American internet users can also go directly to non-U.S. news outlets. Some high-profile British outlets have established a large American following. The BBC News website, for example, attracts more monthly visitors than a host of U.S. outlets (Thurman, 2007). In

2005, according to Nielsen/NetRatings, a monthly average of 5.6 million American internet users visited the BBC News website, compared with 5.5 million for *Fox News*, 3.8 million for *USA Today*, 3.3 million for the *LA Times,* and 2.5 million for the *Wall Street Journal*. There were particular surges around the London terrorist bombings in July of that year (Project for Excellence in Journalism, 2006; Thurman, 2007). It is said that the British newspaper the *Guardian* has more online readers in New York than Birmingham, England (The *Guardian*, 2006), a point supported in part by a recent study which found that the *Guardian*'s website had an average monthly audience of 3 million U.S. visitors (Thurman, 2007; see also ComScore, 2007a). The London *Times* attracted an average monthly audience of 1.6 million, more than the *Star Tribune*, the *Miami Herald*, and the *Seattle Post Intelligencer* (Thurman, 2007). The *New York Times* and *Washington Post* also have a growing number of readers from outside the United States, estimated at between 20 and 30 percent (Project for Excellence in Journalism, 2006; Thurman, 2007).

There is little research to date on why British news sites prove popular with U.S. audiences, though in addition to brand strength and credibility, it seems obvious to suggest that it might be related to cultural or linguistic affinities. Such links can also be seen in other examples. Arabic news channel *Al-Jazeera* claimed to have gained an audience of four million among Europe's Arabic speaking population during the invasion of Iraq in 2003 (Stanyer, 2004). The organization recently launched an online English language news service online aimed at the Muslim diaspora in Europe and North America. Similarly, Hispanic audiences in the United States are not reliant on English-language news sources but may access the Spanish-language websites of central and Latin American news organizations.

In summary, therefore, while there is now greater choice, the majority of net users regularly consume news packaged by the traditional outlets directly or via news aggregators, with smaller numbers visiting the sites of niche providers. Interestingly, a significant number of American web users choose to visit non-U.S. websites for news on a regular basis.

Website ownership and diversity in online news

The previous sections have revealed that although there are more news providers the most popular sites tend to belong to the traditional news organizations and news aggregators. Research also shows that many of these outlets also belong to large media chains, in some cases transnational conglomerates (see McChesney, 2004; Sparks, 2000). There has been a spate of high-profile acquisitions and mergers between online and offline businesses, perhaps the most visible being the multi-billion dollar merger between AOL and Time Warner in 2000. Offline media companies have also been quick to purchase high-profile internet-only news sites.

Table 15.3 shows that the most popular news websites are owned by the largest U.S. media corporations. Time Warner is the parent company of the third and

fourth most popular sites, CNN.com and AOL News, while the second most frequently visited site is a joint venture between computer giant Microsoft and NBC (Project for Excellence in Journalism, 2006). While this picture reveals the dominance of media conglomerates such as Time Warner, it also suggests that change may be occurring. If one looks at the largest media corporations (1–10), then the table shows their ownership of the most popular news websites has fallen by 17 percent between 2003 and 2006. Similarly, the popular sites owned by the top 100 media corporations have also fallen by 11 percent over the same period. Whether these trends will continue in the long term remains to be seen.

Some have observed that there is little diversity in the sources of news used by corporate-owned sites (see Paterson, 2006). Take the example of international news. While there is a wide variety of alternatives most of the American public gain their international news through the most popular big-brand news sites (as shown in Table 15.2) and these sites rely on a few key information sources. Paterson (2006) argues that when it comes to international news the diversity of views is largely illusory, as most of the news on leading sites comes from just two agencies—Associated Press and Reuters. His study measured the "average verbatim

Table 15.3 Ownership of the top 25 most popular news websites in the United States, by size of media corporation 2003–6 (percent)

Media corporations[1] / Year	2003[2]	2005	2006
Media corporations ranked 1–10	42	25	21
Media corporations ranked 11–20	27	35	26
Media corporations ranked 21–100	15	20	26
Media corporations not on the list	15	20	26

Source: Nielsen/NetRatings cited in Project for Excellence in Journalism (2004, 2006, 2007).

Notes:
1 = as determined by domestic media revenues;
2 = 2003 figures show ownership of the top 20 news websites.

challenges for mature democracies
h as the United States. The emergence
the internet has meant that there are
w more news outlets available for citiens to choose from than ever before.
While most American internet users still
visit the websites of the main news outlets, a substantial proportion regularly visit
non-U.S. news sites or niche sites such as
news blogs, and news aggregators often
take them to such sites (Thurman, 2007).
The growth of such outlets has been
beneficial for minorities of various kinds
who have felt that the main offline U.S.
news providers cater for majority tastes or
use the majority language and fail to
accommodate them. For example, diasporas are able to access news outlets with
which they have a cultural or linguistic
affinity (see Chapter 20). A similar point
could be made for those with particular
ideological views. The radical media have
always been part of society (Downing,
2001), but they have never been more
accessible as they are today via the net.

This chapter has also shown that internet news sites provide more opportunities
for citizens to exercise their voice and
contribute to the news. Citizens are able
to supply material and shape news content with greater ease than before. Open-
source news, for example, means readers
can direct content, or post their own
stories. Citizens are no longer confined to
being spectators, monitoring news from
the sidelines, but are able to contribute to
its focus and production, and become
citizen journalists.

But despite the potential for new
developments to enable a more informed
and active citizenry, it is important to
remain critically aware of the challenges
still faced. There may be more choice but
large media chains still exercise power in
the online news environment. They still
own the bulk of the established brand
outlets on which a large proportion of
internet users tend to rely. Research has

shown that the diversity of views on these
branded sites may be largely illusory with
most of the news coming from Associated
Press and Reuters (Paterson, 2006). These
profit-hungry corporations are also interested in charging citizens for additional
news services at the same time as engaging in cost cutting that may well undermine the quality of output on which
citizens depend. And citizens' online
behavior is increasingly subject to surveillance by news corporations interested in
building up information on their tastes
and habits (MacGregor, 2007).

New opportunities to interact and
produce content may also be exaggerated.
Some interactive developments have been
given a lukewarm response by the public
and journalists (Lowery and Anderson,
2005). News editors have continued to
exercise control over much of what is
contributed. In addition, the issue of
unequal access to the internet has
remained. Internet users tend to be wealthier, educated, and young, and this is
also true in relation to the adoption of
new communication technologies such as
cell phones (Chadwick, 2006; ComScore,
2007). These groups are more likely to
post content. According to a recent Pew
survey of bloggers in the United States,
54 percent were under the age of 30, 37
percent had a college degree, and 38
percent were knowledge-based professional workers (Lenhart and Fox, 2006).
These groups are also more likely to use
the internet to access news and information. For example, another Pew survey
conducted during the 2006 mid-term
elections, found that 44 percent of those
who went online to gain campaign information earned over $75,000, 49 percent
had a college degree, and 71 percent were
under the age of 49 (Rainie and Horrigan,
2007).

The current transformation of the news
environment provides new opportunities
and new challenges for democratic

news agency use" in a small sample of
international news stories in 12 of the
leading news websites in the United
States and the United Kingdom. The
results reveal that of the stories examined
on the most popular sites many were
simple copies of the news agency material. For example, in 2006, 97 percent of
the content of Yahoo's international news
was lifted from news agencies, 94 percent
of AOL's international news, 91 percent
of ABC's news, 81 percent of MSNBC's
news, and 59 percent of CNN's news.
Paterson suggests that despite the growth
in the volume of information on news
websites, when it comes to international
news, the transnational news agencies, as
before, remain the dominant voice.
However, he does note that the *New York
Times*, and the BBC, both popular outlets
too, exhibited the least reliance on news
agency copy, with their average verbatim
news agency use being 32 percent and 9
percent respectively (Paterson, 2006).

Financial uncertainty and cross-subsidy

The online news environment is financially precarious and news websites have
so far been largely unprofitable (Freedman,
2006). Audiences have been unwilling to
pay for news online and so few outlets
have been able to charge as a traditional
newspaper or cable station would. Indeed,
in the United States in 2006, of 1456
newspapers online, only 1 national, and
40 small regionals, charged their readers
(Project for Excellence in Journalism,
2006). Many of the news providers have
adopted a strategy of "modulated experimentation," separating off certain content
and charging for it (Scott, 2005). For
example, breaking news is provided free,
but visitors are sometimes asked to pay for
additional services, such as access to
archives, and specialist material, like

classifieds. Many also provide free bespoke
services, such as e-mail alerts and breaking
news alerts, services that outlets hope
consumers will be prepared to pay for in
the future (Scott, 2005).

At the same time, with the lack of
agreed standard measures for audience
numbers, and therefore no way of knowing
whether adverts have been seen and by
whom, news sites have often struggled to
generate significant advertising revenues.
Early metrics such as page views and hit
rates proved unreliable measures of who
had seen adverts and advertisers have been
generally skeptical about the returns of
large ad spends. Not surprisingly, news
sites still command a small share of the
total ad spend in the United States (4
percent in 2005, and projected to be 9
percent of total advertising dollars in 2008)
(Ahlers, 2006). This figure is higher though
in the United Kingdom, where the internet
accounted for 11.4 percent of the national
ad spend in 2006, topping for the first
time the proportion spent on newspaper
ads (Allen, 2007). The switch away from
paid subscription access at the *New York
Times* in the autumn of 2007 indicates
that that online advertising revenues are
beginning to take off in the United States.

With audiences less captive, advertisers
are increasingly interested not just in hit
rates but also in the type of audience that
visit a news site. There is pressure on news
outlets to gain more information about
customer habits and tastes (MacGregor,
2007). Software increasingly allows news
providers to track the audience's online
behavior, including interactions with ads,
or how many times ads are viewed and for
how long—information that can be fed
back to the advertisers themselves (Project
for Excellence in Journalism, 2006).

The reality of online journalism is that
the main news providers have cross-
subsidized their online operations. While
the financial subsidies have been a major
drain on resources they have allowed the

development of web presence. The traditional news providers have invested heavily in the latest technology to enable them to supply news direct to variety of platforms (see Scott, 2005). Corporations like CBS in the United States, and the BBC in the United Kingdom, have sunk millions of dollars in their online news operations (Project for Excellence in Journalism, 2006). Smaller less wealthy news providers are unable to match these levels of investment, with the result that they often cannot offer the quality of output or the services of their larger rivals.

The big players also have the funds to purchase exclusive rights to user-generated content. For example, user-generated footage of the 2004 East Asian tsunami, the aftermath of Hurricane Katrina, the London bombings in 2005, and the campus shootings at Virginia Tech in 2007, was purchased by news outlets in the United States and around the world. Bidding wars are not uncommon, with the main outlets competing for the rights to video footage with specialist rights resellers such as Scoopt, Splash, Cash4yourpics, and news wholesaler Reuters. In the United Kingdom, in 2006, there was fierce competition between news organizations for amateur footage of a police raid on terrorist suspects in north London, with ITN and the *Daily Express* allegedly paying $120,000 for the film.

The picture emerging is of a gap between the online operations of traditional news organizations and those of internet-only news providers. The traditional news operators are part of a chain, able to cross-subsidize their online operations, pay for and provide exclusive access to content that attracts large numbers of visitors, while the smaller news sites of internet-only niche providers often have less capital to invest and less to spend. The financial clout of the leading players often reproduces the existing asymmetry of the offline news environment.

Audience input and its limitations

A key criticism of offline newspapers and news bulletins is that audience input has been too tightly restricted (Richardson and Franklin, 2004). The emergence of news websites and the development of Web 2.0, it is argued, has changed this situation (Twist, 2006). The space for audience debate is no longer limited and the voice of the audience is less reliant on the editor and journalist for exposure. However, while there clearly are greater opportunities for audiences to communicate their views and contribute to the news, some argue that the reality is somewhat different from the hype (see Deuze, 2003; Singer, 2005). News outlets still exercise control of messages posted on their sites and remove comments deemed inappropriate from message boards and blogs. A study of the extent to which online audiences engaged with news websites found that only 15 percent used chat rooms and 13 percent e-mailed journalists (Lowery and Anderson, 2005; see also van der Wurff, 2005). Similarly, a survey by Nielsen/NetRatings found that only a minority of visitors to leading newspaper websites in the United States looked at journalists' blogs. In December 2006, of a unique audience of 30 million, 13 percent visited the blog pages of an online newspaper (Nielsen/NetRatings, 2007).

It is not just the public that shy away from interaction, Lowery and Anderson (2005) found that only a minority of journalists pursued contact through news blogs. Another survey discovered that most journalists in the United States saw responding to e-mail as part of their job but just over half did so—and did so only occasionally (Pavlik, 2004). Indeed, in a study of interactivity Chung (2007: 48) found that although most site producers recognized the "importance of incorporating ... interactivity" they were cautious

about it, especially those inside the established news organizations. These respondents often pointed to the increase in workload in maintaining interactive features (Chung, 2007).

Others have observed that the more radical potential of the technology, for example, in allowing for open-source journalism, has remained just that—potential. While there is greater feedback, some argue that most news organizations encourage little more than comment—the attitude is still very much "we write, you read" (Deuze, 2003). Lowery and Anderson (2005) found there was a limited support among journalists for participatory news. The traditional news outlets largely encourage audience input, not out of a sense of civic obligation, but as another way to gather information that they can then repackage. Many outlets have introduced audience-editors, to read and respond to reader e-mails and to follow up story leads (Project for Excellence in Journalism, 2006). For example, in the United Kingdom, the national daily newspaper, the *Sun,* recently launched its message board MySun. The reason, the assistant editor of the *Sun* online noted, was to gain information and tips on the issues that concerned their audience most, to boost circulation (Gibson, 2006).

The impact on the profession

While some observe that the internet brings new opportunities for the professional journalist (see Pavlik, 2004), others argue that it has an adverse impact (Lowery and Anderson, 2005). One negative effect is news room convergence (see Scott, 2005). Over the last five years or so many of the traditional news players have begun to merge their online and offline news operations. An early example is the tie-up between the *Tampa Tribune,* WFLA-TV, and Tampa Bay Online, who process news

through a centralized m[...] desk (Scott, 2005). In the [...] the *Daily Telegraph* and the [...] merged their online and [...] operations. In addition, c[...] partnerships between differen[...] and between the websites [...] outlets have emerged (Scott, 20[...]

This process of convergence [...] number of consequences. Deadli[...] sures have increased. Journalists w[...] deadlines once or twice a day offline [...] find they have rolling deadlines throu[...] out the day: 78 percent of journal[...] working in U.S. online news outlets [...] 2003 reported that their deadline pres[...] sures had grown (Pew Research Center, 2003). There is more pressure to refresh and repackage material during the day. The same survey of journalists found that a great deal of time was devoted to repackaging news stories; in fact, 71 percent of those sampled said they were doing more repackaging of news compared to 48 percent of those working offline (Pew Research Center, 2003). The need to repackage may well increase as the volume of user-generated content rises.

The precarious position of the news professional has been exacerbated by cost cutting across the industry. As Alhers (2006) observes, with news sites attracting relatively small revenues when compared with offline news media, reducing costs has become key for news organizations. Indeed, 62 percent of online journalists in the Pew survey of 2003 reported that the number of people working in their online news operation had decreased over time (Pew Research Center, 2003). This points to a future in which journalism may become increasingly casualized.

Conclusion

The developments outlined in this chapter provide new opportunities and pose

communication. In the long term, whether these changes enable a more informed and active citizenry or facilitate increasingly interest-driven news consumption remains to be seen, but what is certain is that news will never be the same again.

Guide to further reading

There is a rapidly growing body of literature on the online news environment. Broad overviews can be found in books by Allan (2006) and Gunter (2003), in edited collections by Li (2006), and in shorter length journal articles by Scott (2005) and Deuze (2003). All of these works are easily accessible to the non-specialist reader. More critical accounts can be found in Freedman (2006) or McChesney (2004). These interventions show that there is little consensus on the impact of the internet, and serve as a reminder of the power of large multinational corporations and media chains to influence the online news environment.

With books dating quickly, a useful, regularly updated source of information on the online news environment is provided by Project for Excellence in Journalism's annual state of the news media survey, produced by the Columbia School of Journalism (see www.stateofthe newsmedia.com). These annual reports, together with occasional reports produced by the Pew Internet and American Life Project (see www.pewinternet.org), are an excellent resource for those looking for more empirical detail about the latest developments.

In addition to the general overviews, there are studies with a more specific focus. Bruns (2005) and Pavlik (2004) provide a detailed account of how journalistic roles are being redefined by the net. These studies are complemented by detailed research conducted by Lowery and Anderson (2005) and Singer (2005); together these show that journalists often resist change brought about by the internet. There are also numerous studies of how the internet is shaping news consumption patterns. These range from descriptive data in the Pew Internet surveys to the more detailed studies of consumption by Ahlers (2006) and Thurman (2007).

Part 3

Identities

16

The internet and the changing global media environment

Brian McNair

This chapter describes current trends in the global media environment, with a focus on their impli-cations for the management of public agendas and political processes. It assesses the extent to which trends such as the growth of the blogosphere, "citizen journalism," and other forms of user-generated content, have complicated and problematized news and agenda management as engaged in by both media and political elites. It argues that, in large part due to the rise of the internet and the pro-liferation of online producers of information and commentary, alongside 24-hour news channels such as CNN and Al Jazeera, political and social actors today face a much more complex, chaotic communication environment than ever before, an environment characterized as one of cultural chaos. Having outlined the roots of this trend in the emergence of an expanded, globalized public sphere, the chapter goes on to ask if elite control over the political agenda has been eroded, and if it has, what the consequences for government and the exercise of power might be. Can author-itarian regimes in China, the Middle East, and elsewhere survive the onset of internet-fueled global journalism, for example? In a political environment where public opinion is driven and buffeted by news coverage of unprecedented speed and volume, can democratic governments retain sufficient control over decision- and policy-making processes to enable competent social administration and political management? Can the citizens of contemporary democracies use the emerging media envir-onment to enhance elite accountability and strengthen the democratic process? The chapter concludes that the changing global media environment has the potential to strengthen democratic processes, though there is no single template for the impact of the internet and other new media on specific countries.

The media environment within which political actors must operate has been in a state of constant evolution ever since the invention of the printing press and the first newspapers. As democratic polities developed in early modern Europe, poli-tical media played a key role in the articulation of public opinion and debate. They emerged not just as reporters of information, but as watchdogs and scruti-neers over power, partisan advocates of competing political positions and ideolo-gies, and representatives of the citizen before elites. They did so in contexts such as providing a platform for the publication of readers' letters, phone-in contributions to a radio talk show, or a TV studio debate. Whether one examines the origins and outcomes of the English Civil War, the French Revolution, or the American War of Independence, the media emerge as important actors in the evolution of democratic politics (Hartley, 1996; Conboy, 2004; Starr, 2004). These aspects of the media's democratic role remain valued today, cited as guiding principles by the journalists and editors of Al Jazeera as much as those of the BBC or the Wall Street Journal. As Vladimir Putin, George W. Bush, Tony Blair, and his successor Gordon Brown have all discovered, politicians in societies that aspire to be democratic must pursue their activities against the backdrop of media, which, in theory, should be free from and independent of state authority and commercial pressure (private media pursue private interests, of course, but it is generally acknowledged that in a pluralist democracy there should be ideological diversity of news outlets, and no overwhelming "bias" towards one view or another). Democratic politicians must seek legitimacy at the ballot box, by communicating with their potential voters through the media. Not only do the media provide channels of communication from aspiring governors to those in whose name they will govern, they should hold governors to account by critical scrutiny of their performance, including the representation and championing of citizens before elite power.

The media that performed these democratic functions and that formed the first public spheres were, from the seventeenth century, newspapers and periodicals. In the 1600s coffee house cultures emerged in the capital cities of Europe, where men of property and education would debate the issues of the day. As democratic institutions developed in the course of the seventeenth century and into the next, the importance of the existence of a common communicative space, within which citizens could be informed, advised, and exhorted to think and act politically, came to be a key element of what we would today call deliberative democracy—a democracy of informed citizens, acting rationally on the basis of information received from political media, then tested in debate.

More than two hundred years after the launch of the first daily newspaper in England in 1702, the print media were joined in an expanding public sphere by radio in the early twentieth century, and television broadcasting in the late twentieth. By then, democracy had also expanded, with universal suffrage having been achieved in most advanced capitalist societies by the outbreak of World War II. Universal education had encouraged the growth of literate mass publics, served by popular "tabloid" media (Engel, 1996). By the end of the twentieth century, and the end of the cold war, which brought with it the end of authoritarian power in the Soviet Union and eastern Europe, the world was by most objective standards a more democratic place than it had ever been. Where in 1900 there were on the planet precisely *no* fully democratic countries (meaning those in which every adult had a vote, and was free to choose which, if any party, they wished to support), by the end of the century nearly two thirds of the world's population, living in 121 out of 190 recognized nation states, enjoyed "free" or "partly free" democratic politics. "Partly free," as the U.S.-based thinktank Freedom House puts it, recognizes that many of these democracies were imperfect, characterized by "some restrictions on political rights and civil liberties, often in a context of corruption, weak rule of law, ethnic strife, or civil war" (Freedom House, 2007). Putin's Russia, one might observe, is a "partly free" democracy, in sometimes painful transition from the authoritarianism of the Soviet era, and not yet free of that regime's censorial and intimidatory habits (not least in respect of political journalism). Iran is a democracy, but again only partly free, in so far as religious theocracy continually clashes with competing demands for liberalism and pluralism. Democracy has expanded globally, then, in recent decades, but is not yet a completed project. On the contrary, democratization at the global level, and within nation states, is an ongoing process subject to blockages and reversals.

One can also say that the process of democratization has been paralleled by the expansion of the media and the public sphere. That there is a precise, measureable causal relationship between the rise of mass media and the spread of universal suffrage is difficult to prove in the conventional sense (as are all media–effects hypotheses), but there is clearly a correlation between the two trends. And why should there not be? The media have fueled political debate and democratic participation since the seventeenth century, expanding their audiences and enabling their engagement with expanded democratic structures. The two sets of institutions are inherently linked. Without a free and independent media, accessible to the people who rely upon it as their main source of political information, there can *be* no democracy worthy of the name.

But mass media, like political institutions, are imperfect vehicles for democracy. Print and broadcast media of the traditional type have been and remain centralized, vertically hierarchical, top-down channels of communication, allowing only limited opportunities for public feedback, and then in circumstances closely controlled by media professionals. Readers' letters and callers to phone-in shows are screened, with only a small minority of contributions making it through, according to the criteria of the medium in question (political viewpoint, level of articulacy of the contributor, willingness or ability to adopt the communicative etiquette required, such as no racist abuse on the BBC). This was a necessary and inevitable gatekeeping exercise, given the limited availability of column inches and airtime, designed to ensure that those voices that made it though the various filtering processes in operation were at one and the same time representative of the public as a whole,

relevant to the issues under debate at any given time, and sufficiently well-formulated to engage the rest of the audience. Opportunities for access to, and participation in, the public spheres of the nation state were, for the three-and-a-half centuries or so that separated the English Civil War from the outbreak of the "war on terror," strictly limited, and awarded by the media, reasonably perhaps, only to those deemed to have something worthwhile to say. Members of the public were in this respect structurally subordinate to the professionals of the media, dependent on them for access to the public sphere.

Access was also restricted by the fact that media have traditionally been expensive to set up and maintain; highly capital-intensive, and thus almost entirely restricted to big business. There have been independent, radical media in existence throughout the history of most democracies, but usually existing on the margins, financed by political donations or other non-commercial means. Otherwise, and with the exception of publicly funded organizations such as the BBC, the vast majority of the media of capitalist societies have taken the form of business enterprises, owned by corporations and wealthy entrepreneurs.

This top–down, centralized, industrially organized media apparatus was relatively easy for political elites and other actors to manage, manipulate, and control. What Walter Lippmann called in his 1922 book *Public Opinion* "the art of creating consent among the governed" (quoted in McNair, 2007), and the "control of affairs" by "persuasion" was relatively easy in a media environment of few outlets where the possibilities of feedback and rapid public response were limited. No politician could ever guarantee a good press, of course, and rulers from Charles II employed what we would today call spin doctors to try to ensure the best possible coverage in the media of their times (Charles II had the diarist Samuel Pepys to look after his image). As soon as there were democratic elections in place, and public opinions that mattered, political elites were obliged to pursue persuasive communication strategies. The lavishly resourced public relations apparatuses of today's political parties, governments, and campaigning groups have their roots in the early twentieth century recognition that in mass-mediated democracies the management of public opinion and, dare one say it, the manufacture of consent, could not be left to chance, but should henceforth be the province of a recognized category of communication professional (McNair, 2007).

In the days where the political media comprised only print and analog broadcasting, however, there were fewer channels to manage, and information flowed more slowly, determined by the level of communication technology deployed. Politicians had days, weeks, months, and even years to react to stories that might be damaging. They could preserve confidentiality, censor, cover up bad news, not only because there were fewer media outlets to control, but because they inhabited a culture of public deference towards elites in general, based on the authoritarian traditions of absolute monarchy and church, further elaborated by the class and status distinctions that emerged in bourgeois society as a means of maintaining social hierarchy. Thus, if a prime minister or a president refused to give an interview to a journalist—the first such interviews took place in the late nineteenth century (Silvester, ed., 1993)—this was accepted as a reasonable exercise of executive detachment, necessary to preserve the dignity and authority of power. Journalists, like citizens in general, routinely deferred to the presumed authority of political elites, and rarely challenged their prerogative to dictate the style and content of political communication.

This deference began to erode after World War II, in the U.K. perhaps most rapidly, as journalists such as Robin Day on the commercial channel ITV pioneered more aggressive, interrogatory interviewing styles, and as journalism in general became more intrusive. Between the 1950s and the turn of the millennium the barriers that had traditionally existed between private lives and public affairs, between the personal politics of politicians and their political personas, were steadily eroded. Thus, while in the 1960s the White House press corps knew about and even participated in John F. Kennedy's swimming pool dalliances with starlets and models, but never reported them (Hersh, 1997), three decades later Bill Clinton's sex and family life became a central theme in reportage of his presidency. Where Winston Churchill could dismiss the value of appearing in the media to address the British people, and expect no objection from a compliant journalistic profession, Tony Blair and his contemporaries entered office in the certain knowledge that everything they did or had done, be it smoking a joint at university, having affairs and getting divorced, or buying a second home for the use of a child going to university, would be under intense and constant scrutiny by a media hungry for stories and increasingly fearless in its determination to uncover everything.

As deference declined in the post-war era, however, it did so in the context of a top–down media system, which remained relatively easy to control. Press officers and media advisers helped politicians such as Harold Wilson to lobby editors and cultivate media loyalties, but these efforts were small scale by comparison with the political public relations operations of modern politics. A handful of radio and TV stations, a dozen or so newspapers and periodicals of influence—

these were the political media faced by any political actor. In the twenty-first century, by contrast, political elites face a transformed media environment, and an immeasurably more complex agenda and opinion management challenge. To put it another way, political actors now face an environment characterized by the loss of control, and the onset of communication chaos (McNair, 2006).

The rest of this chapter explores the roots and causes of this trend, which I will group into four categories.

Expanded information flow

There are now many more media outlets, producing much more information than at any previous time in human history. The expansion has been gradual over a period of centuries since the invention of print, accelerating in the twentieth century with the invention of broadcasting, and exploding in the 1980s and 1990s with the appearance of the first 24-hour news channels. CNN in 1980, Sky in 1989, BBC News 24 in 1997—each new entrant to the real-time news market added more hours to the total of journalistic discourse in the public sphere than had previously been provided by all terrestrial channels put together. In the U.K., when this writer was commencing his Ph.D. in 1981, the quantity of broadcast news approximated five hours per day across four TV and one radio channel. By September 11, 2001 there were three U.K.-based 24-hour news channels available to the British viewer, as well as CNN and several other overseas-based services (McNair, 2006). As this essay went to press these included Al Jazeera, which launched an English-language service in 2006, and a growing number of non-English speaking services in the Middle East, Asia, and Latin America (Chalaby, ed., 2005).

The internet

From the late 1990s, following the launch of Netscape's Mosaic browser and the beginning of the development of the internet as a mass medium (by which I mean a communication channel accessible to and used by the general population, as opposed to specialist or elite segments of it) real-time news channels were joined by a rapidly growing number of online news and information outlets: websites set up by newspapers and TV companies such as Guardian Unlimited and BBC Online; online publications such as Slate; sites dedicated to commentary and comment, run by individual journalists such as Andrew Sullivan, and also by amateurs such as the Drudge Report. Personal weblogs (blogs), many of them devoted to news and commentary on the news, emerged as a visible feature of the internet at the turn of the millennium, proliferating after the events of September 11, 2001. By 2005, there were millions of blogs operating all over the world, the number increasing all the time (McNair, 2006). In 2005–6 online social networking services such as YouTube, MySpace, Bebo, and Facebook emerged, allowing individuals to spread and share information in the form of video, text, and audio files.

All of this amounted to an information environment of practically infinite size, from the point of view of the individual. Where in the pre-internet era there had been a large, but finite, public sphere comprising print and broadcast media, by the time of this writing there was a vast universe of publicly available data within easily searchable reach of anyone on the planet with a computer and an internet connection (of whom there were more than a billion, with internet access and usage figures rising all the time). Those who sought to track the expansion of this data flow talked not of gigabytes but terabytes and petabytes—quantities unimaginable

221

to the human mind, just as we find it hard to visualize just how many stars there are in the known universe.

These data included everything from individual e-mails to huge, multi-layered websites devoted to government information and official business, such as the reports of the U.S. 9/11 Commission and the Hutton inquiry, which explored the circumstances behind the death of a U.K. government scientist and the U.K. government's decision to participate in the invasion of Iraq. It included professional journalism, amateur punditry in the form of blogs, academic research, online editions of books and papers, most of it downloadable at the touch of a mouse button. Much more data, in short, than any individual could ever hope to master. Information had gone from being a scarce resource to one freely available in unlimited quantities. The child of the early twenty-first century had access not just to his or her local library, or to the learning of a teacher or parent, or to documentaries on TV and radio, but to the whole universe of accumulated human knowledge (that proportion of it, at least, that was digitized), for the price of a PC and a broadband connection (by 2007, in a country such as the U.K., barely more than the annual cost of a mobile phone contract). The expansion of internet access was a marked trend, moreover, not merely in the relatively affluent advanced capitalist world, but in the developing countries of China, India, and Africa, where its educational and economic benefits were among the factors revolutionizing rates of growth and enabling countries such as India to aspire to superpower status.

Accelerated information flow

Not only has the internet made more information publicly available than ever

before in human history, it has accelerated the rate of flow of that information, and the speed at which all kinds of knowledge are disseminated. If, during the English Civil War for example, it took days and perhaps weeks for news about a battle to be widely disseminated, in the era of the internet, information travels around the world at the speed of light, spread along horizontal vectors and decentralized hubs. The networked structure of the internet (Watts, 2003) enables rapid dissemination of information to any and every point on the network. Real-time news, meanwhile, reports newsworthy events as they are actually happening, and often before the journalists, or anybody else, understand their meaning or significance. Those who witnessed the Twin Tower attacks unfold on CNN, no matter where in the world they were at the time (I tuned in from a remote part of tropical Australia, just in time to see the second plane hit the towers) will recall the confusion of journalists as they struggled to make sense of events. Was it an accident caused by a fire or a light aircraft; a cruise missile fired by a hostile power; a terrorist attack? No-one knew for sure, and for quite some time, even though the whole world was watching.

And as real-time news transmitted pictures and commentaries to the world, the internet came alive with bloggers and e-mailers spreading the news, sometimes from the heart of Manhattan. There was, in short, practically no gap between the event happening and its being reported, then commented on and debated by millions of people all over the world. In the case of 9/11 this collapse of the gap between happening and reportage, which had previously been a structural constraint on journalism, was facilitated by the fact that CNN and other organizations' cameras were on the scene from the outset, perched on roof tops only a short distance from the towers. Even if those conditions have not always been present, however, a similarly accelerated cycle of event–reportage–commentary has accompanied subsequent events such as the invasion of Iraq in 2003, the July 7 bombings in London, and the Beslan siege of September 2004. The whole world watched the tragic end of the Beslan siege, though no-one knew with any certainty what was going on amidst the chaos of a rescue operation gone wrong.

The speed of flow of information on the internet, coupled with its relative uncensorability, alongside the advent of real-time news, has encouraged the collapse of what Anthony Giddens (1990) describes as time–space distantiation. After many centuries of gradual erosion of the gap between the places where events happen and the places where we read about or watch them in our news media, we are suddenly in the era of reportorial instantaneity, or something very close to it. Whether an event happens in Darfur or Caracas, New York or Bali, we have the potential to access live coverage of it in our front rooms, on TV, and then to follow the story on the internet, sharing information, alerting others, accessing the online sites of print and broadcast news outlets. The boundaries of time and space are dissolved through technology, which allows information to be packaged digitally and then to travel anywhere in the world.

The rise of interactivity and mass participation

Adding to the qualitative shift that this emerging environment represents is the fact that it is uniquely accessible to the people who wish to use it. Assuming that the members of a society can afford to buy the necessary hardware (and the proportion of the world's population with internet access is rising all the time, as

already noted), they can produce as well as consume the information that flows on the internet. Blogs, e-mails, personalized websites on MySpace and YouTube—all involve an unprecedented degree of inter-activity and participation. The sharing of information and debating of its significance with anyone, anywhere on the planet, has in a few short years become a commonplace of cultural life. We upload information, many of us, as readily as we download it.

Media organizations have sought to reflect the growth of interactivity and participatory media by establishing platforms for the posting of videos, text, and other contributions from members of the global public. "Citizen journalism," though a misleading term in so far as most such contributions are submitted by amateurs unversed in professional journalistic skills and practices, and user-generated content have become prominent elements in the global media environment. The quality of these contributions varies hugely, as one would expect, but that they exist at all is a significant causal factor in the increasingly chaotic information environment confronted by political actors. The images of torture and abuse taking place in Abu Ghraib prison in Iraq, for example, were made available to the mainstream media by U.S. soldiers at the scene, from where they generated a major political crisis for the Bush administration.

From control to chaos

All of this—expanded, accelerated information flow, which crosses borders of time and space and is relatively difficult to police, and which is easily accessed by the individual constituted as a participant–producer and not merely a consumer—amounts to a globalized public sphere of a new type; a diffuse network of information sources, horizontally organized rather than vertically hierarchical like the top–down media of old. The internet was originally designed to be robust in the face of military attack, with a high degree of redundancy built into its components (Naughton, 1999). As a consequence of this feature of the internet, and when combined with the velocity and geographical reach of the information that flows down its myriad pathways, it is relatively difficult to control and censor. Newspapers could easily be closed down by an authoritarian regime, and still are in countries such as Zimbabwe and Iran. Terrestrial TV stations can be closed down too, as occurred in Venezuela in 2007, or their transmissions blocked, with relative ease. Real-time news channels on satellite are harder to control within the boundaries of a nation state, but can be policed by banning satellite dishes or otherwise criminalizing the consumption of undesirable material. States such as Saudi Arabia and China have compelled broadcasters such as the BBC and CNN to curtail their activities within their national boundaries, leading directly, in the former example, to the establishment of Al Jazeera by disgruntled Arab journalists seeking an outlet for their journalism (Zayani, ed., 2005).

Such tactics can also be used against the internet, as Google discovered when trying to break into the Chinese market in 2006. To widespread protest from its global user base the online search company accepted restrictive Chinese government terms in return for permission to operate in the country. Google subsequently reversed its decision, in order to repair its damaged reputation, but the incident was a cautionary reminder to those of a more utopian view that the internet *can* be controlled, whether by means of commercial, technological, or political instruments. Debate on the means and justifications for future regulation of the internet continues to occupy the international

community, focused on how best to control the medium while preserving its unique communicative properties, and addressing the problems of racist or sectarian hate speech, terrorism, pedophilia, copyright theft, and others.

The difference, however, between contemporary attempts at control, for whatever reason they are pursued, and those of the pre-internet era, is that the former rapidly become part of the global public debate. The Chinese, fearful of the effect of freely flowing information on their authoritarian control regime, may seek to censor internet companies such as Google, but as bloggers and others in the media hear the news and begin to share it with their online networks, from where it breaks into the mainstream news agenda, the act rapidly becomes common knowledge, inside and out of the country, and impacts on China's other goals, such as holding a successful Olympics, or obtaining most favored nation status with the U.S. Control of the internet *is* possible, and in relation to some content desirable (child pornography, racist hate speech, and so on), but the costs of political censorship, in terms of global reputation, trade, and influence, not to mention the impact on internal pressures for reform, are much higher than they were in the past. Some countries—some of those in south east Asia, for example—have combined strict control of the internet with political stability and economic success (Atkins, 2002). Others, such as Iran under the fundamentalists, struggle to persuade their young people in particular, and what is to a considerable extent a liberal, cosmopolitan population in general, that banning their access to the internet and satellite TV is good for their morality or the security and stability of the country.

The leaders of the U.S.S.R. could get away with this kind of logic during the cold war, and were able to quarantine their population from the outside world quite effectively for the best part of seventy years. As early as the 1980s, however, as fax and video were becoming commonplace communicative tools in the U.S.S.R., and CNN was becoming available to Soviet TV viewers, the communists under Mikhail Gorbachev recognized that the game was up in terms of authoritarian information control, and introduced the policy of *glasnost* (openness). This did not prevent the collapse of the Soviet state in 1991, and may have accelerated that process, but it was a sign of the increasing degree of difficulty involved in any state seeking to police the media-consumption habits of its people, once those people had even a limited knowledge of what they were missing. Two decades later, in an online world, no matter how reluctantly it is conceded by the Chinese, the Cubans, the Iranians, or any other regime, the difficulty is immeasurably greater. Censorship is far from impossible to repeat, but it is much more problematic as a governing strategy unless, as appears to be the case in North Korea, people are so completely isolated from the outside world that they have little or no understanding of the globalized media environment that is emerging, and thus no substantial basis on which to compare their internal situation.

The internet and politics

Does this loss of control matter to the exercise of political power? Does it strengthen democracy where it already exists, and increase the potential for it to emerge in the authoritarian societies that remain? Anderson and Ward's (2007) recent edited volume points to the loss of elite communicative control that the internet has produced.

> Potentially it could be argued that the internet provides a channel through

which news provision can be truly democratized. Despite his enormous power and influence within the print and broadcast media, for example, Rupert Murdoch's newspapers and television stations can find their view of the news world challenged and contradicted by anti-capitalist news sites on the web that people all over the world are able to view whenever they want and without charge.

(Anderson and Ward, 2007: p. 15)

Murdoch himself, in a 2006 speech to a London audience made less than a year after his company had paid $580 million for the social networking site MySpace, reflected on the transformed media environment, and what it meant to global media barons such as him. "Power is moving away from those who own and manage the media to a new and demanding generation of consumers—consumers who are better educated, unwilling to be led and who know that in a competitive world they can get what they want, when they want it" (McNair, 2006). And who can, as already noted, contribute through blogs and other means to the globalized public sphere, participating to an unprecedented degree in the emergence and evolution of news stories, and the impact they have on public opinion at both local and global level.

Evaluating the globalized public sphere

On the face of it, with other things remaining equal, these trends should enable a strengthening of the democratic process, in so far as they widen and deepen access to the means of communication, from the perspectives of both consumption and production. On the other side, it is argued that, notwithstanding the explosion of the blogosphere and the emergence of millions of people world-wide who through access to the internet actively contribute to the globalized public sphere, the quality of debate is low. Oliver Kamm, himself a blogger of some influence in the United States, concedes that blogging is "a democratic medium, allowing anyone to participate in political debate without an intermediary, at little or no cost." There is a downside, how-ever. "It is a direct and not deliberative form of democracy. You need no com-petence to join in" (Kamm, 2007). Blogs are frequently inaccurate, opinionated without being authoritative, and add little to the stock of knowledge in the public sphere. For Kamm, the democratic con-tribution of the blogosphere is undermined by the fact that:

> Blogs are providers not of news but of comment. This would be a good thing if blogs extended the range of available opinion in the public sphere. But they do not; paradoxically, they narrow it. This happens because blogs typically do not add to the available stock of commentary: they are purely parasitic on the stories and opinions that traditional media provide. In its paucity of coverage and predictability of conclusions, the blogosphere provides a parody of democratic deliberation.
>
> (Kamm, 2007)

This somewhat pessimistic conclusion has substance, but then, haven't much of the old media been accused of precisely the same flaws—that they add little that is new to political debate, and trade instead on opinions, polemic and bias? In recent times the established political media in both Britain and the U.S. have been accused of "corrosive cynicism" and "hyperadversarialism" respectively (Lloyd, 2004; Fallows, 1996a), implicated in the

development of a public sphere that is raucous and noisy, aggressive and con-frontational, but lacking in the quantity and quality of information required by a truly informed citizenry. If the blogger functions in a globalized, digitized media environment, and if there are many mil-lions of them competing for attention, their articulations on the issues are no different, in essence, from those of the tabloid columnist or the radio shock jock.

On the other hand, the sheer size and complexity of the online environment presents a challenge to the normative public sphere. How does the reader sift and sort the wheat from the chaff, the unsubstantiated rant from the insightful analysis? There are several answers to that question. First, the "old," established media brands take on an enhanced role as gatekeepers, identifying and highlighting online voices that are, for one reason or another, worthy of attention. Bloggers such as Salam Pax, the "Baghdad blogger" who emerged during the build-up to and execution of the invasion of Iraq in 2003, broke through into the mainstream, with a column for the *Guardian* and a book collecting his blog entries, not merely because he was a rare independent source on the ground in Baghdad as the war began, but because he was a good writer and a courageous reporter in the best tra-dition of foreign correspondents. Norman Geras, the former Marxist intellectual, found his Normblog picked up by the mainstream print media in 2005 because of the eloquence and passion with which he, as a Marxist, defended the coalition intervention to remove Saddam Hussein from power. There is, in short, a compe-titive environment for bloggers and other online contributors, in which success, meaning influence and reach beyond the still relatively narrow networks of blog-gers, extending to the mainstream media and their audiences, depends on a variety of criteria, from the quality of writing to the originality of perspective. The digitized media environment is noisy, to be sure, and may well be conceived as a communicative tower of Babel, but it is an environment in which quality rises to the top of the pile, while the mediocre and the rubbish sink to the bottom, never to be heard of again. Millions talk, but only a few are listened to.

Cultural globalization and its critics

Aside from the question of the quality of the contributions that an expanding, active global citizenry (and many who are not citizens) make to the globalized public sphere, the concept of globalization itself continues to be contentious, particularly in the sub-field of critical media studies. Angus Stewart observed in 2001 that the dominant usage of "globalization" in scholarly writing was "to invoke chaotic or irresistible social forces and convey a powerful sense of uncontestable … political fatalism" (Stewart, 2001: p. 124). For this writer "the historical reality of the current phase of capitalist modernity is one of extreme fragmentation" (Stewart, 2001: p. 93). These themes persist in the writings of sociologists such as Paul Virilio (1997) and Zygmunt Bauman (2002), who has described a world under siege from the relentless flow of information. Virilio has written of "the sudden bewildering Babel clamor of the world-city, the untimely mix of the global and the local" (Virilio, 1997, p. 57).

Samuel Huntington's influential *Clash of Civilisations*, published in 1996 and anticipating the resurgence of global religious conflict long before 9/11 opened full-scale holy war on the west, observed that "little or no evidence exists to support the assumption that the emergence of pervasive global communications is providing significant convergence in attitudes and beliefs" (Huntington, 1996: p. 59). A globalized public sphere does not imply a rational, deliberative debate on global political issues, in short. It may indeed inflame and intensify conflicts that might otherwise have remained marginal and localized. The media image of Al Qaida's jihad, and the widespread perception that the small group of disaffected Muslim men who actively participate in it represent a serious global threat to countries that defeated the industrial might of fascism in World War II, is the product of skillful media management by the Islamists on the one hand, and structural features of the global news media on the other. Audacious attacks such as 9/11 and the July 7 London bombings are designed and executed precisely to command the news agenda, to spread fear and panic, and to amplify the salience of the issues that drive their perpetrators. Beheading a hostage on camera and sending the footage to Al Jazeera for broadcast to the world is more than an act of religious sadism—it is political communication, designed to terrorize and intimidate a variety of constituencies.

Adam Curtis' documentary *The Power of Nightmares*, broadcast by the BBC in 2005 and in many other countries since, argues persuasively that the perception of Al Qaida as a global threat is exaggerated, not merely by the neo-conservative ideologues who have wielded, some would say, disproportionate and pernicious influence on the Bush administration and have an interest in threat inflation, but by the unintended consequences of pervasive, global media coverage of the Islamists' activities. The "war on terror" is in this context a media construction, fueled by the panicked responses of political elites and then global publics as they watched the twin towers fall, or the people of Madrid emerge from their blasted train carriages, or the Australian clubbers in Bali mourning their dead friends. Compared with the millions who died in the 1939–45 war against fascism, or the half million massacred in Rwanda in 1994, or the atrocities committed by the Serbs in the former Yugoslavia, the crimes of Al Qaida are small in scale (if no less offensive to humanity than those of the Nazis or the ethnic cleansers of Serbia). They loom large in the global public imagination, however—inhabiting our nightmares, indeed—because of the speed and spread of their dissemination across the planet. The consequences of this threat inflation for national and global politics have been clear—not merely the war in Iraq, which would probably have happened anyway, at some point in the future, but also the vast expense and other costs for civil liberties of airline security and other measures designed to protect us from a handful of fanatical young men and women on suicide missions. The perception of a global terror threat, built not by conspiracy but by the mere fact of terrorist incidents being reported intensively, has generated a global response that may in time come to be seen as overdone, indeed damaging to democracy in other respects. The U.S. Patriot Act, the introduction of ID cards in the U.K., the treatment experienced in many countries by innocent Muslim citizens because of the perceived threat caused by the Islamists—all these can be related, at least in part, to the perceptions of risk and threat encouraged by a globalized, digitized media culture.

Conclusion

The changed global media environment described above *is* making a difference to the conduct and management of politics on every level, and in every arena. Accelerated, expanded, increasingly interactive and uncensorable information flows present political elites in democratic societies with new challenges in the sphere of information and media management. Bill Clinton's presidency was almost (if not quite) destroyed by the media storm that engulfed his administration in the wake of the Monica Lewinsky scandal. The story was broken by the online Drudge Report, when traditional "old" media such as Newsweek decided that they could not take the risk. When the news broke, and in the months following, CNN's feeds of the president's testimony to the Starr commission and other twists demonstrated in sharp relief the uncontrollable, chaotic nature of contemporary political media, and the speed at which stories that would once have been kept secret, often with the complicity of journalists, become part of the globalized public sphere.

George W. Bush faced comparable information management challenges with the emergence from Iraq of atrocity stories, such as the human rights abuses and torture occurring in Abu Ghraib prison. As is well known, digital photographs of the torture of Iraqi prisoners by U.S. servicemen and women made their way into the investigative journalism of Seymour Hersch, and thence on to Al Jazeera and other international media outlets. The widespread outrage that resulted, both in the United States and overseas, compelled the president to make a public apology to the Iraqi people, live on Arab-speaking television. The success of this attempt to limit the damage caused by Abu Ghraib, and to restore some order to the chaos of the global media environment, was limited, in so far as the war in Iraq subsequently intensified and the American occupation grew ever less popular with both the Iraqis and the American people, but it would not have occurred, nor would it have been necessary, thirty or forty years ago.

In conclusion, then, it is possible to argue that the globalized public sphere that has been brought into being by the combination of 24-hour news channels and the internet, has generated a political environment that is harder for elites and other social actors to control than may have been the case in the past. News stories rise and fall unpredictably, rapidly cascading into damaging media storms because of images taken on mobile phones, or off-the-record speeches recorded and then posted on a blog. In March 2007, U. S. Republican presidential candidate John McCain was recorded at a dinner singing, to the tune of the Beach Boys' Barbara Ann, "bomb, bomb, bomb, bomb, bomb Iran." A joke, he insisted, and not in particularly good taste, but transferred by the communicative power of the blogosphere into a global controversy requiring public contrition. CNN news editor Eason Jordan was "exposed" on a blog when he asserted at an off-the-record news conference that U.S. forces deliberately targeted journalists in Iraq. He was required to resign as a result. U.S. senator Trent Lott was recorded making racist remarks. In the digitized media environment, nothing is secret for long, and there is no such thing as "off the record." Political actors must adapt to this new reality, or perish under the weight of hostile public opinion, fanned and fueled by bloggers, online pundits, net-savvy campaigners, and the rest.

Uncomfortable as it may be for those who are the targets of such scrutiny, from a normative perspective it enhances the potential for the media to exercise accountability over power. The internet, and its gradual convergence with the established print and broadcast media, has produced greater elite visibility and transparency. In democratic societies where the media are free to say more or less whatever they like, this has led to some excesses, in which politicians may be thought to have been unfairly traduced for "crimes," which though they may fascinate the blogosphere, have little to do

with the performance of public duty. On balance, though, democracy is stronger when power and its exercise is transparent, even insecure, before the court of global public opinion. Better out than in, one might say. The democratic predisposition should be to more rather than less openness and transparency, a stance that the emergence of the internet makes difficult to resist.

In the declining number of authoritarian societies, on the other hand, the trends appear to be in favor of movement towards democratization, and if there is no obvious or simple cause-and-effect relationship between the pressure for democratic reform in for example Cuba and China, or Singapore, or Saudi Arabia, control of the media environment within the boundaries of the nation-state becomes as a general rule ever more problematic. How long these societies can hold out against the demands of young, internet-literate populations eager to participate in globalized media culture will depend on the sociocultural specifics of each case, and the extent to which economic success can be combined with the control of information. There is no single template for how the internet will react with and impact on the conduct of politics in different countries. But that there has been and will be reactions and impacts, everywhere the hardware is available to people, is inevitable.

Guide to further reading

For further reading on the impact of new communication technologies on authoritarian regimes see Kalathil and Boas (2003). Maltby and Keeble's (2007) edited collection explores the impact of digital media on war and conflict reporting, and on military decision-making. McNair (2007) provides an overview of the changing media environments.

229

17

The virtual sphere 2.0

The internet, the public sphere, and beyond

Zizi Papacharissi

This chapter first traces dominant narratives on private and public opinion, beginning with an overview of the public sphere, examining models that oppose or supplement the public sphere, and leading into work that examines the internet as a public sphere. As a second step, distinct conditions that moderate the democratizing impact of the internet are identified and explicated. First, the self-centered nature of online expression lends a narcissistic element to political deliberation online, which is distinct from the objectives of the public sphere. Second, patterns of civic engagement online suggest selective uses of online media to supplement the representative model of democracy and mobilize subversive movements. Finally, the proliferation of online public spaces that are part commercial and part private suggests a new hybrid model of public spaces, where consumerist and civic rhetoric co-exist. These three recent developments are used to question whether the public sphere is the most meaningful lens from which to evaluate the democratizing potential of online technologies.

"Technology is neither good nor bad, nor is it neutral."

(Melvin Kranzberg, 1985: p. 50)

"Technology is a mirror of society, not a 'neutral' force that can be used for good or evil."

(Lasch, 1987: p. 295)

The potential of online media generates a multitude of responses and reactions. Most are centered around the ability of digital and online media to simultaneously restrict and empower individuals as they interact with each other in public life. Thus, the use of the internet, the operative medium here, as it converges and sustains multiple technologies, becomes an asset or a detriment, depending on how it is put to use. The internet, from this point of view serves as a tool, and does not contain the agency to effect social change. Individuals, on the other hand, possess differing levels of agency, based on which they can employ the internet to varying ends,

effects, and gratification. While it is important to avoid the deterministic viewpoint that online technologies are able to, on their own, "make or break" a public sphere, it is also necessary to understand that technologies frequently embed assumptions about their potential uses, which can be traced back to the political, cultural, social, and economic environment that brings them to life. Therefore, it is not the nature of technologies themselves, but rather, the discourse that surrounds them, that guides how these technologies are appropriated by a society. Both Kranzberg's (1985) and Lasch's (1987) descriptions of technology as "non-neutral" or a "mirror of society," acquire meaning as they position technology within a particular discourse. Kranzberg (1985) recognizes technology as a historically relative construct that possess neither evil nor good inherent characteristics, but at the same time is not neutral; it is actualized by and within the historical context that delivered it. Lasch (1987) frames technology as the mirror that exposes the inadequacies, the merits, and the hopes of a society. Thus, individuals are likely to respond to technologies, but even more so, to the discourse that surrounds them. The future of technology rests on the metaphors and language we employ to describe it (Gunkel and Gunkel, 1997; Marvin, 1988).

The discourse surrounding the political potential of online news media could be located in the tension between the "private" and the "public," as articulated in contemporary democracies. Online media lend themselves to several uses, but they acquire agency as they enable the renegotiation of what is considered private and what is considered public in public life. Thus, a political opinion posted on a blog or a video parody posted on YouTube present an attempt to populate the public agenda, and a potential, privately articulated challenge, to a public agenda determined by others. In the truest form of democracy, negotiation of that which is considered public and that which is considered private takes places within the public sphere. As defined by the architect of the concept, Jurgen Habermas, the public sphere presents "a realm of our social life, in which something approaching public opinion can be formed" (Habermas, 1974: 49).

Quite distinct from, but reliant on, the constructs of the public, public space, and public opinion, the public sphere facilitates rational discourse of public affairs directed toward the common good, and it operates autonomously from the state and/or the economy (Garnham, 1990; Habermas, 1974). The modern public sphere, according to Habermas, plagued by forces of commercialization and compromised by corporate conglomerates, produces discourse dominated by the objectives of advertising and public relations. Thus, the public sphere becomes a vehicle for capitalist hegemony and ideological reproduction. Naturally, a digital medium such as the internet, with an infrastructure that promises unlimited and unregulated discourse that operates beyond geographic boundaries, would suggest a virtual reincarnation of the public sphere.

Utopian rhetoric habitually extols the democratizing potential of media that are new (e.g., Bell, 1981; Davis *et al.*, 2002; Johnson and Kaye, 1998; Kling, 1996; Negroponte, 1998). Dystopian rhetoric conversely cautions against enthusiasm regarding the democratizing potential of medium that currently operates on a 17 percent global penetration rate (World Internet Usage and Population Statistics, www.internetworldstats.com/stats.htm, accessed April 2007). Others characterize the democratizing potential of the internet as simply vulnerable (e.g., Blumler and Gurevitch, 2001). This chapter examines the democratizing potential of online media, as articulated through relevant theory, research, and online practices.

This essay first traces dominant narratives on private and public opinion, beginning with an overview of the public sphere, examining models that oppose or supplement the public sphere, and leading into work that examines the internet as a public sphere. As a second step, distinct conditions that moderate the democratizing impact of the internet are identified and explicated. First, the self-centered nature of online expression lends a narcissistic element to political deliberation online, which is distinct from the objectives of the public sphere. Second, patterns of civic engagement online suggest selective uses of online media to supplement the representative model of democracy and mobilize subversive movements. Finally, the proliferation of online public spaces that are part commercial and part private suggests a new hybrid model of public spaces, where consumerist and civic rhetoric co-exist. These three recent developments are used to question whether the public sphere is the most meaningful lens from which to evaluate the democratizing potential of online technologies.

The premise of the public sphere

Academic discussions of civic engagement typically pay tribute to the concept of the public sphere, as conceptualized by Jurgen Habermas (1967/74) in his seminal work. The public sphere presents a domain of social life in which public opinion is expressed by means of rational public discourse and debate. The ultimate goal of the public sphere is public accord and decision-making, although these goals may not necessarily routinely be achieved. Agreement and rational deliberation are desirable outcomes; however, the value of the public sphere lies in its ability to facilitate uninhibited and diverse discussion of public affairs, thus typifying democratic traditions.

The public sphere must not be confused with public space. While public space provides the expanse that allows the public sphere to convene, it does not guarantee a healthy public sphere. The public sphere also serves as forum for, but is conceptually distinct from, the public, public affairs, or public opinion. According to Habermas (1974), "public opinion can only come into existence when a reasoning public is presupposed," and that is what distinguishes it from individuals expressing mere opinions, or mere opinions about public affairs, opinions expressed within

simple proceedings that are made public, or a public consisting of individuals who assemble. Because, according to Habermas, the public sphere has been compromised to the point where its actual existence is in doubt, it is best understood as a metaphor for "a sphere which mediates between society and state, in which the public organizes itself as the bearer of public opinion, accords with the principle of the public sphere—that principle of public information which once had to be fought for against the arcane politics of monarchies and which since that time has made possible the democratic control of state activities" (Habermas, 1973: p. 351).

The historical context evoked by this definition places the public sphere at odds with feudal authorities, and in the modern era, with the state. Within the liberal model of the public sphere, mass media play a critical part in informing and directing public opinion, especially since mass society simultaneously abridges gender/class/race borders and renders direct communication among varying public constituencies more difficult. It is Habermas' argument that the commercialized mass media have turned the public sphere into a space where the rhetoric and objectives of public relations and advertising are prioritized. Commercial interests, a capitalist economy, and mainstream media content have colonized the public sphere and compromised rational and democratic public discourse extinct, with television frequently playing a vanguard role (Habermas, 2004).

This point of view resonates with leading communication scholars. Carey (1995), for instance, articulated how a capitalist economy and the private sector may further amass commercial culture that crowds out the democratic objectives of a public sphere. Specifically relating to the mass media, Putnam (1996) examined a variety of institutional "suspects" responsible for the decline of civic engagement in the U.S., to conclude that television is responsible for displacing time previously devoted to civic affairs and promoting passive involvement with politics. Similarly, Hart (1994) argued that some media, such as television, "supersaturate viewers with political information," and that as a result, "this tumult creates in viewers a sense of activity rather than genuine civic involvement" (Hart, 1994: p. 109).

Additional conditions associated with the transition to industrial and post-industrial modern and postmodern society contribute to a deteriorating public sphere and declining interest in politics. For instance, in contemporary representative models of democracy, politicians, opinion leaders, and the media frequently rely on aggregations of public opinion obtained through polls, as opposed to the rational exchange of opinions fostered by the public sphere. Herbst (1993) refers to such aggregations of public opinion as "numbered voices," thus pointing to the substitution of individual and detailed personal opinion on public affairs with a concentration of viewpoints usually expressed in the bipolarity of the yes/no polling response format. Thus, deliberation of public affairs within the public sphere is postponed as citizens are called upon to express agreement or disagreement with prescribed options.

Such re-appropriation of the public sphere, combined with mainstream media narratives that commodify or simplify complex political issues, conjure up public skepticism among citizens who already have narrowly defined ways of becoming involved in public affairs within a representative democracy model. So, it is not simply that the media crowd the public sphere with commercial rhetoric, it is also that when they do choose to focus on public affairs they do so using frames that prioritize politicizing an issue rather than encouraging rational deliberation of it (Fallows, 1996b; Patterson, 1993). One argument suggests that the prospect of civic participation is de-emphasized and skepticism is reinforced through negative or cynical coverage in the mass media, growing cynicism spreads in a spiraling manner (Cappella and Jamieson, 1996, 1997), producing a public that is further detached from the public sphere.

Several scholars find that the malaise over the public sphere overestimates civic engagement in past societies and civilizations, or the value of public agreement for a healthy democracy. For instance, Lyotard (1984) argued that Habermas overemphasized rational accord as a condition for a democratic public sphere, and argues that it is anarchy, individuality, and disagreement that have and can lead to genuine democratic emancipation. Lyotard's dissent was founded in Derrida's (1997) deconstructivist approach, who emphasized undecidability as the necessary constant in any form of public deliberation. Mouffe (2000, 2005) explicitly connected these ideas to contemporary, pluralist, democracy and posed the concept of agonistic pluralism as a more realistic alternative to the public sphere. Mouffe's (2000) critique is based on the impossibility of true plurality within a modern or postmodern deliberative democracy. Thus, she proposed agonistic pluralism, as a "vibrant clash of democratic political positions," guided by undecidability, and more receptive to the plurality of voices that develop within contemporary pluralist societies than the deliberative model (Mouffe, 2000: p. 104). Specifically, the "agonistic" approach acknowledges the real nature of its frontiers and the forms of exclusion that they entail, instead of trying to disguise them under the "veil of rationality or morality" (Mouffe, 2000: p. 105). Mouffe's (2000, 2005) emphasis on the agonistic foreshadows modes of political expression that have been popularized through the internet, including blogging, YouTube privately produced content, and discussion on online political boards.

The notion of exclusion from the public sphere is also present in Fraser's (1992) work, who suggested that Habermas' examples of past, romanticized public spheres excluded women and non-propertied classes and proposed a post-industrial model of co-existing public spheres or counterpublics, which form in response to their exclusion from the dominant sphere of debate. These multiple public spheres, though not equally powerful, articulate, or privileged, exist to give voice to collective identities and interests. Schudson's (1998) historical review of past political activity further questioned the actual existence of a public sphere, and argued that public discourse is not the main ingredient, or "the soul of democracy," for it is seldom egalitarian, may be too large and amorphous, is rarely civil, and ultimately offers no magical solution to problems of democracy (Schudson, 1997).

Perhaps it is more meaningful to view the public sphere as a metaphor that suggests a mode and ideal for civic participation and interaction, as Habermas originally intended. Within this context, online media, including the internet, could host a virtual sphere or revitalize the public sphere. Several scholars have looked into this question and examined how online media serve as political discussion forums, encourage deliberative or direct models of democracy, and ultimately revive civic participation in public affairs.

The virtual sphere 1.0

Scholarship examining the public sphere potential of the internet has been typically divided into utopian and dystopian visions, which praise civic participation online or question the actual impact of online deliberation, or do both. In these scholarly examinations, researchers tend to be concerned with the following three aspects of online communication, as they directly affect the social and political capital generated by online media: *access* to information, *reciprocity* of communication, and *commercialization* of online space (e.g., Malina, 1999; Papacharissi, 2002; Sassi, 2000).

Access to information

While the internet and surrounding digital technologies provide a public space, they do not necessarily provide a public sphere. Greater *access* to information, enabled by online media, does not directly lead to increases in political participation, or greater civic engagement, or trust in political process (Bimber, 2001; Kaid, 2002). The advantages of the internet as a public space can be enjoyed only by the select few who have access to it, thus harboring an illusion of an open public sphere (Pavlik, 1994; Sassi, 2005; Williams and Pavlik, 1994; Williams, 1994). With the global digital diffusion presently at 17 percent (North America: 70 percent, Oceania: 54 percent, Europe: 39 percent, Asia: 11 percent, Africa: 4 percent, Latin America: 17 percent, Middle East: 10 percent) it might be more appropriate to discuss local, regional, or national public spheres over a global public sphere. Moreover, while digitally enabling citizens (Abramson *et al.*, 1988; Grossman, 1995; Jones, 1997; Rash, 1997), online media simultaneously reproduce class, gender, and race inequalities of the offline public sphere (Hill and Hughes, 1988). Finally, the information access the internet provides also typically results in entertainment uses of the medium (Althaus and Tewksbury, 2000; Shah *et al.*, 2001), the public sphere relevance of which is arguable (Moy *et al.*, 2005; Dahlgren, 2005).

Access can also be understood as greater access to political elites that shape the public agenda, and the ability for these elites to communicate directly with the electorate. Thus, in addition to enabling access to information, online media make it possible for privately motivated individuals and groups to challenge the public agenda (e.g., Grossman, 1995; Rash, 1997), connect the government to citizens, and allow for two-way communication, through interactive features (e.g., Abramson *et al.*, 1988). Still, greater access to information and communication channels does not ensure increases in civic engagement, and could simply generate the illusion of "a sense of activity rather than genuine civic involvement" (Hart, 1994: p. 109). Online political conversations can be as easily dominated by elites as offline ones. Access to information does not guarantee that information will be accessed. Similarly, access to information does not render an electorate more active or efficacious.

Reciprocity

Online media enable conversations that can transcend geographic boundaries. They also allow for relative anonymity in personal expression, which could lead to empowered and uninhibited public opinion. Still, the technological potential for global communication does not ensure that people from different cultural backgrounds will also be more understanding of each other (e.g., Hill and Hughes, 1998). The deliberative model may either be globalized or tribalized, based on the motivations of the political actors that put it to use. Several scholars argue that in order for online discussion to be democratizing, meaning that it must involve two-directional communication, cover topics of shared interest, and be motivated by a mutually shared commitment in rational and focused discoursed. These

elements afford online conversations a degree of *reciprocity,* which can truly help connect citizens of democracies, rather than reproduce fragmented spheres of conversation.

Specifically, online discussion of public affairs can connect citizens sharing similar motivations but may also reproduce and magnify cultural disparities (e.g., Mitra, 1997a, 1997b; Schmitz, 1997). Scholars routinely point to online political discussions that are too amorphous, fragmented, dominated by few, and too specific to live up to the Habermasian ideal of rational accord. While relative anonymity enables political expression online (Akdeniz, 2002), that expression does not always result in discussion of greater substance or political impact (Jones, 1997; Poster, 1995; Schement and Curtis, 1997). Online communication typically takes place among people who already know each other offline (Uslaner, 2004). Research conducted by Jankowski and van Selm (2000) indicated that online discussions seemed to be dominated by elites and seldom extended to the offline sphere of interaction. Other analysis of online political deliberation revealed that collective use of the internet can lead to greater political participation, but only when it is characterized by trust and reciprocity (e. g., Kobayashi *et al.*, 2006). Studies examining the connection between online political talk and social capital found that the social connections people make online do not necessarily promote trust; on the contrary, evidence suggests that online forums frequently bring together mistrusting people (Uslaner, 2004).

Commercialization

Finally, *commercialization* presents a primary concern for researchers who examine the potential of the virtual sphere. The internet has gradually transitioned into an online multi-shopping mall and less of a

235

deliberative space, which influences the orientation of digital political discussion. As a medium constructed within a capitalist context, the internet is susceptible to the profit-making impulses of the market, which do not traditionally prioritize civic participation or democratization (O'Loughlin, 2001; Schiller, 1999, 2006). While equipped with an open architecture that resists commercialization (Lessig, 2006) it is not immune to commercial objectives (McChesney, 1995; Newhagen and Rafaeli, 1996). For instance, in a study of how an online democracy project measured up to the public sphere ideal, Dahlberg (2001) demonstrated how such projects, while partially successful, ultimately are unable to attract a sizeable portion of the population and are frequently "marginalized by commercial sites, virtual communities of common interest, and liberal individualist political practices" (Dahlberg, 2001: p. 615). Employing the Habermasian concepts of colonization and juridification, Salter (2005) showed how mainstream legal tendencies may restrict the democratizing potential of the internet. More importantly, the internet is unable to single-handedly "produce political culture when it does not exist in society at large" (McChesney, 1995: p. 13). Scholars also argue that the content featured online has yet to become distinct from that provided by traditional mass media or to draw in the average citizen in the manner traditional media do (Bimber and Davis, 2003; Margolis *et al.*, 1997; Scheufele and Nisbet, 2002). Finally, through collaboration and mergers with media conglomerates, creative factions of the internet are colonized by the commercial concerns that standardize the content of traditional media (Davis, 1999; Margolis and Resnick, 2000).

Therefore, scholarly examinations of the internet as a public sphere all point to the conclusion that online digital technologies create a public space, but do not

inevitably enable a public sphere. Research so far has shown that *access* to information, *reciprocity* of communication, and *commercialization* are the three primary conditions that prohibit the transition from public space to public sphere. A new public space is not synonymous with a new public sphere, in that a virtual space simply enhances discussion; a virtual sphere should enhance democracy. Similarly, given the nature of online deliberations, it would not be appropriate to even use the term virtual commons; the technologies at hand generate common space, but do not constitute "commons." However, this should not be interpreted as a predicament or a failure. It is not online technologies that fail the public sphere test; rather it could be the other around. This does not necessarily suggest a failure of the online political apparatus; it could merely suggest that the language we use to describe online technologies routinely underestimates their potential.

The virtual sphere 2.0

As individuals become more comfortable with online media, newer appropriations of the internet suggest interesting trends that pull us farther away from the public sphere ideal to a direction that is meaningful, but not what we may have expected. The remainder of this chapter examines these trends and how they articulate the democratizing potential of the internet in a way that has little in common with the Habermasian public sphere but more in common with contemporary public impulses and desires.

On the benefits of civic narcissism

Personalization, that is, the ability to organize information based on a subjective order of importance determined by the self, presents an operative feature of online media such as the internet. Popular features of the internet, such as blogs or MySpace personal/private spaces thrive on personalization. In *The Culture of Narcissism*, Christopher Lasch (1979) described a self-centered culture that emerged following the political turmoil of the sixties, focused on self-improvement, "wrapped in rhetoric of authenticity and awareness," and signifying "a retreat from politics and a repudiation of the recent past" (p. 4–5). Lasch was not describing historical trends that have escaped other historians. Media scholars have also picked up on and analyzed how the consequences and failures of sixties alternative politics have impacted the current relationship individuals have with media or the tendency of contemporary media to abandon historical perspective (e.g., Hart, 1994; Gitlin, 1980, 1983; Patterson, 1993; Putnam, 1996; Schudson, 1998). Moreover, social and political scientists have visited the lasting impact social, economic, cultural, and economic changes brought on by modernity have had on value and belief systems. Inglehart and Welzel (2005) have taken a comparative look at modernity, cultural changes, and democracy across developed and developing societies, to conclude that post-industrialization has ratified a transition from existential to self-expression values. Self-expression values are connected to the desire to control one's environment, a stronger desire for autonomy, and the need to question authority. Self-expression values are not uncivic, and have frequently lead to subversive or collective action movements on environmental protection, fair trade, and gender equality.

It is within a postmodern culture that emphasizes self-expression values that this particular breed of civically motivated narcissism emerges. It should be clarified at this point that the term narcissism is not employed in a pejorative manner or in its pathological sense, which would imply a personality disorder. Narcissism here is employed to understand the introspection and self-absorption that takes place in blogs and similar spaces, and to place these tendencies in historical context. Lasch's work, over psychological research on narcissism as a personality disorder, serves an apt starting point. Narcissism is defined as a preoccupation with the self that is self-directed, but not selfishly motivated. Narcissism is referenced as the cultural context within which blogs are situated, and not as a unilateral label characterizing all blogs.

Blogs are defined as web pages that consist of regular or daily posts, arranged in reverse chronological order and archived (Herring *et al.*, 2004). Initially heralded as a groundbreaking development in the world of reporting and media, blogs bear considerable democratizing potential as they provide media consumers with the opportunity to become media producers (Coleman, 2005a, 2005c). However, despite the audience and public pulpit that blogs provide, they typically regress to self-confessional posts that resemble diaries, with few exceptions that engage in journalistically informed punditry (Papacharissi, 2007). Research has shown that blogs can broadly be divided into A-list blogs (popular publicized blogs); blogs that are somewhat interconnected; and the majority of sparsely socially connected and less conversational blogs (Herring *et al.*, 2005). At the same time, there are many instances in which bloggers exerted sizeable influence over mainstream media, usually by creating noise over issues or political candidates initially marginalized by mainstream media (Kerbel and Bloom, 2005; Tremayne, 2006). Several major news outlets, including CNN, use blogs as "a finger on the pulse of the people" substitute and routinely feature stories or content on what "the blogs" are reporting on a given day. Other mainstream outlets, like the *New York Times*, have incorporated blogging into their traditional reporting, and use it to provide in-depth reporting and/or indulge specific journalist story interests. Varied and diverse as they may be, news blogs frequently function as gateways for mainstream media coverage.

Blogs, video blogs (vlogs), and similar expressions present an articulation of what Scammell (2000) terms "consumer-style critique" (p. 354). Within this context, they are symptomatic of a hedonistic and materialistic culture, which, in Althusserian sense, "interpellates" its citizens as consumers. Political thoughts expressed on blogs are narcissistically motivated in that they are not created with the explicit purpose of contributing to a public sphere, the commons, or heightening civic engagement. While it is true that occasionally they impact mainstream media and public opinion in a sizeable manner, blog content is determined by subjective inclinations and tendencies based on a personal evaluation of content. Quantitative analysis of blogs finds them to be largely self-referential (Papacharissi, 2007) and motivated by personal fulfillment. Even news oriented, A-list blogs present a mélange of public and private information that is subjectively arrived to and removed from western standards of the journalistic profession (objective or partisan). Bloggers blog because they simply want to.

This particular breed of political expression is self-serving and occasionally self-directed, but should not be mis-characterized as selfish. Similarly, Lasch understands narcissistic behavior as structured around the self, but not motivated by selfish desire. Ironically, narcissistic behavior is motivated by the desire to connect the self to society. Lasch acknowledges the insecurity embedded in narcissism, but proceeds to place that narcissism within the "sense of endless possibility" pitted against "the banality of the social order"

contemporary Americans find themselves overcome with (p. 11). According to Lasch, the self-preoccupation associated with the culture of narcissism "arises not from complacency but from desperation" with a society that does not provide a clear distinction between public and private life (p. 26). In moments of variable insight bloggers engage in typical secondary strategies of the narcissist: "pseudo self-insight, calculating seductiveness, nervous, self-deprecatory humor" (Lasch, 1979, p. 33). The new Narcissus, according to Lasch (1979), gazes at his/her own reflection "not so much in admiration as in unremitting search of flaws, signs of fatigue, decay," structuring a performance of the self that is reminiscent of the theatrical, as explicated by Erving Goffman (1959) in the seminal *The Presentation of Self in Everyday Life*. On blogs, the expression of public opinion on private forums (or the expression of private opinion on a public forum—the blogger constantly plays with this distinction) becomes a carefully orchestrated performance with the other in mind.

This particular breed of narcissism has a democratizing effect. The subjective focus of blogs and similar forums encourages plurality of voices and expands the public agenda. While narcissistically motivated, blogs are democratizing in a unique manner. As Bimber (2000) argues, while online technologies "contribute toward greater fragmentation and pluralism in the structure of civic engagement," their tendency "to deinstitutionalize politics, fragment communication, and accelerate the pace of the public agenda and decision making may undermine the coherence of the public sphere" (pp. 332–3). With their focus making a private agenda public, blogs challenge the established public agenda in an anarchic manner. This lack of coordination or concentrated civic objective limits the contribution to the public sphere, and exemplifies how online technologies enhance democracy in ways tangential to, but not directly connected with, the public sphere. While blogs and similar vehicles (e.g., YouTube.com) dilute the agenda-setting function of traditional news sources, they still present personalized media environments (Swanson, 2000), and as such, have a limited contribution to the greater good objectives of the public sphere.

Atomized uses of online media by individuals in their homes do not constitute a public or a public sphere (Dahlgren, 2005), but they do successfully make the political environment more "porous" (Blumler and Gurevitch, 2000). Blogging should not be mistaken for journalism, nor should it be mistaken for a public sphere. Its value lies in demonstrating the conflict between what is private and public; a venerable and timeless conflict that is stressed by online technologies. The type of self-absorption we see on blogs is a play, a constant game with what others define as public or private and what the blogger believes should be defined as public or private. This online user and citizen is interested in challenging what is defined as private and what is defined as public. Priorities here lie in broadening and overlapping private and public agendas; not reviving the public sphere.

Direct representation and subversion: pluralistic agonism

Initial reaction to the democratizing potential of online media was filled with the hope that citizens would employ the media for the deliberative discourse of public affairs that is emblematic of the public sphere. The inherent assumption was that digital media would inject our representative model of democracy with a healthy dose of direct democracy. Recent research on how citizens make use of online media worldwide, however, indicates

that, while political use of new media is vast, it does not fit the mold of the Habermasian public sphere and promotes direct democracy selectively. Specifically, while citizens are increasingly drawn to digital media, they are attracted mostly to interest group and non-partisan websites (Cornfield et al., 2003). Digitally connected citizens still prefer websites of major media outlets or TV for information on public affairs over internet based news organizations (Kohut, 2003).

Additional research indicates that political party websites are successful in reaching out to young voters, but are unable to connect with people who have so far remained aloof toward politics (Jensen, 2003; Boogers and Voerman, 2003). Availability of information alone is unable to sustain and encourage civic engagement (Marcella et al., 2002). Those connected enjoy participating in online polls and circulating political jokes and cartoons, but are not drawn to conventional formats of political content online (such as news releases and endorsements) (Cornfield et al., 2003).

On the opposite end, politicians employ digital media mostly to conduct political research, enhance two-step flow communication with other media and opinion leaders, invite donations to political causes, and publicize news releases and endorsement (Cornfield, 2004a). Online political discussions that feature politicians do enjoy greater participation, but are frequently dominated by politicians who employ them to advocate for their agendas (Jensen, 2003). Uses of digital media by politicians and the media tend to be one-directional and do not sustain feedback channels for the digital public or enable substantive citizen involvement.

Additional research points out the capacity of digital media to connect and sustain subversive movements. Subversion of mainstream political objectives by alternative movements, while not built in to the traditional Habermasian model, presents an operative aptitude of digital media. The role of the internet in shaping the anti-globalization movement specifically highlights this aptitude, and better fits within Fraser's model of counterpublics that compete to articulate a voice within the public sphere. The Zapatistas' use of the internet for political subversion presents a renowned example (e.g., Langman, 2005). Anti-globalization websites are instrumental to (a) establishing movement formation, (b) shaping movement collective identity, and (c) mobilizing movement participants and organizations in a fluid manner (Van Aelst and Walgrave, 2002). Simone (2006) found similar consensus and mobilization use of the internet by CODEPINK, a self-identified women's movement for peace. Pickard (2006) explicated the centrality of the internet in Seattle's Indymedia activist efforts. To this point, Davis (1999) found that the internet reinforces existing patterns of political participation, which primarily serve traditional activists and/or citizens active beyond the norm. Similarly, the internet is essential to non-profits and community associations seeking access to the mainstream media agenda (Jensen *et al.*, 2007; Kenix, 2007). Average voters and politically disinterested citizens employ the internet in a less goal-directed manner. Typically, online media succeed in mobilizing political expression and serving as complements or alternatives to traditional media (Shah *et al.*, 2005).

In societies that are undergoing political transition, access to alternative media online becomes important. For instance, for users in Russia and the Ukraine, sites of online-only newspapers are of primary importance and online versions of offline news outlets, along with politician websites, only minimally used (Semetko and Krasnoboka, 2003). Similarly, in a study of advocacy blogs in Kyrgystan, a former Soviet republic of Central Asia, Kulikova

and Perlmutter (2007) found that samizdat (unofficial) blogs provided information not available through mainstream media, but essential in articulating vocal opposition to the republic's leadership and supporting the "tulip revolution."

Through this exemplary review of recent studies, it becomes obvious that citizens go online to complement or substitute their uses of traditional communication and directly represent their opinions, when possible and necessary. Politicians and media institutions, on the other hand, make use of digital media to supplement their own agendas and objectives, as they see fit. This model of use may ultimately have a democratizing effect, but does not bear a direct resemblance to the public sphere. Moreover, digital media prove adept at furthering mobilization and subversive action. These types of uses evoke Schudson's (1998) model of monitorial citizens, who "scan (rather than read) the informational environment … so that they may be alerted on a variety of issues … and may be mobilized around those issues in a large variety of ways" (p. 310). Not to be mistaken as inactive or uninformed, monitorial citizens are "defensive," rather than "proactive," surveying the political scene, looking "inactive, but [poised] for action if action is required" (p. 311). In the same vein, and adapted to the context of the internet, Bimber's (1998) model of "accelerated pluralism" presents a more accurate portrayal of the democratic role of the internet as contributing "to the ongoing fragmentation of the present system of interest-based group politics and a shift toward a more fluid, issue-based group politics with less institutional coherence" (p. 135).

Contemporary uses of the internet suggest citizen confusion in directly engaging the public sphere. Some of the confusion is associated between the paradox of civic engagement in representative democracy, labeled by Mouffe (2000), among others, as the "democratic paradox." Mouffe (2000) argues that "Democracy requires the existence of homogenous public sphere, and this precludes any possibility of pluralism" (p. 51). Most political scientists subscribed to the more tempered viewpoint that, while civic engagement in representative democracy is not an impossibility, it is, nonetheless, a compromise (e.g., Coleman, 2005c). For instance, Coleman's (2005c) conceptualization of the "directly-represented" citizen presents a compromise between direct and representative democracy. Direct representation, enabled through online media, Coleman argues, "offers many of the same benefits as direct democracy, but fewer of the burdens," thus allowing "citizens the prospect of representative closeness, mutuality, coherence, and empathy without expecting them to become full-time participating citizens." With the incorporation of subversive activities enabled by the internet to this model, we are left with a set of online digital media that do not revive the public sphere, but inject a healthy dose of plurality to a maturing model of representative democracy.

In the same vein, the examples of online activity reviewed here reflect a challenge to authority and the need for the expression of individual political identity. Acts of online mobilization and subversion are aligned with Inglehart and Welzel's (2005) model of human development, which suggests that as societies are able to cater to the existential needs of individuals, citizens then progress to individual autonomy, thus emphasizing self-expression values more. Rising self-expression values do not lead to decline in all civic activities, but they do promote new political habits, "linked with higher levels of political action, focused on making elites more responsive to popular demands" (p. 194). Contemporary political uses of the internet reflect these tensions.

To this point, several argue that models of politics structured around collective identities present an inadequate way of understanding political activity in a more "reflexive," or "liquid" society (e.g., Bauman, 2005; Beck et al., 1994; Giddens, 1990). Diminished participation in the public sphere, online or offline, reflects a move to newer modes of civic engagement, which might be understood better through Mouffe's (2005) proposal of agonistic pluralism and agonistic confrontation. Agonistic pluralism is formulated in contrast to the dialogic pluralism of the public sphere, and is aimed at radically transforming existing power relations. Mouffe (2005) employed the concept in a different context, to specifically call for the reinsertion of right and left into everyday politics, yet the concept is useful in understanding the effect of online subversive movements on democracy. While not all instances of subversion described here have successfully destabilized the existing power structure, they originated as adversarial, possess elements of what Mouffe (2005) terms a "conflictual consensus," and attempt a real confrontation based on a shared set of rules and despite disparate individual positions (p. 52). Mouffe (2005) defined agonism as a "we/they relation" where the conflicting parties, although acknowledging that they are adversaries, operate on common symbolic ground and see themselves as belonging to the same association. In this context, "the task of democracy is to transform antagonism into agonism" (p. 20). While agonists do not function outside the spectrum of the public sphere, they are less concerned with public accord and more with self-expression and voicing disagreement. Thus, the direct representation and subversive capabilities of online media enable agonistic expressions of dissent that do not necessary empower the public sphere, but enhance democracy.

Commercially public spaces: a model of hybrid influence

Early speculation on the democratizing impact of the internet addressed the possibility of online forums being subsumed by corporate entities and interests (McChesney, 1995; Schiller, 1999, 2006). From a political economy perspective, it is inevitable that as information technologies enter the capitalist market, they become commodified so as to enter the mainstream or perish to the margins. Within this context, several online forums emerge as alternatives to mainstream media, but easily forfeit their singularity as they merge with larger corporate entities and become corporate brands themselves. Numerous companies have gone through such cycles, including AOL being bought by Time Warner and gradually losing its unique place on the market, Excite being merged into AT&T and failing to retain its competitive share of the market, and Napster first being sued by music conglomerates, then eventually partnering with entertainment and telecommunications companies to launch a semi-successful online music venture.

More recently, Google, the on-again-off-again auctioning of Facebook, the YouTube/Google partnership, and the incorporation of MySpace.com into News Corporation present some of the latest ventures currently being valuated in the present market cycle (and will likely have undergone significant transformations by the time this chapter goes to print). Like their predecessors, these companies gain stature by challenging conventional media business and attracting new audiences. Media scholars ascertain that as new ventures become commodified, they transition from public spaces to commercial spaces, and thus compromise their democratizing potential. However, this cycle is not that simple or predictable, and conceptualizing market dynamics through the dualities of

marginal and mainstream, while not inaccurate, frequently detracts from observing important trends.

For instance, the recent examples of online music vendors running Tower Records offline stores out of business, or Blockbuster being forced to adopt a half offline, half online model so as to compete with NetFlix, indicate that the influence of online ventures on traditional media has a more far-reaching and long-term effect than expected. Viacom's current ongoing suit of YouTube on digital copyright reveals not only outdated regulatory and market mentalities about copyright law, but also how deeply threatened media giant conglomerates are by smaller, but more flexible, online entities. The recent marketing decision of all major networks to make primetime shows available through their own websites, shortly after they air on TV presents a formal recognition of changes to the market and audience structure effected by entities offering on demand content, for free (peer-to-peer file exchange) or nominal charges (iTunes, Tivo).

Thus, the rigid model of mainstream conglomerates subsuming the smaller marginal firms is being gradually replaced by a model of hybrid influence. This should not suggest that marginal online ventures and the alternative interests they represent are no longer commodified, or that the larger conglomerates are being subverted. However, through a gradual process, which unfolds over the long term, the dynamics of the market are actively challenged and conglomerates are being forced to adopt a more flexible structure that can more easily adapt and serve an audience that has become more selective, elusive, and whimsical. This development produces conglomerates with a more fluid and transient structure; firms that must not only include, but adopt, the practices of the marginal firms they buy out so as to survive. What does this imply for the democratizing potential of online media? Online public spaces do not become immune to commercialization. However, they become adept at promoting a hybrid of commercially public interaction that caters to audience demands and is simultaneously more viable within a capitalist market.

The case of YouTube presents such an example of a commercially public space. YouTube contains vast amounts of audiovisual content, presented in an amorphous format that makes the site virtually impossible to monitor or regulate. Some of this content violates copyright, in that it blatantly reproduces content already copyrighted by other entities. Other types of content present creative re-workings of media content in ways that endorse the audience member as media producer, and promote political satire and dialog. Finally, YouTube also features original content that serves a variety of purposes, ranging from catching a politician in a lie to impromptu karaoke. This blend or hybrid of commercial and public interest is interesting enough to sustain audiences and viable enough to scare off conglomerates (YouTube was recently bought out by the more fluid-structured, medium-sized, Google and consequently sued by Viacom, who saw versions of its copyrighted content featured on YouTube web space). These commercially public spaces may not render a public sphere, but they provide spaces where individuals can engage in healthy democratic practices, including keeping a check on politicians, engaging in political satire, and expressing/circulating political opinions. These spaces are essential in maintaining a politically active consciousness that may, when necessary, articulate a sizeable oppositional voice, in response to concentrated ownership regulation (as described in McChesney, 2004) or U.S. foreign policy (as described in Hands, 2006). While distinct from the public sphere of the past, these tendencies

may present a more accurate reflection of contemporary and postmodern public needs and wants.

Conclusion

The public sphere, in its many forms and conceptualizations by a variety of scholars, presents a concept that allows us to understand civic engagement in historical context. As a construct, the public sphere also helps explicate the influence of the mass media on public discourse, in mass societies that employ varying models of capitalist markets and representative democracy. Research on the political potential of the internet is frequently rapt in the dualities of determinism, utopian and dystopian. In reviewing literature on the role of the internet in political life, Howard (2001) characteristically concluded that the first set of scholarship was "too favorable," the latest "too somber" (p. 949). Scholarly research does not lend support to a virtual sphere, modeled after the public sphere. Moreover, uses that the public spontaneously invents for the internet are removed from the ideal of the public sphere, counter-publics, or similar conceptualizations. As Noam (2005), among others, argued, the internet is not "Athens, nor Appenzell, nor Lincoln-Douglas. It is, if anything, less of democracy than those low-tech places. But of course, none of these places really existed either, except as an ideal, a goal, or an inspiration" (p. 58).

Models that emphasize the plurality enabled by digital media (Bimber, 1998), contemporary citizen needs and wants (Schudson, 1997), and the ability of the internet to amplify political processes (Agre, 2002) present more realistic assessments of online media potential. Romanticized retrospectives of past and future civic engagement often impose language and expectations that curtail the true potential

243

of technologies of the present. The public sphere can be helpful in critiquing and contextualizing the political role of online media, but not in prescribing that role.

Public sphere rhetoric set aside, the question of the democratic relevance of online media remains. The trends identified in this essay capture more recent tendencies in online deliberative spaces. These tendencies are situated in narcissistically derived, civically beneficial expressions of political opinion present in blogs; subversive actions articulated in discourse that emphasizes plurality and agonism; and, finally, privately generated narratives published in commercially public spaces. These tendencies form as an extension of previous dimensions of the virtual sphere, identified as access, reciprocity, and commercialization. But, in both recent and earlier appropriations of online media, the tension between the "public" and the "private" is prevalent. The common thread among all these tendencies can be located in the individual, who operates civically in a political sphere that is founded about the tension between that which is considered public and that which is considered private. Participating in a moveon.org online protest, expressing political opinion on blogs, viewing or posting content on YouTube, or posting a comment in an online discussion group represents an expression of dissent with a public agenda, determined by mainstream media and political actors.

Strikingly, these potentially powerful acts of dissent emanate from a private sphere of interaction, meaning that the citizen engages and is enabled politically through a private media environment located within the individual's personal and private space. Whereas in the truest iterations of democracy, the citizen was enabled through the public sphere, in contemporary democracy, the citizen acts politically from a private sphere of reflection, expression, and behavior. Within

this private sphere, the citizen is alone, but not lonely or isolated. Connected, the citizen operates in a mode and with political language determined by him or her. Primarily still monitorial in orientation, the citizen is able to become an agonist of democracy, if needed, but in an atomized mode.

The private sphere is empowering, liquid, and reflexive. But, what happens to the public sphere, when all political action retreats to the private sphere? This transition from the prominent public realm to private spaces could equal alienation, in which "the specific and usually irreplaceable in-between which should have been formed between the individual and his fellow men" is lost (Arendt, 1968: p. 4). It is precisely this "in-between," which, as individuals act civically from the locus of the private sphere, is filled in by online digital media. Unlike offline digital media, online technologies possess "reflexive" architecture, responsive to the needs of multiple private spheres, which would be isolated were it not for the connectivity capabilities of online media.

Guide to further reading

As we look for contemporary metaphors and new language with which to describe and understand the political potential of online media, it is necessary to contextualize our assessments within human development. For those interested in the internet as a public sphere (or not, as I argued here), readings beyond the obligatory public sphere literature, should include a balanced combination of pontification and data reflecting social, political, economic, and cultural trends. Habermas (2004), in his recent writings (e.g., *The Divided West*), refers less to the public sphere, and more to concepts like cosmopolitanism, which could inform how a "global" citizen functions in an online digital environment. Toby Miller's (2007) *Cultural Citizenship* traces the transition of citizenship from the political to the cultural realm, presenting an argument that could explain several behaviors we observe on online public environments. Zygmunt Bauman, in any of his books on liquid modernity (he typically publishes two every year), synthesizes contemporary social and political theory to provide a lively and accurate depiction of public life in the age of modernity and beyond. Any work by Manuel Castells sets the standard for interdisciplinarity, and the complex interaction of socio-cultural factors to be considered as we interpret the meaning of contemporary technology. Inglehart and Welzel's (2005) more recent set of data and accompanying analysis trace a progression of human values that we all notice in our everyday lives, but lack the vocabulary with which to discuss. Finally, for a proper understanding of how social, political, economic, and cultural trends converge, I like to read the work of architects, and anything by Rem Koolhaas presents a good starting point.

18

Identity, technology, and narratives

Transnational activism and social networks

W. Lance Bennett and Amoshaun Toft

Social movement research often regards collective identity and collective action frames as central for movement development or decline. Yet the social fragmentation experienced by younger generations in late-modern societies suggests a decline in formal memberships and collective identities, and rising participation in loose-tie networks. Narratives play important roles in structuring these networks, but they may or may not operate as collective action frames brokered by leading organizations. Many action stories are open to highly personalized and diverse interpretations, enabling flexible relationships between individuals and organizations. In other cases, narratives flow through gatekeeping nodes in networks such as planning committees or network support organizations. Such narrative gatekeeping by leading network organizations can affect the diffusion of identity cues across networks, resulting in structural coherence or tensions. We examine three cases that suggest different contributions of communication technologies and narrative flow to the relationships among organizations and individual activists in mobilization networks: the global anti-war protests against the Iraq war; the planning and cancellation of a regional social forum; and a comparison of fair trade networks in the U.S. and the U.K.

The changing organization of social activism in post-industrial societies has received considerable attention, from the study of "new" social movements (Buechler, 1995; Melucci, 1994), to exploring information networks in transnational advocacy (Keck and Sikkink, 1998), to the examination of self-organizing properties in technology-enabled *permanent campaigns* (Bennett, 2003). We are interested in how networking technologies operate in different social activism contexts. Social technologies do not offer magic solutions in the formation of activist networks, nor do they often replace organizations, meetings, or rallies as means of building solidarity. We begin with this point as a caution against thinking that persistent,

large-scale activist networks, such as those associated with the recent surge of transnational activism, occur effortlessly online. Our interest is to determine where information technologies fit into the conventional gamut of protests, campaigns, and endless meetings that bring people into direct contact. At the same time, many forms of activism—particularly those that cross national and cultural boundaries—blur easy distinctions between on- and offline behavior. The difficult question is to locate the connective elements that enable people to travel across interpersonal and digital pathways, and in the process, cross individual, organizational, and network levels of action. We suggest that the uses and flows of narratives in the organization of political action illuminate the interplay between technology and human interaction, while providing links among different levels of analysis required for understanding protest organization.

The junctures and disjunctions in the composition of networks can be thought of as choices at different levels (e.g., individual, organization, and network-wide) about what to identify with and how strongly. Stories often embody and calibrate those identifications at different levels of analysis. For example, if we focus on the organizational level in protest networks, identifying the uses of narrative quickly takes us to the nexus between individuals and organizations: what organizational stories enable which individuals to identify with them, leading them to form what kinds of relationships (e.g., from formal membership to loose affinity) with which organizations? The ways in which stories join or separate individuals and organizations may affect how network ties are established and how easy they are to sustain.

Stories also may become elemental in the flow or blockage of information across internet connections among individuals and organizations. Some degree of the linking in most contemporary protest networks is electronic—machines communicating with people and with other machines. Not only are costs of organization potentially reduced by digital linking, but various technology links may well become part of organizational structure themselves. Stories are relatively easy to embed, whether in whole or in part, in digital media, from action alerts in e-mail lists, to the mission statements and "get involved" pages of websites, to electronic forums that enable members to tell and share stories about their concerns. Pentland and Feldman (2007) suggest that technologies, alone, do not organize social networks apart from the stories that people share through and about those

technologies—including their reasons for, and their ways of using them.

We propose to explore how technology and narrative organization play out in three different contexts in which activist relationships form and become expressed: *protests, campaigns,* and *social forums.* Each type of activity represents a different slice of activist life, and each arguably requires the others in order to create sustainable and effective movements. Protest events such as marches, vigils, and demonstrations draw dramatic attention to causes, and give activists opportunities to vent and publicly express emotional concerns. Campaigns target larger audiences with more detailed information about why they might want to join in protest against offending campaign targets. And forums provide opportunities for the activist community to reflect, learn, plan, and celebrate their causes. This analysis examines a case of each type of activity with an eye to how narratives travel over networks and either enable or inhibit the loose-tied relationships that social technologies can help establish.

Our first case explores the "World Says No to War" protests on February 15th, 2003, when 15–20 million people took to the streets in opposition to the impending U.S. invasion of Iraq. In what many regard as the largest coordinated mobilization in human history, activists and organizations working on a wide range of issues showed their support for a common political demand—"No War on Iraq," a frame of such breadth that millions of individuals and organizations could raise their own narrative versions of the issue within it. That broad narrative freedom enabled many individuals to develop flexible relationships with sponsoring organizations, resulting in the broad use of digital media to activate diverse personal political networks (Bennett, Breunig, and Givens, 2008).

Our second case, which may be generally described as centered on a long-running

247

campaign (surrounded by various protest events and forums), compares fair trade networks in the U.S. and the U.K. Those networks consist of individuals and various types of organizations seeking fair compensation for the producers of commodities such as coffee, tea, and cocoa in the global south. While both the U.S. and the U.K. campaign networks are transnational in character and dedicated to a common cause, the lead national "gatekeeping" organizations differ substantially in the stories they promote about how individuals, companies, and, ultimately, nations can best engage with fair trade. The national certification and labeling organization in the U.K. (the Fairtrade Foundation) emphasizes a layered narrative that encompasses both individual conscientious consumption and collective (including national and transnational policy) commitments to principles of social and economic justice in trading relationships. The relatively radical collective action story of global economic exploitation has been widely publicized through a national *trade justice campaign* in which the Fairtrade Foundation joins most other major fair trade groups to mobilize public action for fairer national and international trade policies. Thus, narratives about exploitation and justice sit comfortably alongside more personalized, less explicitly political narratives about reasons for responsible consumption, all of which are given room for expression in web forums, e-mail lists, and other media affordances such as events calendars. By contrast, the U.S. certification and labeling organization (Transfair USA) emphasized the individual "conscientious consumer" version of the fair trade narrative to the near exclusion of the trade justice story, creating tensions with many other actors in the U.S. network who would prefer elevating the justice story, which they see as part of a larger narrative whole. The relative

narrative harmony in the U.K. and the tensions in the U.S. are clearly reflected in the distances and clusters in the structure of web linkages in the two networks (Bennett *et al.*, 2007).

Our third case looks at the organization and cancellation of the Northwest Social Forum (NWSF) in the northwestern United States and southwestern Canada. Social forums have emerged as valuable tools in building cross-issue and transnational collaboration and solidarity by providing spaces for speakers, workshops, films, and social networking to explore issues, strategies, and social divisions. The organizers of the NWSF set explicit narrative goals to empower traditionally disempowered groups such as people of color and indigenous groups. However, the broadly shared narrative of an open participatory organizing process ultimately clashed (in the view of many participants) with an adopted planning committee process aimed at building personal relationships with disempowered groups. This process was accompanied by decisions to reject more technology-based, loose tie networking strategies for organizing and communicating with participants in the forum. The inability to create strong tie relationships in a short time led to the last minute cancellation of the event, followed by critical and often personally hostile narratives expressed on the list serve, and the collapse of the Forum process (Toft *et al.*, 2007).

Narratives and frames as distinct analytical constructs

Our cases indicate that the framing of action (Entman, 1993; Benford and Snow, 2000) still matters, but often in surprising ways that do not always fit easily alongside the conventional social movement notions of collective identity frames being the *sine qua non* of movement building and stability. In fact, our research indicates that there may be advantages to looking at narrative processes as distinct from the ever-popular communication concepts of frames and framing. Several distinct advantages may be revealed in separating narratives from frames as analytical constructs.

First, some frames may be shorthand references for clear and commonly shared underlying narratives, while others may not. Consider the Iraq war protest frame of "No War in Iraq," which is a frame that traveled around the globe and drew millions of protesters. Yet, within that frame, were gathered untold numbers of stories that differed as to why the war was wrong (another case of U.S. imperialism, ill considered policy, attacking the wrong country, lack of diplomatic initiatives, etc.) and what should be done in its stead (sanctions, diplomacy, more limited military action, nothing, etc.). Thus, identifying an organizing frame may not lead to much understanding of the underlying narratives that give it meaning, much less help us understand how those underlying narratives affect the organization of protest networks.

Second, in some networks multiple frames can be embedded comfortably within the same commonly accepted story, while in other comparable networks the same frames may be viewed as constituting competing or incompatible narratives about the rationale for action. Thus the lead organizations in the U.K. fair trade coffee network appear generally to agree that personal consumer choices are one part of a larger fight for national and international trade justice, making the two frames of responsible consumer choice and trade justice easy elements of the same grand narrative. In the U.S., by contrast, some leading organizations are careful to emphasize consumer choice while avoiding trade justice in the context of a larger market-oriented, business-friendly narrative about fair trade being good for businesses that sell certified products. The narrative split in the U.S. is reflected in tensions in the larger network that affect the capacity of the movement to undertake various kinds of collective action.

Third, even when frames are commonly accepted across a broad spectrum of a network, communication practices may inhibit the kinds of narrative co-production (through actions and story sharing) that people need to verify and affirm the underlying meanings of frames. As a result, frames that may be passionately embraced as general principles may end up being experienced in particular networks as empty slogans, or contested on grounds of betrayal by one faction against others. For example, the frames of openness and inclusiveness were unassailable bywords for most who planned to attend the Northwest Social Forum. Yet the thick-tie (low tech) strategy pursued by the planning committee to draw in disempowered groups ultimately failed, leaving many outside the planning committee to doubt the credibility of the process, asking how an open and inclusive process could be canceled by a committee; to which many on the inside argued that those who later expressed criticism could have joined the process.

These examples of how narratives and frames can be usefully separated as analytical concepts are not exhaustive of the reasons for keeping the concepts distinct. However, they suggest important ways in which narratives operate in relation to frames via various social mechanisms and communication technologies that help them travel across networks. It is to these technological features of narrative networking that we now turn.

Activist networks and technology

Accounting for the presence or absence of different types of social technologies in activist networks involves thinking about choices available to individuals and organizations. Both organizations and individuals make choices as they *join*, *organize*, and *leave* networks, producing different sorts of collective action. Some of those choices are enabled or limited by technology access, resources, and skills. For instance, large portions of the world's population still have little or no real access to the internet. Sometimes the networking choices are more strategic, reflecting fundamental conceptions about the kinds of relationships organizations want with their members and affiliates, or that individuals seek with organizations and each other. For example, election campaigns in many nations today could turn over substantial levels of content production and decision-making to large numbers of supporters by joining them through interactive networking technologies (Chadwick, 2006). However, few parties, candidates or, more importantly, their political consultants are willing to abandon the so-called *war room*, centrally organized model of campaigns (Center for Communication and Civic Engagement, 2004). In contrast to elections, other kinds of campaigns are much more decentralized, and more driven by technologically facilitated relationships among actors. For example, many so-called *logo campaigns* pressing companies for greater social responsibility in environment, labor, or trade practices have been relatively self-organizing, even (and perhaps especially) when disparate players possess only the barest of organizational resources (Bennett and Lagos, 2007). Some of these predominantly internet-based campaigns have proved remarkably sustainable, while offering players—both organizations and individuals—a great deal of autonomy in how and when to participate. While highly managed campaigns like elections restrict bottom–up interactivity in order to act strategically, decentralized campaigns can have the opposite problem of coordinate strategies, protest actions on and off (Ben. 005).

Allowing an integral role for technology choices in the analysis of activism means that social software and the devices that run them can be understood as non-human *actants* in complex networks, to borrow a term network theory (Latour, 2005) thinking of networks only as of human actions, this approach us to see how elements of the physical environment (from fair trade pels on coffee bags, to social networking software and the platforms that run it) contribute independently to the scale, speed, or durability of networks. The presence or absence of basic technology features such as calendars, open forums, or links can inhibit or facilitate the sharing of stories along networks, and affect the identifications and action choices among potential participants.

Identity, narratives, and network dynamics

Affiliation with an online activist organization such as *MoveOn* in the U.S. entails receiving e-mail or text message alerts and calls to action, which often include requests to send them along to friends. This social networking often involves sharing a personal story or message. These personal accounts may then be fed back to the network as examples of how others, who remain complete strangers, have framed their participation. At any level of analysis, from the individual, to the organization, to the network, stories locate actors in relationship to action: Who am I? What do I think about this protest? What do I do? Who am I with? Do I belong to their group? Who are they? What do they do? How do they do it? Why?

Just as narrative elements help us move analytically from individuals, to organizations, to personal networks, we can also start at other points in network formations and travel along other paths. For example, we can look at how organizations signal to individuals and to other organizations: Who are we? What do we do? Who do we do it with? How do we act? What do we ask from you? Such identifying story elements can be found in websites under familiar tabs such as About Us, Get Involved, What You Can Do, Mission Statement, and so on.

By moving among individuals and organizations, narratives thus play a central role in the formation of the ties that constitute networks. Polletta (1998, 2006) argues that the development of narratives about the reasons for action contributes significantly to participants' self-conceptions and ultimately the ways that they institutionalize those experiences. Once organizations generate mission inspiring narratives, they may develop into strategic "collective action frames" that "assign meaning to and interpret, relevant events and conditions in ways that are intended to mobilize potential adherents and constituents, to garner bystander support, and to demobilize antagonists" (Snow and Benford, 1988: 198).

Whether collective action frames emerge, or whether more open framing permits action based on diverse individual and organizational narratives, understanding the properties of resulting networks may be enhanced by examining the technologies through which frames and underlying narratives flow. Consider, for example, what may be revealed about a network in the weblinks among organizations. In- and out-linking in technologically enabled networks may reflect perceptions on the part of organizations that others share concerns about issues or problems (Rogers, 2002). Failure to return links may signal that an in-linking party is seen as being too small a player in an organization's scheme to warrant attention; alternatively, the relationship may be close, but too controversial to acknowledge publicly. As elements of narratives join individuals and organizations in dynamic networks, the relatively *open* or *closed* nature of the stories—that is, the willingness of individuals and organizations to share ownership and control over them—helps determine the size and degree of distributed or centralized structure of the network. For example, as noted earlier, the main fair trade labeling (narrative gatekeeping) organization in the U.S. promotes a business-friendly consumer story while downplaying a more radical trade justice narrative, contributing to a network with relatively large path distances among organizations. One result is that a few social justice nongovernmental organizations (NGOs) must take on a disproportionate share of the influence work, as reflected in a high volume of out-linking to other organizations to help keep the network together.

Organizations not only negotiate with each other to find suitable action frames that accommodate their respective stories, but those stories are also in play with individuals who can form various kinds of relationships with organizations in the mobilization process. Where individual level identity properties may have been relatively less important in the era of mass media and mass social membership, digital media both reflect and enhance the capacity of individuals to communicate in personalized ways. Far from being a technologically deterministic process, we prefer to think about them as an interaction between the development of communication technologies and patterns of social change.

The capacity for collective action in fragmenting (Beck, 1999, 2000; Putnam, 2000) and increasingly personalized societies (Giddens, 1991; Bennett, 1998) increasingly

251

hinges on the formation of networks around lifestyles and the personal political values of individuals who often do not wish to cede authority to, or otherwise conform to, the membership requirements of conventional political organizations. As a result of the shifting nature of social identification and organization, many conventional political interest organizations are replacing formal membership requirements with more entrepreneurial relationships that reduce various costs and conditions of collective action (Flanagin, Stohl, and Bimber, 2006). Social movements attempting to span geographical (particularly national political) spaces and social differences may reflect these changes most clearly. For example, della Porta (2005) talks about the *flexible identities* that are drawn to global justice networks where much of the bridging and bonding is done at the individual level.

All of this suggests that the nature of network relationships and their technological management play out along two dimensions of identity-related tensions:

- At the organization level: organizational pressures for *collective identification* lead to more centralized strategic management of inter-organizational relationships and individual membership requirements, generally resulting in less deployment of interactive technology and participation in the production of narrative content. By contrast, an emphasis on *inclusiveness and diversity* is likely to lead to a greater use of interactive technology that invites bottom–up action initiatives and accompanying narration.
- At the network level: collective identification pressures typically result in preferences for *strong tie coalitions,* with the attendant problems of high maintenance and limits on growth. The preference

for more inclusive organizations fueled by co-production of narratives via networking technologies favors (indeed, defines) *weak tie networks*. Weak ties empower individuals to mobilize their own diverse political networks.

These propositions help explain a good deal about network dynamics. For example, it is not surprising that the lack of a binding narrative definition for the inclusive "No War in Iraq" frame of the global protests enabled considerable grass-roots technology deployment and a high level of personal-level network activation (perhaps accounting for the speed and scale of the mobilization). By contrast, the strain between the inclusiveness and diversity frames and the relatively centralized, low-tech planning of the social forum may account for both the shock expressed at its cancellation and the fact that list traffic actually increased in terms of the number and diversity of posts after the event was canceled. The following sections explore these two dimensions of networks in more detail.

Collective identification versus inclusiveness and diversity

As we enter an era marked by public reaction to evolved global economic and state-level political arrangements, many new forms of political and cultural associations are forming across borders and issues (Clark, 2003; Cohen and Rai, 2000; della Porta and Tarrow, 2005; Garrido and Halavais, 2003; Kaldor, 2003). Movements are organizing in the transnational arena, connecting geographically disconnected groups with common issues and targets of protest. As a result, many single-issue movements are developing capacities to organize across issues, as evident in the connections among environmentalism, shade-grown coffee, organic production, and some branches of the fair trade movement. In the process, collective identity requirements for membership and belonging are relaxed, personal narratives are easier to publicize, and technology applications are coded to facilitate networks in more diverse and creative ways.

Information and communication technologies (ICTs) have created a capacity to aggregate audiences by linking dense networks of personal, "micro media" such as e-mail, personal blogs, and text messaging, to "middle media" channels such as issue blogs, NGO sites, or Indymedia, offering activists unprecedented channels of communication (Peretti, 2001, 2003). The growth of large and less centrally organized networks populated with large numbers of upstart organizations and "direct activists" may repel old line social movement organizations working on particular issues, making them reluctant to give up or share control of political narratives and strategies. Research on social movements has begun to reflect this shift, supplementing the traditional focus on collective identity as a defining quality of movement organizations and networking dynamics (McCarthy and Zald, 1977; Tilly, 1978), with greater attention to "meaning creation" (Eyerman and Jamison, 1991: 55) and the contestation of "codes" in modern informational societies (Melucci, 1996).

While it is clear that organizations still play an important role in building and networking modern social movements (Fisher et al., 2005), the role of information technologies has had a significant impact on the form and function of political mobilization. In some cases ICT applications allow large and diverse populations to find common cause in networks that challenge conventional organizational structures and capacities. A variety of networking technologies, have enabled these so-called "weak tie" networks to shape participation in a wide range of cross-issue movements (Bennett, 2003).

Weak ties versus strong coalitions in networks

As a result of the distribution of opportunities and demands for collective or more inclusive identification with organizations and causes, networks take on different organizational forms, with varying mixes of strong-tie relationships between individuals and groups, to weaker affinity ties that enable greater individual choice over the terms of engagement. Granovetter (1973) measured these differences in the strength of relationship ties in terms of "the amount of time, the emotional intensity, the intimacy (mutual confiding), and the reciprocal services which characterize the tie" (1361). By creating a triad categorization scheme consisting of *strong ties*, *weak ties*, and *absent ties*, Granovetter (1973) outlined a theoretical basis for understanding the social organization of strong cohesive groups and broader loose networks something that is particularly relevant to social movement research. The persistent issue campaigns that surround companies like Starbucks, McDonald's, Shell, Monsanto, Microsoft, and Nike exemplify weak-ties networks of individuals and organizations sharing resources but often engaging in autonomous activity. The explosion of "parallel summits" (Pianta, 2003) like social fora have provided spaces for disseminating public information, proposing alternative policies, and networking among civil society organizations through loose ties operating under common umbrella themes such as globalization (Pianta and Silva, 2003; della Porta, 2005; Diani, 2003; Galaskiewics and Wasserman, 1993; Garrido and Halavais, 2003; Scott, 2000; Whitaker, 2004).

What distributed networks lack in terms of traditional organizational resources they often gain in networking capacities through the use of social technologies to facilitate the maintenance and activation of weak ties (Bennett, 2003). Bimber (1998) expanded Granovetter's (1973) strong and weak ties analysis to the impact of communication technologies on social organization, hypothesizing that "the Net is accelerating the process of issue group formation and action"—something he calls "accelerated pluralism" (Bimber, 1998: 136). This trend exhibits "a shift toward a system of more rapidly changing issue groups, with less stability and less dependence on private and public institutional structures" (Bimber, 1998: 155). Such a move towards fluid parallel information structures (Kidd, 2003), alongside existing institutions, facilitates the development of myriad weak ties between individuals, and loose collectivities of specialized issue groups.

These developments suggest that technologies can do more than reduce organizational costs: they can greatly enhance the capacity of individuals to organize weak-tie networks, enabling the contribution of information by single actors to a "collective good" (Marwell and Oliver, 1993; Rogers, 2004; Bimber, Flanagin, and Stohl, 2005: 372). In other words, at some point on this spectrum of organizational types, *the communication process becomes the organizational structure*, making technology inseparable from the social network itself. However, we also caution against sweeping generalizations regarding the role of technology in political mobilization. Clearly not all situations tap the interactivity and networking potential of digital media. We find that when identity requirements (formal membership, ideological commitment, collective framing) are relaxed so that individuals can find social ties and narrative connections that are personally comfortable, technology networks have the potential to do considerable organizational work. When organizations, or powerful factions within them, fight for control over the collective agenda and try to set the terms of political

engagement (i.e., create collective frames and master stories), the role of technology, beyond simply reducing communication costs, is often more limited.

Narratives, identities, and technology networks: three cases

We illustrate these intersections of identity, narrative, and technology with brief elaborations of the three cases introduced earlier: the global anti-war protests against the Iraq war in 2003; a comparison of fair trade networks in the U.S. and the U.K., and the organization and cancellation of a regional social forum in the northwest U.S. and southwest Canada.

No war in Iraq

The planning of the February 15, 2003 global anti-war protests can be traced to the European Social Forum meetings in the summer of 2002. The Forum displayed its rapid networking capacity with the mobilization of a half million demonstrators in the streets of Florence. While some observers worried that the shift in focus from global justice to anti-war might sidetrack and deplete the energy of the globalization movement, it turned out that the existing emphasis on weak ties and flexible identities enabled focus-shifting with relative ease. Subsequent regional meetings leading to the World Social Forum gathering in January of 2003 resulted in remarkable consensus around sharing the broadest possible action frame: "No War in Iraq"—a frame within which many other narratives could fit, including imperialism, peace, anti-racism, and global justice, among others. Subsequent protest cycles after the war was launched continued to invite diversity of personal and organizational narratives, a fact that often confounded mass media journalists looking for "the story" about the protests. Resulting news coverage often focused on the chaos or incoherence of the movement itself, themes that have also characterized news framing of globalization protests (Bennett *et al.*, 2004). Looked at differently, the case of the Iraq protests suggests that the openness of the framing shared by the sponsoring organizations (including some strongly ideological groups) was key to the broad activation of weak-tie networks.

A survey of 6753 demonstrators in 8 nations (Germany, the U.K., Spain, Switzerland, Belgium, Netherlands, Italy, and the U.S.) showed that many different kinds of organizations were involved, and that there was considerable diversity in activist profiles, from first-time demonstrators, to single-issue advocates, to activists with diverse issue commitments and protest histories (Walgrave and Rucht, 2008). While there were national differences in the demographic composition of the demonstrators, one notable feature characterized all the national samples: activists who had the most diverse personal political network identifications also tended to manage their information and communication activities with digital media. Diversity of network identification was measured in several distinct ways: individual-level sympathy and strength of identification with the global justice movement (which tends to favor inclusiveness and diversity among its narrative frames), the number of different organizational memberships logged for each demonstrator, and the number of different issues for or against which each respondent had demonstrated in the past. Each of these measures was associated with dominant e-media use (high reliance on e-mail, lists, websites, and low reliance on mass media) for obtaining and sharing information about the demonstrations, for promoting social change, and for obtaining general political information.

Even more interesting is that activists with more diverse network identifications also tended to be more likely to have some affiliation with organizations involved in helping to coordinate the demonstrations. Both association with sponsoring organizations and holding diverse personal political networks turn out, after statistical analysis, to be strong predictors of dominant e-media use even when entered in the same regression equation and controlling for various demographic variables. This suggests that organizations continue to play a role in rapid, large-scale mobilization such as demonstrations, but the key to the scale and speed of mobilization is whether lead organizations are open to action stories that allow individuals to activate their own networks to magnify the turnout. While we cannot definitively connect all the links in this complex chain of inference, we tentatively propose that chains of weak ties from organizations, to individuals, to their personal social and issue networks were managed by digital information technologies in ways that contributed to the scale of the protests (both numbers of participants and geographic dispersion of sites) and the speed (a matter of months) with which they were organized. While the flow of narratives in such a complex mobilization is difficult to document, the continuing openness among lead organizations to an inclusive story surely helped activate the broadest reach of those weak-tie networks (Bennett, Givens, and Breunig, 2008).

Buyer be fair: a tale of two nations

Our second case involves comparing two large-scale fair trade networks in the U.S., and the U.K. This case illustrates the effects of different narrative flows on organization and technology deployment in those networks. Recall that the fair trade story most evident in the U.S.

emphasizes individual consumer choice to create market demand to persuade large companies such as Starbucks to be more socially responsible in their buying and marketing of products. In the U.K., consumer choice stories also exist, but they are generally embedded in broader narratives that include more radical social justice scripts about inequality, injustice, and sustainable development policies. These social and economic justice narratives often invite individuals to go beyond buying fair trade coffee or chocolate, and to organize their towns, schools, and offices, or contact their member of parliament, the U.K. trade minister, or the president of the European Union to advocate trade justice policies. By contrast, there are few invitations to contact government about policy issues in the U.S. The heavily consumer framing more often encourages individuals to ask for fair trade products and avoid radical political messages that might offend businesses. Organizations that promote more radical stories in the U.S. often sit at the margins of the main network, sometimes even promoting different schemes for certifying products and the companies that sell them.

The distributions of narratives across these networks are reflected in the linking patterns among organizations. For example, organizations in the U.S. network that favored a trade justice narrative tended to have greater path distances from the more consumer/market oriented sites, requiring considerably greater out-linking efforts by a small number of centralized organizations (such as Global Exchange) to keep the network together. By contrast, the U.K. network contained considerably smaller path distances among organizations, with more organizations sharing the out-linking load in network influence. An important source of these different network structures are the pronounced narrative differences on the sites of the

national labeling organizations Transfair USA and the Fairtrade Foundation in the U.K., which exert gatekeeping influence over the network due to control of the certification process and dispensing the trademarks that populate the physical environment with clear signals about products and the stores and brands selling them. Due to the greater agreement on the combined consumer and justice narrative, the U.K. network displayed more closeness, less brokerage or path distance, and more coherence in the mobilization of individual actions beyond buying fair trade products. In addition, the U.K. network organization websites offered individuals more opportunities to contribute their own content, along with encouragement to contact different levels of government to pressure for change in trade policies. The U.S. network organizations (including many of the NGOs in the network) offered fewer opportunities to contribute content, fewer points of contact with government, and far greater opportunities to buy products (Bennett *et al.*, 2007).

Canceling a forum: building on success, learning from failure

The World Social Forum (WSF) has established itself as a global justice icon gathered under a simple frame: "Another World is Possible" (Schönleitner, 2003). The presentation of such an open frame, has functioned as an umbrella, allowing a diverse array of narratives to develop (Fisher and Ponniah, 2003). This flexibility has also impacted the spread of the WSF model, and dozens of local social forums have taken root across the globe, often borrowing and adapting its 14-point Charter of Principles (Olivers, 2004; Pleyers, 2004). The Northwest Social Forum (NWSF) would have been the second social forum in the U.S., following the Boston Social Forum.

The NWSF was developed as an ambitious project, spanning a broad range of issues across a significant geographical area. While the initial event was scheduled for October of 2004, many of the individuals and organizations involved saw the Social Forum as a ten-year process of building strong-tie relationships across cultures and geography, and creating communication spaces where ideas and issues could be worked out for a common cause. However, in the last two months of planning, a narrative of discord between the inclusive social justice framing of the Forum and key participant experiences in the organizing process began to emerge, with several groups pulling out. Less than two weeks before it was scheduled to occur, the Planning Committee (the main organizing body) cancelled the event, and the organizing infrastructure dissolved. In order to understand how the network structure proved so fragile, we conducted an analysis based on archived copies of the organizing website, 243 discussion list e-mail messages, 42 responses to an online survey, and 21 in depth interviews.

Organizing narratives were modeled after the WSF and informed by local indigenous protocol around respect and consensus. Early organizers conceived of a diverse planning committee that put the most disadvantaged at the center of the organizing process. Efforts were made to invite participation from marginalized populations and establish strong relationships before making an open call for participation in the Social Forum. One participant noted the great excitement about "the commitment to indigenous wisdom and worldview and to youth and people of color in leadership." However, it soon became clear that organizers lacked the staffing, time, and resources to effectively carry out the agreed upon strong-tie process in such a short timeline.

With only a few months to organize the event after an opening planning retreat, meetings became more constrained and it became difficult to achieve meaningful, consensus-based participation. As one participant put it, "[people] signed on for a consensus process and for being at the center of the process, and then the whole end-focused process, driven by the deadline, happened. And that was all lost." Despite the narrative of openness and diversity, some participants felt that the exclusionary tendencies of the dominant culture were inscribed invisibly into the tight time frame and the imperative to forge fast, strong-tie coalitions: "[all] that is a very western, very white, very male, and a very traditional normal non-profit approach—we are very end driven in this country: the ends justify the means." The tension between an open, consensus-based process and the realities of planning an event on a short timeline became too great and one of the core constituencies began calling for postponing the conference—a request that was denied, and the group pulled out. Once the Indigenous Planning Committee pulled out, others followed suite and organizers decided to cancel the forum in the hopes of reconciling differences and moving forward later on with a more open process.

The narrative emphasis on racial justice in the organizing vision led to an emphasis on strong-tie networking and a decision early on not to introduce more sophisticated social networking technologies beyond e-mail and the website into the organizing process. Instead, organizers focused their energies on building face-to-face relationships with those communities most severely affected by economic and social inequalities. Among organizers of the forum, there was a sense that there is often too heavy a reliance on technology for outreach, and they wanted to counter this trend. One member of the Planning Committee commented that, "if you are especially talking about electronic networks there are a whole bunch of people that you cannot reach at all and I think that the people who are most likely to be left out are older poor people of color. It is going to be a much narrower group."

Of the digital tools that were made available, the discussion list was the most used, but mostly for posting announcements of offline activities. As noted earlier, the uses of the list changed drastically once the event was cancelled. Almost overnight, the list went from a low-traffic announcement platform with very few authors (only four authors posted 47 percent of all e-mails) to a popular discussion platform (accounting for 47.3 percent of all sent messages) with 24 participants posting their comments or ideas for the first time. The number of posts per thread shifted from a pre-cancellation mean of 1.4 to 2.5 afterward. Many posts questioned the decision to cancel and wanted to know what had happened; others provided their assessment of the situation or helped organize an emergency meeting. However, this flurry of activity was short lived, and subsequent spaces for open dialog had not emerged by the time of this writing nearly three years later.

The NWSF was an ambitious attempt to organize thick-tie networks based on collective identity formation around an anti-racist social justice narrative. As a result, despite the short time frame, strategic decisions were made to de-emphasize the kind of social networking technologies that often facilitate weak-tie networks based on more open narrative formation. While adopting more open narrative and technology-assisted networking strategies may have strengthened parts of the network, the capacity to bridge race, class, and locality in the global justice movement may still have remained an elusive goal.

Conclusion

One conclusion from these studies is that large-scale rapid networking is facilitated by relatively open stories that enable both organizations and individuals to rely on social networking technologies to activate dense interorganization and individual-level networks. Yet even when stories seem open and inclusive, their capacity to travel across particular technological and social divides may be limited by a combination of organizational form, network boundaries, and trust across social (e.g., racial) or cultural (e.g., tribal custom) differences. The organizers of the NWSF may have been right in thinking that thick-tie networks were more appropriate to their goals by building trust between individuals across social divides, but the implementation of a time-intensive thick-ties approach based around a pre-figurative anti-racist organizational narrative did not work well with the short timeline constraints imposed by an impending event. Perhaps employing a combination of thin- and thick-tie organizing approaches with sensitive applications of networking and online discussion technologies could bridge the gap between building long-range personal relationships and short-term affinity-based mobilization.

Beyond the strategic applications of technology, the role of organizations in networks remains important to study. For example, the fair trade networks suggest the importance of gatekeeping organizations in exercising power across a network. Gatekeeper stories may introduce structure into networks as various organizations choose to strategically link to each other or not. Moreover, as individuals and organizations begin to plant elements of their narratives in the physical and social environments in which people work, shop, live, and protest, those elements further constrain or echo the various dominant narratives that may flow through networks. For example, the relatively uniform adoption of the national fair trade trademark in the U.K. on goods certified by the Fairtrade Foundation provides substantial environmental affirmation of the common story about trade justice. By contrast, a number of small companies and NGOs have broken with the primary fair trade network in the U.S. over conflicts about whether to elevate trade justice to a more dominant story. The result is that the social environment contains a proliferation of small competing trademarks and labels that may confuse consumers about what sort of certification a product has, which, in turn, may lead to a reluctance by some companies to add contested trademarks to their branded packages (Bennett *et al.*, 2007). The various breaks and path distances in the U.S. web network reflect these disputes over the narrative. Those digital breaks and distances are coded in the lived environment in the jumble of different trademarks and certification schemes that define what fair trade means to different activists.

As these cases suggest, the idea of narratives as networking devices offers a useful mechanism for understanding how individuals and organizations actually construct social ties: they tell and exchange stories, and play with physical elements of them in their social environments. In our view, the more popular academic concept of *framing* continues to be useful for describing broad organizational alliances, calls to action, and media representations. Beyond this, it becomes important to grasp how narratives weave together social relationships by providing the interpretive contexts for frames. In the process of negotiating meaning, stories travel across various communication channels, both digital and personal, leaving their traces in technology affordances, in personal consciousness, and in the built human environment. As these pieces of

plot and action populate the communication context, they provide resources to help individuals move among—or set limits on—personal, organizational, and network levels of affiliation.

Guide to further reading

There is a vast literature on identity and social change, with implications for changing forms of political association. Good places to start are Giddens (1991), Bennett (1998) and Beck (1999, 2000). della Porta (2005) suggests that these changes encourage "flexible identities" in recent global justice organizing.

The focus on symbolic linkages in much of the social movement literature has been on framing. Snow and Benford (1988) and Snow *et al.* (1986) are two seminal works that outline the field of collective action framing research. A more recent assessment of the field by Benford and Snow (2000) makes an interesting companion.

Work on narratives in social movements is fairly new to the field. Polletta's (1998, 2006) work on activist narratives and storytelling provides valuable insight into the ways that stories shape activists' conceptions of themselves and others.

For more general work on meaning and social movements we recommend Eyerman and Jamison (1991) and Melucci (1996). Both works present a compelling account of the way that social movements are adapting to larger changes in the role of information in industrialized countries and the role of meaning contestation in social change. Similarly, Keck and Sikkink's (1998; Sikkink, 2002) work on transnational advocacy brings an analysis of "soft power" in global governance activism around human rights and development to discussions of meaning and movements.

A crucial starting point for thinking about networks and collective action is

Granovetter's (1973) analysis of thick- and thin-tie networks.

The role of technology in activist networks is a burgeoning field. We recommend reading Rogers (2002) for his account of issue networks on the web, Bennett (2003) for an assessment of decentralized digital activist campaigns, and Pentland and Feldman (2007) for their account of narratives in technology-assisted networks.

The authors would like to acknowledge the support of the Belgian Science Policy Foundation in funding the studies described in this chapter. The input and support of Stefaan Walgrave has been particularly valuable.

19

Theorizing gender and the internet

Past, present, and future

Niels van Doorn and Liesbet van Zoonen

The growth of the internet has been accompanied by a profound academic interest in its gendered features and contexts. This chapter first discusses how studies of the relationship between gender and the internet have been articulated through the use of two conceptions of gender common within a feminist theoretical framework: "gender as identity" and "gender as social structure." Yet, as we will demonstrate, studies in these domains often have gender-essentialist and technological-determinist tendencies and ignore the positioned and embodied everyday interactions with internet technologies. We therefore continue with an assessment of approaches that counter essentialism and determinism by focusing on the mutual shaping of gender and technology in situated practices and spaces. We conclude by discussing whether the current prevalence of user-generated content referred to as Web 2.0 raises new questions for research about gender and the internet.

As early as 1993, well before the proliferation of the web, Sandra Herring investigated differences between men and women in their use of language in asynchronous computer-mediated communication (CMC) such as bulletin boards, newsgroups, and discussion lists. Barely 15 years later, research on gender and the internet has burgeoned. The online sphere, with its mixture of information, entertainment, and communication modalities and its convergence of audiovisual technologies requires multidisciplinary theoretical and methodological lines of inquiry. Psychologists, for instance, often examine gender differences in the online behavior of women and men; anthropologists and sociologists regularly investigate how women build communities on the internet; feminist political scientists tend to look at the way women use it to mobilize for social and political causes;

cultural studies scholars have a recurring interest in the virtual performance of gendered identities in, for instance, online games; and sociolinguists mostly discuss gendered language patterns in various online contexts. Given this plethora of approaches, any attempt to write about this subject is bound to be incomplete and partial. Nevertheless, we organize our account around what we see as the key conceptual contours of the social science literature in this area.

Gender as identity

Differences

Gender differences online have been a central area of concern in studies of gender as identity. In her pioneering study, Herring (1993) identified two separate discourses online: a feminine discourse encompassing a more "personal" style of communication, characterized by apologetic language use and the prevention of tension; and a masculine discourse, typified as being more "authoritative" and oriented towards action, and characterized by challenging and argumentative language use. When these two discourses met in a "mixed gender" online environment, the masculine discourse dominated: men tended to introduce more subjects and ignored or ridiculed the input of female participants (Herring, 1993). These results led Herring to conclude that the internet perpetuates everyday linguistic inequalities between men and women (Herring, 1995, 1996a, 1996b, 1999; Herring et al., 1995). Similar research, such as a study of newsgroups by Savicki et al. (1996), concluded that newsgroups with predominantly male participants could be characterized as containing a large amount of fact-related exchange and impersonal speech, while female-dominated newsgroups featured conflict-avoiding speech and high levels of "self-disclosure." Jaffe et al. (1995) found that women tend to display textual patterns of social interdependence more than men do in both real-name and pseudonymous online conferences, while Kendall (1998) demonstrated that the interactions between "male" and "female" characters in MUDs (Multi User Dungeons—an early type of online fantasy game) were largely predicated on stereotypical gender relations, even though these provided what appeared on the surface to be an anonymous and disembodied environment.

Some research has shown how male dominance is violently reinforced online through the sexual harassment of women in different online contexts (Herring, 2002, 2001, 1999, for an overview see Li, 2005). These studies make clear how gender and sexual identities are mutually constitutive and how, for heterosexual men, the position of the former is strengthened by the oppressive explication of the latter through the use of sexually demeaning language targeted at women.

On the other hand, a detailed analysis by Nancy Baym (2000) of the participants in the online fan community of the U.S. daytime soap *All My Children* reveals that it is not only the gender of participants that explains particular feminine communicative styles, but also the topic of conversation (in this case a soap) and the offline contexts of the participants. Baym's study suggests that gender cannot be considered the sole explanatory factor for "gender differences" online—a result supported by a small number of others that have found reversed gender patterns. For example, in an experimental study by Jaffe et al. (1999) men abandoned dominant behavior and approached others in a socially aware and helpful way, while Witmer and Katzman (1997) found that women actually uttered more conflictual speech than men. Similarly, Can's (1999) investigation of the language styles in two feminist Usenet newsgroups, alt.feminism and soc.feminism, showed that exclusionary rhetorical techniques can also be found in online environments dominated by women.

Whether these "difference" studies emphasize the reiteration or the reversal of stereotypical gender relations in CMC, they leave the "male/female" dichotomy unchallenged because they focus on generalized types of "male" and "female" communicative behavior. They find evidence for the claim that the internet reconfirms and exaggerates traditional gender relations.

Yet, just as in feminist theory more generally, gender differences are not only a source of women's oppression, but are also seen by some scholars as a source of power. Influenced by Donna Haraway's "cyborg theory," the radical French feminism of Luce Irigaray, and Freudian psychoanalysis, British author Sadie Plant (1995, 1996, 1997) argues that the "digital revolution" marks the decline of masculine hegemonic power structures, as the internet constitutes a non-linear world that cannot be ordered or controlled. Plant's "cyberfeminist" vision conceptualizes the web as a fractured and diffuse structure— one that is uniquely aligned with women's fluid identities and that deconstructs the traditionally patriarchal character of technology. According to Plant, women have a "natural" affinity with new digital technologies because they allow them to explore a multitude of gender identities in a virtual environment where the relation between gender and the body is a contingent construction.

Although Plant's utopian view certainly serves as an encouraging theoretical source for young women who are increasingly immersing themselves in new technologies, it also has a rather peculiar way of combining conceptions of femininity as universally different from masculinity with a view of female identity as fragmented and diffuse. In an awkward effort to merge the two notions, Plant reconciles her version of biological essentialism with the technologically determinist claim that the internet constitutes the key to women's liberation because it allows female multiplicity to flourish. This tension leads Wajcman (2004) to oppose this position, by suggesting that the claim that internet technology is essentially feminine Plant pre-empts the need for feminist political action.

Experimentation

In an effort to break out of this traditional gender binary and further investigate the liberating potential of cyberspace, another strand of research shifts the focus from gender differences to gender experimentation. In early research about "gender bending" the absence of the body in text-based CMC plays a central role. Due to the fact that cyberspace offers an environment in which gender can be disconnected from one's physical body, the possibilities for creating different gender identities become abundant. Studies by Reid (1993) and Danet (1996) examined the construction of gender at the moment in which participants enter "virtual space." For example, Reid (1993) argued that internet relay chat (IRC) users construct their gender identities through the choice of their nickname. "Nicks" may express masculinity, femininity, or even gender ambiguity. "MUDders" are able to choose gendered, gender-neutral, or gender-plural characters when they join. This provides them with an opportunity to actively create their gender (or lack thereof) in virtual space.

Perhaps the most influential examination of gender bending online is Sherry Turkle's *Life on the Screen*. Turkle contends that the internet has become "a significant social laboratory for experimenting with the constructions and reconstructions of self" (Turkle, 1995: 180). In contrast with other studies, Turkle approaches this from a socio-psychological perspective, by investigating the participants' personal reasons for engaging in experimentation with gender and sexual identity, as well as the social context in which these performances take place. This approach places strong emphasis on the relation between online and offline selves. In Turkle's view, online experiments with gender and sexuality are useful tools for the rethinking not only of one's "virtual" gender identity, but also of one's "real-life" gendered and sexualized self (Turkle, 1995). This last point is made especially clear in the book's chapter on "cybersex", in which it is argued that cyberspace offers a risk-free environment where people can engage in the intimate relationships they desire but are afraid to initiate in the real world. The possibilities of online gender bending fit well with poststructuralist theories about identities as non-essential discursive performances that open up space for negotiation (Butler, 1990). In addition, these notions have helped the political struggles of feminists trying to escape the "prison-house of gender."

Yet, notwithstanding its theoretical and political popularity, several empirical studies have suggested that gender bending is uncommon, or is most often conducted for fun or specific game-related advantages rather than to break out of the gender dichotomy (e.g., Wright *et al.*, 2000; Van Doorn *et al.*, 2007). A further problem with these theories is that their focus on escaping the offline confines of gender causes them to ignore the impact of embodied everyday experience on online performances. Turkle herself believes that ultimately the gendered self is rooted in the physical, offline world, even though cyberspace provides us with profound experiences that can lead to "personal transformation" and a reconfiguration of how we perceive ourselves (Turkle, 1995).

This concern about the offline self is shared, for example, by Jodi O'Brien (1999), who also stresses the importance of embodied experience. O'Brien argues that "gender categories evoke a deeply entrenched cognitive–emotive script for who we can be and how we should relate to others," and these make it doubtful whether "cyberspace will be a realm in which physical markers such as sex, race, age, body type and size will eventually lose salience as a basis for the evaluative categorization of self/others" (O'Brien, 1999: 77). Through a reliance on "classification schemes," which cause one to make continual references to the body as connected to the self even though this body is not physically present, the body provides us with a common point of reference that structures our disembodied communication and gives it meaning (O'Brien, 1999). From this perspective, the internet could hardly be considered a site that facilitates the creation of totally fluid gender identities.

Despite their different perspectives, both the "difference" and the "experimentation" approaches focus on gender as identity: a discourse in which individuals engage and through which they assume agency while being simultaneously shaped and disciplined by it. The "difference" studies distinguish between feminine and masculine language patterns and behaviors and conclude that the internet does not change traditional relations of dominance between women and men, femininity and masculinity. In these works gender is perceived as a foundational property, with its internal truth or logic located in the sexed body. It is what makes women and men who they are and it determines human interactions, even in an online context. In contrast, the "experimentation" works implicitly perceive the internet as the determining force, since its facilitation of disembodied communication is said to enable individuals to break out of the traditional confines of socially constructed gender relations. Not only are both perspectives thus rather determinist (favoring either gender or technology as the deciding factor) they also tend to ignore social contexts and structures. One reason for this is that empirical studies on "gender as identity" have mainly focused on the interpersonal online practices of CMC (chat, bulletin boards, online gaming, and so on) while mostly discarding the socio-economic framework in which these practices take place. Although these studies have at times incorporated a notion of embodiment, with the notable exception of Turkle's this is rarely related to a focus on the actual lives of users in everyday social contexts—in other words, gender as a social structure that locates women and men in particular roles in society is usually ignored. We now turn to another field of research that has examined how the internet is engaged in the negotiation of socio-political positions by women and men.

Gender as social structure

Marketing "the feminine" online

A number of feminist researchers have interrogated the internet's commercial spaces. Women online are now routinely addressed in their traditional role as consumers (Van Zoonen, 2002). Market research has produced ever more studies about the online differences between women and men in order to find ways to promote women's online consumption (for example, Parasuraman and Zinkhan, 2002; Rodgers and Harris, 2003; Van Slyke *et al.*, 2002).

Feminist scholars have looked upon these developments with suspicion. Leslie Regan Shade (2002), for instance, warns against the increasing tension "between e-commerce applications directed towards women as consumers and the usage of the internet as a locus for citizen-oriented activities" (Shade, 2002: 10). According to Shade, digital capitalism's rising interest in women as a viable consumer market has decreased the number of online spaces where women can engage in non-profit cultural or political practices, while corporate websites that aim to profit from women's supposed needs and interests have proliferated (Shade, 2002). Similarly, Gustafson (2002) explores the concept of the "feminization" of community online through the interrogation of three popular commercial women's sites (iVillage, Oxygen, and Women.com). Gustafson suggests that "while women are a growing internet population, they are being discursively constructed on the internet as

community-seekers and as consumers—traditionally feminine roles" (Gustafson, 2002: 169). Consalvo (2002) also suggests that community and consumption have been coded as "feminine" traits in metaphors used in popular discourse about women and the internet. And while women are now equal to men in their online consumption, they remain far behind when it comes to the production and design of the web and other information technologies (Whitehouse, 2006; Wajcman, 2007).

Internet pornography: from the abject to the everyday?

While women are increasingly targeted as consumers in many of the web's commercial spaces, the single largest commercial enterprise on the internet is still mainly directed at a male audience. The porn industry was one of the first to take its business online and since then has expanded exponentially in size and profit, simultaneously figuring as a further catalyst for the technological innovation that facilitated its growth and pervasiveness (Lane, 2000; Cronin and Davenport, 2001; Lillie, 2004). According to Lillie, there are four general perspectives from which "cyberporn" has been studied. First, behavioral-psychological studies have examined uses and addictions, and have established an agenda for research that describes a range of "healthy" and "unhealthy" online behaviors, while providing possible remedies for "compulsive" uses of online porn. Second, the "effects" tradition of empirical media research has mainly concerned itself with the exposure of children to cyberporn. This has usually recommended policies on increased parental guidance and surveillance or filtering software. The third perspective adopts a political economy approach, studying the many facets of the online porn industry and its development in a broader social context, while the fourth focuses on how different social groups use cyberporn in their everyday lives and is mainly indebted to the traditions of cultural studies and CMC research.

Feminist analyses of online pornography were initially structured around the polarizing debates between radical "anti-porn" feminists and liberal "free speech" or "pro sex" feminists, which took place during the 80s and 90s, mainly in the United States. The most well-known anti-porn feminists of this time, Andrea Dworkin and Catherine MacKinnon, have argued that pornography functions as a system for male domination, where male power is established through the violent degradation of women. Thus, the goal for feminist activists is to dismantle this system of domination. In contrast, next to the rather obvious free speech arguments that have been raised, "pro sex" feminists have applauded pornography for undermining and subverting our culture's repressive attitude to sexuality in general, and female sexuality in particular. What these debates make clear is how discourse about pornography is inextricably linked to conceptions of gender, sexuality, and power (Allen, 2001).

Yet for all the theoretical and ideological discussions concerning pornography in general, there is remarkably little feminist scholarship on online sex. The few studies that do exist generally align themselves with the "established" areas of media research. Feminists working within the "media effects" and "political economy" traditions have tended to center on the hazards of internet pornography for women and children (e.g., Adam, 2002; Burke et al., 2002; Hughes, 1999, 2004), while those with a cultural studies background have focused their attention on online cultures and how they may be redefining the standard gendered codes of porn and sexual practices (Kibby, 2001; Kibby and Costello, 2001; Waskul, 2004).

This last area of feminist scholarship has been gaining currency over the past few years, with studies extending the scope of analysis by paying specific attention to the situated and everyday contexts of internet porn consumption. For instance, Lillie has argued for a need for "porn reception" studies that investigate "the truths of the architecture of knowledge and technologies of sexuality, which pornography as a participant in the construction of the subject's desire and sexual identity works within." An important location for these kinds of studies would be what Lillie terms "the moral economy of the networked home" (Lillie, 2004: 53, 58).

New communication technologies have played a crucial role in the production, distribution, and consumption of pornography, both as visually explicit material and in terms of the accompanying discourses of gender, sex, and sexuality (Paasonen, 2006; Paasonen et al., 2007; Attwood, 2002; Cronin and Davenport, 2001; O'Toole, 1999). To a large extent, the internet can be credited for spreading a "diversity of pornographies" in today's media environment, contributing to the omnipotence, normalization, and increased acceptance of sexualized imagery in mainstream cultural products. In fact, this trend is slowly positioning women as another viable consumer market for pornographic content, however unlikely this might seem (Cronin and Davenport, 2001; McNair, 2002; Schauer, 2005). It is in such environments, on- and offline, that sexuality and gender are performed and negotiated, and this makes them a primary target for further feminist research.

Web of empowerment

Despite the previously mentioned efforts to commercialize the concept of "community," it has also played an instrumental role in a variety of feminist activities to empower women in their everyday on-

and offline lives. Many women's groups and feminist activists have approached the internet as an international platform for such diverse goals as creating support networks, challenging sexual harassment, discussing feminist politics, creating spaces for sexual self-expression, and rallying against social injustices. In this sense, community is strongly attached to a commitment to social change, and resists commercial appropriation by market actors.

Feminist scholars have devoted considerable attention to these social movements, documenting the everyday efforts of women to exercise their rights as citizens in an online environment. Aside from offering a critical look at the efforts by multimedia conglomerates to "feminize" the internet in order to exploit women's consumer potential, Shade (2002) also provides an overview of how women have used the same internet for feminist communication and activism. She describes, for instance, how mailing lists were one of the earliest and most successful tools for building international women's networks, creating hundreds of online discussion groups covering a multitude of topics related to feminism and women's everyday lives. More specifically, Shade illustrates how the internet was used to organize and coordinate the Fourth World Conference on Women, held in Beijing in 1995, and how it enabled Zapatista women to wage a social "net war" against the Mexican government and inform and educate the Western world about their cause. In a similar vein, Kensinger (2003) presents a critical perspective on how the internet was used for promoting social activism and solidarity with women in Afghanistan during the Taliban regime and the subsequent war in the region.

Aside from investigating how the internet can be used for organizing feminist social activism in various "offline" contexts, scholars have also paid attention

to women's and girls' online strategies for cultural criticism and self-expression. The so-called "cybergrrls" movement has been the subject of extensive academic enquiry. Of particular interest is how techno-savvy young women negotiate and deconstruct the consumerist messages encoded in their everyday pop cultural environment (Driscoll, 1999; Kr--kke, 2003; Yervasi, 1996). However, according to some critics, a focus on this kind of "postfeminist" cultural renegotiation neglects basic gender inequalities concerning internet access and work-related issues (Wilding, 1998).

As some scholars have pointed out, an important area where women have been working to empower themselves is in the internet sex industry, where they have become increasingly visible as active consumers and producers of pornographic content (Podlas, 2000; Cronin and Davenport, 2001; Attwood, 2002; Smith, 2007). Through this process of emancipation, women are gradually redefining the idea of pornography as an exclusively masculine domain in which women are treated as passive sex objects, in favour of a realm in which they enjoy porn on their own terms and in which they are in control of their sexual practices. This is not only taking place on a symbolic level, for instance through the resignification of "female sexuality" in live webcam shows or in pornographic stories produced and published by women, but also on a material level, with more female entrepreneurs starting their own online business and making profits from pornographic productions (Podlas, 2000; Ray, 2007). Thus, while the porn industry has so far remained a predominantly masculine environment, and sexist representations of women are unlikely to decrease in the future, the internet is for some a tool for women's sexual and economic freedom.

These studies all share a concern with women's agency in relation to the internet, whether it is through the creation of networks for political activism, producing female-friendly pornography, or the feminist reappropriation of digital capitalism's consumer culture. While some see this agency as eroding due to the increasing dominance of male corporate presence online, others emphasize women taking matters into their own hands, effectively using the net to engage in various forms of socio-political action. More generally, internet research that approaches gender as a social structure is effectively concerned with the material-semiotic relation between gender and power at a macro level. Meanwhile, the internet itself functions as an unbiased, ahistorical, and gender-neutral technological instrument that can be used by and against women in the struggle for material and symbolic power. At the same time, gender also appears to be a stable entity in the majority of these studies, principally aligned along the man–woman binary and seemingly untouched by the technology that facilitates these feminist practices. Thus, the biological essentialism and technological determinism witnessed in the "gender as identity" approach tends to resurface here once again in the context of the "gender as social structure" debate (Wacjman, 2004).

Situated practices and spaces

In response to these shortcomings, some feminist research on gender and the internet has started to shift its emphasis from the "identity vs. social structure" dichotomy to the manifold interactions between gender and internet technology, paying special attention to their situated offline/online articulations. Some authors in the field of science and technology studies (STS) have argued that because the experience of ourselves is so thoroughly mediated through our everyday interactions with technological artifacts, we cannot meaningfully study gender without taking into account its intricate relationship with technology (Akrich, 1995). Influenced by this notion, feminist scholars have approached gender as something that is both shaping and shaped by technology. This "mutual shaping" approach generally looks at the intersections of gender and technology on three different, yet interrelated, levels: structural, symbolic, and identity related (Harding, 1986; Cockburn and Ormrod, 1993). Mutual shaping research investigates how these three dimensions of gender are articulated within the web's techno-social spaces, which are themselves gendered in the process. According to this approach, techno-social spaces are not only shaped by their use, but also through the design and production of their technological infrastructure (Wajcman, 2004, 2007). These practices are dependent on many different socio-technical factors, such as the interplay of commercial and institutional interests. Technological change, then, is never the linear result of "techno-*logical*" decision-making, but the outcome of a contingent process.

Research that follows this approach ideally takes into account the whole techno-cultural circuit including the design, development, marketing, consumption, and domestication of specific technologies (e.g., Cockburn, 1992). However, in practice STS scholars mostly conduct detailed case studies that focus on specific elements of this circuit. We will now briefly discuss three such studies, two from a Dutch perspective and one situated in the Norwegian context.

Els Rommes (2002) examines how implicit presumptions about gender roles among the design team worked to exclude and alienate women as users and designers of Amsterdam's *Digital City*—one of the first Dutch experiments with the internet in 1994. Adopting a "gender script" approach, she demonstrates how the desire of the predominantly male design team to experiment with state-of-the-art technology made it hard for less tech-savvy users to participate in the Digital City. Rommes calls this a typical example of the "I-methodology" found among ICT developers, or taking one's own preferences and capacities as the starting point for designing technology. Since most ICT workers are male, user scenarios implicit in ICT production are severely gendered. The masculine gender scripts that informed the design and development of the Amsterdam Digital City produced a pioneering online space that received international acclaim but it did not attract a diverse group of users. Ultimately, Rommes suggests, the masculine gender scripts implemented in the Digital City's techno-social fabric contained a set of normative assumptions that favored high-tech male users, while alienating other, especially female, users. Only those who already owned a computer with an internet connection, or who had sufficient financial and social capital to purchase one, could get access to the Digital City. Since ownership of a computer and internet access were, and still are, unequally distributed along gender lines in Dutch society, this favored male users (Rommes, 2002). Further, Rommes shows that while women did have access to a computer in their home, they often did not use it because they viewed the device as something that belonged to their male partner.

While Rommes' study centers its attention on the design/development side of the mutual shaping process, other mutual shaping studies focus on how the gendered meanings of the internet arise in the context of usage, and how usage interacts with everyday constructions of gender. Van Zoonen (2002) examines how internet technology is domesticated within everyday practices in Dutch households. Contrary to common claims that the internet constitutes an essentially masculine or feminine environment, gendered meanings of the internet arise, especially at the moment of domestication. Through in-depth interviews with young couples she demonstrates how the "social," "symbolic," and "individual" dimensions of gender interact with the everyday negotiations of technology use among heterosexual partners living together. Four types of negotiations among the partners emerged from the interviews, constituting "traditional," "deliberative," "reversed," and "individualized" use cultures. While male usage primarily determines these types, the interviews show that this does not automatically result in the construction of a masculine domain in the household, but instead opens up space for shared and feminine appropriations. For instance, a "deliberative" use culture involves explaining the negotiation of domestic computer use in collective terms and is instrumental in constructing a sense of togetherness among the partners: a shared techno-social domain (Van Zoonen, 2002). Technology is effectively gendered through the process of domestication as masculine- and feminine-coded practices mutually add meaning to the artifact. At the same time, the computer and the internet present the members of a household with a techno-social environment in which their gender roles can be renegotiated. This can occur when the computer is identified with work-related tasks, as is shown in some of the study's interviews. In these cases, work or studies are more valued than surfing or gaming and thus get prioritized. In effect, this priority turns out to be male-biased in the context of Dutch households, where men are still the main "provider." As a consequence the domestication of the computer in the household leads, in these cases, to a reiteration of traditional gender roles.

While Van Zoonen's study focuses on the gendered domestication of technology

269

in the home, Lægran (2004) examines internet cafés as "gendered techno-social spaces." Influenced by the actor-network theory of Bruno Latour (2005), she considers technologies, spaces, and gender as mutually constructed in situated processes that involve material and symbolic articulations, as well as both human and non-human actors. Following Latour, technological artifacts are seen as "actants," which are able to acquire agency in the production of space by means of how they are integrated in actor networks. By extending the concept of agency from human to non-human actors, Lægran opens up new possibilities for the analysis of gendered spaces and technologies. Through the inspection of the relation between the two, and by considering both as agents producing meaning alongside human actors, she is able to analyse the material-semiotic processes in which technology and spaces are reciprocally gendered in a physical realm. Instead of creating a space where the masculine connotation of ICT can be deconstructed through the material and symbolic presence of feminine use cultures, internet cafés favor one culture over the other (usually the masculine culture). This leads Lægran to conclude that the internet café, with its female visitors largely invisible, remains "just another boys' room." While mutual shaping research usually takes into account the multiple dimensions in which gender interacts with technology, this study draws our attention to the inter-relations of gender, space, and internet culture on a symbolic level. This is effective in showing how offline spaces acquire meaning as a gendered realm, an area that is generally overlooked in traditional research on gender and the internet.

As the three examples above show, mutual shaping theory necessitates a case study approach to examining gender and the internet, in which the manifold dimensions that make up particular gendered practices can be studied in detail. The phenomenon of I-methodology (Akrich, 1995) in the design phase has been taken up as a useful concept in diverse case studies, such as the gendered design of digital games (Kerr, 2002), smart-building projects (Aune et al., 2002), or gendered ICT use in the workplace (Sefyrin, 2005). Also, the concept of gendered domestication has been well developed in theoretical terms (e.g., Cockburn and Dilić, 1994) and has been applied in several studies of old and new media use (Haddon, 2006).

New web, new questions, new outcomes?

Having discussed the main areas of research on gender and the internet, the question for the future is how far the existing approaches can function as adequate theoretical tools for the investigation of new developments—the emerging era of Web 2.0 typified by an increasing number of users producing and sharing their own content.

According to many, Web 2.0, with its non-hierarchical modes of content production and dissemination, has replaced the top–down structure of the so-called Web 1.0. As part of this Web 2.0 buzz, *Time* magazine named "You" their Person of the Year in 2006: a tribute to the "common people who transformed the way we socialize, gather information, and do business on the internet" via rapidly growing web applications and platforms such as MySpace, Facebook, and YouTube. While we should not lose sight of the fact that user-generated content of all kinds has long been a feature of online life, it is worth exploring the implications of Web 2.0 for gender politics.

Given the fact that these new web applications have only recently become the focus of gender-informed research, any attempt to predict outcomes is necessarily precarious. Nevertheless, we can theorize how the previously discussed approaches might be able to provide new and interesting insights in the field of gender and internet research. How are the existing approaches able to come to terms with the present internet landscape, dominated by applications that facilitate novel forms of user-generated content?

Dealing first with the "gender as identity" approach, it is most likely that studies investigating gender differences in internet use will continue to find these differences in the way that men and women design their weblogs, provide information on their MySpace profiles, or contribute to a discussion about a video posted on YouTube. These gender differences find their origins in the embodied everyday experiences of internet users and are thus unlikely to be easily altered by any specific ICT application. For this reason, we contend that this kind of "difference" research is continuously reinventing the wheel.

Turning to "experimentation" research, it does not seem plausible that future studies will find much evidence of gender experimentation that transcends or disrupts binary gender discourse. Contemporary internet applications incorporate new and improved visualization technologies, which constitute both a response to and a perpetuation of our preoccupation with the exhibition of everyday "reality." Whereas the "virtual" was once believed to form an alternative to the "real," a space where users could engage in disembodied communication Web 2.0 has definitively collapsed this dichotomy because people upload an increasing number of photographs and home-made videos onto the web, transporting the "real" and "authentic" into cyberspace. One of the realms in which this phenomenon is evident is the "reality porn" niche, which has expanded significantly over the past few years

(Barcan, 2002; Ray, 2007). In response to YouTube's policy of not allowing nudity, websites such as PornoTube and RedTube are now providing a platform where users can upload pornographic video material (either actually home made or purporting to be) to which other users can respond by leaving comments. Most of these videos focus on the everyday reality of people engaged in sexual practices. Consequently, this dynamic has strongly reaffirmed the "real body" on the screen, which can now be visually tracked to its physicality. It thus seems unlikely that Web 2.0 will cater to much gender bending, with continuous visual scrutiny causing users to be extremely aware of their bodies and those of their peers.

Away from the mainstream, however, the general increase in internet access in the Western world, coupled with considerably lower thresholds for creating personalized content online, do certainly open up possibilities for marginalized gender and sexual identities to be exposed to a larger audience. The visualization technologies that may reaffirm gender and body norms in a mainstream context could also be used by queer and transgender people to deconstruct traditional images of gender, embodiment, and sexuality, in addition to simply increasing their visibility. This could cause a grassroots disruption of what counts as "the real body." Thus, contemporary research on gender as identity should further examine how gender, sexuality, and embodiment are experienced and performed through visualization technologies such as the webcam and internet video software. A relevant question would be how this "body-technology" constellation is affecting our conceptions of embodied gender and the ways it can be mediated online.

When considering the "gender as social structure" approach it is clear that this will remain valuable. As previously noted,

271

multinational corporations have collectively jumped on the Web 2.0 bandwagon and have bought into the current hype around user-generated content. Surely this will have repercussions for how present and future Web 2.0 applications can be experienced and used, with designs now under increasing corporate control, and marketing divisions eager to benefit from the possibilities of new personalized advertisement techniques. This raises the issue of the increased prevalence of pervasive marketing schemes directed at specific groups of female users, in addition to a more general concern about privacy issues. On the other hand, the previously mentioned low thresholds for participation and production that characterize Web 2.0 could have positive effects on the level of women's participation in political activism and opinion formation online. As research in this novel area is still in its infancy, future studies need to investigate the dimensions of women's political efficacy in these new social spaces. However, even if the number of politically active women grows over the next few years, it seems unlikely that the gendered inequalities identified by Herring and others will dissolve solely through an increase in women online.

Further questions in this area revolve around the extent to which users actually have control over the content they are encouraged to produce and how this may be delimited by corporate design teams. To what extent do these new user communities allow for women to engage in politically radical activities, when the -cultural environment of websites like MySpace and YouTube seems to be predominantly concerned with the consumption of entertainment and lifestyles? How "political" can a book discussion on Amazon.com be? Does the type of interaction taking place on the main Web 2.0 sites require a reinterpretation of what it means to be "politically active?" These

are by no means new questions, but it is vital to reformulate them in the different contexts of a constantly transforming landscape in which economic, cultural, and political interests will continue to shape the way that people use the internet.

Mutual shaping research on the relation between gender and the various technosocial spaces of Web 2.0 will prove to be an important tool for showing how situated practices of gendered content producers are related to their everyday lives and concerns, with the internet constituting an extension of everyday practices rather than a disruptive alternative to it. Future studies should continue to focus on the occurrence of the I-methodology in the design of current websites featuring user-generated content, as well as examining whether and how traditional gender patterns are reinstated in the domestication of popular Web 2.0 applications. In our own research on the gendered constitution of blogs, for instance, we found that they are on the one hand extensions of the traditionally feminine act of diary writing, and imbue the blogosphere with feminine codes and rituals, while on the other they redefine the act of diary writing as a "technological" practice, enabling men to share in it as "bloggers." This as a clear case of gender and technology shaping each other mutually, with repercussions both for the traditional relations of women with technology, and of men with self-expression. Nevertheless, we also observed male and female bloggers making gender stereotypical choices of blogging content, mode of address, layout, and hyperlinks in order to create clear masculine and feminine spaces (Van Doorn et al., forthcoming). The mutual shaping of gender and Web 2.0 is, and will continue to be, a fragmented process contingent upon a multitude of situated practices featuring a constant interpellation between particular groups of users and the technologies with which they interact.

Conclusion

We started this chapter by acknowledging that the different academic disciplines each have their own perspectives on the articulation of gender in relation to the internet. We identified two initial approaches: "gender as identity" and "gender as a social structure." The internet has been shown to both confirm existing differences between women and men and to enable transgressions of the stereotypical codes of femininity and masculinity. Research has also demonstrated how internet marketing exploits women's social positions by addressing them merely as consumers, while other studies have shown how many women use the net to engage in activism and feminist networking. Whichever of these contradictory possibilities occur depends very much on particular articulations of design, development, use, and users that take place around internet applications. We therefore discussed the mutual shaping approach, which assumes that gender and technology mutually influence each other, with neither gender nor technology as the determining force. Gender and technology are considered "actants" in a network of users and producers whose continuous negotiations and contestations propose specific articulations of gender and technological artifacts. Studies of gender and the internet conducted from such a perspective have identified influential processes such as the I-methodology in the development of internet applications, in which designers and developers (mostly men) adopt their own preferences and capacities as the standard for creating new technological applications, and the domestication process, which refers to the way the internet is integrated in the everyday gendered lives of domestic users.

We concluded by anticipating some research questions that the three approaches could produce when applied to the current social spaces of Web 2.0, and argued that the "gender as identity" studies should focus on the experience of embodied identity as the nexus of gendered techno-social practices; that the "gender as social structure" studies will find an increasingly interesting research field, which demands an emphasis on the tension between user agency and commercial interest; and that the mutual shaping studies will be able to illustrate the situated and diverse articulations of gender and technology in the context of those Web 2.0 applications that facilitate user-generated content. Rather than causing a schism in the established research tradition on gender and the internet, the social and technological features of Web 2.0 are more likely to evoke questions similar to those asked before. Yet these will require a reformulation commensurable with the current socio-technical environment and its foundation in today's political economy.

Guide to further reading

While this chapter has presented the reader with an overview of the past, present, and possible future of research on gender and the internet, it is by no means an exhaustive account. Shade's (2002) feminist analysis of the opportunities and threats that women face when engaging with the internet serves as a solid introduction to the socio-political aspects of women's internet use. Consalvo and Paasonen (2002) also focus on the politics of women's everyday interactions with the web, but broaden the scope of their book through the additional investigation of more "cultural" issues such as identity construction, embodiment, and discourse. More generally, Poster (2001), Bell (2001), and Trend (2001) all provide insightful analyses on gender identity and the internet from a critical cultural studies perspective, while Schaap (2002) and Campbell (2004) offer two of the most interesting and detailed case studies in this area of research.

For those looking for an elaborate discussion of the relationship between science and technology studies and feminist analysis, Judy Wajcman's (2004) *TechnoFeminism* is an indispensable work, as is the collection of Norwegian case studies edited by Lie (Lægran 2004). Though it might now be considered somewhat dated, Cockburn and Ormrod's (1993) seminal book is sure to remain of interest to anyone curious about the multidimensional relations of gender and technology. Turning to technology's connection to sex and sexuality, O'Toole's (1999) *Pornocopia* offers a vivid account of how porn is consumed and the technological innovations that foster its consumption. Likewise, Waskul (2004) presents a collection of essays, which will prove to be of great use to those with an interest in the political and cultural dimensions of sexual practices in the online environment. These are just a few suggestions for further reading, which will help the reader navigate a path through the growing landscape of gender and internet research.

20

New immigrants, the internet, and civic society

Yong-Chan Kim and Sandra J. Ball-Rokeach

This chapter discusses the role of the internet in the new immigrant identity negotiation process and its implications for civic engagement. New immigrants have options that were difficult at best to create in earlier eras. For example, communication technologies and especially the internet, can offer ways for the new immigrant to negotiate pressures toward assimilation. The ease and contemporaneous nature of communication with the home country is a feature that makes immigration today a different experience from immigration in the pre-internet era. We suggest that there are four possibilities open to new immigrants in terms of the primary way(s) the internet is incorporated into their everyday political lives: the internet can be used for (1) connecting to there (home society), (2) connecting to here (host country), (3) connecting to neither here nor there, and (4) connecting to both here and there. We label each of these internet use types as assimilation, transnational, virtual, and hybrid. We discuss various cases illustrating each of these types. We also discuss research issues related to individual and contextual factors that are likely to shape and modify the internet use type/civic engagement relationship.

In this chapter, we explore the intriguing case of the internet and new immigrants. Most studies of the social implications of the internet concern settled populations within the borders of a community, city, region, or nation state. New immigrants in contemporary contexts may be regarded as part of a grounded notion of globalization where migration and immigration are part of the process. Movements of populations within and between nation states are flows over spaces that have different implications from the migrations and immigrations of earlier eras, such as that studied by the Chicago School in the 1920s and 30s. New immigrants have options that were difficult at best to create in earlier eras. For example, communication technologies, and especially the internet, can offer ways for the new immigrant to

negotiate pressures toward assimilation (Appadurai, 1996). The ease and contemporaneous nature of communication with the home country is a feature that makes immigration a different experience from what it was in earlier eras.

In contrast to settled populations whose immigrant memories, if any, afford stories in family or community history, internet-connected first- and second-generation immigrants may engage in storytelling practices that speak to the present and future. These stories are constructed and communicated in a dynamic milieu of options for situating identity. Whereas settled populations deploy internet connections for identity exploration and confirmation (Morley and Robins, 1995; Holmes, 1997), even more fundamental considerations of identity are likely in the new immigrant case. While there is consensus in scholarly circles that linear assimilation models no longer apply (Zhou and Cai, 2002), scholars have not yet fully understood the ways in which new immigrants are appropriating internet technologies to manage the negotiation of identity prompted by the immigrant experience (Hall, 1994).

While identity negotiations are important in and of themselves, they also have important implications for how new immigrants engage the host country. This connection has been a major theme in the worlds of research and policy. In many host countries, there were serious concerns about societal integration extant at the time of heightened immigration. It is, thus, not surprising that the coincidental occurrences of new communication technologies (especially the internet) and heightened immigration have produced anxiety about how new immigrants will relate to the communities of their host country.

In this chapter, we review threads of evidence that researchers have created in their attempts to understand the role of the internet in the new immigrant identity negotiation process and its implications for civic engagement. As in most attempts to catch a process in mid air, we quickly gain an appreciation of complexity. For example, we cannot assume that the experience of new immigrants to the United States is the same as those of immigrants to France due to their different immigration histories and policies. Similarly, we cannot assume that all immigrants from a country will have the same experience, as there are individual and group differences they bring with them that also affect the nature of the experience in the host country (Myers, 1999). Also, our focus on internet connections leaves us open to myopia as these connections are part of a larger communication ecology of traditional media and interpersonal communication (Ball-Rokeach et al., 2001; Kim and Ball-Rokeach, 2006).

Typologies often serve as early building blocks of theory. In that spirit, we will present a typology of internet uses as one way of capturing the literature and what it has to say about the range of identity negotiations that new immigrants are creating in their everyday lives. Following a discussion of the internet uses typology with reference to civic engagement concerns, we will extend the discussion to the individual and contextual factors researchers have identified as being implicated in the new immigrant identity negotiation process.

Internet use and civic engagement

As a backdrop for comparison with new immigrants, we can first summarize the literature on the civic engagement outcomes of internet connections on settled populations. This literature runs the gamut of outcomes, ranging from positive, negative, or minimal effects of internet use on civic engagement. The most common finding is that internet use has positive outcomes. These include civic or community engagement (Wellman and Gulia, 1999; Preece, 2000; Uslaner, 2000; Lin, 2001), participation in community activities (Gibson et al., 2000; Kraut et al., 2002), political participation (Gibson et al., 2000), neighborhood belonging (Hampton and Wellman, 2000; Matei and Ball-Rokeach, 2001), contact with families and friends (Katz and Aspden, 1997; Franzen, 2000; Rainie and Kohut, 2000; Howard et al., 2001b; Katz et al., 2001), political interest (Johnson and Kaye, 1998; Bucy et al., 1999), political behavior, such as voting (Hill and Hughes, 1998), and trust in government (Kim et al., 2001; Shah, Kwak, and Holbert, 2001). Other researchers observe negative effects of internet use on civic engagement.

These include lower levels of involvement with family members and social circles (Kraut *et al.*, 1998; Nie and Erbring, 2000), loneliness and depression (Kraut *et al.*, 1998), political distrust (Johnson and Kaye, 1998), and less neighborhood belonging (Katz *et al.*, 2001). Finally, some studies find no direct effect of internet use on civic engagement, neighborhood belonging, or participation in public affairs (Katz and Aspden, 1997; Kohut, 2000; Putnam, 2000).

Scholars working from a social shaping of technology perspective have sought to resolve these seemingly contradictory findings by examining how the internet is incorporated into specific contexts of individual, household, and community life. These studies find that the relationship between internet use and civic engagement is conditional on other variables such as degree of access to social, political, or technological resources (Howes, 2002), motivations for internet use (Norris, 1998; Bimber, 2000; Kavanaugh and Patterson, 2001; Shah, McLeod, and Yoon, 2001), and the geo-ethnic environment of community life (Matei and Ball-Rokeach, 2001; Kim *et al.*, 2002).

Building upon the social construction of technology approach and its emphasis upon social context, we examine how internet use is incorporated into specific social, political, and cultural contexts of new immigrants' lives. New immigrants' lives can be characterized as a "confused positioning between the host country, the originating country and any other identities felt unaddressed by these two" (Hirji, 2006). The implications of the internet in their everyday lives are largely shaped by how they manage and negotiate such tensions. Unlike internet and civic engagement studies dealing with settled populations, researchers studying immigrant groups will be faced with the challenge of answering one fundamental question: civic engagement in which place?

A contingent model of new immigrants' use of the internet for civic engagement

It used to be that research on human migration, especially immigration, was based on what we may call a "disconnect–reconnect" paradigm. In this linear assimilation way of thinking, immigrants who migrated from one place (the sending country) to the other (the receiving country) disconnected from their social relationships in their homelands and reconnected by building new social relationships in the host country. More recently, scholars have argued that there is a loosening link between locality and sociability due to new communication and transportation technologies. As Anthony Giddens suggested with the concepts of "disembeddedness" and "reembeddedness" (Giddens, 1991) and Manuel Castells illustrated in his notion of the "network society" (Castells, 2000), where we live, where we communicate, and where we belong do not necessarily correspond. Barry Wellman and colleagues' concept of "network individualism" is particularly relevant for the discussion of the disjuncture of physical locality and social networks. They suggest that the internet is incorporated by individuals as a tool to strengthen locally-based social connectedness, but also to develop and maintain global connectedness. Thus, individuals may use the internet to form their own social networks across local and global geographical boundaries. Even those who live in the same geographical place can live in very different, specialized communities constructed around shared interests, identity, and history. While most of this genre of research focuses upon settled populations, there is no reason why new immigrants could not also become both global and local e-citizens in a highly individualized "pseudo community" (Howard *et al.*, 2001b).

In applying this way of thinking, we suggest that there are four possibilities open to new immigrants in terms of the primary way(s) the internet is incorporated into their everyday political lives: the internet can be used for (1) connecting to *there* (home society), (2) connecting to *here* (host country), (3) connecting to neither *here* nor *there*, and (4) connecting to both *here* and *there* (Figure 20.1).

When the primary use of the internet is as a tool to settle in and establish associations in the host society, we call it an "assimilation" use. When the internet is used primarily as a connection to the home country (there), then it is not likely that internet use will contribute to civic engagement at home (host country). We call this case "transnational" internet use because the internet is a vehicle for connecting to *there* from *here*. In the case where the internet is primarily a tool for the construction of an imagined community that belongs neither to *here* or *there*, then we call it a "virtual" internet use. Finally, the most challenging and interesting case from the point of view of identity and civic engagement is "hybrid" internet use. In this case, new immigrants use the internet to simultaneously maintain significant connections to the home country and to build and expand connections to the host community.

As with any typology, these are "ideal types" or analytical categories useful in making theoretically relevant distinctions. In reality, connecting and disconnecting to a place is a matter of degree. It is important to note that we are not classifying individuals per se, but their internet uses. Individuals' internet use patterns should be viewed as dynamic and fluid rather than static. Critical turning points such as changes in immigration policies in the host society, socio-political disasters (e.g., the 9/11 terrorist attacks or the wars in Iraq and Afghanistan), or changes in the diplomatic relation between the host society and the home country could transform one type of internet use into another. Another point is that the division of host society and home country becomes more problematic as we move from new immigrants to settled populations. Generally, first and second generations are considered new immigrants and settled populations include the third generation and beyond (Myers, 1999). These qualifiers aside, we suggest that the analytical distinctions between these four categories have implications for new immigrants' civic engagement.

		Host Society	
		Connect	Disconnect
Home Country	Connect	Hybrid	Transnational
	Disconnect	Assimilation	Virtual

Figure 20.1 Four ideal types of new immigrant internet use.

Assimilation internet uses, connecting to "here"

In the early days, it was expected, with both trepidation and excitement, that the internet would free individuals from the tyranny of geography, and enable them to build space-free relations in technologically simulated "social" spaces called cyberspace. However, many empirical studies have found that local residents use the internet to bond with, rather than escape, their immediate environments. The University of Toronto's Netlab study of digital neighborhood *Netville* demonstrates that internet users are more strongly connected to their neighborhood than non-users (Hampton and Wellman, 2001). Likewise, the internet has the potential to be incorporated into new immigrants' lives by offering short-cuts in their efforts to establish new social relations, engage in civic activities in their new neighborhoods, and get civically or politically assimilated to the host society.

New immigrants can use the internet to familiarize themselves with the new social, political, and cultural environments. One case is *MissyUSA.com*, an online community. Korean female immigrants or short-term visitors including foreign students or family members visit this website and share a variety of topics related to living in American society. Topics include children's education, real estate, immigration issues, and entertainment. In many respects, this website functions as a bridge between old and new worlds for new immigrants from South Korea, smoothing the transition from their homeland to their new "home" in the United States. Siapera (2005: 516) calls such online spaces "communities of care." She analyzed 18 U.K. websites constructed to provide refugees and exiles—such as Armenians, Cameroonians, Sudanese, and Rwandans—with practical information regarding immigration, welfare, emotional needs, education, employment, and cultural events. Siapera suggests that such websites play "pre-political" functions constructing "a community of care and support and creating a common world among or within a refugee public which then can be summoned or enacted as a public." *MissyUSA.com* for Korean immigrants in the United States and websites for refugees and exiles in the U.K. offer an "entrance to the public sphere" in the host society.

Another assimilation-oriented internet use concerns having a space to articulate a group identity as *immigrants*, an identity that is en route to participation in identity politics in the host society. For example, in a case study of websites for non-resident Indians in the United States, Mitra (2005) observed that they offer a "discursive safety zone" where new immigrants "negotiate the identity tension and dissonance" that they experience in their new lives in the United States. It is a political process in which new immigrants talk about who they are and who they should be in their host society. For Mitra (2005), this is a "cybernetic space which is produced by the combined voices of many people who occupy different physical spaces" (p. 380). In this space, immigrants' identities, deconstructed in the move to their host society, are reconstructed to adapt to their new social environment.

In addition to talking with fellow immigrants about who they are, the internet also provides a forum where new immigrants can actively resist host society stereotypes of them. For example, Brouwer (2006) found that Dutch Moroccan youth use websites to correct negative public images of Moroccans in the Dutch mainstream media, providing them with a chance to be heard despite lack of access to mainstream institutions. Mitra (2001) observed that in cyberspace, indistinct individual voices can converge

279

into a specific discourse for a specific group. Such acts of resistance may serve as antidotes to the tendency towards downward assimilation for new immigrants (Portes and Sensenbrenner, 1993; Ostergaard-Nielsen, 2003).

Talking to the host society through the internet does not necessarily take the form of resistance. Sometimes, new immigrants try to enlighten the host society about their unique situations. Siapera's (2005) case study of African refugees in the United Kingdom shows that new immigrants try to get the host society's support and understanding by "providing complex socio-historical explanations for the current exile," and building "an alliance with the general public, resting on the common understanding sought through these websites" (p. 515).

Finally, there are instances of new immigrants using the internet to gain political empowerment by participating in civic and political activities in the host country. Siddiquee and Kagan's (2006) study of the Community Internet Project in the United Kingdom found that refugee women who are more technologically competent are more motivated to participate in their local community. In a University of Southern California Metamorphosis Project study of community technology centers (CTCs) in Los Angeles, Hayden and Ball-Rokeach (2007) found that the majority of the CTCs are serving new immigrant populations, most of whom do not have internet access at home. In other Metamorphosis Project studies of Los Angeles' new immigrant communities, the researchers found that new immigrants from East Asia, Mexico, and Central America have low levels of civic engagement in their host communities (Ball-Rokeach et al., 2001) and that their internet use does not operate as a facilitating factor in community engagement (Matei and Ball-Rokeach, 2001). However, such studies also found that when the

CTC has positioned itself as an important part of the community communication infrastructure, immigrants may learn to use the internet to learn about their new environment (Hayden and Ball-Rokeach, 2007). They can develop neighborhood storytelling skills that motivate participation in civic activities that bridge them (Putnam, 2000) to the larger community (Ball-Rokeach et al., 2001; Kim and Ball-Rokeach, 2006).

Transnational internet uses, connecting to "there"

Benedict Anderson (1991) observed that newspapers and other national language print media symbolically construct national boundaries and nationalism. These days, the internet and other ICT technologies (e.g., satellite TV, mobile phones, fax, and so on) afford a new boundary for nationalism, by allowing for transnational networking that can be mobilized to collectively (re) imagine the homeland. Such collective imagining is a political process that begets a terrain of struggle among the participants in transnational communities. This collective imagining does not necessarily reflect the reality of the homeland, as it can take on an idealistic, fundamentalist, or essentialist form. As Appadurai (1996) notes, "the homeland is partly invented, existing only in the imagination of the deterritorialized groups, and it sometimes becomes so fantastic and one-sided that it provides the fuel for new ethnic conflicts." Participation in such collective transnational imagining of homelands may discourage or slow the process of new immigrant assimilation into a host society.

Chan provides an illustrative case of Chinese students studying in Singapore Universities and their collective imaging of the homeland. They constructed websites that imagine their homeland as a super-power (Chan, 2005). These transnational migrants acted as representatives of their "imagined" country of origin, using online imagery of China as a tool of resistance against the United States in the global context and against the discipline of the host community.

New immigrants may also use the internet to maintain access to social, economic, human, and cultural resources in their home country. A Dutch Moroccan interviewee in Siddiquee and Kagan's (2006) study said that e-mail was a lifeline for "maintaining quick, cost effective connections to [their] geographically distant ... country of origin." Flourishing matrimonial websites for non-resident Indians of the United States are another example of how new immigrants remain tightly connected to resources in their country of origin (Adams and Rina, 2003).

By using online news media, new immigrant groups are now able to participate in the public sphere of their home country. In a survey conducted in 2003, home country news was the most read or watched news among Korean Americans in Los Angeles (Kim and Ball-Rokeach, 2003). The internet and traditional ethnic media were the main sources of this type of news. The net also has made it easier for new immigrants to participate in the opinion formation process in the home country (Kaldor-Robinson, 2002). They can contact politicians, news media, or government agencies in their homeland to register their opinions about homeland issues, especially emigration policies. Political participation can involve direct support to political groups in the homeland, even participation in "netwars" supporting politically dissident or rebellious groups. Two examples of such networks are the support of the Liberation Tigers of Tamil Eelam in Sri Lanka by the Tamil diaspora (Tekwani, 2003) and "guerilla sites" constructed by Zapatista supporters outside Mexico (Froehling, 1999).

Virtual internet uses, connecting to neither "here" nor "there"

In the preceding sections, we discussed two ideal types of new immigrant internet use, assimilation into the host society and reinforcement of transnational connections to the homeland. In this section, we discuss a third possibility; namely, an internet use that connects new immigrants to an alternative socio-political space whose gaze is focused neither on the home country nor the host society. New immigrants may deploy this to explore both personal (Turkle, 1995) and collective identities (Rheingold, 1991).

Two of the more common collective identity spaces are religious and diasporic virtual networks. Some religiously oriented new immigrants use the internet to construct a virtual community that has no direct reference either to *here* or *there*. These include Muslim networks (Schiffauer, 1999) and Hindu online groups (Brasher, 2004). Some diasporas, especially those who can be categorized as exiles or refugees forcefully uprooted from their homeland, have constructed online networks. One example is PALESA (Palestinian Scientists and Technologists Abroad), which was set up by Palestinian professionals overseas who have been disconnected from their homeland since the installation of the Palestinian National Authority (Hanafi, 2005). This network's geographical reference is weak because it refers to the Palestinian Territories which constitute only a "fragile center of gravity" for the Palestinian diaspora. Hanafi comments that new media can be an important tool "for connecting these communities to each other without having to go through the center" (596).

As we mentioned earlier, immigrants' internet use patterns are often dynamic and fluid. Immigrants may change their internet use pattern from one type to another following a decisive shift in the host or home country. Virtual uses of the internet, based on religious or professional networks without a particular geographical reference, can soon be transformed into assimilation or transnational uses due to events such as, to mention some recent examples, the immigration law reform protests during 2006 in the United States, or socio-political disasters such as the September 11th terrorist attacks and the subsequent wars in the Islamic countries. These critical turning points can lead immigrants toward place-based political engagement, such as using networks to organize protests, encourage voting, or the mobilization of resources for neighborhood development, *here* and/or *there*.

Hybrid internet use, connecting to both "here" and "there"

Unlike the 1920s and 30s' sociological descriptions of assimilation as a zero-sum game, we are now observing the possibility for new immigrants to leverage their social, economic, political, and cultural resources. Disconnecting from a homeland is not a necessary precondition for assimilation into the host society (Thompson, 2002). Hybridity or the construction of identities across *here* and *there* was previously regarded as problematic (Naficy, 1993) or as just an intermediate rite of passage from "separation" from their homeland to complete "incorporation" into the host society. But as Castles and Davison (2000) have suggested, cross-cultural competence that entails adaptation to multiple social spaces can be desirable in networked societies (Castells, 2000). In a global world, hybridity can be considered cultural intelligence (Hoogvelt, 2001): new immigrants can use it to connect to multiple social and political resources.

Internet use can be one facilitator in the process through which new immigrants develop multi-local attachments. The internet is used by some new immigrant groups to manage their social contacts *here* and *there* (Chan, 2005). Many of their social networks cross over local or global boundaries, revealing a form of networked individualism (Wellman *et al.*, 2003). For example, one recent study of Turkish and Moroccan immigrants to the Netherlands and Belgium found that their e-mail contacts were evenly distributed between the home and host countries (d'Haenens *et al.*, 2007). Adams and Rina (2003) have introduced the concept of "bridgespace" to capture a space where non-resident Indians in the United States leverage their connections to diverse resources from both the United States and India, describing it as "a virtual space that supports flows of people, goods, capital and ideas between South Asia and North America."

The internet use type/civic engagement relationship

While we have drawn the typology of new immigrant uses of the internet around issues of civic engagement, we are unable to make confident predictions about civic engagement outcomes on this basis alone. Ideal types are useful only to the extent that they capture broad differences between groups. Personal and social contexts influence both internet use and civic engagement. The next step, then, is to account for differences in both the intensity and the geographical focus of new immigrants' civic engagement, and how this relates to the four types of internet use we have just sketched out: assimilation, transnational, virtual, and hybrid. We turn now to theorizing the individual and contextual factors that are likely to modify the internet use type/civic engagement relationship.

Individual-level factors

Class

Classical studies of cultural assimilation or acculturation have suggested that upward mobility of immigrants is positively related to an increased level of assimilation into the host community and a decreased level of connection to the home country. However, recent studies have found that middle class and professional immigrants are more likely to take advantages of available resources, including new communication technologies, to leverage social, cultural, or economic capital from both *here* and *there* (Portes and Zhou, 1992). Østergaard-Nielsen (2003) observed that among Kurds in the United Kingdom, lower class immigrants could not find the time to attend rallies for better social, political, and legal conditions for asylum seekers in the U.K. because they were already mobilized around homeland political agendas. These limited observations suggest that higher class levels may be associated with hybrid internet use, while low-income migrants, when they have access to the internet, are more likely to use the internet to maintain their connection to the homeland.

Education

Some studies suggest that high levels of education help immigrants to quickly learn the language of the host society and, therefore, to assimilate faster than the less educated (Alba and Logan, 1991; Hechter and Okamoto, 2001). But other studies have shown that education increases political participation not only in the immediate social environments but also around more global issues, including homeland politics (Tarrow, 1998). We can speculate that education increases the likelihood of hybrid internet use.

Gender

Past studies have found that female immigrants more easily shift their orientation toward the host society than their male counterparts (Jones-Correa, 1998). Some suggest that this is due to the fact that males are more likely to experience downward mobility than females when they migrate from the homeland to the host country (Guarnizo *et al.*, 2003). These very limited findings suggest that females may be more likely to develop assimilation internet uses, while males may be more likely to develop transnational uses.

Reasons for immigration

The decision to immigrate is influenced by various push and pull factors but only a limited number of studies examine the relationship between reasons for immigration and civic engagement. A few studies compared the two major drivers (political and economic) and found that political motivations tended to be more positively related to civic or political participation in the host society than economic motivations (Agurrie and Saenz, 2002; Doerschler, 2006). Immigrants who were forced to leave their home country for political reasons tended to have lower expectations of going back home. Thus, they may have relatively high motivation to invest their time, money, and efforts in the host country political process. Immigrants who came to their host communities primarily for finding better economic opportunities (jobs, education, and so on) usually wish to go back to their country of origin as soon as their goals are achieved. Unlike politically motivated immigrants, they usually do not have enough time and other resources to invest in developing new political skills and interests.

Based on these limited empirical findings, we propose the hypothesis that politically motivated immigrants would more likely display an assimilation type of internet use (if they have access to political capital in the host community) or a virtual type of internet use (if they do not have access to political resources in the host community). We would also expect that economically motivated immigrants would be more likely to develop a transnational pattern of internet use. Relationships between immigration motivations and internet use types would be either mediated or moderated by other factors such as age, gender, immigration generation, language skill, education, and income.

Length of residence and immigration generation

The traditional view is that the longer immigrants are in a host country, the more likely it is that they will engage with it and disconnect from the homeland. The corollary prediction was made for immigration generation; that is, that the second generation would be less connected to the homeland than the first generation, and so on. A few recent studies suggest that these predictions may no longer hold. Guarnizo *et al.* (2003) found that length of residence in the host society does not significantly decrease interest or involvement in homeland politics. Several studies have shown that second-generation immigrant children do have substantial interest in their and their parents' homeland (d'Haenens, 2003; Hiller and Franz, 2004). These studies suggest that we may not find assimilation internet uses to be as prevalent as they once were. This opens up the possibility of hybrid internet uses, in which people develop civic interest both *here* and *there*.

Religion

In most contemporary immigrant communities, religious institutions play multiple roles. They help immigrants integrate into the receiving society, while providing them with the institutional, social, cultural, or psychological resources to remain connected to the country of origin. Religious membership also provides immigrants with opportunities to withdraw from matters related to either their host community or their country of origin and to construct private, spiritual spaces. Roles vary among religious institutions. For example, observing Salvadoran immigrant communities in U.S. metropolitan areas, Menjívar (2003) found that Catholic churches put more emphasis on community-building efforts and the integration of Salvadoran immigrants into their host communities than evangelical churches that emphasized individual spiritual experiences. The features of religious institutions that might affect their role in their affiliates' internet use type may include their place orientation (*here*, *there*, neither-*here*-nor-*there*, or both-*here*-and-*there*); whether the religion has strong transnational or global networks; and whether it is in the mainstream of the host society (for example, Christianity in most western countries).

Internet connectedness

Any type of internet use for political engagement requires internet access and will be affected by the level of internet skill. Metamorphosis Project studies of new immigrant groups in Los Angeles have shown that different groups of new immigrants in different places vary in terms of having internet access, internet use skills, and internet use goals (Jung *et al.*, 2001; Kim *et al.*, 2002; Gibbs *et al.*, 2006). Internet access and a certain level of skill is an obvious pre-condition for internet use for civic engagement. What may not be so obvious is that not all new immigrant groups meet this pre-condition (Jung *et al.*, 2007). Also, it will be important in future studies to know the full range of goals that are implicated in internet use. We hypothesize that when immigrants use the internet generally for social and self-understanding goals, they are more likely to develop hybrid internet uses.

Contextual factors

The political environment of the host society

The political environment in the host society can be an important contextual factor in the uses that new immigrants make of the internet. Societies and communities with high levels of social capital (Putnam, 2000) afford a conducive environment for new immigrants. Similarly, new immigrants living in communities with strong communication infrastructures will have greater opportunities to become engaged than those living in communities with fragmented communication infrastructures (Kim and Ball-Rokeach, 2006). Accordingly, both of these political environments should foster assimilation and/or hybrid internet uses.

Host society's immigration policies

The host country's immigration policies are features of the environment that are likely to affect how new immigrants deploy the internet. As Østergaard–Nielsen (2003) observed, in countries like Germany and many East Asian countries where migrants are categorized as foreigners and excluded from full access to political rights, new immigrants are more likely to use the internet for either connecting or reconnecting to their country of origin (transnational uses) or for finding a "third space" that belongs to neither here nor there (virtual uses). On the other hand, in a society emphasizing multiculturalism such as the Netherlands or the United States, where there are many resources and spaces available for civic life as immigrants (such as ethnic media or immigrant organizations) (Vertovec, 2001; Østergaard-Nielsen, 2003), the internet is more likely to be used for strengthening new immigrants' connections to the host society (assimilation uses) or bridging between the host society and the country of origin (hybrid uses).

Socio-economic difference between new comers and the host society

Previous studies of migration and assimilation have found that socio-economic divisions between newcomers and members of the host society is a factor in the pace of assimilation (Guarnizo et al., 2003). When new immigrants have lower socio-economic status, the bigger the gap, the slower the pace of assimilation. This suggests that new immigrants will be less likely to develop assimilation or hybrid internet uses when they enter a society where they are toward the bottom of the socio-economic ladder.

Home country emigrant policies

States vary in their policies toward those who leave. Some, such as Haiti, try to maintain hegemony over emigrants. Some states encourage dual citizenship, while others do not. Those that reach out to their emigrants should foster more durable civic connections and this is more likely to promote either the transnational or hybrid patterns of internet use.

Immigrants' communication environment

Different immigrants live in different communication environments (Kim and Ball-Rokeach, 2006). Having access to transnational news channel such as *Al Jazeera* for immigrants from the Middle East, or

Telemundo for Latinos, and satellite TV networks for Asian immigrants (e.g., *Arirang TV* for Koreans overseas) affords transnational connections to the home country. Local ethnic media have flourished in many immigrant communities around the world. These have the potential to promote immigrants' civic participation in their host societies. But studies have also found that ethnic media play a limited role in this regard (see Ball-Rokeach *et al.*, 2001). When new media such as the internet come into an individual's or a community's communication environment, their social meanings and roles are largely shaped by the characteristics of the existing communication environment (e.g., Jung *et al.*, 2007). We propose that immigrants' internet use types (assimilation, transnational, virtual, or hybrid) are influenced by the kinds of communication environments they experience. For example, if an immigrant community has a local storytelling network encouraging integration into the host society, assimilation internet use is more likely. If immigrants live in a communication environment discouraging engagement in the host community, their internet use is likely to be of either the transnational or virtual type.

Conclusion

Considerations of how the internet is woven into immigration processes and immigrants' lives are not sufficiently theorized in communication studies. We have presented an internet uses typology formulated around the issue of new immigrants and civic engagement. It will serve its intended purpose if this typology spurs other internet politics researchers to incorporate new immigrants into their studies. As this chapter illustrates, incorporation means more than adding new immigrants to sample frames or study

groups. Rather, it requires expansion of the theory to allow for the case of civic engagement over multiple spaces. Such expansion is fully consistent with the larger need to grasp aspects of the globalization process that include immigration flows.

Much of the research that bears upon individual and contextual factors that may shape new immigrants' internet uses is based upon case studies. While these are useful, we have a long way to go in creating theory-driven, multi-method inquiry. Comparative studies will be especially helpful in building theory. For example, studies of the same ethnic immigrant group in different places, and immigrants of different ethnicities in the same place may generate insights into how immigrants operating under different personal and contextual conditions form their internet uses.

These issues matter because new immigrant decisions on media use are likely to reflect and to intensify the identity negotiations that have substantial implications for civic engagement. Immigration flows are not likely to lessen in the foreseeable future; we need to conduct social science research on the internet in a way that incorporates this trend, and to allow for the possibility of internet-related civic engagement *here* and *there*.

Guide to further reading

Castles and Davidson (2000) provides a nice overview about the issues regarding migration and civic engagement in both global and historical contexts. Appadurai (1996), Giddens (1991), Hall (1994), and Morley and Robins (1995) also offer useful conceptual tools to understand the multiplicity of issues around migration, communication technologies, and place attachment in the globalizing world. For recent discussions about transnationalism, we recommend Vertovec (2001) and Guarnizo *et al.* (2003). In his introductory article in *Journal of Ethnic and Migration Studies,* Vertovec offers very useful summaries of conceptual issues and criticisms about transnational approaches to migration and immigration. Guarnizo *et al.* (2003) is an important article for anyone interested in the factors influencing immigrants' political actions in multiple social spaces. For recent discussions about immigrants' assimilation, Zhou and Cai (2002) provide an excellent overview of different approaches and recent developments.

Most of the previous works on immigrants' internet use are based on case studies. Among them, we recommend Mitra (2001), D'Haenens *et al.* (2007), Østergaard-Nielsen (2003), and Siddiquee and Kagan (2006). The works from the Metamorphosis Project at the University of Southern California (Hayden and Ball-Rokeach, 2007; Jung *et al.*, 2007; Kim *et al.*, 2007; Matei & Ball-Rokeach, 2001) provide contextual knowledge about how the internet is woven into existing communication environments and community life among new immigrants.

21

One Europe, digitally divided

Jan A. G. M. van Dijk

The digital divide in Europe still is a problem, and the goal of universal access to computers and internet connections has yet to be achieved. In this chapter the extent of the problem will be analyzed in terms of user access, and the public policy options for solving the problem will be reviewed. A comprehensive description will be made of the current status of the digital divide in Europe, highlighting the gaps between Northern and Southern, Western and Eastern Europe and the gaps between population groups within these countries. The description will follow a fourfold model of access: motivation, physical access, digital skills, and usage.

Access for all is important for internet politics in the world. This certainly goes for Europe where at least the policy texts of the European Union abound with phrases such as "an information society for all" and "e-inclusion." Yet, reality shows otherwise, as even in the latest Eurobarometer statistics persistent large access gaps appear between Northern and Southern or Eastern and Western European countries and between people with different social class, education, age, and gender within all these countries.

The second part of the chapter will deal with policy issues. What solutions have been proposed and practiced in the European Union? What are the prospects of solving this presumed problem in an environment of increasing global economic and informational inequality? What are the political implications when the digital divide problem in Europe, and elsewhere, is not sufficiently solved?

But first of all, we have to take a closer look at the core concepts of digital divide, universal access, or simply access to computers and the internet. The digital divide commonly refers to the gap between those who do and those who do not have access to new forms of information technology. Most often these forms are computers and their networks but other digital equipment such as mobile telephony and digital television are also included by some users of the term.

The term digital divide probably has caused more confusion than clarification. According to Gunkel (2003) it is a deeply ambiguous term that is caused by the sharp dichotomy it refers to. Van Dijk (2003, 2005) has warned of a number of pitfalls of this metaphor. First, the metaphor suggests a simple divide between two clearly divided groups with a yawning gap between them. Second, it suggests that the gap is very difficult to bridge. A third misunderstanding might be the impression that the divide is about absolute inequalities between those included and those excluded. In reality most inequalities of access to digital technology observed are of a relative kind. A final wrong connotation might be the suggestion that the divide is a static condition while in fact the gaps observed are continually shifting. Both Gunkel and van

Dijk have emphasized that the term echoes some kind of technological determinism. It is often suggested that the origins of the inequalities referred to lie in the specific problems of getting physical access to digital technology and that achieving such access for all would solve particular problems in the economy and society. In the last suggestion not only a technological bias but also a normative bias is revealed.

The great merit of the sudden rise of the term digital divide at the turn of the century is that it has put the important issue of inequality in the information society on the scholarly and political agenda. Between the years 2000 and 2004 hundreds of scientific and policy conferences and thousands of sessions on regular conferences have been dedicated to this issue under the call of the term digital divide. In the years 2004 and 2005 attention has started to decline. In terms of policy and politics many observers, particularly in the rich and developed countries, reached the conclusion that the problem was almost solved. After all, a rapidly increasing majority of their inhabitants obtained access to computers, the internet, and other digital technologies.

From a scientific point of view the concept ran into difficulties; ever more expressions such as "redefining the digital divide" and "beyond access" appeared. However, this does not mean that the concept has become an empty cover. On the contrary, it is more of a container concept carrying too many meanings. Therefore, one should carefully distinguish between different kinds of digital divide. In this chapter this will be done by a distinction of four types of access.

Universal access also has been defined rather differently. We have to observe that the developed and the developing countries try to realize this principle of (tele)communication policy in different ways. In the developed countries universal access usually means household

access for all. For those not connected at home, public access and public service in community and government buildings, libraries, telecenters, and internet cafés are the second option. In developing countries household access is a luxury that is far beyond reach. There public access is the first option; access in public buildings, community centers, and commercial telecenters or cafés is the only achievable aim of access in a short or medium term.

However, the biggest conceptual problem is caused by the term access itself. Usually access is equated with physical access. This narrow definition causes many problems. It does not sufficiently explain the diversity of phenomena that are related to inequality concerning the use of digital technology. It is no surprise that all conceptual elaborations of the terms digital divide and technology access of the last five years have tried to extend the concept of access or to go beyond access narrowly defined. My own research is characterized by a model with four successive and accumulative types of access that mark the steps to be taken by individual users in the process of appropriating digital technology. The first type is motivation or motivational access. The second is material access, particularly physical access. Then comes skills access: a number of "digital skills" required to work with digital technology. The last type of access is the purpose of the whole process of technology appropriation: usage.

This model of access (Figure 21.1) will serve as a framework for the current state of the many digital divides in Europe to be described in the following large section.

The digital divide in Europe

Motivation

Acquiring the motivation to use a computer and to achieve an internet connection

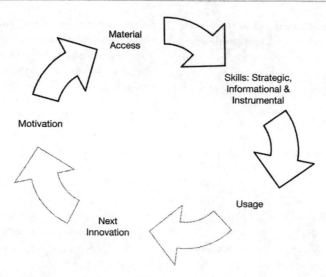

Figure 21.1 A cumulative and recursive model of digital technologies access.

is the first step to get access to these digital technologies. Many of those who remain at the "wrong" side of the digital divide have motivational problems. It appears that there are not only have-nots, but also "want-nots." Probably, the motivational divide has become smaller in the last two decades, at least in developed societies. In Europe it is increasingly taken for granted that people have a computer and internet connection if they do not want to become marginalized in society. Also, it seems that the phenomena of technophobia and anxiety that usually accompany the advent of a new, perhaps frightening, technology have diminished. In the 1980s and early 1990s, large parts of the European and American populations showed signs of technophobia, computer anxiety, and distrust in a world dominated by computers in nationwide surveys.

However, fears and dislikes have not disappeared. They are surprisingly persistent. According to a representative UCLA survey in 2003 more than 30 percent of new American internet users reported that they were moderately to highly technophobic and the same applied to 10 percent of experienced internet users (UCLA, 2003: p. 25). German and Dutch surveys from 1999 to 2006 revealed that about half of those not connected to the internet explicitly refused to obtain such a connection (ARD-ZDF, 1999; van Dijk, Hanenburg, and Pieterson, 2006).

The main reasons for not wanting a home internet connection mentioned by European inhabitants in a large-scale European survey of 2005 (Eurostat, 2006) in percentages between brackets are: does not want internet, content is not useful (41), equipment costs are too high (25), lack of skills (24), access costs of telephony etc. too high (23), and has access elsewhere (18). Eight percent do not want the internet because content is harmful etc.; privacy and security reasons are called by 6 percent and 13 percent mention other reasons.

The factors explaining motivational access are both of a social or cultural and a mental or psychological nature. A primary social explanation is that "the internet does not have appeal for low-income and low-educated people" (Katz and Rice, 2002: p. 93). To dig deeper into the reasons for this lack of interest it seems appropriate to complement the large-scale surveys with qualitative studies in local communities and cultural groups. Those who did discovered the importance of culture, ethnicity, and particular lifestyles for the motivation to obtain and use digital technology (van Dijk, 2005: pp. 35–9).

However, most pronounced are mental and psychological explanations. Here the phenomena of computer anxiety and technophobia come to the fore. Computer anxiety is a feeling of discomfort, stress, or fear experienced when confronting computers (Brosnan, 1998; Chua, Chen, and Wong, 1999; Rockwell and Singleton, 2002). Technophobia is fear of technology in general and distrust in its beneficial effects. Computer anxiety and technophobia are major barriers of computer and internet access, especially among seniors, people with low educational level, and a part of the female population. These phenomena do not completely disappear with a rise in computer experience.

Material and physical access

The following type of access is the one that draws all attention in digital divide research, opinion, and policy. Many people think that the problem of the digital divide is solved as soon as (almost) everybody has a computer and internet connection. That this assumption is wrong forms the tenor of this chapter. In this section we first have to make a distinction between physical access, that is having a computer and internet connection, whether at home or in a public place—provisions at work are not supposed to be used for every purpose—and material access. This is the broader concept that includes all expenses for computer and network hardware, software, and services. While computers and internet connections on their own are getting cheaper every year, total expenses for these media are not dropping according to

most consumer expenditure surveys. Among these expenses are subscriptions, the growing number of computer peripheral devices, the rising prices for primary products such as ink, paper, and electricity, and, in general, the accelerating obsolescence of computer hardware and software.

The current state of the physical access divide in Europe can be described in terms of the gap between European countries or regions, and the gap of relevant demographics such as age, gender, educational level, type of employment, and ethnic minorities. The question posed in this section is whether these gaps are narrowing or widening at the time of writing.

In Northern and Western Europe the physical access divide in terms of computers and internet connections has started to close after the year 2000. This means that the upper strata in terms of education and income were no longer adopting these digital media at a faster rate than the lower strata. On the contrary, people with lower education and income, and seniors have been catching up since that time. The physical access divide of gender in Northern and Western Europe already closed before 2000. (See annual Eurobarometer research summarized in GESIS, 2004.)

However, in Southern and Eastern Europe the physical access divide has still grown after the year 2000. Only recently it can be observed that particular countries in Southern Europe slowly enter the phase of a closing divide (Eurostat, 2006). See Figure 21.2. This goes for Spain and Cyprus, where computer possession in 2006 rose above 50 percent and internet connections at home became available for more than a third of the population in that year. However, Greece and Portugal were still running behind.

Figure 21.2 shows that there are large gaps between Northern and Southern and between Western and Eastern European countries considering household access to computers, the internet, and broadband connections. Inside Eastern Europe differences are very large. Countries such as Slovenia and Estonia already have access figures around the EU average, while countries such as Romania and Bulgaria run very far behind with access figures of a Third World country.

What explains these North–South and West–East divides? Generally, they are ascribed to the economic wealth and the level of development of nations. However, the causes are deeply entrenched features of each country's economic, cultural, and political character: the availability and cost of digital technology in a country; a country's general level of literacy and education; the language skills of a country's population, speaking English in particular; the level of democracy (freedom of expression); the strength of policies to promote the information society in general and access in particular; a culture that is attracted to technology, computers, and computer communication (van Dijk, 2005: p. 57).

Cultural factors might be more important than usually thought. One of the factors explaining lower access rates in Southern Europe is a lifestyle of living outdoors and on the streets more than in cold Northern Europe. Here people spend a large part of leisure time at home, among others behind their computer screen.

Except for the disparities at the country level and the regional level—within European countries there are pronounced differences between city and rural regions with rural regions often lacking broadband access (see Eurostat, 2005)—one can observe access differences at the level of organizations with some organizations and categories of employees having more access than others—that are not discussed here—and at the individual or household level. Individual-level disparities in Europe touch the same social categories as in all other continents of the world. Those with senior age, lower educational level, positions outside the labor market or educational institutions, and to a lesser extent with female sex and ethnic minority

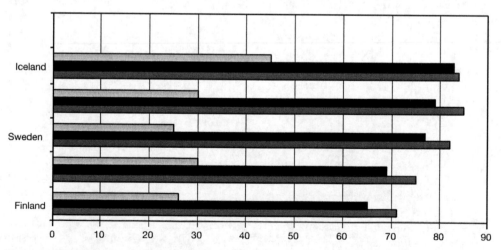

Figure 21.2a Personal computers, internet access, and broadband speed in the European Union, by region, 2006: Northern Europe.
Source: Eurostat (2006).

Note: Data for 26 European Union members from 2005, data for Norway and Iceland from 2006.

origin, have less physical and material access to computers and the internet. As a general proposition one can maintain that these social category digital divides are more pronounced in countries with lower social and economic development and a lower rate of diffusion of information and communication technology (van Dijk, 2005). Taking into account that Europe on average has a relatively high position globally on both rates (development and diffusion) the social category digital divides in Europe still are very articulate. Table 21.1 shows broad divides of age, level of education, and occupational position. In 2005, 61 percent of Europeans between 55 and 74 years of age had never used a computer and 81 percent did not regularly use the internet. Among the youngest adult age group (16–24) 9 percent never used a computer and 32 percent no internet. Europeans with low education had a proportion of 57 percent

with no computer use and 71 percent with no internet use while these percentages were only 8 and 28 percent for Europeans with high education. Finally, Table 21.1 shows large differences of physical access between European students, employees, and the self-employed on the one side and European unemployed, retired, and inactive people at the other.

The gender gap of physical access in Europe has closed for the youngest age group of 16–24, but not for older age groups. Gender differences are biggest in the age group of 55–74. The general physical access figure for the 25 EU counties in 2004 for computer access was 58 percent for males and 51 percent for females, and regarding internet access it was 51 percent for males and 43 percent for females.

Physical and material access to computers and the internet of ethnic minorities,

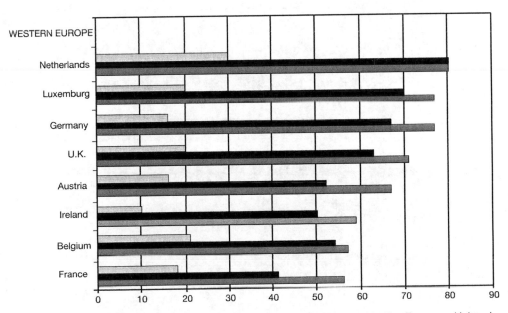

Figure 21.2b Personal computers, internet access, and broadband speed in the European Union, by region, 2006: Western Europe.

Source: Eurostat (2006).

Note: Data for 26 European Union members from 2005, data for Norway and Iceland from 2006.

most often migrants from other continents, usually is very much lower than that of the ethnic majority in a particular country. Evident problems are a lack of employment, material resources, and understanding of the official language in a country, or the knowledge of English. The ethnic composition of European countries is so different that general ethnic majority and minority access figures cannot reasonably be conveyed here.

Skills access

After having received the motivation to use computers and some kind of physical access to them, one has to learn to manage the hardware and software. Here the problem of a lack of skills might appear according to the model in Figure 21.1. This problem is framed with terms such as "computer, information, or multimedia literacy" and "computer skills" or

"information capital". Steyaert (2000) and van Dijk (1999, 2003, 2005) introduced the concept of "digital skills" as a succession of three types of skill. The most basic are *operational skills*, the capacities to work with hardware and software. These skills have acquired much attention in the literature and in public opinion. The most popular view is that skills problems are solved when these skills are mastered. However, many scholars engaged with information processing in an information society have called attention to all kinds of information skills required to successfully use computers and the internet. *Information skills* are the skills to search, select, and process information in computer and network sources. Two types of information skills can be distinguished: formal information skills (ability to work with the formal characteristics of computers and the internet, e.g., file and hyperlink structures) and substantial information skills

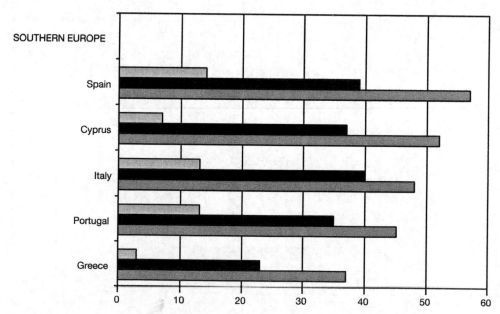

Figure 21.2c Personal computers, internet access, and broadband speed in the European Union, by region, 2006: Southern Europe.
Source: Eurostat (2006).

Note: Data for 26 European Union members from 2005, data for Norway and Iceland from 2006.

(ability to find, select, process, and evaluate information in specific computer and network sources following specific questions).

Finally, we can distinguish *strategic* skills. They can be defined as the capacities to use computer and network sources as the means for particular goals and for the general goal of improving one's position in society. An example of a strategic skill on the internet is the task to find the nearest hospital with the shortest waiting list (means) for a particular knee operation (particular goal). Usually, strategic skills

both require knowledge of computer and network skills and some substantial knowledge of the field under consideration, for example understanding the way the labor market, the government bureaucracy, or hospitals work and knowing particular laws and regulations.

Empirical research of all kinds of digital skills is scarce. Actually, the only data are about the command of operational skills. Institutions offering computer courses sometimes record the achievements of course takers. Some national surveys that

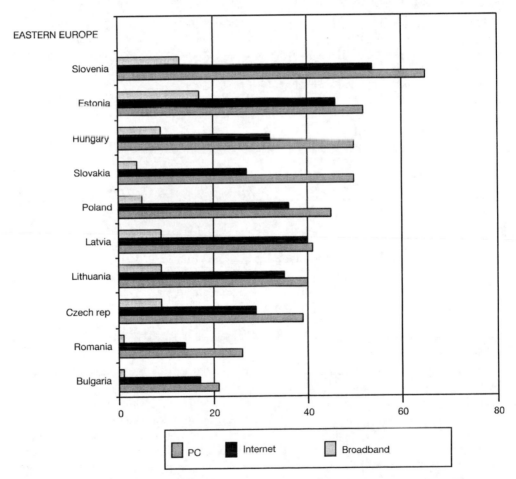

Figure 21.2d Personal computers, internet access, and broadband speed in the European Union, by region, 2006: Eastern Europe.
Source: Eurostat (2006).

Note: Data for 26 European Union members from 2005, data for Norway and Iceland from 2006.

Table 21.1 Computer and internet non-use, and skills among selected demographics in 25 EU countries, 2005

Demographics		*Not regularly using the internet*	*Never used a computer*	
Age	16–24 years old	32	9	
	25–54 years old	51	27	
	55–74 years old	81	61	
Education	Low education	77	57	
	Middle education	53	25	
	Higher education	28	8	
Employment	Students	22	4	
	Employees and self-employed	46	22	
	Unemployed	68	36	
	Retired, inactive, other	84	64	
Total	Average across 25 EU countries	57	34	

Computer skills		*Never*	*Low*	*Medium*	*High*
Education	Low education	65	10	15	10
Age	55–64 years old	61	13	16	10
	65–74 years old	83	7	7	3
Employment	Retired, inactive, other	73	11	11	5
	Unemployed	44	14	23	19
Total	Average across 25 EU countries	41	13	24	22

Internet skills		*Never*	*Low*	*Medium*	*High*
Education	Low education	67	17	12	4
Age	55–64 years old	65	26	8	1
	65–74 years old	85	12	3	0
Employment	Retired, inactive, other	76	17	6	1
	Unemployed	48	27	19	6
Total	Average across 25 EU countries	43	31	20	6

Source: Author's calculations based on data available from Eurostat (2006).

ask population samples to report about their computer and internet skills are available (for example van Dijk *et al.*, 2000; Park, 2002; UCLA, 2001, 2003). Mostly, they only pay attention to the command of hardware and software, not to information skills.

The latest estimation of computer and internet skills, in this case also mainly operational skills, of the European population were made in the Community Survey on ICT use in Households and by Individuals (Eurostat, 2006). Table 21.1 also portrays the overall low computer and internet (operational) skills of the European population in 2006, emphasizing the even worse situation of the poorly educated, the senior users, and the retired.

Analyzing the data of this survey, it appears that all three social demographics—age, educational level, and gender—are significantly related to the level of computer and internet (operational) skills but that age is most important, educational attainment second, and gender third.

Measuring computer and internet skills with general surveys poses two fundamental problems: a measurement problem and the problem that only operational skills and not information and strategic digital skills are considered. The first problem is the validity of survey measurement for this purpose: are self-reports valid measurements of actual skills possessed? Many people have difficulties in judging their own skills. It is well-known that males and young people give higher self-estimations than females and seniors. Moreover, in the surveys referred to, including the Eurostat survey, it is asked whether a particular operation has ever been executed, not whether it was performed well. This goes among others for the use of a search engine. Probably most people are very bad in using search engines. However, this can only be validly determined by performance tests in a controlled environment. Most measures of computer literacy or digital skills have an educational background; they are the tests finishing computer classes or courses. One of the few attempts to give performance tests of actually mastered computer and internet skills in a controlled experimental environment that have been reported, is the experiment of the American sociologist Esther Hargittai. For her dissertation she conducted a series of experimental tests with American user groups charged with tasks of finding particular information on the internet (Hargittai, 2002, 2003, 2004). In this way, she also measured some formal and substantial information skills. Subjects were selected and matched according to age, sex, and education. Enormous differences were found in the measure of accomplishment and time needed to finish these tasks. Only half of the experimental group was able to complete all tasks in the first experiment, but for some subjects time required for a particular task was a few seconds while others needed 7 to 14 minutes (Hargittai, 2002). Another attempt was made by Ulla Bunz of Florida State University. She compared the actual versus the perceived "computer-, e-mail-, and web fluency," as she calls the digital skills, of a group of 61 first-year students (Bunz et al., 2006). Considering the command of skills she found no gender differences of actual fluency. Females only revealed a lower level of perceived fluency than males. However, she focused on

computer anxiety and there she observed that the less computer anxiety subjects reported, the higher they perceived their fluency while not showing lower actual fluency.

An investigation with performance tests of digital skills in a media lab comparable to that used by Hargittai, is presently being done by myself and a Ph.D. student at the University of Twente in the summer of 2007. A stratified random sample of a hundred Dutch residents, age 18 to 70, is invited to perform a series of tests to measure the level of operational skills (formal and substantial), information skills, and strategic skills separately. The sample is stratified in four age groups, three educational attainment groups, and two sexes.

Two general hypotheses still waiting for conclusive evidence in surveys and performance tests of digital skills are (1) that the divides of skills access are bigger than the divides of physical access, and (2) that while physical access gaps are more or less closing in the developed countries, the (relative) skills gaps tend to grow, the gap of information skills and strategic skills in particular.

Usage access

Actual usage of digital media is the final stage and ultimate goal of the total process of appropriation of technology that is called access in this chapter. Having sufficient motivation, physical access, and skills to apply digital media are necessary but not sufficient conditions of actual use. Usage has its own grounds or determinants. As a dependent factor it can be measured in at least four ways: usage time; usage applications: number and diversity; broadband or narrowband use; more or less active or creative use.

One of the gravest errors in statistics of computer and internet diffusion is that the possession of a computer and access to the internet are conflated with actual use.

Some people have a computer but rarely or even never touch it. At least 20 percent of those having formal access to the internet at home in Europe and North America are not using this medium themselves, but one or more housemates do. Those really using a computer and the internet can do this for a few minutes a week or they can use them everyday and all day long. Usage time might be a better indicator of the digital divide than dichotomous physical access (yes/no). Eurostat measures frequency of internet use in a number of categories (once a day, a week, etc.) and for several demographics (see Eurostat: http://epp.eurostat.cec.eu.int/portal). Generally, the same disparities can be observed here as with physical access and skills access mentioned above.

However, the most valid and reliable estimations of actual usage time are made in detailed daily time diary studies that measure all daily activities to the minute. For example, the Dutch Social and Cultural Planning Agency measures detailed home usage times for computers and the internet every five years.

Sometimes they lead to surprising results. In 2000, this Agency found that the number of weekly hours of computer and internet use of males at home was double as compared to that of females (SCP, 2001). In 2005 the distribution was still the same: males used the computer and internet at home 5.2 hours and females 2.4 hours a week. The gender physical access gap may have been almost closed in the Netherlands, but this certainly does not apply to the usage gender gap.

Usually, the average *number* of internet applications used overall, such as the twelve applications mentioned in Table 21.2, is between two and six (van Dijk, 2007). However, experienced users, people with high education, and young users use considerably more applications than inexperienced users, people with low education, and senior users. The same goes for people with broadband access as compared to narrowband and dial-up access (van Dijk, 2007). Comparable results appear in surveys relating the *diversity* of usage applications to demographic characteristics of users (for the U.S. see

Table 21.2 Internet activities of Europeans, by age and education subgroups, 2005

Internet activities	Age Group								
	16–24 Level of education			25–54 Level of education			55–74 Level of education		
	Low	Medium	High	Low	Medium	High	Low	Medium	High
Information from public authorities	19	29	43	–	37	51	–	32	40
Information on health and food	21	25	29	–	40	44	36	41	40
Information on goods and services	63	74	85	77	83	86	71	76	79
Reading online papers and magazines	26	36	41	24	33	47	–	29	37
Training and education	37	48	34	–	28	35	–	20	28
Travel and accommodation	22	42	54	–	51	61	–	55	60
Financial services	13	28	44	–	43	53	–	39	45
Selling goods and services (auctions)	11	16	16	16	19	18	–	–	12
Playing and downloading games and music	61	57	50	28	29	30	–	15	15
Chat and instant messaging	65	57	53	28	26	28	–	14	14
Web-radio and web-TV	32	31	31	17	18	25	–	10	14

Source: Eurostat, 2006.

Note: Includes people in 27 European Union countries who have used the internet in the last three months.

Howard *et al.*, 2001a, Horrigan and Rainie, 2002a; UCLA Center for Communication Policy, 2003 for Europe see Eurostat, 2006 and Table 21.2). Evidently, specific social categories of users prefer different kinds of applications. The studies just referred to all show significant differences among users with different social class, education, age, gender, and ethnicity. Table 21.2 also portrays the differences among the two most important categories: age and education.

This table shows a generation gap in playing and downloading games and music, in chatting or instant messaging, and in receiving web-radio and web-TV as the youngest age group uses these applications much more; conversely, internet users with middle and high ages benefit more from information on health and food, financial services, and travel or accommodation services. However, disparities between people with different levels of education, an important indicator of social class, are much bigger. This also goes for the youngest generation that has grown up with digital media.

In this context some investigators (van Dijk, 1999, 2000, 2003, 2004; Bonfadelli, 2002; Park, 2002; Cho *et al.*, 2003) perceive a so called *usage gap* between people with different social class and education that is comparable to the phenomenon of the knowledge gap that has been observed from the 1970s onwards. While the knowledge gap is about the differential derivation of *knowledge* from the *mass media*, the usage gap is a broader thesis about a differential use of *computer and internet* applications as a whole in *all kinds of activities*. I have observed "the first signs of a usage gap between people of high social position, income, and education using the advanced computer and internet applications for information, communication, work, business, or education and people of low social position, income, and education using more simple applications for information, communication, shopping, and entertainment" (van Dijk, 2005: p. 130).

Bonfadelli (2002) has shown that in Switzerland, in the year 2000, 72 percent of internet users with low education used entertainment types of internet applications as compared to 35 percent of users with high education. Further, 64 percent of users with high education employed information types of application and 45 percent transaction services, as compared to 53 percent information applications and 31 percent transaction applications by users with low education. I have observed the same tendency in 2005 in the Netherlands (van Dijk, 2007). Users with high education used significantly more applications of information, news and current affairs, jobs and vacancies, internet banking, buying and selling goods, and the use of government websites than users with low education. On the other hand users with low education used significantly more applications of gaming and downloading or exchanging music and videos, chatting and entertainment as a whole. The situation of Europe as a whole in 2006 shows the same pattern. Table 21.3 reveals that internet users with low education perform less activities of information retrieval, text communication (both e-mail and reading newspapers and magazines), financial services, and services of mobility (travel and accommodation) than users with medium and high education. Simultaneously, they perform more entertainment activities: playing and downloading games and music, chatting and instant messaging, and web broadcasting.

Other digital divide considerations

Usage of narrowband versus broadband connections appears to have a strong effect on usage time and on the type and range of applications. People with broadband connections take much more advantage of the opportunities of the new media. They are much less deterred by the costs of connection time; they use much more applications and for a longer time. This has been observed in the U.S. (Horrigan and Rainie, 2002b; UCLA, 2003). Unfortunately, Eurostat only supplies data for household broadband access per country in Europe, not individual demographics. However, most likely in Europe a "broadband elite" also exists that uses the connection for ten or more online activities on a typical day (Horrigan and Rainie, 2002b). As a matter of fact, broadband also stimulates a much more active and creative use of the internet (Horrigan and Rainie, 2002b).

Despite its image of being interactive, most internet usage, apart from e-mailing, is relatively passive and consuming. Active and creative use of the internet, that is, the production of internet content by users themselves still is a minority phenomenon despite all contemporary promises of Web 2.0 and the rise of participatory media perspective. Active contributions are publishing a personal website, creating a weblog, posting a contribution on an online bulletin board, newsgroup or community, and, perhaps, in a broad definition, exchanging music and video files. From the Eurostat data it appears that people with lower age and social class or education are exchanging music and video files more often than people with middle and senior age and high social class and education, but that the distribution is opposite for people with high education in creating web pages and posting messages to chat rooms, newsgroups, or online discussion forums.

A first general conclusion of many investigations is that, increasingly, all familiar social and cultural differences in society are reflected in computer and internet use (van Dijk, 2005). A second conclusion is that these differences tend to be reinforced by computer and internet use. In most, if not all, spheres of societal participation (economical, social, political, cultural) and citizenship, those already occupying the strongest positions tend to benefit more from access and usage of ICTs as potentially powerful tools than those occupying the weakest positions (van Dijk, 2005). This is sometimes called the rich are getting richer effect or the Matthew effect, a term first coined by the sociologist Merton in 1968 referring to the Gospel "For to everyone who has, more shall be given" (Matt. 25: 29, New American). Without necessarily defending an instrumentalist view of technology it can be claimed that computers and the internet can be used as tools to strengthen one's position in society. The better one commands this tool the better it can be used for this purpose.

If this proposition is true, it could lead to a dark perspective for policies to reduce the digital divide of skills and usage access as types of relative inequality. Every measure one could take would benefit those in the strongest positions more than those in the weakest positions. Is this perspective inevitable, or are there other, more focused policy options that only or primarily benefit people in the weakest positions? What digital divide policies are available anyway? What has Europe done to close the digital divide? Are European digital divide policies special, for example as compared to U.S. policies? These questions will be discussed in the following sections.

Policies to solve the digital divide in Europe

There are two main reasons for countries to develop policies that help to reduce the digital divide. The first is economic development or innovation, and the second is social inclusion or the reduction of a level of inequality that tends to become too high. Traditionally, the first reason is more important for governments and corporations, though legitimizing digital divide policies usually is framed more in terms of social inclusion and access for all. Clearly, a persisting digital divide reduces the potential of the labor force and of innovation. Advanced high-tech societies cannot afford to exclude about a third of this potential labor force and of all hidden talents for innovation it contains. Moreover, information and communication technology is considered to be a growth sector in the economy that should be supported in global competition.

With regard to economic development and innovation the digital divide statistics in the former section are a matter of grave concern for the European Union. In its Lisbon 1999 declaration, the EU has launched a strategy to become the most innovative economy in the world by the year 2010. In the year 2007, it has to acknowledge that a very large proportion of the European population has never even used a computer and internet connection. At the level of countries, the EU should be concerned about the enormous disparities of physical access between Northern and Southern, Western and Eastern member states.

In all documents of the EU of the last 15 years that dealt with access to the information society, both the issues of economic development or innovation and of social inclusion and participation of all Europeans in the information society were present.

Officially and ideologically, the European Union (27 member states from January 2007 onwards) is very much occupied with an all-inclusive information society. Documents with titles like *An Information Society for All* have abounded since the middle of the 1990s. However, like the U.S. the EU adopts a market orientation in technological innovation and diffusion.

This strongly applies to ICTs. Here the prime strategic orientation is the liberalization of telecommunications. The construction of new infrastructures and their general diffusion is left to the market. The EU and its member states try to stimulate and direct development with innovation funds and to correct by regulation.

First policy phase: emphasizing physical access

During the second half of the 1990s and the first years after the year 2000, when the digital divide first appeared as a policy problem for governments, the European Union and its member states were very much preoccupied with the diffusion of the technology and the achievement of physical access to computers and the internet for as many Europeans as possible. This was enacted by the principles of universal and public access and of universal service. In this context these principles mean that every citizen or inhabitant should either have a private connection to a computer and the internet, preferably at home, but also students at schools and employees in working places (universal access) or a public connection in a public place such as a library and a community access centre (public access).

The principle of universal *service* was defined by the European Commission as "access to a defined minimum service of specified quality to all users independent of their geographical location and, in light of specific national conditions, at an affordable price" (Commission of the European Communities, 1996: p. 22). Here it was accepted that physical access itself is not sufficient and that the price, quality, and geographical availability of services should be safeguarded and kept under some regulatory control. This is an instance of the broader concept of material access and it requires a particular distribution of material resources. In the U.S. this has taken the form of the Universal Service Fund that reaps a small part of the tariffs of telecom users to afford connections, computers, and other resources in (primarily) schools. The EU has not seriously tried to create such a fund. Instead the EU attempts to realize universal service by regulation (Commission, 2003). A large number of obligations have forced telecom operators to interconnect their networks, to open up their connections for access to the internet and other digital media by telephone subscribers, and to provide some pubic access points.

In the first phase additional steps were made to provide extra resources focused on disadvantaged groups in Europe. They were hardware and connection cost subsidies to schools in poor neighborhoods or regions and additional means in publicly accessible buildings and community access centers, for example staff to guide new users and to give computer courses. In some European countries yet another further step was made: to supply hardware, software, and training for the unemployed to increase their chances on the labor market.

Second policy phase: emphasizing skills, usage, and motivation

In the action plan *eEurope 2005: An information society for all* (Commission, 2002) the emphasis was still on the rollout of (broadband) infrastructure, new services, and content. However, here first mention was made of the necessity to re-skill adults for the knowledge society outside formal education for mainly young people. In 2005, a long-term strategy was announced in the context of so-called *i2010* that could be framed as a new digital divide policy: "In i2010 strong emphasis is given to full participation and to providing people with basic

digital competence." (Commission, 2005: p. 9).

This new policy was summarized in the *Riga Declaration* of 2006. The background of the policy shift was explained in a 2007 working document: "It focused on three facets of eInclusion: the access divide (or 'early digital divide') which considers the gap between those with and without access; the usage divide ('primary digital divide') concentrating on those who have access but are non-users; and the divide stemming from quality of use ('secondary digital divide') focusing on differentials in participation rates of those people who have access and are users" (European Commission Staff, 2007: pp. 33–4).

In the Riga Declaration (Ministers of the EU, 2006) six broad policy areas for inclusion are defined: older workers and elderly people; the geographical digital divide; eAccessibility and usability; digital literacy; cultural diversity in relation to inclusion; inclusive eGovernment. In the Riga Declaration very ambitious targets are expressed: "the differences in internet usage between current average use by the EU population and use by older people, people with disabilities, women, lower education groups, unemployed and 'less-developed' regions should be reduced to a half, from 2005 to 2010."

Here, for the first time, EU digital divide policy is explicitly focused on the elderly and on the countries and regions with low access to computers and the (broadband) internet. To close the geographical divide the EU now aims broadband coverage to reach at least 90 percent of the EU population in 2010. So-called eAccessibility and usability mean better and more user-friendly software and services to be obtained by voluntary industry commitments and by EU-legislation for particular standards where they are appropriate. According to the Declaration this also means that "attention must be paid to further improve user motivation towards ICT use, as well as trust and confidence through better security and privacy protection. Furthermore, greater gender balance in the information society remains a key objective." (Ministers of the EU, 2006: p. 2).

Another new focus is on digital literacy and competence. Here actions also are tailored to the needs of groups at risk of exclusion: "the unemployed, immigrants, people with low education levels, people with disabilities, and elderly, as well as marginalised young people" (p. 4). Here the EU ministers want to cut the gaps of literacy by half in 2010 but, evidently, they do not know what they are talking about as it is admitted that operational definitions of this type of literacy still have to be made.

Cultural diversity in relation to inclusion means "fostering pluralism, cultural identity and linguistic diversity in the digital space" (p. 4). This is supposed to stimulate European cultural diversity and the participation of immigrants and minorities in the information society. As many eGovernment applications are not yet accessible for EU citizens a final Declaration aim is to "promote the accessibility of all public websites by 2010, through compliance with the relevant W3C common web accessibility standards and guidelines" (p. 4).

Two things are striking in this new policy direction. First, a shift is made from an emphasis on physical access with a hardware and services orientation to skills and usage access stressing digital literacy and applications that enable people to participate in the information society. This move echoes more recent analyses of the digital divide as a multifaceted phenomenon or as a problem that goes "beyond access." A second shift is the transition from a general policy of universal access and service to a much more focused approach for particular social categories and European regions lagging behind.

This double shift is also made in some other countries of the world that previously also emphasized physical access. It is conspicuous that it is not made in the United States. After the installation of the Bush administration in 2001 the digital divide was no longer a government policy problem. The U.S. was heading to be *A Nation Online: How Americans are Expanding Their Use of the Internet* (National Telecommunications and Information Administration, 2002). So, the assumption was that the problem was already being solved. The Bush administration concluded that government action was no longer needed. It proposed to terminate programs like the CTC (Computer Technology Centers) program and the TOP (Technology Opportunities Program). Of course, this does not mean that there is no government policy in terms of the diffusion of ICTs and the spread of digital literacy, or that American civil organizations will not call attention to digital divide issues. Only, that currently there is no concerted government action. Karen Mossberger will analyze the digital divide in the U.S. in Chapter 13 of this handbook.

Conclusion

The general implication of the digital divide is social exclusion of large sections of the population in several fields of society: the economy, politics, culture, education, community life, mobility and transport, social and sexual relationships, and even citizenship (Warschauer, 2003; van Dijk, 2005). In politics it means more or less disenfranchisement. Currently, this has started to take a modest form, but when the digital divide problem is not solved, ultimately citizens will even be disenfranchised as voters.

The modest forms we witness today all are disadvantages for citizens and voters that appear because in their provisions governments and politicians increasingly expect that people have computers and internet access and are able to work with these media. In this chapter it was shown that these are erroneous assumptions. Yet, most current innovations in the field of politics and government are spent on information and communication technology. Those with access are able to benefit from them, and those without are not. This is not only caused by a lack of physical access but also by insufficient digital skills. It even goes for usage access where those already politically involved have proven to benefit much more from the new digital opportunities than those less interested.

Contemporary examples of modest disenfranchisement are valuable e-government services, online voting guides, online political and government information, campaign news, online petitions and discussions, the opportunity to send e-mails to politicians and civil servants, and many other internet applications that cannot be used by digitally excluded citizens. Additionally, one of the main venues for European citizens to be informed about the EU project and EU policies so far away for many Europeans, EU websites would only be available for an elite among them.

In the mean time the election process also is digitized step by step. Electronic voting with computers in poll stations has become common practice in many developed societies. Electronic voting from home, though contested, is a potential future step. In that case those without access would certainly be disadvantaged. Of course, they would be offered alternatives for a long time to come. But with each of these innovations it appears that step by step those at the wrong side of the digital divide are pushed to the margins of political and citizen participation.

In this chapter the policies of the EU have received much attention. For the

EU not closing the digital divide would mean an even more divided Europe, contrary to its mission. While actually, the "information society for all" project clearly has been one of the main unifying and legitimizing projects for the EU as an institution; failing in this respect would lead to even larger regional disparities between Northern and Southern, Western and Eastern Europe.

Guide to further reading

Current and old policy documents of the European Union regarding information society access and the digital divide are available at the EU Information Society Thematic Portal: http://ec.europa.eu/information_society/policy/ecomm/index_en.htm. Statistical data regarding access are available in a freely accessible database called Eurostat Data Navigation Tree: http://ec.europa.eu/information_society/policy/ecomm/index_en.htm. Summarized data over many years (archive) are available at GESIS: http://www.gesis.org/en/data_service/eurobarometer/. Specific country reports of all EU countries and Norway and Turkey are available at: http://countryprofiles.wikispaces.com.

The conceptual background of this chapter is elaborated in van Dijk (2005) and (2006). The latter book also contains a comparison of the general information society policies of the European Union, the United States, and East Asia. Additionally, comparisons of digital divide policies of the European Union and the United States can be derived from Mossberger et al. (2003) and Wilhelm (2004). Comparisons of digital divide policies worldwide, focusing on developing countries are available in Warschauer (2003).

22

Working around the state

Internet use and political identity in the Arab world

Deborah L. Wheeler

Whereas the internet is an increasingly common tool used in Arab everyday life, only a handful of scholars have studied what impact internet use is having on Arab societies. This study remedies this lacuna by providing an analysis of the relationship between internet diffusion and democratization; the role that IT diffusion plays in economic growth and development; and the extent to which internet access enhances individual agency and empowerment (especially in terms of gender and social class, and given authoritarian information environments). It argues that in spite of government attempts to censor and police the network, individual citizens manage to work around the state, constructing a wide range of internet meanings and practices, which often challenge norms. The cumulative, long-term effects of these subversions will alter the ways in which people live their lives in the region, but may not on their own transform authoritarian states.

In the Middle East, as in all regions of the world, the internet and its constituency evolve daily. In spite of this flux, key patterns in regional internet culture are clearly visible, and it is these regional themes that form the foundation for this analysis of the internet and Arab political identity. It is estimated that most of the Arab public's use of the internet happens in a community access point, yet surprisingly, few scholars if any have analyzed what goes on in internet cafés and community telecenters throughout the region. This article attempts to fill this gap by analyzing recent data collected in internet cafés in Jordan and Egypt to illustrate the subtle changes in the politics of everyday life in the Arab world.

The Arab world is a compelling field site for testing many of the competing explanations of the internet's global diffusion and meaning. It is a middle-ranked economic region (Kane, 2007); it is a place with one of the fastest internet diffusion rates on the planet (2000–7), and it is a region with a mostly literate population where computer literacy is often encouraged by state and society. At the same time, the Arab world is a place with distinct security challenges, both for state and individual (Eid, 2004; Bellin, 2005). It is a place where authoritarianism rules and information environments are historically not prone to free flow and openness (Noland, 2005; Kalathil and Boas, 2003). It is also a region with significant gaps between haves and have nots, urban dwellers and rural inhabitants, men and women. These conditions provide a good environment for examining the relationship between internet diffusion and democratization; the role that IT diffusion plays in economic growth and development; the extent to which internet access enhances individual agency and empowerment (especially in terms of gender and social class, and given authoritarian information environments). Moreover, a study of internet diffusion and identity issues in the Arab world enables us to see the ways in which the technology's meanings are, in part, socially constructed.

Over the past ten years the author has performed ethnographic studies of the internet's meanings in Arab contexts including studies of culture in Kuwait (Wheeler, 2006b), Egypt (Wheeler, 2003a, 2003b), Jordan (Wheeler, 2006a), Oman, Tunisia, and Morocco. These in-depth case studies were supplemented by short research trips to Syria, Turkey, and the United Arab Emirates. This chapter synthesizes this research in light of competing explanations to produce a bird's eye view of the internet and its multi-colored meanings in the Arab world. It looks at different levels of analysis, focusing upon the varying responses to the internet by states and societies in the Arab world. It asks the fundamental question of whether or not the internet is transforming identity and politics in the Arab world. The analysis maintains the possibility that the internet, instead of being transformative, is simply a vehicle for relationships that already exist in real life. One thing we know for sure is that the prophecies about the internet undermining authoritarianism and ushering in a period of Athenian-style democracy worldwide have not come true (Gore, 1994). This does not mean, however, that the internet is insignificant. The following pages explore a handful of reasons why. In the end, this chapter makes an argument for why the internet matters in the Arab world.

Internet diffusion in context: a look at the Arab world

Internet diffusion has been increasing exponentially in the Arab world over the past few years. This high rate of diffusion contrasts sharply with the early years of the internet's regional spread. Some of the earliest adopters of the technology include Tunisia (1991—NSFNET connection), Cypress and Kuwait (1992), Egypt, Turkey, and UAE (1993), Jordan, Morocco, Algeria, and Lebanon (1994). In the early years, diffusion was slowed by state concerns about losing an information monopoly, low public awareness and demand for the technology, high cost of access, limited computing skills among the population, and sparseness of Arabic-language web content. For example, in 2000, it was estimated that internet users in the Arab world constituted 2,474,800; in other words, less than 1 percent of the population. By 2007, however, the number of internet users in the Arab world has risen to approximately 39,777,500 (according to Internet World Stats), which means that access has increased 15-fold. In some oil-rich Gulf countries, internet access rates have reached an all-time high of just over 35 percent penetration (UAE). But even in countries such as relatively cash-poor Morocco, internet penetration has reached a surprising 15 percent of the population. This represents an astounding seven-year growth rate of 4,500 percent for Morocco's internet users, 1,500 percent for the region as a whole.

As illustrated in Table 22.1, there are gross differences among countries in the Arab world in terms of internet use and access. Scholars have explained this diversity in terms of a country's per capita income, literacy rates, PC and telephone penetration rates (Kirchner, 2001; Ghareeb, 2000; Warshauer, 2003). A state's attitude towards the technology also shapes internet diffusion. For example, in the Syrian and

Saudi cases in the early years of regional adoption, both of these governments initially banned the technology, greatly slowing diffusion. Only after it was clear that their populations were going to have access to the internet—perhaps illegally, through foreign dial-up accounts—did they slowly introduce the technology. Even today, Syria has a low internet penetration rate, but the rapid increase in users from 2000–7, growing at more than 3,500 percent, illustrates that even if the state wants to block internet access for its own security concerns, it cannot afford to be technologically cut off from the rest of the region and the world, mostly for economic reasons.

To show that economic prosperity is not robust enough an indicator by itself to predict internet penetration consider Table 22.2. In only 3 countries out of 17 is there symmetry in terms of per capita income and internet penetration: the UAE, Qatar, and Syria. In the UAE and Qatar, where per capita income is high, internet penetration is also high. In Syria, where per capita income is low, internet penetration rates are also low. In Morocco, Jordan, and Lebanon, however, per capita income is relatively low, and internet penetration rankings are relatively high. Thus, some variable beyond per capita income must be influencing internet penetration rankings, especially in non-oil-producing states.

Table 22.2 shows that literacy rates as well are not a sufficient variable with which to explain internet penetration. For example, the top four countries for internet penetration—the UAE, Qatar, Kuwait, and Bahrain—all fail to make it into the top four countries for regional literacy. Moreover, all four of the top countries for literacy—Palestine, Jordan, Lebanon, and Libya—rank 11th, 7th, 5th, and 15th respectively for internet penetration. This chapter seeks to explore some of the contextual variables at play in

Table 22.1 Internet connectivity and growth in the Arab world, 2000–7

Country	Total population, 2007	Internet users, 2007 (%)	Percent change in internet users 2000–7
Algeria	33,506,567	6	3,740
Bahrain	738,874	21	288
Egypt	72,478,498	7	1,011
Iraq	27,162,627	0	188
Jordan	5,375,307	12	295
Kuwait	2,730,603	26	367
Lebanon	4,556,561	15	133
Libya	6,293,910	3	1,950
Morocco	30,534,870	15	4,500
Oman	2,452,234	12	217
Palestine	3,070,228	8	594
Qatar	824,355	27	630
Saudi Arabia	24,069,943	11	1,170
Syria	19,514,386	6	3,567
Tunisia	10,342,253	9	854
United Arab Emirates	3,981,978	35	90
Yemen	21,306,342	1	1,367
Total	268,939,536	16	1,500
North America	334,538,018	70	115
European Union	493,119,161	52	171

Source: Internet World Stats (2007).

Table 22.2 Information access, income, literacy, and freedom in the Arab world

Country	Daily newspapers per 1,000 people (2002)	Percentage of households with TV (2004)	Personal computers per 1,000 people (2004)	Number of internet cafés (2004)	Income per capita (2004)	Literacy rate percentage male/female over 15 (2004)	Freedom (2006)
Algeria	27	98	9	3,000	7700	78.8/61.0	not free
Bahrain	–	–	–	90	25300	91.9/85.0	not free
Egypt	31	95	32	400	4200	68.3/46.9	not free
Iraq	–	–	8	50	2900	55.9/24.4	not free
Jordan	74	97	55	500	4900	95.9/86.3	partially free
Kuwait	–	95	183	300	21600	85.1/81.7	partially free
Lebanon	63	93	113	200	5500	93.1/82.2	partially free
Libya	14	–	24	700	12700	92.4/72.0	not free
Morocco	29	76	21	2,150	4400	64.9/39.4	not free
Oman	–	79	47	80	14100	83.1/67.2	partially free
Palestine	–	94	48	60	1500	96.3/87.4	partially free
Qatar	–	–	–	80	29400	89.1/88.6	not free
Saudi Arabia	–	99	354	200	13800	84.7/70.8	not free
Syria	–	80	32	600	4000	89.7/64.0	not free
Tunisia	19	90	48	300	8600	83.4/65.3	not free
United Arab Emirates	–	86	116	191	49700	76.1/81.7	not free
Yemen	–	43	15	120	900	70.5/30.0	not free

Source: Daily newspapers per 1,000 people in 2002, percent of households with TV in 2004, personal computers per 1,000 people in 2004, income per capita in 2004, and literacy rate ability to read and write for males and females over 15 years old in 2004.

shaping internet diffusion in the Arab world.

The question remains, why should we care about internet diffusion (and other IT access) in the Arab world? International aid organizations are fond of arguing that "Information technology has become a potent force in transforming social, economic and political life globally. Without its incorporation into the information age, there is little chance for countries or regions to develop" (Hafkin and Taggert, 2001: 1). But do Arabs themselves place any value on these technologies? Is their value an imported concept, driven into local culture and state politics by rhetorical promises of improved human and economic development by outsiders?

Some scholars of new media diffusion in the Middle East have argued for the importance of satellite TV over the internet as a technology capable of re-shaping Arab identity in a mass way. They base such arguments on the assumption that more people in the region have regular access to satellite TV than to the internet. They also argue that illiteracy is not a barrier to accessing satellite TV programming, whereas with the internet, literacy (being able to read and type) and computer literacy (familiarity with using a computer and surfing the net) are keys to successful internet access and use. For example, Jon B. Alterman observes, "Assessing the impact of the information technology revolution in the Middle East solely in terms of internet use would be a huge mistake. A number of technological innovations are poised ... to have an even greater impact in the years to come" (Alterman, 2000: 23). Satellite TV, for instance, reached "between 20–30 percent of the region's population" by 2000 (Alterman, 2000: 23). During that same year, the internet reached less than 1 percent of the population in the Arab world, thus, one can understand Alterman's point.

Ambassador William Rugh, reinforcing Alterman's position, does not include the study of the internet in his revised classic on Arab mass media, claiming that the technology "does not reach a mass audience in the Arab world" (Rugh, 2004: xiii). Instead he focuses on radio, television, and print media.

Rather than try to rank the importance of one IT mode over another, this chapter views the internet as part of a process of IT diffusion that is more widespread and important than the internet in isolation. For the sake of analytical clarity, however, this chapter looks at the internet as representative of this IT diffusion process, understanding that the technology has not yet reached the critical mass that TV or radio has. Given the rapid growth rates of internet access, however, this article argues that it is just a matter of time until the internet will be a mass based technology. The number of internet cafés, especially in countries with supposedly low penetration rates, suggests that even for those who cannot afford a PC, or their own IP address, internet access is available, and demand is growing. More than likely, the growth rates and percentage of penetration figures above fail to accurately reflect the number of internet users, especially the high percentage of the region's population that goes online at a community access point (café or telecenter). One observer estimates that close to 80 percent of all internet use in the Arab world takes place in a community access point (Rochidi, 2004). These narratives suggest that it does make sense to look at the impact of the internet on everyday citizens' lives.

Among Middle East specialists studying IT diffusion in the Arab world, high expectations and value are placed on the regional diffusion of new media technologies. For example, as Marc Lynch observes, new media (from fax machines to mobile phones, newspapers to satellite

TV, the internet and beyond) are together creating "a new kind of Arab public and a new kind of Arab politics" (Lynch, 2006: 2). These technological transformations are enabling citizens to construct "the underpinnings of a more liberal, pluralist politics rooted in a vocal, critical public sphere" (Lynch, 2006: 3). Several years earlier, Jon B. Alterman, observed, "Change brought on by [this] new technology does seem certain" (Alterman, 1998: 68). Dale F. Eickelman and Jon W. Anderson outline a potential explanation for what kind of change can be expected. As a result of increasing "access to contemporary forms of communication that range from the press and broadcast media to fax machines and audio and video cassettes and from the telephone to the internet," Eickelman and Anderson argue that "increasingly open and accessible forms of communication play a significant role in fragmenting and contesting political and religious authority" (Eickelman and Anderson, 1999: 1–2). The key to their argument is that "the state is powerless to limit their [new media] use without disrupting the economy" (Eickelman and Anderson, 1999: 3).

The following pages consider two levels of analysis, the state and societal uses of the internet to decipher the ways in which new media technologies are shaping Arab identity and politics, to see if the internet matters, and if so for whom, and why. Augustus Richard Norton argues that internet use, and other forms of horizontal communication, are producing the "slow retreat of authoritarianism" in the Muslim World (Norton, 1999: 27). The Egyptian government's recent arrest and sentencing of a blogger to four years in prison illustrates the Arab state's calculated response to the threat of person-to-person forms of opposition (Associated Press, 2007b: A6). Some Egyptian blogs publicly raise doubts about the legitimacy of Hosni Mubarak's regime. In this case the state responded with a grave punishment for the brave and vocal critic. The response is designed to intimidate would-be opposition. Another move, which calls into question the retreat of the state in new media environments, is the government's recent call to revise the Egyptian constitution in order to extend the powers of the presidency (Slackman, 2007a: 11). The vote was boycotted by dissidents. It was reported in the press that the vote was likely rigged by the regime. The new laws introduced by this vote have been interpreted by several international organizations as the worst violation of human rights in the past 26 years of Egyptian politics (Slackman, 2007b: A7). The new legislation, which passed with "overwhelming public approval," gives Hosni Mubarak the legal right to "dissolve parliament without holding a referendum, to suspend civil protections in cases the president deems associated with terrorism and to limit the role of judges in monitoring future elections" (Slackman, 2007c: p. A5). This expansion of state power comes as internet use in Egypt has expanded more than one thousand percent over the past seven years. This situation in Egypt illustrates the complexities of determining how and why the internet matters in the Arab world. Mixed messages are ripe in the region, as states expound the values of the Information Age for their societies, their commitment to democracy, and openly acknowledge the need for reform, as demonstrated for example, in President Mubarak of Egypt's speech to the Arab Reform Conference in 2004 (Mubarak, 2004). In spite of the rhetoric, states in the region, including Egypt, often arrest citizens for openly criticizing the regime and resist the tides of reform by more heavily entrenching state power and controls over public life. Making some sense of these mixed messages is the goal of the following sections.

Arab states and the internet: friend or foe? A top–down approach to the internet and its meanings

Concern over the increasing gaps between haves and have nots in the information age are being exasperated by the advent of internet led globalization and the rise of the knowledge economy. This process of creating an information rich class and an information poor class has created a fundamental transformation in international aid policy, Arab state economic policy (at least in theory or at the rhetorical level), and the perceived value of IT locally (in the Arab world) and beyond. The goal of stimulating IT led development is a common feature of regional leaders' speeches, official documents, and projects. For example, King Abdullah of Jordan on his official website states:

> Jordan is rapidly emerging as a hub for technology investment in the region. E-leadership through a strong public–private sector partnership, an educated and talented workforce, local and foreign direct investment, and world-class infrastructure are enabling the development of a competitive Information and Communications Technology (ICT) industry
>
> (King Abdullah, 2007).

According to the website, the King and his advisors identified that:

> "information" had become a source of wealth in its own right, and immediately set out to enable industries associated with the manipulation, storage, transmission, or retrieval of information, better known as ICT. As a nation with little "natural resources," the focus of King Abdullah II was to leverage Jordan's qualified "human resources" to work for the creation of knowledge-based industries.
>
> (King Abdullah, 2007)

In the UAE, the country with the highest internet penetration in the region (35.1 percent), information technology has been viewed by the state as a path to economic development. Epitomizing this strategy are the Dubai Internet City project and the Media Free Trade Zone. Both of these Dubai-based IT and economic development initiatives have "attracted both venture capitalists and foreign direct investment in industries related to information technology" (Rosenthal, 2007). At the societal level, the UAE has worked to introduce youths to IT and computing from a young age. The UAE's 2007 Yearbook explains that it is a part of government education policy to spur IT awareness and economic development through education. For example, the Yearbook explains, "one of the government's goals is to provide a computer for every 10 children in kindergarten, every 5 pupils in primary schools, every 2 students in preparatory school and one computer per student at university" (*UAE Yearbook,* 2007).

Egyptian President Hosni Mubarak has been an advocate for his country's IT revolution, and has sought to expand the role of Egypt as a regional IT hub, competing with Jordan and the UAE for foreign direct investment in the IT sector. In 2000, Hosni Mubarak made an official visit to the United States designed to create greater cooperation between the IT sector in the U.S. and Egypt. During his visit, the President of Egypt chose to release the following speech to the American people via the AOL server. He observes:

> Egypt, as one of the world's fastest growing markets for the Information industry, promises unlimited potential of cooperation with the United

States in this field. I therefore chose to extend this digital message directly to the American people through the largest online community in the world, to highlight some of Egypt's views on the Information age.

(Mubarak, 2000).

To expand on those views, President Mubarak in his letter to the American people observes:

The technology that portrays itself to be global needs to be truly so not only in terms of reach, but more importantly in terms of equal access and mutual benefit. That is not necessarily the case in many instances; which lays down a salient task to be undertaken by the world community, as a whole. These new technologies need to be geared towards the advancement of the developing world. The countries, previously known as the Third World, can not afford to miss what is currently known as the Third Wave. Every effort must be made to utilize the new technologies to support leapfrog development strategies. Technology transfer is the only vehicle to make sure that the world, now coming together by technology, does not fall apart by inequality and the neglect of the basic needs of the world's poor.

(Mubarak, 2000)

Egypt made its commitment to building an IT revolution along the Nile transparent when Ahmad Nazif, former Minister of Communication and Information Technology was made Prime Minister during a summer of 2004 cabinet reshuffle. In spite of these changes and strategies, Egypt remains a country with severe development challenges including growing poverty, unemployment, a youth bulge, one of the highest illiteracy rates in the region, and increasingly vocal opposition movements. Egypt also has an internet penetration level of only 6.9 percent. The fact that Egypt is one of five Middle Eastern countries listed on the "Internet Enemies" list also calls into question the sincerity of the state's commitment to empowering all Egyptians with IT (Reporters without Borders, 2006).

In spite of the rampant and elative state rhetoric regarding the celebrated powers of the internet and other information technologies for building opportunities across the social spectrum, what has lagged in the region is the delivery on promises for real change in the structure of wealth and power in Arab societies. For example, in 2000, Egypt's e-government project made it possible to order train tickets online and to download and print the documents needed to renew one's driver's license. In 2004, the Jordanian government partnered with Intel Corporation to implement a high-profile initiative called the e-Education project. The idea was to create a series of "discovery schools" throughout Jordan, with each school wired to high-speed bandwidth and operating an e-math, e-science and other e-based curricular transformations. While all of this may sound like progress, in actuality what it produces is a confusing gap between state rhetoric and social impact. Raising a child's knowledge of computing does not solve the problem of extremely high youth unemployment; moreover, being able to order train tickets online is only useful for those elite few who own a computer, a printer, a phone line, an internet connection, and need to (and have the means to) ride by reserved train coach (Economic and Social Commission for Western Asia, 2002).

It is not by accident that Arab states commonly look to Singapore, China, and other Asian Tigers for inspiration for their IT led economic goals. It is not uncommon to hear Jordan, for example, refer to its development goals and transition to the information economy as a desire to become the Singapore of the Middle East (Ang, 2004). In Asia, high human development has been achieved, without democratization. Contrary to the Washington Consensus, political liberalization does not have to precede or accompany economic liberalization, as the case of Singapore illustrates. The goal of the Arab state has been to use IT as a tool for enhancing economic growth opportunities, while at the same time maintaining a tight grip on society's use of the internet for political change. To illustrate the effectiveness of this strategy, consider that the two countries with the highest level of internet penetration, the UAE and Qatar are rated by Freedom House as "not free." Table 22.1 suggests that there is a freedom gap in the Arab world, in spite of the growing spread of the internet (United Nations Development Program, 2004). The governments in the region have been able to run the IT "revolution" as they please, adding information capabilities to a growing percentage of the population, attracting new economic investment, while at the same time retaining a tight grip on the reins of state power. Economists argue, however, that if the region is going to continue to grow, it is going to have to allow for more freedom, at least for the potential entrepreneurs. For example, the most recent *World Competitiveness Report* observes:

> Today, the Arab world is at a critical juncture. The region's economies are currently very dynamic and offer tremendous business opportunities; there is no doubt that improvement to national competitiveness and closer integration with the global economy and within the region are necessary if this growth momentum is to be sustained.
>
> (Schwab, 2007: p. 1)

The 2007 version of the report stresses the necessity for a profound change in mindsets to realize the region's full potential. Entrepreneurship, an element that is often cited as the key to unlocking the potential of the Arab economies, can only take root in societies where freedom of thought, enthusiasm for inquiry, and critical thinking are popular values (el-Diwany, 2007: p. 1).

A tension clearly exists in the Arab world between the concepts of freedom, security, and economic growth. Ideally, Arab states would like to increase economic growth, while stifling political transformation. The question is, can increasing access to the internet and other potentially empowering communication technologies open up new spaces for entrepreneurialism without stimulating innovative political experimentation in the Arab world? Elsewhere I have analyzed attempts to create an IT enabled entrepreneurial class in the Middle East (Wheeler, 2003a, 2003b, 2001a). This chapter focuses instead on the residual political and social experimentation that occurs in spite of state efforts to control the information revolution and its meanings. For the past ten years the author observed a growing critical mass of dissenting voices emerge to challenge restrictive political and social practices in the Arab world. Gal Beckerman calls this discursive shift the emergence of "A new Arab conversation" which "reflects a new culture of openness, dialogue and questioning" (Beckerman, 2007: p. 1). Beckerman continues:

> Whether it is a Jordanian student discussing the taboo subject of the monarchy's viability or a Saudi woman writing about her sexual experiences or an Egyptian commenting with sadness at an Israeli blogger's description of a suicide bombing, each of these unprecedented

acts is one small move toward opening up these societies.

(Beckerman, 2007: p. 1)

Part of what makes this picture complex is the way in which the Arab state puts security above freedom, and in the end, above economic growth and entrepreneurialism. Jordan may have its REACH initiative, which is designed to spur ICT led development in Jordan, but this does not mean that the state is not above using its coercive power to stop citizens from adapting technologies that are good for business, to technologies which empower oppositional imaginations (*Jordan Times* 11 July, 2000). In Jordan, in spite of clear state efforts to build an economically motivated information society, with a thriving ICT industry, citizens still face prison time if they publish things "considered 'harmful to the country's diplomatic relations' or to do with the king and the royal family" (Reporters without Borders, 2007a). Similarly, in Egypt, "a national plan developed by the Ministry of Information and Communication Technologies" attempts "to link national development with global forces using ICTs" (el-Sayed and Westrup, 2003: p. 77). At the same time, Egypt remains one of five Middle Eastern countries on Reporters Without Borders' "List of Internet Enemies," defined by the organization as "a roll of shame reserved for countries that systematically violate on-line free expression" (Reporters without Borders, 2007a). The five states included on this list include Egypt, Saudi Arabia, Tunisia, Iran, and Syria.

If Arab states wish to take full advantage of the global economy they will have to change their policies of attempting to muzzle opposition and manipulate economic opportunity so as to co-opt the entrepreneurial class (Heydemann, 2004). Both freedom of expression and freedom to innovate are keys to building an information economy.

Blogs and chat: Arab societies' internet use and constructions of meaning

The Arab blogosphere

In spite of state attempts to control information environments in the Arab world, the following section demonstrates the ways in which internet access is shaping public life, facilitating critical thinking, free thought, and entrepreneurialism. Participants in this social "revolution" are aware of the power of these contestations to shape identity, even if institutions, especially those of the state, are proving impervious to such public interventions. Ahmed Zewail, an Egyptian scientist and Nobel Laureate, recently described how the internet was creating a pathway towards a Muslim renaissance. He explains:

> Now, with the internet, ambitious young people in Egypt or Morocco can go to the internet cafes and see what is going on in Los Angeles or Kuala Lumpur—or even Qatar, which now has a GDP per capita close to the U.S.—but they can't seem to get it [income] themselves. That feeds their frustration. When we can convert that frustration into positive energy, there will be hope for the young Arab Muslims who now see a different future.
>
> (Zewail, 2004: p. 2)

Imagining, discussing, and implementing a new future for the Arab world is the goal of many regional bloggers. From all across the political spectrum, young Arabs narrate their visions for a new Middle East. For example, Egyptian blogger Abdul-Moneim Mahmud, whose blog is called Ana Ikhwan (www.ana-ikhwan.blogspot.com), reports "arbitrary arrests and acts of torture by the [Egyptian state] security services" and criticizes the excesses of state coercion. He was arrested by Egyptian authorities on April 14, 2007. Similarly, Egyptian Abdel Kareem Nabil Suleiman has used his blog (www.karam903.blog spot.com) to "condemn the government's authoritarian excesses." He was recently arrested for his outspokenness. Another Egyptian blog, "From Cairo with Love," explains the importance of blogs when the author observes:

> Its really different to read a piece of news, opinion, or thought on a weblog than on a "traditional" news site. The difference I guess is that they mostly reflect personal opinions, provide lots of freedom for everyone to voice their opinion, and to hear opinions and news those are not channeled through mainstream media. They also allow for contribution where everyone is actually contributing to the news delivery.
> (From Cairo with Love, 2005: p. 1)

In terms of the regional impact of blogging, Gal Beckerman explains that in the Arab world:

> The historical and the personal slam up against each other daily ... This gives even mundane musings elevated significance. Bloggers are writing about their lives. But those lives are taking place in environments in which politics and history cannot be perceived as mere elements on the margins. For the twenty-somethings growing up in Riyadh, writing resentfully about the power of the religious authorities, the questions are fundamental ones about the state of her society. For the Egyptian blogger, the brutal suppression of a demonstration can make the difference of whether he chooses

to stay in the country or leave. This urgency makes the commentary more complex and interesting
> (Beckerman, 2007: p. 4).

When thinking about the meaning of blogs in the Arab world, obvious questions emerge. Who is blogging? How widespread is blogging? Do blogs have any political significance? Are they instituting the "slow retreat of the state" (Norton, 1999a: p. 27)? While data is not really available to answer these important questions at this stage, some initial responses can be obtained by looking at regional and local portals, and by doing some content analysis of the blogs themselves.

The initial results of this investigation suggest that blogging is new, but gaining momentum. In its present state, it seems mostly to be young people who blog, and these young people seem to be mostly urbanites. Moreover, their blogs reveal that they are generally from the regional upper classes. There are strategies to translate blogging into a vehicle for political change, as evidenced by "meet-ups" and strategies to take blogging to the grassroots. Moreover, blogs are increasingly quoted in the world media and even presidential speeches, as authentic voices from the region and representative of views beyond state propaganda. All of these indicate something about the potential of blogging, even if we are not yet seeing the retreat of the state.

In his book the *Politics of Small Things*, Jeffrey C. Goldfarb examines "the power of the powerless in dark times" by observing that "daily life shapes the economy, the polity and civilization itself." His text is an exploration of the ways in which "people make history in their social interactions" (Goldfarb, 2006: p. 1). In some small ways, bloggers are making history with their narratives. Through their blogs they are creating new forms of social interaction, and expanding the realm

315

of public discourse to include open, frank, and challenging narratives. When bloggers overstep certain boundaries of the permitted, they are publicly punished in disproportionate ways. The brutality of the Arab state in these matters is both a demonstration of its monopoly on the use (not necessary legitimate) of coercive resources to preserve the status quo.

At the same time, this extreme response to freedom of expression and public opposition to the status quo reveals the precarious nature of the state's monopoly on power. Hannah Arendt observed several decades ago, that when states have to resort to violence, torture, repression, this is when legitimacy has died, and power is on the wane. Blogs reveal to us the process through which "members of subordinated social groups invent and circulate counter-discourses to formulate oppositional interpretations of their identities, interests and needs" (Fraser, 1991: p. 123). The question remains, how will these counter-narratives be institutionalized, if at all? Do they matter? The following section demonstrates how internet access matters in the lives of internet café users, most of whom are from the middle to lower classes.

Internet café users in Jordan and Egypt

The data analyzed for this section was collected during five months of internet café research in Jordan and Egypt, January–May 2004. The goal of this study was to uncover whether or not the internet was an important part of everyday life for the average or below average citizen in the Arab world. Also key in the study was to identify the ways in which the internet mattered to their lives. Those interviewed were not prompted to think of the internet as a political tool. Rather, they were asked, in an open-ended fashion, to narrate how the internet may have

changed their lives. The answers to this question in particular provided a rich canvas against which to understand the draw of the lower and middle classes to the technology. Together, their responses tended to coalesce around one of three main themes: (1) developing a political consciousness; (2) building social networks and knowledge capital; and (3) transgressing boundaries, especially lines of gender, nation, and social class. Each of these themes, and a selection of the narrative samples that created them, are examined in more detail below.

By conducting interviews in internet cafés, this study provides windows on the "grass-roots" of internet use in the region. This approach takes the focus away from the cosmopolitan elite, and replaces it with views from the lower and middle classes. In general, the data gathered for this case study suggest that individuals who use internet cafés as their main source for access don't have a computer and internet access at home. If they are employed (many are not) and have access at work, they are not high enough on the hierarchy to be able to use the technology freely for personal use. Moreover, many internet café users do not use the technology in their work environments (carpenters, sales people in small- and medium-sized enterprises, tea boys, students, customer service representatives, housewives), nor do they typically have any formal training in using computers. internet café users in Jordan and Egypt tend to have learned to use the technology in an internet café, and they tend to be taught to use the tool by a family member or a friend. In most cases, these café users have subsequently taught a friend, family, or community member to use the internet, thus demonstrating a form of civic engagement whereby knowledge once attained is shared with others through informal networks. Moreover, many became internet users to reduce the news agency use" in a small sample of international news stories in 12 of the leading news websites in the United States and the United Kingdom. The results reveal that of the stories examined on the most popular sites many were simple copies of the news agency material. For example, in 2006, 97 percent of the content of Yahoo's international news was lifted from news agencies, 94 percent of AOL's international news, 91 percent of ABC's news, 81 percent of MSNBC's news, and 59 percent of CNN's news. Paterson suggests that despite the growth in the volume of information on news websites, when it comes to international news, the transnational news agencies, as before, remain the dominant voice. However, he does note that the *New York Times*, and the BBC, both popular outlets too, exhibited the least reliance on news agency copy, with their average verbatim news agency use being 32 percent and 9 percent respectively (Paterson, 2006).

Financial uncertainty and cross-subsidy

The online news environment is financially precarious and news websites have so far been largely unprofitable (Freedman, 2006). Audiences have been unwilling to pay for news online and so few outlets have been able to charge as a traditional newspaper or cable station would. Indeed, in the United States in 2006, of 1456 newspapers online, only 1 national, and 40 small regionals, charged their readers (Project for Excellence in Journalism, 2006). Many of the news providers have adopted a strategy of "modulated experimentation," separating off certain content and charging for it (Scott, 2005). For example, breaking news is provided free, but visitors are sometimes asked to pay for additional services, such as access to archives, and specialist material, like classifieds. Many also provide free bespoke services, such as e-mail alerts and breaking news alerts, services that outlets hope consumers will be prepared to pay for in the future (Scott, 2005).

At the same time, with the lack of agreed standard measures for audience numbers, and therefore no way of knowing whether adverts have been seen and by whom, news sites have often struggled to generate significant advertising revenues. Early metrics such as page views and hit rates proved unreliable measures of who had seen adverts and advertisers have been generally skeptical about the returns of large ad spends. Not surprisingly, news sites still command a small share of the total ad spend in the United States (4 percent in 2005, and projected to be 9 percent of total advertising dollars in 2008) (Ahlers, 2006). This figure is higher though in the United Kingdom, where the internet accounted for 11.4 percent of the national ad spend in 2006, topping for the first time the proportion spent on newspaper ads (Allen, 2007). The switch away from paid subscription access at the *New York Times* in the autumn of 2007 indicates that that online advertising revenues are beginning to take off in the United States.

With audiences less captive, advertisers are increasingly interested not just in hit rates but also in the type of audience that visit a news site. There is pressure on news outlets to gain more information about customer habits and tastes (MacGregor, 2007). Software increasingly allows news providers to track the audience's online behavior, including interactions with ads, or how many times ads are viewed and for how long—information that can be fed back to the advertisers themselves (Project for Excellence in Journalism, 2006).

The reality of online journalism is that the main news providers have cross-subsidized their online operations. While the financial subsidies have been a major drain on resources they have allowed the

209

development of web presence. The traditional news providers have invested heavily in the latest technology to enable them to supply news direct to variety of platforms (see Scott, 2005). Corporations like CBS in the United States, and the BBC in the United Kingdom, have sunk millions of dollars in their online news operations (Project for Excellence in Journalism, 2006). Smaller less wealthy news providers are unable to match these levels of investment, with the result that they often cannot offer the quality of output or the services of their larger rivals.

The big players also have the funds to purchase exclusive rights to user-generated content. For example, user-generated footage of the 2004 East Asian tsunami, the aftermath of Hurricane Katrina, the London bombings in 2005, and the campus shootings at Virginia Tech in 2007, was purchased by news outlets in the United States and around the world. Bidding wars are not uncommon, with the main outlets competing for the rights to video footage with specialist rights resellers such as Scoopt, Splash, Cash4yourpics, and news wholesaler Reuters. In the United Kingdom, in 2006, there was fierce competition between news organizations for amateur footage of a police raid on terrorist suspects in north London, with ITN and the *Daily Express* allegedly paying $120,000 for the film.

The picture emerging is of a gap between the online operations of traditional news organizations and those of internet-only news providers. The traditional news operators are part of a chain, able to cross-subsidize their online operations, pay for and provide exclusive access to content that attracts large numbers of visitors, while the smaller news sites of internet-only niche providers often have less capital to invest and less to spend. The financial clout of the leading players often reproduces the existing asymmetry of the offline news environment.

Audience input and its limitations

A key criticism of offline newspapers and news bulletins is that audience input has been too tightly restricted (Richardson and Franklin, 2004). The emergence of news websites and the development of Web 2.0, it is argued, has changed this situation (Twist, 2006). The space for audience debate is no longer limited and the voice of the audience is less reliant on the editor and journalist for exposure. However, while there clearly are greater opportunities for audiences to communicate their views and contribute to the news, some argue that the reality is somewhat different from the hype (see Deuze, 2003; Singer, 2005). News outlets still exercise control of messages posted on their sites and remove comments deemed inappropriate from message boards and blogs. A study of the extent to which online audiences engaged with news websites found that only 15 percent used chat rooms and 13 percent e-mailed journalists (Lowery and Anderson, 2005; see also van der Wurff, 2005). Similarly, a survey by Nielsen/NetRatings found that only a minority of visitors to leading newspaper websites in the United States looked at journalists' blogs. In December 2006, of a unique audience of 30 million, 13 percent visited the blog pages of an online newspaper (Nielsen/NetRatings, 2007).

It is not just the public that shy away from interaction, Lowery and Anderson (2005) found that only a minority of journalists pursued contact through news blogs. Another survey discovered that most journalists in the United States saw responding to e-mail as part of their job but just over half did so—and did so only occasionally (Pavlik, 2004). Indeed, in a study of interactivity Chung (2007: 48) found that although most site producers recognized the "importance of incorporating ... interactivity" they were cautious about it, especially those inside the established news organizations. These respondents often pointed to the increase in workload in maintaining interactive features (Chung, 2007).

Others have observed that the more radical potential of the technology, for example, in allowing for open-source journalism, has remained just that—potential. While there is greater feedback, some argue that most news organizations encourage little more than comment—the attitude is still very much "we write, you read" (Deuze, 2003). Lowery and Anderson (2005) found there was a limited support among journalists for participatory news. The traditional news outlets largely encourage audience input, not out of a sense of civic obligation, but as another way to gather information that they can then repackage. Many outlets have introduced audience-editors, to read and respond to reader e mails and to follow up story leads (Project for Excellence in Journalism, 2006). For example, in the United Kingdom, the national daily newspaper, the *Sun*, recently launched its message board MySun. The reason, the assistant editor of the *Sun* online noted, was to gain information and tips on the issues that concerned their audience most, to boost circulation (Gibson, 2006).

The impact on the profession

While some observe that the internet brings new opportunities for the professional journalist (see Pavlik, 2004), others argue that it has an adverse impact (Lowery and Anderson, 2005). One negative effect is news room convergence (see Scott, 2005). Over the last five years or so many of the traditional news players have begun to merge their online and offline news operations. An early example is the tie-up between the *Tampa Tribune*, WFLA-TV, and Tampa Bay Online, who process news

through a centralized mt desk (Scott, 2005). In the the *Daily Telegraph* and the merged their online and operations. In addition, cc partnerships between differen and between the websites c outlets have emerged (Scott, 2C

This process of convergence l number of consequences. Deadlin sures have increased. Journalists wl deadlines once or twice a day offline find they have rolling deadlines throu out the day: 78 percent of journal working in U.S. online news outlets i 2003 reported that their deadline pressures had grown (Pew Research Center, 2003). There is more pressure to refresh and repackage material during the day. The same survey of journalists found that a great deal of time was devoted to repackaging news stories; in fact, 71 percent of those sampled said they were doing more repackaging of news compared to 48 percent of those working offline (Pew Research Center, 2003). The need to repackage may well increase as the volume of user-generated content rises.

The precarious position of the news professional has been exacerbated by cost cutting across the industry. As Alhers (2006) observes, with news sites attracting relatively small revenues when compared with offline news media, reducing costs has become key for news organizations. Indeed, 62 percent of online journalists in the Pew survey of 2003 reported that the number of people working in their online news operation had decreased over time (Pew Research Center, 2003). This points to a future in which journalism may become increasingly casualized.

Conclusion

The developments outlined in this chapter provide new opportunities and pose challenges for mature democracies h as the United States. The emergence the internet has meant that there are ow more news outlets available for citiens to choose from than ever before. While most American internet users still visit the websites of the main news outlets, a substantial proportion regularly visit non-U.S. news sites or niche sites such as news blogs, and news aggregators often take them to such sites (Thurman, 2007). The growth of such outlets has been beneficial for minorities of various kinds who have felt that the main offline U.S. news providers cater for majority tastes or use the majority language and fail to accommodate them. For example, diasporas are able to access news outlets with which they have a cultural or linguistic affinity (see Chapter 20). A similar point could be made for those with particular ideological views. The radical media have always been part of society (Downing, 2001), but they have never been more accessible than are today via the net.

This chapter has also shown that internet news sites provide more opportunities for citizens to exercise their voice and contribute to the news. Citizens are able to supply material and shape news content with greater ease than before. Open-source news, for example, means readers can direct content, or post their own stories. Citizens are no longer confined to being spectators, monitoring news from the sidelines, but are able to contribute to its focus and production, and become citizen journalists.

But despite the potential for new developments to enable a more informed and active citizenry, it is important to remain critically aware of the challenges still faced. There may be more choice but large media chains still exercise power in the online news environment. They still own the bulk of the established brand outlets on which a large proportion of internet users tend to rely. Research has

shown that the diversity of views on these branded sites may be largely illusory with most of the news coming from Associated Press and Reuters (Paterson, 2006). These profit-hungry corporations are also interested in charging citizens for additional news services at the same time as engaging in cost cutting that may well undermine the quality of output on which citizens depend. And citizens' online behavior is increasingly subject to surveillance by news corporations interested in building up information on their tastes and habits (MacGregor, 2007).

New opportunities to interact and produce content may also be exaggerated. Some interactive developments have been given a lukewarm response by the public and journalists (Lowery and Anderson, 2005). News editors have continued to exercise control over much of what is contributed. In addition, the issue of unequal access to the internet has remained. Internet users tend to be wealthier, educated, and young, and this is also true in relation to the adoption of new communication technologies such as cell phones (Chadwick, 2006; ComScore, 2007). These groups are more likely to post content. According to a recent Pew survey of bloggers in the United States, 54 percent were under the age of 30, 37 percent had a college degree, and 38 percent were knowledge-based professional workers (Lenhart and Fox, 2006). These groups are also more likely to use the internet to access news and information. For example, another Pew survey conducted during the 2006 mid-term elections, found that 44 percent of those who went online to gain campaign information earned over $75,000, 49 percent had a college degree, and 71 percent were under the age of 49 (Rainie and Horrigan, 2007).

The current transformation of the news environment provides new opportunities and new challenges for democratic

Table 22.3 Examples of attempts by authoritarian regimes to discourage cyber-dissidence

Country	Charge
Algeria	Ahmed Fattani, journalist, was arrested on the 13th of October, 2003 for "posting articles online while the paper he edited, Expression, was officially suspended."
Bahrain	Galal Olwi was arrested in March of 1997 and detained for 18 months. The charge was sending information via the internet to, "The Bahrain Liberal Movement."
Syria	Abdel Rahman Shagouri was arrested on the 23rd of February, 2003 for e-mailing a newsletter Lavant News from the banned website www.thisissyria.net. He is still being held on charges that he "endangered Syria's reputation and security."
Tunisia	Zohair al-Yahyaoui, journalist, was arrested June 4th, 2004 and sentenced to 28 months in prison for "disseminating false news" on the internet through his website TUNISIANE

Arab states. It is not possible for the knowledge economy to take root, grow, and spread opportunity without more open information environments emerging. So, the economic incentive to foster a culture of discursive openness is strong in Arab societies. At the same time, enabling new communications environments could also encourage more organized demands for democratic change in the region.

Conclusion

This chapter has analyzed the ways in which Arab states try to regulate the internet, and internet-enabled Arab publics try to create change in spite of state controls. The persistence of Arab state attempts to police cyberspace, to publicly punish cyber dissidents who go too far with their new freedoms of expression, and to filter the web give pause to optimism and temper expectations for institutionalizing political change in the region. The state, however, may ultimately be fighting a losing battle. The global pressure to join the knowledge economy means that states in the region can no longer afford to keep their publics digitally muzzled and blindfolded. Future economic opportunities in the region will be built upon the backs of entrepreneurs, and agents bent upon creating change

through and with digital technologies. And in part, such changes will be constructed out of the voices and visions of those trained to use digital technologies in the pursuit of economic growth. Just as in the past it has proven difficult to liberalize without democratizing, in the same way, it is hard to sustain freedoms to be creative and entrepreneurial economically, while at the same time, keeping these same concepts and tools from being used to re-engineer political and social life, from the family, to the community, to the state. As A. Richard Norton has observed, "Programs of liberalization are not easily contained: as press controls are loosened, demands for accountability emerge. Controls on associational life may be selectively lifted. But, even so, the right to organize freely is hard to contain" (Norton, 1999b: 37). We see similarly that internet experimentation can help to foster a political consciousness and civic engagement, the tides of which states are unlikely to control fully. It seems reasonable to expect that like other contexts (Indonesia, China, and Latin America) life online will have spill-over effects on the practice of everyday life.

Guide to further reading

In addition to the works cited for this chapter, interested readers may want to consider Marcus Franda's (2001) work *Launching into Cyberspace: internet development and politics in five world regions*, especially the sections on the Middle East. In terms of more specialized studies of the internet's impact in the Arab world, *Middle East Journal* in the Summer of 2000 offered a special issue on the impact of the information revolution in the Arab world. If readers are interested in starting at the beginning of scholarly interest in the internet in the Middle East, then they would need to read the work of Jon Anderson. Anderson pioneered the study of the internet in the Arab world, way back in 1995. See his article "Cybarites, knowledge workers and new creoles on the information superhighway," *Anthropology Today* 11(4): 13–15, 1995 (Anderson, 1995). He also wrote an important Occasional Paper for the Emirates Center for Strategic Studies entitled "Arabizing the Internet" (Anderson, 1998). For one of the most recent studies of the impact of the internet in the Middle East readers may wish to consult Emma Murphy's (2006) article "Agency and space: the political impact of information technologies in the Gulf Arab states."

Part 4

Law and policy

23

The geopolitics of internet control

Censorship, sovereignty, and cyberspace

Ronald J. Deibert

What is the impact of the internet on state sovereignty, and in particular on states' ability to control information flows across their borders? Whereas once the internet was presumed to be a borderless world of free-flowing information, today countries and corporations alike are carving it up in a bewildering array of filtered segments, often with major unintended consequences. The motivations for these practices range widely, from concerns over national security, cultural sensitivities, and protection of social values, to rent seeking and the protection of economic monopolies. Whereas once it was conventional wisdom to believe that the internet's technological infrastructure was immune to control, today states and corporations are applying an ever-increasing level of skill and technological sophistication to precisely that mission. The result is that rather than being a single seamless environment, the internet a user connects to and experiences in Canada is far different than an internet a user experiences in Iran, China, or Belarus. This chapter provides an overview of the geopolitics of internet control, and in particular state efforts to control information flows across borders, with comparative data from over 22 countries.

In early 2007, the online mapping service Google Earth provided a feature on the ongoing political crisis in the Darfur region of Sudan. Not long afterwards, however, an aid worker based inside Sudan reported not being able to properly load the map, receiving an error message in his browser stating "This product is not available in your country." Upon further inspection, the source of the inaccessibility was Google itself—filtering access to its own services based on the "geolocation" of the computer's IP address making the request. Google was not permitting IP addresses based within Sudan from connecting to its service in order to comply with U.S. export restrictions against the sale or export of informational products to the country (Geens, 2007).

Earlier the same year, Tunisian authorities filtered the popular video-streaming service, DailyMotion. DailyMotion is known to carry a wide range of political videos, including many satirical videos of the Tunisian government's record on human rights. Many inferred that Tunisia had blocked the website because of those videos, following its known track record of blocking access to opposition and human rights websites (Reporter Without Borders, 2007). However, Tunisia uses (but does not openly admit to doing so) the U.S. commercial filtering product, Smartfilter, to block its citizens' access to information (OpenNet Initiative, 2005a). DailyMotion was, perhaps mistakenly, categorized within the Smartfilter database as "pornography"—a category apparently selected by Tunisia for blocking. After reports of the DailyMotion block surfaced, Smartfilter apparently corrected the categorization error, and access to the DailyMotion website from within Tunisia was gradually restored.

The source for much of the evidence and illustrations used in this chapter comes from the research of the OpenNet Initiative (ONI)—collaboration among the Citizen Lab at the University of Toronto, the Berkman Centre for Internet and Society at Harvard Law School, the Cambridge Security Programme, U.K., the Oxford Internet Institute, and partner non-governmental organizations (NGOs) worldwide.[1] The aim of the ONI is to document empirically patterns of internet censorship and surveillance worldwide using sophisticated means of technically interrogating the internet directly. The ONI's tests are carried out both remotely from North America and the U.K., and in-field by dozens of local researchers. Our reports over the last several years have documented a disturbing increase in the scale, scope, and sophistication of internet censorship practices worldwide.[2] This chapter summarizes some of the main findings of this research and draws connections to wider implications for global politics, security, and human rights. The main questions addressed by this chapter are: how many states are filtering access to information on the internet? What are the types of content that these states are targeting for filtering? What are the most effective methods used by states that filter? What is the range of transparency and accountability practices among states that filter? Are states open about their practices? And, what are some of the wider implications of these practices? As will be described in this chapter, the picture of the internet that emerges from this research is of a hotly contested and deeply politicized realm.

Beneath the surface of internet communications

What happens to a request when a user clicks on a link to a website or sends an e-mail? For most surfers, the internet experience begins and ends with what happens on the computer screen in front of them. However, if surfers follow that e-mail or web request as it leaves a computer and passes down the fiber optic cable to the servers and routers of a local internet service provider (ISP), through the internet exchange points (IXPs), international gateways, and on to the undersea trunk cables of tier 1 telecommunication companies, they will find a complex and largely hidden infrastructure of filters and chokepoints.

Most people assume that the internet's vast infrastructure is an open, decentralized, network of networks through which information flows freely along a shared routing protocol. While this description has some basis in the historical evolution of the internet, and captures parts of what makes it unique, it also obscures some of the details that structure internet communications beneath the surface. While it is true that there is no single node through which all traffic passes on the internet, and thus no form of centralized control, there are thousands of nodes that parse out and filter information and act as gateways. Each of these nodes and gateways—from routers to IXPs to autonomous systems—present opportunities for authorities to impose order on internet traffic through some mechanism of filtering and surveillance. Some of this control takes place for technological reasons; some of it takes place for cultural, political, and economic reasons. Instead of a network of networks, therefore, it is perhaps more accurate to characterize the internet as a network of *filters and chokepoints*.

The means by which content is blocked or filtered on the internet vary widely in terms of complexity, effectiveness, and intent. Furthermore, not all of the means by which states attempt to control the internet are technological. In some cases, regulations are employed to supplement technical controls, which can create a climate of self-censorship among internet users. The following section defines some of the central terms associated with internet content filtering and surveillance before turning to specific examples of accountability and transparency issues.

Internet content filtering is a term that refers to the techniques by which control is imposed on access to information on the internet (Deibert and Villeneuve, 2004). Content filtering can be divided into two separate techniques: address blocking techniques and content analysis techniques. Address blocking techniques refer to particular router configurations used to deny access to particular internet protocol (IP) addresses and/or domain names, or specific services that run on particular port numbers. For example, a state may run a blocking filter at the international gateway level that restricts access from within the country to websites that are deemed illegal, such as pornographic or human rights websites.

Content Analysis refers to techniques used to control access to information based on its content, such as the inclusion of specific keywords on a website or the address of a URL. Because parsing mechanisms employ keywords to block access, they are often the source of mistaken or unintended blockages. Unintended blocking can occur as a result of IP based blocking as well, however, as it is not uncommon for many domain names to share the same IP address. Filtering that aims to block access to a specific website by blocking its IP address, in other words, can result in the collateral filtering of potentially thousands of unrelated sites sharing the same IP.

Depending on need and circumstance, different approaches to filtering can be implemented:

Inclusion filtering: users are allowed to access a short list of approved sites, known as a "white list," only. All other content is blocked.

Exclusion filtering: restricts user access by blocking sites listed on a "black list." All other content is allowed.

Content analysis: restricts user access by dynamically analyzing the content of a site and blocking sites that contain forbidden keywords, graphics, or other specified criteria.

The mechanisms used to do these types of filtering vary considerably. Routers act as junctions between networks, passing information packets back and forth, and thus routers are the main (though not only) nodes where such blocking takes place in the form of instructions written into the routing tables. However, filtering software can be implemented into virtually any node throughout the internet's system. As a consequence, the level at which filtering can be implemented varies widely too. Filtering can take place on an individual's personal computer, an office local area network (LAN), an internet café, an ISP, a wireless network, an SMS system, at the backbone or international gateway level, or some combination of all of these levels. Not surprisingly, national-level internet content filtering can vary dynamically, and across ISPs within a single country (Anderson and Murdoch, 2007).

Although filtering traditionally takes place by blocking requests for information from either reaching their destination or returning the requested information at information chokepoints, other non-filtering mechanisms can be employed that achieve the same ends. After all, filtering is simply denial of access to information.

As is described below, new forms of blocking access to information are emerging based on the use of distributed denial of service attacks. Such attacks bring web servers down by overwhelming them with requests for information, thus "filtering" information at its source and denying access to all users equally. The same type of denial of service can (and occasionally does) take place by cutting off power to the building where web servers are located, or misconfiguring routing tables to cause what appear to be network errors, but which in fact are deliberate attempts to shut off communications at the source.

As the Google Earth example demonstrates, filtering can also take place through reverse geolocation—that is, the server hosting websites can refuse to take requests from users based on the geographical origin of their computer's IP address. The ONI has documented numerous instances of this type of reverse geolocation filtering, including by the website georgewbush.com during the 2004 U.S. Presidential Elections (ONI, 2004).

Methods of investigating censorship

Although filtering practices are widespread, knowledge of their use by states has tended to be limited. In part, this is a function of a lack of accountability and transparency among states that block access to information. In part, however, it is also a function of the lack of empirical evidence about such practices. Up until recently, the majority of reports on internet filtering tended to emerge from users, news reports, or advocacy organizations. Not surprisingly, they tended to be unsystematic and sometimes even unreliable. Moreover, because of the complex and varied ways in which filtering can be implemented, as noted earlier, reports

have often been made in error or have contained contradictory information.

The aim of the ONI has been to overcome these shortcomings by developing a systematic way to investigate empirically internet filtering practices from within state borders over an extended period of time. The project employs a unique methodology that combines in-field investigations by partners and associates who travel to or live in the countries concerned, and a suite of technical interrogation tools that probe the internet directly for forensic evidence of content filtering and filtering technologies.[3] These tools work from the "inside out" of the internet, probing parts of the information infrastructure not generally apparent to the average user. The methods range from automating connecting requests to servers hosting websites simultaneously from within the country under investigation and a control location in a non-filtered location, to using tracing and other network mapping tools to interrogate the location of and technologies used to do the filtering. Tests for accessibility to internet content were based on categorized lists of websites.[4] These categories were meant to cover as comprehensively as possible the likely targets for filtering by states while allowing for as precise as possible identification of content categories singled out for filtering. While most states that filter target pornographic content, as will be shown later a wide range of non-pornographic, political content—such as opposition parties or minority rights, for example—is now being targeted as well by several states.

This method allows for a comprehensive picture of internet content filtering in a particular country by probing all aspects of the national information infrastructure (internet cafés, ISPs, wireless networks, backbone gateways) and over an extended period of time testing accessibility in both English and local languages to lists of thousands of websites in each of these categories.[5]

Since 2002, the project has produced detailed reports on 11 countries—Belarus, Yemen, Tunisia, Burma, Singapore, Iran, China, Bahrain, United Arab Emirates, Vietnam, and Saudi Arabia. More recently, in 2006 the ONI conducted extensive tests over several months in more than forty countries worldwide. The following sections highlight some of the main trends and findings emerging from this research.

The globalization of online censorship

In 2002, only a handful of countries were known to engage in internet content filtering, most prominently China, Iran, and Saudi Arabia. By 2007, 26 of 40 examined countries were found to engage in internet filtering practices to some degree. China is still the world's most notorious and sophisticated censoring regime (ONI, 2004, 2005a, b, c, d; Dowell, 2006; Li, 2003; Li, 2004). Its filtering system comprises multiple levels of legal regulation and technical control, the latter implemented primarily at the backbone level using specially configured Cisco routers. The system involves numerous state agencies and thousands of public and private personnel, and a dense web of ever-thickening legal restrictions.

The range of information that China seeks to limit and control from within its borders is broad. China targets content for filtering across every major category tested, including human rights, opposition and independence and secessionist movements, minority faiths, pro-democracy groups, search engines, free e-mail and webhosting services, anonymizers and circumventors, pornography and sexually explicit material, and others.

However, China is not alone. Although many countries justify their censorship practices as a way to block access to pornography or other culturally sensitive material, our research has documented a large and growing swathe of content beyond pornography that is targeted for filtering. At least 14 countries blocked access to content that spans the major categories of *political*, *social*, and *conflict/security* content, including Burma, China, Ethiopia, Iran, Oman, Syria, Thailand, Tunisia, United Arab Emirates (UAE), Uzbekistan, Vietnam, Pakistan, Saudi Arabia, Sudan, and Yemen (See Figure 23.1).

Some of the countries in which we found evidence of content filtering in each of these major categories began by blocking only a few select sites in one category, usually pornography. After a period of time, however, the scope of content targeted for filtering began to increase to other content areas. In Thailand, for example, what started out as an effort to block pornography has been gradually broadened to include politically sensitive websites as well, particularly since the September 2006 military coup. In addition to pornographic content, Thailand blocks access to the popular video streaming service, YouTube.com, ostensibly in response to a single video posted on the service satirizing the deposed King. Pakistan began filtering websites that contain imagery offensive to Islam, and now targets all sites related to the Balochistan independence movement as well. The Thai and Pakistan cases are illustrative of what may be a more general trend: that is, once the tools of censorship are put in place, the temptation for authorities to employ them secretly for a wide range of ulterior purposes may be large—particularly in circumstances where there is little civilian oversight or accountability—a phenomenon we refer to as internet censorship "mission creep."

A number of other countries were found to be engaged in less pervasive forms of internet filtering, typically concentrated around a single content area or contentious internet service. For example, in addition to blocking some gambling and pornographic sites, ISPs in South Korea block access to all websites related to North Korea. India blocks access to websites related to extremist and militant groups, particularly those associated with Hindu and Islamic extremism. A number of Middle Eastern and Gulf Countries, including Syria, Jordan, UAE, Bahrain, and Saudi Arabia, block access to the entire Israeli (.il) domain (see also Warf and Vincent, 2007). Though having strict controls over traditional media and heavy penalties for libel, Singapore blocks access only to a small handful of pornographic websites (see also Rodan, 1998). Following the Thai and Pakistani

examples above, we might hypothesize that over time these states will likely use their filtering systems to block a growing body of content.

Increasing censorship sophistication

Not surprisingly, the methods used to do internet content filtering have become more sophisticated, as states and the firms that sell censorship and surveillance technologies continually refine them. There are several examples of increasing sophistication. First, authorities are becoming increasingly adept at targeting newly developed modes of communication, such as blogs, SMS, chat, and instant messaging

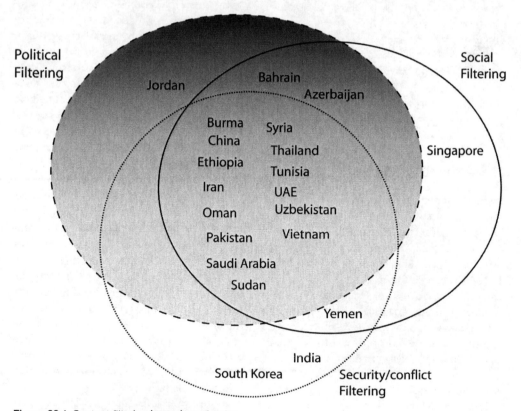

Figure 23.1 Content filtering by major category.
Source: Faris and Villeneuve, 2006.

protocols, and voice over internet protocol (VOIP) services. In the past, such newly devised methods of information sharing could be used as a means to circumvent internet censorship. However, today authorities are becoming more adept at targeting new media and developing methods particular to such services. Second, although content filtering is prone to overblocking and error, there are examples where authorities have been able to use such technologies with precision.

A good example is China's targeting of the specific string of codes embedded in the URL of the Google cache function. The latter is a service provided by Google whereby users can connect to archived information from websites stored on Google's servers, rather than on the servers of the original website. The service was designed to provide a way to access information through redundancy, but it is also a very simple and effective way to get around content filtering. Since users connect to Google servers rather than to the blacklisted servers, they bypass the content filters. Upon learning of this technique, China implemented a blocked string on their backbone/gateway routers that prevented *any* use of the Google cache function from within China.

A third example of increasing sophistication of content filtering is the targeting of local languages and websites of opposition movements and dissidents particular to a specific national context. Tests from within China comparing the top 100 Google search results for keywords in English and Chinese show a very significant disproportionate amount of keywords are filtered when they are searched for in Chinese as opposed to English (ONI, 2005b). For example, a search for the terms "Chinese Labor Party" in Chinese yields a 93 percent inaccessible rate when compared to the same search performed in English, which yields only a 20 percent inaccessible rate. Iran, in

2005, showed a similar relationship among English and local language filtering (ONI, 2005c). In the case of Iran, many of the blocked websites in various categories had a higher percentage of inaccessibility in Farsi as opposed to English. Overall, 80 percent of the Farsi-language websites tested were inaccessible whereas 45 percent of English-language sites were inaccessible. Such *localization* filtering—where "international" sources of information are left accessible while local variants are blocked—may at first seem counterintuitive. However, there are two potential explanations. First, localization filtering targets those groups that matter most to regime stability and power, such as local opposition movements and dissident groups presenting contentious information in languages spoken by citizens within the country. Second, the disproportionately open access to English-language international sites can give the impression that access to global information is wide open, particularly to foreign journalists who do not speak local languages. Authorities can point to contentious human rights and news sites and say that they allow access to information while blocking relatively more obscure sites from a global perspective that matter most in local politics.

The tests conducted across 40 countries in 2006 provided further confirmation that state content filtering tends to concentrate on local content and websites. Table 23.1 shows the percentage of websites blocked by country in the local and global content categories respectively. For each country, two baskets of websites were used for comparison: a local list, which includes categorized websites related to the particular context of each country in question; and a global list, which is a control list of categorized websites tested for accessibility in every country. The local list contains mostly local-language content of each country in question (e.g., Farsi for Iran) while the global list contains English-language content. The percentage of blocked websites in the local category was higher than in the global category for many countries in which filtering was found. When pornographic-related content is removed (which tends to be mostly global in character and filtered as a default by many countries using commercial filtering applications), the percentage of local content targeted for filtering is even higher. Among countries found to be engaging in content filtering, UAE, Bahrain, China, Ethiopia, India, Iran, Korea, Libya, Myanmar, Pakistan, Saudi Arabia, Syria, Thailand, Tunisia, Uzbekistan, and Vietnam all blocked relatively more local- than global-related content. What this suggests is that states who filter the internet tend to concentrate on social and political content that matters most within their local country context.

Use of commercial filtering technologies

The increased sophistication of internet content-filtering practices can be attributed, in part, to the services provided by western (mostly U.S.-based) software and internet service firms. Whereas once the best and brightest of Silicon Valley were associated with wiring the world, connecting individuals around the globe, and opening up access to vast stores of information, today they are just as likely to be known for doing the opposite.

Although Microsoft, Cisco, Yahoo, Skype, and Google have all come under scrutiny for colluding with China's internet

Table 23.1 Percent of tested websites blocked in 21 countries, by type of local and global content, 2006

Country	Blocked websites, all		Blocked political websites	
	Local	Global	Local	Global
Azerbaijan	2	98	0	100
Bahrain	62	38	86	14
China	80	20	92	8
Ethiopia	95	5	95	5
India	100	0	100	0
Iran	43	57	87	13
Libya	100	0	100	0
Myanmar	62	38	89	11
Oman	15	85	0	100
Pakistan	94	6	96	4
Saudi Arabia	22	78	68	32
Singapore	43	57	–	–
South Korea	81	19	100	0
Sudan	7	93	0	100
Syria	84	16	95	5
Thailand	81	19	100	0
Tunisia	32	68	73	27
United Arab Emirates	17	83	58	42
Uzbekistan	80	20	92	8
Vietnam	94	6	98	2
Yemen	10	90	22	78

Notes: Local websites are those designed for users in a specific country, and are usually in that country's national language. Global websites are primarily English language content, and include pornography.

330

censorship practices, perhaps the most significant, serious, and yet overlooked contribution to internet censorship by Western corporations comes from the manufacturers of the filtering software used to block content.

Internet security companies, like Fortinet, Secure Computing, and Websense, create off-the-shelf filtering products that block access to categorized lists of websites. While these products are primarily marketed to businesses, they have been readily employed by censoring states like Tunisia (Secure Computing), Iran (Secure Computing), Myanmar (Fortinet), and Yemen (Websense) to block access to politically-sensitive content.

Just like businesses that do not want their employees to view gambling or sport sites on company time, these governments simply tick off those categories of websites they do not want their citizens to access, such as "advocacy groups" or "militancy and extremist groups"—two categories in Websense's database. The former is defined by Websense as "sites that promote change or reform in public policy, public opinion, social practice, economic activities, and relationships," while the latter is defined as "sites that offer information about or promote or are sponsored by groups advocating anti-government beliefs or action" (Websense, 2007). As the Tunisia example listed in the introduction illustrates, however, the block lists used by these companies can contain categorization errors leading to untended blockages of websites.

Digital deceit

One troubling trend is been the lack of accountability and transparency over internet content-filtering practices by states that censor. While there is certainly a legitimate debate to be had about the balance between a state's right to cultural

sovereignty and the free flow of information raised by internet censorship, unfortunately most states do not allow such a debate to take place prior to filtering, and have been shown to be deceitful about the content they block and the filtering practices they employ.

There are accountability and transparency issues around the disclosure of filtering practices. Among states that filter, few are willing to admit the full scope and scale and precise nature of their filtering systems. For example, Saudi Arabia provides a substantial level of detail about their filtering practices in published reports, including an acknowledgment on the block page it sends back to users' computers, as does the UAE. Other countries are not so open, and some engage in deceptive practices. For example, in China when users make a request for a website that is banned, the request is blocked at the router level and an error message is sent back to the user's machine effectively penalizing that machine's IP address from making further http requests for a varying period of time. From the user's end, the penalization appears as a "time-out" error with no explanation (Clayton et al., 2006). Tunisia uses the same commercial product as Saudi Arabia—Smartfilter—but alters the block page functionality of that program to deliver a false error indication to users. When users attempt to access blocked content, they receive a page that appears to be a "File not found" error page but is in fact a block page designed to deceive users. In Uzbekistan, block pages sent back to users explain a site is blocked because it contains pornography even though the sites blocked are not pornographic but political in nature. Additionally, some Uzbeki ISPs redirect requests for banned content to unrelated sites or sites that are disguised to appear like the original site but which third parties operate and which contain false or misleading information. As countries that censor are generally sensitive about it being known that they block access to political information, they tend to be opaque and/or deceptive about their filtering practices. Only very rarely do states fully disclose their filtering behavior.

As outlined in Table 23.2, most countries lack transparency and accountability when it comes to processes around internet filtering practices. Very few openly acknowledge filtering at all. Concealed filtering reflects either efforts to conceal the fact that filtering is occurring or the failure to clearly indicate filtering when it is occurring. Decentralized filtering is any blocking that occurs at the sub-national level, although this study does not include filtering at the institutional level, e.g., cybercafés, universities, or businesses. Transparency considers the presence of concealed filtering, provisions to appeal or report instances of inappropriate blocking, and open acknowledgement of filtering policies. Consistency measures the variation in filtering within a country across different ISPs.

Table 23.2 also shows the variation in filtering practices among countries in terms of relative centralization of content filtering methods and consistency among ISPs within the country. Many states defer the implementation of internet content filtering to individual ISPs, some of whom do not fully comply with authorities or choose their own methods or software products to perform the filtering. The result is that accessibility to internet content within certain countries, such as Azerbaijan, Burma, Iran, and Vietnam, for example, can vary widely depending on the ISP to which a user connects. When combined with a low

Table 23.2 Centralized, decentralized, concealed, transparency, and consistency of website filtering in 22 countries, 2006

Country	Centralized filtering at national level	Decentralized filtering at sub-national level	Filtering concealed from user	Transparency of filtering policies	Consistency across country ISPs
Azerbaijan		×		low	low
Bahrain		×	×	low	high
Burma		×		medium	low
China	×	×	×	low	medium
Ethiopia	×		×	low	high
India		×		high	medium
Iran		×		medium	medium
Jordan				low	high
Libya				low	high
Oman	×			high	high
Pakistan	×	×	×	high	medium
Saudi Arabia	×			high	high
Singapore		×		high	high
South Korea		×		high	high
Sudan	×			high	high
Syria		×		medium	high
Thailand		×		medium	medium
Tunisia	×			low	high
United Arab Emirates	×			medium	low
Uzbekistan	×		×	low	high
Vietnam		×	×	low	low
Yemen		×		medium	high

Source: Faris and Villeneuve, 2006.

degree of transparency and accountability, such a lack of consistency can be a vexing experience for users within the country who are unaware of what content is being denied to them and experience different forms of censorship depending on the ISP to which they connect.

Blocking by computer network attack and DNS tampering

Rather than blocking access to a site, entire websites can be forced offline and essentially silenced by attacks that overwhelm the servers that host the websites. For example, during elections in Kyrgyzstan, several opposition newspapers came under simultaneous distributed denial of service attacks. The opposition websites were moved to a hosting service at the Citizen Lab in Toronto for analysis. The attacks were carried out by a hacker or group of hackers known as "shadow team" based in the Ukraine, and although no conclusive proof could be obtained, the Kyrgyz authorities cannot be ruled out as being responsible. In addition to the attacks on the opposition websites, other attacks temporarily suspended access to all websites on two Kyrgyz ISPs (Elcat and AsiaInfo) (ONI, 2005d).

The same pattern of disruption during election periods was observed in Belarus in April 2006. Although no evidence of state-directed filtering or sponsorship of denial of service attacks could be found, there were several suspicious events:

- 37 opposition and media websites were inaccessible from the state-owned Beltelecom network on March 19 (election day), although they were accessible within Belarus from a different ISP network as well as from the external control location;

- the internet was inaccessible to subscribers using Minsk Telephone access numbers on March 25 (the day of a major demonstration, where riot police were used to disperse and arrest protestors);

- the website of the main opposition candidate, Aleksandr Milinkevich, was "dead" on March 19 and experienced access issues on March 21–22, (the post-election protest period); and

- an opposition website (Charter 97) was only partially accessible between March 19–25.

The internet is likely to be targeted by subtle methods of information disruption that are not so easily tracked and traced as are more traditional forms of filtering and surveillance. Moreover, the participants in these contests over information space are likely to include more than just state authorities, such as NGOs and activists, who benefit politically (with the outside world) by being able to claim they are under attack just as much as authorities may benefit by having their information kept offline (ONI, 2006).

The trends towards offensive computer network attacks as methods of filtering are even more significant in the context of the role the U.S. military is playing in setting doctrinal examples and establishing norms of acceptable practices in areas like information warfare. The recently declassified "Information Operations Roadmap" makes it clear that the U.S. and its regional allies intend on taking the war on terrorism to the internet, using a variety of means ranging from taking down "illegal content" through to using the internet as a means to "deter, deny and destroy terrorist groups" (U.S. Department of Defense, 2003).[6] Such militarization of cyberspace could legitimize the type of denial of service actions that occurred in Kyrgyzstan and Belarus, and open up dynamics of competitive state and non-state offensive activities aimed at bringing down the sources of online information through "active," offensive means. Certainly the lessons have not been lost on the Chinese and Russian militaries, which are also supportive of a free-ranging scope for military action over the internet. Taken together with the shift in U.S. strategic policy towards preemption of threats "before they are fully formed," this stance has effectively opened the door for states to use computer network operations as a means to act unilaterally and extra-territorially to combat self-defined threats to national security emanating from the internet. As a consequence, computer network operations and information warfare are amongst the most secretive and fastest growing areas of investment for military, security, and signals intelligence organizations worldwide. Moreover, as the recent revelation concerning the U.S. National Security Agency's extralegal tapping of domestic communications (including the internet) suggest, even open and democratic societies are undertaking covert internet surveillance. The impact that these doctrinal shifts will have on the internet environment is likely to be substantial, and will make the challenges around accountability and transparency even more substantial.

Conclusion

Over the last several decades, the internet has enabled new, nimble, and distributed challenges to states worldwide, manifest in vigorous, mobilized opposition movements, protests, and in some cases, even revolutionary changes to political authority. Although these challenges have presented the most serious problems for non-democratic and authoritarian regimes, even among democratic states, the internet has presented serious challenges insofar as it empowers militant, terrorist, and criminal networks. Whereas once the promotion of new information and communication technologies were widely considered benign public policy, today states of all stripes have been pressed to find ways to limit and control the internet as a way to check their unintended and perceived negative consequences.

As the research shows, these efforts to control internet content are growing in scope, scale, and sophistication worldwide. Moreover, the methods used by states to filter content demonstrate a systematic lack of accountability and transparency. Although at first glance these policies and practices may be attributed simply to the strategic interests of states to control information flows across their territorial borders, the policies and practices of internet content filtering—in particular the use of computer network attacks and offensive information warfare—suggest a much deeper geopolitical struggle over the internet's architecture that is only beginning to unfold. Just as the domains of land, sea, air, and space have all been gradually colonized, militarized, and subject to inter-state competition so too is the once relatively unencumbered domain of cyberspace.

Of course these efforts by states to intervene in global internet communication flows are not going uncontested. The growth of state content-filtering practices has generated a burgeoning grass-roots transnational social movement around the protection and preservation of the internet as an open commons of information (see Deibert, 2003; Deibert and Rohozinski, 2007). The movement includes major NGOs, such as Amnesty International and Reporters without Borders, and efforts directed at multiple levels, from the construction of censorship circumvention technologies and other "hacktivist" tools to lobbying for the promotion of norms of openness and access to information at international levels.

These developments should make scholars of world politics and the internet rethink assumptions about not only the character of the internet but the social and political implications that flow from it. Although it is true that the internet helped unleash non-territorial forces and flows that have helped redefine the landscape of global politics, the internet's architecture is now being hotly contested and an object of competing discourses and practices of securitization. Almost certainly a new set of implications, many of them unintended, will flow as its architecture undergoes political transformation as a result of this competition.

Guide to further reading

In light of the fact that it is such a recent issue, there is relatively little scholarship about internet censorship and content filtering practices (outside of the work of the OpenNet Initiative outlined in this chapter). The latter is covered comprehensively in Deibert and Rohozinski (2007) with overviews of 41 countries and 8 regions, as well as several analytical chapters on the legal, social, and political implications of internet filtering. Those interested in exploring general issues of state control of internet communications might begin with Deibert (2003), Drezner (2004), as well as Goldsmith and Wu (2006), Goldsmith (1998), Lewis (2006), and Kalathil and Boas (2003). Villeneuve (2006) and Wu (2006) deal with some of the general issues concerning internet content filtering. There is a growing scholarship on internet content filtering in specific country and regional contexts, including Turkey (Altintos, 2002), China (Dowell, 2006; Hachigian, 2001; Lacharite, 2002; Li, 2003; Li, 2004), Singapore (Rodan, 1998), the Middle East (Goldstein, 1999), and Iran (Granick, 2005). Human Rights Watch (2006) did a major study

on corporate complicity in internet censorship practices in China. Those interested in exploring some of the topics raised in this chapter concerning information warfare practices will find a much larger set of studies. Arquilla (1995, 1996), and Arquilla and Ronfeldt (2001) are essential background, with Adams (2001), Berkowitz (2003), Cohen (1996), Denning (1999), Der Derian (2000), Libicki (1998), Nye and Owens (1996), and Rattray (2001) all highly recommended as well.

Notes

1 OpenNet Initiative. http://opennet.net/
2 For additional detail on the analysis presented here, see Ronald J. Deibert, John G. Palfrey, Rafal Rohozinski and Jonathan Zittrain, (eds.) *Access Denied: the practice and policy of global internet filtering*, (MIT Press: 2008).
3 Those familiar with intelligence practices will recognize the combination of human and technical intelligence methods. The adoption of these methods, as well as other aspects by which the ONI operates, from intelligence-derived approaches has been deliberate. The ONI's researchers take considerable personal risks to carry out the tests, and great effort is taken to minimize those risks by securing group communications and employing compartmentalized information techniques. The latter means that researchers and experts consulted about or in a particular country may not know the identity of the testers in that country, and vise versa. Testing in some countries has been hampered by personal security considerations. In several instances, ONI researchers have been apprehended and interrogated by authorities for their activities.
4 Multiple categories of websites have been subject to internet filtering, including websites on a range of topics, from a range of site producers, or offering a range of services: free expression and media freedom; political transformation and opposition parties; political reform, legal reform, and governance; militants, extremists and separatists; human rights; foreign relations and military; minority rights and ethnic content; women's rights; environmental issues; economic development; sensitive or controversial history, arts and literature; hate speech; sex education and

family planning; public health; gay and lesbian content; pornography; provocative attire; dating; gambling; gaming; alcohol and drugs; minority faiths; religious conversion, commentary and criticism; anonymizers and circumvention; hacking; blogging domains and blogging services; web hosting sites and portals; voice over internet protocol (VOIP); free e-mail; search engines; translation; multimedia sharing; peer-to-peer file sharing; groups and social networking; commercial sites.

5 We group these categories themselves into four major categories: political, social, conflict/security, and internet tools.

6 The Pentagon document was written in October 2003, but recently obtained and released by a Freedom of Information request from the National Security Archives at George Washington University. It can be obtained from: http://www.gwu.edu/~nsarchiv/NSA EBB/NSAEBB177/info_ops_roadmap.pdf

24

Locational surveillance

Embracing the patterns of our lives

David J. Phillips

This chapter discusses three prevalent systems of locational surveillance. The surveillance of mobility is facilitated by many different technical systems. Mobile phones, closed circuit television (CCTV), and radio frequency identification tags all can signal the changing location of physical objects. Standardized addresses, sophisticated maps, and analytic software make this movement legible. The chapter then examines the economic and legal pressures that shape access to those systems. Finally, it suggests avenues for intervention into the development of new technologies of mobility.

Many different political and historical tensions shape the contours of surveillance practice. Nevertheless, two factors occur consistently in these developments. First, global corporations or national governments control significant portions of the surveillance infrastructure. Second, the dichotomy of security versus privacy occurs again and again as a discursive device to frame the stakes and implications of surveillance. These two organizing structures contribute to the development of surveillance systems that are always more or less useful for large organizations to control and manage large populations. To counteract this trend, to encourage the development of surveillance practices that are small scale, grass-roots, and local, and to grasp the social and political implications of such practices, policy-makers should look to legal theories of common carriage and intellectual commons. Sociologists and system designers should look to the processes by which identity and place arise out of communication and situated interaction.

Techniques and practices of locational surveillance

Mobile phones, emergency response, and location-based services

Mobile telephone carriers have emerged as primary generators of locational data. In one sense, this is obvious—carriers must locate the call's recipient in order to route the call. Yet, especially in the U.S., the locational capacity of mobile phone networks has become both sophisticated and standardized. This is due to a nation-wide mandate to integrate mobile phone networks within the existing emergency response system (ERS).

Originally ERS was designed to auto-matically open a direct voice line between the caller and a public safety answering point (PSAP) whenever the caller dialed 911. The PSAP operator would then, in conversation with the caller, dispatch the appropriate response team. In the 1980s U.S. Federal Communications Commission

(FCC) supported upgrading the ERS system so that it automatically delivered to PSAPs not just the call itself, but also the phone number and address of the caller. To aid dispatching, local authorities disambiguated and normalized street names and addresses, especially in rural areas.

In the late 1990s the FCC mandated that mobile phone carriers make their networks compatible with this system. It ordered that mobile carriers be able to determine the location of any phone calling 911 to deliver that location, along with the phone number and the call itself, to the nearest PSAP. A standard infrastructure of location determination and delivery has evolved in response to this mandate. During a 911 call, the carrier locates the phone using either terrestrial triangulation, in which the caller's voice signal is located by reference to nearby antennas, or using the global positioning system (GPS). In this latter case, the phone polls orbiting satellites for their positions and forwards that data to the carrier, which performs the triangulation calculations to locate the phone. Usually GPS devices perform that calculation locally, but phone carriers and manu-facturers have off-loaded the calculation, in part to make the handsets lighter. Thus in either case the carrier is the first holder of the locational data. The carrier then forwards that locational data and the caller's number to a specialized geographic data-base, which determines the nearest PSAP. The carrier transfers the call and continues to update the geographic database, which the PSAP accesses to track the caller. In the PSAP itself, specialized mapping and dispatching software help make visual sense of the locational data.

Development of this infrastructure has required many types of expertise, includ-ing the ability to locate calls, operate geographic databases to determine such qualities as "nearness," route calls based on geographic conditions, link voice

channels with auxiliary data channels, and provide mapping tools and other inter-faces. As neither the wireless nor the wireline carriers are expert in all of these, alliances among carriers and with third-party developers have become common. Throughout, demands for interoperability among current and future institutions and technical structures have prompted the transformation of the U.S. emergency response system from a special-purpose, local, emergency communication system into a generic, modular, national, locational surveillance system. In particular, there has been a strong incentive to implement that modularity and interoperability through the use of internet protocols, rather than telephony switching protocols.

This infrastructure is useful not only for the provision of emergency services, but also for many other location-aware appli-cations. Typically, these services operate under a paradigm very similar to the ERS system. Mobile phone carriers determine a phone's location, and deliver that loca-tion to a location-based service (LBS) provider. The LBS provider then makes geographic sense of the locational data, perhaps triggering alarms if the phone is traveling at a certain speed, or is outside a prescribed area, or is near a particular location of interest.

The subscribers to these services may not be the person using the phone. For example, TeleNav, in cooperation with mobile carriers and phone manufacturers, offers a service to managers of mobile workers. Each worker carries a phone that regularly reports its location, via the mobile carrier, to TeleNav's servers. TeleNav records and maps this data, and triggers alarms when workers enter or leave certain areas, or spend more than a specified amount of time at a location. The employer accesses these maps and alarms through a web interface, and communicates with the workers through specialized Java applets in their phones

(TeleNav, 2007). Sprint offers Family Locator, which alerts parents when their children near a specific location. Verizon's Chaperone sends an alarm to the parent when their children leave a "geo-fenced" area. Another service, soon to be offered by Sprint, alerts the user whenever a "buddy" is near (Magid, 2007).

Closed circuit television systems

Closed circuit television systems, in their simplest form, may consist simply of a video camera recording the activity in a single location, perhaps a till or a store entrance. The system operators, perhaps the store owner or manager, would probably watch these recordings only after some anomalous event, such as a robbery. But in the past few decades, CCTV systems have grown in complexity so that, for example, a single guard can watch a building's several entrances simultaneously. By far the most sophisticated, extensive, and pervasive CCTV systems are in the U.K., where over 4 million cameras are in use, often covering entire downtown areas and monitored by central police stations (Edwards, 2005).

A standalone CCTV camera will only tell you whether someone is present at a particular location; coordinated CCTV systems can be used to track individuals' movements. In practice, this tracking is usually retroactive. That is, after a crime occurs, police consult recorded CCTV images to view the scene of the crime and trace suspects' movements backwards as they leave and enter cameras' fields of vision.

Newer CCTV systems are augmented with software that can automatically recognize objects within their field of vision and respond appropriately in real time. The most common such systems are used for the collection of road tolls. Roads and highways in central London and elsewhere are lined with CCTV cameras linked to software that captures the text of the license plates within the video image. The system then collates various appearances of that license plate, calculates each car's road usage, and sends a bill to the car's owner. While the system's primary purpose and justification is toll collection, the system operators will alert police when unregistered or unlicensed vehicles appear. They will also, upon police request, watch for and forward data regarding "suspect" license plate numbers. Of course, these systems also provide for more extensive retrospective surveillance.

Radio frequency identification

Radio frequency identification (RFID) systems consist of three parts: tiny short-range transmitters (tags) that emit a unique digital code, readers that activate the tags and receive their signals, and the databases and administrative processes that are activated upon their receipt. Radio frequency identification systems are quite common; in general, any card that one waves at a reader, rather than swiping through a reader, probably contains an RFID tag. Common RFID applications include automatic toll collection (for example, the EZPass system in the U.S.) and building access cards.

Because the tags are short-range transmitters, RFID systems are in a way inherently locational. If the reader has read the tag, then the tag was near the reader. Initial applications were concerned with taking the action appropriate at a particular place—assess this toll, open this door. But multiple readers linked to common databases offer a vantage point from which to note movement of a particular tag from reader to reader. This kind of tracking is becoming perhaps the predominant use of RFID tags. Retailers such as Wal-Mart are requiring their suppliers to tag products in order to track inventory through the supply chain. Currently, Wal-Mart's tagging is done at the pallet level and tracking stops when items are stocked on the shelves. But item-level tagging is increasingly common. Michelin embeds a unique tag in each tire it manufactures (Michelin, 2006). Airports use RFID to track baggage (Friedlos, 2007). A U.S. Department of Agriculture project uses RFID tags to track feed animals from birth to slaughterhouse (U.S. Department of Agriculture, 2007).

This sort of lifetime product tracking involves coordination of readings as the tagged item moves through institutions: manufacturer, shipper, and retailer, at the very least. Verisign, the U.S. company that manages two of the internet's thirteen root name servers, as well as the .com and .net domains, has developed a system to facilitate this sort of global RFID tracking, creating "a unified view of sightings of individual … tags" (Juels, 2006: 383).

It is a short hop from tracking objects and animals to tracking people. In some cases, locating an object effectually implies locating a person. One can reasonably assume, for example, that if an RFID equipped car passed a toll booth, then the car's driver passed it too. But developers are also offering RFID applications specifically designed to track or locate people. Usually such tags are embedded in a worn object, for example a bracelet worn by a child at an amusement park, an inmate in a prison, or a patient in a hospital (Bennet and Crow, 2005; Bushell-Embling, 2007). However, some companies are offering subcutaneous tagging for dementia sufferers likely to wander from their caregivers (Penn, 2007).

Convergence

These are not the only techniques available for locational surveillance. For example, laptop computers can be programmed to calculate their position by triangulating local WiFi signals, then report that position to a third party (Magid, 2007). But GPS, cell phone location, CCTV, and RFID are the most pervasive, institutionalized, and standardized location techniques. They are mature enough that the infrastructures supporting their use have begun to merge and interact. The U.K. is planning to integrate satellite positioning into its road pricing system, especially as that system extends beyond the dense urban areas most amenable to CCTV surveillance (Oliver, 2007). Bermuda and the U.K. both plan to embed RFID tags in license plates (Ferguson, 2007).

Police are also growing more sophisticated in their analysis of the vast amounts of data produced by locational surveillance systems, and can integrate other types of data into that analysis. In the U.K., police use i2 Analyst's Workstation, which integrates license plate data with other data sources and provides an interface to visualize temporal, geographic, or associative patterns in the data. That is, the operator can map the path of a particular vehicle, highlight areas frequented by suspicious vehicles, or note the regular appearance of a cohort of vehicles (i2 Inc, 2007).

Research is underway on systems to integrate face recognition and other biometric data into CCTV and RFID systems. The RFID based secure alert tracking system will not only inform casino managers of their employees' locations, it will also let managers know if the employee's heart is racing (Swedberg, 2007). Researchers in Europe are developing a system to monitor every airline passenger through CCTV cameras installed in the backs of seats, and automatically recognize suspicious activities, like lip-licking, blinking, or rapid eye movements (Leake, 2007).

Police agencies and global corporations are not the only ones to take advantage of the growing sophistication, maturity, and interoperability of these techniques. Grassroots organizations, individuals, and small businesses are also taking them up. Radio frequency identification readers and satellite positioning receivers are relatively cheap. Cell phones are practically ubiquitous in some communities. Google has published the specifications that permit relatively unsophisticated users to create "mash-ups" that link databases to maps. So, for example, one need only go to www.housingmaps.com to see a map with "pins" stuck in it marking the location of available apartments. Click the pin and you are shown the ad for that apartment. The Institute for Applied Autonomy has developed a web-based service mapping the locations of CCTV cameras in Manhattan, and allowing users to plot "paths of least surveillance" (Institute for Applied Autonomy, 2007). Nokia offers a phone with a built-in RFID reader, making possible applications where the RFID tags are stationary and the readers mobile (Nokia, 2007). Thus, the phone user can wend her way around an unfamiliar city, referring to databases about locations, rather than having the operators of those locations refer to databases about her.

While nothing in the technologies themselves necessitates a top–down, panoptic structure of locational surveillance, certain trends are nevertheless apparent. The infrastructure is controlled, maintained, and used by governments and large corporations. Telephone companies, especially, are important players, in that they produce and control the locational data regarding the phones on their system. Closed circuit television systems are expensive to deploy and coordinate, and are generally operated on a large scale only by those for whom they can produce income (as with toll collection systems) or when they are supported by a tax base (as with public police surveillance).

Radio frequency identification technology is relatively inexpensive in itself, though its supporting infrastructure has evolved to satisfy the needs of global trade, and is operated by the most powerful communications corporations in the world.

Huge global corporations are also implicated in these infrastructures as individual locational data is supplemented by other sources of personal data. ChoicePoint, which operates the systems allowing U.K. police to quickly link license plate numbers with other sources of data, had revenues of over a billion dollars in 2006 (ChoicePoint, 2007). Google and Microsoft, two behemoths in the computing industry, are the primary providers of maps and mapping services used in ad hoc mash-ups.

A further trend is that these systems are used not only for the tracking of individual people or items, but for geographic sense-making and pattern analysis. These applications require sophisticated and expensive software generally available only to those with deep pockets.

The following section investigates further the laws, policies, and economic arrangements that act to structure access to locational surveillance infrastructures, and so order social relations and distribute social power.

Structuring the order of surveillance

In general, there are two phases of the configuration of access to locational surveillance resources. The first is the configuration of the technical infrastructure that makes certain practices possible. The second is the legal, economic, and cultural infrastructure that constrains and shapes actuations of that potential. Nowhere is this dual structuring more apparent than in the configuration of police access to locational data.

The E911 system in the U.S. is the result of very specific, articulate, and well-funded

341

policy mandates to provide the technical capacity for locational surveillance. There is no opt-out of the system. All telephony carriers must provide a 911 service, locate their callers, and deliver that location to the PSAP. Having extended this mandate from wired to wireless carriers, the FCC is again extending it to voice over internet protocol (VOIP) carriers. Every internet telephony service provider who is capable of receiving calls from, or making calls to, the public switched telephony network, must also be able to interconnect with the E911 system and deliver a "registered location" to the PSAP. For now, this location is relatively static. The user provides it to the VOIP carrier when first signing up for the service. However, the FCC is also considering requiring VOIP operators to institute real-time, automatic location determination (Federal Communication Commission, 2005).

Laws requiring data collection and retention are another policy mechanism through which police and security agents attain potential access to locational data. Many countries have enacted legislation to require mobile phone carriers to obtain identification from all of their clients, making anonymous pre-paid mobile phone cards illegal (Centre for Policy Research on Science and Technology, nd). European lawmakers have proposed to make it illegal to provide false information when opening a web or e-mail account (Shannon, 2007). A new law in New York City mandates video surveillance of entrances and exits of nightclubs (Rivera, 2007), and a proposed law in the U.K. would require all CCTV operators to produce images of sufficient clarity to identify their subjects (Johnston, 2007).

All of these are specifically intended to make the technical infrastructure of surveillance efficiently available to police and security agencies. Of course, that access can be constrained by non-technical

regulations, and it is to these that we now turn.

Data protection in the EU

The Data Directive of 1995 (European Union, 1995) required EU countries to pass laws regulating the processing of personally identifiable information. These laws are intended to protect personal privacy of individuals, and must instantiate certain principles of data protection. Thus, in general, across Europe, data subjects have the right to know when data is collected about them, to opt out of that collection, and to access and correct that data.

Certain tensions and ambiguities have arisen as regulators attempt to apply these principles to modern surveillance practices. For example, the principles are explicitly intended to protect individual privacy. But often the purpose of surveillance is to discover or create usable patterns in vast amounts of data, rather than to isolate or act upon any particular individual. Any social, rather than personal, implications of that sort of knowledge production are orthogonal to the principles' intent.

Moreover, since the principles apply only to "any information relating to an identified or identifiable natural person," regulators are forced to tackle the question of what it is to "relate" to an individual, and what it is for an individual to be "identifiable." Green and Smith (2003) note that British mobile phone carriers have taken advantage of this ambiguity. Clearly, when those carriers market the locational data of the cell phones in their system, they act as though that data is related to an individual. After all, it is the link between the cell phone and its user that gives that locational data its monetary value. Yet, until recently, regulators refused to apply privacy principles to that data, viewing the cell phone's location as a non-individuated, non-personal bit of information "on par with a bus ticket" (Green and Smith, 2003: p. 580).

The prevalence of RFID surveillance, where the link to the individual is more tenuous, but the granularity of tracking potentially more pervasive, has brought these questions before policy-makers with greater urgency. In response, an EU policy team has recommended that data be subject to privacy regulations if it "is used to determine or influence the way in which [a] person is treated or evaluated" (European Union, 2005). This would certainly seem to cover, for example, mobile carriers supplying marketers with anonymized locational data that would nevertheless permit the marketers to deliver location-specific messages to mobile phones. However, the recommendations specify that the data be used to influence a "person," and it is not clear that it would apply to the wholesale use of large quantities of anonymized locational data if that information were used in ways that affected the lives of many people (for example, in siting billboards or road blocks), so long as none of them were targeted individually.

Privacy law in the U.S.

Unlike the EU, the U.S. has taken a sectoral approach to informational privacy, where each type of data (for example financial records, health records, or video rental records) is subject to a different policy mechanism. Locational data, especially that generated by mobile phone systems, enjoy the highest legislative protection.

As was mentioned earlier, the software, networks, and expertise involved in emergency response systems are also useful in commercial location-based services. But while the locational infrastructure may be generally available to non-emergency services, access to the locational data itself is highly restricted. Carriers are forbidden to disclose a customer's location except with the customer's "express prior consent" (P.L. 106–81 (5)(2); 47 U.S.C. 222 (f)). This requirement for consent is waived in several cases. First, of course, is in the provision of emergency services. It is also waived if the carrier is presented with a court order for disclosure. There are also populations who are deemed unable to consent or who have had their right to consent revoked. Consent also can be coerced. We will discuss these situations in turn.

Police agents have been eager to avail themselves of the locational data generated in mobile telephony. Until recently, courts were generally ready to assist them in this, by classifying that data as routing information, the release of which, under U.S. law, is subject to a very low level of judicial review. Since 2005, however, judges in several jurisdictions have denied such requests. In doing so, they have accepted the argument that the use of such routing information turns the cell phone into a tracking device, the use of which by police agents is subject to the very highest level of judicial scrutiny (Savin, 2006). These rulings are recent, local, and contested and they apply only to real-time surveillance. It remains unclear what judicial standards apply to retrospective access to locational phone records (Schwartz et al., 2006).

The unquestioned necessity for potential police access is one principle underlying both European and U.S. data regulation. Consent is another. Both the EU and the U.S. data protection regimes, to varying degrees, require that individuals be given the opportunity to consent to the collection and use of their personal information. The actual implementations of that right to consent are too varied and intricate to be reviewed here. Nevertheless, certain issues arise whenever consent is an operating principle.

One issue is that consent, to be meaningful, must be informed. Individuals must know the likely results of their decision to consent. But that sort of prognostication is impossible, either for the data subject or the operator of the surveillance system, especially since surveillance is used not to act upon a particular individual, but to fashion social edifices like market segments or political districts. Nor is withholding consent particularly effective. While each individual may regard the establishment of a surveillance state with distaste or alarm, it is not clear that the actions of any individual will do much to prevent it.

Another issue is that certain populations—children and the mentally incompetent for example—are deemed unable to consent. And other populations, like prisoners, are deemed to have forfeited their right to consent. It is not surprising that these—children, hospital patients, Alzheimer's sufferers, and prisoners—are among the first human targets of RFID tracking.

Ideally, consent is freely given and uncoerced. Yet every decision occurs in relations of power. This is especially true in another of the most common practices of human tracking, workplace surveillance. In recognition of these power differentials, different regulatory regimes come into play in the workplace.

Labor law and workplace regulation

Mobile phone based employee tracking systems, such as the Navtrak system are extensions of a long line of electronic surveillance of mobile workforces, starting first with the trucking industry (Lappin, 1995). In the U.S., union resistance to workplace surveillance has historically been feeble (Townsend and Bennett, 2003). However, resistance is growing as more workers in more fields—cab drivers, case workers, and hospital employees, for example—are subject to finer observation and control.

Some of this resistance is in the form of legislative lobbying. This tends to be more successful in the EU, with its established and expansive regimes of data protection. There, employers are required to disclose and justify all monitoring activity (Townsend and Bennett, 2003). Legislative initiatives are more difficult in the U.S. Even though the U.S. sectoral approach does grant high protection to locational data, that protection is trumped by consent, and workers are legally deemed to consent by taking (or keeping) the job. Instead, U.S. workers must either explicitly bargain for contractual limits on surveillance, or argue before labor relations boards that surveillance constitutes a significant change to established working conditions.

Bennett and Crow (2005) report that U.S. unions are addressing employee tracking more frequently in their contract negotiations, and sometimes have called strikes to resist the imposition of tracking during a contract period. Though increasingly common, these efforts have met with mixed success. Appeals to labor relations boards have generally failed, with the board holding that surveillance in the workplace is simply a reasonable automation of managerial prerogative. However, two new arguments are being formulated. The first holds that surveillance and communication systems do not merely operate within the work environment but that they *are* the work environment. They "are the primary tools through which an employee accomplishes his or her work, [and] also ... a primary mediator of employees' interactions with coworkers and clients. As such, information and telecommunications systems [define] both the nature of the work and the social environment in which it occurs" (Townsend and Bennett, 2003: 196). The second nascent argument is that the permanence of the records of surveillance constitutes a material shift in the relations between employers and employees, if for no other reason than that these records become available to police under subpoena.

Access to maps

Individual location only makes sense in a geographic context. Maps form the backdrop against which mobility is understood. Access to maps is influenced by a host of regulatory, economic, and historical conditions. This confusion is especially evident in the U.S., where national E911 emergency response initiatives generated a lot of local mapping activity. Sometimes local authorities compiled these maps from existing utility company data. In other cases, localities commissioned entirely new maps using aerial photography and satellite positioning systems. As localities adopted policies regarding public access to those maps, they had to take into account their contracts with data providers, the local and regional "sunshine" laws regarding access to government documents, and cost recovery policies. Localities also negotiate national security issues as they make mapping data available.

Similar tensions among issues of intellectual property, economic policy, and security are played out across the globe. In the U.S., the government does not hold copyright to any of the information it compiles and cannot collect royalties. However, one political trend is to assess access fees to recover the cost of data collection, processing, and delivery. Another trend is to outsource data gathering to private companies, allowing those companies to retain copyright and paying them for government use of the data.

In the EU and Canada, governments generally can and do hold copyright. However, across the EU, the regulatory trend is to encourage the free availability of government maps, in the hope that such availability will spur economic development through new location-based services.

Copyright issues are also at play among private purveyors of geo-data. In North America and Europe, Navteq and Tele Atlas are the two dominant private providers of geo-coded data. Google licenses this data for their Google Maps and Google Earth services. In providing interfaces to these mapping systems, Google facilitates the generation of ad hoc, community-oriented locational surveillance systems such as the mash-ups mentioned earlier. However, all creators of Google mash-ups are subject to Google's licensing agreements. These forbid the bulk download of geographic data, as well as the integration of Google's maps with "any products, systems, or applications installed or otherwise connected to or in communication with vehicles capable of vehicle navigation, positioning, dispatch, real-time route guidance, fleet management or similar applications" (Google, 2007). They also require that the services be non-commercial and limited to 50,000 page views per day. In effect, while Google and their map providers seek to encourage experimentation and novel developments in mapping practice, that encouragement guides those applications into a market logic, and protects market domination where it already exists.

To circumvent the restrictions of both private and state control of geographic data, some groups like OpenStreetMap are trying to generate open source or "wiki" maps. These use open protocols to generate useful geo-coded databases using either public domain maps or, ideally, new data generated by users with personal geopositioning devices (OpenStreetMap, 2007).

Social movements

The open source mapping movement is not the only ground-swell reaction to increasingly pervasive, regularized, and institutionalized locational surveillance practice. This reaction is, however, mixed.

While polls indicate that most U.S. mobile phone users worry about locational privacy (Harris Interactive, 2007), there has been little organized resistance to CCTV surveillance, though perhaps resistance will be piqued by "talking" video cams, which allow CCTV station operators to verbally chide litterers and loiterers in real time. Resistance to nation-wide vehicle surveillance in the U.K. seems to be geared toward the road tolls that the system facilitates, rather than to the surveillance itself (Oliver, 2007).

Radio frequency identification technologies, on the other hand, have excited some effective opposition. In part due to organized backlash, retailers have had to delay or defend their plans for RFID tagging (Wolinsky, 2003). Several U.S. states have banned forced RFID implants in humans. The U.S. Senate recently responded to public distrust of RFID systems by stipulating that the mandatory anti-counterfeiting protection on consumer pharmaceuticals must be visual and may not include readers or scanners (S. 1082 Sec 514(2)(A)(i)).

Conclusion

Dominant and entrenched institutions, especially police agencies, telecommunication corporations, and global manufacturers and retailers, have the political and economic capital to instigate expansive infrastructural changes in locational surveillance. As new techniques and practices develop, regulators, policy-makers, or activists respond to those novelties, generally to make sure that emerging infrastructures are adaptable to their interests. The reactive response calls on previous regulatory regimes, especially privacy and data protection law, but also telecommunication, media, and labor law.

This reaction tends to be fragmentary, and limited to the attributes of a particular technical or social configuration. There is little overall reconceptualization of the political stakes and or the long-term social implications of locational surveillance. There are exceptions to this. European Union policy-makers, especially, are engaged in far-sighted attempts to broadly reconsider qualitative changes in surveillance practice (Commission of the European Communities, 2007; European Union, 2005, 2007). Some legal scholars are beginning to apply the insights of critical geography—that is, the idea of places as constructed, not merely monitored, by surveillance practice—to labor law and privacy law.

But the broadest, deepest, most entrenched and prevalent exception to the fragmentary approach is the dominance of two paradigms: the security paradigm manifested in the explicit articulation of the interests of police and security agencies into every aspect of regulatory infrastructure, and the privacy paradigm with its individualist rather than collectivist understandings of the threats of surveillance.

The legal, economic, and technical infrastructure of locational surveillance is developing in a way that makes its resources most readily available to large-scale police and corporate entities. Those entities use the locational infrastructure to organize and administer populations and processes, whether workforces, traffic flows, urban crowds, or manufactured goods. While this involves noting and responding to the actions of individuals, its primary focus is efficiency and normalization. This normalization entails a "God's eye view" and the imposition of a matrix against which individual actions are measured and analyzed.

Regulatory responses to surveillance are framed by the concepts of security and privacy. Security is the most powerful of these framing devices, in part because it encompasses the entire surveillance process and understands the control of populations. The privacy framing, on the other hand, tends to be quite restricted in its purview. Privacy and data protection regimes protect individuals rather than communities. They only peripherally protect the ability to interact in public, to create and use public spaces, or to engage in the production of social order. Yet the production of order is exactly the purpose of surveillance.

New theoretical approaches are necessary in order to effectively engage with and counter the expanse of surveillance as a mechanism of normalization and control. The relatively new discipline of surveillance studies is making great strides in this direction, especially in the articulation of surveillance as "social sorting" (Lyon, 2002; Haggerty and Ericson, 2006). While that theoretical and empirical work has helped to elucidate the processes and implications of surveillance, there remains a great need for concrete policy or regulatory guidance.

Some legal theorists have suggested that the regulation of oversight technologies be geared not to protect privacy per se, but to protect the "contextual integrity" of social activities (Nissenbaum, 2004). While this is a welcome direction, it must also be abetted by a constructivist understanding of context and activity as mutually constitutive. As Dourish puts it, context "is an achievement, rather than an observation; an outcome, rather than a premise" (Dourish, 2004: 22). The central policy question then becomes how to "support the processes by which context is continually manifest, defined, negotiated, and shared" (Dourish, 2004: 26). Moreover, to counteract a tendency toward monolithic normalcy, context creations should be messy, overlapping, dissonant, and mutually productive.

The Urban Tapestries project offered an excellent ethnographic venture into the processes of geographic context creation, and the policies that might support

them. Many of these policy suggestions recommend that the underlying infrastructure of surveillance—the data sources and networks of exchange—be kept open and available to action from the peripheries rather than constrained by the economic and political interests of corporations and governments. In particular, they suggest that telecommunication policy require openness, interconnection, and interoperability among data and telephony networks (Lane and Thelwall, 2005). European Union policy documents extend this principle, recommending an open service for tracking RFID tags (Commission of the European Communities, 2007).

Urban Tapestries also recommend that geo-data be publicly available. Further, they suggest that many forms of locational knowledge be integrated. That is, to recognize that people make sense of where they are not only by latitude and longitude, but also by signage, architectural style, and the fashion sense of passersby (Lane and Thelwall, 2005).

Most importantly, Urban Tapestries recognized that while people are eager to share and create locational knowledge, this desire is tempered by questions about how and by whom the knowledge would be used (Lane and Thelwall, 2005). This is an important policy issue regardless of how locational surveillance capacity is distributed. Grass-roots locational knowledge production is no more inherently benevolent than state or corporate surveillance. Mash-ups pinpointing the homes of gynecologists working at family planning agencies are of ambiguous social value. The new dynamics of social visibility raise ethical, social, and legal questions that are only beginning to be articulated.

But these are exactly the questions that must be addressed. Unless we do, awe will be thrown back on the dichotomy of security (defined always as national security, the security provided by police and armies) versus privacy, and individuals will be managed, to a greater or lesser extent, by overbearing organizations.

Guide to further reading

Norris and Armstrong (1999) provide a classic study of public CCTV systems in the U.K. Though the technical configuration of the systems they study is already somewhat quaint, their ethnographic and political economic insights are enduring. For more on the development of mobile phone tracking and location-based services in North America, see Phillips (2005) and Bennett and Crow (2005). Thorough analyses of the policy implications of RFID have recently been published (Commission of the European Communities, 2007; European Union, 2005, 2007). Dourish (2004) offers brief and persuasive arguments for articulating context creation into the design of pervasive computing systems. Finally, Haggerty and Ericson's (2006) *The New Politics of Surveillance and Visibility* is a brilliant collection of the best current theoretical and empirical research on surveillance.

25

Metaphoric reinforcement of the virtual fence

Factors shaping the political economy of property in cyberspace

Oscar H. Gandy, Jr. and Kenneth Neil Farrall

Understanding the political economy of the internet requires a comprehensive assessment of the strategic resources that interested actors bring to bear at critical points of engagement with those institutions that identify, assign, and enforce the rights and responsibilities that define it. This chapter is focused on the role of the U.S. Supreme Court and the appellate courts that help to set its agenda in defining the nature of property in cyberspace. An analysis of the strategic use of metaphor by justices, judges, plaintiffs, defendants, and a rapidly growing pool of "friends of the court," reveals the ways in which boundaries are drawn, fences are raised, and rules regarding their height, density, and inviolability are set into place. While legal scholars assume that some logic governs the use of particular metaphors, such as those that reflect an internal or users' perspective rather than an external or engineering orientation, the fact is that it is strategic impact, rather than logic or allegiance to a particular community of interest, that governs their use. Although continuing tension between property and liberty interests has marked the development of cyberspace, appellate courts have tended to use a broad array of metaphoric constructions to justify reinforcing limits on access to virtual property. The future of cyberspace will be shaped, explained, and justified through the strategic use of metaphors and analogies. The challenge will be to understand how their use reflects and reinforces existing distributions of power.

Fences are both a technical and a symbolic force when marshaled by those who seek to announce and defend their property interests. Fences are also seen as a constraint on the freedom of others to make use of public or collective resources. Although the ultimate status of a particular bit of fence was often determined through the use of deadly force (Anderson and Hill, 1975), the resolution of these conflicts at a more general level came to depend upon the establishment, interpretation, and enforcement of the rule of law (McFerrin and Wills, 2007).

Laws defending the use of barbed wire in the American West had much in common with Section 1201 of the Digital Millennium Copyright Act (Herman and Gandy, 2006). Each served to reinforce the claims of property rights holders who were engaged in the development of new frontiers.

The power of law is magical. It has the ability to establish as fact, things that we know in our hearts are not so (Madison, 2005). As Balkin (2003: 8) puts it, law "is a form of cultural software that shapes the way we think about and apprehend the world." Legal doctrines establish facts as well as systems of rights and responsibilities associated with the social actors and objects that are created along with those facts (Tiller and Cross, 2005). Development and change in the nature of what we treat as right or wrong is the product of a complex interaction of socio-technical factors that include the strategic efforts of social actors seeking to maintain or establish power or advantage over others (Etzioni, 1988). These actors bring a variety of resources to bear in their attempts to shape the law and its influence over behavior. We have chosen to focus on the use of metaphor and analogy as resources in the discursive construction of the regime of rights and responsibilities that helps to determine the character of cyberspace.

Political economy and the transformation of cyberspace

Cyberspace is more than the internet, although its infrastructure provides the matrix within which its countless transactions and interactions take place. The number and variety of communicative interactions that determine the character of cyberspace continue to expand as a function of socio-technical factors (Garrie, 2005) that both shape, and are shaped by, transformations in the global economy (Spar, 2001).

Although there are ongoing debates about whether the emergence of global markets for information goods and services represents a fundamental change in the nature of the market system (Webster, 2002), there is little doubt that the commodification of information has been a driving force in its transformation.

This process of commodification has been especially troubled, however, by the immaterial nature of information, and the associated difficulties of establishing and defending property interests in these intangible goods. A substantial increase in legislative and judicial activity has been a largely ineffective response to this growing uncertainty (Landes and Posner, 2004).

We focus our attention in this chapter on the ways in which conflicts between property and liberty interests in cyberspace have been pursued within the U.S. appellate court system. The appellate courts serve as the final authority on the meaning of legislative acts designed to establish rights as well as to control the behavior of cyberspace residents and guests. And, although the production of influence within the appellate court system differs in important ways from its production within the legislative arena (Baumgartner and Jones, 1993), the pursuit of group interests in both venues shares much in common.

Although judicial decisions are constrained to a certain extent by professional norms and expectations regarding the influence of legal doctrine and precedent, we are also mindful of the fact that jurists' interpretations of the law will be shaped to some degree by their own moral, ethical, and ideological commitments (Balkin, 1991).

The metaphoric construction of cyberspace

In 1690 philosopher John Locke wrote the following about metaphor:

> … all the art of rhetoric, besides order and clearness; all the artificial and figurative application of words eloquence hath invented, are for nothing else but to insinuate wrong ideas, move the passions, and thereby mislead the judgment; … And therefore, however laudable or allowable oratory may render them in harangues and popular addresses,

they are certainly, in all discourses
that pretend to inform or instruct,
wholly to be avoided …
(Locke, 1959: 146)

Locke's concern about the misleading
aspects of metaphor has been particularly
salient within legal discourse. Susan
Tiefenbrun (1986: 118–19) notes "Students
of law are taught early in law school to
avoid the use of emotive or metaphoric
language in legal brief writing. Despite
the generally held belief in this convention, however, metaphors are commonly
found in cases." Further, as Haig Bosmajian
(1992) demonstrates, it is the metaphors
(or "tropological passages") in court opinions that are likely to be quoted in
subsequent decisions.

That metaphors may, in fact, play a
critical role in legal discourse where clear
logical thinking is paramount, should no
longer come as a surprise given recent
work in the philosophy of language.
Certainly, George Lakoff and Mark
Johnson's (2003) seminal work, *Metaphors
We Live By*, helped scholars across academic discourses gain a greater appreciation for the vital, central role of metaphor
in human cognition and communication.

In Lakoff and Johnson's framework,
metaphor is constructed of a source and
target domain. The source domain is one
in which the communicating agents are
assumed to be familiar (or at least to share
knowledge of certain relative characteristics) while the target domain is the less
familiar area, where understanding can be
increased via association with the source
domain. The act of communicating in
metaphor is an invitation to the receiver
to consider the less familiar in terms of
the more familiar. The familiar aspects of
the source domain are its entailments.
The entailments inherent in metaphoric
expressions mean that certain aspects of
the target domain are highlighted while
others are hidden.

To say that the internet is a library or a
town square are metaphorical constructions that involve key entailments of a
source domain (library, town square) that
the receiver of the message can then map
on to the target domain (the internet). In
the case of cyberspace, the entailments of
this source domain, other than that it is
some form of space, do not emerge from
common experience. People derive their
sense of the meaning of cyberspace from
its usage in popular culture, mass media,
and other extant discourses.

The cyberspace metaphor has had a
tortuous history. While the word as first
used was associated with freedom, independence, and new frontiers (Barlow,
1996; Post and Johnson, 2006), its overt
spatial entailments came to be seen as
playing into the hands of established
interests and the march of global capitalism (Cohen, 2007). Far too often, from
the perspective of some, courts have
tended to oppose the treatment of cyberspace locales as equivalent to spaces in the
material world, in part because it might
subject service providers to additional
burdens under equal accommodations laws
(*Access Now* v. *Southwest Airlines*, 2002).
Today, the term seems to have lost much
of its power (both positive and negative)
and is instead just one of the words one
might pull from a thesaurus to avoid the
stylistic *faux pas* of repeating the word
internet or network one too many times.

Metaphor as a twin-edged sword

There is considerable disagreement in the
legal literature as to the specific role of
metaphor in the development of cyberspace. Hunter (2001) suggests that metaphor, when used to understand the
internet, often clouds and constrains the
thinking of the court. McGowan (2005),
however, through careful readings of the
cyber-trespass case law, makes a compelling

351

counter-argument that judges are more sophisticated in their reasoning than the metaphoric blinders' criticism suggests. Further, as McGowan (2005: 4) points out, focusing exclusively on metaphorical constraint "trivializes judicial opinions without engaging them."

While McGowan is persuasive, Balganesh (2006) shows us that jurists can still be led astray. This can happen when a chain of case decisions, beginning with instrumental, rather than truly conceptual uses of metaphor, becomes locked into a conceptual path that ends up corrupting the core concepts along the way. Deference to precedents activated by familiar metaphors means that discursive course corrections become more and more difficult. This outcome is quite clear in the case of decisions regarding the definition of property and trespass as they relate to intangibles (Balganesh, 2006: 316).

The troubles, according to Balganesh (2006: 282–3), began in earnest when a court needed to provide a rationale to justify its attempt to curb the actions of spammers.

The *CompuServe* court reasoned that electronic interference with a server could be equated with a tangible invasion, and thus it was appropriate to apply the doctrine of trespass to transactions in cyberspace. The rhetorical stance selected by the court was not without consequence for subsequent cases involving troublesome access and use of internet resources. In his view, the "doctrinal ambiguities and inconsistencies" that have followed the *CompuServe* decision (Balganesh, 2006: 267) may make recovering from its discursive mis-steps exceedingly difficult due to the nature of associated path dependencies.

Metaphoric dominance and distortion

The fact that metaphors both highlight and hide has led to much criticism of particularly dominant legal metaphors such as the "marketplace of ideas" (Ingber, 1984). The phrase, first coined by Justice Holmes in his dissenting opinion in the 1919 case *Abrams* v. *United States,* has become the dominant metaphor in free speech cases. On the other hand, although the importance of the marketplace of ideas metaphor is beyond debate, its actual impact on legal discourse is harder to gauge. Cass Sunstein (1993) has criticized the metaphor for what it hides, for obscuring important aspects of free speech in a democracy. In his view, "Aggregative or marketplace notions disregard the extent to which political outcomes are supposed to depend on discussion and debate, or a commitment to political equality, and on the reasons offered for or against alternatives" (Sunstein, 1993: 249).

Philip Napoli's (1999) examination of the use of the marketplace metaphor in the Federal Communications Commision (FCC) policy discourse over a period of 33 years showed that it had been used with two very distinct sets of entailments in mind: the economic dimension, which Sunstein criticizes above, and the democratic theory dimension, which is much more focused on the role of free speech in democratic self-government.

Napoli's analysis suggests that the FCC has not consistently associated specific kinds of regulatory policy-making with particular interpretations of the marketplace of ideas concept. Thus, although this metaphor typically has been used to justify deregulation of the communications industry, these decisions have been predicated almost as much upon democratic theory principles as they have upon the goal of promoting economic efficiency and consumer satisfaction (Napoli, 1999:164).

Napoli's observations help to underscore a number of key issues that arise in the study of metaphor and legal discourse.

How does metaphor affect legal reasoning? What motivates its use? How does metaphor help jurists to understand new and unfamiliar legal contexts? In what cases can metaphor constrain reasoning in ways that negatively impact the public interest?

The strategic use of metaphor

In order to answer these questions, we must first recognize that metaphors are instrumental resources, used strategically by plaintiffs, defendants, and a host of interested parties in an effort to influence the outcome of a court's deliberation. These discursive resources are deployed at critical moments through well-established channels and means that include briefs, direct testimony, and the majority and dissenting opinions of the court.

Courts (and judges) issue finely crafted opinions that are woven throughout with analogies and metaphors that have been selected because of their likely effect in making judicial reasoning available to others as both justification and guidance (Berger, 2002). When, as is quite likely in the case of cyberspace transgressions, there are competing doctrines that are arguably relevant to the facts at hand, opinions are likely to make use of a metaphor that foregrounds a particular doctrine that supports a preferred behavioral or policy outcome (Cass, 1995). A carefully constructed opinion that uses a familiar, or an especially powerful, metaphor to justify a particular doctrinal choice allows the court to appear principled, when it may in fact be pursuing a political end (Tiller and Cross, 2005).

Friends of the court (amici) are active, and increasingly important, participants in appellate decision-making (Kearney and Merrill, 2000). Their involvement is limited primarily to the provision of formal arguments, or amicus briefs. The nature of the interests that amici might pursue are quite varied, but they include the defense of institutional interests, such as those represented by members of some professional group such as librarians or engineers. On occasion, members of Congress or representatives of administrative agencies offer briefs in support of prior decisions that have been challenged.

Paul Collins (2006) suggests that the arguments presented by pressure groups have had a measurable impact on the policy decisions reported by the Supreme Court. Amici play a role in the courts similar to that played by lobbyists seeking to influence the legislature—they provide information, including information about the preferences of other interested parties and the public more generally (Spriggs and Wahlbeck, 1997). While the informational component of amicus briefs often contains "alternative and reframed legal arguments," what Collins (2006: 11) sees as particularly important is the way these arguments are used to illustrate the "broader social ramifications of the case."

While the influence of amicus briefs is difficult to determine precisely, in part as a function of the nature of the dependent measures chosen by analysts (Songer and Sheehan, 1993), as well as by a rather dramatic increase in the number of amicus briefs being submitted, most observers conclude that the ideological bias of the courts determines the extent to which a court will highlight arguments drawn from an amicus brief (Kearney and Merrill, 2000). Indeed, legal scholars suggest that when a court is politically unified, even established legal doctrine will be ignored if it is in conflict with the policy preferences of the court's majority (Tiller and Cross, 2005).

Property versus liberty interests

Among the more troublesome issues in the development of cyberspace law and policy is the nature of property, and the meaning of property rights as they relate to theft, unauthorized access, or trespass (Loughlan, 2006). Conflicts over objects and interactions in cyberspace tend to arise as individuals and institutions seeking to protect their interests come to define those interests in terms of property (Radin, 2006).

In order to convince the courts that property rights in information, or in the infrastructures that enable the exploitation of those rights have been abridged, plaintiffs have to establish parallels between crimes against property in the material world and crimes against property in cyberspace (Lipton, 2004).

A difficult problem of representation emerges in those cases where the theft or misappropriation of property is based on unauthorized access to some facility. Here, the challenge is to describe this property in such as way as to make the law of trespass seem appropriate. Within the common law in the United States, important distinctions have been made between trespass to real property and trespass to chattels (McGowan, 2005).

Often in cases in which the nature of the link between tangible property and theft is difficult to establish, petitioners will deploy metaphors that they hope will influence the characterization of those charged with misbehavior. Persons who derive benefit from the creative labor of others are compared with those who would "reap without sowing." Such a construction is less menacing than the image of lawless and dangerous criminals that is evoked by reference to pirates (Loughlan, 2006: 218). Nissenbaum (2004:199) identifies recent decisions by the courts as contributing to the characterization of hackers as the "white-collar criminals and terrorists of the Information Age." Because they have been constructed rhetorically as criminals, it is difficult for the uninvolved and uninformed to treat cases of hactivism as

being similar to other forms of civil disobedience (Kreimer, 2001), or to accept well-publicized hacks of supposedly secure systems as a form of whistle-blowing (Jordan and Taylor, 1998: 773).

Another difficulty in cases involving crimes against property is the demonstration and assessment of the harm caused to the plaintiff or the plaintiff's interests. The problems involved in this determination are quite substantial when the property is intangible, or the harm or loss is speculative or potential, rather than documented. Still, we find courts willing to grant that a plaintiff has met the requisite demonstration of harm even when the burden is as insignificant as an increase in the number of electrons flowing through a system, some temporary loss of the full functionality of a server, or the distraction of otherwise productive workers by unauthorized e-mail (*Intel Corp.* v. *Hamidi*, 2003). The courts' assessments of these burdens are rarely based upon any readily agreeable standard of measure; instead they reflect the courts' evaluation of the relative worth of an imagined class of victims and the agents who might cause them harm. Well-chosen metaphors help to establish and reinforce the impressions that their sponsors desire.

The tyranny of perspective: internal versus external

The ways in which a court might interpret the facts of a particular cyberspace case may depend upon whether the discourse focuses on the ways in which users perceive their interactions or transactions, or on the ways in which an engineer might describe them. A users' perspective might reflect a kind of virtual reality that can be readily distinguished from the physical reality of computers, peripherals, and network infrastructure. Orin Kerr (2003: 357) labels these two perspectives internal and external, and he suggests:

"many of the disputes within the field of 'cyberlaw' boil down to clashes between internal and external perspectives."

As Kerr (2003) observes, judges and other participants move easily between internal and external perspectives, depending upon the nature of the argument they seek to make. He suggests that in our efforts to apply the laws of the physical world to those of the virtual world we tend to look for analogies or metaphors that support the application of particular doctrines. On the other hand, those who oppose constraints on the imagined freedoms of cyberspace challenge the appropriateness of those metaphors (Froomkin, 1995). Legal scholars, such as Lawrence Lessig, who frequently intervene as friends of the court, often reveal well-established preferences for one perspective over another. Kerr (2003: 374) identifies Lessig's famous declaration that "Code is law" as the basis for his belief that "because external code is internal law, we should regulate external code from an internal perspective."

We are not in a position to suggest which perspectives should determine the outcome of cases and the future of cyberspace; instead we seek to characterize the ways in which these perspectives, inherent in the metaphors chosen to convey them, have been used strategically by the competing interests that come before the court.

Central cases and their metaphors

We have identified three cases that we believe mark critically important turning points in the path-dependent development of cyberspace. We have also been attracted to these cases because of the ways in which the deployment of metaphors reflects fundamental tensions between property and liberty interests.

The judges who decide these cases arguably seek to achieve an appropriate balance between the interests of property holders and a host of other interests and values that are placed at risk as property rights are extended or reinforced. We understand many of these risks as threats to freedom and autonomy. We see the search for a morally and politically defensible balance between property and liberty interests as being at the heart of the judicial construction of cyberspace. We review these cases in chronological order because each provides a framework against which the subsequent cases are likely to be compared.

Universal City Studios v. Reimerdes: *hyperlinks as the ties that bind*

We examined the case of *Universal City Studios v. Reimerdes* (2000) because of the ways in which a fundamental feature of cyberspace navigation was explicitly challenged. The U.S. Court of Appeals affirmed the decision of a lower court that barred the publication of a computer program, or the provision of hypertext links to other websites publishing the program because of its likely use for copyright infringement.

The *Reimerdes* (later *Corley*) case attracted a large number of amici representing both property and liberty interests (*Universal City Studios* v. *Corley*, 2001). First Amendment interests were involved because the defendant, Eric Corley, was a publisher whose website often contained material related to stories printed in his magazine. In this particular case, the site included a copy of the decryption program, DeCSS, so named because it was routinely used to circumvent CSS, the software that the motion picture industry was using to prevent unauthorized viewing and copying of its films. Corley's site also included links to other websites that had posted the program. Following a decision by the District Court in NY to grant an injunction against Corley, he appealed to the 2nd Circuit. Although the Court explicitly recognized the complex policy concerns that required the balancing of access and fair use aspects of communications and technology policy against copyright interests, they chose to sidestep these issues and define the provision of hyperlinks as the equivalent of trafficking in dangerous contraband.

There were two ways in which hyperlinks were discussed within the courts. One, which we would characterize as an internal construction, emphasized the transportation of the user to some place; the other, which was also presented from the users' (internal) perspective, emphasized the transportation of text, or image, or in this case a computer program, to the user. External constructions focused on the actions of users, and the technology involved in the transfer. In noting the distinction, the Circuit Court revisited the explanation offered by the District Court judge:

> In applying the DMCA to linking (via hyperlinks), Judge Kaplan recognized, as he had with DeCSS code, that a hyperlink has both a speech and a nonspeech component. It conveys information, the internet address of the linked web page, and has the functional capacity to bring the content of the linked web page to the user's computer screen (or, as Judge Kaplan put it, to "take one almost instantaneously to the desired location").
>
> (*Universal City Studios* v. *Corley*, 2001: 455–6)

The American Civil Liberties Union (ACLU) and its colleagues offered an extended metaphor describing the internet as "a vast library" where "links serve as both its card catalog and its digital footnotes"

(ACLU *et al.*, 2001: 21–2). The brief also suggested "linking effectively ties the entire web together into a single interconnected body of knowledge made up of all individually published web pages of different users around the world." Like many of the participating computer scientists, these amici sought to challenge the court's arguments regarding functionality by suggesting that if an annotated bible and Thomas Acquinas' commentaries were shelved near each other on a library's shelves, this enhanced access should somehow lessen the constitutional protection that those commentaries would ordinarily have enjoyed (ACLU *et al.*, 2001: 22–4). They also challenged the court's assertion that linking to a site with the DeCSS program was the "functional equivalent" of providing the program more directly.

The U.S. government also saw this case as being of particular importance, and participated as an intervenor in support of copyright interests. The government's brief repeated the district court's evocation of an internally oriented transportation metaphor to characterize the function of hyperlinks as a way to "transfer the user to another web page." In the government's view, the "sole function of a link is to 'take one almost instantaneously to the desired destination (on the internet) with the mere click of an electronic mouse" (United States, 2001: 60–1).

On the other hand, the government rejected the characterization of code as speech, suggesting instead that hyperlinks are "the technological bridges that connect different internet websites for myriad purposes." Further they argued that for "those who use internet links to join with others who share their beliefs, the act of linking might be said to constitute association in cyberspace" (United States, 2001: 64). By emphasizing the associative function of hyperlinks, the government sought to invoke the application of First

Amendment principles that relate to associational contact, rather than speech and the press. Arguably this was because associations whose purpose is unlawful would not enjoy the same level of constitutional protection as the speech of those whose views are merely unpopular.

The Court noted that the defendants and their allies focused on speech, while assiduously avoiding consideration of the functional aspects of hyperlinks. In discussing this transparently strategic use of metaphor and analogy, the Court noted that the:

> Appellants' supplemental papers enthusiastically embraced the arguable analogy between printing bookstore addresses and displaying on a web page links to websites at which DeCSS may be accessed. ... Like many analogies posited to illuminate legal issues, the bookstore analogy is helpful primarily in identifying characteristics that distinguish it from the context of the pending dispute
> (*Universal City Studios* v. *Corley*, 2001: 457)

For the Court, the distinction that mattered was that the "digital world" ensured that "the materials are available for instantaneous worldwide distribution before any preventive measures can be effectively taken" (*Universal City Studios* v. *Corley*, 2001: 457).

Despite its implications for First Amendment interests and concerns, this Court acted to defend copyright interests against what it came to see as a never-ending series of technologically enabled threats.

United States *v.* American Libraries Association: *filtering the public sphere*

The second case we have selected differs in critical ways from the other two because its fundamental conflict over cyberspace technology pits public libraries against the federal government, and does not directly involve a struggle over exploitative rights.

In its long-term struggle to erect fences or technological barriers that would prevent children from gaining access to pornography or other dangerous content, the U.S. Congress sought to require libraries to install filters that would screen out objectionable material with the Children's Internet Protection Act 2000 (CIPA). The American Library Association (ALA) argued that the imposition of a filtering requirement was an unconstitutional limit on the rights of adult users of the library. While the ALA had been successful in convincing a District Court that internet access in a library was a public forum, and therefore entitled to substantial First Amendment protections, the Supreme Court majority was not so easily persuaded.

The metaphoric struggles in this case were focused on the characterization of a public library's activities with regard to the internet. The first, and perhaps most important, issue was the extent to which the provision of internet access for its clients was the same as, or equivalent to, the establishment of a public forum. The second issue was related to a comparison of filtering with other routine decisions about which books and periodicals the library would acquire for the benefit of its clients.

The majority argued that the provision of internet access did not create a designated public forum because libraries did not introduce internet terminals to "create a public forum for web publishers to express themselves, any more than it collects books in order to provide a public forum for the authors of books to speak" or to "encourage a diversity of views from private speakers." They agreed with Congress that the internet was "no more than a technological extension of the book stack" (*U.S.* v. *ALA*, 2003: 206–7).

With regard to petitioner's arguments about the lack of discretion over which websites would be blocked or screened out, the majority focused on the rapidly evolving character of the internet, and the virtual impossibility of librarians making informed decisions about which content to block. What really mattered to the majority, however, was whether the use of blocking software could be equated with other decisions that libraries made about their collections. The majority held that "a library's decision to use filtering software is a collection decision, not a restraint on private speech" (*U.S. v. ALA*, 2003: 209).

In their dissents, Justices Souter and Ginsburg engaged the distinction between decisions about which materials to acquire, and the blocking of content from all of the library's public terminals. Their rejection of equivalence is explicit and extensive:

> At every significant point, however, the internet blocking here defies comparison to the process of acquisition. ... deciding against buying a book means there is no book ... but blocking the internet is merely blocking access purchased in its entirety ... The proper analogy therefore is not to passing up a book that might have been bought; it is either to buying a book and then keeping it from adults lacking an acceptable "purpose," or to buying an encyclopedia and then cutting out pages with anything thought to be unsuitable for all adults.
>
> (*U.S. v. ALA*, 2003: 236–7).

Although neither Souter nor Ginsburg credit any of the amici for the metaphors they use in their dissent, the core of their argument can be found in the brief submitted by the American Publishers Association:

> CIPA takes such decisions away from libraries and delegates them to software filtering companies whose proprietary criteria for blocking material are completely hidden from public scrutiny. This is in no way analogous to a decision by libraries to acquire a book on Mark Twain rather than one on rap music, for example. It is, instead, analogous to the scissoring by a government contractor of important articles from a magazine to which the library subscribes and to which library patrons expect full access.
>
> (APA, 2003: 3)

The majority appears to have been convinced, or at least supported by the metaphoric constructions included in the brief submitted by the state of Texas, and from a group of legislators who had sponsored the original legislation.

As a counter to the criticism of the imprecision of available filters, the legislative supporters of CIPA suggested that: "The fundamental question presented, then, is whether public libraries, merely by providing internet access, are constitutionally required to relinquish all editorial discretion over what is permitted in the library ... simply because current technology does not permit them to exclude such material with mathematical precision" (Lott *et al.*, 2003: 4).

The court majority based its rejection of the public forum designation on an assumption about the kinds of discretion that librarians, like public broadcasters, have to exercise over what to acquire and make available to the public. The fact that requiring librarians to delegate that responsibility to third-party vendors of blocking software would have the same effect apparently did not give the majority pause. The majority also rejected the public forum designation because the internet, as a novel resource, could not be equated with public parks and sidewalks because "the doctrines surrounding traditional public forums may not be extended to situations where such history is lacking" (*U.S.* v. *ALA*, 2003: 206).

The majority also appeared concerned that there was some risk involved in their application of the public forum doctrine to the internet so early in its development, because of the implications of such a doctrinal shift for future decisions. They expressed this concern early in the process through a series of pointed questions about other settings in which the public forum designation might or might not be applied. The response of the ALA's representative, while on point, was apparently not sufficient to satisfy the court's majority:

> Well, Your Honor, if you allow the Government to define its forum as all content under the sun ... ever invented by mankind except the piece that they don't like, then I submit that ... will be the end of the public forum doctrine because there will never be any situation in which the Government will be constrained in any way to censor out a particular piece of content ... from the public forum.
>
> (Smith, 2003: 35–6)

The metaphors and analogies that dominated the discussion in the *U.S.* v. *ALA* case were almost entirely internal, reflecting the views of internet users. Although there was some attention paid to the mechanics of blocking, the fact that this technology was proprietary served to limit discussion to the consequences, rather than the details of its use, and the fact that no one had "presented any clearly superior or better fitting alternative" (*U.S.* v. *ALA*, 2003: 219).

MGM *v.* Grokster: *safe havens and the engineer's crystal ball*

This final case involved a set of decisions with the potential to shape the future of network technology. The U.S. Supreme Court rejected the decision of a lower court and created great uncertainty about the extent to which software distributors could be held liable for contributory infringement, despite the fact that their network resources could be used for substantial and socially important non-infringing uses (*MGM* v. *Grokster*, 2005). The case was seen as challenging an earlier and more liberal doctrine established by the *Sony* court (*Sony* v. *Universal City*, 1984). Without the benefit of the doubt previously granted to new information technology by *Sony*, many saw the future for technological innovation as far more unsettled and uncertain.

Of all the cases we examined, this intellectual property case drew the highest level of involvement by friends of the court. Fifty-five amicus briefs were filed, and the greatest proportion of these briefs (47.2 percent) supported the respondents (Grokster *et al.*) or the lower court's favorable decision rejecting the charge of contributory infringement.

Briefs were presented by coalitions of academics, representing a variety of disciplines from intellectual property law to media studies and computer science. Briefs were also presented by coalitions of authors, music publishers, broadcasters, motion picture studios, as well as venture capitalists, and telecommunications service firms. Public interest organizations on the right and the left formed a loose coalition in support of the respondents, while the U.S. government submitted a brief in support of MGM. A coalition of 39 state governments, excluding California, also supported the copyright interests. They were joined by a group of high-profile economists including Kenneth Arrow, Gary Becker, William Landes, and Steven Levitt who charged the lower courts with encouraging inefficiency in markets (Arrow *et al.*, 2005: 7–8).

Information service providers used a variety of metaphors to describe the status of a market in which a cloud of uncertainty hung over its participants. Where advocates of free speech were likely to talk about the chilling effect of a court's decision, investors and venture capitalists tended to talk about the risky and dangerous environment for entrepreneurs. Representatives of the copyright industries offered similarly gloomy images of the economic landscape they would face in the future without a favorable decision by the court.

Grokster amici frequently challenged the accuracy of the doomsday scenarios offered by their opponents. In its brief, the National Venture Capitalist Association (NVCA) accused the entertainment industry of "crying wolf for a century, ever since John Philip Sousa claimed that the player piano spelled the end of music in America" (NVCA, 2005: 11). They suggest that the industry is "like the drunk searching for his key under the street lamp because the light is there" when they "focus their attacks on the inventors, investors, and entrepreneurs who create the technologies that make the many acts of infringement so easy to commit" rather than on those who actually infringe (NVCA, 2005:14).

Because the *Grokster* case was so fundamentally concerned about the making of unauthorized copies, it was in the interest of those seeking to avoid restrictions on the use peer-to-peer (P2P) technology to underscore the fact that digital technology in general, and the internet in particular functioned by making copies. They relied upon metaphors and analogies based on an external perspective in order to inform the court about how this technology actually worked. They argued that the current operation of the internet could not be imagined without widespread copying.

The brief from the Intel Corporation reminded the court that "to access information from a book, one opens the book.

But information stored digitally can be accessed only by copying it from stored memory … " (Intel Corp., 2005: 22). In the oral arguments phase of the case, Grokster's representative, Richard Taranto, suggested that nearly every component of the infrastructure, and nearly every participant in the process of internet communication make digital copies. He concluded that the challenge for the court was determining just "which pieces, if any, and under what standard, get singled out for a judicially fashioned secondary copyright liability doctrine" (Taranto, 2005: 36).

The proposed tests that would determine whether a new technology was capable of substantial non-infringing uses came in for numerous pointed critiques. Intel suggested that the test would "require an innovator to have a crystal ball" because it would "require innovators to anticipate often unforeseeable infringing uses to which their inventions … might be put" (Intel Corp., 2005: 16–17).

The antidote to uncertainty among innovators and entrepreneurs was thought to reside in the *safe harbor* that *Sony*, "the 'Magna Carta' of the information technology industry" had established (Intellectual Property Professors, 2005: 10). Although the motion picture and copyright industry petitioners argued for a revision of the *Sony* safe harbor, with a standard more in line with that established by the Digital Millennium Copyright Act (DMCA) (MGM Reply Brief, 2005: 12), the Court was not yet ready to take that step. Although Justices Ginsburg and Breyer joined their colleagues in reversing the lower court's decision on the basis of evident criminal intent, they divided their colleagues with regard to the nature of the evidence that there was, or could be substantial non-infringing usage of P2P technology. Justices Breyer, Stevens, and O'Connor expressed support for the more forward looking meaning of "capable," while the conservative majority seemed ready to condemn the technology on the basis of its early troublesome use (*MGM* v. *Grokster*, 2005).

Conclusion

In 1997, the Supreme Court rejected the Communications Decency Act as a tenable solution of the problem of children gaining access to pornography (*Reno* v. *ACLU*, 1997) in part because its survival also depended upon compelling demonstrations of awareness and intent on the part of likely defendants. More critically, the barriers to access that it would establish threatened the future of cyberspace. Indeed, the court expressed the belief that if the CDA were allowed to stand, they would be doing more than "burning the house to roast the pig"; their inaction would threaten to "torch a large segment of the internet community" (*Reno* v. *ACLU*, 1997. 882). The internet was too new, and potentially too important to the emerging information economy for the Court to allow it to be placed at risk in this way.

In 2003, however, the court approved the government's alternative (CIPA), despite the obvious flaws in its technology. They did so in part because of the identity and character of its behavioral target: the nation's public librarians. Despite charges of imprecision by amici and dissenting justices, the majority offered a tortured definition of informed choice to justify the installation of a technological fence. In claiming that a decision to use filtering technology was a collection decision, the court majority engaged in strategic misdirection: first by ignoring the fact that the use of filters was a requirement of funding, and a delegation of decision-making to the providers of filtering software, and second, by limiting the definition of speech to expression, ignoring the public's interest in access to information.

We observed greater consistency in the appellate courts when the contending interests could be defined more clearly. The battle of good against evil set the copyright industry against pirates and those who would assist them. In its defense of copyright interests, the Court of Appeals upheld a lower court's decision to ban the direct and indirect provision of software that could be used to gain unauthorized access to commercial media content. While there was considerable academic interest surrounding the extent to which computer software was speech, and therefore entitled to greater protection, the courts' decisions were primarily based on the ways in which this speech actually functioned in cyberspace.

The courts' commitment to defending copyright interests, however, would not be well served by an emphasis on an engineer's understanding of hypertext. Instead, the Court of Appeals focused on the ways in which either users, or the content of interest to users, could be transported around the globe well before the publishers or legitimate content distributors could act to defend their property interests. In the *Reimerdes* case, the courts were little swayed by the efforts of amici to define the court's ruling as imprecise, and a threat to the future of cyberspace. The court was willing to risk weakening the central infrastructure of global network in order to reinforce the links in copyrights' virtual fence.

In the *Grokster* case, the determination of the court to defend copyright interests against the threat of cyberspace technology led them not only to overturn the decision of a lower court, but also to invite a frontal assault on established precedent at the highest level. In one sense, we might understand the driving force behind the challenge to P2P technology as an attempt to mine the safe harbor for innovators that *Sony* had provided.

Rather than rejecting *Sony* directly, however, the *Grokster* court argued that the lower court misunderstood its meaning. Future courts will determine the meaning of *Sony's* safe harbor unless a revision of the DMCA by the legislature provides a more agreeable solution to the conflict between the copyright industries and the developers of cyberspace.

On the horizon, battles over the commoditization of personal, especially transaction-generated, information will be fought using some of the metaphors that have been field tested in the cases we have reviewed in this chapter. More will be required.

Given the role of the legal fiction of property in protecting personal privacy in the course of U.S. history, it is still worth attending to the concept of property in the hopes of affecting some form of course correction within the courts. Approaches to privacy that construct it as an ongoing process of boundary negotiation rather than a stable condition or social good to be conserved (Margulis, 2003) have not gained much traction within political economy or surveillance studies. At the same time as communication and social practice increasingly shift to the electronic, networked world, people lose both the legal and physical affordances of privacy that have been associated with real property. Yet, as Balganesh (2006) has shown, the courts have been reluctant to create any new doctrines of online territoriality that would extend the concept of real property and the private spaces it affords to the internet.

It will not be easy to construct a new language of the online boundary, yet we cannot ignore a growing sense that we have somehow lost our ability to negotiate our personal boundaries. The resources we once had, in particular the walls, windows, doors, and fences of our private spaces, no longer hold sway, as it were, in cyberspace. This is a problem desperately in need of scholarly attention.

Guide to further reading

For those interested in further exploring the nature of metaphor and analogy from a range of disciplinary perspectives, Ortony's (1993) edited book is a good start. Within cognitive science, Fauconnier and Turner's (2003) work on conceptual blending offers a rigorous theoretical model that explains how the juxtaposition of dissimilar concepts can generate powerful insights and fuel the evolution of language.

Blavin and Cohen (2002) provide a useful chronological overview of three dominant internet metaphors: information superhighway, internet as novel space (cyberspace), and internet as real space. Work by Hunter (2003) and Lemley (2003) provide important and oft-cited critiques of the use of spatial metaphors in internet law, in particular how the cyberspace as place metaphor and its application to trespass to chattels doctrine has enabled a second enclosure movement, a period of expanding property interests that Heller (1988) has called an "anticommons." Benoliel (2005) takes a different approach to the issue of space and property online, suggesting the construction of online locales as a legal fiction could more easily facilitate the translation of territorial privacy rights to the internet. Cohen (2007) moves beyond the debates about what cyberspace is, and instead focuses on the social construction of the term and the emergent, contested relationship between embodied space and networked space.

Lessig's (1999, 2001, 2004) series of books provides the most thorough introduction to the dangers of the copyright regime and the increasing propertization and commoditization of information, in particular its negative impact on creativity, innovation, and culture. Benkler (2006) offers a detailed picture of the emerging structure of the "networked information economy" and demonstrates how its productivity and value can and does flourish without proprietary rights in the information it produces. While technically not a metaphor, Zittrain's (2006) new turn of phrase, the "generative internet," is rife with linguistic entailments that challenge well-established assumptions about the open architecture of the internet and its support for the production and diffusion of innovations.

26

Globalizing the logic of openness

Open source software and the global governance of intellectual property

Christopher May

In an age of so-called global information abundance, disputes over intellectual property are central to politics. This chapter explores the tension and conflicts between openness and property in the realm of computer software. First, the context of global governance that underpins the making of knowledge and information into property is established as the global political economic background to this increasingly important issue. The chapter then sets out the impact these political structures have had on the realm of digital technologies and the internet. The discussion focuses on the development and utilization of free and open source software as a reaction to the attempts by information capitalists to control their (now digitized) knowledge assets through the deployment of digital rights management technologies. Although this conflict between openness and ownership is often depicted as taking place predominantly in North America and Europe (the developed areas of the global system), it is developing in much more important ways in sub-Saharan Africa and elsewhere in the developing world, where the fruits of the information revolution have yet to be fully enjoyed. The chapter concludes that the fight to establish open digital systems is central to the global political economy.

However one might view the claims about the arrival of the information age, it seems clear that more people than ever before are aware of the existence (and importance) of intellectual property rights (IPRs). In this chapter I seek to briefly establish the context of global governance that underpins the making of knowledge and information into property, and explain the impact these political structures have had on the realm of digital technologies and the internet. This leads me to focus on the development and utilization of free and open source software as a reaction to the attempts by information capitalists to control their knowledge assets through digital rights

management technologies. Although this conflict between openness and ownership is often depicted as taking place predominantly in North America and Europe, its more profound impact can be found in sub-Saharan Africa and elsewhere in the developing world.

More generally, I will suggest that the attempts at the beginning of this new millennium to continue or even expand control over information through commoditization and digital rights management have engendered a political response that we can call "openness." While IPRs are unlikely to wither away any time soon, a social balance is being (re)established between property and openness; these are not unconnected and separate realms, but rather encompass a range of political positions about how we should value and exchange knowledge and information, and the services and products dependent to a large part upon them.

The nature of intellectual property rights

The most important role of IPRs is in the formal construction of scarcity—where none necessarily exists—in matters related to knowledge and information use. Unlike material things, knowledge and information are not necessarily rivalrous. Coincidental usage does not detract from utility. With certain exceptions, such as the use of trademarks to identify makers of goods, the deployment of knowledge and information resources by multiple users does not reduce their usefulness, nor does it diminish the quality or quantity of such resources. In this sense, usually knowledge, before it is made property, does not exhibit the characteristics of material things before they are made property: knowledge is not naturally scarce in the same way materially existing things are. Where there are information asymmetries, advantage may be gained by keeping information "scarce" (i.e., reducing its circulation), but this seldom serves the wider social good. Thus, because it is difficult to extract a price for the use of non-rival knowledge goods, a legal form of scarcity—intellectual property—is introduced.

Although predicated on the notion of individual creators' and innovators' rights, most IPRs are owned and exploited not by innovating individuals but by commercial enterprises. Moreover, many of the rights intellectual property is intended to establish are not the freedoms for an individual owner to do something or not

to have something done to them, but rather the "right" to halt certain rights-infringing behavior by others. Intellectual property rights establish the right of owners to halt the actions of others at a distance, even when such actions produce no actual loss to the *social* utility for owners. Infringements of IPRs *can* have a commercial impact, but this is not always obviously the case. While limitations on use imposed by IPRs have always been constrained by the assertion of public benefits in most IPR legislation, the remaining enforceable rights still have a significant effect on the freedom of action of others. For example, there is a clear tension between the rights of AIDS patients to receive life-extending treatment and the rights of multinational pharmaceutical companies to receive financial rewards for the utilization of their patents to produce those medicines when patients or their governments cannot afford the price demanded by patent holders for their drugs.

Given that this is a state of affairs that non-owners of intellectual property might resist, especially when this is related to vast differences in wealth, the developed countries, who own and control most of the world's IPRs, have spent much diplomatic effort establishing a global governance regime to protect the rights of the corporations domiciled in their countries, on a global scale. Before turning to the impact of IPRs and the open alternatives, I shall briefly introduce the intellectual property governance regime that has been established in the last decades.

The global governance of intellectual property

Since 1995, IPRs have been subject to the Trade Related Aspects of Intellectual Property Rights (TRIPs) agreement overseen by the World Trade Organization

(WTO). The agreement represents an undertaking by members of the WTO to uphold certain minimum standards of protection for IPRs and to provide legal mechanisms for their enforcement. To be clear: the TRIPs agreement is not a model law that must be adopted by national legislation, nor an international law that directly enforces IPRs; rather it requires that national legislation must produce the enforcement effects that the agreement sets out. However, and most importantly, the WTO's stringent dispute-settlement mechanism encompasses international disputes about IPRs, and can be used to ensure national laws *do* bring about the effects required. Prior to 1995, there were longstanding multilateral treaties for the international recognition and protection of IPRs, overseen by the World Intellectual Property Organization (WIPO) (May and Sell, 2005; May, 2007). However, the governments of the U.S. and various members of the EU, as well as many multinational corporations (MNCs) based in these countries, regarded these agreements as toothless in the face of "piracy" and infringement. This prompted a number of MNCs to play a major role in the negotiations that resulted in the inclusion of the TRIPs agreement within the structure of the WTO (Sell, 2003: 96–120). These companies therefore had a significant impact on the rights supported by the TRIPs agreement, and it is no surprise that the TRIPs agreement's conception of information (as noted in the title of the agreement itself) is "trade related."

The TRIPs agreement builds on principles that are central to the WTO: national treatment; most-favored nation (MFN) treatment; and reciprocity. Although reciprocity does little to change the intellectual property regime (due to a long history of bilateral arrangements), the introduction of MFN (under article 4 of TRIPs) has transformed the international

governance of IPRs. This treatment ensures that any agreement in favor of a specific country must be extended to *all* other trading partners. Previously, under the auspices of WIPO, a diverse group of conventions with different sets of signatories shaped the international relations of intellectual property, alongside a complex pattern of bilateral treaties. Now, under TRIPs, and due to MFN, all undertakings apply to all members of the WTO. Furthermore, favoritism accorded domestic inventors or prospective owners of IPRs relative to non-nationals is halted; national treatment (article 3 of TRIPs) stipulates that foreign individuals and companies must be treated no worse than domestic companies. This is an important shift as many national IPR systems had previously favored domestic "owners" either through legislative or procedural means.

Overall the TRIPs agreement facilitates a significant international extension of the rights of the owners of intellectual property. Although the TRIPs agreement is a complex and wide-ranging multilateral instrument, here I shall only focus on aspects of the governance of IPRs that are related to computer software, as this has a direct relevance to the political economy of the internet and the expansion of "openness" as a political movement being discussed here.

Despite calls for a "new world information and communication order" in the 1980s, during the Uruguay Round of multilateral trade negotiations the full potential of the internet had not yet been fully appreciated. While this round of negotiations, concluding in 1994 with an agreement to establish the WTO, did establish a number of mechanisms that developing countries could deploy to counter the domination and economic power of the richest countries in global markets, this shift was notably absent in intellectual property, especially as related to digital technologies (May and Sell, 2005: chapter seven). Indeed, for many national negotiating teams the issue of intellectual property was seen more as an item for horse-trading and bargaining in the overall trade negotiation rather than anything that would have an immediate impact on a country's ability to access and use technologies to pursue both development and social welfare. However, since the establishment of the WTO, with TRIPs as one of the key elements of the "single undertaking" required by all members in the wake of the final settlement of the Uruguay Round, the control of software through IPRs has become a much more evident concern for developing countries seeking to utilize new information and communications technologies, and for those in the developed countries who reject the commoditization of software and information or knowledge more generally.

Like other elements of the TRIPs agreement, the spur towards a multilateral governance settlement for the protection of IPRs in software was initiated by U.S. corporations. In 1980 the U.S. Congress passed the Copyright Act that defined software programs as literary works, and protected them through copyright, including operating systems, their object, and source code. This entrenched a view of software as an individualized creative process (amenable to commoditization), and willfully ignored the collective processes of software development that until then had been prevalent in the industry (Halbert, 1999: 52–4). The difficulty of fitting software into traditional modes of copyright subsequently suggested to some companies that patent protection might better serve their needs. Thus, in the new millennium there have been a number of attempts to secure patents for specific software tools. However, at the time of the Uruguay Round negotiations, the Japanese government managed to secure a

limitation of the protection for software under TRIPs to copyright, and software ideas, procedures, or methods of operation and mathematical concepts were excluded from the agreement (Sell, 2003: 114). Thus, the TRIPs agreement extended international copyright protection to cover software, as the U.S. Congress had similarly extended the scope of U.S. copyright 15 years earlier.

Under article 10.1 of the TRIPs agreement "Computer programs, whether in source code or object code shall be protected as literary works under the Berne Convention (1971)." The question of patents for software was left unsettled, although more recent discussions at the WIPO suggest that, if achieved, the Substantive Patent Law Treaty is likely to include protection for software. Nevertheless, by protecting software under copyright, its form (as language) was given precedence over its use as a tool. This afforded it the longest protection period possible and removed the registration procedure required for protection. Conversely, the advantage of patents is that the function of software is protected, even if the actual code has been modified sufficiently to avoid copyright infringement. However, while there may be industry pressures to recognize software patents in specific jurisdictions, and software patents *have* been established in the U.S. and elsewhere, this is not currently *required* by any countries' multilateral commitments at the global level. Thus, in the last decade the international market for software has enjoyed the increasingly robust protection available through copyright. As countries have become TRIPs-compliant, so the ability of software companies to protect their IPRs internationally has been enhanced. This may not go as far as many corporations would like, but the market for software is one that is now largely patterned by IPRs.

This protection has been further enhanced by the development of technical means of protection or digital rights management (DRM) to enforce copyright. The legal position of these new protection technologies was not firmly mandated by the TRIPs agreement, therefore in 1996 the WIPO adopted the WIPO Copyright Treaty. This introduced the anti-circumvention principle for DRM into the multilateral governance of IPRs. Recognizing that technological fixes are seldom permanent, the Treaty sought to establish a legal layer of protection for these technologies' digital mechanisms. This legal innovation subsequently was enacted in the U.S. Digital Millennium Copyright Act (DMCA) and the EU Copyright Directive. Both sets of legislation, among other things, made the avoidance of these technical limitations ("circumvention") illegal. Ironically, while these laws recognize that there may be a "fair use" or "fair dealing" justification for access to encoded information, to gain legal access without authorization is rendered impossible by the complete prohibition on any modification of the technological controls of DRM programs. This expanded legal protection underpins the effectiveness of DRM systems, and embodies the clash of values that is the focus of the rest of this chapter.

Intellectual property and digital technologies

In recent years DRM has been extensively deployed in the realm of software, digital entertainment products, and digitally stored information goods of all kinds. When your computer refuses to install a specific piece of software until you have downloaded the most recent version of Microsoft Explorer, this is DRM at work. The most notorious recent example of DRM came in 2005, when Sony Corporation included a "rootkit" on some of their commercial CDs. Once loaded onto a computer to be played, this installed software onto the users machine allowing Sony or their agents unfettered access to the hard disc, via the internet, to monitor usage for illegal activity. This was widely condemned as a DRM-initiated security risk and an invasion of privacy. Software that prohibits certain functions, such as copying, or amending files in e-book readers, again is driven by the logic and practices of DRM, as in a more reactive way are click-through licenses that require you to agree to terms and conditions that are both extensive (including your acceptance of the vendor's complete denial of *any* liability for problems with their software) and opaque. Perhaps most obviously in the realm of digital music players, DRM ensures that downloads from one vendor (such as iTunes) will only play on certain MP3 players, ensuring you are locked in to a certain company's technology (although at the time of writing, resistance to this lack of interoperability, has prompted Apple to remove DRM from some iTunes music files).

The early history of DRM in the software sector was a period of experimentation, with successive software limitations being "hacked," and broken by those who wished to retain some flexibility of use, or who relished the challenge of cracking the software. More recently, the continuing deployment of DRM in software has prompted not only complaint, critique and hacking, but also long-running *legal* "resistance" in the form of a turn to open-source and free software, and open access to information. DRM is now politicized.

Although, computing itself has a long and often-told history (Ceruzzi, 1997; Winston, 1998), this need not detain us here. The story presents the information society as partly the result of individual efforts to free computing from the domination of the mainframe, and partly the fulfilling of computing's characteristic destiny as an individualized technological tool; a narrative of individual freedom, against which (intellectual property owning) corporations have continually had to struggle in their need to "own" their important digital assets.

The establishment of a non-technical, non-specialist market for software was largely driven by IBM's development of the PC, the advance of Microsoft, and the dominance of the Windows operating system by the late 1980s. Given the growing ease of copying complex computer files, even by technically unsophisticated users, once large companies began to see the profit potential from a mass market in software, the need to protect products from unauthorized duplication became a key strand of research and development. Indeed, as the effort to create software has always far outweighed the effort required to copy it, this issue arose almost from the beginning of the software *industry*, as a separate sector.

Contemporary forms of DRM constrain users of PCs and other devices and may also adversely affect the security of their hardware. Digital rights management systems in software can deny or at least constrain interoperability. This control allows market segmentation and price discrimination, because DRM can easily halt the emergence of secondary markets for protected products. Although historically copyright has included a "first-sale" doctrine that has allowed a vibrant second-hand market to emerge alongside the market for new items, in software this is constrained by license conditions, sellers' DRM restrictions on the hardware on which software will run, and the rapid product cycles for upgrades that are characteristic of the information technology industry.

Increasingly the use of surveillance systems within DRM allows suppliers to both limit and reveal user activities and practices, enabling software providers to discriminate between various users, for instance through single user and multiple users site licenses. While many economists may celebrate this ability to run more accurately priced parallel markets, for users there is a considerable cost in the realms of privacy and control, costs that are borne not by the companies that benefit from price discrimination but by the subjects of surveillance and the limitations on use.

Partly because the potential for this control and surveillance was obvious to some from the start, the early stages of the commercialization of software prompted the first moves towards an alternative: open source working and the campaign for free software. The non-proprietary model of software development shaped the early, non-commercial period of computer development, during which computing source code was routinely shared, and development work collaborative and essentially "unowned." However, after the U.S. Department of Justice prosecuted IBM for anti-trust violations in the 1970s, software and hardware provision was split, prompting the development of a separate software industry, which sought to "own" code as a means of profiting from it. As a response to the widening scope of this model of "ownership," Richard Stallman and others established the Free Software Foundation to support a positive and explicit movement to keep software free from ownership.

Stallman, with some legal advice, then produced what he regards as his "greatest hack"; the GNU General Public License (GPL) sometimes referred to as "copyleft" (reproduced in Annex 1 of UNCTAD 2003). The GPL permits the user to run, copy, or modify a software program's source code, and if they so wish, to distribute versions of the program.

369

However, it does not allow them to add rights-related restrictions of their own. Often termed the "viral clause" of the GPL, the license compels subsequent programs utilizing aspects of GPL licensed software to be fully compatible with the GPL. Crucially the license utilizes copyright law to ensure it is both included in any derivative works as well as ensuring the GPL itself remains unchanged; to change the license terms included in the software is to violate the copyright of the software and invite prosecution. While this guarantees that GPL-protected programs are never commoditized, it has also undermined the development of hybrid free/proprietary software tools.

While there are philosophical differences between the "free software" and "open source" software movements, both are based on what I term a "logic of openness." The use of the term "free and open source software" (FOSS) tries to paper over these differences to allow those interested in promoting free software *and* open source software, to focus on the key joint endeavor: the establishment of a logic of openness as the defining practice of the information society; a practical and often formally articulated critique of the controlling logic of IPR enforcement in digital goods and services.

The appeal of the open approach is perhaps best exemplified by the success of the Firefox web browser. After the dismemberment of Netscape and the "triumph" of Internet Explorer, the developers of Netscape, though now dispersed across various other computer companies, kept developing their browser and released an open source version (Firefox) that has recently become the main threat to Internet Explorer, gaining market share as more and more people become disenchanted with the Microsoft product (and indeed forcing Microsoft to copy some of Firefox's innovations in the latest version of its web browser).

However, while this is certainly an interesting and important development, perhaps the greatest impact of openness will be not in the developed countries, whose entry into the information age has been relatively unproblematic, but rather in the developing countries, where wealth effects can severely inhibit access to informational goods and services. It is in sub-Saharan Africa especially where we can see both the appeal and utility of openness for those who are disadvantaged in the information society. It is also where we can see the strength of the campaign by corporations to maintain ownership of their resources, despite the high social costs. Here, the tipping of the long-term balance between private rights and public goods, in favor of the former is clear and its effects difficult to dismiss.

Making a difference: open source software in Africa

Across sub-Saharan Africa the ability to take advantage of any sort of computing is unevenly distributed on the basis of wealth and education but the continuing spread of community computing centers, alongside access via mobile telephony, has ensured that while still uneven, connectivity is no longer clustered overwhelmingly in a few major urban centers. The character of the internet, however, allows owners of operating systems and other key software protected by proprietary rights to enjoy monopoly rents when these technologies become industry standards. As the domination of computer operating systems by Microsoft demonstrates, the considerable network effects of a communications infrastructure have allowed a near monopoly to be established in some software products. Moreover, the trade in software in sub-Saharan Africa can be easily characterized as rent-taking by owners who have already fully recovered their costs of development and made significant profits in developed country markets.

Across Africa, the policy problem of intellectual property has so far been sidestepped due to the easy availability of pirated software in urban centers. The savings from piracy, of course, remain dwarfed by the vast financial transfers established by the current IPR system from consumers on the continent to predominantly U.S. software corporations. And considerable political pressure is being brought to bear, both bilaterally and through the WTO, for countries to properly enforce the rights mandated by the TRIPs agreement, as a means of curtailing piracy. Mass participation by Africans in the global information society remains far in the future in the context of this policy regime.

Under previous national legislation the high social costs of IPRs have usually prompted recourse to some form of "fair use" provision, according to which copyright is ignored in specific circumstances that served a wider social good. However, such strategies have been severely constrained under the TRIPs agreement, and in any case the move to DRM limits by technological means any unauthorized distribution. Furthermore when the source code of software is protected, reverse engineering of specific programs for local modification is inhibited by TRIPs-compliant law. This further restrains development as reverse engineering in the past allowed local innovators to improve off-the-shelf technologies to reflect local conditions, and by doing so familiarize themselves with these new technologies.

Not only are the tools that are central to "informational development" expensive, previous methods for taking advantage of them are being withdrawn under immense political pressure from the U.S. and the EU to maintain the developed world's competitive advantage (Wade, 2002).

Ironically, the European Commission has funded research, published in 2007, that noted the savings for organizations in the public and private sectors of switching to open software based products (BBC News Online, 2007), and it is becoming clear that this switch to openness need not merely be a minority pursuit. Unlike the developed countries where there is already a vast base of Windows-installed machines (with billions of stored files), across sub-Saharan Africa, and other areas of the majority world, PCs and other digital devices are only now starting to be deployed in growing numbers: for many users the choice between FOSS and proprietary products remains very much a genuine one, still largely unencumbered by issues of backwards compatibility.

This is why both proprietary companies and FOSS developers are trying to capture the next generation of users, and as more users come online across the African continent so their choices over the programs they use will become crucial to African countries' domestic software sectors. Recognizing that its use can play a "key role to extend and disseminate human knowledge" UNESCO's support for FOSS includes an extensive website that provides access to information about FOSS, access to developer tools or software, and extensive background materials. UNESCO has also worked with the New Zealand *Digital Library Project* and *Human Info* from Antwerp to develop the Greenstone Digital Library software package that enables the development of open source digital libraries of scientific, educational, and cultural resources predicated on open access and public domain information. The Regional Information Society Network for Africa, responsible for aiding the migration to low-cost FOSS hardware and software by public sector and civil society organizations, is also supported by UNESCO (Barry and Dauphin, 2003).

There are many practical advantages to the utilization of FOSS in developing countries (not least of all substantial long-term cost savings) but here I will briefly focus on the wider political implications of this move to openness.

The clearest political advantage of FOSS for developing countries is the potential to establish independent national capacity in one of the key strategic technologies of today. Indeed, for some commentators the adoption of FOSS (specifically LINUX) is a counter-hegemonic strategy against the domination of the Microsoft based mode of establishing information society linked development (e.g., Sum, 2003). Late entrants face significant challenges, as they do in all industrial sectors, but FOSS offers a strategy for side-stepping the most significant monopoly in the sector, the domination of operating systems by Microsoft Windows. Certainly the software industry remains remarkably concentrated, dominated by the developed countries' companies, but as the recent emergence of both Indian and Chinese software development sectors has amply demonstrated this is not necessarily fixed. Although one should not underestimate the locational path dependency in software development and deployment—Silicon Valley remains a major center of software development after all—neither are the opportunities for breaking into these markets as narrow as Microsoft's domination of operating systems might suggest.

As internet usage expands across the continent, the promotion of FOSS could be utilized as an infant industry support strategy for informational and digital services. The danger is that this may also ghettoize African software companies, if export markets do not also shift significantly to FOSS programs. However, governments across the developing world that are suspicious of the involvement of U.S. companies in public sector procurement

have begun to promote the use of FOSS products to establish greater technological independence. Many national and regional governments are at various stages of establishing a major role for FOSS in the public sector. Policy-makers have become concerned about ceding too much control over their central communicative functions to a single (foreign) software supplier. As Peruvian Congressman Edgar Villanueva stressed in a widely publicized exchange of letters with Microsoft Peru in 2002: "to guarantee free access by citizens to public information, it is indispensable that the encoding and processing of data not be tied to any single provider ... the usability and maintenance of software should not depend on the goodwill of suppliers or on conditions imposed by them in a monopoly market" (quoted in UNCTAD, 2003: 111). This issue has also been recognized in Europe, where a number of governments currently either utilize or are investigating open source solutions to particular computer projects, having become increasingly disenchanted with expensive proprietary contracts.

A significant difficulty is that the costs of switching once expertise has been gained and files generated and archived are high, and may deter even those who assume that FOSS programs are superior. This has been compounded in the past by development agencies configuring tendering requests for aid project contracts around proprietary software. The ability to access sought-after funds and support has often required the adoption of specific software platforms for the convenience of the donor/supporting agency. Many non-governmental organizations (NGOs) and other agencies seem unaware, or do not prioritize, developments in computing and software. Equally, as developers in Africa admit, the FOSS community has been slow to bridge this gap (Bridges, 2004: 10–12). As in many ways the underlying political perspectives of many NGOs fit quite snugly with the social developmental aims at the center of the FOSS movement there is at least significant potential for collaboration. Indeed the celebration of openness and access would seem already to figure quite widely in NGO campaigns, although the link with the enforcement of IPRs is most often made in the realm of AIDS medicines and biotechnology.

If the TRIPs agreement has often been a mechanism for consolidating the grip of companies in developed countries on high technology markets, a developmental strategy that stresses FOSS programs may be more suitable for countries that are technological "followers." This has the clear advantage of allowing countries in sub-Saharan Africa to fully comply with their multilateral obligations under TRIPs, while also supporting the development of a potentially competitive industry in one of the key technologies of this new century. Thus, if African countries can enhance their software development communities, and specifically the scope of FOSS-related skills in the labor force, then they will also have started to develop sales opportunities for customized software to these and other potential users (UNCTAD, 2003: 120). That non-U.S., non-EU software companies can become globally competitive has already been adequately demonstrated by the software sector based in Bangalore, India. At the same time, the relative preponderance of mobile telephony in sub-Saharan Africa has undermined Microsoft's potential desktop domination, with many new hand-held devices from Symbian and Palm to Nicholas Negroponte's "100 dollar laptop" all already running, or potentially able to run, non-proprietary software.

The central issue is whether a critical mass of FOSS users can be established that will act as an alternative gravitational pole for users about to enter the world of the internet. If it can, this may produce new markets for software in developed countries for companies based in Africa offering FOSS-based programs. Utilizing FOSS could enable developing countries to establish new forms of valuable expertise, while at the same time freeing themselves (at least partly) from dependence on the developed countries for information and digital manufacturing and services. This can be achieved while complying with their multilateral commitments under the TRIPs agreement.

Bounded openness

The developments noted above and elsewhere in the majority world, where participation in the information society is patterned by wealth effects, are paralleled by developments in the U.S. and Europe, where a similar desire to sidestep proprietary software and other limitations on openness has become a growing response to the attempts to maintain and expand control over digitized informational content and tools. Eric von Hippel has detected a move to openness across many sectors through what he terms the democratization of innovation. This encompasses developer-led openness of the sort typified by open software, and aspects of customer-generated innovation and adaptation, which is then commercialized by companies. As von Hippel points out this notion of unorganized innovation requires a shift from a property logic in knowledge and information to an open, or commons, logic, where exclusion is not the default position (von Hippel, 2005: 112–15).

While von Hippel's observations are important, openness is not merely about commercial activity. One of the key areas where the logic of openness has become prominent is in the access to, and distribution of, knowledge and information.

Here, openness maps on to the desire to establish open access, which itself has become a major project both within the university (and science) sector (Jacobs, 2006; May, 2005) and more widely with the current A2K (access to knowledge) campaign, which seeks to link a wide range of concerns about the commoditization of information. This campaign attempts to draw together the political momentum discussed in the previous section, and the high-profile campaign around the wealth effects of IPRs in the health sector (most obviously, but not exclusively, related to AIDS medicines), and link these campaigns to others around open science (and access to scientific research), as well as demands to limit the effects of DRM and expand the "knowledge commons." This movement reflects a logic of openness that also finds its expression in the increasing popularity of weblog publishing and other open digital initiatives of which one of the best known has been the development of Wikipedia.

Wikipedia, while overseen by a group of editors led by the project's founder Jimmy Wales, remains a collective endeavor, mostly open to all willing to contribute and share (Benkler, 2006: 70–4). To be sure openness here (as with the role of Linus Torvalds in the LINUX community—see Moody, 2001) does not indicate an absence of controlling authority. Rather, the editorial intent at the Wikipedia is to *maintain* an open resource, which sometimes (due most often to ideologically driven "vandalism" of contentious pages) requires absolute openness to be (perhaps temporarily) constrained. Thus, here the advantage of openness is balanced by the disadvantage of assuming that collective contributions will be in good faith. Certainly, multiple and continuing peer scrutiny may strip out many invasive and ill-meant contributions, but the logic of openness, at its limits, sits uncomfortably with the idea of a hierarchy

of guidance, of some more able to control content than others.

What might be termed "bounded openness" indicates that the project of openness itself cannot be a totalizing demand, but rather a recognition that in many cases, openness may have some clear social benefits that need to be accorded weight in the face of the controlling logic of IPRs. This bounded openness implies, as Sandra Braman has forcefully argued, that the erosion of the ownership of knowledge may also bring with it the parallel erosion of confidence in the information accessed (Braman, 2006). This suggests that other forms of authority will need to be established within the open realm to substitute for the authority that flows from defined ownership. Here the strategy of peer production of relevance and accreditation information, perhaps best exemplified by Web 2.0 ranking systems such as Digg, or Google's more mechanical PageRank algorithm that identifies how many other pages link to relevant pages thrown up by searches to establish a rank, may offer one path out of this dilemma (Benkler, 2006: 76–7). In other words, a key challenge for the openness movement is to find ways of delivering the quality-related quick and ready assessments that previously were delivered via proprietary modes of establishing information and knowledge.

Conclusion

As the above indicates, rather than an either/or proposition, we can see a more fluid set of possibilities, reflecting pragmatic choices between property and openness, within the socio-economic relations of the global information society (Carlaw *et al.*, 2006). Openness can act as a countervailing force, balancing the more outlandish and excessive claims to property rights. The key to developing something that resembles the early positive ideas of the information society, and thus reigns in the more pernicious aspects of a rampant information capitalism, may be the conjunction of ownership and "openness" in an ongoing dialectical relationship, each modifying and depending on the other.

This recognizes both the continuing strength of the dominant regime of IPRs, as well as understanding the challenge represented by openness; the dialectic between these two poles may be volatile and subject to political challenge and contest, but this in itself may be its main appeal. A continual (re)balancing, seen as a process, and not as an end, allows shifts in social needs and interests to be articulated and mediated. This is preferable to the domination of the "one-size-fits-all" logic of IPRs, but also reflects the historical development of the limitations to the rights accorded intellectual property owners.

Although earlier commentary on the internet and its possibilities tended to assume that there was some sort of technological inevitability that would free information from the shackles of property, the last decade has demonstrated that the protection and expansion of the information commons is a political project requiring extensive agency.

The supporters of openness are going to have a fight on their hands. Indeed, openness is the contemporary manifestation of a historical tendency within the political economy of intellectual property for resistance to emerge when the privileges and rights claimed by owners inflict onerous and unacceptable costs and duties on non-owners (May and Sell, 2005). The notion of sharing rather than owning, of open access rather than digital control, has nonetheless begun to establish a social presence. This suggests, at the very least, that it will offer a clear alternative to the commoditization that currently dominates innovation and knowledge creation.

Guide to further reading

Much has been written about the rise of open source software. The majority of this literature is quite populist. The best of these popular treatments is Moody (2001). For a more recent and more detailed social scientific analysis either Weber (2004) or Benkler (2006) can be recommended. Neither of these books deals with the technical side in any great detail but both attempt, utilizing different methodologies, to explain its appeal and sustainability. Jacobs (2006) is a good place to start if you are seeking to explore the technical issues that surround the move to digital openness. For those seeking accounts that develop a more political argument von Hippel (2005) offers a view of open innovation from the perspective of business, while Halbert (2005), Perelman (2002), and Strangelove (2005) seek to place the free software and open source software movements in a political context of resistance. Here, the anti-capitalist potential is emphasized in direct contrast to von Hippel's more pragmatic perspective. For those wishing to place intellectual property in a much longer historical context, my book with Susan Sell (May and Sell, 2005) attempts to establish a two-and-a-half millennia history behind the contemporary battles to make knowledge and information into property, while Winston (1998) offers a longer history of digital technologies than is normally found. Lastly, for a guide to up-to-date arguments about the open source community, there is no better place to start than Wikipedia, an artifact of openness itself.

27

Exclusionary rules?

The politics of protocols

Greg Elmer

Is internet governance an oxymoron? What are the political implications of internet software standards, and how are such software settings used for political ends? Obviously there are political interests when it comes to engineering decisions and standards setting for internet infrastructure. But even after those decisions are made, not only do ideological perspectives appear in internet content, but these perspectives continue to influence design decisions that effect who can see which content, when. This chapter looks at internet protocols as distinct political artifacts, tools in effect that political actors use to supplement their more traditional communication strategies. The chapter makes particular reference to the Bush White House's use of the robots.txt commands, a technique for excluding website content from search engine databases. The chapter subsequently tracks the emergence of the proposed robots.txt protocol as an instance of informal internet governance and regulation to its integration into software offered by search engine giant Google. In the last instance, the chapter highlights how adoption of internet protocols, with little to no public debate or scrutiny, can impact upon access to public information and harness the work of internet users for the benefit of information aggregators like Google.

The international network of computers has posed a series of challenges to legislators worldwide.[1] Attempts to regulate, censor, and otherwise police the internet face complex decentered and distributed architectures that often present multiple opportunities for unregulated communication and networking. The internet is, however, not without its historical and technological forms of governance, and since its days as a wing of the U.S. military (ARPANET) it continues to be defined and refined. This chapter is thus concerned with the set of technological rules, standards, and protocols that provide for common functions and software platforms on the internet. This digital commons is distinct, however, in its particular form of techno–governmentality. In part because of the rapid development and deployment of the internet—historically speaking—the network's standards continue to be overseen by a set of engineers and computer scientists who first initiated its common protocols, namely TCP/IP.[2] What results is a complex mix of self-regulatory ethics defined by university researchers, research and development (R&D) departments from the new media sector, and public sector policymakers—many of whom routinely move in and out of these three spheres.

While much has been written about new regulatory bodies charged with overseeing the global governance of the internet (Kahin and Keller, 1997; Mueller,

2002), in addition to the controversies that such bodies have of late been adjudicating (internet addresses, standards, regulations, and protocols) (Pare, 2003; Galloway, 2004), studies of the internet's distinct technological forms of governmentality (in and through code) remain underdeveloped. To limit our understanding of internet governance to such institutions as the Internet Society, the Internet Engineering Task Force, or the World Wide Web Consortium (W3), would significantly downplay the synergistic forces that have come to produce other internet conventions that similarly attempt to regulate practices of internet connectivity and networking. This chapter focuses on one such convention, robots.txt exclusion commands, to outline the contours of internet governmentality on the peripheries of the regulatory bodies.

Exclusion commands offer both familiar yet unique perspectives on debates over internet governance and politics. To start, the commands are meant to exclude web content from internet search engines, a practice that raises questions about security, censorship, and the representativeness of search engine databases—all issues that have been dealt with at length by the aforementioned bodies. Robots.txt commands were also, at one time, subject to review by the Internet Society, though to date the convention has not been adopted as a formal protocol by the Engineering Taskforce. The point being of course that the exclusion commands serve a governmental role without having been formally recognized as such through the internet's governmental bodies.

This chapter begins with a historical and technical overview of robots.txt commands, making note of its relationship to industry insiders/engineers, the protocol governance process through the Internet Society, and most importantly the rather banal language used to frame the need for—and functionality of—such

commands. The chapter then focuses on the broader public articulation and rationale of robots.txt commands made in response to a political controversy. Latour (2005) makes a compelling argument that studies of social systems should begin by "feeding off controversies" in an effort to locate its central actors, and discursive characteristics, formats, reach, and intensity, in lieu of assuming a priori the legitimacy and centrality of traditional political institutions. Since the internet is such a dispersed, content rich environment, however, we see in the example of robots.txt commands that information controversies often erupt at the very highest level, for the simple fact that they expose contradictions in traditional, hierarchical centers of government. Information controversies are made more broadly public (to less "wired" worlds), in other words, as *mass mediated* controversies. Furthermore, information controversies, as we shall see, are also often articulated as political controversies, particularly on the web where libertarian ethics still prevail in certain circles.

We therefore begin by mapping the political controversy that erupted on the internet over the White House's use of robots.txt exclusion commands to reportedly keep content related to Iraq from being included in search engine databases. The controversy refutes the fallacy that data cleaning and formatting are simply attempts at making information retrieval more relevant, useful, and aesthetically pleasing. Rather, the chapter argues that robots.txt commands serve to expand proprietary spaces and ideologies of the web, even where no explicit forms of security—or password protected domains—exist.

The remainder of the chapter focuses on Google, both as governmental archive and self-regulatory space. Earlier in the chapter it is noted that the shear paucity of public information on robots.txt exclusion commands has amplified the monopolistic tendencies of Google's ranking of information on this topic. The "inventor" of robots.txt commands dominates the top-ranked Google pages on the topic. Moreover, in addition to centralizing and amplifying the language of the informal protocol's inventor, Google has also sought to develop new tools to yet again highlight the unruly and unmanageable robots.txt commands and files. The chapter concludes with a discussion of how Google's own web management systems and software have incorporated the robot exclusion convention in an effort to increasingly standardize—and make search-engine ready—the formatting of web content via web management tools.

Commanding a standard

The robots.txt exclusion command is an informal internet rule or convention that attempts to restrict search engine robots from crawling and archiving specific files on a website. The robot exclusion command was discussed in parallel with the deployment of the first automated search engine indexing robots and the web browser. Like many protocols and standards developed for implementation on the internet and the web, discussions about limiting the reach of web robots was conducted in informal online communities that worked in large part by consensus, itself a metaphor—if not a model—for internet governmentality. Much of the documentation on robot exclusion protocols has been compiled by Martijn Koster, a former employee of the early search engine company Webcrawler (owned by America Online). Koster developed robot exclusion policies in conjunction with a dozen or more researchers housed at computer science faculties at major American, British, Dutch, and German universities.[3] Early discussions

about the exclusion policy and the manner in which it would in effect exclude search engine robots from archiving content and hyperlink architectures of websites, can be traced back to June 1994.

By December of 1996 Koster had developed a draft policy on robot exclusion for consideration by the Network Working Group, a committee of the Internet Engineering Taskforce. To date the draft remains the most comprehensive technical document in broad circulation (Koster, 1997). For reasons unknown, Koster's proposal was not adopted by the group as an official standard. The document provides a number of rationales for the development of a standard and a shared technique for restricting access of web content—and in effect limiting the scope and reach of search engines. Koster (1996) offers four reasons why web-masters may want to respect access to their site. Koster's language implies a sense of privacy and proprietorial interest, but in general makes few clear statements about the transparency, control, or publicity of the net in general. Rather in clinical language he writes: "Robots are often used for maintenance and indexing purposes, by people other than the administrators of the site being visited. In some cases such visits may have undesired effects which the administrators would like to prevent, such as indexing of an unannounced site, traversal of parts of the site which require vast resources of the server recursive traversal of an infinite URL space, etc."

Koster's website of robots—which includes extensive information on robots.txt exclusion scripts, history, and advice—is, consequently, like much of the technical literature on the topic, decidedly vague. In a brief description of the use of robot exclusion, for instance, Koster's site notes that, "Sometimes people find they have been indexed by an indexing robot, or that a resource discovery robot has visited part of a site that for some reason shouldn't be visited by robots."[4] Like much of the internet's governance and history for that matter, the robots.txt protocol offers a seemingly innocuous technical rule, developed by engineers, that offered few if any hints or discussions about their possible implication for the broader circulation and accessibility of information on the web. Indeed, while Koster's work and robots.txt information site still tops Google's ranking of resources on the subject, his home page in the spring of 2006 offered few clues about his involvement in the process, rather, the site offered visitors a number of images from the Star Wars films.[5] Such informalities, however, while providing some insight into the cultures of internet production and regulation, technologically speaking, stand in stark contrast to the protocol's emergence as an increasingly professionalized and universal—though some might say secretive—technique that has the potential for excluding access to large amounts of web content.

The White House robots.txt files

The debate over the Bush White House use of the exclusion protocol in 2003, however, provides a stark contrast to the vague and purposefully broad discussions of web exclusion standards outlined in the technical and governmental literature. Yet, at the same time this particular example of robots.txt use, while seemingly under the glare of the mass media, politicians, and bloggers worldwide, further highlighted the protocol's evasiveness, its ability to confuse and defuse accusations of information control and censorship. The protocol that was developed with little discussion or explanation, with regards to its ability to filter or exclude content from the net-publics eye,

in other words, would later be explained as an innocuous piece of code that merely gave individuals some control over what to publish on the web and other banal forms of digital housekeeping.

In October 2003, with the United States slipping further into political crisis with an increasingly unpopular war in Iraq, bloggers and then mainstream media began to report that the White House had been using the robot exclusion tags within their website to exclude a number of files from search engine indexing. Approximately half of all White House web files excluded from search engine indexing included the term "Iraq," assuring the story extra attention.[6] Not surprisingly a series of articles and web posts questioned the use of such strategies as a means of censorship. More generally, of course, the use of robot commands by the White House also raised broader concerns about the use of this technology as a means of filtering potentially controversial content from the public eye, at least as indexed through the major internet search engines. The robot controversy also highlighted a little-known fact among the broader public, that search engines are in effect constructed databases that reflect choices and biases of search engines, their search logics, and robot archival strategies (Introna and Nissembaum, 2000).

Unlike other censorship stories that have largely focused on the corporate sector (Google and China for example), the White House website robot exclusion controversy also focused attention on the relationship between technology, publicity, and the writing of history. The controversy was heightened by the accusation that the White House was using the exclusion protocol to manipulate the historical record. In May of 2003 the *Washington Post* reported that the White House had issued a press release with the title "President Bush announces combat operations in Iraq have ended." Some months later, however, the same press release was found on the White House site with a new title: "Bush announces *major* combat operations in Iraq have ended" (emphasis added).[7] On his blog, Stanford professor Larry Lessig wrote in response to the controversy, "Why would you need to check up on the Whitehouse, you might ask? Who would be so unAmerican as to doubt the veracity of the press office? ... if you obey the code of the robots.txt, you'll never need to worry."[8] Lessig's last point here is crucial: the robot exclusion protocol has the potential of removing public documents from archival platforms such as Google and other web archives, calling into question their status as reliable—and ultimately unchangeable—forms of the "public record."

It should be noted, however, that while the White House did change the wording of a previous released public statement, the use of the robot exclusion protocol's role in the matter was widely contested and debated. When confronted by accusations of rewriting e-history, the White House argued that its use of robot exclusion commands merely intended to avoid the duplication, or the retrieval, of multiple copies of the same content.[9] Some online critics agreed that in fact the White House could have merely been using the protocol as a means of managing its web content.[10] Questions still abound, however, most obviously, why were so many files stamped "Iraq" on the White House's exclusion list? And intentional or not, did the act of excluding content on the White House website facilitate the "revision" of previously released statements to the media and public?

Regardless of the White House's intent, the controversy offers a unique perspective on new techniques in information management on the web. While concerns about the multiplicity of authors, versions of documents, the suitability of posts, appended comments, and hyperlinks have all been replayed since at least Ted Nelson's Xanadu hypertext vision/manifesto (the debate over Wikipedia being the most recent), the robot exclusion protocol focused the debate about virtual knowledge once again (as was the case with web cookies) on the control over—and management of—PC, server, and remote hard drives in a networked infoscape (Elmer, 2002). If the White House did not want files to be archived why were they not kept in private folders, on another server, or in an unpublished folder? Part of what this exclusion protocol calls into question then is the creation of files that are relatively accessible for those with knowledge of the system,[11] but are excluded from third-party search engines archives.

Google's symbiotic business model: site maps

The legal status of web code, internet content, and the regulation of crawlers and search engine bots is of course big news for new media big businesses. Search engine industry leader Google now considers robots exclusion to be a significant obstacle for their business of indexing and ranking web content and pages. Part of their concern stems from the haphazard organization of robots exclusion tags that are typically attached to specific web pages, and not sites as a whole. There are a number of ways in which webmasters can control or exclude robots from archiving their respective content. First, a webmaster can insert a tag, or short script, in the server log file that hosts the website. This exclusion file then tells robots not to archive specific files on a server. The following example tells all robots to avoid archiving the file that begins with the name /911:

User-agent: *
Disallow: /911/sept112002/text[12]

Having to determine and then write code to exclude specific files on a site can be a terribly complicated and, moreover, time-consuming process.[13] Consequently, proponents of robot exclusion have also developed a second more efficient technique for excluding robot indexing. Webmasters can insert the tag within the HTML header instructing robots not to index or crawl links on that specific page. The benefit of this technique is that webmasters do not need to have access to their server, rather they can exclude robots much more easily by making changes directly within the code of their websites.

Consequently, with patches of content on sites and now across the web being tagged as "out of bounds" for robot archiving, the search engine industry is faced with the possibility of users increasingly limiting access to their lifeblood and main resource—unfettered access to all of the internet's content and structure. A parallel might be drawn from the television industry's concern with digital video recorders, which, when first introduced, were able to cut out or fast forward through the industry's main source of revenue, advertisements (Boddy, 2003).

Google responded to the threat of large-scale excluded content by treating it as a broader concern about website management, including of course the promotion of one's website through their own page-rank search engine ranking algorithm. Google's solution, Site Maps, a free software suite for webmasters, offered a number of web management tools and services, most of which assist in managing the content, structure, and interactive functions of their website. In a published discussion and interview with Google's Site Maps team a broad overview and rationale for the tool was articulated. Of particular interest (historically speaking

with regards to the development of the internet) is the manner in which Site Maps attempts to offer a universal technical support platform for webmastering. The team for example characterizes Site Maps as "making the Web better for Web masters and the users alike."[14] The realization of this vision in effect means going beyond Google's initial vision of the search engine business to create suites of tools that facilitate a symbiotic management platform between the Google databases and individual webmasters. In many respects the Site Maps platform represents Google's attempt to provide easily downloadable (crawled and archived) "templates" of websites. The tool is, from the perspective of the webmaster, also quite alluring. Site Maps clearly helps manage a website, providing one window that would summarize the overall structure and functionality of hyperlinks and code, in effect making it easier to keep a site up to date. From the webmaster's perspective, the tool also benefits from indexical efficiency, specifically by having their site ranked higher with Google's results list. Site Maps thus offers a parallel window or interface for the webmaster, with html and site management on one site inherently linked through a convergence of coding and indexing conventions (or "templates").

In February 2006 Google announced the inclusion of a robot exclusion management tool for Site Maps. This new tool also conforms to the symbiotic function of Site Maps, providing users—and of course Google—with a common platform where robots.txt commands can be input, edited, and reviewed. While the Site Maps program is still a relatively new technology, there are obvious questions about its treatment of information, its impact upon the privacy of webmasters, and of course its overall impact upon the accessibility of information through their search engine. Site Maps, in addition to providing management tools also serves an aggregation function, bringing together data of immense interest to a search engine company. The simple structure or architecture of sites, for example, would offer a great deal of information for Google, information which the search engine giant could use to then prompt its *Site Maps* users to revise or amend to fit into its web archiving goals. Another potential concern is the user base for *Site Maps*. While the tool is fairly user-friendly one could assume that more advanced webmasters, or at least those with more complex websites, would form its user base. The symbiotic effects of the relationship between such users and Google might further skew the links-heavy, "authoritative" logic of its search engine.[15] One might speculate that more established or resource-heavy businesses or organizations are also much more apt to adopt such technology. Lastly, as the technology becomes more widely adopted as a tool for managing website content, it is not inconceivable that this tool may start to regulate and even define best practices for excluding content or not excluding content from the eyes of the search engine.

Conclusion

Since the protocol has never been adopted by the Engineering Taskforce or other larger regulatory bodies such as the Internet Society, one could argue that the protocol merely replicates a questionable history of informal and professional conventions that few outside of computer science departments and R&D units have debated. The protocol is in effect entirely voluntary, respected by those actors who can harness it for commercial purposes (search engine optimization), and rejected by others who themselves seek to mine internet data for a less respected yet

similar profit-seeking rationale (e-mail spam bots, for example). There are, of course, other examples of protocols that have automated the collection of personal information from individuals with little or no notice. Thus, given the proliferation of surveillance and user tracking protocols on the internet, such as web cookies (Elmer, 2002), web bugs, and other state-hosted programs such as the National Security Agency's Internet surveillance program in the United States that automatically collect personal information in hidden—and for some—undemocratic ways, the monitoring of robots.txt excluded content might be viewed as a justified form of counter-surveillance—and an important democratic practice.

Moreover, as we increasingly rely upon information aggregators and search engines to make visible the contents of the internet, the limits of their archives should become important public concerns and not simply opportunities to forge more symbiotic business models. Robots.txt excluded documents constitute one of the most important sites of new media research as they both articulate and attempt to structure the very limits and scope of the internet—not only the access to information, but also the economic, legal, proprietorial, and ethical claims to new cyberspaces. The governance of such spaces, commands, and excluded lists, are equally worthy of counter-surveillance, that is to say, such web artifacts—if reverse engineered or otherwise laterally mapped—highlight the rather informal nature of internet governance.

Thus, a protocol proposal rejected (or left to expire) by the committees of the Internet Society has, through the indexical and content formatting strategies of companies like Google, become a rather formalized informal protocol. The paucity of information on the proposed robots exclusion protocol has also created, through Google's own search engine ranking algorithm, a near monopoly of information on robots.txt commands, further restricting or marginalizing critiques and questions of their applicability, legal status, and potential impact upon publicly accessible online archives and political communications.

Guide to further reading

This chapter is largely inspired by a subset of new media studies referred to as "software studies." A broad survey of this approach, which typically questions the political and social aspects of software innovation and artifacts, would be best served by reading Wardrip-Fruin and Montfort's (2003) brilliant edited collection *The New Media Reader*. While the Reader offers an excellent historical perspective on the place of software in new media studies, Hawk, Rieder, and Oviedo's (2008) *Small Tech* collection offers more traditional individual essays that highlight case studies of software. Conversely, a more sustained discussion and exposition of the tenets of software studies is probably best served by Matthew Fuller's (2003) readable—though at times tangential—*Behind the Blip: essays on the culture of software*. A more consistent contribution to the software studies literature, which builds on the importance of software code and formats, is offered by Adrian Mackenzie's (2006) *Cutting Code: software and sociality*. Theoretically speaking, however, I still recommend Alex Galloway's (2004) *Protocol*, a frustrating read, but one that successfully challenges the reader to think about laws, conventions, and rules encoded in layers of computer and internet software. Finally, see Elmer (2004) for a broad treatment of technologies associated with profiling and surveillance.

Notes

1 The author would like to thank the following individuals for their assistance in preparing this chapter: Phil Howard, Andrew Chadwick, Zach Devereaux, and Ganaele Langlois. The research was made possible by grants from the Canadian Media Research Consortium and the Social Science and Humanities Research Council of Canada.

2 Vint Cerf, for example, remains active in developing protocols for the net and in September 2005 joined Google as an advisor, or "Chief Evangelist." See: www.google.com/press/pressrel/vintcerf.html [accessed April 9, 2007].
Cerf also serves on the board of the internet Corporation for Assigned Names and Numbers (ICANN).

3 An archive of the listserv that discusses the formulation of the exclusion standard can be found at: www.robotstxt.org/wc/mailing-list/robots-nexor-mbox.txt

4 www.robotstxt.org/wc/exclusion.html [accessed June 12, 2006].

5 By the fall of 2006, though, Koster had uploaded a more conventional home page that included links to the robots.txt resource pages and a page that listed his other major technical contributions to the early days of the web.

6 www.bway.net/~keith/whrobots

7 www.washingtonpost.com/ac2/wp-dyn/A11485–2003Aug18?language=printer

8 www.lessig.org/blog/archives/001619.shtml

9 www.2600.com/news/view/print/1803

10 www.2600.com/news/view/print/1803

11 The keywords "white house" together with "robots" in Google, for instance, return an exclusion list from the White House server.

12 www.whitehouse.gov/robots.txt [accessed October 9, 2006].

13 The protocol does, however, provide for the exclusion of all robot crawling: # go away User-agent: *
Disallow: /
http://www.robotstxt.org/wc/norobots.html [accessed October 9, 2006].

14 www.smart-it-consulting.com/article.htm?node=166&page=135

15 www.db.stanford.edu/~backrub/google.html [accessed October 9, 2006].

28

The new politics of the internet

Multi-stakeholder policy-making and the internet technocracy

William H. Dutton and Malcolm Peltu

The internet grew with the support of standardization, management, and other governance procedures. These involved mainly technically oriented groups and the network's initial sponsor, the U.S. government. However, demands for widening this policy-making base have grown as more stakeholders have understood the internet's enormous potential to transform activities throughout societies and across the world. The UN's World Summits on the Information Society (WSIS) in 2003 and 2005 were a significant and controversial recognition of this growing global importance. A key WSIS characteristic was its commitment to multi-stakeholder global internet policy-making. But was this just a symbolic gesture with little lasting impact, or did it signal a shift away from the internet technocracy in the political dynamics shaping internet developments and their social implications? This chapter seeks answers to these and related questions by critically assessing the WSIS experience to identify any ways its multi-stakeholder model could contribute to enduring internet governance processes, as well as its limitations. After an introductory overview, the nature and outcomes of WSIS multi-stakeholder processes and procedures are examined, as are differing perceptions of their value and limits. An analytical framework for understanding the underlying dynamics of internet governance is also proposed.

The internet is often viewed as a primarily technical project, centered on information and communication technologies (ICTs).[1] However, from its initiation in the 1970s as the U.S. Department of Defense's Arpanet project (e.g., see Leiner *et al.*, 2003) a "politics of the internet" has shaped its development. In its early phases, this was governed primarily by an internet technocracy: technical experts and constituencies, with financial support. Oversight was provided from the U.S. government, which generally took a hands-off approach to its operation and technical evolution albeit with the potential to intervene.

The changing politics of internet policy-making

As the internet's capabilities, reach, and impacts across all sectors of society around the world have grown, other nations and stakeholders have sought to play a growing role in formal and informal processes determining the internet's direction. For example, many more national governments have sought to exert influence, from filtering internet content to demanding a greater role in the internet governance policy-making processes that determine how the internet's infrastructure is actually managed and operated. Meanwhile, global commercial companies have sought more control over certain sectors, while end users have continued to exercise their own controls, such as by creating and disseminating key innovations at the edges of this network of networks.

The fact that there have always been such structures of control and influence over the development and use of the internet has been a point missed by those who have sought to promote—and decry—more recent efforts to develop "internet governance" as a new concept tied to a set of emerging structures (e.g., see Dutton *et al.*, 2007). The call for internet governance should therefore be more accurately viewed as an effort to transform the politics of the internet by internationalizing and diversifying the structures of political control and accountability that have been governing this technology. Is this occurring? Is a new politics of the Internet emerging in a substantial way?

Two related issues might signal a transformation from the "old" technocratic and U.S.-centric politics of the internet towards a more global and pluralistic "new" politics. One of these issues is the growing debate over global internet governance. Is it a vital step forward? Or is it a misdirected, potentially dangerous, development that puts the future of the internet at risk? The other issue concerns the ways in which wider stakeholder groups can become involved in the new forms of multi-stakeholder policy-making that have been articulated increasingly since the late 1990s across a variety of public policy sectors.[2] One of the key aspects of this is the crucial need when enlarging the base of stakeholders involved in internet politics and policy-making to avoid alienating key traditional players, particularly the essential commitment of technical experts.

The World Summit on the Information Society (WSIS)[3] is a significant example of the multi-stakeholder approach, as it was one of the first major UN events to embody a multi-stakeholder model as a basic principle determining its aims, organization, procedures, and outcomes. This chapter focuses on this aspect of WSIS to explore how an understanding of its successes and failures can help to raise and illuminate questions about the changing nature of internet governance more generally.

The governance challenge posed by the WSIS

The WSIS was controversial because the central multi-stakeholder element in its strategy challenged the received wisdom of those who regarded it as dangerous to define the debate so broadly. The fear is that this could undermine the delicate—and largely successful from a technical perspective—processes that have evolved to enable experts to govern technical standards by consensus, without interference from commercial or other special interests. Some view policy-making by a much broader range of stakeholders to be an impractical ideal in this field, of no more than symbolic value. This view regards technical innovation and developments as the prime factor governing the future of the internet and the information society, not public policies (Zittrain, 2006).

However, there are also those who looked to the WSIS as a vital attempt to translate into practice a genuinely valuable new structure of accountability. From this perspective, internet policy-makers will need to prioritize a multi-stakeholder approach at some point in order to protect the future of the internet from a wide range of threats to its security and continued growth (e.g., see Cave *et al.*, 2007).

The sharpness of debates about the significance of the WSIS indicates it might have touched a nerve at a key transition point towards a new structure of political control of the internet. Contrary to warnings

385

of the pessimists, this chapter draws on evidence to suggest that the multi-stakeholder processes typified by the WSIS could be a valuable means of widening the base of influential internet political processes. This could lead to the erosion of the formerly strong—almost autonomous—influence exerted by technical experts. It could also internationalize control by reducing the relative dominance of the U.S. in internet governance. For better or worse, or better and worse, is the politics of the internet undergoing a radical change?

To investigate these issues, the chapter explores the WSIS as an exemplar of the shape of any emerging new politics. An analysis of its processes is used to explore their relevance to traditional and new internet governance structures, including initiatives that grew from the WSIS and thereby inherited the multi-stakeholder ethos. It offers an analytical framework, the "ecology of games" and an internet issue classification, to help understand the underlying social dynamics affecting the politics of the internet in general. The analysis draws on a growing base of research on internet policy and multi-stakeholder collaboration,[4] interviews with key participants, and a series of seminars reflecting on civil society participation in the WSIS, and two international forums on internet governance[5] (see Dutton and Peltu, 2005; Dutton *et al.*, 2007).

The WSIS: a case study of global multi-stakeholder policy-making

A waste of time, or an exemplar of a new policy-making paradigm?

Many doubt that moves in internet governance towards the kind of multi-stakeholder processes exemplified by the

WSIS will be influential. It is therefore useful to clarify the concept of multi-stakeholder policy-making in relation to the WSIS.

The broad aim of the WSIS, held in two phases (culminating in major events in Geneva in 2003 and Tunisia in 2005), was to harness the potential of ICTs to promote international development ambitions, such as to meet the UN Millennium Development Goals (see www.un.org/millenniumgoals). These grand social and economic ambitions led many to question the relevance and effectiveness of the WSIS. At one end, a set of views depict the WSIS as a waste of time or a risky venture that should be ignored. At the other end of the spectrum are those who see it as the start of an important new era in multi-stakeholder global policy development. In between is the view that valuable steps were taken towards creating a wider and more informed debate about the information society, although there is no agreement about which were the best steps forward or where they are leading.

Those who saw the WSIS as misguided or largely a waste of time highlight the astounding success of the internet. They emphasize its dependence on a continuing stream of technical innovations and standards-setting processes that have been enabled, they argue, by the absence of control by elected politicians, regulators, and public agencies. These critics point to what was not achieved at WSIS. For instance, no significant policy remedies were produced for major issues, such as how to provide adequate financing mechanisms to sustain ICT for Development (ICT4D) initiatives that could close economic, cultural, age, gender, ICT access, and other "digital divides." There was also no agreement on whether the internet should be regulated or, if so, by which international bodies, beyond a general acceptance of the evolution of the Internet Corporation for Assigned Names and Numbers (ICANN) towards more international accountability (Dutton and Peltu, 2005). The wide range of conflicting interests, perceptions, and values among the diverse stakeholder groups involved in the WSIS was also seen to make the search for agreements or consensus extremely difficult.

Many of those who recognize the substantive value of key aspects of the summit also acknowledge the assessment encapsulated in the title of a WSIS Civil Society (2005) statement: *Much More Could Have Been Achieved*. For instance, the Digital Solidarity Fund (see www.dsf-fsn.org) was first articulated in the WSIS (2003) Declaration of Principles, as a means of bridging digital divides by contributing 1 percent of certain public ICT contracts to the fund. However, there has been strong opposition to such initiatives within industry and many developed nations. The UN backing of the WSIS helped to signal the significance of the internet as an issue of global importance. At the same time, media coverage and general public awareness of the Geneva and Tunis events were relatively limited and indicated that many still did not appreciate its significance.

Nevertheless, the relatively high profile of the WSIS has helped to redefine the internet policy agenda and create a greater awareness and understanding at many levels of the substantial breadth and magnitude of potential ICT4D impacts and of the key global issues of internet governance affecting attempts to spread as widely as possible the benefits tied to the internet's use. The gain in understanding was highlighted by one experienced senior international official who commented that at the first Geneva event many people were not even sure what "the internet" meant and why it should be significant to them—let alone what a concept like "internet governance" signifies. Yet the 2003 Geneva phase led to

the establishment by the United Nations of the Working Group on Internet Governance (WGIG, see WGIG, 2005 and www.wgig.org) and subsequent Internet Governance Forum (IGF, see www.intgovforum.org). The IGF offers a tangible legacy from the WSIS as a notable part of the global internet policy-making arena open to a broad range of stakeholders (Drake, 2005).

Civil society as a key stakeholder in the WSIS

The multi-stakeholder origins of the WSIS

The WSIS was organized by UNESCO and the International Telecommunication Union (ITU). The origin of this event generated much skepticism from the start, since critics viewed this as an attempt by the ITU to broaden its scope beyond telecommunications to include the internet, and also to create a platform for civil society participation.

The presence and participation of civil society in the WSIS lay in the summit's origin in UN Resolution 56/183, adopted in December 2001. This encouraged "intergovernmental organizations, including international and regional institutions, non-governmental organizations, civil society and the private sector to contribute to, and actively participate in, the intergovernmental preparatory process of the Summit and the Summit itself" (UN, 2001: 2). It is therefore a relevant case for examining wider multi-stakeholder political processes, particularly those at a global level. Here, civil society is increasingly being recognized as a significant new policy-making actor involved in a dialog with business, non-governmental organizations (NGOs), global entities (such as the UN and ITU), and state, regional, and local government bodies.

This wider relevance is shown by a report to the UN Secretary-General on strengthening UN systems, prepared by a panel headed by Fernando Henrique Cardoso, the former President of Brazil. This concludes: "The rise of civil society is indeed one of the landmark events of our times. Global governance is no longer the sole domain of Governments. The growing participation and influence of non-State actors is enhancing democracy and reshaping multilateralism. Civil society organizations are also the prime movers of some of the most innovative initiatives to deal with emerging global threats" (Cardoso, 2004: 3). The WSIS could be viewed as setting a precedence that could illuminate potentialities and shortcomings of this new approach to multi-stakeholder politics in which the role of civil society is more formally acknowledged.

Participants at the WSIS in Geneva and Tunis came from a cross-section of stakeholders (Table 28.1). For a global event of the stature and ambitions of the WSIS, however, noticeably low-key or negligible roles were played by many relevant major global players, such as larger Western countries, private enterprises, and NGOs with a development rather than information and communication orientation. For example, the U.S. delegation of 66 at the Geneva summit was the same size as that from Gabon.

The sparseness of many big players at the WSIS has two-edged implications for the summit as an exemplar of global political activity. Although this lessened the event's overall authority and potential practical significance, it also freed more space in which active civil society participants could seek to shape its agenda and outcomes. This makes it particularly suitable as a case that can help elucidate the role of civil society as an active partner in policy-making.

The WSIS Executive Secretariat created a Civil Society Division with responsibility for civil society participation. Formal rules were introduced to support this goal. For example, Rule 55 of the WSIS (2002) procedures establishes the conditions within which representatives of NGOs, civil society, and businesses accredited by the WSIS Executive Secretariat can sit as observers at public meetings of the WSIS Preparatory Committee and its subcommittees (Cammaerts and Carpentier, 2005). Such observers could make oral statements on questions in which they had special competence. If requests to speak were too numerous, the civil society entities could have requested to form themselves into constituencies whose views were articulated through spokespersons.

Was the multi-stakeholder approach a success or failure in the WSIS?

Assessments made of the success of civil society participation have often depended on the degree and nature of involvement in WSIS of those making the judgments.

Table 28.1 Participants at the WSIS phases in Geneva and Tunis

Type	Number of participants			Number of entities represented		
	Geneva 2003	Tunis 2005	% change	Geneva 2003	Tunis 2005	% change
State	4,590	5,857	+28	176	174	−1
International organizations	1,192	1,508	+27	100	192	+92
NGOs and civil society entities	3,310	6,241	+89	481	606	+26
Private enterprises	514	4,816	+837	98	226	+131

The civil society groups and individuals most closely involved seemed to feel they made a difference, but not enough to feel fully represented within the summit's outcomes. The main overall influence of civil society was probably in reinforcing and prioritizing human-centered issues in the summit's information society agenda (e.g., see Padovani and Tuzzi, 2005). This is expressed in the final WSIS (2005:1) Tunis Commitment as: "We reaffirm our desire and commitment to build a people-centered, inclusive and development-oriented Information Society, premised on the purposes and principles of the Charter of the United Nations, international law and multilateralism, and respecting fully and upholding the Universal Declaration of Human Rights, so that people everywhere can create, access, utilize and share information and knowledge, to achieve their full potential and to attain the internationally agreed development goals and objectives, including the Millennium Development Goals."

A major practical success for many civil society participants was their establishment of new and better informal processes of networking among such groups and activists. On the other hand, unrealistic expectations raised by the imprecise promise implied by the notion of participation seemed to be at the root of more pessimistic views of the outcome. Both the formal WSIS rules and the practices of those actors with most real-world power substantially limited the scope of what participation could achieve in affecting the decisions made by those with access to government policy-makers.

For example, restrictions were placed on the right of civil society actors to vote. In addition, the WSIS Executive Secretariat could act as gatekeepers in excluding or allowing in particular groups by deciding to withhold or grant official accreditation (Cammaerts and Carpentier, 2005). The way the WSIS Civil Society Division could subdivide civil society into different caucuses and working groups was resented by some participants, including objections to the inclusion of some local government entities as civil society actors.

On a broader front, inequalities in the distribution of financial resources and institutional, technological, and transport infrastructures were among the strongest restraints on civil society participation. This affects both virtual access to ICT-related capabilities and physical access to location-specific events and activities. For instance, 17 percent of the active participants in physical WSIS meetings were from Africa but 40 percent of civil society organizations showing earlier interest came from that continent (Cammaerts and Carpentier, 2005). Sufficient funds for transport, translation services, and meeting places to support civil society groups are also required to build and sustain meaningful engagements with policy processes.[6]

Different civil society interests at times clashed with each other, as well as with those of government or business. Civil society representatives from some countries seemed to be putting forward restrictive views on freedom of speech and access that were much closer to those of governments with traditions of state censorship than to openness advocated by information and communication activists (e.g., the Communication Rights in the Information Society (CRIS) campaign, see www.crisinfo.org). Extremists within some political and religious movements are also part of civil society, but often have views on freedom of speech that clash directly with those of more libertarian groups.

On the other hand, the diversity represented by civil society helped to put on the WSIS agenda a wide range of topics that might otherwise have been ignored. These include issues such as: free and open source software; the ICT4D needs of minority communities (e.g., indigenous peoples); technological waste; alternatives to largely Western commercial concentration of media power (e.g., see Dutton, 2005); and the empowerment of local communities through knowledge gained from an open "information commons" (e.g., see Kranich, 2004).

One reason why the WSIS participation from development NGOs was relatively low is indicated by the way many non-technical participants found it difficult to engage with more technically oriented issues. This could have led many NGOs to fail to see how the main WSIS focus on the information society could address their own economic, social, and health concerns. This could have led these NGOs to attend the summit in only token numbers, or primarily through their ICT specialists.

Despite these divisions and conflicts, the WSIS process exemplified distinctive characteristics of a process that differed substantially from earlier internet policy-making processes (Table 28.2). Traditionally, governments represent all relevant groups and interests within their constituencies, including the diversity of interests within the business and civil society sectors. In contrast, the WSIS had an explicit commitment to a multi-stakeholder approach in which governments would come to the table with representatives of business and civil society. In practice, this led to significant variations from more traditional patterns of public policy-making processes. Government representatives to the WSIS played a central role, such as in the final stages of negotiation at the summit, but in comparison to more traditional forums, a range of more marginal actors became active participants alongside government representatives. Instead of technical issues being handled reasonably efficiently by committees and groups with much technical expertise, the number of lay participants involved in discussions

with high technical content often made it difficult to engage in dialogs leading to productive outcomes. And rather than working within a set of well developed procedures and processes, actors spent much time on developing rules and procedures for managing and sustaining a range of inputs and the resolution of differences. Table 28.2 provides a summary comparison of the multi-stakeholder processes adopted by the WSIS with more traditional patterns of internet governance.

Will the WSIS multi-stakeholder model characterize a new phase in internet governance?

The multi-stakeholder approach of the WSIS has been inherited by the WGIG and IGF global internet governance initiatives, which were among the most concrete outcomes of the summit. But is this a signpost to a significant new "third phase" direction in the evolving history of internet governance developments, moving away from the internet technocracy that has characterized the first two phases?

The first two phases of internet governance (1960s to 2000)

The multi-stakeholder approach adopted by the WSIS challenges the autonomy of the more technically dominated standardization and governance arrangements in the first few decades after the emergence of the internet in the late 1960s (see Simonelis, 2005 for details of the history of internet governance bodies). For instance the Internet Engineering Task Force (IETF)[7] was founded in 1986. And the Internet Society (ISOC) was created in 1992 to provide an institutional home and financial support for the internet standards process, which by then had to

Table 28.2 Internet governance: comparison of traditional and WSIS processes

Aspect of internet governance process	Traditional patterns	WSIS multi-stakeholder patterns
Representation	Governments represent legitimate interests	Explicit commitment to a multi-stakeholder approach
Representation of key actors	Major nations and actors play key roles across a number of issues	Low key (or non-existent) engagement by many "big players" (countries, businesses and NGOs)
Legacies and historical dependencies	Legacy of entrenched interests	New area, with few entrenched interests (e.g. compared to other global policy-making arenas such as trade talks)
Incorporation of technical expertise	Delegated to specialized committee structures and bodies, such as standards groups	More technically oriented issues difficult to engage with by many participants (e.g. development NGOs)
Representation of non-governmental, civil society actors	Elected officials and public agencies take on responsibility for aggregating the interests of a pluralistic array of groups	Civil society organizes itself, but sometimes with splits and tensions between civil society participants and difficulties in determining who represents civil society
Indirect v. direct participation	Business and civil society represented by elected officials.	Specific provisions for civil society, including business, to participate directly in formal WSIS processes; but some rules, processes and resource divides restrict participation
Sustainability	Reliance on major institutions, lobbies, and organized groups to maintain access and participation	Difficulties in sustaining virtual and physical participation among some civil society actors

accommodate growing commercial interests in this network of networks.

A second phase began in the late 1990s. Until then, the U.S. government had ultimate control over core internet "root server" files, but their administration tasks were performed by an internet pioneer, the late Jon Postel of the University of Southern California (see Leiner *et al.*, 2003). However, there was a growing feeling in the U.S. government and among some other major stakeholders that such an independent technical mechanism could not take account of the broader range of social, commercial, and political issues that could be substantively affected by technical internet governance decisions. This perception was a key factor in the establishment in 1998 of ICANN, which is an internationally organized not-for-profit corporation based on the laws of California. Its formation signaled a significant step towards the latest phase of wider stakeholder participation in internet governance, which could reduce the autonomy of technical experts and their constituencies. However, the internet technocracy with the support of the U.S. government remained the most powerful participants.

The first two phases of internet governance arrangements worked well as a basis for the internet's phenomenal growth for three main reasons. First, the technical community involved had a commitment to maintaining the founding design principles of end-to-end (E2E) openness, core architectural stability, and independence as a shared resource for the benefit of all. This community was small and homogenous enough to allow for decision-making that was both consensual and reasonably efficient in translating agreed standards into effective technical enhancements, as well as to solve problems within the operational infrastructure. Second, innovation flourished through activities at the edges of the network, with creative users and businesses developing innovations such as the web, browsers, and social networking. This was achieved in ways that maintained a cascading array of innovations. Third, the U.S. government played a largely hands-off role. At the same time, from the outset it has been the ultimate policy authority for key aspects of the internet infrastructure, such as files in the highest level internet root servers that determine vital operational issues like the allocation of web domain names.

The emergence of a third phase

In the twenty-first century, a new phase in internet governance was triggered as the internet's impact as a global socio-economic as well as technical phenomenon was first fully realized. This came about through the wide enactment in everyday life of the much-forecast diffusion and convergence of digital technologies, from multimedia online content to a huge range of mobile consumer devices and an increasing use of embedded sensor networks (e.g., see Dutton *et al.*, 2005). It also stemmed from growing threats to the internet's infrastructure, from amateur hackers and spammers to organized criminal efforts to exploit vulnerabilities in the internet's architecture, such as the ability to mask identities.

A crucial difference in this emerging third phase of internet governance— which could be called the new politics— was triggered by the involvement in the internet of a much wider base of committed stakeholders. This could be a significant departure that lessens the degree of control of the internet technocracy and the U.S. government by stimulating countervailing pressures through the policy-making involvement of other governments, business, international bodies, and civil society stakeholders. This approach has been adopted by the ongoing WSIS-influenced IGF global internet governance initiative.

Technical participants in the initial phases may not even have thought of themselves as being involved in governance activities, as that term is often incorrectly perceived as implying direct government-led regulation. However, they were indeed involved in undertaking governance functions. And the processes they used were inherently political, as for any policy formation effort needing to balance the interests and perceptions of a diverse range of stakeholders. This has been the case even when they have focused on essentially technologically oriented issues, as indicated by the U.S. government's hand on important technical levers such as the internet root servers.

As internet governance processes have moved from being the preserve largely of an internet technocracy towards a wider ownership of the related substantive issues, the politics involved have become more critical, more global, and more diverse. This is indicated by the multi-layered, fragmented, complex, and generally highly distributed nature of internet governance. The internet itself is not one technology, but an assembly of many at different levels. Similarly, governance is not one process, but several at different levels and in overlapping arenas addressing specific issues. This means different government models and agencies involving many different institutional, group, and individual stakeholders, will continue to be needed to address different governance issues.

Can elements of best practice from the past be maintained?

A major challenge for the multi-stakeholder orientation of the third phase of internet governance politics is to preserve and strengthen the so-far successful insulation of the technology's essential core infrastructure from political and commercial manipulation by special interests. Technically creative and elegant designs need to be invented and implemented on a global scale. At the same time, appropriate processes need to be explored to address the diverse range of substantive issues and stakeholder needs raised by the increasing intertwining of internet use with wider social, economic, and political policies and activities.

This is a difficult challenge as it involves pressures from diverse and often conflicting viewpoints and interests, which reflect very different values and cultural and political understandings. For instance, such conflicts include: governments seeking to empower and safeguard or exploit and subjugate their citizens; enterprises wanting to promote locally driven development or dominate and manipulate new markets; users seeking creative benefits or defensive protection from their online connections; and experts striving to maintain the integrity of the architecture or undermine it maliciously.

The impact of real-world political issues in internet governance is illustrated by a debate over what has been called "network neutrality." This fundamental internet design principle has sought to ensure that the network provides E2E routing without inspecting or changing the data being carried. In the U.S., network neutrality became a hotly contested area among telecommunications infrastructure suppliers, Internet Service Providers (ISPs), media

content producers, consumers, regulators, and others (e.g., see Stern, 2006). The dispute arose because some infrastructure suppliers were seen to be seeking tiered services in order to charge differential rates for access to its channels for different types of content (e.g., enabling a revenue stream from on-demand video). Network neutrality became a global issue when regulators sought to anticipate industrial strategies in the U.S. within the potentially lucrative sector of entertainment, but with the relevance of that strategy varying across nations. For example, the high level of competition in the provision of broadband services in the U.K. made this debate less relevant, since the market was well positioned to shape online offerings.

Implications of the multi-stakeholder perspective

The value of incorporating a wider base of stakeholders in internet policy-making and reducing technocratic control to some degree is the way involving more stakeholders from, and representing, developing countries in the WSIS and IGF has helped to move debates on ICT4D away from their traditional focus on a single digital divide in access to ICT infrastructure and systems. Instead, a broader view is emerging of the many important differential impacts of use (Williams, 2005). The IGF is seeking to use the multi-stakeholder model to try to build a new form of internet governance framework that offers light-touch coordination with a broad scope and diverse inputs. The aim is to establish and maintain a "big picture" coherence that can avoid an unmanageable fragmentation of the internet governance mosaic (Dutton and Peltu, 2005).

A previously narrow focus, primarily on the divide in internet access, has led some policy-makers and researchers to claim that "the" digital divide might already be over now, making it seem that there is perhaps little left to do in internet governance to assist development. However social research in this field (e.g., Dutton et al., 2006; Dutton and Helsper, 2007) is increasingly showing that there is not just one divide based on access. Instead, there are many divides along multiple social, economic, cultural, geographic, political, and other dimensions. These follow and reinforce similar existing divides in societies, as well as creating new ones.

The kind of internet governance agenda favored in developed Western countries has generally focused on market liberalization as the prime solution to the divide in access. This is being widened by initiatives such as the IGF to take account of the specific needs of developing countries and regions. For instance, governments in developing countries are often a major source of ICT know-how, infrastructure development, and capacity building, together with the private sector, universities, and NGOs. Such governments also generally view internet access as a key to many economic and social development areas, so it is unrealistic to expect these governments to stand aside from active participation in internet governance processes, as some would prefer. Given the financial, political, cultural, and other constraints faced by developing countries, building a better understanding between them and developed countries within a coordinated internet governance strategy could be valuable in addressing internet-related regulations affecting key non-technical areas, such as freedom of speech, human rights, and intellectual property rights (IPR).

Incorporating multiple stakeholder perspectives in policy-making can also highlight the value that can be gained not only from leading-edge ICTs but also from applying still-relevant older technologies, often in conjunction with the latest ICTs.[8] For example, developing countries often dismiss the internet as a poor replacement for radio, such as in orchestrating health campaigns. However, the internet can be used to support health campaigns through the radio and other mass media by helping to network health officers and program makers across the developing world, enabling access to richer content, and preventing every agency from having to reinvent existing materials. This also illustrates how input from the internet technocracy remains central to developing appropriate solutions to different stakeholder requirements.

Despite these kinds of benefits, the multi-stakeholder model is limited in several respects. There are two main reasons for these constraints: it does not reflect the real diversity of issues and actors; and it has so far failed to incorporate the technocrats effectively into this process.

A major constraint of the multi-stakeholder model is its inability to incorporate the full complexity of the actors and their interplay of objectives and motives that shape choices about the internet. The issues that shape the future of the internet and the information society are many, and arise at multiple levels and in multiple arenas. People do not seek to govern the internet or the information society as such, but aim to achieve more immediate and focused objectives. Multi-stakeholder policy-making also raises critical questions about who represents different stakeholder constituencies—questions that are particularly difficult to answer in an agreed way for the multitude of diverse civil society interests involved. Keeping technical experts committed to, and enthusiastic about, the governance process is also essential to successful outcomes because their advice and knowledge is essential to the successful implementation and operation of any agreed technically related policies.

Understanding the dynamics of multi-stakeholder decision-making

A framework is now proposed to help understand how a multi-stakeholder approach can best be applied to internet governance in a way that addresses its potential flaws and builds on its positive benefits. This has two main elements: a three-part classification of internet issues; and the concept of internet governance being viewed as an "ecology of games" in which many actors are pursuing their own goals through a range of interactions.

The concept of an ecology of games can help to understand the real-world contexts and interactions shaping outcomes from the new politics of multi-stakeholder policy-making, including taking account of the range of issues outlined above (Dutton, 2004). This idea is based on the notion of a game,[9] defined as an arena of competition and cooperation structured by a set of rules and assumptions about how to act to achieve a particular set of objectives. internet governance can then be seen to be the outcome of a variety of choices made by many different players involved in separate but interdependent governance games. Multi-stakeholder policy-making is an example of an ecology of games.

A classification of internet governance issues

Given the different goals and interests of participants in a multi-stakeholder policy-making model, classifying governance issues into areas focused on particular types of outcome can be of much value. Table 28.3 illustrates one such classification based on three categories: internet centric, which is intrinsically focused on the internet, such as domain names; internet-user centric, where rules need to focus on users; and non-internet centric, where rules are shaped by policies in wider related—but distinct—sectors, such as by copyright (Table 28.3). As in an ecology of games, different actors in different arenas seek to address these different issues. The examples in the table relate to some key internet policy-making games.

An illustration of the value of the classification proposed in Table 28.3 is the way in which the WSIS process often artificially separated internet governance from development issues, rather than treating them as separate but interrelated fields (Williams, 2005). As highlighted earlier, this separation created a perception of the summit as being technically oriented and less relevant to development issues. An important role for a coordinating body such as the IGF could be to highlight this interdependence by alerting existing development agencies and affected stakeholders to the internet governance issues of intrinsic relevance to their development activities, but which may be obscured to them by the opaqueness to non-experts of some key innovations in the internet and related digital technologies. Nevertheless, it is important to realize that many people interested in the economic development of a particular nation or locality might well be uninterested in structures governing internet governance issues such as domain names. Different actors are focused on different issues.

In an ecology of games such as those illustrated in Table 28.3, no single set of actors actually seeks to control governance as such, but each player pursues more focused goals in collaboration or competition with other actors. Actual goals could be, for example: to create an equitable market for registering and managing internet names (Type I); enhance socio-economic development by promoting equity of internet access (Type II); or close wealth divides with the help of

Table 28.3 Selected games shaping internet governance for development

Domain	Game	Main players	Goals and objectives
Internet centric	Transnational jurisdictional governance "turf struggles"	Governments, regional entities, internet and other governance agencies, such as IGF, ICANN, WIPO (on IPR-related issues), experts	Participation in governance bodies to gain or retain, limit or expand control over internet resources (e.g. the root servers).
	Names and numbers	Individual experts, ICANN, Registries, ISPs, users	Obtain, sell, allocate domain names, etc. for sites, servers, users.
Internet-user centric	Network neutrality	Telecom infrastructure suppliers, ISPs, content providers, consumers, media businesses, regulators, civil society activists, lawyers, public policy-makers.	Negotiate terms of access to internet content, taking account of different stakeholder views (e.g. on social equity, development, free markets, the internet's open e2e design principle).
	Privacy and data protection	Governments, citizens, regulators, private firms, lawyers, journalists, civil liberties activists	Prevent or seek disclosure of personal data depending on negotiated or imposed criteria.
Non-internet centric	Freedom of expression	Political and religious activists, writers, artists, media rights advocates, news media, bloggers, governments, censors	Individuals, groups, organizations aim to facilitate or constrain the expression and exchange of certain viewpoints.
	Copyright, digital rights management	Legislators and regulators, creative industries and other content providers, telecom suppliers, ISPs, ICT vendors.	Negotiate access and rights to balance players' goals (low-cost access for consumers; highest return on assets for content creators and suppliers).

internet use (Type III). The same actors could own all these goals, while participating in games that could be called "internet names and numbers," "internet diffusion," and "economic development." One of the games illuminated by the WSIS is about the politics underlying the conceptualization of who comprises civil society and the processes determining how different interests are represented.

The politics of participation: who represents civil society?

The multi-stakeholder goals and rules defined by the WSIS process exemplify a "politics of participation" game. Civil society is diverse both in its structures and ideological orientations, ranging from extremely conservative to radically progressive. This leads to numerous competing and complementary interests and interactions between actors in overlapping civil society games. These take place at household, community, state, and other arenas, up to the level of the global ecology of games that characterized the WSIS.

The social dynamics of interactions between grass-roots movements and communication with higher levels often leaves the grass-roots without a voice that fully articulates their particular interests, particularly as there are many inequalities in economic, educational, and other support that militate against the views of the disadvantaged being heard or getting high on policy agendas. Many civil society participants in the WSIS seem to have been largely self-selected and driven by individual commitment. In addition, users as a category are considered most often by designers of systems and artifacts when seeking to create markets for products, rather than as full participants in the design process. Ambiguity over the official status of local authorities and city administrations as civil society actors, and the desire of some governments to represent their citizens—as they are elected to do—further illustrates the lack of clarity in delineating the contours of civil society representation.

The central role of ICANN creates further ambiguity. As a private corporation, rather than a public body, its status as a representative of users is not clear to many stakeholders. Yet it has more financial resources than perhaps any other actor in the internet governance sphere, other than governments themselves (with an annual income in the neighborhood of $50M in 2007). ICANN's rules and procedures are geared towards involving users and other stakeholders, but it has its own approach to aggregating global interests that can be in conflict with those of traditional bodies such as the UN, which rely on negotiation among state representatives. But as a key representative of the established internet technocracy, it is vital to harness ICANN's expertise to any governance process, if that process is to be effective.

Participation in policy-making processes typically demands large amounts of time, effort, and accumulated expertise, as was involved in attending preparatory meetings and analyzing discussions and documents at the WSIS. This can result in relatively few people representing an enormous range of civil society interests. For instance, the wording of the main WSIS Civil Society (2003; 2005) "Declaration of Principles" and "Tunis Statement" was developed by a relatively small core of people. This is not new, or unique, to the internet governance processes, as suggested by Robert Michels' (1915) "iron law of oligarchy." However, there is a danger that civil society representation will not be viewed as legitimate and that some representatives can be "captured" within policy processes, which to some extent can distance them from their constituencies' ongoing experience and evolving views.

Conclusion

The global diffusion of the internet, along with twenty-first-century digital convergence, has accelerated pressures from numerous stakeholders to engage in shaping the design, development, and governance of the internet, as well as in using the technology to meet their diverse needs and aims.

The WSIS was an important event as it had strong institutional backing from key global bodies, such as the UN and ITU, and helped move internet politics towards a more pluralistic process. Even though it failed to achieve its ambitious goals, and probably highlighted more problems concerning its multi-stakeholder model than tangible successes, it was a significant and interesting exemplar of a wider trend (as

397

highlighted, for example, by the Cardoso Report) to develop a new politics rooted in a vision of broad multi-stakeholder participation. This includes a strong civil society presence and seeks to deal with a wide range of social and economic as well as technical policy issues. The establishment of the IGF was a valuable initiative, and continues to offer an arena for examining the issues explored in this chapter.

The WSIS was therefore far from being a waste of time and hasn't had the substantive damaging effects feared by its strongest detractors. In addition to initiatives like the IGF, its main long-term benefits could lie in the network ripples it sent out when bringing together a wide range of groups who learned about each other only through contacts linked to the WSIS, including some who were previously unaware how much their own interests could be well served by taking a keener interest and involvement in internet developments, use, and governance. In addition, as this chapter has argued, analyses of the WSIS processes and outcomes, here and elsewhere (e.g., Servaes and Carpentier, 2005), reveal important insights into the opportunities and difficulties created by an emerging new internet politics.

Civil society is a major new actor in the new politics, which opens a number of important avenues for exploring social research on the new politics, both in relation to the internet and the wider issues highlighted in the Cardoso Report. For instance, analysis of the WSIS raises important issues surrounding the conceptualization and enactment of notions like participation, access, and power that are applicable to wider political arenas. These are illustrated by the description given of the tensions between formal rules of participation, the promise of full participation, and the realities of pluralistic processes that fall short of democratic ideals.

The WSIS multi-stakeholder experience can also help to suggest research directions for investigating how different stakeholder sectors (e.g., civil society, business, government) and groups within a sector (e.g., libertarian civil society advocates versus more restrictive civil society interests) can cooperate more effectively, while acknowledging and addressing conflicting perspectives. This could include examining the factors promoting "real engagement" between multiple stakeholders, where participants in discussions respond directly to each other in productive ways even if they approach the topic from different backgrounds and conflicting values (e.g., see Dutton et al., 2006).

The questions raised earlier about who represents civil society could equally apply to business and NGOs, for instance in differences between larger and smaller entities or between those engaged in different sectors of activity. The WSIS experience and follow-on activities such as the IGF could be further analyzed to seek answers to crucial questions such as: What kinds of people and groups should be called civil society? How are their representatives chosen? What criteria can be used to assess their validity as a legitimate representative voice of those for whom they claim to speak?

There is also a need to clarify who and what other stakeholders represent. For instance, the ambiguous status of local government at the WSIS, and claims by some governments that they speak on behalf of their civil societies, raise pertinent points about the voices articulated by government representatives. The reasons why many development NGOs were not greatly attracted by the summit's information society focus could help to reveal approaches that could make wider constituencies aware of the need to engage more vigorously in policy-making that shapes outcomes tied to convergent digital technologies. Academic researchers can also help to articulate grass-roots user and social requirements to policy-makers and product, system, and service designers and developers.

In meeting such challenges, social research could offer both practical and conceptual insights. Good empirical data and evidence-based analyses would enable researchers to work with policy-makers and practitioners to identify and evaluate the priorities that are most likely to lead to sustainable strategies and institutions to assist disadvantaged areas and groups. In internet governance, issue-based policy research that is likely to be of most value could include empirical studies of actual uses[10] and action research[11] based on a strong scholarly grounding for analyzing experimental uses of the internet. Analytical frameworks from academic research, such as the ecology of games and internet governance issue classification outlined in this chapter, can also help to understand the politics of participation in bodies such as the IGF.

One of the most significant challenges is to explore how the talent and enthusiasm of the internet technocracy, which served the network so effectively since its inception, can feel comfortable working in a multi-stakeholder framework that could empower both experts and the lay policy actors. If this is handled successfully, the technical understanding of all participants could be enhanced, while the technical experts will gain a better understanding of how their knowledge can benefit a wider range of users

Guide to further reading

This chapter works at the intersection of four different topics: the history of the internet; the WSIS; internet governance; and new institutionalist perspectives on politics such as the ecology of games. Each has much to explore, but we suggest the following entry points to each topic. The history of the internet remains controversial, central role of technical experts inventing the internet is conveyed well by Hafner and Lyon (1996). Dutton (2004) provides an overview of issues of the information society dealt with at the WSIS. With respect to internet governance, Bill Drake's (2005) edited compilation of papers by members of the Working Group on Internet Governance offers an insider's perspective on key issues. These can be delved into directly to explore the diversity of viewpoints and issues, as well as ongoing developments, at the IGF's website (www.intgovforum.org). Chadwick (2006: 229–56) provides an analytical perspective on the political stages of internet governance. A key work on the ecology of games is Long's (1958) article.

Notes

1 This chapter arose from research initiated throughout a seminar series on the World Summit of the Information Society (see www.oii.ox.ac.uk), which was supported by a grant (RES-451-26-0295) from the U.K. Economic and Social Research Council. The authors acknowledge the valuable insights and information from these seminars, which they have been able to draw on for this chapter. The contributions of Sonia Liff, Warwick University and former Visiting Fellow, Oxford Internet Institute, and OII Research Officer, Victoria Nash, who coordinated the series with William Dutton, are particularly valued.

2 For example, see the European Multistakeholder Forum on CSR, Review Meeting, December 2006 at http://ec.europa.eu/enterprise/csr/forum_2006_index.htm

3 See www.unesco.org/wsis or www.itu.int/wsis for details.

4 A key account of developments within WSIS and the WGIG is provided by Drake (2005), particularly a section on multistakeholder collaboration, pp. 7–46.

5 Organized in collaboration with the Berkman Center for Internet and Society at Harvard

Law School and sponsored by Afilias, the *Economist*, Nominet U.K., and the Public Internet Registry.

6 For instance, only 7 percent of civil society organizations were involved from start to finish in the 2003 WSIS (Cammaerts and Carpentier, 2005).

7 A large international community of network designers, operators, vendors, and researchers responsible for the development and stability of the internet's architecture.

8 For instance, the Kothmale Community Radio and Internet Project (www.kothmale. org) integrates radio and internet services. This includes allowing listeners to send questions to the radio station. Staff at the station obtain answers from the internet and broadcast them over the radio.

9 The term game is used here only in this sense and should not be seen as trivializing an arena by suggesting it is like a sporting or entertainment game.

10 For example, the World Internet Project covering over 20 countries (www.worldinternetproject.net), including the OII's Oxford Internet Surveys (OxIS) in Britain (www.oii.ox.ac.uk/research).

11 An example of such action research is StopBadware.org, an initiative run by the OII and Berkman Center for Internet and Society to provide practical defenses against malicious software programs (www.StopBadware.org).

29

Enabling effective multi-stakeholder participation in global internet governance through accessible cyber-infrastructure

Derrick L. Cogburn

The global policy processes for internet governance are becoming increasingly complex. A dizzying array of institutions are involved, from the established Internet Corporation for Assigned Names and Numbers, the World Wide Web Consortium, and the Internet Engineering Task Force to the newly emerging set of institutions that arose from around the UN World Summit on the Information Society, the Internet Governance Forum, and the Global Alliance for ICT and Development. One trend evident within these global policy processes is the focus on "multi-stakeholder" participation, designed to create space at the negotiating table for civil society organizations and the private sector alongside governments and international organizations. However, in most cases, the current working methods of internet governance policy processes do not facilitate active participation by developing countries and civil society. Simply allowing non-state actors to register and be physically present at meetings is not sufficient. Using international regime theory as a conceptual framework, this chapter seeks to clarify the structure and relevance of the institutionalized policy processes related to global internet governance. It explores the potential for "cyber-infrastructure" to overcome some of the problems of this emergent regime by enabling more effective participation by developing countries and civil society participants.

As the internet continues to grow in importance, its relationship to commerce, science, government affairs, and political advocacy becomes more evident, as does its global nature. The internet is at once deceptively simple and staggeringly complex. With relative ease, you can click a few buttons on a hand-held device or laptop computer and view highly detailed audio, video, and textual information from nearly every country in the world. Almost effortlessly, you can make a perfect copy of that information and send it to a friend or collaborator six time zones away. The technical protocols, security mechanisms, and underlying infrastructure of the internet, while quite complex, have remained hidden from the average user. The global policy processes that make these possible have become known as "internet governance," and they involve a diverse group of national and international institutions. This chapter seeks to clarify the structure and relevance of these institutionalized policy processes related to global internet governance and to explore the potential for information and communications technologies (ICTs) to enable more effective participation in them by developing countries and civil society participants.

Research questions and theoretical framework

This chapter asks three principal research questions. First, what are the current institutionalized policy processes related to global internet governance and how are they structured to include multi-stakeholder participants? Second, in what ways are ICTs being used to include multi-stakeholder participants? Finally, could the scientific concept of "cyber-infrastructure" be harnessed to enable the institutionalized policy processes of global internet governance to better include multi-stakeholder participants, especially those with geographical and physical limitations?

Two approaches drive this chapter. The first approach, which covers the first and second research questions, involves a theoretically driven analysis of six important entities within the internet governance regime. However, with the third research question, the study switches to an "action research" approach (Lewin, 1946; Freire, 1970; Davison, Martinsons, and Kick, 2004), by exploring the degree to which ICTs might enhance the ability for diverse multi-stakeholder groups to participate in global governance processes.

While contemporary international public policy seems to be wrestling with the concept of global governance, there is already a significant academic literature exploring this phenomenon. Much of the literature emerging from international relations focuses on addressing the "anarchy problematique." If the world-system comprises sovereign and equal nation-states, as well as a range of critically important non-state actors, all operating in a global environment devoid of any semblance of a world government, how are decisions made and enforced, resources allocated, and stability and order maintained? This fundamental problem of international coordination and collaboration has been studied by a wide range of scholars (Keohane, 1984; Axelrod, 1985; Oye, 1986; Keohane and Nye, 1989; Ostrom, 1990; Rosenau and Czempiel, eds., 1992).

Much of the literature on global governance is dominated by realist or neorealist approaches to international relations, which focus on the interactions of powerful state actors and the interplay of their strategic interests around international conferences and negotiations. The biggest contender to these approaches is sometimes called the idealist or neoliberal institutionalist approach, which focuses on the role of international organizations in creating a just and fair world order.

In recent years, state primacy in international negotiations has been challenged by the emergence of far more heterogeneous stakeholder groupings in nearly all of these processes—transnational civil society organizations. Individual citizens, represented by non-governmental organizations and transnational networks, have been increasingly recognized as important stakeholders in global governance. The UN has even commissioned studies to understand how it might redesign its relationship with civil society (Cardoso Report, 2004). These civil society organizations represent a new energy and dynamism that is seen as critical to the growth and development of the information society.

International regimes, knowledge, and networks

The term international regime draws explicitly on the canonical definition developed by Krasner (1983), which refers to "sets of implicit or explicit principles, norms, rules and decision-making procedures around which actors' expectations converge in a given area of international relations." internet governance is essentially about the international regime formation processes illuminated by Krasner's definition. However, unlike Krasner's approach, which focused mostly on states, this study takes a broader perspective to include non-state actors in what is known as a "multi-stakeholder" regime formation process. Such multi-stakeholder processes ostensibly create space at the international negotiating table for non–state actors such as civil society organizations (Cogburn, 2005) and the private sector (Haufler, 2001), along with the more traditional state actors—governments and international organizations.

International conferences play a critical role in global governance and specifically regime formation (Cogburn, 2004b). They serve as focal points for contestation of the norms, principles, values, and decision-making procedures of the emergent regime. They also serve to nurture global networks of recognized policy experts and epistemic communities. Policy-actors interact at these global forums and practice "conference diplomacy" in an attempt to influence outcomes (Kaufmann, 1968).

Unfortunately, simply allowing non–state actors to register for a conference does not necessarily create an environment in which these individuals and organizations can effectively participate and influence policy outcomes. After all, developing countries have participated in international negotiations for decades, and in most cases have failed to significantly influence the outcomes.

The formulation of an equitable international regime requires the active and effective participation of multiple stake-holders who can adequately represent their own interests. One key to this may be active membership in transnational policy networks and significant linkages with like-minded epistemic or knowledge-producing communities. The current working methods of most international policy processes do not take full advantage of geographically distributed networks and require restructuring in order to facilitate active participation.

Internet governance

The term internet governance refers to the making of collective policies and standards for the global internet community. In practice, much of internet governance boils down to who actually manages the internet's system of unique identifiers, such as domain names (for example, www.nytimes.com), generic top-level domains (such as .edu, .com, .net), country code top level domains (.uk, us), IP addresses (128.230.84.47), the underlying software protocols and databases that tie it all together (e.g., IPv4, IPv6, TCP/IP, Whois), and the procedures for handling disputes within this system. In 1998, the U.S. government established an innovative approach to internet governance when it subcontracted many of the technical functions formerly assigned to Department of Defense contractors to a private, not-for-profit corporation with relatively broad-based international participation: the Internet Corporation for Assigned Names and Numbers (ICANN). Currently, ICANN administers the domain name system (DNS) and performs such important tasks as introducing competition among domain name registrars and managing a system of dispute resolution for domain name trademark conflicts (Mueller, 2002). In addition to ICANN, other institutions that play an important role in internet governance include the World Wide Web Consortium (W3C), and the Internet Engineering Task Force (IETF).

ICANN and these other organizations are supposed to have a "narrow" technical mandate. However, technical decisions also have social and political consequences. ICANN makes collective policies that touch the lives of people around the world. However, it is now facing serious challenges.

UN World Summit on the Information Society

When the United Nations General Assembly agreed to convene the two-phased

World Summit on the Information Society (WSIS) held between 2003 and 2005, it was not clear that it was a deliberate attempt to challenge the existing internet governance order. However, that is precisely what happened.

The WSIS brought together the world's governmental, private sector, and civil society leaders in a discussion about the uses of information and communication technologies in the development of a global information society. The ITU, a specialized agency of the UN focusing on the technical and developmental aspects of telecommunications, organized the WSIS and had a clear interest in its outcomes. It saw the WSIS as an opportunity for it to regain a central role in telecommunications policy, since telecommunications, and indeed the internet, which itself is underpinned by telecommunications infrastructure, plays a critical role in the information society.

The WSIS was explicitly "multistakeholder," and established a significant precedent within the UN for the involvement of non-state actors in policy formulation (Klein, 2004). With new stakeholders come new policy perspectives. The WSIS brought together diverse actors from around the world, in developed and developing countries, to focus on an incredible array of policy issues, from infrastructure financing and development to multi-lingual content creation. While it is quite appropriate to criticize the outcomes of the WSIS, as many have done (see Franklin, 2007), there is no doubt that it unleashed a dynamic for change in the existing global internet governance regime. This new multistakeholder dynamic has emerged to challenge the existing internet governance mechanisms organized around ICANN.

In many ways, the WSIS was an overt attempt to create the principles, norms, and values necessary for the global governance of an international issue area

(Klein, 2004; Cogburn, 2004b). However, while the WSIS was praised for its multistakeholder participation, its implementation of the idea left a lot to be desired. For example, one of the central components of the first phase of the WSIS was the negotiation of text for a *Declaration of Principles* and an *Action Plan* (WSIS, 2003a, b). In the UN context, this negotiation around text is a lengthy process. Each document is endlessly debated, page by page, paragraph by paragraph, and word by word. Participants in the negotiation process suggest specific text, known as "language," that usually reflects their own parochial interests in the issue in question. This often takes place in a very large plenary session. In this critical process during the WSIS, civil society was limited in its inputs to the first five minutes of each morning or afternoon session (the same was true for the private sector). During this time, they had to offer their suggested language for every issue planned to be negotiated during that session. In stark contrast, governments (all governments, both developed and developing) had free reign during the session to take the floor, offer language, and respond to other suggestions. Civil society and the private sector delegates had no such opportunities. These structural limitations were pervasive throughout the structure of the WSIS, greatly reducing the impact of civil society on its outcomes.

Dynamics of change

In the course of the WSIS debates internet governance emerged as one of the thorniest ICT policy issues. The crux is the following question. If the internet is going to serve increasingly as the underlying infrastructure for nearly all the applications that enable the global information society, who should control the allocation of scarce resources relating to it, and what should be its overall global governance mechanisms? On one hand are the proponents of ICANN, who argue that ICANN is already a functioning, complex, multi-stakeholder global institution, based on the principles of internationalization and privatization of governance. It has numerous institutional structures already in place, and a relatively proven set of mechanisms.

On the other hand, this position is heavily criticized by those who ask: should the future of such a valuable resource as the internet be determined by ICANN, a not-for-profit corporation registered in the United States, which is still overseen by a contractual relationship with the U.S. government, or should a more global, independent, and representative institution evolve to assume these responsibilities? Again, the ITU is seen by many, but certainly not all, as just such an international mechanism and one that provides a role for the UN system in internet governance. The continued dominance of states, and in some cases the relative strength of developing countries within the ITU, is a significant negative for some policy activists. But many of the proponents of the UN-based approach argue that ICANN is too politically beholden to the U.S., and will bend to its political will.

The most interesting recent illustration of this pressure came when significant lobbying from the U.S. conservative religious right was applied to the Bush Administration's Department of Commerce to oppose the proposal for ICANN to approve an .xxx domain (Westerdal, 2007). The ICANN board determined in June 2005 that the proposal met all of its requirements and initiated a process to begin a contractual relationship with ICM, the proposing company, which was approved in final form on August 1, 2005. Shortly after, domestic political mobilization against the decision began in the U.S., and the government officially announced its opposition to ICANN's decision.

In response, ICANN put the implementation of the new domain on hold. Even with the support of the chair and numerous board members, the .xxx decision was voted down in May 2006 (Westerdal, 2007). For many, this turn of events shows the substantial influence—both latent and actual—of the U.S. on what is supposed to be a global, independent, and neutral technical body.

The second significant element of these debates concerns the tension between freedom and control. Some states, some but not all of which are authoritarian, want to ensure that they have the capability to control the internet within their own countries. While this is frequently presented as the desire to "protect" their citizens, the reality is that it allows them to exert significant censorship and surveillance of their citizens' online activities. Many of these types of governments see the UN environment as much more amenable to their individual or collective influence than the current "U.S.-dominated" ICANN structures. For them, the WSIS presented an alternative to raise these issues and try to shift the debate to familiar UN territory.

After all of the international wrangling between these warring camps and the creation of a new Working Group on Internet Governance (WGIG) following the Geneva WSIS in 2003, these issues were still unresolved with the conclusion of the WSIS at the 2005 Tunis summit. As a result, two new follow-on mechanisms were born, the Internet Governance Forum (IGF) and the Global Alliance for ICT and Development (GAID). In particular, the IGF is designed to continue the process of UN-led global discussion on the future of internet governance.

Enabling participation?

The preceding section addressed the first research question by outlining the contours of internet governance. The second research question asks: in what ways are ICTs being used to include developing countries and civil society participants in these regime formation processes?

Numerous obstacles exist to the effective participation by multiple stakeholders in global policy formulation. At the international level, MacLean (2004) has identified the lack of easy, affordable, and timely information; the structure, functioning, and working methods of international forums; and the ineffective use of financial resources available for participation as some of the primary factors. At the national level, he identifies a lack of awareness among decision-makers, lack of technical and policy capacity on ICT issues, and weaknesses in national and regional ICT policy processes and institutions.

Internet governance organizations have barely begun to tap into the potential of the internet to overcome some of these obstacles and to enable remote participation and geographically distributed collaboration. This section compares some of the efforts to date.

ICANN

Without a doubt, ICANN is still the central organization in global internet governance. Through its public meetings and complex organizational structure, ICANN touts its role in maintaining the "ongoing security and stability" of the internet through its various multi-stakeholder policy and decision-making processes.

Although the structure of ICANN has changed since its inception in 1998, several of the same basic elements are still in place. These attempt to honor the goal of bringing together the technical community, the commercial constituency, the non-profit constituency, individual users, and governments. Each of these constituencies has an organizational role within the ICANN structures. For example, there

is an Address Supporting Organization, a Country Code Domain Name Supporting Organization, a Generic Names Supporting Organization, an AT-Large Advisory Committee, and a Governmental Advisory Committee (GAC). A Board of Directors oversees this structure, as well as a President who oversees the ICANN Staff. All of these structures have well-developed and in most cases multi-lingual and accessible websites that provide background information, membership applications, announcements, blogs, listservs, and many other information distribution features.

In November 2007, ICANN held its 39th public meeting in only its ninth year of existence. On average, it holds about four public meetings a year, and like most other international meetings, they are in exciting destinations (for example, Singapore, Berlin, Santiago, Los Angeles, Cairo, Yokohama, Melbourne, Stockholm, and Montevideo, to name just a few). All of these meetings are open to the public, and are advertised on its well known website. Here one may also find information about how to register for a meeting, background documents, and other preparatory materials. As early as March 2000, in its fifth meeting, ICANN was already using a variety of techniques to enable some level of remote participation in its meetings. For example, it would make a transcript of the main plenary sessions available online in almost real time, and would take questions and comments from the internet.

The WSIS

From the perspective of enabling multi-stakeholder participation, the WSIS presents numerous analytical challenges. The UN General Assembly resolution that created the WSIS explicitly stated that civil society groups would be equal participants in the process. However, it was apparent from the outset how difficult it is to put this desire into practice.

To begin, the WSIS was a very elongated policy formulation process. Not only did it have two distinct phases (Geneva 2003–Tunis 2005), it also had a number of fairly complicated regional and preparatory rounds. From an international regime formation perspective, these were in many ways far more important than the summit itself. The sheer number, geographical distribution, and duration of these meetings were overwhelming. It was almost impossible for any developing country or civil society organization to be active participants in all of the WSIS preparatory rounds. For those fortunate few who could attend each of the meetings, at significant financial expense, fully active participation was yet another hurdle.

The formal Preparatory Committee meetings (PrepComs) were held mostly in Geneva (with one in Tunisia), and each lasted two weeks. For many people, "participation" in these conferences meant physically traveling to Geneva, staying in a hotel for two weeks, and traveling every day to the conference center to sit through the PrepCom meetings. After all this expense, time, and effort to get to Geneva to attend the PrepCom, what "participation" actually meant for civil society organizations was being able to contribute to a "collective" civil society statement that could be made at the opening five minutes of the morning session, and again at the opening five minutes of the afternoon session. Other than that, there was no official mechanism for civil society input into any of the actual deliberations and negotiations being conducted on the various policy issues and draft documents.

Even if we accept the argument that these meetings and their subsequent documents are important to regime formation, it is difficult to accept that participating in this manner was cost-effective

and efficient. If this was to be the extent of civil society participation—while governments could take the floor as frequently as they liked to negotiate on every single sentence and paragraph being debated—then there is a clear need for alternative mechanisms.

The primary focus of the use of ICTs during the WSIS was on the dissemination of information. From the official WSIS website, anyone with internet access could download nearly every document under formal discussion (in multiple languages), and could access webcasts of the formal plenary sessions. While these uses of information technology are helpful, they allow for very little (if any) interactivity, and focus on passive receipt of information as opposed to enabling remote participants to engage in a deliberative process.

WGIG

The WGIG was organized as a multi-stakeholder working group after the close of the first phase of the WSIS, when the internet governance issues remained intractable. Unlike the structural limitations described above in the WSIS preparatory meetings, the WGIG members were all able to participate relatively equally in the WSIS processes, albeit mostly behind closed doors. One aid to this process was the decision to organize the WGIG using Chatham House rules, meaning that while members were free to use the information discussed during meetings, no member was allowed to attribute anything to any individual member or their institution. This well-known rule is designed to stimulate a free-flowing exchange of information and ideas—crucial in difficult policy areas.

Since most of the WGIG procedures were behind closed doors, it is difficult to assess the extent to which ICTs were used to support their processes and the degree

407

to which remote participation was encouraged or used. However, it seems likely that e-mail listservs were the dominant technology. Transcripts of public consultations were made available, as well as submissions from various groups. Very little effort was made to accommodate members that could not physically attend meetings.

IGF

Building upon the structural innovations of the WGIG, the IGF has introduced more innovative mechanisms for multistakeholder participation and has gone further than nearly any other internet governance institution in terms of facilitating remote participation.

The IGF does not have a selective "membership" structure like the WGIG. It is an open and multi-stakeholder venue for discussion. At its 2006 inaugural meeting in Athens, the IGF gave birth to yet another innovation, the "Dynamic Coalition," which was supposed to be a bottom–up self-organizing mechanism for multi-stakeholder interest groups to convene. However, at the same time, some of the selective participatory elements from the WGIG were incorporated into the IGF as the secretariat appointed what it called a "Multi-stakeholder Advisory Group." This was designed to be the highest advisory grouping to support the decision-making processes of the IGF. The IGF also supported the creation of a parallel academic body called the Global Internet Governance Academic Network (GigaNet) to allow for scholars and academics to organize around the IGF meetings.

More importantly from the perspective of this chapter, however, was the decision to facilitate interactive, geographically distributed, multi-stakeholder participation in the IGF. In Athens, this happened on at least two levels: the plenary sessions, and the workshops. In the plenary sessions,

a nearly verbatim transcript was made available in real-time to the public from the IGF website. This complemented the multiple webcasts and multi-lingual audio feeds. The secretariat set up a team of experts to receive e-mail responses and questions from remote participants, and the panel moderators were instructed to integrate those questions and comments into their session moderation. Particularly illustrative of this approach was the session moderated by Ken Cukier of the *Economist*, who skillfully integrated the remote participants into the physical session. In addition to this e-mail based interactivity, the IGF secretariat organized two mobile phone lines for receiving caller questions and comments, a blog for conference participants, and a free wireless network (though the latter broke down at various stages).

UN Global Alliance for ICTs and Development

The remaining WSIS follow-on activity, the UN Global Alliance for ICTs and Development (GAID) is important due to its focus on the development aspects of the internet and the information society, and on getting developing countries more actively involved in the process.

The GAID held its inaugural meeting in Kuala Lumpur in June 2006. It invited multi-stakeholder activists from around the world. They organized a steering committee, a high-level panel of advisors, and champions' networks, all chaired by Craig Barrett, chief executive officer of Intel Corporation. In February 2007, the Global Alliance held its second meeting at the headquarters of Intel in Santa Clara, the heart of Silicon Valley. But at neither of these meetings did the GAID make any attempt to use ICTs to better engage civil society or participants from developing countries. As with many of the other post-WSIS initiatives, the GAID has mostly

used its website to disseminate information to the public about events, with
some background information on how
the organization is structured and governed.

The comparative analysis of these
organizations and forums shows that in
nearly all of the cases, there has been some
effort to use ICTs to facilitate remote
participation. The usage is varied and
occasionally patchy. Clearly, the dominant
technology is still e-mail and listservs. This
is followed by audio and video webcasts,
which allow remote participants to follow
what is going on in meetings, frequently
in multiple languages. Often, text-based
transcripts of meeting discussions support
these webcasts. However, most of these
approaches are still one-way broadcasts,
and do not promote much interactivity
and participation.

Emergent participatory practices

As the discussion has shown, there is a
desire on the part of most institutions
involved in global internet governance to
enable some form of remote participation.
Unfortunately, most of these approaches
take a "broadcast" approach, and focus on
allowing remote participants to read, see,
and/or hear what is going on at the
meetings. These approaches are mostly
not highly interactive, and fail to capture
the essential knowledge, expertise, and
involvement of most of the remote participants. More importantly, this approach
continues to highlight and reinforce the
reality that the "physical" meetings are
really the most important, and where the
"action" really occurs.

But in common with most contemporary international gatherings, official meetings in the internet governance policy
area have often been accompanied by a
number of "unofficial" experimental participatory mechanisms. During the WSIS,

for example, ICTs were a key aspect of
the *Global Deliberative Dialogue on Internet
Governance*, established by a consortium
led by the Center for Research on
Collaboratories and Technology Enhanced
Learning Communities (COTELCO) at
Syracuse University, of which the author
is Director. Timed to coincide with the
WSIS Tunis PrepCom 3 in 2005, this
used synchronous and asynchronous
technologies to bring together interested
parties from governments, international
organizations, the private sector, and
civil society to debate the internet governance policy issues being addressed on
the ground in Geneva. Given that most
of the physical participants in the
PrepCom were usually passive spectators
in the conference room, watching other
people—mostly governments—present and
debate text, they had significant time to
be able to participate in the dialog. It also
created an opportunity for experts, both
on the ground in Geneva and around the
world, to help educate novice participants
about the substantive and fundamental
issues. This blended approach, taking
synchronous and asynchronous communication and collaboration tools, and further blending participation on the ground
with geographically distributed individuals, was seen by most participants as
tremendously powerful.

Similarly, outside of the main plenary
sessions of the IGF in Athens in 2006,
additional innovations occurred in the
workshops. The Internet Governance
Project (2004, 2005) used workshops to
demonstrate the broader potential of
remote participation. Both of the projects'
panels used web-conferencing technologies to allow remote participants to deliver presentations, watch and hear the
presentations of others, and ask questions.
Finally, the Internet Governance Project
and COTELCO organized a tri-partite
web-conference linking the Athens IGF
with the Caribbean Internet Forum and a

gathering of faculty and students at Syracuse University. Speakers at each location were also able to interact with participants not located at any of the three sites.

The success of these initiatives indicates the potential for enhanced participation in global policy processes through cyber-infrastructure and policy collaboratories. If multi-stakeholder policy processes are to be successful, what kinds of mechanisms are required to enhance the participation, influence, and ownership of these international regime formation processes by transnational civil society organizations and developing countries? The chapter's final research question asks: could the concept of cyber-infrastructure be integrated into the institutionalized policy processes of global internet governance to better include developing countries and civil society participants?

Enabling multi-stakeholder participation with collaboratories and cyber-infrastructure

In the field of computer-supported cooperative work important literature has focused on a new and highly innovative institutional form called a "collaboratory." A collaboratory blends the words "collaborate" and "laboratory," and emerged out of the U.S. National Science Foundation in the mid 1980s. In 1989, William Wulf argued at an NSF-sponsored workshop that a collaboratory was "a center without walls, in which the nation's researchers can perform their research without regard to geographical location" (Wulf, 1989: p. 2; NAS, 1993: p. vii). Collaboratories can be found in scientific fields as diverse as oceanography, space physics, and molecular biology.

An NSF-funded project called the *Science of Collaboratories* has identified three distinct functions of a collaboratory.

These three functions include: (1) people-to-people; (2) people-to-information; and (3) people-to-facilities (Science of Collaboratories, 2007). A set of collaboration tools and social practices supports the functioning of an effective collaboratory. For example, in the *people-to-people* category, a collection of tools would support the ability for members of the group to remain aware of and in touch with the various members of the research team. Regarding *people-to-information* functions, a collaboratory would use content management systems and other tools to ensure that there was sufficient access to the digital libraries and other knowledge and information required by the members. Finally, certain collaboration tools such as web-conferencing and application sharing would be used to provide remote access to facilities, such as conference rooms.

Some pilot studies have introduced the concepts of collaboratory and cyber-infrastructure into existing networks active in the WSIS (see Cogburn, Johnsen, and Battacharrya, 2008). However, the overarching question is how relevant are these concepts to the structure, functioning, and needs of the global internet governance process? This involves examining each component of the collaboratory concept to see how it might apply to the practices required by current internet governance processes. The hypothesis is that the insertion of a policy collaboratory into global governance processes can enhance the ability for policy actors from developing countries and transnational civil society groups to participate in these conferences by facilitating their interaction in geographically distributed epistemic communities. This hypothesis has been tested in the context of action research. The author designed, developed, deployed, and evaluated the application of collaboratory approaches to the international ICT policy domain within the processes of the World Summit on the Information Society.

It is possible to work collaboratively with geographically distributed policy actors to enhance the following areas: administrative capacity, policy development capacity, deliberative capacity, density of social networks; and degree of engagement with epistemic communities. For example, it would be possible to use the policy collaboratory to hold geographically distributed seminars and panel presentations on key themes, both to raise awareness of the themes, and to conduct substantive training. These training sessions can include panelists from around the world sitting in their own organization, and participants from around the world sitting in a virtual plenary room. Following the seminar discussion, participants can be moved into multiple virtual breakout rooms. This infrastructure can also be used to hold robust issue debates, strategy sessions, and to conduct administrative business. Evaluation and iterative redesign are critical components of a policy collaboratory.

Presence awareness

Presence awareness functionalities in a collaboratory include such applications as instant messaging; easy to use person-to-person voice, video, and data transfer; and e-mail listservs and archives. When people are co-located, it is common to drop in on someone else's office or bump into someone in the hallway or coffee room. Further, it is usually easy to tell whether the other person is available for an interruption or is too busy. This kind of informal interaction is critical to collaboration. It is also very difficult to do at a distance, and indeed research has shown that it introduces considerable delay into processes that require interaction among dispersed participants (Herbsleb *et al.*, 2000). A number of research projects have attempted to provide such awareness at a distance. Some have used elaborate video or audio hook-ups that are always on to create virtual hallways or virtual shared offices.

Digital repositories

The digital repository functionality of collaboratories facilitates document storage, digital library resources, shared data and archives, as well as photo directories of members, and so on. Projects inevitably generate lots of digital artifacts, such as data sets, drafts of manuscripts, proposals, planning documents, schedules, contact lists, recordings of sessions, photos, and many more. An emerging body of research shows that online photo directories may help to develop and strengthen social capital within distributed communities (Resnick, 2001; Resnick and Shaw, 2003). A project intranet is a web-accessible repository of these materials and can be developed with certain levels of public viewing and access, while maintaining strict security to control access. Security at several different levels of granularity can be provided, starting with something as simple as a login with password. Being able to share material across sites is extremely valuable. There are now numerous open source content management systems, such as Dotnetnuke, Plone, or Mambo, that can be used to build these content management systems.

A further challenge of coordinating a geographically distributed group is the scheduling of activities and shared access to calendars. A number of software applications are now available to collaboratory planners that facilitate easier scheduling of formal and informal joint activities, and awareness of other distributed collaboratory members. Various methods can be used to control access to information from such calendars.

Web-conferencing and application sharing

Finally, within collaboratories, web-conferencing and application-sharing functionalities allow for virtual seminar rooms, with voice and video over internet protocol, multimedia content, whiteboards, polling and decision-making tools, and real-time application sharing. Web-conferencing substantially facilitates interactions among researchers involved in a project. At present most of the interactions in the WSIS processes take place either face to face, which requires expensive air travel and lodging, or via e-mail lists (Cogburn, 2005). Internet-based web-conferencing tools make possible audio and video interactions, with the advantage that these are much less expensive and frequently more efficient than long-distance teleconferencing or traditional video-conferencing.

An important companion to web-conferencing is application sharing. The ability to share any software applications open on one computer with the members of the web-conference presents numerous opportunities. Using these technologies, researchers can collaboratively edit documents, review data sets, run and interpret statistical calculations, observe remote video cameras, and much more, all in real time from the comfort of their own home or office. Application sharing allows all participants access to the editable object (with appropriate floor control protocols), and to jointly annotate work material such as charts, photos, and presentation slides. In short, a high degree of real-time interactivity is possible. Further, these materials can be archived and replayed, an especially useful capability for long-distance education. In a number of prior collaboratories this set of capabilities has turned out to be one of the most useful features. By combining conferencing and application sharing, it is possible to carry out a variety of both formal, scheduled sessions like lab meetings, colloquia, or seminars, and more informal interactions among a small group of researchers.

The potential of cyber-infrastructure in internet governance

Given this background to collaboratories and cyber-infrastructure, the chapter will briefly explain how these ideas and tools might be successfully integrated into the existing practices of the internet governance institutions, specifically the IGF and ICANN.

To begin, presence awareness packages could be used in a variety of innovative ways. For example, the informal practice of the secretariat sharing their instant messaging addresses could be formalized. The secretariats could hold virtual office hours if they did not wish to make themselves too available or visible by being constantly online. In addition, the various working groups and committees organized within ICANN and IGF could use these to help strengthen relationships. These tools could also be used when it is necessary to bring small numbers of participants together for meetings, or to involve them in a small working-group session being held physically.

Some of the internet governance institutions are already using digital repositories in the form of content management systems. However, in nearly all cases, they are not using these to their full potential, such as in supporting the needs of multiple and sometimes overlapping teams by allowing granular control and access to resources. In some cases, the user-management features of these sites are not even activated. Much more attention should be paid to the specific use of these sites to build trust and cohesion within subgroups.

Finally, perhaps one of the most important contributions cyber-infrastructure could make to the existing internet governance institutions comes in the form of interactive remote participation in all meetings, large and small, formal and informal. As I have mentioned, many of the UN institutions have done a fairly good job of webcasting audio and video from their meetings, though ICANN has done far less of this. However, the one-way audio and video broadcast promotes a passive approach to remote participation. Through the use of web-conferencing, large numbers of remote participants could not only hear and see events at the meetings, they could participate actively by raising their hands and getting into the queue to speak. They could ask questions of the speakers, and even speak themselves, give presentations, and make comments from wherever they happen to be located.

Conclusion

This chapter has ended by sketching out a vision for multi-stakeholder democratic participation in global information and communication policy processes. Drawing on international regime theory, it suggested that the WSIS and its follow-on mechanisms were an explicit attempt to formulate the principles, norms, and values of an emergent international regime to govern the information society in general, and the internet specifically. Given the broad reach of the internet and its implications and potential for socio-economic development around the world, it is critical that the broadest diversity of ideas and talents be included in the debate and discussions around its development. However, the point is not just to have those voices included in the meetings, but also to ensure that developing countries and civil society organizations are genuine partners in the process, and are not merely used as pawns to project a false image of multi-stakeholderism.

Pursuing this inclusive approach to internet governance is an important step towards increasing awareness of and adherence to the regime's principles, norms, values, and rules. Such an approach will certainly increase the legitimacy of the internet governance process. However, it requires the active and effective participation of multiple stakeholders. Effective participation must go beyond one or two face-to-face meetings per year.

Key to this effective participation are transnational policy networks and epistemic communities. Empirical evidence shows that these already exist in developing countries and civil society organizations (Cogburn, 2005). The working methods of international policy processes, especially internet governance, need to be restructured in order to facilitate their active participation. In order to overcome the current limitations, institutional mechanisms to strengthen geographically distributed collaboration among the multiple stakeholders should be pursued. The institutional mechanism of a policy collaboratory provides a model.

Guide to further reading

This chapter has covered a range of issues and has drawn on interdisciplinary literatures. Four primary themes—global governance, multi-stakeholder participation, internet governance, and collaboratories and cyber-infrastructure—form its spine.

The literature on global governance is quite voluminous and varied. Readers interested in global governance should start with Keohane (1984). In addition, see Ruggie's (1993) classic book, which explains the role of international institutions in maintaining stability and world order.

After these foundations, readers could work their way up to the perspective drawn upon most heavily in this chapter: international regime theory. The canonical work is Krasner's (1982) article that lays out the accepted definition of international regimes. For the alternative perspective, Susan Strange's classic confrontation with international regime theory is included in the same special issue of the journal *International Organization* which contains Krasner's piece. Peter Cowhey's (1990) work on the roots of high-technology regimes explores the evolution of the international telecommunications system.

For multi-stakeholder participation in global policy processes and deliberative democratic practices, see the special UN review of its relationship with civil society organizations (Cardoso, 2004). For deliberative democracy, start with the roots deep in the Habermasian (1989) literature on the public sphere, then move to the recent analysis of the use of information technology to support deliberative democracy found in Button and Ryfe (2005).

On internet governance, one of the best texts for a complete overview of the technical, economic, and policy issues, is Mueller (2002). In addition, see Goldsmith and Wu (2006), which staunchly supports a realist perspective and highlights the important role states continue to play in this area.

Finally, in the field of collaboratories and cyber-infrastructure, it would be best to start with the National Academy of Science (1993) report, which takes much of the previously disparate work in this area and focuses it into a clearly written treatise on the subject. Then, read the more recent 2003 report on cyber-infrastructure, a report of the Blue-Ribbon Commission (Atkins *et al.*, 2003) to explore the further expansion of the collaboratory concept.

30

Internet diffusion and the digital divide

The role of policy-making and political institutions

Kenneth S. Rogerson and Daniel Milton

As governments, businesses, and society tackle the digital divide, understanding why the divide persists and whether it is widening or is narrowing is crucial. This chapter analyzes attempts to make policy and implement programs relating to the internet and the diffusion of technology in four constitutionally democratic countries. The aim is to generate hypotheses regarding the potential role of institutions in this process. Each case—Brazil, Estonia, Singapore, and the United States—is a recognized leader in technological diffusion in its region. While the literature on the digital divide emphasizes the very real impact of economic and societal forces, political institutions and policy processes are also important drivers of technology diffusion.

A number of studies provide theoretical explanations for how and why the digital divide persists and whether it is widening or narrowing. These explanations can be synthesized into three categories: economic, societal, and political.

Norris comes to the conclusion that "the root cause of unequal global diffusion of digital technologies is lack of economic development" (Norris, 2001b: p. 233). As countries find the economic resources to provide citizens with access to the internet, the divide will narrow. Norris acknowledges that with economic development must also come a change in the political will of governmental institutions to address these issues through traditionally overlooked societal groups, such as "poorer neighborhoods and peripheral rural areas, the older generation, girls and women, ethnic minorities, and those lacking college education" (Norris, 2001: p. 234). Notwithstanding the acknowledgment of these other minor variables, Norris clearly signals economic development as the key catalyst to bridging the digital divide.

The second argument is societal in nature. In order for societies to bridge the gap, people must learn more about the internet and how to use it. These arguments run along a spectrum. At one end is the position that knowing more about technology enables individuals to utilize it to increase their economic and political participation: "The higher the educational background, the more people use the internet in an instrumental way" (Bonfadelli, 2002: p. 81). The other end of the spectrum is that technical knowledge in and of itself is not enough to bring people to a point at which the technical knowledge gives them greater power and influence in the political and economic systems in which they live (Bonfadelli, 2002; Neuman and Celano, 2006). There are too many other necessary factors, like socio-economic status or political opportunity.

The third argument states that political factors are really the underlying force driving change. It is the formulation of new regulations and policies, or changes and adaptations in existing ones, that make a difference in how the digital divide is addressed. Though economic or societal catalysts for change have an impact, a flexible and adaptable internet policy environment can make or break digital divide initiatives. While media use patterns are shaped by technical, economic, and social factors, the impact of regulatory and policy-making factors is understudied and underestimated, especially in light of Guillén and Suárez's view that "Governments can implement specific policies that would make this medium more widely used by the population" (Guillén and Suárez, 2005: p. 697). They suggest that countries that understand this can have "the largest effects in terms of magnitude" on the bridging of the digital divide.

Ernest Wilson (2004: 56) makes a similar argument. Successful technological diffusion depends upon a democratic institutional culture. In order to effectively integrate technology into a society, Wilson proposes that political institutions play a strong, pivotal role in technology policy. In fact, a central tenet of his research "is that the information revolution is an institutional and political revolution more than a technical one" (Wilson, 2004: p. 56).

Democratic governments and bridging the digital divide

Does government type matter in the formulation of technology policies? Kalathil and Boas (2003) describe similar types of authoritarian governments but very

different ways in which computer networking is used by governments and citizens. They suggest that there is no relationship between government type and technology use. For example, although there is some censorship in all authoritarian governments, they do not attempt to suppress information flows over the internet in the same ways or to a similar extent.

The question driving this chapter is whether this same conclusion holds true with technology-related policy in constitutionally democratic political systems. We focus on national political institutions to identify their role in the formulation and implementation of technology-related policy. Which institutions have an impact on information technology policy at a national level, and how?

In contrast with the approach of Kalathil and Boas (2003), what follows is a comparative case study of four democracies of varying types. These countries are drawn from different regions of the globe. In each case we focus on policy related to the digital divide and to privacy, security, and online risks. More importantly, each country has been chosen because it has exhibited a global reputation for technological initiative in its region, both in matters of technical development and in information policy (see Table 30.1).

Country profiles

Brazil has been at the forefront of technological experimentation in politics. Its constitution, completed in 1988, gave the country its current parliamentary republican system. Executive power is vested in a president, who is both the chief of state and head of government. Various ministries operate under the direction of the president. The Ministry of Science and Technology is the bureaucracy charged with the prime responsibility for regulation

Table 30.1 Internet diffusion trends

Country (2006 Population)	2005–6	2000
Brazil (188,078,227)		
Internet users	25,900,000	5,000,000
Percentage online	13.8	2.9
Estonia (1,324,333)		
Internet users	690,000	366,600
Percentage online	52.1	25.6
Singapore (4,492,150)		
Internet users	2,241,800	1,200,000
Percentage online	53.9	28.9
United States (298,078,227)		
Internet users	205,326,680	124,000,000
Percentage online	68.8	44.1

Source: Authors' compilations from Central Intelligence Agency (2007) and Internet World Stats (2007).

and expansion of IT infrastructure. The legislature is comprised of a Federal Senate with 81 seats, and a Chamber of Deputies with 513 seats. Power in the legislature is diluted among a number of the country's main political parties. The highest level of the judiciary is the Supreme Federal Tribunal, with 11 ministers appointed by the president and confirmed by the Senate.

Estonia is a former communist system and an emerging democracy often held up as a leader in IT development in eastern Europe. Estonia formalized its constitution in 1992 after the collapse of the Soviet Union. The executive power in Estonia, unlike Brazil, is split between a president and a prime minister. Under the prime minister is the Council of Ministers, composed of various heads of the bureaucratic arm of the government. Various ministries have made strides in the technology policy sector, the leading body being the Ministry of Economic Affairs and Communications, which has been charged with the coordination of the government's IT activities. The Ministry of Justice deals with internet crime and security, while the Ministry of Education and Research plays a minor role in various technology education initiatives. The legislature is a unicameral parliament with 101 seats, with no single

political party holding more than 30 percent of the seats. The National Court is headed by a chairman appointed by parliament for life.

Singapore is a democratic country according to its constitution but in practice it is semi-authoritarian. It prides itself on its level of networking and technological development. Under Singapore's 1965 amended constitution, the president and prime minister share executive power. The president appoints heads of the individual ministries and the heads are responsible to the parliament. The Ministry of Information, Communication, and the Arts is responsible for technology policy. The Infocomm Development Authority of Singapore (IDA) is responsible for technology diffusion and infrastructure maintenance within Singapore. There are 84 seats in the unicameral Parliament, although 82 of these seats are in the hand of the People's Action Party (PAP). The president, in consultation with the prime minister, appoints the chief justice, and in turn consults with the chief justice in appointing other members. Singapore has the basic features of a liberal democracy but the PAP dominates parliament. In addition, the prime minister wields considerable power and is able to limit political participation by opposition groups.

This power of control over certain types of activity also extends to the mass media and the internet (Rodan, 1998: p. 65; Kluver, 2004: p. 449).

The oldest of the democracies in the study is the United States, which ratified its constitution in 1787. The president is both head of government and chief of state. With the consent of the Senate, the president appoints secretaries to lead the federal bureaucracies. A number of federal agencies have a hand in technology policy, ranging from National Technology and Information Administration in the Department of Commerce, the Federal Communications Commission, and the Federal Trade Commission to the Department of Homeland Security. There are two chambers in the Congress, the Senate having 100 seats and the House of Representatives having 435. Within the chambers of the Senate and House, there are congressional committees that deal with specific areas of legislation. The highest level of the judiciary in the United States is the Supreme Court. Members of the court are appointed by the president, with the advice and consent of the Senate.

For each country we present a snapshot of the recent principal technology policy discussions in the areas of the digital divide and privacy and security. These stem from proposals in legislatures (some of which may have become law), programs within executive branches being implemented by bureaucracies, and other proposals from societal groups.

Brazil

Brazil has been at the forefront of technology adoption in South America. For example, in 2005, president Luiz Inacio Lula da Silva went on record encouraging all government ministries and schools to use open source software as a means of reducing costs and improving access. This vision is fueled by the fact that less than 15 percent of Brazilians identify themselves as internet users.

Brazil's government has played an active role in increasing public access to information technology. The government's "Computers for All" program, completed in late 2006, aimed to make computers available to people from all social classes by helping finance over 450,000 machines for distribution to citizens (Yan, 2006). Another program, the $4 million Casas Brazil project, involved the construction of 75 computer centers to provide internet access to poorer areas (Yan, 2006).

However, despite the government's investment in financing the purchase of computer equipment for lower- to middle-income Brazilians, some citizen groups have complained that the programs do not go far enough in helping the people with newly purchased computers to take the next step and connect to the internet. Internet service provider costs are not defrayed by the government programs and consequently most of those with new computers remain unconnected (Yan, 2006: p. 1).

Brazil's legislators have been active in proposing regulations to enable the monitoring of internet users. One senator in the Brazilian legislature recently noted that while the internet is a tremendous asset to Brazilian society, it also offers the potential for criminals to extend their enterprise. A current legislative proposal will allow the government to gather information on internet usage (Chang, 2007: p. A18). The Brazilian government has also mounted a legal challenge against Google to force the handover of information on users of Google's Orkut social networking site as part of an effort to stem the tide of child pornography flowing through the country. The appellate court ruled that the Brazilian prosecutor's office did not have a right to the information (Chang, 2006: p. 1).

These initiatives have drawn criticism from public interest groups. One group, iCommons, claims that the Brazilian authorities still have a long way to go in protecting freedoms and better regulating the online industry. The group cites a lack of legislative leadership as an explanation for the Brazilian judiciary's heavy hand when it comes to online freedoms (Chang, 2007: p. A18).

Estonia

Many nations of the former Soviet bloc have spent the last decade rediscovering ethnic identity and rebuilding economies. Estonia has quickly gained a reputation for being a leader in technological diffusion and innovation. For example, Skype, a popular online telephony program, was created there. In 2007, the country became the world's first to allow voting in a national parliamentary election via the internet.

Diffusion of technology in Estonia has increased dramatically over recent years and its current internet user rate rivals other developed countries. By early 2007, 95 percent of Estonian schools had access to broadband internet connectivity (though surveys show that only about 20 percent of teachers actually use it in the curriculum (Archdeacon, 2007)). One of the programs credited with igniting the technology push in Estonia was a government initiative that set up 500 public-access computer centers across the country (Swartz, 2003). The Estonian government has continued to emphasize public access to broadband and has assigned this responsibility to the Ministry of Economic Affairs and Communications of Estonia (2006: p. 9).

Estonia has been particularly active in developing policy on internet-related crime. In 2005, it created a task force of public and private sector representatives to create the guiding principles underlying the government's information technology security policy. This outlines the need for cooperation between the public and private sectors, as well as the need to protect basic human rights in the process of securing information systems (Ministry of Economic Affairs and Communications of Estonia, 2006: pp. 33–4).

In the bureaucratic arena, several ministries have proposed and enacted policies on information security. In 2005, the government established the Computer Emergency Response Team of Estonia (CERT Estonia) to help protect citizens from online threats from viruses. CERT Estonia also provides incident response in the event of an attack on the country's networks (Ministry of Economic Affairs and Communications of Estonia, 2006: pp. 35–6). In addition, the Ministry of Economic Affairs and Communication established a task force that will constantly draft, review, and update policies on the protection of "technology assets." This government organization provided key services to both the public and private sector during the April and May 2007 denial-of-service attacks on Estonia's internet infrastructure. The team was able to isolate the source of some of the attacks and filter out all traffic from Russia, as well as limit online users to those in the Baltic states and Scandinavia (Finn, 2007: p. A1).

The Estonian legislature has extended various protections to guard against identity theft and misuse of personal information. In May of 2004, the legislature revised the Personal Data Protection Act, updating several antiquated provisions and establishing a committee of security experts to review and propose amendments to the Act as necessary (Ministry of Economic Affairs and Communications of Estonia, 2006: p. 71). The legislature has also enacted a proposal to better integrate the government's information systems (Ministry of Economic Affairs and Communications of Estonia, 2006: p. 68).

Despite its relatively poor economic status, Estonia has prioritized its resources for technology innovation and diffusion. The evidence suggests that technology policy forms an important component of activity within the government and the legislature.

Singapore

Singapore has long been regarded as a technologically advanced nation. In the mid 1990s, the country began its "paperless" initiative to make all government records electronic in form. Its population is highly connected, and this reflects the fact that in the mid 1990s the government established policies to open internet access to all citizens through, for example, its SingaporeONE program. Government has worked closely with private companies to achieve its goals (Burton and Williams, 2005: p. 10). By 2006, 56 percent of all households that had internet access connected via broadband (Ministry of Finance, Government of Singapore, 2006).

Singapore's government has sought to exercise greater control over the internet. In 1998, the Computer Misuse Act became law. It was revised in 2003, granting the government the power to monitor online activities and act preemptively to prevent criminality (Yun, 2004). While the government promised that all information gathered about innocent citizens would be protected, and that the new powers will only be used for national security threats, civil liberties groups such as Think Centre and some legislators have argued that it will lead to greater political oppression (Burton, 2003: p. 2).

The government has also moved to establish better security measures to protect its technological investment. The Infocomm Development Authority (IDA), the government's technology policy arm, has recently enacted a cyber-watch center to monitor and protect the personal data

gathered in more than 1,600 online government services (Singapore to set up cyberwatch, 2006). The purpose of the center is to monitor, in real-time, threats to government information systems.

Singapore is an interesting case. It is a *de jure* democracy and a *de facto* authoritarian system. Government has moved to regulate and restrict internet use by opposition parties. But as the cyber crime law examples shows, there is genuine legislative discussion about the appropriate limits of such policies.

The United States

A variety of branches of the U.S. government have a stake in the internet and technology policy areas on which we focus. Policy relating to the digital divide has been haphazard, but present in one form or another since the mid 1990s.

On February 2, 2000, then U.S. President Bill Clinton introduced a proposal to help bridge the digital divide. In creating $2 billion in tax incentives, Clinton encouraged the expansion of access to technology, increased education and training, and the promotion of online content. Additionally, Clinton's initiatives included means to increase the funding of Community Technology Centers. The funding for these centers and other technology development programs were administrated through the Technology Opportunities Program office (TOP), which lost its funding in 2005. Other programs focused on education included the E-rate program, which provided discounted technology to educational institutions.

In the United States, policy debates about government's role in regulating online privacy have focused on content such as pornography, pedophilia, extreme violence, and gambling. Congress has debated over various proposals in all of these areas, and several bills have become law since 1995.

420

As part of the broader Telecommunications Act of 1996, Congress passed the Communications Decency Act (CDA). The CDA was designed to create penalties for individuals who transmit indecent or patently offensive information online. Though the intention was to keep improper information out of the reach of children, the law was criticized for being overly vague and ran into problems with the First Amendment. It was judged unconstitutional by the U.S. Supreme Court in 1997.

When it became clear that broadly defined legislation would not pass the test in the courts, other, more specific, routes were attempted. The 105th Congress passed the Children's Online Privacy Protection Act. This limited the type of information that an operator of a website or online service could collect from a child without parental consent. Also, in 1999, senators proposed the Children's Internet Protection Act (CIPA), which called for an amendment to the Communications Act of 1934 to make libraries, elementary and secondary schools ineligible to receive federal funds if the institution's internet access does not have government-approved internet filters. The courts have ruled that this law also violates the rights of library patrons. In June 2003, however, the U.S. Supreme Court upheld CIPA, saying that it did not violate individual rights because each library had the discretion to adapt the law to local needs, and filters could be lifted by request. Interestingly, both liberals and conservatives have been interested in issues of online content.

An important category of internet and technology policy comes as a result of the terrorist attacks on the United States on September 11, 2001. Legislation such as the U.S. Patriot Act (2001) has had an impact on internet-related issues, especially in the area of surveillance systems to investigate and combat terrorism. One of the most heated legislative topics in the 107th Congress was how to regulate the internet to protect homeland security.

In November 2002, President Bush signed a Homeland Security Bill that had far-reaching implications for computer security and internet privacy. The bill includes a provision that "shields internet service providers (ISPs) from customer lawsuits if providers share private subscriber information with law enforcement authorities" (Krebs, 2002: p. 1). The information industry welcomed the exemption in the bill, which paved the way for companies to cooperate with the government and share sensitive information.

Internet policy and democratic institutions

We return now to our original question: how might we hypothesize the potential role of institutions in shaping technology policy? Some trends can be discerned from the preceding discussion that may be helpful in this regard.

First, we can hypothesize that legislatures matter. They have the ability to prescribe programs, provide resources, and set the agenda. The persistent U.S. Congress has repeatedly tried to pass legislation to protect children from what it considers inappropriate internet content. A caveat is that whereas some countries seem to be able to respond to changes in technology relatively quickly, the gridlock in the U.S. Congress may hinder timely policy responses to technology-related issues (see Neuman, McKnight, and Solomon, 1998).

Second, executive leadership could also be a factor. Wilson (2004: 366) discusses information champions: "individual leaders who recognize and seize opportunities and make things happen." Sometimes that leadership can derive from the public sector as with Brazil's president Luiz Inacio Lula da Silva's and U.S. President

Bill Clinton's emphases on bridging the digital divide. Leadership could also come from the commercial sector, international organizations, or societal groups, but these groups are often dependent upon government intervention to achieve their aims such as subsidies, funding for a new program, or legal enforcement (such as the internet security community calling on Estonia's CERT team to help with the cyber attacks on the private sector). In addition, while every country has a ministry or sub-ministry devoted to the internet and technology, their utilization is relative to executive attention and the prominence of other agenda items.

Third, we may hypothesize that ideological divisions do not have a strong influence on technology-related policy. In fact, in the United States, "High-tech issues enjoy broad bipartisanship," as Marc Brailov, a spokesman for the American Electronics Association put it (Mosquera, 2001). In the Estonian legislature, multi-party consensus means that there is little ideological gridlock on issues of technology policy.

Fourth, the impact of civil society groups will play a role. Milner (2006) argues that the ability of societal groups to influence democratic institutions has the strongest influence on technological diffusion. Shuler and Day (2004) present a volume full of examples of how civil society organizations have a positive impact in technology policy-making for social change. However, they acknowledge that "most information society policy development of the past decade has occurred to the exclusion of civil society in the policy processes" (Schuler and Day, 2004: 354). In Brazil, for example, groups "encountered repeated disputes and roadblocks in building out the architecture of the Brazilian internet backbone and defining the rules of access to it" (Wilson, 2004: 329). But, at the same time, policy there has been forged from the interplay between Brazilian interest groups and the government. Even

in the semi-authoritarian Singapore, there was some public opposition to the Computer Misuse Act. While the impact of the opposition is not easily discernible, its existence is intriguing and worth further examination.

Finally, older political institutions can also be said to exert historical influences. Estonia had the benefit of being the home of the Soviet Cybernetics Institute for Computer Studies, a unit of government bureaucracy that remained after the fall of the Soviet Union and which continued to play an important role in the development of information technology policy (Lander, 2005).

Conclusion

Klapper (1960) famously observed that it is difficult to isolate the effects of different forms of mass communication because they interact with so many other "mediating factors and influences" (p. 11). The nature of policy-making is one of those mediating factors—one that has arguably been neglected. While most literature on the digital divide emphasizes the very real impact of economic and societal forces, political institutions and policy processes are also important drivers of technology diffusion.

Guide to further reading

Much has been written about the diffusion of technology and the digital divide. Early important works on technological diffusion include Everett Rogers' (2003) *The Diffusion of Innovations* and Daniel Lerner's (1962) *The Passing of Traditional Society*.

Norris (2001) provides a well-written empirical examination of the digital divide. Other works include Castells and Himanen (2002), Wilson (2004), and Wilson and

Wong (2007). These projects are focused on cases, countries, and the impact of institutions.

Kalathil and Boas (2003) treat issues within authoritarian systems. Two good edited volumes, Hacker and van Dijk (2000) and Ferdinand (2000), address the issues of how technology helps or hinders democratization. For a more anecdotal discussion on the role of civil society groups see Schuler and Day (2004), Hajnal (2002), and Hick and McNutt (2002).

Finally, some of the underlying assumptions in this chapter address questions of whether politics drives technology or whether technology drives politics. These arguments are laid out very succinctly in Street's (1992) book *Politics and Technology*.

31

Conclusion

Political omnivores and wired states

Philip N. Howard and Andrew Chadwick

Over the last decade, the internet has emerged as an important source of political information for many people around the world. A growing portion of the populations of developed countries have omnivorous appetites for political news: they regularly choose multiple media and multiple news sources, and they produce and consume political content. In developing countries, the internet has significantly extended the organizational capacity of civil society actors, political parties, and nation states. The authors in this collection have analyzed many important trends in contemporary patterns of political communication. This chapter summarizes their findings, and identifies some of the issues, contexts, and research challenges that scholars of internet politics are likely to face in the near future.

Over the last decade an important new medium for political communication has emerged, a tool unlike other media in its capacity for distributed and targeted interactivity. To understand contemporary politics, the theoretical reach of communication analysis must be expanded to include our assumptions about new patterns of political behavior, and our awareness of new and different policy challenges (Chaffee and Metzger, 2001; Howard, 2005; Chadwick, 2006).

The findings in this collection

Overall, the goal of this volume is to analyze the impact of new information and communication technologies on our political lives. The impact and implications are immense, with positive and negative outcomes in terms of both the capacities and constraints for political action. Yet the contributors to this collection are mostly upbeat. Some offer evidence of the clear positive effects of internet use on voter sophistication, institutional transparency, and political deliberation. And even those who are critical of the ways in which new information technologies are used for political manipulation, surveillance, and social control suggest interventions to counter these negative effects.

Positive roles

In several important ways, the internet is playing a positive transformative role in our political lives. McNair (Chapter 16) charts significant shifts in the global media environment, driven by the proliferation of online news and citizen-produced reporting, the overall effect being a discomfiting shift for national and global political elites. Bimber *et al.* (Chapter 6) identify and theorize the wide variety of collective political action possible in an era of extraordinary technology-enabled organizational fecundity. Online discussion, according to Brundidge and Rice (Chapter 11), seems to expose people to diverse political perspectives. The internet has fast become a crucial fact checking tool according to Hardy *et al.* (Chapter 10), and those who use it seem better equipped to distinguish between the true and false claims of political campaigns. Moreover, with the rising number of referendums as a tool for deciding on major public policy issues, Wells and Reedy (Chapter 12) find that internet use seems to drive up voter knowledge during referendums at the sub-national, national, and transnational levels. Davis *et al.*'s (Chapter 2) analysis of U.S. elections reveals a growing willingness among politicians and citizens to create internet-fueled, decentralized, distributed campaign organizations, while Coleman (Chapter 7) suggests that the aura of impenetrability and secrecy that surrounds legislative institutions is in the process of being dismantled by the emergence of a new political culture of citizen assertiveness.

In a similar vein, Margetts (Chapter 9) makes a claim for a new framework for public sector bureaucracies that serves as an explanation for technology-driven change and as a normative ideal for more responsive, citizen-centric and holistic governance. Dutton and Peltu (Chapter 28) offer a critique of the recent international events surrounding the World Summit on the Information Society, but also argue that the new multi-stakeholder process has evolved into a significant opportunity for civic influence on the global public policy deliberations over internet standards and governance. Cogburn (Chapter 29) suggests how global internet governance might benefit from the use of online tools to facilitate genuinely inclusive policy deliberation. Bennett and Toft (Chapter 18) make a convincing argument that political narratives shape online

mobilization networks; those networks that use internet tools to allow for a greater range of "action stories" or which invoke the need to connect a specific issue with citizen action are more likely to be successful than those that focus on tight ideological integration and strong ties in offline interaction. Rogerson and Milton (Chapter 30) draw attention to how national political institutions and policy shape the digital divide.

Negative roles

In several important ways, the internet is playing a negative transformative role. Given the challenges of internet access, whether in the form of personal motivation, physical access, digital skills, and actual use, political inequalities are being reinforced as many are unlikely to become digital citizens without a concerted public commitment. Van Dijk (Chapter 21) confirms this for the countries of the European Union, Mossberger (Chapter 13) for the United States, and Wheeler (Chapter 22) for the Arabic-speaking countries. Brundidge and Rice (Chapter 11) find that the information rich get richer as they use the internet, and that the positive impact of internet use on political sophistication is larger for those who are already information literate. Brundidge and Rice's research suggests that online discussion exposes people to diverse opinions, but Tewksbury and Rittenberg (Chapter 14) find that heavy reliance on online news is likely to create a fragmented public. Deibert (Chapter 23) exposes the variety of ways in which states filter online content, though he also identifies the key ways in which citizens can work around such censorship. Elmer (Chapter 27) exposes how political actors can significantly shape the public record of online content by constraining the way it is archived and accessed by what are clearly the internet's most powerful gatekeepers: search engines. Phillips (Chapter 24) tracks the use of mobile technologies for surveilling public movements, a technological development that is far from accidental but deliberately shaped by economic and legal interests.

Surprising roles

Several chapters in the handbook had findings of institutional transformation that were neither positive nor negative, but which can most simply be described as surprising. Foot et al.'s (Chapter 4) study of 19 global elections found that even though these elections occurred in countries with distinct governance systems and political cultures, the web strategies of candidates for election, government agencies, political parties, news media, and civic groups were remarkably consistent across countries. Ward and Gibson (Chapter 3) isolate changes in the inter- and intraorganizational spheres of parties and groups, but suggest that many of these derive from long-running trends towards individualization and political fragmentation. Anstead and Chadwick (Chapter 5) explain national differences in online election campaigning between the United States and the United Kingdom as well as contradictory tendencies within each country through an analysis of the character of existing political institutions as catalysts or anti-catalysts. Gandy and Farrall (Chapter 25) reveal the surprising impact of metaphor in distributing legal power and shaping the way to conceptualize—and regulate—the internet. Papacharissi (Chapter 17) develops a cogent argument that political life online has taken such an unusual form that the well-worn concept of the public sphere does not really illuminate its main features. This distinct virtual public sphere is narcissistic, selectively mobilizing, and a hybrid of civic and consumerist features.

The theme of hybridity (cf. Chadwick, 2007) is strongly developed in Kim and Ball-Rokeach's (Chapter 20) treatment of the complexities of immigrant communities' internet use. Similarly, Stanyer (Chapter 15) identifies contradictory trends in journalism: as old media corporations adapt to the online environment and face competition from new media players the internet also reshapes patterns of newsroom production, erodes some of the authority of news professionals, but creates uncertain effects in a context of unequal capacity on the part of citizens to produce news and hold politicians to account. May (Chapter 26) suggests that the growing strategic importance for developing countries of the internet and its related software is likely to lead to a complex pattern of resistance to Western dominance in the global political economy of intellectual property, while Van Doorn and van Zoonen (Chapter 19) argue for a mutual shaping approach to technology, which recognizes the contradictory ways in which the internet intersects with everyday gender relations. Finally, Fountain (Chapter 8) traces the ways in which the structures of classical Weberian bureaucracy have shaped the adoption of e-government in the United States, but also how dominant organizational models are being reconfigured by the introduction of massive information flows across government bodies.

Studying internet politics

What does this handbook tell us about the nature of internet politics as an area of social scientific inquiry?

Multiple domains

The contributions herein clearly establish that the internet has a role in multiple domains of politics. The volume is structured around four overarching themes: institutions, behavior, identities, and law and policy. Within these themes are several cross-cutting domains of research, including public administration, political theory, political economy, comparative politics and area studies, international relations, electoral politics, gender politics, and cultural politics.

The political analysis of the internet clearly integrates many subfields. Margetts and Fountain situate e-government in the context of public administration research. Phillips, Elmer, Dutton and Peltu, and Cogburn analyze politics at the site of technology engineering, standards setting, and design. Some contributions, such as those from Mossberger and van Dijk, Coleman, and Rogerson and Milton interrogate political inequality and public policy options. Some pieces, such as those from Phillips, Elmer, Bimber *et al.*, Bennett and Toft, and Papacharissi, are political theory, concerning themes such as individual freedom vs. state surveillance, prospects for collective action, or the features of contemporary public discourse online. Contributions from May, Gandy and Farrall, and Stanyer adopt a political economy approach. Wheeler, van Doorn and van Zoonen, and Kim and Ball-Rokeach tackle in different ways the cultural politics of identity online. Foot *et al.*, Gibson and Ward, and Anstead and Chadwick, insist on the importance of a comparative approach, while the chapters by Deibert, Dutton and Peltu, McNair, May, and Cogburn fall into the domain of international relations. Several of the chapters investigate changes in political learning of various kinds: Brundidge and Rice, Hardy *et al.*, Reedy and Wells, Tewksbury and Rittenberg.

Diversity of methodologies and evidence

This volume features a diverse range of methodologies and an equally diverse

range of qualitative, quantitative, and comparative evidence. Davis *et al.* adopt an evolutionary approach to electoral campaigning. Fountain's chapter on e-government uses policy analysis and organizational theory. In-depth interviews give Wheeler insight into the impact of the internet in the political lives of young men and women in several Arab cultures. Archival work and participant observation allow Elmer, Dutton and Peltu, and Cogburn to study the work of policymakers and politically engaged computer hobbyists. A case study approach was useful for Anstead and Chadwick, Margetts, Deibert, Foot *et al.*, and Wells and Reedy. It allowed for, respectively: the construction of hypotheses relating to national differences in online campaigning; charting the rise of digital era governance; typologies of state censorship strategies; political actors' websites; and political learning at different levels of political organization. Finally, Gandy and Farrall, Elmer, and Phillips employ various critical and rhetorical tools for locating the power behind discursive choices in law, policy, and the justifications for technology design.

In all, more than a dozen different quantitative data sets are analyzed in this volume and these reflect the diversity of levels of analysis: from the sub-national and national, to the regional and international. Several data sets from the Pew Internet and American Life Project provided survey insight into trends on internet use. For U.S. elections, Hardy *et al.* use the 2004 National Annenberg Election Survey, Rice and Brundidge use survey data from the Cornell University Survey Research Institute, while Reedy and Wells use the Washington Poll in their analysis of learning in a sub-national referendum. Data from the World Bank and the International Telecommunications Union provide some of the base indicators used by several contributors. The

427

UN's Human Development Index, the World Values Survey, Freedom Forum, and Van Hannen's democracy rankings help to provide context on political culture in contributions from Wheeler, and Foot *et al.* The rich Eurobarometer and Eurostat data sets enabled the analyses of Gibson and Ward, Reedy and Wells, and van Dijk.

Critiquing and creating

Researching internet politics is exciting for many different reasons but one of these is the way in which many scholars not only critique evolving systems of political communication but also conduct creative public scholarship that simultaneously collects data and contributes to fixing the problems they identify. Perhaps because of the nature of the object of study, several researchers have designed from scratch research projects that allow for data collection in the unique media environments online. These purpose-built projects often have a public scholarship goal, seeking to study behavior and ultimately change it for the better. Factcheck. org (www.factcheck.org) (see the chapter by Hardy *et al.*) investigates and assists with the public's use of the internet to confirm campaign claims during elections. The OpenNet Initative (http://opennet. net/) (see the chapter by Deibert) was founded to study the ability of governments to censor the internet, investigate initiatives to overcome such censorship, and facilitate dialog between civic stakeholders. The Global Deliberative Dialogue on Internet Governance (see the chapter by Cogburn) was created to bring NGOs, governments, international organizations, and scholars together to discuss the future direction of the World Summit on the Information Society. The Metamorphosis Project (see the chapter by Kim and Ball-Rokeach) was established to analyze and shape policy on the role of new communication technologies in the experience of immigrant communities in urban environments.

Many of the chapters in the volume have clear implications for public policy. For example, Mossberger develops suggestions for tackling political inequality; Bennett and Toft draw conclusions about why collective mobilization involving underprivileged communities may succeed or fail; van Doorn and van Zoonen's critique points to the need for greater involvement by women in the design and delivery of internet technologies and content; Coleman suggests that political representatives should adopt the participatory mechanisms of Web 2.0; Dutton and Peltu encourage us to learn lessons from the experience of the WSIS; Phillips points out how threats to privacy in electronic surveillance may be resisted by citizens; May calls for the wide dissemination of open source software applications in Africa and the developing world, while van Dijk's critique of policies on the digital divide points the way to a new EU-wide agenda for change. The study of politics online is both a critical and creative endeavor.

In the years ahead, scholars of the internet and politics will face many challenges in their research. The remainder of this chapter focuses on two: the fluid and unfinished nature of technologies themselves and the increasingly omnivorous civic diet for political information; and the problematic globalization of trends already identified in advanced democracies.

The rise of political omnivores in the advanced democracies

The internet is often treated like mass communication media such as television, radio or the press, primarily through survey or experimental research that explores particular software applications. But the internet consists of a wide range of informational tools that allow citizens not only to consume political content but also produce their own. While studies of broadcast news can look for patterns in audience reception, studying internet news habits, for example, often requires studying political engagement. Interrogating political content online is different from watching television news. This makes it difficult to study the social uses of the internet, and many scholars tend to focus on only one of these aspects at a time: either the choice of internet media in comparison with other media, the kinds of sources people have in their news diet, or the ways people interrogate political news and information.

There is a significant amount of debate over the role of the internet in news consumption. Some initially argued that the news online was simply reproductions and transcripts of content developed for print, radio or television (Thalheimer, 1994). But more recently it has been argued that news organizations and political campaigns develop unique content for the internet, in fact reorganizing their production systems to ensure that their online news is fresh and detailed, with print, radio, and television being the summary of selective stories (Boczkowski, 2004a).

Elsewhere, it has been argued that an analytical frame for the internet should avoid two assumptions: first, that it is an object of study that is a bounded and finished technology; and second, that it is an object of study linked to patterns of behavior and social contexts that are presumed to be constant across cultures (Howard, 2004). Within this "embedded media perspective" the internet is not a discrete, bias-free tool for exchanging information. Instead, internet use, and more specifically the political use of the internet, is grounded in social contexts

that explain why some people have more or less access, and others get more or less out of it. In important ways, the internet is more deeply embedded in the lives of users than newspapers, radio, and even television. It co-exists with other technologies that save and consume our time each day. Contemporary newspaper, radio, and television programming frequently reference website content. While news websites offer streaming access to the content produced for print and broadcast, they increasingly offer content that is exclusively produced for internet access.

Table 31.1 summarizes some of the most interesting trends in news consumption during elections in the contemporary United States. Each year, around election time, the U.S. adult population is surveyed on media choice. Many analysts just report the primary media choice or aggregate media choices by category, and doing so suggests that television is still the dominant media of choice. While this is true, it obfuscates interesting changes in the pattern of primary and secondary choices for election news. In recent years, television has been reported as the primary media preference for news, but its dominance has slipped over time. More recently, a growing portion of the population reports that newspapers, radio, or the internet are their primary media. From another perspective, during the 2000 election season about a quarter of the adult population did *not* offer television as their primary source of political news, and by 2004 about a third of the adult population did not do so.

In these surveys, interviewers are instructed to probe for a secondary choice if a respondent only reveals one response. In 2000, fully 64 percent of the U.S. adult population offered no secondary media choice. But by 2004 there was a dramatic change, with only 40 percent of the population not offering a secondary media choice even after the same probing

Table 31.1 The internet and omnivorous information habits during elections in the United States, 1996–2006

	1996	1998	2000	2002	2004	2006
How have you been getting most of your news about the presidential election campaign? Answered "Television."	–	–	78	–	67	59
Respondent reports a secondary source of media, either television, radio, newspaper, the internet or magazines	–	–	36	–	60	46
The internet is either the primary or secondary source of political news and information	–	–	9	–	17	23
Did you get ANY news or information about the [current] elections on the internet or through e-mail?	6	6	10	13	30	25
Yesterday, did you look online for news or information about politics or the campaign? Answered "yes."	7	9	9	8	17	–
When you go online to get information about the elections, do you ever do any of the following things? Responded doing at least 25% of the offered options.	–	6	5	16	22	–
Unweighted N	4,360	3,184	13,343	2,745	4,524	5,758

Source: Reproduced from Howard (2005). Data from 2006 from the Pew Internet and American Life Project (2006).

Notes: Each year, respondents were queried about whether they participated in some of the popular online political activities of that election season. Since this list changed (grew longer) over time, this figure is the proportion of people having completed at least 25 percent of the activities suggested by the interviewer that year: looking for news or information about politics or the campaign; having gone online to get news or information about the elections; participating in online discussions or "chat" groups about the elections; registering their own opinions by participating in an electronic poll; getting information about a candidate's voting record; getting information about when and where to vote; sending e-mail supporting or opposing a candidate for office; receiving e-mail supporting or opposing a candidate for office; contributing money to a candidate running for public office through his or her website; looking for more information about candidates' positions on the issues; getting or sending e-mail with jokes about the campaigns and elections; getting or sending information about getting people out to vote; finding out about endorsements or ratings of candidates by organizations or groups; visiting websites that provide information about specific issues or policies that interested the respondent, such as the environment, gun control, abortion, or health care reform; visiting partisan sites, such as those run by the political parties, a candidate, or a campaign; visiting nonpartisan sites, such as those run by the League of Women Voters; participating in online discussions, signing petitions online, or donating money online; subscribing to candidate or party e-mail notices; volunteering online for campaign service; learning about ballot initiatives or races for presidential, Senate, House, governor, or local offices; finding out how candidates are doing in the public polls; checking the accuracy of politician's claims with online sources; watching political video clips online; following election returns online.

questions from interviewers. A 2000 study of student media choices suggested that widespread internet use was unlikely to diminish the use of traditional news media (Althaus and Tewksbury, 2000). Moreover, the segment of the population that avoids politics probably does so because of the limited appeal of news from television, radio, and newspapers (Doppelt and Shearer, 1999; Fallows, 1996a). The national survey data presented in Table 31.1, however, suggest that there have been some interesting structural changes in media choice. Between 2000 and 2004, television's dominance as the primary medium of choice for news about the presidential election declined slightly and a significant portion of the population went from relying on one medium to relying on multiple media.[1]

In 2000, one fifth of the adult population identified something other than television as their primary source of political news and information, and by 2004 a third of the population did so. In other words, one in ten U.S. adults stopped identifying television as their primary medium for getting news and information about the presidential elections. In 2000, over a third of the U.S. adults had a secondary medium for getting this kind of information, but by 2004 almost two thirds of the population had taken on secondary media. What explains the changing distribution of primary media choice, and the dramatic rise in secondary media? If internet diffusion has drawn people away from other media, has it also had a role in diversifying the range of media options people consult for political news? What impact do changes in the structure of media choice have on choices of news sources and forms of interaction?

Political omnivores are people who increasingly consume news and information over multiple media. They often treat the internet as a key primary or supplementary source for checking facts, drilling deeper into stories, researching candidates and issue positions, and consuming news in new spatial and temporal contexts. In the coming years, it may be less meaningful to call this domain of study "internet politics," given the changing features, content, and use of communicative technologies. In fact, during the 2006 election one in eight adults reported consuming political news and information through one of a number of convergent technologies. This small but growing population reported "listening to news radio" by streaming the content from a website; they "read a newspaper" but did so online; they "watched the news," but reported doing so with a computer, cell phone, iPod, or PDA.[2]

Many people use more than one medium for news and have done so for decades, employing combinations of radio news, television news, newspapers, and news magazines. Chaffee's work in the 1980s revealed the importance of treating news on a Guttman scale—beginning with television, then television and newspapers in combination, and peaking with television news, newspapers, and news magazines. In other words, those who read newspapers tend to watch TV news as well, but those who watch TV news do not necessarily read the newspapers (Chaffee and Schleuder, 1986). While it is reasonable that people who consume lots of political information through one medium might try to do so through the internet, adding the internet to a Guttman scale would have low concept validity. The concept of the Guttman scale relies on users' and respondents' distinction between types of media. It is not simply that the internet can replace radio or newspapers as the third or fourth most popular choice of media. The internet replicates and integrates content—text, audio, video—from both new and traditional sources, through interactive informational tools. Most contemporary research on internet use for political news and information tends to treat media choice, source choice, and interactivity habits as distinct areas of inquiry.

Omnivorous news habits may also take different forms. Some people prefer the name-brand news organizations as sources, but choose to use internet media over television. Others will only ever use television, preferring to try different sources but only on television. Still others will actually learn most of their political information interactively, moving between media on particular stories, and learning from candidates and issue groups instead of traditional news sources. The distinction between producers and consumers of news is further blurred by the growing number of blogs and other types of user-generated content characteristic of Web 2.0. Blogs break news stories, offer opinion pieces, and are an important part of the "shared text" of the public sphere, especially for journalist elites. The distinction between news organizations is also increasingly blurred, with local news television channels providing website content through transcripts of stories, and major national newspapers providing online editions. These online news stories are sometimes assembled by different news teams, and at other times are assembled by the print news team but structured in such a way as to provide more depth and interactivity than allowed in print.

There are several important reasons for conceptualizing political news and information in this way. First, while many scholars continue to use analytical categories like television, newspaper, and internet, it is increasingly clear that people who consume political news and information do not make the same distinctions. A growing number of people rely on blogs, special interest groups, and political candidates for their news. Government agencies have long been important sources of news for citizens and have designed their online presence with this in mind (Chadwick, 2001). Television and newspaper stories often refer to further details online, while many internet users seem to prefer visiting the websites of established offline news organizations. A significant amount of political learning is done through information networks that bridge or bond communities (Norris, 2002). It is not simply that there is a new medium—the internet—in our toolkit for consuming news. It is important to theoretically distinguish between the types of choices people face when pulling from this modern toolkit: choices of which media to use, which sources to rely on, and the level of interaction to pursue.

The rise of wired states and political parties around the world

The second research challenge will come in comparing the trends around the world, as new information and communication technologies diffuse. Much of the literature in our field has developed through the study of advanced democracies. How well will these theories and approaches transport to other types of regimes and levels of development?

Table 31.2, taken from data gathered by the World Information Access Project, reveals some interesting trends in the globalization of the political internet. In all, the proportion of political parties with a website has increased since the turn of the millennium. In 2006, 39 percent of the world's political parties had a website, and by 2007 48 percent of the world's political parties did. But there are differences between the use of the internet by political parties in developed and developing countries. The vast majority of political parties in wealthy countries have an online presence, and while the level of use in developing nations has risen, by 2007 only 38 percent of the 2,351 sampled parties in the developing world had a website.

But it is often forgotten that there is an important difference between having a website and having the indigenous capacity to maintain content online. Among the rich countries, 57 percent of the 738 parties surveyed had the technical capacity to maintain their own information infrastructure within their country. The rest contracted out hosting services to other countries, usually the United States. Among the political parties in developing countries, only 5 percent had the capacity to maintain their website infrastructure in their own country.

A similar story can be told about the different government information infrastructures among nation states. Overall, 82

Table 32.2 Wired political parties and governments around the world

Region		2000	2005	2007
Developing countries	Number of political parties sampled	1,022	1,362	2,351
	Percent with a website	27	40	38
	Percent with capacity to host their own website	–	–	5
	Percent of countries with websites for five major government agencies	–	–	64
	Percent of countries with capacity to maintain own websites for five major government agencies	–	–	18
Developed countries	Number of political parties sampled	262	250	733
	Percent with a website	85	83	78
	Percent with capacity to host their own website	–	–	57
	Percent of countries with websites for five major government agencies	–	–	100
	Percent of countries with capacity to maintain own websites for five major government agencies	–	–	75
All countries	Number of political parties sampled	1,284	1,668	3,084
	Percent with a website	39	46	48
	Percent with capacity to host their own website	–	–	17
	Percent of countries with websites for five major government agencies	–	–	82
	Percent of countries with capacity to maintain own websites for five major government agencies	–	–	44
N of countries		141	166	210

Source: World Information Access Project (2006, 2007).

Note: For major government agencies in 2007, 196 countries were sampled.

percent of countries surveyed in 2007 had websites for five major government bodies: executive branch, foreign affairs, taxation and revenue, justice, and legislative branch. But only 44 percent of countries have the informational capacity to maintain government information infrastructure within their country. All of the wealthy countries surveyed in 2007 had website portals for these government agencies, and three quarters of the wealthy countries maintained their own government infrastructure in-country. In sharp contrast, developing countries' governments are much less likely to have a full complement of informational resources for their state institutions, and only 18 percent of the developing countries surveyed maintained an in-country

informational infrastructure. So not only are political parties and nation states in the developing world less wired, they are more dependent on the informational infrastructure of wealthy countries.

Much of the research on internet politics so far has been conducted in and based upon experience in the wealthier countries. Which assumptions will need to be abandoned and which new theories will need to be endogenously formed from lived experience in developing countries?

Conclusion

The *Handbook of Internet Politics* covers a huge range of material. It is impossible to

433

cover all of the theoretical and empirical advances in this conclusion. However, contributions can be organized by their broadly positive interpretation of the internet's role in political change, those with a negative interpretation, and those that reveal contradictory, counter-intuitive, and surprising findings. In addition, looking back on the collection has revealed three distinctive facets of the study of internet politics: the multiple domains of inquiry; the diversity of methodologies and evidence; and the combination of scholarly critique and creation. Finally, two intriguing challenges for future research come to light.

It seems that more people are using the internet and are treating it as an important source of political news and information. Internet use extends omnivorous news habits, making our news diet more diverse. In a small but significant way, the Internet experience may activate omnivorous news habits, and omnivorous news habits may activate political engagement. Moreover, there are clear patterns of inequality in the global supply of information infrastructure available to political actors as nation states and political parties. As scholars, how should we best approach the increasingly convergent digital technologies that seem to have a role in omnivorous diets for political news and information? How should we best investigate dependences in the global information society, which seem to have differential impacts on the capacities of states and political parties around the world?

It is time to treat new information and communication technologies as widespread and not really so new—they are an integral part of communication and learning in our contemporary political information environment. With this handbook, readers will extend their capacity for understanding the internet and politics.

Notes

1 This trend may have been subject to interviewer effects as some interviewers would have probed more deeply than others. However, interviewers were given the same set of instructions each year. They were required to note a primary media choice, and asked to probe for a secondary media choice. They were not instructed to rotate options, however, and offering television first may have biased the response rate for that answer option upwards.
2 Author's calculations from the Pew Internet and American Life Project, "Daily Tracking Survey—November 2006," (Pew Research Center for the People and the Press, 2006).

Bibliography

6 P., Leat, D., Seltzer, K. & Stoker, G. (2002). *Towards Holistic Government: the new reform agenda.* Basingstoke: Palgrave.

—— (2004). Joined up government in the western world in comparative perspective: a preliminary literature review and explanation. *Journal of Public Administration Research and Theory,* 14(1), 103–38.

Abramson, J. B., Arterton, F. C. & Orren, G. R. (1988). *The Electronic Commonwealth: the impact of new media technologies on democratic politics.* New York, NY: Basic Books.

Accenture (2001). *Egovernment Leadership: rhetoric vs. reality – closing the gap.* London: Accenture.

—— (2002). *Egovernment Leadership: realizing the vision, the government executive series.* London: Accenture.

—— (2003). *Egovernment Leadership: engaging the customer, the government executive series.* London: Accenture.

—— (2004). *Egovernment Leadership: high performance, maximum value, the value, the government executive series.* London: Accenture.

—— (2005). *Leadership in Customer Service: new expectations, new experiences, the government executive series.* London: Accenture.

Acevedo, M. & Krueger, J. I. (2004). Two egocentric sources of the decision to vote: the voter's illusion and the belief in personal relevance. *Political Psychology,* 25(1), 115–34.

Adam, A. (2002). Cyberstalking and internet pornography: gender and the gaze. *Ethics and Information Technology,* 4(2), 133–42.

Adamic, L. & Glance, N. (2005). *The political blogosphere and the 2004 US election: divided they blog.* Retrieved November 22, 2007, from www.blogpulse.com/papers/2005/Adamic GlanceBlogWWW.pdf

Adams, J. (2001). Virtual defense. *Foreign Affairs,* 80(3), 98–112.

Adams, P. C. & Rina, G. (2003). India.Com: the construction of a space between. *Progress in Human Geography,* 27(4), 414–37.

Adkins, R. E. & Dowdle, A. J. (2002). The money primary: what influences the outcome of pre-primary presidential nomination fundraising? *Presidential Studies Quarterly,* 32(2), 256–75.

Agre, P. E. (2002). Real-time politics: The internet and the political process. *Information Society,* 18(5), 311–31.

Aguirre, B. E. & Saenz, R. (2002). Testing the effects of collectively expected durations of migration: the naturalization of Mexicans and Cubans. *International Migration Review,* 36(1), 103–24.

Ahlers, D. (2006). News consumption and the new electronic media. *Harvard International Journal of Press/Politics,* 11(1), 29–52.

Ahrens, F. (2006a, September 24). New-media richcraft invites priceless comparisons. *Washington Post.*

—— (2006b, October 31). With tribune on block, LA times circulation down 8% drop is steepest among major US newspapers. *Washington Post.*

Akdeniz, Y. (2002). Anonymity, democracy, and cyberspace. *Social Research,* 69(1), 223–37.

Akrich, M. (1995). User representations: practices, methods and sociology. In: A. Rip, T. J. Misa & J. Schot (eds.), *Managing Technology in Society: the approach of constructive technology assessment.* London: Pinter Publishers.

435

Alba, R. D. & Logan, J. R. (1991). Variations on two themes: racial and ethnic patterns in the attainment of suburban residence. *Demography,* 28(3), 431–53.

Albrecht, S. (2006). Whose voice is heard in online deliberation? A study of online participation and representation in political debates on the internet. *Information, Communication and Society,* 9(1), 62–82.

Aldrich, J. H. (1995). *Why parties?: the origin and transformation of political parties in America.* Chicago: University of Chicago Press.

Alexa Web Service (2007). *Top 100 sites: US.* Retrieved November 22, from www.alexa.com/site/ds/top_sites?cc=US&ts_mode=country&lang=none

Allan, S. (2006). *Online News: journalism and the internet.* Maidenhead: Open University Press.

Allen, A. (2001). Pornography and power. *Journal of Social Philosophy,* 32(4), 512–31.

Allen, K. (2007, March 28). Online advertising share overtakes newspapers. *The Guardian.*

al-Saggaf, Y. (2004). The effect of online community on offline community in Saudi Arabia. *Electronic Journal of Information Systems in Developing Countries,* 16(2), 1–16.

Alterman, J. (1998). *New Media, New Politics: from satellite television to the internet in the Arab world.* Washington, DC: Washington Institute for Near East Policy.

Alterman, J. (2000). Middle East's information revolution. *Current History, January,* 21–26.

Althaus, S. L. (1999). Toward a theory of information effects in collective preferences, *Annual Conference of the International Communication Association.* San Francisco: International Communication Association.

Althaus, S. L. & Tewksbury, D. (2000). Patterns of internet and traditional media use in a networked community. *Political Communication,* 17(1), 21–45.

—— (2002). Agenda setting and the "new" news: patterns of issue importance among readers of the paper and online versions of the New York Times. *Communication Research,* 29(2), 180–207.

Altintas, K. (2002). Censoring the internet: the situation in Turkey. *First Monday,* 7(6).

Alvarez, R. M. & Hall, T. E. (2004). *Point, Click and Vote: the future of internet voting.* Washington, DC: Brookings Institution Press.

Alvarez, R. M. & Nagler, J. (2002). The likely consequences of internet voting for political representation. *Loyola of Los Angeles Review,* 34 (3), 1115–53.

American Library Association (1989). *Presidential Committee on Information Literacy.* Retrieved May 23, 2002, from www.infolit.org/documents/89Report/htm

Anderson, B. (1991). *Imagined Communities.* New York: Verso.

Anderson, C. (2006). *The Long Tail: how endless choice is creating unlimited demand.* London: Random House.

Anderson, J. (1995). Cybarites, knowledge workers and new creoles on the information superhighway. *Anthropology Today,* 11(4), 13–15.

—— (1998). *Arabizing the Internet.* Abu Dhabi: Emirates Center for Strategic Studies.

Anderson, K. (2006). *The Long Tail: why the future of business is selling less of more.* New York: Hyperion.

Anderson, P. J. & Ward, G. (2007). *The Future of Journalism in the Advanced Democracies.* Aldershot: Ashgate.

Anderson, R. & Murdoch, S. (2007). Tools and technology of internet filtering. In: R. J. Deibert, J. G. Palfrey, R. Rohozinski & J. Zittrain (eds.), *Access Denied: the practice and policy of global internet filtering.* Cambridge, MA: MIT Press.

Anderson, T. & Hill, P. (1975). The evolution of property rights: a study of the American west. *Journal of Law and Economics,* 18(1), 163–79.

Andrejevic, M. (2002). The work of being watched: Interactive media and the exploitation of self-disclosure. *Critical Studies in Media Communication,* 19(2), 230–48.

Ang, I. (2004). *Jordan and Singapore sign a free-trade pact.* Retrieved May 17, 2004, from www.bilaterals.org/article.php3?id_article=142

Anon. (1988, September 8). Bush trips in speech. *New York Times.*

Appadurai, A. (1996). *Modernity at Large: cultural dimension of globalization.* Twin City: University of Minnesota Press.

Archdeacon, T. S. (2007, 14 February). Baltic schools behind in computer use. *The Baltic Times.*

ARD/ZDF-Arbeitsgruppe Multimedia (1999). Nichtnutzer von online: Einstellungen und zugangsbarrieren. Ergebnisse der ARD/ZDF-offline-studie 1999 [Online non-users: attitudes and access barriers. Results of the ARD/

ZDF offline study 1999]. *Media Perspektiven*, 415–22.

Arendt, H. (1958). *The Human Condition*. Chicago: University of Chicago Press.

—— (1968). *Between Past and Future: eight exercises in political thought*. New York: Viking.

—— (1970). *Man in Dark Times*. New York: Harcourt Brace.

Arieanna (2005). *Text messaging lets Iraqis tip authorities to attacks from a safe distance*. Retrieved November 22, 2007, from http://blog.ipipi.com/blog/_archives/2005/1/21/270942.html

Arquilla, J. (1995). Welcome to the revolution in military affairs. *Comparative Strategy*, 14(2), 331–41.

—— (1996). *The Advent of Netwar*. Santa Monica, CA: RAND.

Arquilla, J. & Ronfeldt, D. F. (2001). *Networks and Netwars: the future of terror, crime, militancy*. Santa Monica, CA: RAND.

Ashby, W. (1956). *An Introduction to Cybernetics*. London: Chapman Hall.

Associated Press (2007a). *Blogs transform Middle East social dialogue*. Retrieved February 10, 2007, from www.msnbc.msn.com/id/17070982

—— (2007b, March 13). Egypt: 4-year sentence for blogger upheld. *New York Times*.

Atkins, D. E., Droegemeier, K. K., Feldman, S. I. et al. (2003). *Revolutionizing Science and Engineering through Cyberinfrastructure: report of the blue-ribbon advisory panel on cyberinfrastructure*. Washington, DC: National Science Foundation.

Atkins, W. (2002). *The Politics of South East Asia's New Media*. London: RoutledgeCurzon.

Attwood, F. (2002). Reading porn: the paradigm shift in pornography research. *Sexualities: Studies in Culture and Society*, 5(1), 91–105.

Aune, M., Berker, T. & Sorensen, K. H. (2002). *Needs, Roles, and Participation: a review of social science studies of users in technological design*. Trondheim: NTNU, Department of Interdisciplinary Studies of Culture.

Axelrod, R. (1985). *The Evolution of Co-operation*. New York: Basic Books.

Ayres, R. U. & Williams, E. (2003). The digital economy: where do we stand? *Technological Forecasting and Social Change*, 71(4), 315–39.

Balganesh, S. (2006). Common law property metaphors on the internet: the real problem with the doctrine of cybertrespass. *Michigan Telecommunications and Technology Law Review*, 12(2), 265–333.

Balkin, J. (1991). Ideology as constraint. *Stanford Law Review*, 43(5), 1133–69.

—— (2003). The proliferation of legal truth. *Harvard Journal of Law and Public Policy*, 26 (Winter), 5–16.

Ball-Rokeach, S. J., Kim, Y. C. & Matei, S. (2001). Storytelling neighborhood: paths to belonging in diverse urban environments. *Communication Research*, 28(4), 392–428.

Barber, B. (1984). *Strong Democracy: participatory politics for a new age*. Berkeley: University of California Press.

—— (2004). Which technology and which democracy. In: H. Jenkins & D. Thorburn (eds.), *Democracy and the New Media*. London: MIT Press.

Barber, B., Mattson, K. & Peterson, J. (1997). *The State of "Electronically Enhanced Democracy": a survey of the internet*. New Brunswick, NJ: Walt Whitman Center.

Barcan, R. (2002). In the raw: "home-made" porn and reality genres. *Journal of Mundane Behavior*, 3(1).

Barlow, J. P. (1996). *A declaration of independence of cyberspace*. Retrieved November 22, 2007, from http://homes.eff.org/~brlow/Declaration-Final.html

Barnhurst, K. G. (2002). News geography and monopoly: the form of reports on US newspaper and internet sites. *Journalism Studies*, 3(4), 477–89.

Barry, B. & Dauphin, J. (2003). Unesco activities in the field of free and open source software (Foss). Paper presented at the ACT 2003 The Fifth Annual African Computing and Telecommunication Summit.

Barsoum, G. F. (1999). *Jobs for "wilad al-nas" the Jobs Dilemma of Female Graduates in Egypt*. American University, Cairo.

Bartels, L. (1996). Uninformed voters: information effects in presidential elections. *American Journal of Political Science*, 40, 194–230.

Barzelay, M. (2000). *The New Public Management: improving research and policy dialogue*. Berkeley, CA: University of California Press.

Baum, J. & Oliver, P. (1992). Institutional embeddedness and the dynamics of organizational populations. *American Sociological Review*, 57(4), 540–59.

Bauman, Z. (2002). *Society Under Siege*. Cambridge: Polity Press.

—— (2005). *Liquid Life*. Cambridge: Polity Press.

Baumgartner, F. R. & Jones, B. D. (1993). *Agendas and Instability in American Politics*. Chicago, IL: University of Chicago Press.

Baumgartner, F. R. & Leech, B. L. (1998/2001). *Basic Interests: the importance of groups in politics and in political science*. Princeton, N.J.: Princeton University Press.

Baumgartner, J. C (2000). *Modern Presidential Electioneering: an organizational and comparative approach*. Westport, Conn.; London: Praeger.

Baym, N. K. (2000). *Tune In, Log On: soaps, fandom, and online community*. New York: Sage.

BBC News Online (2005). *Dutch say "no" to EU constitution*. Retrieved November 22, 2007, from http://news.bbc.co.uk/2/hi/europe/4601439.stm

—— (2007). *Open source gets European boost*. Retrieved January 17, 2007, from http://news.bbc.co.uk/go/pr/fr/-/1/hi/technology/6270657.stm

Beck, U. (1999). *World Risk Society*. London: Blackwell.

—— (2000). *What is Globalization?* Cambridge, UK: Polity Press.

Beck, U., Giddens, A. & Lash, S. (1994). *Reflexive Modernization*. Cambridge: Polity.

Becker, L. B. & Dunwoody, S. (1982). Media use, public affairs knowledge and voting in a local election. *Journalism Quarterly*, 59, 212–18.

Becker, L. B. & Whitney, D. C. (1980). Effects of media dependencies: audience assessments of government. *Communication Research*, 7, 95–120.

Beckerman, G. (2007). The new Arab conversation. *Columbia Journalism Review, January/February*.

Beckert, J. (1999). Agency, entrepreneurs, and institutional change. The role of strategic choice and institutionalized practices in organizations. *Organization Studies*, 20(5), 777–99.

Bekkers, V. (2004). Virtual policy communities and responsive governance: redesigning online debates. *Information Polity*, 9, 193–203.

Bell, D. (1981). The social framework of the information society. In: T. Forester (ed.), *The Microelectronics Revolution*. Cambridge, MA: MIT Press.

—— (2001). *An Introduction to Cybercultures*. New York: Routledge.

Bellamy, C. & Taylor, J. A. (1998). *Governing in the Information Age*. Buckingham: Open University Press.

Bellin, E. (2005). Coercive institutions and coercive leaders. In: M. P. Posusney & M. P. Angrist (eds.), *Authoritarianism in the Middle East: regimes and resistance*. Boulder, CO: Lynne Rienner Publishers.

Benford, R. D. & Snow, D. A. (2000). Framing processes and social movements: an overview and assessment. *Annual Review of Sociology*, 26, 611–39.

Benkler, Y. (2006). *The Wealth of Networks: how social production transforms markets and freedom*. New Haven: Yale University Press.

Bennett, C. J. & Crow, L. (2005). *Location based services and the surveillance of mobility: an analysis of privacy risks in Canada*. Retrieved November 22, 2007, from http://web.uvic.ca/polisci/bennett/pdf/lbsfinal.pdf

Bennett, L. (2001). *News: the politics of illusion*, 4th edn. New York: Harlow: Longman.

Bennett, L., Pickard, V., Iozzi, D., Schroeder, C., Lagos, T. & Caswell, C. (2004). Managing the public sphere: journalistic construction of the great globalization debate. *Journal of Communication*, 54(3), 437–55.

Bennett, L. & Serrin, W. (2005). The watchdog role. In: G. Overholser & K. H. Jamieson (eds.) *Institutions of American Democracy: the press*. Oxford: Oxford University Press.

Bennett, W. L. (1998). The uncivic culture: communication, identity, and the rise of lifestyle politics. *Political Science and Politics*, 31(4), 41–61.

—— (2003). Communicating global activism: strengths and vulnerabilities of networked politics. *Information, Communication and Society*, 6(2), 143–68.

Bennett, W. L., Breunig, C. & Givens, T. (2008). Crossing political divides: Communication, political identification, and protest organization. In: S. Walgrave & D. Rucht (eds.), *Protest Politics: anti-war mobilization in Western democracies*. Minneapolis, MN: University of Minnesota Press.

Bennett, W. L., Foot, K., Werbel, L. & Xenos, M. (2007). *Strategic conflicts in advocacy networks: how narrative frames shape relations among US and UK fair trade organizations*. Paper presented at the Annual Conference of the International Communication Association, San Francisco, CA.

Bennett, W. L. & Lagos, T. (2007). Logo logic: the ups and downs of branded political communication. *Annals of the American Academy of Political and Social Science,* 611, 193–206.

Bennett, W. L. & Manheim, J. B. (2001). The big spin: strategic communication and the transformation of pluralist democracy. In: W. L. Bennett & R. M. Entman (eds.), *Mediated Politics: communication in the future of democracy.* Cambridge: Cambridge University.

Benoliel, J. (2005). Law, geography and cyberspace: the case of territorial privacy. *Cardozo Arts and Entertainment Law Journal,* 23(1), 125–96.

Berelson, B. (1952). Democratic theory and public opinion. *Public Opinion Quarterly,* 16(3), 313–30.

Berger, B. L. (2002). Trial by metaphor: rhetoric, innovation, and the juridical text. *Court Review,* (Fall), 30–38.

Berkowitz, B. D. (2003). *The New Face of War: how the war will be fought in the 21st century.* New York: Free Press.

Berry, J. M. (1984). *The Interest Group Society.* Boston, MA: Little, Brown.

Best, S. J., Chmielewski, B. & Krueger, B. S. (2005). Selective exposure to online foreign news during the conflict with Iraq. *Harvard International Journal of Press/Politics,* 10(4), 52–70.

Bimber, B. (1998). The internet and political transformation: populism, community, and accelerated pluralism. *Polity,* 31(1), 133–60.

—— (1999). The internet and citizen communication with government: does the medium matter? *Political Communication,* 16(4), 409–28.

—— (2000). The study of information technology and civic engagement. *Political Communication,* 17(4), 329–33.

—— (2001). Information and political engagement in America: the search for effects of information technology at the individual level. *Political Research Quarterly,* 54(1), 53–67.

—— (2003). *Information and American Democracy: technology in the evolution of political power.* Cambridge: Cambridge University Press.

Bimber, B. & Davis, R. (2003). *Campaigning Online: the internet in US elections.* New York: Oxford University Press.

Bimber, B., Flanagin, A. J. & Stohl, C. (2005). Reconceptualizing collective action in the contemporary media environment. *Communication Theory,* 15(4), 365–88.

Blavin, J. H. & Cohen, I. G. (2002). Gore, Gibson, and Goldsmith: the evolution of internet metaphors in law and commentary. *Harvard Journal of Law and Technology,* 16(1), 265–85.

Blears, H. (2007). *Speech to the Fabian Society.* Retrieved May 10, 2007, from http://fabians.org.uk/events/blears-party-07/speech

Blumler, J. G. & Gurevitch, M. (2000). Rethinking the study of political communication. In: J. Curran & M. Gurevitch (eds.), *Mass Media and Society,* 3rd edn. London: Arnold.

—— (2001). The new media and our political communication discontents: democratizing cyberspace. *Information, Communication and Society,* 4(1), 1–13.

Boase, J., Horrigan, J. B., Wellman, B. & Rainie, L. (2006). *The Strength of Ties.* Washington, DC: Pew Internet and American Life Project.

Boczkowski, P. (2002). The development and use of online newspapers: what research tells us and what we might want to know. In: L. A. Lievrouw & S. Livingstone (eds.), *The Handbook of New Media.* London: Sage.

—— (2004a). *Digitizing the News: innovation in online newspapers.* Cambridge, MA: MIT Press.

—— (2004b). The processes of adopting multimedia and interactivity in three online newsrooms. *Journal of Communication,* 54(2), 197–213.

Boddy, W. (2003). Redefining the home screen: Technological convergence as trauma and business plan. In: D. Thorburn & H. Jenkins (eds.), *Rethinking Media Change: the aesthetics of transition.* Cambridge, MA: MIT Press.

Bogdanor, V. (1984). Introduction. In: V. Bogdanor (ed.), *Parties and Democracy in Britain and America.* New York: Praeger.

Bolter, J. D. & Grusin, R. (1999). *Remediation.* Cambridge, MA: MIT Press.

Bonfadelli, H. (2002). The internet and knowledge gaps: a theoretical and empirical investigation. *European Journal of Communication,* 17 (1), 65–84.

Boogers, M. & Voerman, G. (2003). Surfing citizens and floating voters: results of an online survey of visitors to political websites during the Dutch 2002 general elections. *Information Polity,* 8(1–2), 17–27.

Bosmajian, H. A. (1992). *Metaphor and Reason in Judicial Opinions.* Carbondale: Southern Illinois University Press.

Boubakar, B. & Dauphin, J. (2003). *UNESCO activities in the field of free and open source software.*

Paper presented at the The Fifth Annual African Computing and Telecommunication Summit, Abuja, Nigeria.

Bowers-Brown, J. (2003). A marriage made in cyberspace? Political marketing and British party websites. In: R. K. Gibson, P. Nixon & S. Ward (eds.), *Political Parties and the Internet: Net Gain?* London: Routledge.

Bowler, S. & Donovan, T. (1998). *Demanding Choices: opinion, voting, and direct democracy.* Ann Arbor: University of Michigan Press.

—— (2002). Do voters have a cue? Television advertisement as a source of information in citizen-initiated referendum campaigns. *European Journal of Political Research,* 41(6), 777–93.

Bowler, S., Donovan, T. & Tolbert, C. (1998). *Citizens as Legislators: direct democracy in the United States.* Columbus: Ohio State University Press.

Bradley, C. D. (1993). Access to US government information on the internet. *Interpersonal Computing and Technology: An Electronic Journal for the 21st Century,* 1(4).

Braman, S. (2006). Tactical memory: the politics of openness in the construction of memory. *First Monday,* 11(7).

Branton, R. P. (2003). Examining individual-level voting behavior on state ballot propositions. *Political Research Quarterly,* 56(3), 367–77.

Brasher, B. E. (2004). *Give Me That Online Religion.* New Brunswick, NJ: Rutgers University Press.

Bretschneider, S. (2003). Information technology, e-government, and institutional change. *Public Administration Review,* 63(6), 738–41.

Bridges.org (2004). *Straight from the Source: perspectives from the African free and open source software movement.* Cape Town: Bridges.org.

Brint, S. & Karabel, J. (1991). Institutional origins and transformations: the case of American community colleges. In: W. W. Powell & P. J. DiMaggio (eds.), *The New Institutionalism in Organizational Analysis.* Chicago: University of Chicago Press.

Broder, D. (2000). *Democracy Derailed: initiative campaigns and the power of money.* Orlando: Harcourt.

Broder, J. (2007, February 9). Edwards learns blogs can cut 2 ways. *New York Times.*

Brody, R. (1978). The puzzle of political participation in America. In: A. King (ed.), *The New American Political System.* Washington, DC: American Enterprise Institute.

Brosnan, M. J. (1998). The impact of computer anxiety and self-efficacy upon performance. *Journal of Computer Assisted Learning,* 14(3), 223–34.

Brouwer, L. (2006). Dutch Moroccan websites: a transnational imagery? *Ethnic & Migration Studies,* 32(7), 1153–68.

Browning, G. (2001). *Electronic Democracy: using the internet to transform American politics,* 2nd edn. Medford, NJ: CyberAge Books.

Brundidge, J. S. (2006). *The contribution of the internet to the heterogeneity of political discussion networks: does the medium matter?* Paper presented at the International Communication Association Annual Conference, Dresden.

Bruns, A. (2005). *Gatewatching: collaborative online news production.* New York: Peter Lang.

—— (2007). Methodologies for mapping the political blogosphere: an exploration using the issue crawler research tool. *First Monday,* 12(5).

Bucy, E. P., D'Angelo, P. & Newhagen, J. E. (1999). The engaged electorate: New media use as political participation. In: L. L. Kaid & D. G. Bystrom (eds.), *The Electronic Election: perspectives on the 1996 campaign communication.* Mahwah, NJ: Erlbaum.

Budge, I. (1996). *The New Challenge of Direct Democracy.* Cambridge: Polity Press.

Buechler, S. (1995). New social movement theories. *The Sociological Quarterly,* 36(3), 441–64.

Bunz, U., Curry, C. & Voon, W. (2006). Perceived versus actual computer-email-web fluency. *Computers in Human Behavior,* 23(5), 2321–44.

Burke, A., Sowerbutts, S., Blundell, B. & Sherry, M. (2002). Child pornography and the internet: policing and treatment issues. *Psychiatry, Psychology and Law,* 9(1), 79–84.

Burkhalter, S., Gastil, J. & Kelshaw, T. (2002). A conceptual definition and theoretical model of public deliberation in small face-to-face groups. *Communication Theory,* 12(4), 398–422.

Burnett, R. & Marshall, P. D. (2003). *Web Theory: an introduction.* New York: Routledge.

Burnham, D. (1983). *The Rise of the Computer State.* New York: Random House.

Burt, E. & Taylor, J. (2001). When virtual meets value: insights from the voluntary sector. *Information Communication and Society,* 4(1), 54–73.

Burt, R. S. (2005). *Brokerage and Closure: an introduction to social capital.* Oxford: Oxford University Press.

Burton, C. (2003, November 1). Singapore tightens control over internet cyber-threat. *Financial Times*.

Burton, J. & Williams, F. (2005, March 10). Singapore overtakes US to lead world in new IT. *Financial Times*.

Bush, J. (2005, February 27). Worried you don't understand the rules of the Euro game? You'd be more worried if you did. *Independent on Sunday*.

Bushnell-Embling, D. (2007). *Australian prisoners chipped as part of a new RFID trial, plans to integrate tags with CCTV*. Retrieved June 26, 2007, from www.computerworld.com.au/index.php?id=774240213

Butler, D. & Ranney, A. (1994). *Referendums Around the World: the growing use of direct democracy*. Washington, DC: AEI Press.

Butler, J. (1990). *Gender Trouble*. New York: Routledge.

Button, M. & Ryfe, D. (2005). What can we learn from the practice of deliberative democracy? In: J. Gastil & P. Levine (eds.), *The Deliberative Democracy Handbook*. San Francisco: Jossey-Bass.

Buxton, N. (2002). Dial-up networking for debt collection and development. In: S. Hick & J. McNutt (eds.), *Advocacy, Activism and the Internet: community organization and social policy*. Chicago: Lyceum Books.

Cammaerts, B. & Carpentier, N. (2005). The unbearable lightness of full participation in a global context: WSIS and civil society participation. In: J. Servaes & N. Carpentier (eds.), *Towards a Sustainable Information Society: deconstructing WSIS*. Bristol: Intellect.

Campaign for Freedom of Information (1995, October 16). Press release.

Campbell, A. A., Converse, P. E., Miller, W. E. & Stokes, D. E. (1960). *The American Voter*. Chicago: University of Chicago Press.

Campbell, J. (2000). *The American Campaign, U.S. Presidential Campaigns and the National Vote*. College Station, TX: Texas A&M University Press.

Campbell, J. E. (2004). *Getting it on Online: cyberspace, gay male sexuality, and embodied identity*. Binghampton: Harrington Park Press.

Can, F. (1999). Feminist rhetoric in cyberspace: the ethos of feminist usenet newsgroups. *Information Society*, 15(3), 187–97.

Cappella, J. & Jamieson, K. H. (1996). News frames, political cynicism, and media cynicism. *Annals of the American Academy of Political and Social Science*, 546, 71–85.

—— (1997). *Spiral of Cynicism: the press and the public good*. New York: Oxford University Press.

Cappella, J., Price, V. & Nir, L. (2002). Argument repertoire as a reliable and valid measure of opinion quality: electronic dialogue during Campaign 2000. *Political Communication*, 19(1), 73–93.

Cappella, J. N. & Jamieson, K. H. (1997). *Spiral of Cynicism: the press and the public good*. New York: Oxford University Press.

Cardoso, F. H. (2004). *We the Peoples: civil society, the United Nations and global governance*. New York: United Nations.

Carey, J. (1995). The press, public opinion, and public discourse. In: T. Glasser & C. Salmon (eds.), *Public Opinion and the Communication of Consent*. New York: Guilford.

Carlaw, K., Oxley, L., Walker, P., Thorns, D. & Nuth, M. (2006). Beyond the hype: intellectual property and the knowledge society/knowledge economy. *Journal of Economic Surveys*, 20(4), 633–90.

Cass, R. A. (1995). Judging: norms and incentives of retrospective decision-making. *Boston University Law Review*, 75, 941–96.

Cassidy, W. P. (2005). Variations on a theme: the professional role conceptions of print and online newspaper journalists. *Journalism and Mass Communication Quarterly*, 82(2), 264–81.

Castells, M. (1996). *The Rise of the Network Society*. Oxford: Blackwell Publishers.

—— (2000). *The Rise of the Network Society*, 2nd edn. Oxford: Blackwell.

Castells, M. & Himanen, P. (2002). *The Information Society and the Welfare State: the Finnish model*. Oxford: Oxford University Press.

Castles, S. & Davison, A. (2000). *Citizenship and Migration: globalization and the politics of belonging*. New York: Routlege.

Cave, J., Marsden, C., Klautzer, L., Levitt, R.., van Oranje-Nassau, C., Rabinovich, L. *et al.* (2007). *Responsibility in the Global Information Society: towards multi-stakeholder governance*. Santa Monica, CA: Rand.

Ceasar, J. W. & Busch, A. E. (2005). *Red over Blue: the 2004 elections and American politics*. Lanham, MD: Rowman and Littlefield.

Center for Communication and Civic Engagement (2004). *The digital election: 2004.* Retrieved November 22, 2007, from http://depts.washington.edu/ccce/civicengagement/digitalelections.html

Centre for Policy Research on Science and Technology (nd). *Prepaid in the news.* Retrieved November 22, 2007, from www.sfu.ca/cprost/prepaid/news.htm

Ceruzzi, P. (1997). An unforeseen revolution: computers and expectations 1935–85. In: A. H. Teich (ed.), *Technology and the Future*, 7th edn. New York: St. Martin's Press.

Chadwick, A. (2001). The electronic face of government in the internet age: borrowing from Murray Edelman. *Information Communication and Society*, 4(3), 435–57.

—— (2006). *Internet Politics: states, citizens, and new communication technologies.* New York: Oxford University Press.

—— (2007). Digital network repertoires and organizational hybridity. *Political Communication*, 24(3), 283–301.

Chadwick, A. & May, C. (2003). Interaction between states and citizens in the age of the internet: "E-government" in the United States, Britain, and the European Union. *Governance*, 16(2), 271–300.

Chaffee, S. H. (2001). Studying the new communication of politics. *Political Communication*, 18(2), 237–44.

Chaffee, S. H. & Frank, S. (1996). How Americans get political information: print versus broadcast news. *The Annals of the American Academy of Political and Social Science*, 546(1), 48–58.

Chaffee, S. H. & Kanihan, S. F. (1997). Learning about politics from the mass media. *Political Communication*, 14(4), 421–30.

Chaffee, S. H. & Metzger, M. J. (2001). The end of mass communication? *Mass Communication and Society*, 4(4), 365–79.

Chaffee, S. H., Nichols, M., Graf, J., Sandvig, C. & Hahn, K. (2001). Attention to counter-attitudinal messages in a state election campaign. *Political Communication*, 18(3), 247–72.

Chaffee, S. H. & Schleuder, J. (1986). Measurement and effects of attention to media news. *Human Communication Research*, 13(1), 76–107.

Chaffee, S. H., Zhoa, X. & Leshner, G. (1992). Political knowledge and the campaign media of 1992. *Communication Research*, 21, 305–24.

Chalaby, J. K. (2005). *Transnational Television Worldwide*. London: I.B. Tauris.

Chan, B. (2005). Imagining the homeland: the internet and diasporic discourse of nationalism. *Journal of Communication Inquiry*, 29(4), 336–68.

Chan, J. K. C. & Leung, L. (2005). Lifestyles, reliance on traditional news media and online news adoption. *New Media and Society*, 7(3), 357–82.

Chang, J. (2007, January 14). Order to ban YouTube ignites Brazil firestorm. *Seattle Times*.

Chen, P. (2002). Virtual representation: Australian elected representatives and the impact of the internet. *Journal of Information Law and Technology*, 3.

Cho, J., de Zúñiga, H., Rojas, H. & Shah, D. (2003). Beyond access: the digital divide and internet uses and gratifications. *IT and Society*, 1(4), 46–72.

Choi, J. H., Watt, J. H. & Lynch, M. (2006). Perceptions of news credibility about the war in Iraq: why war opponents perceived the internet as the most credible medium. *Journal of Computer-Mediated Communication*, 12(1).

ChoicePoint (2007). *2006 Annual Report*. Alpharetta, GA: ChoicePoint.

Chua, S. L., Chen, D. T. & Wong, A. F. L. (1999). Computer anxiety and its correlates: a meta-analysis. *Computers in Human Behavior*, 15(5), 609–23.

Chung, D. S. (2007). Profits and perils: online news producers' perceptions of interactivity and uses of interactive features. *Convergence*, 13(1), 43–61.

Clark, J. (2003). Introduction: civil society and transnational action. In: J. Clark (ed.), *Globalizing Civic Engagement: civil society and transnational action.* London: Earthscan Publications Limited.

Clarke, J. & Themudo, N. (2003). The age of protest: internet based dot-causes and the anti-globalization movement. In: J. Clarke (ed.), *Globalizing Civic Action.* London: Earthscan.

Clayton, R., Murdoch, S. J. & Watson, R. N. M. (2006). *Ignoring the great firewall of China.* Paper presented at the 6th Workshop on Privacy Enhancing Technologies Robinson College, Cambridge, UK.

Clinton, W. J. (1996). *Address before a joint session of the Congress on the state of the union.* Retrieved November 22, 2007, from http://frwebgate.access.gpo.gov/cgi-bin/getdoc.cgi?

dbname=1996_public_papers_vol1_text&docid=
pap_text-54

CNN (2006). *American votes 2006: US Senate –
Virginia.* Retrieved November 22, 2007, from
http://edition.cnn.com/ELECTION/2006/
pages/results/states/VA/S/01/index.html

Cobb, R. W. & Elder, C. D. (1983). *Participation
in American Politics: the dynamics of agenda-
building,* 2nd edn. Baltimore: John Hopkins
University Press.

Cockburn, C. (1992). The circuit of technology:
Gender, identity and power. In: R. Silverstone
& E. Hirsch (eds.), *Consuming Technologie:
media and information in domestic spaces.* London:
Routledge.

Cockburn, C. & Fürst-Dilić, R. (1994). *Bringing
Technology Home: gender and technology in a
changing Europe.* Buckingham: Open
University Press.

Cockburn, C. & Ormrod, S. (1993). *Gender and
Technology in the Making.* Thousand Oaks, CA:
Sage.

Cogburn, D. L. (2004a). Diversity matters, even
at a distance: evaluating the impact of
computer-mediated communication on civil
society participation in the World Summit on
the Information Society. *Information Technology
and International Development,* 1(3–4), 15–40.

—— (2004b). Elite decision-making and epistemic communities: implications for global
information policy. In: S. Braman (ed.), *The
Emergent Global Information Policy Regime.* New
York: Palgrave.

—— (2005). Partners or pawns? Developing
countries and regime change in global information policy governance. *Knowledge, Technology,
and Policy,* 18(2), 52–82.

Cogburn, D., Johnsen, J. F. & Bhattacharyya, S.
(2008). Distributed deliberative citizens: exploring the impact of cyberinfrastructure on transnational civil society participation in global
ICT policy processes. *International Journal of
Media and Cultural Politics,* 4(1), 27–49.

Cogburn, D. L., Mueller, M., McKnight, L.,
Klein, H. & Mathiason, J. (2005). The US
role in global internet governance. *IEEE
Communications Magazine* (December), 12–14.

Cohen, E. A. (1996). A revolution in warfare.
Foreign Affairs, 75(2), 37–54.

Cohen, E. L. (2002). Online journalism as
market-driven journalism. *Journal of Broadcasting
and Electronic Media,* 46(4), 532–48.

Cohen, J. (1997). Deliberation and democratic
legitimacy. In: J. F. Bohman & W. Rehq
(eds.), *Deliberative Democracy: essays on reason
and politics.* Cambridge, MA: MIT Press.

Cohen, J. E. (2007). Cyberspace as/and space.
Columbia Law Review, 107, 210–56.

Cohen, R. & Rai, S. (eds.). (2000). *Global Social
Movements.* London: Athlone Press.

Coleman, S. (2004). Connecting Parliament to
the public via the internet: two case studies of
online consultations. Information. *Communication
and Society,* 7(1), 1–22.

—— (2005a). Just how risky is online voting?
Information Polity, 10(1–2), 95–104.

—— (2005b). New mediation and direct representation: reconceptualizing representation in
the digital age. *New Media and Society,* 7(2),
177–98.

—— (2005c). The lonely citizen: indirect
representation in a age of networks. *Political
Communication,* 22(2), 197–214.

—— (2006). Parliamentary communication in
an age of digital interactivity. *Aslib Proceedings,*
58(5), 371–88.

Coleman, S. & Blumler, J. (2001). *Realizing
Democracy Online: towards a civic commons in
cyberspace.* London: Institute for Public Policy
Research.

Coleman, S. & Hall, N. (2001). E-campaigning
and beyond. In: S. Coleman (ed.), *Cyberspace
Odyssey.* London: Hansard Society.

Coleman, S. & Ross, K. (2008). *Them and Us:
how the media see the public.* London: Blackwell.

Coleman, S., Taylor, J. & Van Donk, W. (1999).
Parliament in the age of the internet.
Parliamentary Affairs, 52(3).

Collins, P. M. (2006). *Interest group influence on
the supreme court: theoretical and methodological
considerations.* Paper presented at the Southern
Political Science Association Annual Conference,
Atlanta, GA.

Commission of the European Communities
(1996). *Communication of the Commission about
universal service for telecommunication* (No. COM
(1996) 96–73). Brussels: Commission of the
European Communities.

—— (2002). *Europe 2005: An information society
for all* (No. COM 263 final). Brussels:
Commission of the European Communities.

—— (2003). *European electronic communications
regulation and markets 2003: report on implementation of the EU electronic communications*

regulatory package (No. COM (2003) 715 final). Brussels: Commission of the European Union.

—— (2005). *I2010-a European information society for growth and employment* (No. COM (2005) 229 final). Brussels: Commission of the European Communities.

—— (2007). *RFID technologies: emerging issues, challenges, and policy options.* Luxembourg: Institute for Prospective Technological Studies.

Compaine, B. M. (2001). *The Digital Divide: facing a crisis or creating a myth?* Cambridge, MA: MIT Press.

ComScore (2007). *Mobile web audience already one-fifth the size of PC-based internet audience in the UK.* Retrieved May 14, 2007, from www. comscore.com

Conboy, M. (2004). *Journalism: a critical history.* London: Sage.

Consalvo, M. (2002). Selling the internet to women: the early years. In: M. Consalvo & S. Paasonen (eds.), *Women and Everyday Uses of the Internet: agency and identity.* New York: Peter Lang.

Consalvo, M. & Paasonen, S. (eds.) (2002). *Women and Everyday Uses of the Internet: agency and identity.* New York: Peter Lang Publishing.

Converse, P. E. (1964). The nature of belief systems in mass publics. In: D. A. Apter (ed.), *Ideology and Discontent.* New York: Free Press.

—— (1990). Popular representation and the distribution of information. In: J. A. Ferejohn & J. H. Kuklinski (eds.), *Information and Democratic Processes.* Chicago: University of Illinois Press.

Cooke, L. (2005). A visual convergence of print, television, and the internet: charting 40 years of design change in news presentation. *New Media and Society,* 7(1), 22–46.

Copsey, N. (2003). Extremism on the internet: the far right and the value of the internet. In: R. K. Gibson, P. Nixon & S. Ward (eds.), *Political Parties and the Internet: net gain?* London: Routledge.

Cornfield, M. (2004a). *Pew Internet Project data memo.* Washington, DC: Pew Internet and American Life Project.

—— (2004b). *Politics Moves Online: campaigning and the internet.* New York: Century Foundation Press.

—— (2004c). *Presidential Campaign Advertising on the Internet.* Washington, DC: Pew Internet and American Life Project.

—— (2006). YouTube and you. *Campaigns and Elections,* 27(8), 43.

Cornfield, M. & Rainie, L. (2006). *The Impact of the Internet on Politics.* Washington, DC: Pew Internet and American Life Project.

Cornfield, M., Rainie, L. & Horrigan, J. (2003). *Untuned Keyboards: online campaigners, citizens, and portals in the 2002 elections.* Washington, DC: Pew Internet and American Life Project.

Corrado, A. (1996). Elections in cyberspace: prospects and problems. In: A. Corrado & C. M. Firestone (eds.), *Elections in Cyberspace: toward a new era in American politics.* Washington, DC: Aspen Institute.

Cowhey, P. F. (1990). The international tele-communications regime: the political roots of regimes for high technology. *International Organisation,* 45(2), 169–99.

Cronin, B. & Davenport, E. (2001). E-rogenous zones: positioning pornography in the digital economy. *The Information Society,* 17(1), 33–48.

Crowley, J. E. & Skocpol, T. (2001). The rush to organize: explaining associational formation in the United States, 1860s–1920s. *American Journal of Political Science,* 45(4), 813–29.

Crowston, K. & Williams, M. (2000). Reproduced and emergent genres of communication on the World Wide Web. *The Information Society,* 16(3), 201–15.

D'Haenens, L., Jankowski, N. & Heuvelman, A. (2004). News in online and print newspapers: differences in reader consumption and recall. *New Media and Society,* 6(3), 363–82.

D'Haenens, L., Koeman, J. & Saeys, F. (2007). Digital citizenship among ethnic minority youths in the Netherlands and Flanders. *New Media & Society,* 9(2), 279–99.

Dacin, T., Goodstein, J. & Scott, R. (2002). Institutional theory and institutional change: introduction to the special research forum. *Academy of Management Journal,* 45(1), 45–56.

Dahl, R. A. (1967). *Pluralist Democracy in the U.S.: conflict and consent.* Chicago: Rand McNally.

—— (1989). *Democracy and its Critics.* New Haven: Yale University Press.

Dahlberg, L. (2001). The internet and democratic discourse: exploring the prospects of online deliberative forums extending the public sphere. *Information Communication and Society,* 4(1), 615–33.

Dahlgren, P. (2005). The internet, public spheres, and political communication: dispersion and deliberation. *Political Communication*, 22 (2), 147–62.

Dahlgren, P. & Gurevitch, M. (2005). Political communication in a changing world. In: J. Curran & M. Gurevitch (eds.), *Mass Media and Society*, 4th edn. London: Hodder Arnold.

Dalton, R. J. (1994). *The Green Rainbow: environmental groups in Western Europe*. New Haven: Yale University Press.

—— (2004). *Democratic Challenges, Democratic Choices: the erosion of political support in advanced industrial democracies*. Oxford: Oxford University Press.

Dalton, R. J. & Wattenberg, M. P. (2000). *Parties without Partisans: political change in advanced industrial democracies*. Oxford: Oxford University Press.

Danet, B. (1996). *Text as mask: gender and identity on the internet*. Retrieved November 22, 2007, from http://Atar.mscc.huji.ac.il/~msdanet/mask.html

Danziger, J. (2004). Innovation in innovation? The technology enactment framework. *Social Science Computer Review*, 22(1), 100–110.

Davidow, W. H. & Malone, M. S. (1992). *The Virtual Corporation: structuring and revitalizing the corporation for the 21st century*. New York: HarperBusiness.

Davis, G. F. (2005). *Social Movements and Organization Theory*. Cambridge: Cambridge University Press.

Davis, G. F., McAdam, D., Scott, W. R. & Zald, M. N. (eds.) (2005). *Social Movements and Organizational Theory*. New York: Cambridge University Press.

Davis, R. (1999). *The Web of Politics: the internet's impact on the American political system*. New York: Oxford University Press.

—— (2005). *Politics Online: blogs, chatrooms, and discussion groups in American democracy*. New York: Routledge.

Davis, R., Owen, D., Taras, D. & Ward, S. J. (2008). *Making a Difference? The internet and elections in comparative perspective*. Lanham, MD: Lexington Books.

Davis, S., Elin, L. & Reeher, G. (2002). *Click on Democracy: the internet's power to change political apathy into civic action*. Boulder, CO: Westview Press.

Davison, R. M., Martinsons, M. G. & Kock, N. (2004). Principles of canonical action research. *Information Systems Journal*, 14(1), 65–86.

de Vreese, C. H. (ed.). (Forthcoming). *The Dynamics of Referendum Campaigns: an international perspective*. Basingstoke: Palgrave Macmillan.

de Vreese, C. H. & Semetko, H. A. (2004a). News matters: influences on the vote in the Danish 2000 Euro referendum campaign. *European Journal of Political Research*, 43, 699–722.

—— (2004b). *Political Campaigning in Referendums: framing the referendum issue*. London: Routledge.

Deibert, R. J. (2003). Black code: censorship, surveillance, and the militarization of cyberspace. *Millennium: Journal of International Studies*, 32(3), 501–30.

Deibert, R. J., Palfrey, J. G., Rohozinski, R. & Zittrain, J. (eds.). (2008). *Access Denied: the practice and policy of global internet filtering*. Cambridge, MA: MIT Press.

Deibert, R. J. & Rohozinski, R. (2007). Good for liberty, bad for security? The internet and global civil society. In: R. J. Deibert, J. G. Palfrey, R. Rohozinski & J. Zittrain (eds.), *Access Denied: the practice and policy of global internet filtering*. Cambridge, MA: MIT Press.

Deibert, R. J. & Villeneuve, N. (2004). Firewalls and power: An overview of global state censorship of the internet. In: M. Klang & A. Murray (eds.), *Human Rights in the Digital Age*. London: Cavendish Publishing.

della Porta, D. (2005). Multiple belongings, flexible identities and the construction of "another politics": between the European social forum and the local social fora. In: D. della Porta & S. Tarrow (eds.), *Transnational Protest and Global Activism*. Boulder, CO: Rowman and Littlefield.

della Porta, D. & Tarrow, S. (eds.). (2005). *Transnational Protest AND Global Activism*. Boulder, CO: Rowman and Littlefield.

Delli Carpini, M. X., Cook, F. L. & Jacobs, L. R. (2004). Public deliberation, discursive participation, and citizen engagement: a review of the empirical literature. *Annual Review of Political Science*, 7, 315–44.

Delli Carpini, M. X. & Keeter, S. (2003). The internet and an informed citizenry. In: D. M. Anderson & M. Cornfield (eds.), *The Civic Web: online politics and democratic value*. Lanham, MD: Rowman and Littlefield.

—— (1996). *What Americans Know About Politics and Why it Matters*. New Haven; London: Yale University Press.

Delli Carpini, M. X. & Williams, B. A. (2001). Let us infotain you: Politics in the new media environment. In: W. L. Bennett & R. M. Entman (eds.), *Mediated Politics: communication in the future of democracy*. Cambridge: Cambridge University Press.

Denning, D. (1999). *Information Warfare and Security*. New York: ACM Press.

Der Derian, J. (2000). Virtuous war/virtual theory. *International Affairs*, 76(4), 771–88.

Derrida, J. (1997). *The Politics of Friendship*. London: Verso.

Dessauer, C. (2004). New media, internet news, and the news habit. In: P. N. Howard & S. Jones (eds.), *Society Online: the internet in context*. Thousand Oaks, CA: Sage.

Deuze, M. (1999). Journalism and the web: an analysis of skills and standards in an online environment. *Gazette*, 61(5), 373–90.

—— (2003). The web and its journalisms: considering the consequences of different types of news media online. *New Media and Society*, 5(2), 203–30.

d'Haenens, L. (2003). ICT in multicultural society: the Netherlands – a context for sound multiform media policy? *Gazette*, 65(4–5), 401–21.

d'Haenens, L., Koeman, J. & Saeys, F. (2007). Digital citizenship among ethnic minority youths in the Netherlands and Flanders. *New Media and Society*, 9(2), 278–99.

Dia, X. & Norton, P. (2007). The Internet and Parliamentary democracy in Europe. *Journal of Legislative Studies*, 13(3), 342–453.

Diani, M. (2001). Social movement networks. In: F. Webster (ed.), *Culture and Politics in the Information Age: a new politics?* London: Routledge.

—— (2003). Networks and social movements: A research programme. In: M. Diani & D. McAdam (eds.), *Social Movements and Networks: relational approaches to collective action*. Oxford: Oxford University Press.

Diani, M. & Donati, P. (2001). Organization change in western European environmental groups: a framework for analysis. *Environmental politics*, 8(1), 13–34.

DiMaggio, P. & Celeste, C. (2004). *Technological careers: adoption, deepening, and dropping out in a panel of internet users (Russell Sage Working Paper)*. Retrieved November 22, 2007, from www.russellsage.org/publications/workingpapers

DiMaggio, P. & Powell, W. (1983). The iron cage revisited: institutional isomorphism and collective rationality in organization fields. *American Sociological Review*, 48(2), 147–60.

—— (1991). Introduction. In: W. Powell & P. DiMaggio (eds.), *The New Institutionalism in Organizational Analysis*. Chicago: University of Chicago Press.

DiMaggio, P. J. (1988). Interest and agency in institutional theory. In: L. G. Zucker (Ed.), *Institutional Patterns and Organizations*. MA: Ballinger.

Dimmick, J., Chen, Y. & Li, Z. (2004). Competition between the internet and traditional news media: the gratification-opportunities niche dimension. *The Journal of Media Economics*, 17(1), 19–33.

Doerschler, P. (2006). Push-pull factors and immigrant political integration in Germany. *Social Science Quarterly*, 87(5), 1100–16.

Doherty, B. (2002). *Ideas and Actions in the Green Movement*. London: Routledge.

Donohue, G., Tichenor, P. & Olien, C. (1975). Mass media and the knowledge gap: a hypothesis reconsidered. *Journalism Quarterly*, 50(4), 652–9.

Doppelt, J. & Shearer, E. (1999). *Nonvoters: America's no-shows*. Thousand Oaks, CA: Sage Publications.

Doppely, J. (1996). *Nonvoters: America's no-shows*. Thousand Oaks, CA: Sage.

Dougherty, M. & Foot, K. (2007). The internet and elections project research design. In: R. Kluver, N. W. Jankowski, K. Foot & S. M. Schneider (eds.), *The Internet and National Elections: a comparative study of web campaigning*. New York: Routledge.

Dourish, P. (2004). What we talk about when we talk about context. *Personal and Ubiquitous Computing*, 8(1), 19–30.

Dowell, W. T. (2006). The internet, censorship, and China. *Georgetown Journal of International Affairs*, 7(2), 111–19.

Downing, J. D. H. (1989). Computers for political change: peace net and public data access. *Journal of Communication*, 39(3), 154–62.

—— (2001). *Radical Media: rebellious communication and social movements*. Thousand Oaks, CA: Sage.

Downs, A. (1957). *An Economic Theory of Democracy*. New York: Harper and Row.

Drake, W. J. (2005). *Reforming Internet Governance: perspectives from the working group on internet governance*. New York: United Nations ICT Task Force.

Drew, D. & Weaver, D. (2006). Voter learning in the 2004 presidential election: did the media matter? *Journalism and Mass Communication Quarterly,* 83(1), 25–42.

Drezner, D. (2004). The global governance of the internet: bringing the state back in. *Political Science Quarterly,* 119(3), 477–98.

Driscoll, C. (1999). Girl culture, revenge and global capitalism: cybergirls, riot grrls, spice girls. *Australian Feminist Studies,* 14(29), 173–93.

Drucker, P. F. (1988). The coming of the new organization. *Harvard Business Review,* 66(1), 45–53.

Dunleavy, P. & Margetts, H. (1999). *Government on the Web*. London: HMSO.

—— (2002). *Government on the Web II*. London: HMSO.

Dunleavy, P., Margetts, H., Bastow, S. & Tinkler, J. (2006a). *Digital Era Governance: IT corporations, the state and e-government*. Oxford: Oxford University Press.

—— (2006b). New public management is dead – long live digital-era governance. *Public Administration Research and Theory,* 16(3), 467–94.

Dutta-Bergman, M. J. (2004). Complementarity in consumption of news types across traditional and new media. *Journal of Broadcasting and Electronic Media,* 48(1), 41–60.

Dutton, W., di Gennaro, C. & Millwood-Hargrave, A. (2005). *The Internet in Britain 2005*. Oxford: Oxford Internet Institute.

Dutton, W. H. (2004). *Social Transformation in the Information Society*. Paris: UNESCO.

—— (2005, 1–2 April). *Hired gun or partner in media reform: high noon for the social scientist*. Paper presented at the Synthesizing Necessary Knowledge for a Democratic Public Sphere Workshop, New York.

Dutton, W. H., Carusi, A. & Peltu, M. (2006). Fostering multidisciplinary engagement: Communication challenges for social research on emerging digital technologies. *Prometheus,* 24(2), 129–49.

Dutton, W. H. & Helsper, E. J. (2007). *The Internet in Britain 2007*. Oxford: Oxford Internet Institute, University of Oxford.

Dutton, W. H., Palfrey, J. & Peltu, M. (2007). *Deciphering the Codes of Internet Governance: understanding the hard issues at stake*. Oxford: Oxford Internet Institute.

Dutton, W. H. & Peltu, M. (2005). *The Emerging Internet Governance Mosaic: connecting the pieces*. Oxford: Oxford Internet Institute.

Dutton, W. H., Shepherd, A. & di Gennaro, C. (2006). Digital divides and choices reconfiguring access: National and cross-national patterns of internet diffusion and use. In: B. Anderson, M. Brynin & Y. Raban (eds.), *Information and Communications Technologies in Society*. London: Routledge.

Duverger, M. (1954). *Political Parties: their organization and activity in the modern state*. London: Methuen.

Dwyer, P., Hof, R. D. & Kerstetter, J. (2004). *The amazing money machine*. Retrieved August 2, 2004, from www.businessweek.com/magazine/content/04_31/b3894011_mz001.htm

Ebbinghaus, B. & Visser, J. (1999). When institutions matter: union growth and decline in Europe 1950–95. *European Sociological Review,* 15(2), 1–24.

Economist (2007). *Special report: constitutional conundrum*. Retrieved March 15, 2007 from www.economist.com/research/articlesBySubject/displaystory.cfm?subjectid=3853071&story_id=8808026

Edmiston, K. D. (2003). State and local e-government: prospects and challenges. *American Review of Public Administration,* 33(1), 20–45.

Edwards, A. (2002). The moderator as an emerging democratic intermediary: the role of the moderator in internet discussions about public issues. *Information Polity,* 7(1), 3–20.

Edwards, J. (2007). *John Edwards for President – social networking*. Retrieved November 22, 2007, from http://johnedwards.com/action/networking/

Edwards, L. (2005). Switching off the surveillance society? Legal regulation of CCTV in the United Kingdom. In: S. Nouwt, B. R. d. Vries & C. Prins (Eds.), *Reasonable Expectations of Privacy? Eleven country reports on camera surveillance and workplace privacy*. The Hague: Asser.

eGovernment News (2005, April 5). UK government launches new digital strategy. *eGovernment News*.

Ehrlich, E. (2003, December 14). What will happen when a national political machine can fit on a laptop. *Washington Post*.

Eickelman, D. F. & Anderson, J. W. (1999). Redefining muslim publics. In: D. F. Eickelman & J. W. Anderson (eds.), *New Media in the*

Muslim World. Bloomington, IN: Indiana University Press.

Eid, G. (2004). *The internet in the Arab world: a new space for repression?* Retrieved November 22, 2007, from www.hrinfo.net/en/reports/net2004

El Diwany, S. (2007). *Arab world competitiveness report 2007 press release.* Retrieved November 22, 2007, from www.weforum.org/en/media/Latest%20Press%20Releases/AWCReportPR

El Sayed, H. & Westrup, C. (2003). Egypt and ICTs: how ICTs bring national initiatives, global organizations and companies together. *Information Technology and People,* 16(1), 76–92.

Eldersveld, S. J. (1982). *Political parties in American society.* New York: Basic Books.

Elmer, G. (2002). The case of web cookies. In: G. Elmer (ed.), *Critical perspectives on the internet.* Boulder: Rowman and Littlefield.

—— (2004). *Profiling Machines: mapping the personal information economy.* Boston, MA: MIT Press.

Engel, M. (1996). *Tickle the Public.* London: Gollancz.

Entman, R. (1991). Framing US coverage of international news. *Journal of Communication,* 41(4), 6–28.

—— (1993). Framing: toward clarification of a fractured paradigm. *Journal of Communication,* 43(4), 51–58.

Epstein, L. D. (1980). *Political Parties and Western Democracies.* New Brunswick, NJ: Transaction.

ESCWA (2002). Youth unemployment in the ESCWA. *The Economic and Social Commission for Western Asia for the Youth Employment Summit.* Alexandria, Egypt: The Economic and Social Commission for Western Asia.

Etzioni, A. (1988). *The Moral Dimension: toward a new economics.* New York: The Free Press.

—— (1997). The end of cross-cultural relativism. *Socialism and Democracy,* 11, 177–89.

Eurobarometer (2004). *62.1: The constitutional treaty, economic challenges, vocational training, information technology at work, environmental issues, and services of general interest.* Brussels: Eurobarometer.

European Commission Staff (2007). *Commission staff working document* (No. COM (2007) 116 final). Brussels: Commission of the European Communities.

European Union (1995). *Directive 95/46/EC of the European Parliament and of the Council on the protection of individuals with regard to the processing*

of personal data and on the free movement of such data. Brussels: European Union.

—— (2005). *WP 105: Working document on data protection issues related to RFID technology. Working party on the protection of individuals with regard to the processing of personal data.* Brussels: European Union.

—— (2007). *WP 135: Opinion 4/2007 on the concept of personal data. Working party on the protection of individuals with regard to the processing of personal data.* Brussels: European Union.

Eurostat (2005). *Statistics in focus issue 38: The digital divide in Europe.* Retrieved August 14, 2007, from http://epp.eurostat.cec.eu.int/portal/page?_pageid=1073,46587259&_dad=portal&_schema=PORTAL&p_product_code=KS-NP-05-038

—— (2006). *Community survey on ICT usage in households and by individuals 2005.* Retrieved August 11, 2007, from http://ec.europa.eu/information_society/eeurope/i2010/docs/annual_report/2006/sec_2006_604_en.pdf

Eveland Jr, W. P. (2001). The cognitive mediation model of learning from the news: evidence from non-election, off-year election, and presidential election contexts. *Communication Research,* 28(5), 571–601.

—— (2002). News information processing as mediator of the relationship between motivations and political knowledge. *Journalism and Mass Communication Quarterly,* 79(1), 26–40.

—— (2003). A "mix of attributes" approach to the study of media effects and new communication technologies. *Journal of Communication,* 53(3), 395–410.

Eveland Jr, W. P., Cortese, J., Park, H. & Dunwoody, S. (2004). How web site organization influences free recall, factual knowledge, and knowledge structure. *Human Communication Research,* 30(2), 208–33.

Eveland Jr, W. P. & Dunwoody, S. (1998). Users and navigation patterns of a science world wide web site for the public. *Public Understanding of Science,* 7(4), 285–311.

—— (2001a). Applying research on the uses and cognitive effects of hypermedia to the study of the world wide web. *Communication Yearbook,* 25, 79–113.

—— (2001b). User control and structural isomorphism or disorientation and cognitive load? Learning from the web versus print. *Communication Research,* 28(1), 48–78.

—— (2002). An investigation of elaboration and selective scanning as mediators of learning from the web versus print. *Journal of Broadcasting and Electronic Media*, 46(1), 34–53.

Eveland Jr, W. P., Marton, K. & Seo, M. (2004). Moving beyond "just the facts": the influence of online news on the content and structure of public affairs knowledge. *Communication Research*, 31(1), 82–108.

Eveland Jr, W. P., Seo, M. & Marton, K. (2002). Learning from the news in campaign 2000: an experimental comparison of TV news, newspapers and online news. *Media Psychology*, 4 (4), 352–78

Eveland Jr, W. P., Shah, D. V. & Kwak, N. (2003). Assessing causality in the cognitive mediation model: a panel study of motivations, information processing and learning during Campaign 2000. *Communication Research*, 30(4), 359–86.

Eyerman, R. & Jamison, A. (1991). *Social Movements: a cognitive approach*. University Park, PA: Pennsylvania State University Press.

Fairlie, R. (2004). Race and the digital divide. *Contributions of Economic Analysis and Policy, 3* (1), 1–35.

Fallows, D. (2005). *How Women and Men use the Internet*. Washington, DC: Pew Internet and American Life Project.

Fallows, J. (1996a). *Breaking the News: how the media undermine American democracy*. New York: Pantheon books.

—— (1996b). Why Americans hate the media. *Atlantic Monthly*, 277(2), 45–64.

Faris, R. & Villeneuve, N. (2008). Measuring global internet filtering. In: R. J. Deibert, J. G. Palfrey, R. Rohozinski & J. Zittrain (eds.), *Access Denied: the practice and policy of global internet filtering*. Cambridge, MA: MIT Press.

Farrell, D., Kolodny, R. & Medvic, S. (2001). Parties and campaign professionals in a digital age: political consultants in the United States and their counterparts overseas. *Harvard International Journal of Press/Politics*, 6(4), 11–30.

Farrell, D. & Webb, P. (2000). Political parties as campaign organisations. In: R. J. Dalton & M. P. Wattenberg (eds.), *Parties without Partisans: political change in advanced industrial democracies*. Oxford: Oxford University Press.

Fauconnier, G. & Turner, M. (2003). *The Way We Think: conceptual blending and the mind's hidden complexities*. New York: Basic Books.

Fearon, J. D. (1998). Deliberation as discussion. In: J. Elster (ed.), *Deliberative Democracy*. Cambridge: Cambridge University Press.

Federal Communication Commission (2005). *FCC 05–116: first report and order and notice of proposed rulemaking adopted*. Washington, DC: Federal Communication Commission.

Ferber, B., Foltz, F. & Pugliese, R. (2005). The internet and public participation: state legislature web sites and the many definitions of interactivity. *Bulletin of Science, Technology and Society*, 25(1), 85–93.

Ferdinand, P. (ed.). (2000). *The Internet, Democracy and Democratization*. London: Frank Cass.

Ferguson, R. (2007). *Bermuda to put RFID in all vehicles on island*. Retrieved November 22, 2007, from www.eweek.com/article2/0,1895,2126991,00.asp

Festinger, L. (1957). *A Theory of Cognitive Dissonance*. Evanston, IL: Row, Peterson.

Fielding, S. (2001). Activists against "Affluence": Labour party culture during the "Golden age" circa 1950–70. *Journal of British Studies*, 40(2), 241–67.

Filzmaier, P. (2004). Information management of MPs: experiences from Austria, Denmark and the Netherlands. *Information Polity*, 9(2), 17–28.

Finn, P. (2007, May 19). Cyber assaults on Estonia typify a new battle tactic. *Washington Post*.

Finnegan, M. (2007, January 29). 2008 candidates, foes rush to roll web video. *Los Angeles Times*.

Fisher, D., Stanley, K., Berman, D. & Neff, G. (2005). How do organizations matter? Mobilization and support for participants at five globalization protests. *Social Problems*, 52 (1), 102–21.

Fisher, W. & Ponniah, T. (eds.). (2003). *Another World is Possible: popular alternatives to globalization at the World Social Forum*. Black Point, NS: Zed Books.

Flanagin, A., Stohl, C. & Bimber, B. (2006). Modeling the structure of collective action. *Communication Monographs*, 73(1), 29–54.

Flavian, C. & Gurrea, R. (2006). The choice of digital newspapers: influence of reader goals and user experience. *Internet Research*, 16(3), 231–47.

Foot, K. M. & Schneider, S. M. (2006). *Web Campaigning*. Cambridge, MA: MIT Press.

Foot, K. M., Schneider, S. M., Kluver, R., Xenos, M. & Jankowski, N. (2007). Comparing web production practices across electoral web spheres. In: R. Kluver, N. Jankowski, K. M. Foot & S. M. Schneider (eds.), *The Internet and National Elections*. New York: Routledge.

Fountain, J. E. (1998). Social capital: a key enabler of innovation in science and technology. *Science and Public Policy*, 25(2).

—— (2001a). *Building the Virtual State: information technology and institutional change*. Washington: Brookings Institution Press.

—— (2001b). Toward a theory of federal bureaucracy in the 21st century. In: E. C. Kamarck & J. S. Nye (eds.), *Governance.Com: democracy in the information age*. Washington DC: Brookings Institution Press.

—— (2002). *Information, Institutions and Government: advancing a basic social science research program for digital government*. Cambridge, MA: National Centre for Digital Government, John F. Kennedy School of Government.

—— (2006). Central issues in the political development of the virtual state. In: M. Castells & G. Cardoso (eds.), *The Network Society: from knowledge to policy*. Washington, DC: Brookings Institution Press.

—— (2007). Challenges to organizational change: Multi-level integrated information structures. In: D. Lazer & V. Mayer-Schoenberger (eds.), *Governance and Information Technology: from electronic government to information government*. Cambridge MA: MIT Press.

Fountain, J. E. & Osorio-Urzua, C. (2001). Public sector: Early stage of a deep transformation. In: R. Litan & A. Rivlin (eds.), *The Economic Payoff of the Internet Revolution*. Washington DC: Brookings Institution Press.

Fox, S. (2005). *Digital Divisions*. Washington, DC: Pew Internet and American Life Project.

Fox, S. & Livingston, G. (2007). *Hispanics with Lower Levels of Education and English Proficiency Remain Largely Disconnected from the Internet*. Washington, DC: Pew Internet and American Life Project/Pew Hispanic Center.

Francia, P. L. & Herrnson, P. S. (2002). The e-campaign: coming to an election near you. In: R. D. Faucheux & P. S. Herrnson (eds.), *Campaign Battle Lines*. Washington DC: Campaigns and Elections.

Franda, M. (2001). *Launching into Cyberspace: internet development and politics in five world regions*. Boulder, CO: Lynne Rienner.

Frank, D. (2002). *IT budget takes on e-gov*. Retrieved February 18, 2002, from www.few.

com/few/articles/2002/0218/cov-budget1-02-18-02.asp

Franklin, B. (2004). *Packaging Politics: political communications in Britain's media democracy*, 2nd edn. London: Hodder.

Franklin, M. I. (2007). NGOs and the "Information society": grassroots advocacy at the UN – a cautionary tale. *Review of Policy Research*, 24(4), 309–30.

Franzen, A. (2000). Does the internet make us lonely? *European Sociological Review*, 16(4), 427–38.

Fraser, N. (1992). Rethinking the public sphere: a contribution to the critique of actually existing democracy. In: C. Calhoun (ed.), *Habermas and the Public Sphere*. Cambridge, MA: MIT Press.

Freedman, D. (2006). Internet transformations: old media resilience in the new media revolution. In: J. Curran & D. Morley (eds.), *Media and Cultural Theory*. London: Routledge.

Freedom House. (2006). *Freedom in the World*. Washington, DC: Freedom House.

—— (2007). *Democracy's Century*. Washington, DC: Freedom House.

Freire, P. (1970). *Pedagogy of the Oppressed*. New York: Herder & Herder.

Frey, D. (1986). Recent research on selective exposure to information. In: L. Berkowitz (ed.), *Advances in Experimental Social Psychology*. San Diego, CA: Academic.

Friedlos, D. (2007). *Heathrow joins trial of RFID scheme*. Retrieved July 5, 2007, from www.computing.co.uk/computing/news/2193486/heathrow-joins-trial-rfid

Frissen, P. (2002). Representative democracy and information society: a postmodern perspective. *Information Polity*, 7(4), 175–83.

Froehling, O. (1999). Internauts and guerilleros: the Zapatista rebellion in Chiapas, Mexico and its extension into cyberspace. In: M. Crang, P. Crang & J. May (eds.), *Virtual Geographies: bodies, space and relations*. New York: Routledge.

From Cairo With Love (2005). *The blogging effect*. Retrieved November 22, 2007, from http://fromcairo.blogspot.com/2005/02/blogging-effect.html

Froomkin, A. M. (1995). The metaphor is the key: cryptography, the clipper chip, and the constitution. *University of Pennsylvania Law Review*, 143, 709–897.

Fulk, J. (2001). Global network organizations: emergence and future prospects. *Human Relations,* 54(1), 91–99.

Fulk, J., Flanagin, A. J., Kalman, M., Monge, P. R. & Ryan, T. (1996). Connective and communal public goods in interactive communication systems. *Communication Theory,* 6(1), 60–87.

Fulk, J., Heino, R., Flanagin, A. J., Monge, P. R. & Bar, F. (2004). A test of the individual action model for organizational information commons. *Organization Science,* 15(5), 569–85.

Fuller, J. E. (2004). Equality in cyberdemocracy? Gauging gender gaps in online civic participation. *Social Science Quarterly,* 85(4), 938–57.

Fuller, M. (2003). *Behind the Blip: essays on the culture of software.* New York: Autonomedia.

Galaskiewics, J. & Wasserman, S. (1993). Social network analysis: concepts, methodology, and directions for the 1990s. *Sociological methods and research,* 22(1), 3–22.

Galbraith, J. R. & Kazanjiam, R. K. (1988). Strategy, technology, and emerging organizational forms. In: J. Hage (ed.), *Futures of Organizations: innovating to adapt strategy and human resources to rapid technological change.* Lexington, MA: Lexington Books.

Gallagher, M. & Uleri, P. V. (eds.). (1996). *The Referendum Experience in Europe.* New York: St. Martin's Press.

Galloway, A. (2004). *Protocol: or how control exists after decentralization.* Cambridge, MA: MIT Press.

Galston, W. A. (2003). If political fragmentation is the problem, is the internet the solution? In: D. M. Anderson & M. Cornfield (eds.), *The Civic Web: online politics and democratic values.* Lanham, MD: Rowman and Littlefield.

Galusky, W. (2003). Identifying with information: Citizen empowerment, the internet and the environmental anti-toxins movement. In: M. McCaughey & M. Ayers (eds.), *Cyberactivism: online activism in theory and practice.* New York: Routledge.

Gans, H. J. (2003). *Democracy and the News.* Oxford: Oxford University Press.

Garnham, N. (1990). *Capitalism and Communication: global culture and the economics of information.* London: Sage.

Garrett, K. R. (2005). Exposure to controversy in an information society (unpublished doctoral dissertation). Michigan: University of Michigan.

Garrido, M. & Halavais, A. (2003). Mapping networks of support for the Zapatista movement: applying social networks analysis to study contemporary social movements. In: M. McCaughey & M. Ayers (eds.), *Cyberactivism: online activism in theory and practice.* London: Routledge.

Garrie, D. B. (2005). The legal status of software. *John Marshall Journal of Computer and Information Law,* 23(Summer), 711–69.

Garrison, B. (2005). Online newspapers. In: M. B. Salwen, B. Garrison & P. D. Driscoll (eds.), *Online News and the Public.* Mahwah, NJ: Erlbaum.

Garud, R., Jain, S. & Kumaraswamy, A. (2002). Institutional entrepreneurship in the sponsorship of common technological standards in the case of Sun Microsystems and Java. *Academy of Management Journal,* 45(1), 196–214.

Gasco, M. (2003). New technology and institutional change in public administration. *Social Science Computer Review,* 21(1), 6–14.

Gastil, J. (2000). *By Popular Demand: revitalizing representative democracy through deliberative elections.* Berkeley, CA: University of California Press.

Gastil, J., Black, L. & Moscovitz, K. (Forthcoming). Group and individual differences in deliberative experience: a study of ideology, attitude change, and deliberation in small face-to-face groups. *Political Communication.*

Gastil, J. & Crosby, N. (2003). *Voters need more reliable information.* Retrieved August 14, 2007, from http://seattlepi.nwsource.com/opinion/147013_uninformed06.html

Gastil, J., Wells, C. & Reedy, J. (Forthcoming). When good voters make bad policies: Assessing and improving the deliberative quality of initiative elections. *Colorado Law Review.*

Gates Foundation (2005). US public libraries providing unprecedented access to computers, the internet, and technology training. Seattle: Gates Foundation.

Geens, S. (2007). *Google Earth ban in Sudan is due to US export restrictions.* Retrieved November 22, 2007, from www.sudantribune.com/spip.php?article21501.

Gelman, A. & King, G. (1993). Why are American election polls so variable when votes are so predictable? *British Journal of Political Science,* 23(4), 409–51.

Gerber, E. R. (1999). *The Populist Paradox: interest group influence and the promise of direct legislation.* Princeton: Princeton University Press.

Gershon, P. (2004). *Releasing Resources to the Front-Line: independent review of public sector efficiency.* London: HM Treasury.

GESIS (German Social Science Infrastructure Services) (2007). *Summary of Eurobarometer data.* Retrieved August 14, 2007, from www.gesis.org/en/data_service/eurobarometer/

Ghareeb, E. (2000). New media and the information revolution in the Arab world: an assessment. *Middle East Journal,* 54(3), 395–418.

Ghoshal, S. & Bartlett, C. (1990). The multinational corporation as an interorganizational network. *Academy of Management Review,* 15 (4), 603–25.

Gibbs, J., Ball-Rokeach, S., Jung, J.-Y., Kim, Y.-C. & Qiu, J. (2006). The globalization of every day life: visions and reality. In: M. Sturken, D. Thomas & S. Ball-Rokeach (eds.), *Reinventing Technology: cultural narratives of technological change.* Philadelpia, PA: Temple University Press.

Gibson, O. (2006). *Have you got news for US?* Retrieved November 6, 2007, from www.guardian.co.uk/media/2006/nov/06/monday mediasection

Gibson, R. K., Howard, P. N. & Ward, S. J. (2000). *Social capital, internet connectedness and political participation: a four-country study.* Paper presented at the International Political Science Association Annual Conference, Quebec, Canada.

Gibson, R. K., Lusoli, W. & Ward, S. J. (2003a). The internet and political campaigning: the new medium comes of age? *Representation,* 39 (3), 166–80.

—— (2005). Online participation in the UK: testing a contextualised model of internet effects. *British Journal of Politics and International Relations,* 7(4), 561–83.

—— (Forthcoming). Italian elections online: 10 years on. In: J. Newell (ed.), *The Italian General Election of 2006: Romano Prodi's victory.* Manchester: Manchester University Press.

Gibson, R. K., Margolis, M., Resnick, D. & Ward, S. J. (2003b). Election campaigning on the www in the USA and the UK: a comparative analysis. *Party Politics,* 9(1), 47–75.

Gibson, R. K., Nixon, P. & Ward, S. J. (eds.). (2003c). *Political Parties and the Internet: net gain?* London: Routledge.

Gibson, R. K. & Rommele, A. (2003). *Regional web campaigning in the 2002 German federal election.*

Paper presented at the American Political Science Association Annual Meeting, Philadelphia.

—— (2005). Truth and consequence in web campaigning: is there an academic digital divide? *European Political Science,* 4(3), 273–87.

Gibson, R. K., Rommele, A. & Ward, S. J. (eds.). (2004). *Electronic Democracy: mobilisation, organisation and participation via new ICTs.* London: Routledge.

Gibson, R. K. & Ward, S. J. (1999). Party democracy online: UK parties and new ICTs. *Information Communication and Society,* 2(3), 340–67.

—— (2002). Virtual campaigning: Australian parties and the impact of the internet. *Australian Journal of Political Science,* 37(1), 99–129.

Giddens, A. (1990). *The Consequences of Modernity.* Cambridge: Polity Press.

—— (1991). *Modernity and Self-identity: self and society in the late modern age.* Stanford: Stanford University Press.

—— (1999). *Runaway World: how globalisation is reshaping our lives.* London: Profile Books.

Giddings, P. J. (2005). *The Future of Parliament: issues for a new century.* New York; Basingstoke: Palgrave Macmillan.

Gil-Garcia, J. R. & Martinez-Moyano. (Forthcoming). Understanding the evolution of e-government: the influence of systems of rules on public sector dynamics. *Government Information Quarterly.*

Gitlin, T. (1980). *The Whole World is Watching: mass media and the unmaking of the new left.* Berkeley, CA: University of California Press.

—— (1983). *Inside Prime Time.* New York: Pantheon Books.

Goffman, E. (1959). *The Presentation of Self in Everyday Life.* New York: Anchor Books.

Goldfarb, J. C. (2006). *Politics of Small Things: the powers of the powerless in dark times.* Chicago: University of Chicago Press.

Goldfarb, Z. A. (2007). *Mobilized online, thousands gather to hear Obama.* Retrieved February 17, 2007, from www.washingtonpost.com/wpdyn/content/article/2007/02/02/AR2007020201233.html

Goldsmith, J. (1998). Against cyberanarchy. *University of Chicago Law Review,* 65(4), 1199–1250.

Goldsmith, J. & Wu, T. (2006). *Who Controls the Internet? Illusions of a borderless world.* New York: Oxford University Press.

Goldstein, B. (1999). *The Internet in the Mid East and North Africa: free expression and censorship*. New York: Human Rights Watch.

Goldstein, K. M. (1999). *Interest Groups, Lobbying, and Participation in America*. Cambridge: Cambridge University Press.

Google. (2007). *Google Maps terms and conditions*. Retrieved August 15, 2007, from http://maps.google.ca/help/terms_maps.html

Gore, A. (1994). Remarks prepared for delivery by Vice President Al Gore. Paper presented at the International Telecommunications Union Conference, 1994. Retrieved June 20, 2007, from www.goelzer.net/telecom/al-gore.html

Graber, D. A. (1984). *Processing the News: how people tame the information tide*. New York: Longman.

—— (1988). *Processing the News: how people tame the information tide*, 2nd edn. New York: Longman.

—— (2006). *Media power in Politics*, 5th edn. Washington, DC: CQ.

Graf, J. & Darr, C. (2004). *Political Influentials Online in the 2004 Presidential Election*. Washington, DC: Institute for Politics, Democracy and the Internet, George Washington University.

Graf, J., Reeher, G., Malbin, J. & Panagopoulos, C. (2006). *Small Donors and Online Giving: a study of donors to the 2004 presidential campaigns*. Washington, DC: Institute for Politics, Democracy and the Internet, George Washington University.

Granick, J. (2005) Middle East. Nixing the news: Iranian internet censorship. *Harvard International Review*, 27(2), 11–12.

Granovetter, M. S. (1973). The strength of weak ties. *American Journal of Sociology*, 78(6), 1360–80.

Grant, A. (2005). The reform of party funding in Britain. *Political Quarterly*, 76(3), 381–92.

Gray, M. & Caul, M. (2000). Declining voter turnout in advanced industrial democracies. *Comparative Political Studies*, 33(9), 1091–1122.

Gray, V. & Lowery, D. (1996). *The Population Ecology of Interest Representation: lobbying communities in the American states*. Ann Arbor: University of Michigan Press.

Green, D. P. & Shapiro, I. (1994). *Pathologies of Rational Choice Theory: a critique of applications in political science*. New Haven: Yale University Press.

Green, N. & Smith, S. (2004). "A spy in your pocket"? The regulation of mobile data in the UK. *Surveillance and Society*, 1(4), 573–87.

Greene, A. M., Hogan, J. & Grieco, M. (2003). E-collectivism and distributed discourse: new opportunities for trade union democracy. *Industrial Relations Journal*, 34(4), 282–89.

Greenwood, R. & Hinings, C. R. (1996). Understanding radical organizational change: bringing together the old and new institutionalism. *Academy of Management Journal*, 21(4), 1022–54.

Greenwood, R., Suddaby, R. & Hinings, C. R. (2002). Theorizing change the role of professional associations in the transformation of institutional fields. *Academy of Management Journal*, 45(1), 58–80.

Greer, J. & LaPointe, M. (2004). Cyber-campaigning grows up: a comparative content analysis of websites for US Senate and gubernatorial races, 1998–2000. In: R. K. Gibson, A. Roemmele & S. J. Ward (eds.), *E-democracy: mobilisation, organisation and participation online*. London: Routledge.

Greer, J. D. & Mensing, D. (2006). The evolution of online newspapers: a longitudinal content analysis, 1997–2003. In: X. Li (ed.), *Internet Newspapers: the making of a mainstream medium*. Mahwah, NJ: Erlbaum.

Grignou, B. & Patou, C. (2004). Attac(k)ing expertise: does the internet democratize knowledge. In: W. van de Donk, B. Loader, P. Nixon & D. Rucht (eds.), *Cyberprotest: new media, citizens and social movements*. London: Routledge.

Grossman, L. K. (1995). *The Electronic Republic*. New York: Viking.

Guarnizo, L. E., Portes, A. & Haller, W. (2003). Assimilation and transnationalism: determinants of transnational political action among contempory migrants. *American Journal of Sociology*, 108(6), 1211–48.

Guillen, M. & Suarez, S. (2005). Explaining the global digital divide: economic, political and sociological drivers of cross-national internet use. *Social Forces*, 84(2), 681–708.

Gunkel, D. (2003). Second thoughts: toward a critique of the digital divide. *New Media and Society*, 5(4), 499–522.

Gunkel, D. J. & Gunkel, A. H. (1997). Virtual geographies: the new worlds of cyberspace. *Critical Studies in Mass Communication*, 14, 123–37.

Gunter, B. (2003). *News and the Net*. Mahwah, NJ: Lawrence Erlbaum Associates.

Gurak, L. J. (1996). The case of Lotus MarketPlace: organization and ethos in a net-based protest. In: S. Herring (ed.), *Computer-Mediated Communication: linguistic, social and cross-cultural perspectives*. Amsterdam: John Benjamins.

—— (1997). *Persuasion and Privacy in Cyberspace: the online protests over Lotus Market Place and the clipper chip*. New Haven, CT: Yale University Press.

Gustafson, K. E. (2002). Join now, membership is free: women's websites and the coding of community. In: M. Consalvo & S. Paasonen (eds.), *Women and Everyday Uses of the Internet: agency and identity*. New York: Peter Lang.

Habermas, J. (1962/1981). *The Structural Transformation of the Public Sphere: an inquiry into a category of bourgeois society* (T. B. W. F. Lawrence, trans.). Cambridge, MA: Cambridge University Press.

—— (1973). *Theory and Practice* (J. Viertel, Trans.). London: Heinemann.

—— (1974). The public sphere: an encyclopedia article. *New German Critique*, 3, 49–55.

—— (1989). *The Structural Transformation of the Public Sphere*. Cambridge, MA: MIT Press.

—— (2004). *The Divided West*. Malden, MA: Polity Press.

Hachigian, N. (2001). China's cyber-strategy. *Foreign Affairs*, 80(2), 118–33.

Hacker, J. S., Mettler, S. & Pinderhughes, D. (2005). Inequality and public policy. In: L. R. Jacobs & T. Skocpol (eds.), *Inequality and American Democracy: what we know and what we need to learn*. New York: Russell Sage Foundation.

Hacker, K. L. & van Dijk, J. (2000). *Digital Democracy: issues of theory and practice*. Sage: London.

Haddon, L. (2006). The contribution of domestication research to in-home computing and media consumption. *The Information Society*, 22 (4), 195–203.

Hafkin, N. & Taggart, N. (2001). *Gender, Information Technology and Developing Countries: an analytic study*. Washington, DC: USAID.

Hafner, K. & Lyon, M. (1996). *Where Wizards Stay Up Late: the origins of the internet*. New York: Simon and Schuster.

Haggerty, K. D. & Ericson, R. V. (eds.). (2006). *The New Politics of Surveillance and Visibility*. Toronto: University of Toronto.

Hajnal, P. I. (ed.). (2002). *Civil Society in the Information Age*. Burlington, VT: Ashgate.

Halbert, D. (1999). *Intellectual Property in the Information Age: the politics of expanding ownership rights*. Westport, CT: Quorum Books.

—— (2005). *Resisting Intellectual Property*. London: Routledge.

Hall, S. (1994). Cultural identity and diaspora. In: P. William & L. Chrisman (eds.), *Colonial Discourse and Post-Colonial Theory*. New York: Columbia University Press.

Hammer, M. & Champy, J. (1993). *Reengineering the Corporation*. New York: HarperCollins.

Hampton, K. N. & Wellman, B. (2000). Examining community in the digital neighborhood: early results from Canada's wired suburb. In: T. Ishida & K. Isbister (eds.), *Digital Cities: technologies, experiences and future perspectives*. New York: Springer-Verlag.

—— (2001). Long distance community in the network society: contact and support beyond Netville. *American Behavioral Scientist*, 45(3), 476–95.

Hanafi, S. (2005). Reshaping geography: Palestinian community networks in Europe and the new media. *Journal of Ethnic & Migration Studies*, 31(3), 581–98.

Hands, J. (2006). Civil society, cosmopolitics and the net: the legacy of 15 February 2003. *Information, Communication and Society*, 9(2), 225–43.

Harding, S. G. (1986). *The Science Question in Feminism*. Ithaca: Cornell University Press.

Hardy, B. W. & Scheufele, D. A. (2005). Examining differential gains from internet use: comparing the moderating role of talk and online interactions. *Journal of Communication*, 55(1), 71–84.

Hargadon, A. & Douglas, Y. (2001). When innovations meet institutions: Edison and the design of the electric light bulb. *Administrative Science Quarterly*, 46(3), 476–501.

Hargittai, E. (2002). Beyond logs and surveys: in-depth measures of people's web use skills. *Journal of the American Society for Information Science and Technology*, 53(14), 1239–44.

—— (2002). The second-level digital divide: differences in people's online skills. *First Monday*, 7(4).

—— (2003). The digital divide and what to do about it. In: D. C. Jones (ed.), *The New Economy Handbook*. San Diego, CA: Academic Press.

—— (2004). *How wide a web? Social inequality in the digital age* (unpublished Ph.D. dissertation). Princeton, NJ: Princeton University.

Hargittai, E. & Shafer, S. (2006). Differences in actual and perceived online skills: the role of gender. *Social Science Quarterly*, 87(2), 432–48.

Hargreaves, I. & Thomas, J. (2002). *New News, Old News*. London: BSC/ITC.

Harmel, R. & Janda, K. (1982). *Parties and their Environments: limits to reform?* New York: Longman.

Harper, C. (1996). Online newspapers: going somewhere or going nowhere? *Newspaper Research Journal*, 17(3–4), 2–13.

Harris Interactive (2007). *Survey shows privacy concerns a major roadblock for the adoption of location-based services and presence technology.* Retrieved August 15, 2007, from www.harris interactive.com/news/allnewsbydate.asp?News ID=1184

Harrison, T. & Falvey, L. (2001). Democracy and new communication technologies. *Communication Yearbook*, 25(1), 1–43.

Hart, R. P. (1994). Easy citizenship: television's curious legacy. *Annals of the American Academy of Political and Social Science*, 546, 109–20.

Hartley, J. (1996). *Popular Reality*. London: Arnold.

Haufler, V. (2001). *Public Role for the Private Sector: industry self-regulation in a global economy.* Washington, DC: Carnegie Endowment for International Peace.

Havick, J. (2000). The impact of the internet on a television-based society. *Technology in Society*, 22(2), 273–87.

Hawk, B., Rieder, D. M. & Oviedo, O. (eds.). (2008). *Small Tech: the culture of digital tools.* Minneapolis: University of Minnesota Press.

Hayden, C. & Ball-Rokeach, S. J. (2007). Maintaining the digital hub: locating the community technology center in a communication infrastructure. *New Media Society*, 9 (2), 235–57.

Healy, A. & McNamara, D. (1996). Verbal learning and memory: does the modal model still work? In: J. Spense, J. Darley & D. Foss (eds.), *Annual Review of Psychology*. Palo Alto, CA: Annual Reviews.

Hechter, M. & Okamot, D. (2001). Political consequences of minority group formation. *Annual Review of Political Science*, 4, 189–215.

Heckscher, C. C. & Donnellon, A. (eds.). (1994). *The Post-Bureaucratic Organization: new perspectives on organizational change.* Thousand Oaks, CA: Sage.

Heeks, R. & Bailur, S. (2007). Analyzing e-government research: perspectives, philosophies, theories, methods and practice. *Government Information Quarterly*, 24(2), 243–65.

Heileman, R. (2007, April 15). Money chooses sides. *New York Magazine*.

Heinz, J. P. (1993). *The Hollow Core: private interests in national policy making*. Cambridge, MA: Harvard University Press.

Heller, M. (1998). The tragedy of the antic-ommons: property in the transition from marx to markets. *Harvard Law Review*, 111, 621–88.

Herbsleb, J. D., Mockus, A., Finholt, T. & Grinter, R. E. (2000). Distance, dependencies, and delay in a global collaboration. In: W. A. Kellogg & S. Whittaker (eds.), *Proceedings of the 2000 ACM conference on computer supported cooperative work*. Philadelphia, Pennsylvania: United States.

Herbst, S. (1993). *Numbered Voices: how opinion polling has shaped American politics*. Chicago: University of Chicago Press.

Herman, B. & Gandy, O. (2006). Catch 1201: a legislative history and content analysis of the DMCA exemption proceedings. *Cardozo Arts and Entertainment Law Journal*, 24(1), 121–90.

Herring, S. C. (1993). Gender and democracy in computer-mediated communication. *Electronic Journal of Communication*, 3(2).

—— (1995). *Men's Language on the Internet*. Nordlyd: Tromso University.

Herring, S. C. (ed.). (1996a). *Posting a Different Voice: gender and ethics in computer mediated communication*. Albany: SUNY Press.

Herring, S. C. (1996b). Two variants of an electronic message schema. In: S. C. Herring (ed.), *Computer Mediated Communication: linguistic, social and cross-cultural perspectives*. Amsterdam: John Benjamins.

—— (1999). The rhetorical dynamics of gender harassment on-line. *The Information Society*, 15 (3), 151–67.

—— (2001). *Gender and Power in Online Communication*. Bloomington: Center for Social Informatics Working Papers.

—— (2002). Cyber violence: recognizing and resisting abuse in online environments. *Asian Women,* 14, 187–212.

Herring, S. C., Johnson, D. & DiBenedetto, T. (1995). This discussion is going too far! Male resistance to female participation on the internet. In: M. Bucholtz & K. Hall (eds.), *Gender Articulated: language and the socially constructed self.* New York: Routledge.

Herring, S. C., Kouper, I., Scheidt, L. A. & Wright, E. (2004). Women and children last: the discursive construction of weblogs. In: L. Gurak, S. Antonijevik, L. Johnson, C. Ratliff & J. Reyman (eds.), *Into the Blogosphere: rhetoric, community, and culture of weblogs.* Minnespolis, MN: University of Minnesota online publication: http://blog.lib.umn.edu/blogosphere/ Retrieved November 23, 2007.

Hersh, S. (1997). *The Dark Side of Camelot.* New York: Little Brown.

Heydemann, S. (ed.). (2004). *Networks of Privilege in the Middle East: the politics of economic reform revisited.* New York: Palgrave.

Hick, S. F. & McNutt, J. G. (eds.). (2002). *Advocacy, Activism and the Internet: community organization and social policy.* Chicago: Lyceum Books.

Hickson, D., MacMillan, C., Azumi, K. & Horvath, D. (1979). The grounds for comparative organization theory. In: C. Lammers & D. Hickson (eds.), *Organizations Alike and Unalike.* London: Routledge and Kegan Paul.

Hickson, D. J., Hinings, C. R., McMillan, C. J. & Schwitter, J. P. (1974). The culture-free context of organizational structure: a trinational comparison. *Sociology,* 8(1), 59–80.

Hill, K. A. & Hughes, J. E. (1998). *Cyberpolitics: citizen activism in the age of the internet.* New York, NY: Rowman and Littlefield.

Hiller, H. H. & Franz, T. M. (2004). New ties, old ties and lost ties: the use of the internet in diaspora. *New Media and Society,* 6(6), 731–52.

Hindman, M. (2005). The real lessons of Howard Dean: Reflections on the first digital campaign. *Perspectives on Politics,* 3(1), 121–28.

Hirji, F. (2006). Common concerns and constructed communities: Muslim canadians, the internet and the war in Iraq. *Journal of Communication Inquiry,* 30(2), 125–41.

Ho, K. C., Kluver, R. & Yang, K. (eds.). (2003). *Asia.Com: Asia encounters the internet.* London: Routledge.

Hobolt, S. B. (2006). Direct democracy and European integration. *Journal of European Public Policy,* 13(1), 153–66.

—— (2007). Taking cues on Europe? Voter competence and party endorsements in referendums on European integration. *European Journal of Political Research,* 46(2), 151–82.

Hodkinson. (2004). Problems @ labour: towards net internationalism. In: R. K. Gibson, A. Rommele & S. Ward (eds.), *Electronic Democracy: mobilisation, organisation and participation via new ICTs.* London: Routledge.

Hoff, J. (2004). The democratic potentials of information technology: attitudes of European MPs towards new technology. *Information Polity,* 9(2) 55–66.

Hoff, J., Horrocks, I. & Tops, P. W. (2000). *Democratic Governance and New Technology: technologically mediated innovations in political practice in Western Europe.* London: Routledge.

—— (2000). Introduction. In: J. Hoff, I. Horrocks & P. W. Tops (eds.), *Democratic Governance and New Technology: technologically mediated innovations in political practice in Western Europe.* London: Routledge.

Hoffman, A. (1999). Institutional evolution and change: environmentalism and the US chemistry industry. *Academy of Management Journal,* 42(4), 351–71.

Hoffman, D. L., Novak, T. P. & Schlosser, A. E. (2001). The evolution of the digital divide: examining the relationship of race to internet access and usage over time. In: B. M. Compaine (ed.), *The Digital Divide: facing a crisis or creating a myth?.* Cambridge, MA: MIT Press.

Hoffman, L. H. (2006). Is internet content different after all? A content analysis of mobilizing information in online and print newspapers. *Journalism and Mass Communication Quarterly,* 83(1), 58–76.

Holbrook, T. M. (1996). *Do Campaigns Matter?* Thousand Oaks, California; London: Sage Publications.

Holmes, D. (1997). Introduction: virtual politics, identity and community in cyberspace. In: D. Holmes (ed.), *Virtual Politics: identity and community in cyberspace.* London: Sage.

Hood, C., James, O. & Scott, C. (2000). Regulation of government: has it increased, is it increasing, should it be diminished? *Public Administration,* 78(2), 283–304.

Hood, C. & Margetts, H. (2007). *The Tools of Government in the Digital Age.* London: Palgrave.

Hoogvelt, A. (2001). *Globalization and the Postcolonial World: the new political economy of development.* Baltimore, MD: Johns Hopkins University Press.

Hopkins, H. (2006). *BBC favoured news source: but Wikipedia and Flickr growing in importance.* Retrieved January 5, 2006, from www.hitwise.co.uk

Hopkins, K. & Matheson, D. M. (2005). Blogging the New Zealand election: the impact of new media practices on the old game. *Political Science,* 57(2), 93–105.

Horrigan, J. (2004). *Broadband Penetration on the Upswing.* Washington, DC: Pew Internet and American Life Project.

—— (2006). *Online News: for many home broadband users, the internet is a primary news source.* Washington, DC: Pew Internet and American Life.

—— (2007). *A Typology of Information and Communication Technology Users.* Washington DC: Pew Internet and American Life Project.

Horrigan, J., Garrett, K. & Resnick, P. (2004). *The Internet and Democratic Debate.* Washington, DC: Pew Internet and American Life Project.

Horrigan, J. & Rainie, L. (2002a). *The Broadband Difference: how online behavior changes with high-speed internet connections.* Washington DC: Pew Internet and American Life Project.

Horrigan, J. B. & Rainie, L. (2002b). *Counting on the Internet.* Washington, DC: Pew Internet and American Life Project.

Houston, F. (1999). What I saw in the digital sea. *Columbia Journalism Review,* (July/August), 34–7.

Howard, P. N. (2001). Can technology enhance democracy? The doubters answer. *Journal of Politics,* 63(3), 949–55.

—— (2003). Digitizing the social contract: Producing American political culture in the age of new media. *Communication Review,* 6(3), 213–45.

—— (2004). Embedded media: who we know, what we know, and the context of life online. In: P. N. Howard & S. Jones (eds.), *Society Online: the internet in context.* Thousand Oaks, CA: Sage.

—— (2005). Deep democracy, thin citizenship: the impact of digital media in political campaign strategy. *Annals of the American Academy of Political and Social Science,* 597, 153–70.

—— (2006). *New Media Campaigns and the Managed Citizen.* Cambridge: Cambridge University Press.

Howard, P. N., Carr, J. & Milstein, T. (2005). Digital technology and the market for political surveillance. *Surveillance and Society,* 3(1), 59–73.

Howard, P. N., Rainie, L. & Jones, S. (2001a). Days and nights on the internet: the impact of a diffusing technology. *American Behavioral Scientist,* 45(3), 383–404.

—— (2001b). Days and nights on the internet: The impact of a diffusing technology. In: B. Wellman & C. Haythornthwaite (eds.), *The Internet in Everyday Life.* Oxford: Blackwell.

Howard, P. N. & World Information Access Project (2006). *World information access report 2006.* Seattle: University of Washington.

—— (2007). *World information access report 2007: wired states.* Seattle: University of Washington.

Howes, M. (2002). Reflexive modernization, the internet and democratic environmental decision making. *Organization & Environment,* 15(3), 328–35.

Huang, Z. (2006). E-government practices at local levels: an analysis of US counties' websites. *Issues in Information Systems,* 7(2), 165–70.

Huckfeldt, R., Johnson, P. E. & Sprague, J. (2004). *Political Disagreement: the survival of diverse opinions within communication networks.* New York: Cambridge University Press.

Huckfeldt, R. & Sprague, J. (1995). *Citizens, Politics, and Social Communication: information and influence in an election campaign.* New York: Cambridge University Press.

Hug, S. (2002). *Voices of Europe: citizens, referendums, and European integration.* Lanham, MD: Rowman and Littlefield.

Hughes, D. M. (1999). The internet and the global prostitution industry. In: S. Hawthorne & R. Klein (eds.), *Cyberfeminism: Connectivity, Critique & Creativity.* Melbourne: Spinifex.

—— (2004). The use of new communications and information technologies for sexual exploitation of women and children. In: D. D. Waskul (ed.), *Net.Sexxx: reading on sex, pornography, and the internet.* New York: Peter Lang.

Human Rights Watch (2006). *Race to the Bottom: corporate complicity in Chinese internet censorship.* New York: Human Rights Watch.

Hume, E. (1996). The new paradigm for news. *Annals of the American Academy of Political and Social Science,* 546, 141–53.

Hunter, D. (2001). Reason is too large: analogy and precedent in law. *Emory Law Journal,* 50 (Fall), 1197–264.

—— (2003). Cyberspace as place and the tragedy of the digital anticommons. *California Law Review,* 91(2), 439–519.

Huntington, S. (1996). *The Clash of Civilizations and the Remaking of World Order.* New York: Simon and Schuster.

i2 Inc (2007). *Denying criminals the use of the roads.* Retrieved November 22, 2007, from www.i2.co.uk/company/press/default.asp?action=view&id=77

Imfeld, C. & Scott, G. W. (2005). Under construction: measures of community building at newspaper web sites. In: M. B. Salwen, B. Garrison & P. D. Driscoll (eds.), *Online News and the Public.* Mahwah, NJ: Erlbaum.

Ingber, S. (1984). The marketplace of ideas: a legitimizing myth. *Duke Law Journal,* 1984(1), 1–91.

Inglehart, R. & Welzel, C. (2005). *Modernization, Cultural Change and Democracy.* London: Cambridge University Press.

Initiative and Referendum Institute (2004). *Ballot watch 2004 election summary.* Los Angeles, CA: Initiative and Referendum Institute, University of Southern California.

Institute for Applied Autonomy (2007). *Institute for applied autonomy.* Retrieved November 22, 2007, from www.appliedautonomy.com/isee.html

International Telecommunication Union (2005). *ICT statistics database.* Retrieved November 22, 2007, from www.itu.int/ITU-D/icteye/Indicators/Indicators.aspx#

—— (2006). *World Telecommunications Indicators Database,* 8th edn. Geneva: International Telecommunication Union.

Internet Governance Project (2004). *Internet Governance: state of play. Working paper.* Retrieved November 22, 2007, from http://dcc.syr.edu/miscarticles/MainReport-final.pdf

—— (2005). *What to do about ICANN: a proposal for structural reform. Working paper.* Retrieved November 23, 2007, from http://dcc.syr.edu/miscarticles/IGP-ICANNReform.pdf

Internet Systems Consortium (2004) *Internet Domain Survey, Jan 2004: number of hosts advertised in the DNS.* Redwood, CA: Internet Systems Consortium.

Internet World Stats (2007). *Internet World Stats: usage and population statistics.* Retrieved November 23, 2007, from www.internetworldstats.com

Introna, L. & Nissenbaum, H. (2000). Shaping the web: why the politics of search engines matters. *The Information Society,* 16(3), 1–17.

Iyengar, S. (1990). Framing responsibility for political issues: the case of poverty. *Political Behavior,* 12(1), 19–40.

Jackson, B. & Jamieson, K. (2004). Finding facts in political debate. *American Behavioral Scientist,* 48, 229–37.

Jackson, N. (2004). Email and political campaigning: the experience of MPs in Westminster. *Journal of Systemics Cybernetics and Informatics,* 2 (5), 1–6.

Jacobs, L. R. & Skocpol, T. (2005). American democracy in an era of rising inequality. In: L. R. Jacobs & T. Skocpol (eds.), *Inequality and American Democracy: what we know and what we need to learn.* New York: Russell Sage Foundation.

Jacobs, N. (ed.). (2006). *Open Access: key strategic, technical and economic aspects.* Oxford: Chandos Publishing.

Jaffe, J. M., Lee, Y., Huang, L. & Oshagan, H. (1995). *Gender, pseudonyms and CMC: masking identities and baring souls.* Paper presented at the Annual Conference of the International Communication Association, Albuquerque, New Mexico.

—— (1999). Gender identification, interdependence, and pseudonyms in CMC. Language patterns in an electronic conference. *The Information Society,* 15(4), 221–34.

Jalonick, M. C. (2006, August 22). YouTube catches candidates in compromising positions. *USA Today.*

Jamieson, K. (1992). *Dirty Politics: Deception, Distraction, and Democracy.* Oxford University Press.

Jamieson, K. & Hardy, B. (2007). Unmasking deception: the capacity, disposition, and challenges facing the press. In: D. Graber, D. McQuail & P. Norris (eds.) *The Politics of News: the news of politics,* 2nd edn. Washington DC: CQ Press, pp. 117–38.

Jamieson, K., Hardy, B. & Romer, D. (2007). The effectiveness of the press in serving the needs of American democracy. In: *Institutions of American Democracy: a republic divided.* New York: Oxford University Press, pp. 21–51.

Jamieson, K. & Jackson, B. (2007). *Unspun: finding facts in a world of disinformation*. New York: Random House.

Jamieson, K. & Waldman, P. (2003). *The Press Effect: politicians, journalists, and the stories that shape the political world*. Oxford: Oxford University Press.

Janda, K. (1993). Comparative political parties: Research and theory. In: A. W. Finifter (ed.), *Political Science: the state of the discipline II*. Washington DC: American Political Science Association.

Jankowski, N. W. & van Selm, M. (2000). The promise and practice of public debate in cyberspace. In: K. Hacker & J. van Dijk (eds.), *Digital democracy: issues of theory and practice*. London: Sage.

Janssen, D. & Kies, R. (2005). Online forums and deliberative democracy. *Acta Politica*, 40 (3), 317–35.

Jenkins, G. S. (2004). *Email marketing and the 2004 election*. Retrieved September 20, 2006, from www.imediaconnection.com/content/4499.asp

Jennings, M. K. & Zeitner, V. (2003). Internet Use And Civic Engagement. *Public Opinion Quarterly*, 67(3), 311–34.

Jensen, J. L. (2003). Public spheres on the internet: anarchic or government-sponsored – a comparison. *Scandinavian Political Studies*, 26 (4), 349–74.

—— (2003). Virtual democratic dialogue? Bringing together citizens and politicians. *Information Polity*, 8(1–2), 29–47.

Jensen, M. J., Danziger, J. N. & Venkatesh, A. (2007). Civil society and cyber society: the role of the internet in community associations and democratic politics. *The Information Society*, 23(1), 39–50.

Johnson, P. E. (1998). Interest group recruiting: finding members and keeping them. In: A. J. Cigler & B. A. Loomis (eds.), *Interest Group Politics*. Washington, DC: CQ Press.

Johnson, T. J., Braima, M. A. M. & Sothirajah, J. (1999). Doing the traditional media sidestep: comparing the effects of the internet and other nontraditional media with traditional media in the 1996 presidential campaign. *Journalism and Mass Communication Quarterly*, 76(1), 99–123.

Johnson, T. J. & Kaye, B. K. (1998a). A vehicle for engagement or a haven for the disaffected? Internet use, political alienation, and voter participation. In: T. J. Johnson, C. E. Hays & S. P. Hays (eds.), *Engaging the Public: how the government and media can reinvigorate democracy*. Lanham, MD: Roman and Littlefield.

—— (1998b) Cruising is believing? Comparing internet and traditional sources on media credibility measures. *Journalism & Mass Communication Quarterly*, 75, 325–40.

—— (2002). Webelievability: a path model examining how convenience and reliance predict online credibility. *Journalism and Mass Communication Quarterly*, 79(3), 619–42.

—— (2004). Wag the blog: how reliance on traditional media and the internet influence credibility perceptions of weblogs among blog users. *Journalism and Mass Communication Quarterly*, 81(3), 622–42.

Johnston, P. (2007, March 27). CCTV cameras get upgrade at police request. *Daily Telegraph*.

Johnston, R., Hagen, M. G. & Jamieson, K. H. (2004). *The 2000 Presidential Election and the Foundations of Party Politics*. Cambridge: Cambridge University Press.

Jones, B. D. (1994). *Reconceiving Decision-Making in Democratic Politics: attention, choice, and public policy*. Chicago: University of Chicago Press.

Jones, B. D. & Baumgartner, F. R. (2005). *The Politics of Attention: how government prioritizes problems*. Chicago: University of Chicago Press.

Jones, S. G. (1997). The internet and its social landscape. In: S. G. Jones (ed.), *Virtual Culture: identity and communication in cybersociety*. Thousand Oaks, CA: Sage.

Jones-Correa, M. (1998). *Between Two Nations: the political predicament of Latinos in New York city*. Ithaca, NY: Cornell University Press.

Jordan, A. G. (1998). Introduction. In: F. F. Ridley & A. G. Jordan (eds.), *Protest Politics: cause groups and campaigns*. Oxford: Oxford University Press.

Jordan, A. G. & Maloney, W. A. (1998). *The Protest Business? Mobilizing campaign groups*. Manchester: Manchester University Press.

Jordan, T. (2001). Hactivism: direct action on the electronic flows of information societies. In: K. M. Dowding, J. Hughes & H. Margetts (eds.), *Challenges to Democracy: ideas, involvement and institutions*. Basingstoke: Palgrave.

Jordan, T. & Taylor, P. (1998). A sociology of hackers. *The Sociological Review*, 46(4), 757–80.

Jordan Times (2000, July 11). Jordan IT industry to launch the reach initiative. *Jordan Times*.

Juels, A. (2006). RFID security and privacy: a research survey. *IEEE Journal on Selected Areas in Communications,* 24(2), 381.

Jung, J.-Y., Ball-Rokeach, S. J., Kim, Y. C. & Matei, S. (2007). ICTs and communities in the twenty-first century: challenges and perspectives. In: R. Mansell, C. Averou, D. Quah & R. Silverstone (eds.), *The Oxford Handbook of Information and Communication Technologies.* Oxford: Oxford University Press.

Jung, J.-Y., Qiu, J. L. & Kim, Y. C. (2001). Internet connectedness and inequality: beyond the "Divide". *Communication Research,* 28(4), 507–35.

Kaestle, D. F., Campbell, A., Finn, J. D., Johnson, S. T. & Mickulecky, L. J. (2001). *Adult literacy and education in America: four studies based on the national adult literacy survey.* Washington, DC: U.S. Department of Education, National Center for Education Statistics.

Kahin, B. & Keller, J. (1997). *Coordinating the Internet.* Cambridge: MIT Press.

Kahn, R. & Kellner, D. (2004). New media and internet activism: from the "Battle of Seattle" to blogging. *New Media and Society,* 6(1), 87–95.

Kaid, L. L. (2002). Political advertising and information seeking: comparing exposure via traditional and internet channels. *Journal of Advertising,* 31(1), 27–35.

—— (2006). Political web wars: the use of the internet for political advertising. In: A. P. Williams & J. C. Tedesco (eds.), *The Internet Election: perspectives on the web in campaign 2004.* Lanham, MD: Rowman and Littlefield.

Kain, J. (1968). Housing segregation, negro employment and metropolitan decentralization. *Quarterly Journal of Economics,* 82(2), 175–97.

Kalathil, S. & Boas, T. C. (2003). *Open Networks, Closed Regimes: the impact of the internet on authoritarian rule.* Washington, DC: Carnegie Endowment for International Peace.

Kaldor, M. (2003). *Global Civil Society: an answer to war.* Cambridge: Polity.

Kaldor-Robinson, J. (2002). The virtual and the imaginary: the role of diasporic new media in the construction of a national identity during the break-up of Yugoslavia. *Oxford Development Studies,* 30(2), 177–87.

Kamalipour, Y. (ed.). (2006). *Global Communication,* 2nd edn. Belmont: Wadsworth.

Kamm, O. (2007, April 9). A parody of democracy. *The Guardian.*

Kane, T. (2007). Economic freedom in five regions. In: Heritage Foundation (ed.). *2007 Index of Economic Freedom.* Washington, DC: Heritage Foundation.

Kasarda, J. D. (1990). City jobs and residents on a collision course: the urban underclass dilemma. *Economic Development Quarterly,* 4(4), 286–307.

Katz, E. (1981). Communications in the 21st century: in defense of media events. *Organizational Dynamics,* 10(1), 68–80.

—— (1996). And deliver us from segmentation. *Annals of the American Academy of Political and Social Science,* 546, 22–33.

Katz, J. E. & Aspden, P. (1997). A nation of strangers. *Communications of the ACM,* 40(12), 81–6.

Katz, J. E., Rice, R. E & Aspden, P. (2001). The internet, 1995–2000: access, civic involvement and social interaction. *American Behavioral Scientist,* 45(3), 404–19.

Katz, J. E. & Rice, R. E. (2002). *Social Consequences Of Internet Use: access, involvement, and interaction.* Cambridge, MA: MIT Press.

Kaufmann, J. (1968). *Conference Diplomacy: an introductory analysis.* Leiden: Martinus Nijhof Publishers.

Kavanagh, D. (1995). *Election Campaigning: the new marketing of politics.* Oxford: Blackwell.

Kavanaugh, A. L. & Patterson, S. J. (2001). The impact of community computer networks on social capital and community involvement. *American Behavioral Scientist,* 45(3), 469–509.

Kaye, B. K. & Johnson, T. J. (2004). A web for all reasons: uses and gratifications of internet components for political information. *Telematics and Informatics,* 21(3), 197–223.

Kaye, K. (2006). *Online political ad spending down from '04 election.* Retrieved March 15, 2007, from www.clickz.com/showPage.html?page= 3623858

Kaylor, C., Deshazo, R. & van Eck, D. (2001). Gauging e-government: a report on implementing services among American cities. *Government Information Quarterly,* 18(4), 293–307.

Kearney, J. D. & Merrill, T. (2000). The influence of amicus curia briefs on the supreme court. *University of Pennsylvania Law Review,* 148 (January), 743–855.

Keck, M. & Sikkink, K. (1998). *Activists Beyond Borders: advocacy networks in international politics.* Ithaca: Cornell University Press.

Kelly, R. (2005). *Election Expense Limits.* London: House of Commons Library.

Kendall, L. (1998). Are you male or female? In: J. O'Brien & J. Howard (eds.), *Everyday Inequalities: critical inquiries*. London: Basil Blackwell.

Kenix, L. (2007). In search of utopia: an analysis of non-profit web pages. *Information, Communication and Society*, 10(1), 69–94.

Kensinger, L. (2003). Plugged in praxis: critical reflections on US feminism, internet activism, and solidarity with women in Afghanistan. *Journal of International Women's Studies*, 5(1), 1–28.

Kenski, K. & Jamieson, K. H. (2006). Issue knowledge and perceptions of agreement in the 2004 Presidential General Election. *Presidential Studies Quarterly*, 36(2), 243–59.

Keohane, R. (1984). *After Hegemony*. Princeton: Princeton University Press.

Keohane, R. & Nye, J. (1989). *Power and Interdependence*. New York: HarperCollins.

Kerbel, M. R. & Bloom, J. D. (2005). Blog for America and civic involvement. *Harvard International Journal of Press Politics*, 10(4), 3–27.

Kerr, A. (2002). Representing users in the design of video games. In: F. Mäyrä (ed.), *Proceedings of computer games and digital cultures conference*. Tampere: Tampere University Press.

Kerr, O. S. (2003). The problem of perspective in internet law. *Georgetown Law Journal*, 91 (February), 357–405.

Key, V. O. (1964). *Politics, Parties and Pressure Groups*, 5th edn. New York: Thomas Y. Crowell.

Kibby, M. (2001). Women and sex entertainment on the internet: discourses of gender and power. *Mots Pluriels*, 19.

Kibby, M. & Costello, B. (2001). Between the image and the act: interactive sex entertainment on the internet. *Sexualities: Studies in Culture and Society*, 4(3), 353–69.

Kidd, D. (2003). Indymedia.Org: a new communications commons. In: M. McCaughey & M. Ayers (eds.), *Cyberactivism: online activism in theory and practice*. New York: Routledge.

Kim, J., Wyatt, R. O. & Katz, E. (1999). News, talk, opinion, participation: the part played by conversation in deliberative democracy. *Political Communication*, 16(4), 361–85.

Kim, J. Y. (2006). The impact of internet use patterns on political engagement: a focus on online deliberation and virtual social capital. *Information Polity*, 11(1), 35–49.

Kim, M. Y., Barbour, J., Hals, M., Lewkowicz, M. & Tewksbury, D. (2001). *Informational and participatory use of the internet and trust in the political system*. Paper presented at the Annual Meeting of the Midwest Association for Public Opinion Research, Chicago, IL.

Kim, Y. C. & Ball-Rokeach, S. J. (2003). *Koreans in Los Angeles: community and market*. Los Angeles: Korea Central Daily.

—— (2006). Civic engagement from a communication infrastructure perspective. *Communication Theory*, 16(1), 1–25.

Kim, Y. C., Jung, J.-Y. & Ball-Rokeach, S. J. (2002). *Ethnicity, place, and communication technology: geo-ethnic effect on multi-dimensional internet connectedness in urban communities*. Paper presented at the International Communication Association Annual Conference. Seoul: Korea.

Kim, Y.-C., Jung, J. E. L., Cohen, E. L. & Ball-Rokeach, S. J. (2004). Internet connectedness before and after 9/11. *New Media and Society*, 6(5), 611–31.

Kim, Y. M. (2007). How intrinsic and extrinsic motivations interact in selectivity: investigating the moderating effects of situational information processing goals in issue publics' web behavior. *Communication Research*, 34(2), 185–211.

Kimber, R. (2005). *UK general election 2005: election blogs and forums*. Retrieved November 22, 2007, from www.psr.keele.ac.uk/area/uk/ge05/electionblogs.htm

Kinder, D. R. (2003). Communication and politics in the age of information. In: D. O. Sears, L. Huddy & R. Jervis (eds.), *Oxford Handbook of Political Psychology*. Oxford: Oxford University Press.

King Abdullah of Jordan. (2007). *Introduction to IT development*. Retrieved November 22, 2007, from www.kingabdullah.jo/main.php?main_page=0&lang_hmka1=1

Kiousis, S. (2002). Interactivity: a concept explication. *New Media and Society*, 4(3), 355–83.

Kirchner, H. (2001). Internet in the Arab world: a step towards information society? In: K. Hafez (ed.), *Mass Media, Politics and Society in the Middle East* Cresskill, NJ: Hampton Press.

Kirsch, I. S., Jungeblut, A., Jenkins, L. & Kolstad, A. (2002). *Adult Literacy in America: a first look at the findings of the national adult literacy survey*. Washington, DC: U.S. Department of Education, National Center for Education Statistics.

Kitschelt, H. (1986). Political opportunity structures: anti nuclear movements in four democracies. *British journal of political science*, 1(16), 57–85.

Klapper, J. T. (1960). *The Effects of Mass Communication*. New York: Free Press.

Klein, H. (2004). Understanding WSIS: an institutional analysis of the UN World Summit on the Information Society. *Information Technology and International Development*, 1(3–4), 3–14.

Kleiner, A. & Lewis, L. (2003). *Internet access in US public schools and classrooms: 1994–2002*. Washington, DC: National Center for Education Statistics, Department of Education.

Kling, R. (1996). Hopes and horrors: technological utopianism and anti-utopianism in narratives of computerization. In: R. Kling (ed.), *Computerization and Controversy*. Boston: Academic Press.

Klingemann, H.-D. (1999). Mapping political support in the 1990s: a global analysis. In: P. Norris (ed.), *Critical Citizens*. Oxford: Oxford University Press.

Klotz, R. J. (2004). *The Politics of Internet Communication*. Lanham, MD: Rowman and Littlefield.

Kluver, R. (2004). Political culture and information technology in the 2001 Singapore general election. *Political Communication*, 21(4), 435–58.

—— (2005). Political culture in online politics. In: M. Consalvo & M. Allen (eds.), *Internet Research Annual*. Newbury Park, CA: Sage.

Kluver, R. & Banerjee, I. (2005). Political culture, regulation and democratization: the internet in nine Asian countries. *Information, Communication, and Society*, 8(1), 30–46.

Kluver, R., Jankowski, N. W., Foot, K. A. & Schneider, S. M. (eds.). (2007). *The Internet and National Elections: a comparative study of web campaigning*. New York: Routledge.

Knobloch, S., Hastall, M., Zillman, D. & Callison, C. (2003). Imagery effects on the selective reading of internet news magazines. *Communication Research*, 30(1), 3–29.

Knobloch-Westerwick, S., Sharma, N., Hansen, D. L. & Alter, S. (2005). Impact of popularity indications on readers' selective exposure to online news. *Journal of Broadcasting and Electronic Media*, 49(3), 296–313.

Kobayashi, T., Ikeda, K. & Miyata, K. (2006). Social capital online: collective use of the internet and reciprocity as lubricants of democracy. *Information, Communication and Society*, 9(5), 582–611.

Kohut, A. (2000). Internet users are on the rise: but public affairs interest isn't. *Columbia Journalism Review*, 38(5), 68–69.

—— (2003). *Perceptions of partisan bias seen as growing – especially by Democrats: cable and internet loom large in fragmented political news universe*. Washington, DC: Pew Internet and American Life Project.

Koster, M. (1997). *A method for web robots control: networking working group, internet engineering task force* from www.robots.txt.org/wc/norobots-rfc.html

Kraemer, K. & King, J. (1986). Computing and public organisations. *Public Administration Review*, 46(6), 488–96.

—— (2006). Information technology and administrative reform: will e-government be different? *International Journal of E-government Research*, 2(1), 1–20.

Kraemer, K. & Kling, R. (1985). The political character of computerization in service organizations: citizens interests or bureaucratic control. *Computers and the Social Sciences*, 1(2), 77–89.

Kranich, N. (2004). *The information commons: a policy report*. New York: NYU School of Law.

Kranzberg, M. (1985). The information age: evolution or revolution? In: B. Guile (ed.), *Information Technologies and Social Transformation*. Washington, DC: National Academy Press.

Krasner, S. (ed.). (1983). *International Regimes*. Ithaca: Cornell University Press.

Krasner, S. D. (1982). Structural causes and regime consequences: regimes as intervening variable. *International Organization*, 36(3), 185–205.

Kraut, R., Kiesler, S., Boneva, B., Cummings, J. & Helgeson, V. (2002). Internet paradox revisited. *Journal of Social Issues*, 58(1), 49–74.

Kraut, R., Lundmark, V., Patterson, M., Kiesler, S., Mukopadhyay, T. & Scherlis, W. (1998). Internet paradox: a social technology that reduces social involvement and psychological well-being? *American Psychologist*, 53(9), 1017–31.

Krebs, K. (2002, November 25). Homeland security bill heralds IT changes. *The Washington Post*.

Kreimer, S. F. (2001). Technologies of protest: insurgent social movements and the first amendment in the era of the internet.

University of Pennsylvania Law Review, 150(1), 119–71.

Kretchmer, S. & Carveth, R. (2001). The color of the net: African-Americans, race, and cyberspace. *Computers and Society,* 31(3), 9–14.

Kriesi, H., Koopmans, R., Duyvendask, J. W. & Giugni, M. G. (1995). *New Social Movements in Western Europe: a comparative analysis.* Minneapolis: University of Minnesota Press.

Kroløkke, C. H. (2003). Grrl explorers of the world wild web. *Nora: Nordic Journal of Women's Studies,* 11(3), 140–48.

Krosnick, J. A. (1990). Government policy and citizen passion: a study of issue publics in contemporary America. *Political Behavior,* 12 (1), 59–92.

Krueger, B. S. (2002). Assessing the potential of internet political participation in the United States. *American Politics Research,* 30(5), 476–98.

—— (2006). A comparison of conventional and internet political mobilization. *American Politics Research,* 34(6), 759–76.

Kulikova, S. V. & Perlmutter, D. D. (2007). Blogging down the dictator? The Kyrgyz revolution and samizdat websites. *Gazette,* 69 (1), 29–50.

Kush, C. (2000). *Cybercitizen: how to use your computer to fight for all the issues you care about.* New York: St. Martin's Press.

Kwak, N., Poor, N. & Skoric, M. M. (2006). Honey, I shrunk the world! The relation between internet use and international engagement. *Mass Communication and Society,* 9 (2), 189–213.

Kwak, N., Williams, A. E., Wang, X. & Lee, H. (2005). Talking politics and engaging politics: an examination of the interactive relationships between structural features of political talk and discussion engagement. *Communication Research,* 32(1), 87–111.

Kyllonen, P. & Christal, R. (1990). Reasoning ability is (little more than) working-memory capacity? *Intelligence,* 14(4), 389–433.

Lacharite, J. (2002). Electronic decentralisation in China: a critical analysis of internet filtering policies in the People's Republic of China. *Australian Journal of Political Science,* 37(2), 333–46.

Lægran, A. S. (2004). Just another boys' room? Internet cafés as gendered technosocial spaces. In: M. Lie (ed.), *He, She and IT Revisited: new perspectives on gender in the information society.* Oslo: Gyldendal Akademisk.

Lakoff, G. & Johnson, M. (2003). *Metaphors We Live By.* Chicago, IL: University of Chicago Press.

Lander, M. (2005, December 14). Tech firms find home in revived Estonia. *The International Herald Tribune.*

Landes, W. M. & Posner, R. A. (2004). *The Political Economy of Intellectual Property Law.* Washington, DC: AEI-Brookings Joint Center for Regulatory Studies.

Lane, F. (2000). *Obscene Profits: the entrepreneurs of pornography in the cyber age.* London: Routledge.

Lane, G. & Thelwall, S. (2005). *Urban Tapestries: public authoring, place and mobility.* London: Proboscis.

Langman, L. (2005). From virtual public spheres to global justice: a critical theory of inter-networked social movements. *Sociological Theory,* 23(1), 42–74.

Lappin, T. (1995). Trucking. *Wired, January,* 119–23.

LaRose, R. & Eastin, M. S. (2004). A social cognitive theory of internet uses and gratifications: toward a new model of media attendance. *Journal of Broadcasting and Electronic Media,* 48(3), 358–77.

Lasch, C. (1979). *The Culture of Narcissism.* New York: Norton and Company.

—— (1987). The degradation of the political arts. In: S. Goldberg & C. Strain (eds.), *Technological Change and the Transformation of America.* Carbondale, IL: Southern Illinois University Press, pp. 79–90.

Latour, B. (2005). *Reassembling the Social: an introduction to actor network theory.* Oxford: Oxford University Press.

Laudon, K. (1974). *Computers and Bureaucratic Reform.* New York: John Wiley and Sons.

Lawson-Borders, G. & Kirk, R. (2005). Blogs in campaign communication. *American Behavioral Scientist,* 49(4), 548–59.

Lazer, D. & Mayer-Schönberger, V. (eds.). (2007). *From E-gov to I-gov: governance and information technology in the 21st century.* Cambridge, MA: MIT Press.

Leadbeater, C. & Mulgan, G. (1997). Lean democracy and the leadership vacuum. In: G. Mulgan (ed.), *Life After Politics: new thinking for the twenty first century.* London: Fontana.

Leake, C. (2007, February, 11). The tiny airline spy that spots bombers in the blink of an eye. *Mail on Sunday,* p. 52.

Lebert, J. (2003). Wiring human rights activism: Amnesty International and the challenges of information communication technology. In: M. McCaughey & M. D. Ayers (eds.), *Cyberactivism: online activism in theory and practice*. New York: Routledge.

Leblebici, H., Salancik, G. R., Copay, A. & King, T. (1991). Institutional change and the transformation of interorganizational fields: an organizational history of the US radio broadcasting industry. *Administrative Science Quarterly*, 36(3), 333–63.

LeDuc, L. (2003). *The Politics of Direct Democracy: referendums in global perspective*. Peterborough, Ontario: Broadview Press.

Lee, E. (1997). *The Labour Movement and the internet: the new internationalism*. London: Pluto Press.

Leib, E. J. (2006). Can direct democracy be made deliberative? *Buffalo Law Review*, 54, 903–25.

Leiner, B. M., Cerf, V. G., Clark, D. D., Kahn, R. E., Kleinrock, L., Lynch, D. C., *et al.* (2003). *A Brief History of the Internet*. Reston, VA: Internet Society.

Lemley, M. A. (2003). Place and cyberspace. *California Law Review*, 91(2), 521–42.

Lenhart, A. (2003). *The ever-shifting internet population: a new look at internet access and the digital divide*. Washington, DC: Pew Internet and American Life Project.

Lenhart, A. & Fox, S. (2006). *Bloggers: a portrait of the internet's new story tellers* Washington, DC: Pew Internet and American Life Project.

Lerner, D. (1962). *The Passing of Traditional Society*. Glencoe, Ill: Free Press.

Lessig, L. (1999). *Code and Other Laws of Cyberspace*. New York: Basic Books.

—— (2001). *The Future of Ideas*. New York: Random House.

—— (2004). *Free Culture*. New York: Penguin Press.

—— (2006). *Code: version 2.0*. New York: Basic Books.

Leston-Bandeira, C. (forthcoming). The Impact of the Internet on Parliaments: a legislative studies framework. *Parliamentary Affairs*.

Lewin, K. (1946). Action research and minority problems. *Journal of Social Issues*, 2(4), 34–46.

Lewis, H. (2006). The wild wild web: international internet regulation. *Harvard Political Review*, 33(1), 12–13.

Li, C. (2004). Internet content control in China. *International Journal of Communications Law and Policy*, 8(1).

Li, Q. (2005). Gender and CMC: a review on conflict and harassment. *Australasian Journal of Educational Technology*, 21(3), 382–406.

Li, X. (1998). Web page design and graphic use of three US newspapers. *Journalism and Mass Communication Quarterly*, 75(2), 353–65.

—— (2006). Introduction. In: X. Li (ed.), *Internet Newspapers: the making of a mainstream media*. Mahwah, NJ: Erlbaum.

Libicki, M. C. (1998). Information war, information peace. *Journal of International Affairs*, 51 (2), 411.

Liff, S. (2004). *Locating civil society participation in WSIS*. Oxford Internet Institute Seminar Paper. Oxford Internet Institute, Oxford.

Lijphart, A. (1984). *Democracies: patterns of majoritarian and consensus government in twenty-one countries*. New Haven, CT: Yale University Press.

Lillie, J. J. M. (2004). Cyberporn, sexuality, and the net apparatus. *Convergence*, 10(1), 43–65.

Lim, J. (2006). A cross-lagged analysis of agenda setting among online news media. *Journalism and Mass Communication Quarterly*, 83(2), 298–312.

Lin, N. (2001). *Social Capital: a theory of social structure and action*. Cambridge: Cambridge University Press.

Lippmann, W. (1922). *Public Opinion*. New York: Free Press.

Lipton, J. (2004). Mixed metaphors in cyberspace: property in information and information systems. *Loyola University Chicago Law Journal*, 35, 235–74.

Lizza, R. (2002, November 18). Head count: how the GOP learned voter turnout. *New Republic*.

—— (2006, August 20). The YouTube election. *New York Times*.

Lloyd, J. (2004). *What the Media are Doing to our Politics*. London: Constable.

Locke, J. (1959). *An Essay Concerning Human Understanding*. New York: Dover.

London, S. (1993). *Electronic Democracy*. Dayton, OH: Kettering Foundation.

Long, N. E. (1958). The local community as an ecology of games. *American Journal of Sociology*, 64(3), 251–61.

Loughlan, P. (2006). Pirates, parasites, reapers, sowers, fruits, foxes. The metaphors of intellectual property. *The Sydney Law Review*, 28(June), 211–26.

Lowrey, W. (2006). Mapping the journalism–blogging relationship. *Journalism and Mass Communication Quarterly*, 7(4), 477–500.

Lowrey, W. & Anderson, W. (2005). The journalist behind the curtain: participatory functions on the internet and their impact on perceptions of the work of journalism. *Journal of Computer-Mediated Communication*, 10(3).

Lowry, R. (2004, November 29). Bush's well-mapped road to victory: how Rove *et al.* pulled it off. *National Review*.

Lupia, A. (1994). Shortcuts versus encyclopedias: information and voting behavior in California insurance reform elections. *American Political Science Review*, 88(1), 63–76.

—— (2001). Dumber than chimps? An assessment of direct democracy voters. In: L. J. Sabato, H. R. Ernst & B. A. Larson (eds.), *Dangerous Democracy? The battle over ballot initiatives in America.* Lanham, MD: Rowman and Littlefield.

Lupia, A. & Matsusaka, J. G. (2004). Direct democracy: new approaches to old questions. *Annual Review of Political Science*, 7, 463–82.

Lupia, A. & McCubbins, M. D. (1998). *The Democratic Dilemma: can citizens learn what they need to know?* Cambridge UK: Cambridge University Press.

Lupia, L. & Sin, G. (2003). Which public goods are endangered? How evolving technologies affect the logic of collective action. *Public Choice* (117), 315–31.

Luskin, R. C., Fishkin, J. S., McAllister, I., Higley, J. & Ryan, P. (2005). *Deliberation and Referendum Voting.* Stanford, CA: Stanford University.

Lusoli, W. & Ward, S. J. (2003). Virtually participating: a survey of party members online. *Information Polity*, 7(4), 1–17.

—— (2004). Digital ranks and file: activists perceptions and the use of the internet. *British Journal of Politics and International Relations*, 7(4), 453–70.

—— (2006). Hunting protestors: mobilization, participation and protest online in the Countryside Alliance. In: S. Oates, D. M. Owen & R. K. Gibson (eds.), *The Internet and Politics: citizens, voters, and activists.* London: Routledge.

Lynch, M. (2005). *Voices of the New Arab Public: Iraq, al-Jazeera, and Middle East politics today.* New York: Columbia University Press.

Lyon, D. (ed.). (2002). *Surveillance as Social Sorting: privacy, risk, and automated discrimination.* London: Routledge.

Lyotard, J. F. (1984). *The Postmodern Condition.* Minneapolis: University of Minnesota Press.

MacAskill, E. (2007, July 11 2007). McCain campaign hits crisis point. *The Guardian.*

MacGregor, P. (2007). Tracking the online audience: metric data start a subtle revolution. *Journalism Studies*, 8(2), 280–98.

Macintosh, A., Malina, A. & Whyte, A. (2002). Designing e-democracy in Scotland. *European Journal of Communications*, 27, 261–78.

Mackenzie, A. (2006). *Cutting Code: software and sociality.* New York: Peter Lang.

Maclean, D. (2004). *Herding Schrodinger's Cats: some conceptual tools for thinking about internet governance.* United Nations Information and Communications Technologies Task Force.

Madar Research. (2002). PC penetration vs internet user penetration in GCC countries. *Journal of Knowledge, Economy and Research on the Middle East*, 1(October), 1–15.

Madden, M. (2007). *Online video – July 2007.* Washington, DC: Pew Internet and American Life Project.

Madison, M. J. (2005). Law as design: objects, concepts and digital things. *Case Western Reserve Law Review*, 56(Winter), 381–478.

Magid, L. (2007, July 19). Global positioning by cellphone. *New York Times.*

Maguire, S., Hardy, C. & Lawrence, T. B. (2004). Institutional entrepreneurship in emerging fields: HIV/AIDS treatment advocacy in Canada. *Academy of Management Journal*, 47(5), 657–80.

Mair, P. & Von Biezen, I. (2004). Party membership in twenty European democracies, 1980–2000. *Party Politics*, 7(1), 5–21.

Malbin, M. J. & Cain, S. A. (2007). *The Ups and Downs of Small and Large Donors: a campaign finance institute analysis of pre- and post-BCRA contributions to federal candidates and parties, 1999–2006.* Washington DC: Campaign Finance Institute.

Malina, A. (1999). Perspectives on citizen democratization and alienation in the virtual public sphere. In: B. Hague & B. Loader (eds.), *Digital Democracy: discourse and decision making in the information age.* New York: Routledge.

Maltby, S. & Keeble, R. (eds.). (2007). *Communicating War: memory, media and military.* Bury St Edmunds: Arima Publishing.

465

Manjoo, F. (2003). *Blogland's man of the people*. Retrieved July 20, 2006, from http://archive.salon.com/tech/feature/2003/07/03/dean_web/index_np.html

—— (2004). *Howard Dean's fatal system error*. Retrieved July 20, 2006, from http://dir.salon.com/story/tech/feature/2004/01/21/dean_internet/index.html

Manovich, L. (2001). *The Language of New Media*. Cambridge, MA: MIT Press.

Marcella, R., Baxter, G. & Moore, N. (2002). An exploration of the effectiveness for the citizen of web-based systems of communicating UK parliamentary and devolved assembly information. *Journal of Government Information*, 29(6), 371–91.

March, J. G. & Olsen, J. P. (1989). *Rediscovering Institutions: the organizational basis of politics*. New York: Free Press.

March, L. (2006). Virtual parties in a virtual world: Russian parties and the political internet. In: S. Oates, D. M. Owen & R. K. Gibson (eds.), *The Internet and Politics: citizens, voters, and activists*. London: Routledge.

Margetts, H. (1997). The National Performance Review: a new humanist public management. In: A. Massey (ed.), *Globalization and Marketization of Government Services: comparing contemporary public sector developments*. Basingstoke: Macmillan.

—— (1999). *Information Technology in Government: Britain and America*. London: Routledge.

—— (2006). Cyber parties. In: R. S. Katz & W. J. Crotty (eds.), *Handbook of Party Politics*. London: Sage.

Margetts, H. & Yared, H. (2003). *Incentivization of E-Government*. London: National Audit Office.

Margolis, M. & Resnick, D. (2000). *Politics as Usual: the cyberspace revolution*. Thousand Oaks, CA: Sage.

Margolis, M., Resnick, D. & Levy, J. (2003). Major parties dominate, minor parties struggle: US elections and the internet. In: R. K. Gibson, P. Nixon & S. J. Ward (eds.), *Political Parties and the Internet: net gain?* London: Routledge.

Margolis, M., Resnick, D. & Tu, C. (1997). Campaigning on the internet: parties and candidates on the world wide web in the 1996 primary season. *Harvard International Journal of Press/Politics*, 2(1), 59–78.

Margulis, S. (2003). On the status and contribution of Westin's and Altman's theories of privacy. *Journal of Social Issues*, 59(2), 411–29.

Martin, C. H. & Stronach, B. (1992). *Politics East and West: a comparison of Japanese and British political culture*. Armonk, NY: M. E. Sharpe.

Marvin, C. (1988). *When Old Technologies Were New*. New York: Oxford University Press.

Marwell, G. & Oliver, P. (1993). *The Critical Mass in Collective Action: a micro-social theory*. New York: Cambridge University Press.

Massey, B. L. & Luo, W. (2005). Chinese newspapers and market theories of web journalism. *Gazette*, 67, 359–71.

Massey, D. S. & Denton, N. A. (1993). *American Apartheid: segregation and the making of the underclass*. Cambridge, MA: Harvard University Press.

Matei, S. & Ball-Rokeach, S. J. (2001). Real and virtual social ties: connections in the everyday lives of seven ethnic neighborhoods. *American Behavioral Scientist*, 45(3), 550–63.

Matsusaka, J. G. (2004). *For the Many or the Few: the initiative, public policy, and American democracy*. Chicago: University of Chicago Press.

May, C. (2005). The academy's new electronic order? Open source journals and publishing political science. *European Political Science*, 4(1), 14–24.

—— (2007). *The World Intellectual Property Organization*. London: Routledge.

May, C. & Sell, S. (2005). *Intellectual Property Rights: a critical history*. Boulder, CO: Lynne Rienner.

Mayo, E. & Steinberg, T. (2007). *The Power of Information*. London: Cabinet Office.

Mayor's Advisory Council on Closing the Digital Divide. (2007). *The City that Networks: transforming society and economy through digital excellence*. Chicago: Office of the Mayor of Chicago.

McCarthy, J. & Zald, M. (1977). Resource mobilization and social movements: a partial theory. *American Journal of Sociology*, 82(6), 1212–41.

McCaughey, M. & Ayers, M. D. (2003). *Cyberactivism: online activism in theory and practice*. New York; London: Routledge.

McChesney, R. (1995). The internet and US communication policy-making in historical and critical perspective. *Journal of Computer-Mediated Communication*, 1(4).

—— (2004). Media policy goes to main street: the uprising of 2003. *Communication Review, 7* (3), 223–58.

McChesney, R. W. (2004). *The Problem of the Media: US communication politics in the 21st century*. New York: Monthly Review Press.

McCombs, M. E., Shaw, D. L. & Weaver, D. L. (1997). *Communication and Democracy: exploring the intellectual frontiers in agenda-setting theory*. Mahwah, NJ: Erlbaum.

McFarland, A. (2007). *Participation as civic innovation*. Paper presented at the Midwest Political Science Association Annual Conference, Chicago, IL.

McFerrin, R. & Wills, D. (2007). High noon on the western range: a property rights analysis of the Johnson County war. *Journal of Economic History, 67*(1), 69–92.

McGowan, D. (2005). *The trespass trouble and the metaphor muddle (University of Minnesota Law School legal studies research paper series)*. Minnesota: University of Minnesota Law School.

McKay, D. (2005). *American Politics and Society*, 6th edn. Oxford: Blackwell.

McLeod, J. M. & McDonald, D. G. (1985). Beyond simple exposure: media orientations and their impact on political processes. *Communication Research, 12*(1), 3–33.

McLeod, J. M., Scheufele, D. A., Moy, P., Horowitz, E. M., Holbert, R. L., Zhang, W. et al. (1999). Understanding deliberation: the effects of discussion networks on participation in a public forum. *Communication Research, 26* (6), 743–74.

McNair, B. (2002). *Striptease Culture: sex, media and the democratization of desire*. New York: Routledge.

—— (2006). *Cultural Chaos: journalism, news and power in a globalized world*. London: Routledge.

—— (2007). *An Introduction to Political Communication*, 4th edn. London: Routledge.

Melucci, A. (1994). A strange kind of newness: what's "new" in new social movements. In: E. Laraña, H. Johnston & J. Gusfield (eds.), *New Social Movements: from ideology to identity*. Philadelphia, PA: Temple University Press.

—— (1996). *Challenging Codes: collective action in the information age*. Cambridge: Cambridge University Press.

Menjivar, C. (2003). Religion and immigration in comparative perspective: Catholic and Evangelical Salvadorans in San Francisco, Washington, DC, and Phoenix. *Sociology of Religion, 64*(1), 21–45.

Merrill, J. C. & Lowenstein, R. L. (1979). *Media, Messages, and Men: new perspectives in communication*, 2nd edn. New York, NY: Longman.

Meyer, J. W. & Rowan, B. (1977). Institutionalized organizations: formal structure as myth and ceremony. *American Journal of Sociology, 83*(2), 440–63.

Meyer, J. W. & Scott, W. R. (1983). *Organizational Environments: ritual and rationality*. London: Sage.

Michelin (2006). *Michelin researcher honored for RFID advancements*. Retrieved August 15, 2007, from www.michelinmedia.com/pressSingle/value=MCH2006042061739

Michels, R. (1915). *Political Parties: a sociological study of the oligarchical tendencies of modern democracy*. New York: The Free Press.

Milbank, D. & Van de Hei, J. (2004, May 31, 2004). From Bush, unprecedented negativity: scholars say campaign is making history with often-misleading attacks. *Washington Post*, p. 1.

Mill, J. S. (1998). *On Liberty and other Essays*. Oxford: Oxford University Press.

Miller, J. (2004, February 9). Online extra: congress rebuffs e-gov fund, centralized hiring site in '04 spending. *Government Computer News*.

Miller, T. (2007). *Cultural Citizenship*. Philadelphia, PA: Temple University Press.

Miller, W. E. & Shanks, J. M. (1996). *The New American Voter*. Cambridge, MA: Boston Press.

Milner, H. (2006). The digital divide: the role of political institutions in technology diffusion. *Comparative Political Studies, 39*(2), 176–99.

Milner, H. V. (2003). *The diffusion of the internet globally: the role of political institutions*. Paper presented at the American Political Science Association Annual Meeting, Philadelphia, PA.

Ministers of the European Union (2006). *Ministerial declaration on e-inclusion (Riga declaration)*. Riga, Latvia.

Ministry of Economic Affairs and Communications of Estonia (2006). *Information technology in public administration of Estonia yearbook 2005*. Ministry of Economic Affairs and Communications of Estonia.

Ministry of Finance Government of Singapore (2007). *Singapore e-government 2006*. Singapore.

Mitra, A. (1997a). Diasporic web sites: ingroup and outgroup discourse. *Critical Studies in Mass Communication, 14*(2), 158–81.

467

—— (1997b). Virtual community: Looking for india on the internet. In: S. G. Jones (ed.), *Virtual Culture: identity and communication in cybersociety*. Thousand Oaks, CA: Sage.

—— (2001). Diasporic voices in cyberspace. *New Media and Society,* 3(1), 29–48.

—— (2005). Creating immigrant identities in cybernetic space: examples from a non resident Indian website. *Media, Culture and Society,* 27, 371–90.

Mobbs, P. (2000). Internet disintermediation and campaign groups: a study of the development of the internet, its effects on grassroots campaigning and larger campaign groups. *Ecos,* 21 (1), 25–32.

Monge, P. R. & Contractor, N. S. (2003). *Theories of Communication Networks.* Oxford: Oxford University Press.

Monge, P. R. & Fulk, J. (1999). Communication technologies for global network organizations. In: G. DeSanctis & J. Fulk (eds.), *Communication Technologies and Organizational Forms.* Thousand Oaks, CA: Sage.

Monge, P. R., Fulk, J., Kalman, M., Flanagin, A., Parnassa, C. & Rumsey, S. (1998). Production of collection action in alliance-based interorganizational communication and information systems. *Organizational Science,* 9, 411–33.

Moody, G. (2001). *Rebel Code: Linux and the open source revolution.* London: Allen Lane.

Moon, M. (2002). The evolution of e-government among municipalities rhetoric or reality. *Public Administration Review,* 62(4), 424–33.

MORI (2001). *Attitudes to voting and the political process survey.* Retrieved November 22, 2007, from www.mori.com/polls/2001/elec_comm.shtml

Morley, D. & Robins, K. (1995). *Spaces of Identity: global media, electronic landscapes and cultural boundaries.* London: Routledge.

Morris, D. (1999). *Vote.Com: how big-money lobbyists and the media are losing their influence, and the internet is giving power back to the people.* Los Angeles: Renaissance Books.

Mosquera, M. (2001). *New Senate balance of power won't change high-tech outlook.* Retrieved November 22, 2007, from http://web.archive.org/web/20030426050718/http://www.internetweek.com/story/INW20010525S0002

Mossberger, K., Kaplan, D. & Gilbert, M. (2006). *How concentrated poverty matters for the*
"digital divide": motivation, social networks, and resources. Paper presented at the American Political Science Association Annual Meeting, Philadelphia, PA.

Mossberger, K., Kaplan, D. & McNeil, R. (2007). *Digital Citizenship: the internet, society and participation.* Cambridge MA: MIT Press.

Mossberger, K., Tolbert, C. & Gilbert, M. (2006). Race, place and information technology. *Urban Affairs Review,* 41(5), 583–620.

Mossberger, K., Tolbert, C. J. & McNeal, R. S. (2008). *Digital Citizenship: the internet, society, and participation.* Cambridge, MA: MIT Press.

Mossberger, K., Tolbert, C. J. & Stansbury, M. (2003). *Virtual Inequality: beyond the digital divide.* Washington DC: Georgetown University Press.

Mouffe, C. (2000). *The Democratic Paradox.* London: Verso.

—— (2005). *On the Political.* London: Routledge.

MoveOn. (2007). *Election 2006: people powered politics.* Retrieved November 22, 2007, from http://pol.moveon.org/2006report

Moy, P., Manosevitch, E., Stamm, K. & Dunsmore, K. (2005). Linking dimensions of internet use and civic engagement. *Journalism and Mass Communication Quarterly,* 82(3), 571–86.

Mubarak, H. (2000). *A message from His Excellency President Mohammed Hosni Mubarak of Egypt.* Retrieved November 22, 2007, from www.mideastinfo.com/documents/Mubarak_letter.htm

—— (2004). *Opening speech by President Hosni Mubarak to the Arab reform conference.* Arab Reform Conference. Alexandria, Egypt

Mueller, M. (2002). *Ruling the Root: internet governance and the taming of cyberspace.* Cambridge, MA: MIT Press.

Mulgan, G. (1997). *Life after Politics: new thinking for the twenty-first century.* London: Fontana.

Murphy, E. (2006). Agency and space: the political impact of information technologies in the gulf Arab states. *Third World Quarterly,* 27(6), 1059–83.

Murray, S. (2006, August 9). Lamont relies on netroots – and grassroots. *Washington Post.*

Mutz, D. C. (2006). *Hearing the Other Side: deliberative versus participatory democracy.* New York: Cambridge University Press.

Mutz, D. C. & Martin, P. S. (2001). Facilitating communication across lines of political difference. *American Political Science Review,* 95(1), 97–114.

Myers, D. (1999). Demographic dynamism and metropolitan change: comparing Los Angeles, New York, Chicago, and Washington, DC. *Housing Policy Debate,* 10(4), 915–54.

Naficy, H. (1993). *The Making of Exile Cultures: Iranian television in Los Angeles.* Minneapolis: Univeristy of Minnesota Press.

Nagel, J. (1981). Politics and the organization of collective: the case of Nigeria, 1960–75. *Political Behavior,* 3(1), 87–116.

Nahapiet, J. & Ghoshal, S. (1998). Social capital, intellectual capital, and the organizational advantage. *Academy of Management Review,* 23 (2), 242–66.

Napoli, P. M. (1999). The marketplace of ideas metaphor in communications regulation. *Journal of Communication,* 49(4), 151–69.

NASCIO (2005). *The states and enterprise architecture: how far have we come?* Lexington, KY: National Association of State Chief Information Officers.

—— (2006). *NASCIO's survey on IT consolidation and shared services in the states: a national assessment.* Lexington, KY: National Association of State Chief Information Officers.

National Academy of Science (1993). *National collaboratories: applying information technology for scientific research.* Computer Science and Telecommunications Board, National Academies Press.

National Performance Review (1993). *From red tape to results: creating a government that works better and costs less. Report of the National Performance Review.* Washington, DC: U.S. Office of the Vice President.

National Republican Senatorial Committee (2007). *Excerpts from the National Republican Senatorial Committee campaign internet guide.* Retrieved November 22, 2007, from www. politico.com/pdf/PPM44_nrscexcerpts.pdf

National Telecommunications and Information Administration (NTIA) (1995). *Falling through the net: a survey of the "have nots" in rural and urban America.* Washington, DC: U.S. Department of Commerce.

—— (1998). *Falling through the net II: new data on the digital divide.* Washington, DC: U.S. Department of Commerce.

—— (2002). *A nation online: how Americans are expanding their use of the internet.* Washington, DC: U.S. Department of Commerce.

—— (2004). *A nation online: entering the broadband age.* Washington, DC: U.S. Department of Commerce.

Naughton, J. (1999). *A Brief History of the Future: the origins of the internet.* London: Weidenfeld and Nicolson.

Ned Lamont For Senate (2006). *On the air!* Retrieved November 23, 2007, from http:// nedlamont.com/blog/168/on-the-air

Nee, V. & Ingram, P. (1998). Embeddedness and beyond: institutions, exchange, and social structure. In: M. C. Brinton & V. Nee (eds.), *The New Institutionalism in Sociology.* New York: Russell Sage Foundation.

Negrine, R. & Papathanassopoulos, S. (1996). The "Americanization" of political communication: a critique. *The Harvard International Journal of Press/Politics,* 1(2), 45–62.

Negroponte, N. (1995). *Being Digital.* New York: Knopf.

—— (1998). Beyond digital. *Wired, December.*

Neu, C. R., Anderson, R. H. & Bikson, T. K. (1999). *Sending Your Government a Message: e-mail communication between citizens and government.* Santa Monica, CA: Rand Corporation.

Neuendorf, K. A. (2002). *The Content Analysis Guidebook.* Thousand Oaks, CA: Sage.

Neuman, S. B. & Celano, D. (2006). The knowledge gap: implications of leveling the playing field for low-income and middle-income children. *Reading Research Quarterly,* 41(2), 176–201.

Neuman, W. R. (1991). *The Future of the Mass Audience.* Cambridge: Cambridge University Press.

Neuman, W. R., McKnight, L. & Solomon, R. J. (1998). *The Gordian Knot: political gridlock on the information superhighway.* Cambridge, MA: MIT Press.

Neustadt, R. E. (1997). The politics of mistrust. In: J. N. Nye, P. D. Zelikow & D. C. King (eds.) *Why People Don't Trust Government.* Cambridge, MA: Harvard University Press, pp. 197–202.

Newell, J. (2001). Italian political parties on the web. *Harvard International Journal of Press/ Politics,* 6(4), 60–87.

Newhagen, J. E. & Rafaeli, S. (1996). Why communication researchers should study the internet: a dialogue. *Journal of Communication,* 46(1), 4–13.

Nie, N. H. (2001). Sociability, interpersonal relations, and the internet: reconciling conflicting findings. *American Behavioral Scientist,* 45, 420–35.

Nie, N. H. & Erbring, L. (2000). *Internet and society: a preliminary report*. Stanford Institute for the Quantitative Study of Society.

Nielsen/NetRatings (2006). *YouTube US web traffic grows 75 percent week over week*. Retrieved March 20, 2007, from http://64.233.167.104/search?q=cache:1PoVUO5z5vwJ:www.nielsen-netratings.com/pr/pr_060721_2.pdf+youtube+unique+visitors&hl=en&ct=clnk&cd=1&gl=us

—— (2007). *Online newspaper blog traffic grows 210 per cent year over year*. Retrieved January 17, 2007, from www.nielsen-netratings.com

Nissenbaum, H. (2004). Hackers and the contested ontology of cyberspace. *New Media and Society*, 6(2), 195–217.

—— (2004). Technology, values, and the justice system: privacy and contextual integrity. *Washington Law Review*, 79, 119–57.

Nixon, P. G., Ward, S. J. & Gibson, R. K. (2003). Conclusions. In: R. K. Gibson, P. Nixon & S. Ward (eds.), *Political Parties and the Internet: net gain?* London: Routledge.

Noam, E. M. (2005). Why the internet is bad for democracy. *Communications of the ACM*, 48 (10), 57–8.

Noguchi, Y. (2006, October 29). In teens' web world, MySpace is so last year, social sites find fickle audience. *Washington Post*.

Nohria, N. & Berkley, J. D. (1994). The virtual organization: bureacracy, technology, and the implosion of control. In: C. C. Heckscher & A. Donnellon (eds.), *The Post-Bureacratic Organization: new perspectives on organizational change*. Thousand Oaks, CA: Sage.

NOI (2006). *Transcript of online strategies in the 2006 election*. Washington, DC: Centre For American Progress Action Fund.

Nokia (2007). *Nokia Europe technical specifications*. Retrieved November 22, 2007, from http://europe.nokia.com/A4307095

Noland, M. (2005). *Explaining Middle Eastern Authoritarianism*. Washington, DC: Institute of International Economics.

Norris, C. & Armstrong, G. (1999). *The Maximum Surveillance Society: the rise of CCTV*. Berg: Oxford.

Norris, D. F. & Moon, M. J. (2005). Advancing e-government at the grassroots: tortoise or hare? *Public Administration Review*, 65(1), 64–75.

Norris, P. (1998). Virtual democracy. *Harvard International Journal of Press Politics*, 3(2), 1–4.

—— (2000). *A Virtuous Circle: political communications in postindustrial societies*. Cambridge: Cambridge University Press.

—— (2001a). A failing grade? The news media and campaign 2000. *Press/Politics*, 6(2), 3–9.

—— (2001b). *Digital Divide: civic engagement, information poverty, and the internet worldwide*. Cambridge: Cambridge University Press.

—— (2002). *Democratic Phoenix: reinventing political activism*. Cambridge: Cambridge University Press.

—— (2003). Preaching to the converted? Pluralism, participation and party websites. *Party Politics*, 9(1), 21–46.

—— (2004). The bridging and bonding role of online communities. In: P. N. Howard & S. Jones (eds.), *Society Online: the internet in context*. Thousand Oaks, CA: Sage.

Norton, A. R. (1999a). Associational life: civil society in authoritarian political systems. In M. Tessler (ed.), *Area Studies and Social Science: strategies for understanding Middle East politics*. Bloomington: Indiana University Press.

—— (1999b). The new media, civic pluralism, and the slowly retreating state. In: D. F. Eickleman & J. W. Anderson (eds.), *New Media in the Muslim World: the emerging public sphere*. Bloomington: Indiana University Press.

Norton, P. (2007). Four models of political representation: British MPs and the use of ICT. *Journal of Legislative Studies*, 13(3), 354–69.

Nye, J. S. & Owens., W. A. (1996). America's information edge. *Foreign Affairs*, 75(2), 20–8.

O'Brien, J. (1999). Writing in the body: gender (re)production in online interaction. In: P. Kollock & M. A. Smith (eds.), *Communities in Cyberspace*. London: Routledge.

O'Toole, L. (1999). *Pornocopia: porn, sex, technology and desire*. London: Serpent's Tail.

Oates, S., Owen, D. M. & Gibson, R. K. (2006). *The Internet and Politics: citizens, voters, and activists*. London: Routledge.

Oberschall, A. (1973). *Social Conflict and Social Movements*. Englewood Cliffs, NJ: Prentice Hall.

Office of the Vice President (1993). *Reengingeering through information technology: National Performance Review accompanying report*. Washington, DC: Office of the Vice President.

Oliver, M. (2007). *Minister says road zones solve privacy problem*. Retrieved March 2, 2007, from www.guardian.co.uk/transport/Story/0,2025299,00.html

Olivers, D. (2004). Counter hegemonic dispersions: the World Social Forum model. *Antipode*, 36(2), 175–83.

O'Loughlin, B. (2001). The political implications of digital innovations: the internet and trade-offs of democracy and liberty in the developed world. *Information, Communication and Society*, 4(4), 595–614.

Olson, M. (1965). *The Logic of Collective Action: public goods and the theory of groups*. Cambridge, MA: Harvard University Press.

Olson, M. & Zeckhauser, R. (1966). An economic theory of alliances. *Review of Economics and Statistics*, 48(3), 266–79.

OpenNet Initiative (2004). *Bulletin 007*. Retrieved November 23, 2007, from www.opennetinitiative.net/bulletins/007/

—— (2005a). *Country report: Tunisia*. Retrieved November 23, 2007, from www.opennetinitiative.net/studies/tunisia/

—— (2005b). *Internet filtering in China in 2004–2005, a case study*. Retrieved November 23, 2007, from www.opennetinitiative.net/studies/china/

—— (2005c). *Internet filtering in Iran in 2004–2005*. Retrieved November 23, 2007, from www.opennetinitiative.net/studies/iran/

—— (2005d). *Special report: election monitoring in Kyrgyzstan*. Retrieved November 23, 2007, from www.opennetinitiative.net/special/kg/

—— (2006). *The internet and elections: the 2006 presidential elections in Belarus*. Retrieved November 23, 2007, from www.opennetinitiative.net/studies/belarus/ONI_Belarus_Country_Study.pdf

OpenStreetMap (2007). *FAQ – openstreetmap*. Retrieved August 15, 2007, from http://wiki.openstreetmap.org/index.php/FAQ

O'Reilly, T. (2005). *What is Web 2.0?Design patterns and business models for the next generation of software*. Retrieved November 12, 2007, from www.oreilly.com/lpt/a/6228

Organization for Economic Cooperation and Development (OECD) (2006). *OECD broadband statistics to December 2006*. Paris: OECD.

Ortony, A. (1993). *Metaphor and Thought*, 2nd edn. Cambridge and New York, NY: Cambridge University Press.

Østergaard-Nielsen, E. (2003). The politics of migrants' transnational political practices. *International Migration Review*, 37(3), 760–86.

Ostrom, E. (1990). *Governing the Commons: the evolution of institutions for collective action*. Cambridge: Cambridge University Press.

Ott, D. (1998). Power to the people: the role of electronic media in promoting democracy in Africa. *First Monday*, 3(4).

Overholser, G. & Jamieson, K. H. (eds.) (2005). *Institutions of American Democracy: the press*. Oxford: Oxford University Press.

Oye, K. A. (1986). Explaining cooperation under anarchy: hypotheses and strategies. In: K. A. Oye (ed.), *Cooperation Under Anarchy*. Princeton: Princeton University Press.

Paasonen, S. (2006). Email from nancy nutsucker: representation and gendered address in online pornography. *European Journal of Cultural studies*, 9(4), 403–20.

Paasonen, S., Nikunen, K. & Saarenmaa, L. (eds.) (2007). *Pornification: sex and sexuality in media culture*. London, UK: Berg.

Padovani, C. & Tuzzi, A. (2005). Communication governance and the role of civil society: words and networks in the World Summit on the Information Society. Reflections on participation and the changing scope of political action. In: J. Servaes & N. Carpentier (eds.), *Towards a Sustainable Information Society: deconstructing WSIS*. Bristol: Intellect.

Page, B. I. (1996). *Who Deliberates? Mass media in modern democracy*. Chicago: University of Chicago Press.

Palser, B. (2004). The online frontier. *American Journalism Review*, 78.

Papacharissi, Z. (2002). The virtual sphere: the net as a public sphere. *New Media and Society*, 4(1), 5–23.

—— (2007). The blogger revolution? Audiences as media producers. In: M. Tremayne (ed.) *Blogging, Citizenship, and the Future of Media*. New York, NY: Routledge.

Parasuraman, A. & Zinkhan, G. M. (2002). Marketing to and serving customers through the internet: an overview and research agenda. *Journal of the Academy of Marketing Science*, 30(4), 286–95.

Pare, D. (2003). *Internet Governance in Transition: who is the master of this domain?* Lanham, MD: Rowman and Littlefield.

Park, H. W. (2002). The digital divide in South Korea: closing and widening divides in the 1990s. *Electronic Journal of Communication*, 12(1–2).

Park, H. W., Barnett, G. A. & Kim, C.-S. (2000). Political communication structure in internet networks: a Korean case. *Sungkok Journalism Review*, 11, 67–89.

Paterson, C. (2006). *News agency dominance in international news on the internet.* Leeds: Centre for International Communications Research, University of Leeds.

Patterson, T. (1993). *Out of Order.* New York: Knopf.

Patterson, T. E. (1980). *The Mass Media Election: how Americans choose their president.* New York: Praeger.

Patterson, T. E. & Seib, P. (2005). Informing the public. In: G. Overholser & K. H. Jamieson (eds.) *The Press.* New York: Oxford University Press.

Pavlik, J. V. (1994). Citizen access, involvement, and freedom of expression in an electronic environment. In: F. Williams & J. V. Pavlik (eds.), *The People's Right to Know: media, democracy, and the information highway.* Hillsdale, NJ: Erlbaum.

—— (2001). *Journalism and New Media.* New York: Columbia University Press.

—— (2004). A sea-change in journalism: convergence, journalists, their audiences and sources. *Convergence,* 10(4), 21–9.

Pederson, K. & Saglie, J. (2005). New technology in ageing parties. *Party Politics,* 11(3), 359–77.

Peng, F. Y., Tham, N. I. & Xiaoming, H. (1999). Trends in online newspapers: a look at the U.S. web. *Newspaper Research Journal,* 20 (2), 52–63.

Penn, I. (2007, July 28, 2007). Invasive IDS? *St. Petersburg Times.*

Pentland, B. & Feldman, M. (2007). Narrative networks: patterns of technology and organization. *Organization Science,* 18(5), 781–95.

Perelman, M. (2002). *Steal this Idea: intellectual property rights and the corporate confiscation of creativity.* New York: Palgrave.

Peretti, J. (2001). *Email correspondence with customer service representatives at Nike.* Retrieved November 23, 2007, from http://shey.net/niked.html

—— (2003). *Culture jamming, memes, social networks, and the emerging media ecology: the Nike sweatshop e-mail as an object to think with.* Retrieved November 22, 2007, from http://depts.washington.edu/ccce/polcommcampaigns/peretti.html

Perloff, R. M. (2003). *The Dynamics of Persuasion: communication and attitudes in the 21st century,* 2nd edn. Mahwah, NJ: Erlbaum.

Pew Internet and American Life Project (2004). *2004 post-election tracking survey.* Washington, DC: Pew Internet and American Life Project.

—— (2005). *Buzz, blogs, and beyond.* Washington, DC: Pew Internet and American Life Project.

—— (2006). *Daily tracking survey—November 2006.* Washington, DC: Pew Internet and American Life Project.

—— (2007). *Internet activities.* Washington, DC: Pew Internet and American Life Project.

Pew Research Center for the People and the Press (2003). *Bottom line pressures now hurting coverage say journalists* Washington, DC: Pew Research Center for the People and the Press.

—— (2004). *News audiences increasingly politicized.* Washington, DC: Pew Research Center for the People and the Press.

—— (2007). *How young people view their lives, futures, and politics: a portrait of generation next.* Washington DC: Pew Research Center for the People and the Press.

Pharr, S. J. & Putnam, R. D. (2000). *Disaffected Democracies: what's troubling the trilateral countries?* Princeton: Princeton University Press.

Phillips, D. J. (2005). Texas 9-1-1: emergency telecommunications, deregulation, and the genesis of surveillance infrastructure. *Telecommunication Policy,* 29(11), 843–56.

Phillips, H. (2007). *Strengthening democracy: fair and sustainable funding of political parties: the review of the funding of political parties.* London: HMSO.

Pianta, M. (2003). Democracy vs globalization: the growth of parallel summits and global movements. In: D. Archibugi (ed.), *Debating Cosmopolitics.* London: Verso.

Pianta, M. & Silva, F. (2003). Parallel summits of global civil society: an update. In: M. Kaldor, H. Anheier & M. Glasius (eds.), *Global Civil Society Yearbook 2003.* Oxford: Oxford University Press.

Pickard, V. W. (2006). United yet autonomous: indymedia and the struggle to sustain a radical democratic network. *Media, Culture and Society,* 28(3), 315–36.

Pickerill, J. (2000). Environmentalists and the net: Pressure groups, new social movements and new ICTs. In: R. K. Gibson & S. J. Ward (eds.), *Reinvigorating Democracy? British politics and the internet*. Aldershot: Ashgate.

—— (2001). Weaving a green web: environmental protest and computer mediated communication in Britain. In: F. Webster (ed.), *Culture and Politics in the Information Age: a new politics?* London: Routledge.

—— (2003). *Cyberprotest: environmental activism online*. Manchester: Manchester University Press.

—— (2006). Radical politics on the net. *Parliamentary Affairs*, 59(2), 266–82.

Piott, S. L. (2003). *Giving Voters a Voice: the origins of the initiative and referendum in America*. Columbia: University of Missouri Press.

Pitkin, H. F. (1967). *The Concept of Representation*. Berkeley: University of California Press.

Plant, S. (1995). The future looms: weaving women and cybernetics. *Body and Society*, 1 (1), 45–64.

—— (1996). On the matrix: cyberfeminist simulations. In: R. Shields (ed.), *Cultures of internet: virtual spaces, real histories, living bodies*. London: Sage.

—— (1997). *Zeros and Ones. Digital women and the new technoculture*. London: Fourth Estate.

Pleyers, G. (2004). The social forums as an ideal model of convergence. *International Social Science Journal*, 56(182), 507–17.

Podlas, K. (2000). Mistresses of their domain: how female entrepreneurs in cyberporn are initiating a gender power shift. *Cyber Psychology and Behavior*, 3 (5), 847–54.

Poindexter, P. M., Heider, D. & McCombs, M. E. (2006). Watchdog or good neighbor? The public's expectations of local news. *Harvard International Journal of Press/Politics*, 11(1), 77–88.

Polat, R. K. (2005). The internet and political participation: exploring the explanatory links. *European Journal of Communication*, 20(4), 435–59.

Polletta, F. (1998). "It was like a fever … " Narrative and identity in social protest. *Social Problems*, 45(2), 137–59.

—— (2006). *It Was Like a Fever: storytelling in protest and politics*. Chicago: University of Chicago Press.

Pollitt, C. (2003). Joined-up government: a survey. *Political Studies Review*, 1(1), 34–49.

Pollitt, C. & Boukhaert, G. (2004). *Public Management Reform: a comparative analysis*. Oxford: Oxford University Press.

Popkin, S. L. (1994). *The Reasoning Voter: communication and persuasion in presidential campaigns*,

2nd edn. Chicago; London: University of Chicago Press.

Porter, D. (1997). Introduction. In: D. Porter (ed.), *Internet Culture*. New York: Routledge.

Portes, A. & Sensenbrenner, J. (1993). Embeddedness and immigration: notes on the social determinants of economic action. *American Journal of Sociology*, 98(6), 1320–50.

Portes, A. & Zhou, M. (1992). Gaining the upper hand: economic mobility among immigrant and domestic minorities. *Ethnic and Racial Studies*, 15(4), 491.

Post, D. & Johnson, D. R. (2006). The great debate: law in the virtual world. *First Monday*, 11(2).

Postelnicu, M., Martin, J. & Landreville, K. (2006). The role of candidate web sites in promoting candidates and attracting campaign resources. In: A. P. Williams & J. C. Tedesco (eds.), *The Internet Election: perspectives on the web campaign in 2004*. Lanham, MD: Rowman and Littlefield.

Poster, M. (1995). The internet as a public sphere? *Wired*, January.

—— (2001). *What's the Matter with the Internet?* Minneapolis: University of Minnesota Press.

Potter, W. J. & Levine-Donnerstein, D. (1999). Rethinking validity and reliability in content analysis. *Journal of Applied Communication Research*, 27(3), 258–84.

Powell, W. (1990). Neither market nor hierarchy: network forms of organization. *Research in Organizational Behavior*, (12), 295–336.

PQMedia (2006). *Media companies to come out winners as 2006 political media spending heads for the record books*. Retrieved November 2, from www.pqmedia.com/about-press-20061109-pmb 2006.html

Preece, J. (2000). *On-line Communities: designing usability and supporting sociability*. New York: Wiley.

Price, V. & Cappella, J. N. (2002). Online deliberation and its influence: the electronic dialogue project in campaign 2000. *IT and Society*, 1(1), 303–29.

Price, V., Cappella, J. N. & Nir, L. (2002). Does more disagreement contribute to more deliberative opinion? *Political Communication*, 19(1), 95–112.

Prior, M. (2003). Any good news in soft news? The impact of soft news preference on political knowledge. *Political Communication*, 20, 149–71.

—— (2005). News vs. entertainment: how increasing media choice widens gaps in political knowledge and turnout. *American Journal of Political Science,* 49(3), 577–92.

Project for Excellence in Journalism (2004). *The state of the news media: an annual report on American journalism 2003.* Washington, DC: Project for Excellence in Journalism.

—— (2006). *The state of the news media: an annual report on American journalism 2005.* Washington, DC: Project for Excellence in Journalism.

—— (2007). *The state of the news media: an annual report on American journalism 2006.* Washington, DC: Project for Excellence in Journalism.

Putnam, R. (1994). *Making Democracy Work: civic traditions in modern Italy.* Princeton: Princeton University Press.

Putnam, R. D. (1996). The strange disappearance of civic America. *American Prospect,* 24, 34–48.

—— (2000). *Bowling Alone: the collapse and revival of American community.* New York: Simon and Schuster.

Putnam, R. D., Feldstein, L. & Cohen, D. (2003). *Better Together: restoring the American community.* London: Simon and Schuster.

Puttnam Commission on the Communication of Parliamentary Democracy (2006). *Members Only? Parliament in the Public Eye.* London: Hansard Society.

Pye, L. W. (1985). *Asian Power and Politics: the cultural dimensions of authority.* Cambridge, MA: Harvard University Press.

Qvortrup, M. (2002). *A Comparative Study of Referendums: government by the people.* Manchester: Manchester University Press.

Radin, M. J. (2006). A comment on information propertization and its legal milieu. *Cleveland State Law Review,* 54, 23–39.

Rainie, L., Cornfield, M. & Horrigan, J. (2005). *The internet and campaign 2004: the internet was a key force in politics last year as 75 million Americans used it to get news, discuss candidates in emails, and participate directly in the political process.* Washington, DC: Pew Internet and American Life Project.

Rainie, L. & Horrigan, J. (2007). *Election 2006 online – January 2007.* Washington DC: Pew Internet and American Life Project.

Rainie, L. & Kohut, A. (2000). *Tracking online life: how women use the internet to cultivate relationships with family and friends.* Washington, DC: Pew Internet and American Life Project.

Rappoport, P. N. & Alleman, J. (2003). The internet and the demand for news: Macro- and microevidence. In: A. M. Knott (ed.), *Crisis in Communications: lessons from September 11.* London: Rowman and Littlefield.

Rash, W. (1997). *Politics on the Nets: wiring the political process.* New York: W. H. Freeman & Co.

Rathmann, T. A. (2002). Supplement or substitution? The relationship between reading a local print newspaper and the use of its online version. *Communications: The European Journal of Communication Research,* 27(4), 485–98.

Rattray, G. J. (2001). *Strategic Warfare in Cyberspace.* Cambridge, MA: MIT Press.

Ray, A. (2007). *Naked on the internet: hookups, downloads and cashing in on internet sexploration.* Emeryville: Seal Press.

Reese, S. D., Rutigliano, L., Hyun, K. & Jeong, J. (2007). Mapping the blogosphere: professional and citizen-based media in the global news arena. *Journalism and Mass Communication Quarterly,* 8(3), 235–62.

Reid, E. M. (1993). Electronic chat: social issues in internet relay chat. *Media Information Australia,* 67, 62–70.

Rennie, D. (2005, January 28). Britons "Ignorant and hostile" Over EU constitution. *Daily Telegraph.*

Reporters Without Borders (2006). *List of 13 internet enemies in 2006.* Retrieved July 11, 2006, from www.rsf.org/print.php3?id_article=19603

—— (2007a). *Annual report 2007.* Paris: Reporters Without Borders.

—— (2007b). *Blogger arrested and held for reporting on torture of detainees.* Retrieved April 17, 2007, from http://allafrica.com/stories/printable/200704180322.html

—— (2007c). *The Dailymotion video-sharing website is accessible again.* Retrieved November 22, 2007, from www.rsf.org/article.php3?id_article=21528

Resnick, D. (1998). The normalization of cyberspace. In: C. Toulouse & T. W. Luke (eds.), *The Politics of Cyberspace: a new political science reader.* New York: Routledge.

Resnick, P. (2001). Beyond bowling together: sociotechnical capital. In: J. Carroll (ed.), *HCI in the New Millennium.* Reading, MA: Addison-Wesley.

Resnick, P. & Shah, V. (2002). *Photo Directories: a tool for organizing sociability in neighborhoods and organizations: working paper.* Ann Arbor, MI: School of Information, University of Michigan.

Rhee, J. W. & Cappella, J. N. (1997). The role of political sophistication in learning from news: measuring schema development. *Communication Research*, 24(3), 197–233.

Rheingold, H. (1991). *Virtual Reality.* New York: Simon and Schuster.

—— (1993). *The Virtual Community: homesteading on the electronic frontier.* Boston, MA: Addison-Wesley.

—— (1995). *The Virtual Community: finding connection in a computerized world.* London: Minerva.

—— (2002). *Smart Mobs: the next social revolution.* Cambridge, MA: Basic Books.

Rhine, R. J. (1967). The 1964 presidential election and curves of information seeking and avoiding. *Journal of Personality and Social Psychology*, 5(4), 416–23.

Richard, M. (2004). Modeling the impact of internet atmospherics on surfing behavior. *Journal of Business Research*, 58(2), 1632–42.

Richardson, J. E. & Franklin, B. (2004). Letters of intent: election campaigning and orchestrated public debate in local newspapers' letters to the editor. *Political Communication*, 21 (4), 459–78.

Rittberger, V. (ed.). (1993). *Regime Theory and International Relations.* Oxford: Clarendon Press.

Rivera, R. (2007, March 1). Council acts to make clubs safer. *New York Times.*

Rochidi, N. (2004). Interview by Deborah L. Wheeler. World Trade Center Building, ICT Dar Project Office Cairo, Egypt.

Rockwell, S. & Singleton, L. (2002). The effects of computer anxiety and communication apprehension on the adoption and utilization of the internet. *Electronic Journal of Communication*, 12(1).

Rodan, G. (1998). The internet and political control in Singapore. *Political Science Quarterly*, 113(1), 63–89.

Rodgers, J. (2003). *Spatializing International Politics: analysing activism on the internet.* London: Routledge.

Rodgers, S. & Harris, M. A. (2003). Gender and e-commerce: an exploratory study. *Journal of Advertising Research*, 43(3), 322–9.

Roe Smith, M. (1994). Technological determinism in American culture. In: M. Roe Smith & L. Marx (eds.), *Does Technology Drive History: the dilemma of technological determinism.* Cambridge, MA: MIT Press.

Rogers, E. M. (1995). *Diffusion of Innovations*, 4th edn. New York: Free Press.

—— (2003). *Diffusion of Innovations*, 5th edn. New York: Free Press.

Rogers, R. (2002). Operating issue networks on the web. *Science as Culture*, 11(2), 191–214.

—— (2004). *Information Politics on the Web.* Cambridge, MA: MIT Press.

Rommes, E. (2002). *Gender Scripts and the internet: the design of Amsterdam's digital city.* Enschede: Twente University Press.

Rosenau, J. N. & Czempiel, E. O. (eds.). (1992). *Governance without Government: order and change in world politics.* Cambridge: Cambridge University Press.

Rosenthal, L. E. (2007). *Information technology in the UAE.* Retrieved November 22, 2007, from www.american.edu/carmel/lr2962a/geographics.html

Ruggie, J. (1993). *Multilateralism Matters: the theory and praxis of an international form.* New York: Columbia University Press.

Rugh, W. (2004). *Arab Mass Media: newspapers, radio, and television in Arab politics.* Westport: Praeger Publishers.

Rutenberg, J. (2004, May 25). Campaign ads are under fire for inaccuracy. *New York Times*, p. 1.

Sabato, L. J. (1991). *Feeding Frenzy: how attack journalism has transformed American politics.* New York: Free Press.

Sakkas, L. (1993). Politics on the internet. *Interpersonal Computing and Technology: An Electronic Journal for the 21st Century*, 1(2).

Salaverria, R. (2005). An immature medium: strengths and weaknesses of online newspapers on September 11. *Gazette*, 67, 69–86.

Salter, L. (2005). Colonization tendencies in the development of the world wide web. *New Media and Society*, 7(3), 291–309.

Sanchez-Franco, M. J. & Roldan, J. L. (2005). Web acceptance and usage model: a comparison between goal-directed and experiential users. *Internet Research*, 15(1), 21–49.

Sassi, S. (2000). The controversies of the internet and the revitalizations of political life. In: K. L. Hacker & J. van Dijk (eds.), *Digital Democracy: issues of theory and practice.* London. Sage.

—— (2005). Cultural differentiation or social segregation? Four approaches to the digital divide. *New Media and Society*, 7(5), 684–700.

Savicki, V., Kelley, M. & Lingenfelter, D. (1996). Gender language style and group

475

composition in internet discussion groups. *Journal of Computer-Mediated Communication,* 2(3).

Savin, R. (2006). Conspectus: major court decisions, 2005–6: in re application of the United States for an order (1) authorizing the use of a pen register and a trap and trace device and (2) authorizing release of subscriber information and/or cell site information, 396 f. Supp. 2d 294 (e.D.N.Y. 2005). *CommLaw Conspectus,* 14, 586.

Scammell, M. (2000). The internet and civic engagement: the age of the citizen-consumer. *Political Communication,* 17(4), 351–55.

Schaap, F. (2002). *The Words That Took Us There: ethnography in a virtual reality.* Amsterdam: Aksant.

Schauer, T. (2005). Women's porno: the heterosexual female gaze in porn sites "for women". *Sexuality and Culture,* 9(2), 42–64.

Schement, J. & Curtis, T. (1997). *Tendencies and Tensions of the Information Age: the production and distribution of information in the United States.* New Brunswick, NJ: Transaction.

Schement, J. R. & Scott, S. C. (2000). Identifying temporary and permanent gaps in universal service. *The Information Society,* 16(2), 117–26.

Scheufele, D. A. (2003). *Media use survey.* Ithaca, NY: Cornell University Survey Research Institute.

Scheufele, D. A. & Nisbet, M. C. (2002). Being a citizen online: new opportunities and dead ends. *Harvard International Journal of Press/Politics,* 7(3), 55–75.

Scheufele, D. A., Nisbet, M. C. & Brossard, D. (2003). Pathways to participation? Religion, communication contexts, and mass media. *International Journal of Public Opinion Research,* 15(3), 300–24.

Scheufele, D. A., Nisbet, M. C., Brossard, D. & Nisbet, E. C. (2004). Social structure and citizenship: examining the impact of social setting, network heterogeneity, and informational variables on political participation. *Political Communication,* 21(3), 315–38.

Schiffauer, W. (1999). *Islamism in the diaspora: the fascination of political Islam among second generation German Turks. Working paper.* Transnational Communities Program, University of Oxford.

Schiller, D. (1999). *Digital Capitalism: networking the global marketing system.* Cambridge, MA: MIT Press.

—— (2006). *How To Think About Information.* Urbana: University of Illinois Press.

Schmitt, M. (2007). *Mismatching funds.* Retrieved November 22, 2007, from www.democracy-journal.org/printfriendly.php?ID=6516

Schmitz, J. (1997). Structural relations, electronic media, and social change: the public electronic network and the homeless. In: S. G. Jones (ed.), *Virtual Culture: identity and communication in cybersociety.* Thousand Oaks, CA: Sage.

Schoenbach, K., de Waal, E. & Lauf, E. (2005). Research note: online and print newspapers. *European Journal of Communication,* 20(2), 245–58

Schönleitner, G. (2003). World social forum: making another world possible? In: J. Clark (ed.), *Globalizing Civic Engagement: civil society and transnational action.* London: Earthscan.

Schudson, M. (1997). Why conversation is not the soul of democracy. *Critical Studies in Mass Communication,* 14(4), 1–13.

—— (1998). *The Good Citizen: a history of American civic life.* New York: Free Press.

Schuler, D. & Day, P. (2004). *Shaping the Network Society: the new role of civil society in cyberspace.* Cambridge, MA: MIT Press.

Schumpeter, J. A. (1976). *Capitalism, Socialism and Democracy,* 5th edn. (new introduction by Tom Bottomore ed.). London: Allen and Unwin.

Schwab, K. (2007). *Arab world competitiveness report press release.* Retrieved November 22, 3007, from www.weforum.org/en/media/Latest%20Press%20Releases/AWCReportPR

Schwartz, A., Flint, L., Mulligan, L. D., Suh, G., Mondal, I. & Dempsey, J. X. (2006). *Digital Search And Seizure: updating privacy protections to keep pace with technology.* Washington, DC: Center for Democracy and Technology.

Science of Collaboratories (2007). *Science of collaboratories website.* Retrieved November 23, 2007, from www.scienceofcollaboratories.org

Sciolino, E. (2005, May 31). The French decision. *New York Times.*

Scott, A. & Street, J. (2001). From media politics to e-protest? The use of popular culture and new media in parties and social movements. In: F. Webster (ed.), *Culture and Politics in the Information Age: a new politics?* London: Routledge.

Scott, B. (2005). A contemporary history of digital journalism. *Television and New Media,* 6(1), 89–126.

Scott, J. (2000). *Social Network Analysis: a handbook* (2nd edn.). London: Sage.

Scott, W. R. (1987). The adolescence of institutional theory. *Administrative Science Quarterly,* 32(4), 493–511.

—— (1995). *Institutions and Organizations: theory and research.* Thousand Oaks, CA: Sage.

Scott, W. R. & Christensen, S. (1995). *The Institutional Construction of Organizations: international and longitudinal studies.* Thousand Oaks, CA: Sage.

Scott, W. R. & Meyer, J. W. (eds.). (1994). *Institutional Environments and Organizations: structural complexity and individualism.* Thousand Oaks, CA: Sage.

SCP (Sociaal en Cultureel Planbureau) (2001). *Trends in de tijd [Trends in time].* The Hague: SCP.

Sears, D. & Chafee, S. (1979). Uses and effects of the 1976 debates: an overview of empirical studies. In: S. Kraus (ed.) *The Great Debates.* Bloomington, IN: Indiana University Press.

Sears, D. O. & Freedman, J. L. (1967). Selective exposure to information: a critical review. *Public Opinion Quarterly,* 31(2), 194–213.

Sefyrin, J. (2005). *Understandings of gender and competence in ICT.* Paper presented at the 6th International Women into Computing Conference, University of Greenwich.

Seifert, J. W. & McLoughlin, G. J. (2007). *State E-Government Strategies: identifying best practices and applications.* Washington, DC: Congressional Research Service.

Sell, S. (2003). *Private Power, Public Law: the globalization of intellectual property rights.* Cambridge: Cambridge University Press.

Semetko, H. A. & Krasnoboka, N. (2003). The political role of the internet in societies in transition. *Party Politics,* 9(1), 77–104.

Servaes, J. & Carpentier, N. (eds.). (2005). *Towards a Sustainable Information Society: deconstructing WSIS.* Bristol: Intellect.

Setala, M. & Gronlund, K. (2006). Parlimentary websites: theoretical and comparative perspectives. *Information Polity,* 11(2), 149–62.

Sey, A. & Castells, M. (2004). From media politics to networked politics: The internet and the political process. In: M. Castells (ed.), *The Network Society: a cross-cultural perspective.* London: Edward Elgar.

Shade, L. R. (2002). *Gender and Community in the Social Construction of the Internet.* New York: Peter Lang.

Shah, D., Kwak, N. & Holbert, R. (2001). "Connecting" and "disconnecting" with civic life: patterns of internet use and the production of social capital. *Political Communication,* 18(2), 141–62.

Shah, D. V., Cho, J., Eveland Jr., W. P. & Kwak, N. (2005). Information and expression in a digital age: modeling internet effects on civic participation. *Communication Research,* 32(5), 531–65.

Shah, D. V., McLeod, J. M. & Yoon, S. H. (2001). Communication, context, and community: an exploration of print, broacast and internet influences. *Communication Research,* 28 (4), 464–506.

Shahin, J. & Neuhold, C. (2007). Connecting Europe: the use of "new" information and communication technologies within European Parliament standing committees. *Journal of Legislative Studies,* 13(3), 388–402.

Shannon, V. (2007, February 20). Europe's plan to track phone and net use. *New York Times.*

Shapiro, C. & Varian, H. R. (1999). *Information Rules: a strategic guide to the network economy.* Boston: Harvard Business School Press.

Shifman, L., Coleman, S. & Ward, S. J. (2007). Only joking? Online humour in the 2005 UK general election. *Information Communication and Society,* 10(4), 464–86.

Shoemaker, P. J. & Reese, S. D. (1996). *Mediating the Message: theories of influences on mass media content.* New York: Longman.

Siapera, E. (2005). Minority activism on the web: Between deliberation and multiculturalism. *Journal of Ethnic and Migration Studies,* 31(3), 499–519.

Siddiquee, A. & Kagan, C. (2006). The internet, empowerment, and identity: an exploration of participation by refugee women in a community internet project in the United Kingdom. *Journal of Community & Applied Social Psychology,* 16(3), 189–206.

Sikkink, K. (2002). Restructuring world politics: the limits and asymmetries of soft power. In: S. Khagram, J. V. Riker & K. Sikkink (eds.), *Restructuring World Politics: transnational social movements, networks, and norms.* Minneapolis, MN: University of Minnesota Press.

Silvester, C. (ed.). (1993). *The Penguin Book of Interviews.* London: Viking.

Simon, H. A. (1962). The architecture of complexity. *Proceedings of the American Philosophical Society,* 106 (December), 467–82.

Simone, M. (2006). Codepink alert: mediated citizenship in the public sphere. *Social Semiotics,* 16(2), 345–64.

Simonelis, A. (2005). A concise guide to the major internet bodies. *Ubiquity,* 6(5), 16–22.

Singer, J. B. (2001). The metro wide web: changes in newspapers' gatekeeping role online. *Journalism and Mass Communication Quarterly,* 78(1), 65–80.

—— (2003). Campaign contributions: online newspaper coverage of election 2000. *Journalism and Mass Communication Quarterly,* 80(1), 39–56.

—— (2005). The political j-blogger: "normalizing" a new media form to fit old norms and practices. *Journalism,* 6(2), 173–98.

—— (2006). Stepping back from the gate: online newspaper editors and the co-production of content in campaign 2004. *Journalism and Mass Communication Quarterly,* 83(3), 265–80.

Singer, J. B. & Gonzalez-Velez, M. (2003). Envisioning the caucus community: online newspaper editors conceptualize their political role. *Political Communication,* 20(4), 433–52

Skowronek, S. (1982). *Building a New American State: the expansion of national administrative capacities.* New York: Cambridge University Press.

Slackman, M. (2007a, March 28). Charges of vote rigging as Egypt approves constitution changes. *New York Times.*

—— (2007b, March 25). Egypt to vote on expanding powers of the presidency. *New York Times.*

—— (2007c, March 27). Foregone conclusion appears to keep Egyptian voters home. *New York Times.*

Smith, C. (2007). *One for the Girls! The pleasures and practices of reading women's porn.* Bristol: Intellect.

Smith, M. A. (2002). Ballot initiatives and the democratic citizen. *Journal of Politics,* 64(3), 892–903.

Snow, D. & Benford, R. (1988). Ideology, frame resonance, and participant mobilization. In: B. Klandermans, H. Kriesi & S. Tarrow (eds.), *From Structure to Action: comparing social movements research across cultures.* Greenwich: JAI Press Inc.

Snow, D., Rochford, E. B., Warden, S. & Benford, R. (1986). Frame alignment processes, micromobilization, and movement participation. *American Sociological Review,* 51(4), 464–81.

Songer, D. & Sheehan, R. (1993). Interest group success in the courts: amicus participation in the Supreme Court. *Political Research Quarterly,* 46(2), 339–54.

Sorauf, F. J. (1992). *Inside Campaign Finance: myths and realities.* New Haven and London: Yale University Press.

South Korea Ministry of Information (2006). *Korea Internet White Paper 2006.* Seoul: South Korea Ministry of Information.

Spar, D. L. (2001). *Ruling the Waves: cycles of discovery, chaos, and wealth from the compass to the internet.* New York: Harcourt.

Sparks, C. (2000). From dead trees to live wires: the internet's challenge to the traditional newspaper. In: J. Curran & M. Gurevitch (eds.), *Mass Media and Society,* 3rd edn. London: Hodder Arnold.

Spriggs, J. F. & Wahlbeck, P. (1997). Amicus curiae and the role of information at the supreme court. *Political Research Quarterly,* 50 (2), 365–86.

Stanley, L. (2001). *Beyond Access.* San Diego, CA: UCSD Civic Collaborative.

Stanyer, J. (2004). Politics and the media: a crisis of trust? *Parliamentary Affairs,* 57(2), 420–34.

—— (2007). *Modern Political Communication: mediated politics in uncertain times.* Cambridge: Polity.

Staples, B. (2003, November 10). Editorial observer: viewing California politics through the lens of a science fiction movie. *New York Times.*

Starr, P. (1982). *The Social Transformation of American Medicine.* New York: Basic Books.

—— (2004). *The Creation of the Media.* New York: Free Press.

Stern, C. (2006, January 22). The coming tug of war over the internet. *Washington Post.*

Stewart, A. (2007). *Theories of Power and Domination.* Thousand Oaks, CA: Sage.

Steyaert, J. (2000). *Digitale Vaardigheden: geletterdheid in de informatiesamenleving (Digital Skills: literacy in the information society).* The Hague, Netherlands: Rathenau Instituut.

Stinchcombe, A. L. (1990). *Information and Organizations.* Berkeley, CA: University of California Press.

Stohl, C. (2005). Globalization theory. In: S. May & D. K. Mumby (eds.), *Engaging Organizational Communication Theory and Research: multiple perspectives.* Thousand Oaks, CA: Sage.

Strangelove, M. (2005). *The Empire of Mind: digital piracy and the anti-capitalist movement*. Toronto: University of Toronto Press.

Street, J. (1992). *Politics and Technology*. New York: Guilford Press.

Stromer-Galley, J. (2000). Online interaction and why candidates avoid it. *Journal of Communication*, 50(4), 111–32.

—— (2002). New voices in the public sphere: a comparative analysis of interpersonal and online political talk. *Javnost – The Public*, 9(2), 23–42.

Stromer-Galley, J. & Baker, A. B. (2006). Joy and sorrow of interactivity on the campaign trail: blogs in the primary campaign of Howard Dean. In: A. P. Williams & J. C. Tedesco (eds.), *The Internet Election: perspectives on the web in campaign 2004*. Lanham, MD: Rowman and Littlefield.

Sum, N.-L. (2003). Informational capitalism and US economic hegemony: resistance and adaptations in East Asia. *Critical Asian Studies*, 35(2), 373–98.

Sundar, S. S. (1999). Exploring receivers' criteria for perception of print and online news. *Journalism and Mass Communication Quarterly*, 76(2), 373–86.

—— (2000). Multimedia effects on processing and perception of online news: a study of picture, audio, and video downloads. *Journalism and Mass Communication Quarterly*, 77(3), 480–99.

Sundar, S. S., Kalyanaraman, S. & Brown, J. (2003). Explicating web site interactivity: impression formation effects in political campaign sites. *Communication Research*, 30(1), 30–59.

Sundar, S. S. & Nass, C. (2001). Conceptualizing sources in online news. *Journal of Communication*, 51(1), 52–72.

Sunstein, C. (1993). On analogical reasoning. *Harvard Law Review*, 106(3), 741–91.

Sunstein, C. R. (2001). *Republic.Com*. Princeton: Princeton University Press.

Swanson, D. (2000). The homologous evolution of political communication and civic engagement: good news, bad news, and no news. *Political Communication*, 17(4), 409–14.

Swartz, N. (2003). Estonia embraces cyberspace. *Information Management Journal*, (July–August).

Swedberg, C. (2007, March 23). New RFID system takes security to heart. *RFID Journal*.

Tanner, E. (2001). Chilean conversations: internet forum participants debate Pinochet's detention. *Journal of Communication*, 51(2), 383–403.

Tarde, G. (1989). *L'opinion et la foule*. Paris: PUF.

Tarrow, S. (1998). Fishnets, internets and cat-nets: globalization and transnational collective action. In: M. Hanagan, L. P. Moch & W. P. Brake (eds.), *Challenging Authority*. Minneapolis: University of Minnesota Press.

Tarrow, S. G. (1998). *Power in Movement: social movements and contentious politics*, 2nd edn. Cambridge: Cambridge University Press.

Taylor, P. (1984, August 13). Mondale says President's joke wasn't funny; Reagan's ad-lib on bombing gives foes ammunition. *Washington Post*.

Tekwani, S. (2003). The Tamil diaspora, Tamil militancy, and the internet. In: K. C. Ho, R. Kluver & K. C. C. Yang (eds.), *Asia.Com: Asia encounters the internet*. New York: Routledge.

TeleNav Inc. (2007). *TeleNav Track Features*.

Tewksbury, D. (2003). What do Americans really want to know? Tracking the behavior of news readers on the internet. *Journal of Communication*, 53(4), 694–710.

—— (2005a). *Online news reader specialization and its boundaries: implications for the fragmentation of American news audiences*. Paper presented at the Annual Conference of the International Communication Association, New York.

—— (2005b). The seeds of audience fragmentation: specialization in the use of online news sites. *Journal of Broadcasting and Electronic Media*, 49(3), 332–40.

—— (2006). Exposure to the newer media in a presidential primary campaign. *Political Communication*, 23(3), 313–32.

Tewksbury, D. & Althaus, S. L. (2000a). An examination of motivations for using the world wide web. *Communication Research Reports*, 17(2), 127–38.

—— (2000b). Differences in knowledge acquisition among readers of the paper and online versions of a national newspaper. *Journalism and Mass Communication Quarterly*, 77(3), 457–79.

Tewksbury, D. & Maddex, B. (2001). *Choosing what's right for you: a study of content personalization on the world wide web*. Paper presented at the Annual Meeting of the US National Communication Association, Atlanta, GA.

Tewksbury, D., Weaver, A. & Maddex, B. (2001). Accidentally informed: incidental news exposure on the world wide web. *Journalism and Mass Communication Quarterly,* 78(3), 533–54.

Thalheimer, M. (1994). High tech news or just "Shovelware"? *Media Studies Journal,* 8(1), 41–51.

Thierer, A. D. (2000). *How Free Computers are Filling the Digital Divide.* Washington, DC: Heritage Foundation.

Thomas, J. C. & Streib, G. (2003). The new face of government: citizen-initiated contacts in the era of e-government. *Journal of Public Administration Research and Theory,* 13(1), 83–102.

Thompson, J. B. (2005). The new visibility. *Theory, Culture and Society,* 22(6), 31–51.

Thompson, K. (2002). Border crossings and diasporic identities: media use and leisure practices of an ethnic minority. *Qualitative Sociology,* 25 (3), 409–18.

Thurman, N. (2007). The globalisation of journalism online: a transatlantic study of news websites and their international readers. *Journalism: Theory, Practice and Criticism,* 8(3), 285–307.

Tiefenbrun, S. W. (1986). Legal semiotics. *Cardozo Arts and Entertainment Law Journal,* 5, 89–156.

Tiller, E. H. & Cross, F. (2005). *What is legal doctrine?* Chicago: Northwestern University School of Law Public Law and Legal Theory Research Paper Series.

Tilly, C. (1978). *From mobilization to revolution.* Reading, MA: Addison-Wesley.

Tkach-Kawasaki, L. M. (2003). Politics@Japan: party competition on the internet in Japan. *Party Politics,* 9(1), 105–23.

Toennies, F. (1980). Gemeinschaft and gesellschaft [community and society]. In: L. Coser (ed.), *The Pleasures of Sociology.* New York: Mentor Books.

Toft, A., Leuven, N. V., Bennett, W. L., Tomhave, J., Veden, M. L., Wells, C. *et al.* (2007). *Which way for the northwest social forum?* Seattle, WA: Centre for Communication and Civic Engagement.

Tolbert, C. & McNeal, R. (2003). Unraveling the effects of the internet on political participation. *Political Research Quarterly,* 56(2), 175–85.

Tolbert, C. & Mossberger, K. (2006). The effects of e-government on trust and confidence in government. *Public Administration Review,* 66 (3), 354–69.

Townsend, A. M. & Bennett, J. T. (2003). Privacy, technology, and conflict: emerging issues and action in workplace privacy. *Journal of Labor Research,* 24(2), 195–205.

Trammell, K. D. (2006). The blogging of the President. In: A. P. Williams & J. C. Tedesco (eds.), *The Internet Election: perspectives on the web in campaign 2004.* Lanham, MD: Rowman and Littlefield.

Trechsel, A. H. & Kriesi, H. (1996). Switzerland: the referendum and initiative as a centerpiece of the political system. In: M. Gallagher & P. V. Uleri (eds.), *The Referendum Experience in Europe.* New York: St. Martin's Press.

Tremayne, M. (2004). The web of context: applying network theory to the use of hyperlinks in journalism on the web. *Journalism and Mass Communication Quarterly,* 81(2), 237–49.

Tremayne, M. (ed.). (2006). *Blogging, Citizenship and the Future of Media.* New York: Routledge.

Tremayne, M. & Dunwoody, S. (2001). Interactivity, information processing, and learning on the world wide web. *Science Communication,* 23(2), 111–34.

Tremayne, M., Zheng, N., Lee, J. K. & Jeong, J. (2006). Issue publics on the web: applying network theory to the war blogosphere. *Journal of Computer-Mediated Communication,* 12(1).

Trend, D. (ed.). (2001). *Reading Digital Culture.* Oxford: Blackwell.

Trippi, J. (2004). *The Revolution Will Not Be Televised: democracy, the internet, and the overthrow of everything.* New York: Harper Collins.

Tuchman, G. (1978). *Making News: a study in the construction of reality.* New York: Free Press.

Tucker, J. (2000). The information revolution. *Middle East Journal,* 54(3), 351–465.

Turkle, S. (1995). *Life on the Screen: identity in the age of the internet.* New York: Simon and Schuster.

Twist, J. (2006). *The year of the digital citizen.* Retrieved November 22, 2007, from http://news.bbc.co.uk/1/hi/technology/4566712.stm

UAE Yearbook (2007). *IT and education.* Dubai: UAE National Media Council.

U.K. Electoral Commission (2005). *Registers.* Retrieved November 22, 2007, from www.electoralcommission.org.uk/regulatory-issues/registers.cfm

U.K. Prime Minister's Strategy Unit and Department of Trade and Industry (2005). *Connecting the UK: the digital strategy.* London: Cabinet Office.

United Nations (2004). *Human development report 2004.* Geneva: United Nations.

United Nations Conference on Trade and Development (2003). *E-commerce and development report 2003*. New York: UNCTAD.

United Nations Development Program (2004). *Arab human development report 2004: freedom and good governance*. Stanford: Stanford University Press.

United Nations General Assembly (2001). *56/183: World Summit on the Information Society*. New York: United Nations General Assembly.

University of California, Los Angeles Center for Communication Policy (2001). *The UCLA internet report 2001: surveying the digital future, year two*. Los Angeles: University of California.

—— (2003). *The UCLA internet report: surveying the digital future, year three*. Los Angeles: University of California.

UNPAN and the Center for Administrative Innovation in the Euro-Mediterranean Region (2004). *Best practices in the European countries: The Netherlands*. New York: United Nations Online Network in Public Administration and Finance.

U.S. Bureau of the Census (2003). *E-stats. measuring the electronic economy*. Washington, DC: U.S. Bureau of Census.

U.S. Department of Agriculture (2007). *The national animal identification system: pilot projects/ field trials summary*. Washington, DC: U.S. Department of Agriculture.

U.S. Department of Defense (2003). *Information Operations Roadmap*. Washington, DC: Department of Defense.

U.S. Executive Office of the President (2001). *The President's management agenda, 2002*. Retrieved November 22, 2007, from www.whitehouse.gov/omb/budget/fy2002/mgmt.pdf

Uslaner, E. M. (2000). Social capital and the net. *Communications of the ACM*, 43(12), 60–4.

—— (2004). Trust, civic engagement, and the internet. *Political Communication*, 21(2), 223–42.

Valentino, N. A., Hutchings, V. L. & Williams, D. (2004). The impact of political advertising on knowledge, internet information seeking, and candidate preference. *Journal of Communication*, 54(2), 337–54.

Van Aelst, P. & Walgrave, S. (2002). New media, new movements? The role of the internet in shaping the "anti-globalization" movement. *Information, Communication and Society*, 5(4), 465–93.

van de Donk, W., Loader, B., Nixon, P. & Rucht, D. (eds.). (2004). *Cyberprotest: new media, citizens and social movements*. London: Routledge.

van de Donk, W., Tops, P. & Snellen, I. (eds.). (1995). *Orwell in Athens: A perspective on informatization and democracy*. Amsterdam: IOS Press.

van der Wurff, R. (2005). The impacts of the internet on newspapers in Europe. *Gazette*, 67, 107–20.

van Dijk, J. (1999). *The Network Society: social aspects of new media*. Thousand Oaks CA: Sage.

—— (2000). Widening information gaps and policies of prevention. In: K. Hacker & J. v. Dijk (eds.), *Digital Democracy: issues of theory and practice*. London: Sage Publications.

—— (2003). A framework for digital divide research. *Electronic Journal of Communication*, 12(1).

—— (2004). Divides in succession: possession, skills and use of the new media for participation. In: E. Bucy & J. Newhagen (eds.), *Media Access: social and psychological dimensions of new technology use*. Hillsdale NJ: Lawrence Erlbaum, pp. 233–51.

—— (2006). *The Network Society: social aspects of new media*, 2nd edn. Thousand Oaks CA: Sage.

van Dijk, J., Hanenburg, M. & Pieterson, W. (2006). *Gebruik van nederlandse elektronische overheidsdiensten in 2006, een enquête naar motieven en gedrag van burgers* [*Usage of Dutch electronic government services in 2006, a survey of the motives and behavior of citizens*]. Enschede: University of Twente, Department of Behavioral Sciences.

van Dijk, J. A. G. M. (2005). *The Deepening Divide: inequality in the information society*. Thousand Oaks: Sage.

—— (2007). De e-surfende burger: Is de digitale kloof gedicht? [The e-surfing citizen: has the digital divide closed?]. In: J. Steyaert & J. de Haan (eds.), *Gewoon digitaal, jaarboek ICT en samenleving*. Amsterdam: Boom.

van Dijk, L., De Haan, J. & Rijken, S. (2000). *Digitalisering van de leefwereld* [*Digitization of everyday life: a survey of information and communication technology and social inequality*]. The Hague: Sociaal en Cultureel Planbureau.

van Doorn, N., van Zoonen, L. & Wyatt, S. (2007a). Writing from experience: presentations of gender identity on weblogs. *European Journal of Women's Studies*, 14(2), 143–59.

—— (forthcoming). A body of text: gender and sexuality in text-based computer-mediated communication. *Feminist Media Studies*.

van Slyke, C., Comunale, C. L. & Belanger, F. (2002). Gender differences in perceptions of web-based shopping. *Communications of the ACM*, 45(8), 82–86.

Vanhanen, T. (2003). *Democratization: the comparative analysis of 170 countries*. New York: Routledge.

Vargas, J. A. (2007a, February 17). Young voters find voice on facebook. *Washington Post*.

—— (2007b, March 2). YouTube gets serious with links to candidates. *Washington Post*.

Vedres, B., Bruszt, L. & Stark, D. (2004). Organizing technologies: genre forms of online civic association in eastern Europe. *Annals of the American Academy of Political and Social Science*, 30, 1–18.

Verba, S., Nie, N. H. & Kim, J.-O. (1987). *Participation and Political Equality: a seven-nation comparison*. Chicago: University of Chicago Press.

Verba, S., Schlozman, K. L. & Brady, H. E. (1995). *Voice and Equality: civic voluntarism in American politics*. Cambridge, MA: Harvard University Press.

Vertovec, S. (2001). Transnationalism and identity. *Journal of Ethnic and Migration Studies*, 27 (4), 573–82.

Villeneuve, N. (2006). The filtering matrix: integrated mechanisms of information control and the demarcation of borders in cyberspace. *First Monday*, 11(1).

Virilio, P. (1997). *Open Sky*. London: Verso.

von Hippel, E. (2005). *Democratizing Innovation*. Cambridge: MIT Press.

Vreese, C. H. d. (2007). *The Dynamics of Referendum Campaigns an International Perspective*. Basingstoke: Palgrave MacMillan.

Wade, R. H. (2002). Bridging the digital divide: new route to development or new form of dependency. *Global Governance*, 8(4), 443–66.

Wajcman, J. (2004). *Technofeminism*. Cambridge: Polity.

—— (2007). From women and technology to gendered technoscience. *Information, Communication and Society*, 10(3), 287–98.

Walgrave, S. & Rucht, D. (eds.). (2008). *Protest Politics: anti-war mobilization in western democracies*. Minnesota, MN: University of Minnesota Press.

Walker, J. L. (1991). *Mobilizing interest groups in America: patrons, professions and social movements*. Ann Arbor: University of Michigan Press.

Wall, D. (1999). *Earth First! And the Anti-roads Movement: radical environmentalism and comparative social movements*. London: Routledge.

Wall, M. (2005). Blogs of war: weblogs as news. *Journalism*, 6(2), 153–72.

Wanta, W. (1997). *The Public and the National Agenda: how people learn about important issues*. Mahwah, NJ: Lawrence Erlbaum.

Ward, S. & Lusoli, W. (2005). From weird to wired: MPs, the internet and representative politics in the UK. *Journal of Legislative Studies*, 11(1), 57–81.

Ward, S. J. (2005). The internet, e-democracy and the election: virtually irrelevant? In: A. Geddes & J. Tonge (eds.), *Britain Decides: the UK general election 2005*. London: Palgrave.

Ward, S. J. & Francoli, M. (2007). Twenty-first century soapboxes? MPs and their blogs. Paper presented at the annual conference of the PSA, University of Bath. April 12–14, 2007.

Ward, S. J. & Gibson, R. K. (2003). On-line and on message? Candidate websites in the 2001 general election. *British Journal of Politics and International Relations*, 5(2), 188–205.

Ward, S. J., Gibson, R. K. & Lusoli, W. (2003). Online participation and mobilization in the UK. *Parliamentary Affairs*, 56(4), 652–68.

Ward, S. J., Owen, D., Davis, R. D. & Taras, D. (2007). Parties and election campaigning online: a new era? In: R. D. Davis, D. Owen, D. Taras & S. J. Ward (eds.), *Making a Difference? The internet and elections in comparative perspective*. Lanham, MD: Lexington Books.

Ward, S. J. & Vedel, T. (2006). Introduction: the potential of the internet revisited. *Parliamentary Affairs*, 59(2), 210–25.

Ward, S. J. & Voerman, G. (2000). New media and new politics. Green parties, intra-party democracy and the potential of the internet (an anglo-Dutch comparison). In: *Jaarboek 1999 documentatiecentrum nederlandse politieke partijen*. Groningen: Universiteitsdrukkerij Rijksuniversiteit Groningen.

Wardrip-Fruin, N. & Montfort, N. (2003). *The New Media Reader*. Cambridge: MIT Press.

Ware, A. (1996). *Political Parties and Party Systems*. Oxford: Oxford University Press.

Warf, B. & Vincent., P. (2007). Multiple geographies of the Arab internet. *Area*, 39(1), 83–96.

Warschauer, M. (2003). *Technology and Social Inclusion: rethinking the digital divide*. Cambridge: MIT Press.

Washbourne, N. (2001). Information technology and new forms of organizing. In: F. Webster (ed.), *Culture and Politics in the Information Age: a new politics?* London: Routledge.

Washington Poll (2006). *Public policy attitudes*. Seattle, Washington.

Waskul, D. D. (ed.). (2004). *Net.Sexxx: readings on sex, pornography, and the internet*. New York: Peter Lang.

Watts, D. (2003). *Six Degrees: the science of a connected world*. London: Heinemann.

Watts, D. & Strogatz, S. (1998). Collective dynamics of a "small world" networks. *Nature*, 393, 440–2.

Weare, C. & Lin, W. (2000). Content analysis of the World Wide Web: opportunities and challenges. *Social Science Computer Review*, 18, 272–329

Webb, P. (2000). *The Modern British Party System*. London: Sage.

Weber, S. (2004). *The Success of Open Source*. Cambridge, MA: Harvard University Press.

Websense Inc. (2007). *URL categories*. Retrieved November 22, 2007, from www.websense.com/global/en/ProductsServices/MasterDatabase/URLCategories.php

Webster, F. (2002). *Theories of the Information Society*. London: Routledge.

Webster, J. G. & Lin, S. F. (2002). The internet audience: web use as mass behavior. *Journal of Broadcasting & Electronic Media*, 46(1), 1–12.

Webster, J. G. & Phalen, P. F. (1997). *The Mass Audience: rediscovering the dominant model*. Mahwah, NJ: Erlbaum.

Weinberger, D. (2007). *Everything is Miscellaneous: the power of the new digital disorder*. New York: Henry Holt and Company.

Welch, E. W., Hinnant, C. & Moon, M. J. (2005). Linking citizen satisfaction with e-government with trust in government. *Journal of Public Administration Research and Theory*, 15 (1), 271–91.

Wellman, B., Quan-Hasse, A., Boase, J., Chen, W., Hampton, K. N., de Diaz, I. I., et al. (2003). The social affordances of the internet for networked individualism. *Journal of Computer-Mediated Communication*, 8(3).

West, D. M. (2000). *Assessing e-Government: the internet, democracy, and service delivery by state and federal governments*. Washington, DC: World Bank.

—— (2003a). *State and federal e-government in the United States*. Providence, RI: Center for Public Policy, Brown University.

—— (2003b). *Urban e-government, 2003*. Providence, RI: Center for Public Policy, Brown University.

—— (2004). *Urban e-government, 2004*. Retrieved November 22, 2007, from www.insidepolitics.org/egovt04city.html

—— (2005). *Digital Government: technology and public sector performance*. Princeton: Princeton University Press.

—— (2006). *State and federal e-government in the United States, 2006*. Retrieved August 17, 2007, from www.insidepolitics.org/egovt06us.pdf

—— (2007). *State and federal e-government in the United States, 2007*. Retrieved August 20, 2007, from www.insidepolitics.org/egovt07us.pdf

Westerdal, J. (2007). *Dot xxx is voted down, dot xxx fires back*. Retrieved March 29, 2007, from http://blog.domaintools.com/2007/03/dot-xxx-is-voted-down-dot-xxx-fires-back/.

Wheeler, D. (2001a). Beyond global culture: Islam, economic development and the challenges of cyberspace. *Digest of Middle Eastern Studies*, 10(1), 1–26.

—— (2001b). New technologies, old culture: a look at women, gender and the internet in Kuwait. In: C. Ess & F. Sudweeks (eds.), *Culture, Technology, Communication: towards an intercultural global village*. New York: SUNY Press, 187–212.

Wheeler, D. L. (2003a). Egypt: building an information society for international development. *Review of African Political Economy*, 30 (98), 627–42.

—— (2003b). Living at e-speed: a look at Egypt's e-readiness. In: I. Limam (ed.), *Challenges and Reforms of Economic Regulation in Mena Countries*. Cairo: University of Cairo Press.

—— (2004). Blessings and curses: women and the Internet Revolution in the Arab world. In: N. Sakr (ed.) *Women and the Media in the Middle East*. London: IB Taurus, pp. 138–61

—— (2006a). *Empowering Publics: information technology and democratization in the Arab world: lessons from internet cafes and beyond*. Oxford: Oxford Internet Institute.

—— (2006b). *The Internet and the Middle East: global expectations and local imaginations in Kuwait*. Albany: SUNY Press.

Whitaker, C. (2004). The WSF as open space. In: J. Sen, A. Anand, A. Escobar & P. Waterman (eds.), *Challenging Empires*. New Delhi: Viveka Foundation.

White, D. M. (1964). The gatekeeper: a case study in the selection of news. In: L. A. Dexter & D. M. White (eds.), *People, Society, and Mass Communications*. New York: Free Press.

Whitehouse, A. (2006). Women, careers and information technology: an introduction. *Labour & Industry*, 16(3), 1–6.

Wiklund, H. (2005). A Habermasian analysis of the deliberative democratic potential of ict-enabled services in Swedish municipalities. *New Media & Society*, 7(5), 701–23.

Wilding, F. (1998). *Where is the feminism in cyberfeminism?* Retrieved November 26, 2007, from www.andrew.cmu.edu/user/fwild/faithwilding/wherefem.pdf

Wilhelm, A. G. (2000). *Democracy in the Digital Age: challenges to political life in cyberspace*. New York: Routledge.

—— (2004). *Digital Nation: toward an inclusive information society*. Cambridge, MA: MIT Press.

Williams, A. (2007, March 18). The future President, on your friends list. *New York Times*.

Williams, A. P. & Tedesco, J. C. (eds.). (2006). *The Internet Election: perspectives on the web in campaign 2004*. Lanham: Rowman and Littlefield.

Williams, F. (1994). On prospects for citizens' information services. In: F. Williams & J. V. Pavlik (eds.), *The People's Right to Know: media, democracy, and the information highway*. Hillsdale, NJ: Erlbaum.

Williams, F. & Pavlik, J. V. (1994). Epilogue. In: F. Williams & J. V. Pavlik (eds.), *The People's Right to Know: media, democracy, and the information highway*. Hillsdale, NJ: Erlbaum.

Williams, H. (2005). Driving the public policy debate: internet governance and development. In: W. J. Drake (ed.), *Reforming Internet Governance: perspectives from the working group on internet governance*. New York: United Nations ICT Task Force.

Wilson, E. J. (2004). *The Information Revolution and Developing Countries*. Cambridge: MIT Press.

Wilson, E. J. & Wong, K. R. (eds.). (2007). *Negotiating the Net in Africa*. Boulder, CO: Lynne Rienner.

Winneg, K., Kenski, K. & Jamison, K. (2005). Detecting the effects of deceptive presidential advertising in the spring of 2004. *American Behavioral Scientist*, 49, 114–29.

Winneg, K. & Stroud, T. (2005). *Using the Internet to Learn about the Presidential Candidates and Issue Positions in the 2004 Presidential Primary and General Election Campaigns*. Paper presented at the American Association for Public Opinion Research Annual Conference.

Winston, B. (1998). *Media Technology and Society: a history from the telegraph to the internet*. London: Routledge.

Wise, C. R. (2002). Special report: organizing for homeland security. *Public Administration Review*, 62(2), 131–44.

Witmer, D. F. & Katzman, S. L. (1997). On-line smiles: does gender make a difference in the use of graphic accents? *Journal of Computer-Mediated Communication*, 2(4).

Witt, L. (2004). Is public journalism morphing into the public's journalism? *National Civic Review, Fall*, 49–57.

Wojcieszak, M. & Mutz, D. (2007). *Online Groups and Political Deliberation: does the internet facilitate exposure to disagreement?* Paper presented at the Political Communication Division.

Wolfinger, R. & Rosenstone, S. J. (1980). *Who Votes?* New Haven: Yale University Press.

Wolinsky, H. (2003, November 9). Chipping away at your privacy. *Chicago Sun-Times*.

Working Group on Internet Governance (2005). *Report of the working group on internet governance*. Geneva: United Nations.

World Summit on the Information Society (2002). *First meeting of the preparatory committee: World Summit on the Information Society* (No. WSIS03/PREP-(Rev.1)-E). Geneva: UNESCO/International Telecommunication Union.

—— (2003a). *WSIS action plan* (No. WSIS-03/Geneva/doc/0005). New York: United Nations.

—— (2003b). *WSIS declaration of principles* (No. WSIS-03/Geneva/doc/0004). New York: United Nations.

—— (2005). *Tunis commitment* (No. WSIS-05/TUNIS/DOC/7-E). Paris: UNESCO and Geneva, ITU.

World Summit on the Information Society Civil Society (2003). *Shaping information societies for human needs*. Paris: UNESCO and Geneva, ITU.

—— (2005). *Much More Could Have Been Achieved*. Geneva: UNESCO/International Telecommunication Union.

World Values Study Group (2000). *World values survey*. Ann Arbor, MI: Institute for Social Research.

Wright, T., Boria, E. & Breidenbach, P. (2000). Creative player actions in FPS online video games: playing counter-strike. *The International Journal of Computer Game Research,* 2(2).

Wring, D. & Horrocks, I. (2001). The transformation of political parties. In: B. Axford & R. Huggins (eds.), *New Media and Politics.* London: Sage.

Wu, H. D. & Bechtel, A. (2002). Web site use and news topic and type. *Journalism and Mass Communication Quarterly,* 79(1), 73–86.

Wu, T. (2006). The world trade law of censorship and internet filtering. *Chicago Journal of International Law,* 7(1), 263–87.

Wulf, W. A. (1989). *The National Collaboratory: a white paper.* Paper presented at the Towards a National Collaboratory Workshop, Rockefeller University, New York, NY.

Xenos, M. & Foot, K. A. (2005). Politics as usual, or politics unusual: position-taking and dialogue on campaign websites in the 2002 US elections. *Journal of Communication,* 55(1), 165–89.

Yan, W. (2006). *Survey: more Brazilians gain access to internet.* Retrieved November 25, 2007, from http://news.xinhuanet.com/english/2006–11/24/content_5369766.htm

Yates, J. & Orlikowski, W. J. (1992). Genres of organizational communication: a structurational approach to studying communication and media. *Academy of Management Review,* 17 (2), 299–326.

Yervasi, C. (1996). Confessions of a net surfer: net chick and grrrls on the web. *Postmodern Culture,* 7(1).

YouTube (2006). *Allen's listening tour.* Retrieved November 26, 2007, from www.youtube.com/watch?v=9G7gq7GQ71c

Yuan, Y., Fulk, J., Shumate, M., Monge, P. R., Bryant, J. & Matsaganis, M. (2005). Individual participation in organizational information commons: the impact of team level social influence and technology-specific competence. *Human Communication Research,* 31(2), 212–40.

Yun, H. K. (2004). Infocomm security: going offline is not an option. *Cisco Security Summit.* Singapore: Cisco Systems.

Zaller, J. R. (1992). *The Nature and Origins of Mass Opinion.* Cambridge: Cambridge University Press.

Zayani, M. (ed.). (2005). *The al-Jazeera Phenomenon.* Boulder, CO: Paradigm Publishers.

Zewail, A. (2004). Roadmap to a muslim renaissance. *New Perspectives Quarterly, Fall.*

Zhou, M. & Cai, G. (2002). Chinese language media in the United States: immigration and assimilation in American life. *Qualitative Sociology,* 25(3), 419–41.

Zhou, Y. & Moy, P. (2007). Parsing framing processes: the interplay between online public opinion and media coverage. *Journal of Communication,* 57(1), 79–98.

Zittel, T. (2003). Political representation in the networked society: the Americanization of European systems of responsible party government? *Journal of Legislative Studies,* 9(3), 32–53.

Zittrain, J. L. (2006). The generative internet. *Harvard Law Review,* 119(7), 1974–2040.

Zoonen van, L. (2002). Gendering the internet: claims, controversies and cultures. *European Journal of Communication,* 17(5), 5–23.

Zukin, C. & Snyder, R. (1984). Passive learning: when the media environment is the message. *Public Opinion Quarterly,* 48(3), 629–38.

Legal cases

Access Now v. *Southwest Airlines,* 227 F. Supp. 2d 1312 (U.S. Dist. 2002).

Arrow, K. *et al.* Brief of Amici Curiae, *MGM* v. *Grokster,* 2004 U.S. Briefs 480 (2005).

Association of American Publishers *et al.* Brief of Amici Curiae, *U.S.* v. *ALA,* 2002 U.S. Briefs 361 (2003).

ACLU *et al.* Brief of Amici Curiae, *Universal City* v. *Corley,* 2000 U.S. 2nd Cir. Briefs 9185 (2001).

Buckley v. *Valeo,* 424 U.S. 1 (1976).

Intel Corp. v. *Hamidi,* 30 Cal 4th, 1342 (Sup. Ct 2003).

Intel Corp. Brief of Amicus Curiae, *MGM* v. *Grokster,* 2005 U.S. S. Ct. Briefs 480 (2005).

Intellectual Property Professors *et al.* Brief of Amici Curiae, *MGM* v. *Grokster,* 2004 U.S. Briefs 480 (2005).

Lott, T. *et al.* Brief of Amici Curiae, *U.S.* v. *ALA,* 2002 U.S. Briefs 361 (2003).

Metro-Goldwyn-Mayer Studios *et al.* Reply Brief, *MGM* v. *Grokster,* 2004 U.S. Briefs 480 (2005).

MGM v. *Grokster*, 545 U.S. 913 (2005).

Multnomah County Public Library *et al.* Brief, *U.S.* v. *ALA*, 2002 U.S. Briefs 361 (2003).

National Venture Capitalists Association, Amicus Brief, 2004 U.S. Briefs 480 (2005).

Reno v. *ACLU*, 521 U.S. 844, (1997).

Smith, P., Testimony, oral argument, *U.S.* v. *ALA*, 2003 U.S. Trans Lexis 20 (2003).

Sony v. *Universal City*, 464 U.S. 417 (1984).

Taranto, R., Testimony, oral argument, 2005 U.S. Trans Lexis 27 (2005).

United States, Brief for Intervenor, 2000 U.S. 2nd Cir. Briefs 9185 (2001).

United States v. *ALA*, 539 U.S. 194 (2003).

Universal City Studios v. *Corley*, 273 F.3d 429 (2nd Cir. 2001).

Universal City Studios v. *Reimerdes*, 111 F. Supp. 2d 294 (U.S. Dist. 2000).

Index